dBASE IV™ Programmer's Reference Guide

RELATED TITLES

dBASE® Mac Programmer's Reference Guide
Edward Jones

The Best Book of: dBASE II®/III®
Ken Knecht

dBASE III Plus™ Programmer's Library
Joseph-David Carrabis

dBASE III Plus™ Programmer's Reference Guide
Edward Jones

Inside dBASE III®
National Training Systems, Inc.
Jay M. Sedlik, PhD., Editor

Managing With dBASE III®
Michael J. Clifford

The Best Book of: dBASE IV™ *(forthcoming)*
Joseph-David Carrabis

The Best Book of: Lotus® 1-2-3®, Second Edition
Alan Simpson

The Best Book of: Microsoft® Works for the PC
Ruth Witkin

The Best Book of: Quattro™
Joseph-David Carrabis

The Best Book of: WordPerfect®, Version 5.0
Vincent Alfieri

WordPerfect® 5.0: Expert Techniques
Kate Barnes

The Best Book of: WordStar® 5.0
Vincent Alfieri

The Waite Group's MS-DOS® Developer's Guide, Second Edition
John Angermeyer, Kevin Jaeger, et al

Advanced MS-DOS®: Expert Techniques
Carl Townsend

dBASE IV™ Programmer's Reference Guide

Edward Jones

HOWARD W. SAMS & COMPANY
A Division of Macmillan, Inc.
4300 West 62nd Street
Indianapolis, Indiana 46268 USA

In memory of mom

FIRST EDITION
FIRST PRINTING—1989

International Standard Book Number: 0-672-22654-5
Library of Congress Catalog Card Number: 89-60254

Acquisitions Editor: *Greg Michael*
Development Editor: *C. Herbert Feltner*
Manuscript and Production Editor: *Amy Perry*
Cover Illustration: *Charlie Largent*
Illustrator: *Ralph E. Lund*
Compositor: *Impressions, Inc.*
Indexer: *Brown Editorial Service*

Printed in the United States of America

Overview

Contents

Preface

I can probably best tell you what this book is about by telling you what it is *not*. This book is not a massive collection of some consultant's favorite programs, which may or may not fit your programming needs. (While there are samples of complete applications at the end of this book, these are not the primary focus of this book.) Nearly all applications written in the dBASE programming language possess certain similarities; they contain routines for adding records to a database, for finding and editing records, for deleting records, for putting records in a desired order, and for printing reports based on selected information.

I strongly feel that you will be far better off knowing how to write code that will perform these basic functions in an efficient manner. Armed with such knowledge, you will be able to write applications that do precisely what you want, instead of modifying someone else's code to be as close as possible to what you had in mind.

dBASE IV is substantially different from its predecessors, dBASE III and dBASE III Plus, and radically enhanced from the parent software, dBASE II. Even if you have mastered the earlier programs, this book should prove invaluable to you because it covers in detail the following new features of dBASE IV:

- Networking commands
- The Applications Generator
- The Query-By-Example system
- The expanded Report Generator

If you're a dBASE III or dBASE III Plus user and you haven't taken advantage of the upgrade offer yet, I suggest you do so. You'll gain much programming flexibility from the added commands and functions. That's not to discourage you from using this book if you do not intend to upgrade your software; there are useful examples of routines for adding and modifying records, and for printing reports that will, for the most part, work with dBASE III Plus and dBASE III. If you use this book with dBASE III or dBASE III Plus, much of what you try that's in this book will still work. But there are a number features and commands that don't work, and you won't gain as much benefit as you would if you were using dBASE IV.

What's in the book? Following a brief introduction to dBASE IV and its capabilities in the first chapter, Chapters 2 and 3 provide the basics of both dBASE IV and the programming language that is an integral part of dBASE IV.

Chapters 4 and 5 outline methods of program control and detailed use of memory variables; Chapter 6 outlines effective steps behind system design; and Chapters 7 and 8 cover methods for getting user input and for adding and modifying records from within a program.

Chapter 9 discusses methods of program output, or reports, in detail, since getting complete reports is a major reason behind the use of dBASE IV. Chapters 10 through 12 provide tips on managing databases, nondatabase files, and the DOS environment supporting the dBASE program.

Chapters 13 and 14 cover debugging techniques and methods for cutting program execution time. Chapters 15 and 16 present programming considerations that must be applied if you are going to write programs for a local area network, and they discuss the quirks of converting dBASE II programs to dBASE IV. Chapter 17 covers the use of the Application Generator, Chapter 18 discusses dBASE IV SQL, and Chapter 19 provides some sample applications.

The four appendixes are quick reference aids for programmers who want a quick summary of dBASE IV commands, functions, error messages, and system memory variables.

Acknowledgments

Like many projects, this work would not be what it is without the help of a number of people. I would like to thank members of Wilmer, Cutler & Pickering's computer support team Jordan Engel, Jennifer Fu Hays, Fereydoon Keshavarz, Bruce Laufer, Yvonne McCoy, Osama Muftah, and Susan Randell, for their "book debugging" and helpful suggestions; Roberto Llames for his use of a large government network that added a "real-world" approach to Chapter 15; and my family, for putting up with my being buried in the basement office for numerous weeknights and weekends in a row while getting this book written. Thanks also to Jordan Engel for the back cover photo.

Trademarks

All terms mentioned in this book that are known to be trademarks or service marks are listed below. In addition, terms suspected of being trademarks or service marks have been appropriately capitalized. Howard W. Sams & Company cannot attest to the accuracy of this information. Use of a term in this book should not be regarded as affecting the validity of any trademark or service mark.

Above Board is a trademark of Intel Corporation.

BRIEF is a trademark of UnderWare, Inc.

CLEAR+ is a trademark of Clear Software.

Clipper is a trademark of Nantucket Corporation.

COMPAQ DESKPRO is a registered trademark of COMPAQ Corporation.

dBIII Compiler is a trademark of Wordtech Systems.

dFLOW is a registered trademark of WallSoft Systems.

dBASE II, dBASE III, and RapidFile are registered trademarks, and dBASE IV, dBASE III Plus, dBRUN, Framework II, Framework III, LAN Packs, and Step IVWard are trademarks of Ashton-Tate.

DisplayWrite is a trademark of International Business Machines Corp.

The Documentor is a service mark of WallSoft Systems, Inc.

dSALVAGE is a registered trademark of Comtech Publishing Ltd.

FoxBASE+ is trademark of Fox Software.

GENIFER is a trademark of Bytel Corporation.

IBM AT® is a registered trademark and IBM® XT is a trademark of International Business Machines Corporation.

Lotus, Lotus 1-2-3, Metro, and Symphony are registered trademarks of Lotus Development Corp.

Microsoft, Microsoft Chart, Microsoft File, Multiplan, Microsoft Word, and MS-DOS are registered trademarks of Microsoft Corporation.

MultiMate is a registered trademark of Ashton-Tate.

Novell is a registered trademark of Novell, Inc.

PCWrite is a registered trademark of Quicksoft Inc.

PFS:File is a registered trademark of Software Publishing Corporation.

Quicksilver is a trademark of Quicksilver Ware, licensed to WordTech Systems, Inc.

RAMpage! is a registered trademark of AST Research, Inc.

R:BASE SERIES is a trademark of Microrim, Inc.

Ready! is a registered trademark of Living Videotext.

SCAN-A-LYZER is a registered trademark of Tech III.

SideKick is a registered trademark of Borland International, Inc.

Smartcom I and Smartcom II are registered trademarks of Hayes Microcomputer Products, Inc.

SuperCalc 2, 3, 4, and 5 are registered trademarks of Computer Associates International.

3Com is a registered trademark and 3+ is a trademark of 3Com Corporation.

WordPerfect is a trademark of WordPerfect Corporation.

WordStar is a registered trademark of MicroPro Corporation.

1

Introduction

This chapter provides a short introduction to dBASE IV and offers tips on getting started with the program, installing the program on a hard disk, and using dBASE IV in its assist and interactive, or *dot prompt,* modes of operation.

dBASE IV is a leading database management system for IBM PC's, XT's, AT's, and compatibles. It also offers a strong programming language, and thousands of dBASE users have put that programming language to extensive use. This book is designed to help you put the programming language behind dBASE IV to effective use in your applications. In this book, you will not find page after page of "canned" programs, showing one programmer's opinion of how to create a particular type of application with dBASE IV. Instead, you will find detailed explanations behind those parts at the "core" of all dBASE programs that programmers use to accomplish tasks. Understand how these core parts work, and you can structure them to build any application you desire.

Enhancements in dBASE IV

dBASE IV offers major advances over its predecessors, dBASE II, dBASE III, and dBASE III Plus. (There was no dBASE I, but that is a long story woven in the annals of micro trivia!) dBASE II became entrenched as the first dominant database manager for microcomputers, but the package had severe limits. It could open only two database files at once, was limited to files with a maximum of 32 fields, was horrendously slow at sorting, and required some convoluted programming to work effectively with dates. dBASE II was limited to databases of up to 65,535 records at a time. As a major improvement, dBASE III offered the ability to work with up to 10 database files at once, with greatly increased field limits of 128 fields per database. dBASE III also provided the theoretical ability to work with a database of one billion records (in practice, an amount that would put a severe strain on the capabilities of any personal computer hard disk on the market). dBASE III maintained the dot prompt as its primary means of interfacing with the user, and while dBASE III offered an "assist" feature, it was somewhat clumsy and not well-received by most users. dBASE III Plus improved upon the assist feature, provided support for local area networks, and added enhanced screen design and query capabilities. The number of programming functions doubled, and 35 new commands were added to the dBASE language.

When Ashton-Tate developed dBASE IV, it improved upon dBASE III Plus by adding the following:

1. A greatly enhanced Report Generator
2. The Query-by-Example feature for visual design of data queries
3. Automatic file and record locking on local area networks
4. A greatly enhanced Applications Generator to aid in program creation
5. New commands for fast design of pull-down ("popup") and horizontal bar menus
6. The ability to define windows for editing or for using browse mode
7. The ability to search memo fields
8. A full debugger for use in debugging programs

dBASE IV is provided in a weighty package consisting of two binders, numerous pamphlets, and nine disks. The Developer's Release has additional disks containing the Developer's Utilities.

The software can be copied to a hard disk with the INSTALL routine that is present on the Installation Disk. To run the INSTALL routine, insert the Installation Disk into drive A, make drive A the default drive, and enter INSTALL at the DOS prompt. Then follow the instructions that appear on the screen.

Recommended Hardware

dBASE IV for a single user requires a hard disk and a minimum of 640K memory. It will run under DOS Version 2.1 and all later versions, and under OS/2 versions 1.0 or above.

Changes to CONFIG.SYS

Before you start dBASE IV, the disk or directory used to start your computer should contain a CONFIG.SYS file. This file should contain the commands,

```
FILES = 99
BUFFERS = 20
```

The CONFIG.SYS file is a text file you can create with any word processor that creates ASCII text files. Or, it can be added using a menu option during the installation process.

If the CONFIG.SYS file is not present, dBASE IV will operate. But when you try to run most programs that you write, you will often encounter a "too many files are open" error message; the only cure is to place the CONFIG.SYS file on the disk you use to start your computer.

Starting the Program

dBASE IV is started by changing to the hard disk subdirectory that contains the program, and entering DBASE from the DOS prompt. A copyright notice will display, then a message asking you to press Return to begin use of the program. If you press Return (or if you ignore the message for long enough), dBASE IV will complete its loading, and if no modifications have been made to a CONFIG.DB file (more on that later), the Control Center will appear, as shown in Figure 1-1.

The Control Center is the default operating mode for dBASE IV users. It is, however, not the mode the software will use to execute programs. The Control Center provides a series of user-friendly, pull-down menus to help novice users perform various operations. Since the Control Center bears no relation to programming with dBASE IV, this book will not cover these menus in any detail. It is probably sufficient for you to know that most dBASE IV commands can be

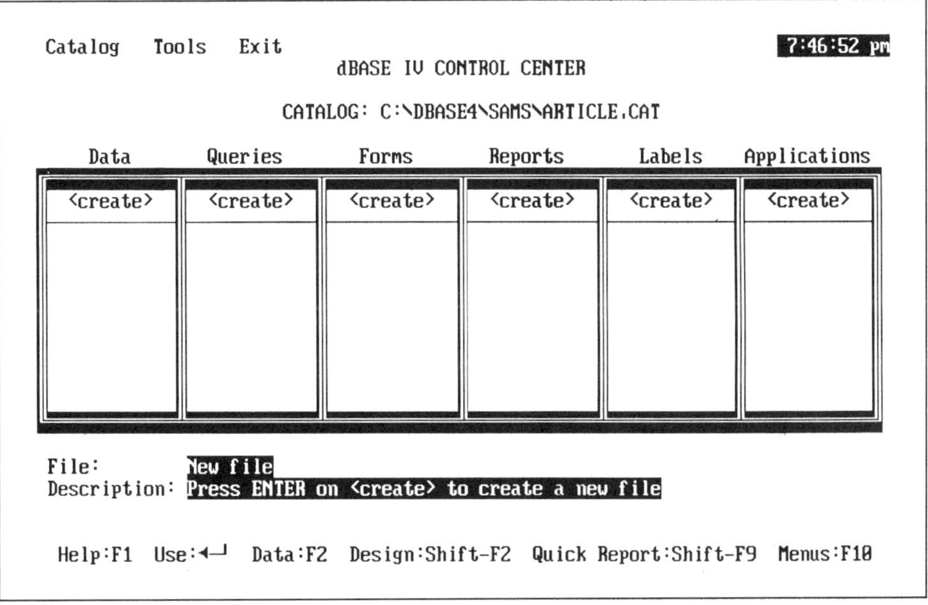

Figure 1-1 Control Center

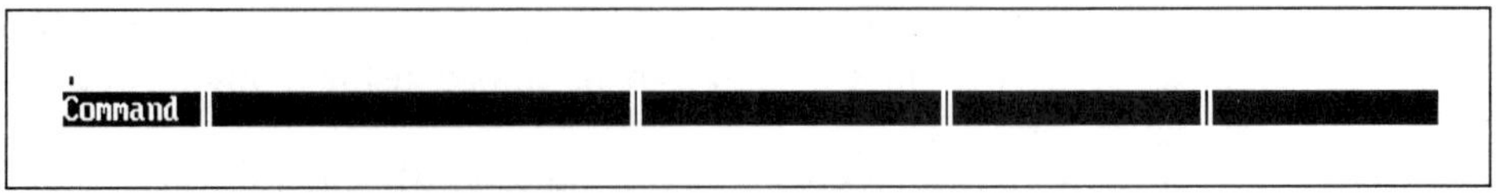

.
Command

Figure 1-2 Dot Prompt Mode

executed by means of the menus within the Control Center, and that a more detailed explanation of the Control Center can be found in the dBASE IV documentation.

dBASE IV can operate in one of three ways: through the Control Center, through the famed *dot prompt,* or through the execution of a dBASE IV program. Pressing the Esc key from within the Control Center will switch dBASE IV to the dot prompt mode. In this mode, a period, or "dot," appears on the screen to indicate that the software is waiting for you to enter an interactive command (Figure 1-2 shows how the screen looks).

After the dot prompt you can enter any valid dBASE IV command. A dBASE IV *command file,* or program, is a file containing a series of dBASE IV commands. Such a file can also be executed from the dot prompt if you enter the DO command, followed by the name of the program.

The way that programs run in dBASE IV is covered in greater detail beginning with Chapter 3; Chapter 2 covers the commands used to perform common operations from the interactive, or dot prompt, mode of dBASE IV. If you are experienced at using dBASE IV, dBASE III Plus, or dBASE III from the dot prompt, you may want to skim over the material in the following chapter, then move into Chapter 3. If you are familiar with other programming languages but are totally new to the dBASE environment, you should cover Chapter 2 thoroughly, as dBASE IV programs are built on a foundation of dBASE commands that can be entered in an interactive mode.

2

dBASE IV Database Basics

This chapter covers hints regarding proper database design, and introduces the commands commonly used to create databases, add data, and view or modify data in a database. Methods of sorting databases and modifying the structure of a database will also be covered. The chapter is designed to aid programmers who are new to the command structure of dBASE IV. If you are new to programming, but are experienced with dBASE IV, dBASE III, or dBASE III Plus, you may want to skim over the material in this chapter.

Effective Database Design

All too often, careful planning is neglected in the design of a database. This is an unfortunate tendency shared by many programmers; most of us find writing program code far more enjoyable than designing databases on paper. The database, however, lies at the heart of every database application. If the users of the program are to gain the most benefit from the system, the design of the database *must* be carefully planned from the start.

When you are planning the design, or structure, of a database, it often helps to first tackle the problem from the output side. The database's output can be reports or responses to queries from users. How do your users want their reports to be formatted? How will the users formulate their queries? Once the desired output has been defined, you can begin to refine the input data necessary to produce the desired output.

While juggling output requirements and input specifications, you must keep in mind that most database management systems will involve the use of multiple files, with varying relationships between those files. As an example, a personnel tracking system might contain a salaries database and a benefits database, with a relationship drawn between common employee identification numbers contained in both files.

To effectively plan a database, list both the output and the input requirements on paper. Then, refer to those requirements as you begin to define the necessary names of fields, types of fields, and sizes of fields. If possible, discuss the revised list of database fields with the future users of the system. They may not know the mechanics of programming, but they will have a good idea of what will work and what will not work when it comes to the design of their database. Implementing a planning process as a part of database design will save *significant* additional effort and frustration later, as major changes to the database structure and dependent applications will be far less likely to occur.

Parts of a dBASE IV Database Structure

The database structure for a dBASE IV database contains some very specific information regarding each field, including the field name, field type, width, and number of decimal places. The field name is precisely that—a name that identifies a particular field. Field names can have up to 10 characters. The first character must be a letter; other characters can include letters, numerals, or underscores. All other characters are illegal.

Fields within dBASE IV can be one of six different types:

- character
- numeric
- float
- logical
- date
- memo

Table 2-1 lists parameters for the field types.

Character fields can store any combination of characters (including numbers, blank spaces, and symbols). The contents of character fields are padded with

Table 2-1 Field Types

Data Type	Length	Acceptable Data
character	1–254	all alphanumeric characters
numeric	1–19	digits 0–9; decimal point; plus or minus signs
float	1–19	digits 0–9; decimal point; plus or minus signs
logical	1	T, t, F, f, Y, y, N, n
date	8	mm/dd/yy (this format can be changed with the SET DATE command)
memo	64K maximum	all alphanumeric characters

blanks, so that a character field with a width of 30 spaces may contain a 16-character name and 14 blank spaces.

Numeric fields store only numbers, which can be whole or fractional (decimal). Numeric fields are normally used for data that will be used in calculations; zip codes and phone numbers should be stored in character fields, as calculations are not normally performed on these values. Numeric fields are right-justified and filled with zeros when necessary. Plus and minus signs can be entered in numeric fields. dBASE IV counts the decimal point (and plus or minus sign, if any is used) as a valid character when figuring the length of the field. So, if you need to display a number with four whole digits and two decimal places, you will need to specify a numeric field with a length of seven.

Float fields are numeric fields with a floating decimal point. As with numeric fields, float fields can store numerals, decimal point, and plus or minus signs.

Logical fields store a single character that indicates a (T)rue or (F)alse condition. Acceptable values for a logical field include T, t, F, f, Y, y, N, and n. Logical fields provide an ideal way to test whether records meet certain true or false criteria, such as:

```
IF SOLD
  DO UPDATE
ENDIF
```

Date fields store a date in any one of a number of international formats. The default format is American, which displays in the mm/dd/yy format. You can use the SET DATE <parameter> command, where <parameter> can be ANSI, AMERICAN, BRITISH/FRENCH, ITALIAN, GERMAN, JAPAN, USA, MDY, DMY, or YMD. The resulting formats for the date fields, when SET DATE is used, will be:

AMERICAN	mm/dd/yy
ANSI	yy.mm.dd
BRITISH/FRENCH	dd/mm/yy
ITALIAN	dd–mm–yy
GERMAN	dd.mm.yy
JAPAN	yy/mm/dd
USA	mm–dd–yy
MDY	mm/dd/yy
DMY	dd/mm/yy
YMD	yy/mm/dd

Limited math operations are possible with the data stored in a date field. You can subtract an earlier date from a later date (the result is the number of days between the two dates), and you can subtract a number from or add a number to a date.

Memo fields are a special form of variable-width character field, and they are used to store large amounts of text (up to a maximum of 64K). The contents of a memo field are stored in an ASCII text file, which is assigned a .DBT extension, rather than in the database. Each memo field uses 10 bytes in the database file.

Creating a Database

The first step in creating a database is entering the CREATE command. The normal syntax of this command is:

```
CREATE <filename>
```

where <filename> is the name of the database to be created. dBASE IV normally assigns an extension of .DBF to the database file, unless you specify otherwise. If no filename is specified, dBASE IV will prompt for the name of a file. Filenames must follow standard DOS naming conventions: they must consist of eight characters or less; the first character must be a letter; and the remaining characters can be letters, numbers, or underscores. Some examples of acceptable filenames include:

SALES12
CLIENTS
BILL_DUE
STUDENTS
A4300

while some examples of filenames not acceptable to dBASE IV are:

SALES 12	(no spaces allowed)
DUE DATE	(no spaces allowed)
PTA:MEMB	(colon is not a valid character in a filename)
3200FILE	(first character must be a letter)

The File Header and File Structure Table

When a database file is initially created by dBASE IV, specific information about the field names, types of fields, and total number of records in the database is stored at the beginning of the file, in an area called the *file header*. Each time a database is updated or the design of the database is changed, dBASE IV automatically updates the header to reflect those changes. This process is transparent to the user, and it is mentioned to emphasize the benefit it offers: flexibility in the design of the database. You can make major changes to the design (structure) of a dBASE database, without substantially altering the design of programs that use the database. This is in marked contrast to most high-level programming languages like BASIC or Pascal.

When you enter the CREATE command, dBASE IV will display the database file structure table shown in Figure 2-1. Five columns are used to display the field name, type of the field, field width, the number of decimal places used (in the case of numeric fields), and whether an index based on the field should be created. The Status Bar, at the bottom of the screen, displays the name of the database file and the disk drive identifier, along with the number of fields defined. When a database is in use, the Status Bar displays how many records are in the database and where you are currently working within the database (details are given about these displays later).

Field names consist of 1 to 10 characters. Up to 256 fields can be placed in a single database; with the relational powers that dBASE IV has to offer, this should be far more than you ever need in a database. (If you need more than 256 fields in any one database, it may be time to go back to the design stage, because the design of the database may be flawed.)

You cannot insert a space between words within a field name (for example, MAY RCTS is invalid), but you can use an underscore as a part of a field name (such as MAY_RCTS).

Field names can be entered in uppercase or in lowercase letters; as the field name entry is completed, dBASE IV will store the letters as all uppercase. Once you enter a name and press Return, the cursor moves to the field type column.

Field types can be any one of the six defined dBASE IV types: character, numeric, float, logical, date, or memo. When the cursor is within the field type column, you can press the Spacebar to toggle through a list of all available field types, or you can type the first letter of the desired type (L for logical, D for date,

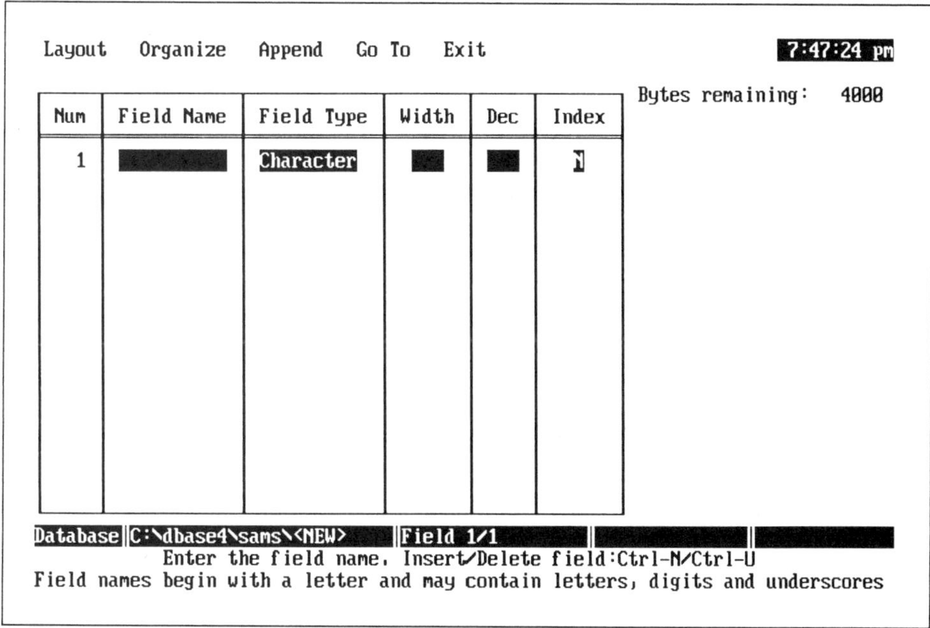

Figure 2-1 File Structure Table

and so on). Press Return after the desired type is displayed, and the cursor will move to the width column.

The width column specifies the width of the field. Character fields can range from 1 to 254 characters in width. Numeric and float fields have a maximum width of 19 characters, but you should keep in mind that dBASE IV is accurate in calculations to only 15 digits of precision. If you are working with advanced scientific applications, this may pose a problem. Widths of the other field types are preset by dBASE IV: logical fields are assigned a width of 1 character, date fields a width of 8 characters, and memo fields a width of 10 characters. (The *width* of a memo field should not be confused with the actual *amount of text* that can be stored in the memo field, as the stored text of a memo field is placed in the corresponding .DBT file.)

If the specified field is a numeric field, when you enter an appropriate width the cursor will move to the decimal places column. The desired number of decimal places for the specific field can then be entered. A Y can be entered in the Index column to designate the presence of an *index tag* based on that field. dBASE IV can keep multiple indexes, or index tags, in a multiple index (.MDX) file. The .MDX file that results when a Y is entered in any Index field during the database design is given the same name as the database file, but with the .MDX extension. Designating a field as an indexed field causes the creation of indexes which will speed data retrieval and ordering of records based on the field's contents.

Once the entry has been made in the Index column, the highlight will move to the next row, and the cursor will be placed within the field name column. All remaining field names, types, widths, and number of decimal places can be added as desired. As an example, a completed database file structure table for the mailing system looks like the one shown in Figure 2-2.

Storing the Database Structure

After the database structure has been defined, you press Control-End. You are prompted for a filename if you entered the CREATE command without specifying a filename. Once you enter a filename (if asked), the database structure will be saved on disk. dBASE IV will then ask,

```
Input data records now (Y/N?):
```

Answering **N** will return you to the dot prompt, while answering **Y** will cause a blank form for data entry to appear. The form is shown in Figure 2-3.

Displaying the Database Structure

The database design, or structure, can be displayed at any time with the DISPLAY STRUCTURE and/or LIST STRUCTURE commands. If you enter DISPLAY

Layout Organize Append Go To Exit 7:49:34 pm

Bytes remaining: 3898

Num	Field Name	Field Type	Width	Dec	Index
1	LAST_NAME	Character	15		Y
2	FIRST_NAME	Character	15		N
3	ADDRESS_1	Character	20		N
4	ADDRESS_2	Character	10		N
5	CITY	Character	15		N
6	STATE	Character	2		N
7	ZIP_CODE	Character	10		N
8	CUSTNO	Numeric	5	0	N
9	COUNTRY	Character	10		N

Database C:\dbase4\sams\MAILER Field 1/9

Enter the field name. Insert/Delete field:Ctrl-N/Ctrl-U

Field names begin with a letter and may contain letters, digits and underscores

Figure 2-2 Database File Structure of a Mailing System

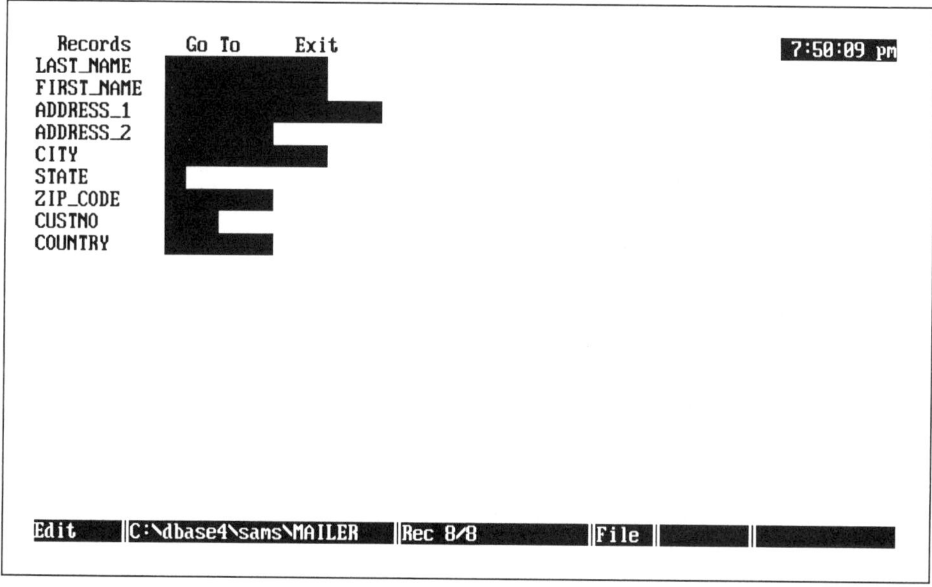

Figure 2-3 Fill-In Form with Blanks Ready for Data Entry

STRUCTURE at the dot prompt, dBASE IV displays the field names, types, widths, decimal places for the database currently in use, and the presence of any index tags. Also displayed will be the number of records presently contained within the database and the date of the last update. The actions of DISPLAY STRUCTURE and LIST STRUCTURE are identical, with the exception that the DISPLAY STRUCTURE command will pause every 24 lines and ask you to press a key to see more screen output. The LIST STRUCTURE command will not pause.

Both commands can be used along with a TO PRINT option when you want to print out the results of the commands on your printer. Or, use a TO FILE <filename> option to store the results in a disk file. When you include the TO PRINT option, the normal format for the command and the resulting display would be as shown in this example:

```
LIST STRUCTURE TO PRINT
```

```
Structure for database: E: \DBASE\MAILER.DBF
Number of data records:       7
Date of last update   : 10/26/88
Field  Field Name  Type        Width    Dec  Index
    1  LAST_NAME   Character      15             Y
    2  FIRST_NAME  Character      15             N
    3  ADDRESS_1   Character      20             N
    4  ADDRESS_2   Character      10             N
    5  CITY        Character      10             N
    6  STATE       Character       2             N
    7  ZIP_CODE    Character      10             N
    8  CUSTNO      Numeric         5             N

** Total **                       88
```

When you include the TO PRINT option, the output device is assumed to be the default printer (usually a parallel printer attached to the DOS device LPT1). If necessary, you can use the dBASE SET PRINTER command to redirect print output to another DOS device, such as COM1, COM2, or LPT2.

Adding Data

The APPEND command is used to add data to an existing database. When APPEND is entered from the dot prompt, a blank form for the next available record of the database appears (Figure 2-3). Pressing Return after each line of data entry moves the cursor to the next field. You can also control cursor movement with the cursor keys. Whenever a field is completely filled, dBASE IV will beep. The beep, which can be annoying when filling in small fields, can be turned off with the SET BELL OFF command.

Data entry in a memo field differs from data entry in other fields of a dBASE IV database. A memo field is accessed by placing the cursor at the location of the field and pressing Control-Home. The dBASE Editor then appears, and you can enter text in the field. When you have typed the text into the memo field, press Control-End to save it. The fill-in form is displayed again. Alternatively, pressing Esc from within a memo field displays a prompt asking if you want to cancel any changes made within the memo field.

If you press Return when the cursor is in the last field of a database, or if cursor movement causes the cursor to exit the last field, the record is stored in memory and the next blank record appears on the screen. When you have entered all the records for a session, you use the Control-End key combination to return to the dot prompt. Alternate methods of terminating the data entry process include pressing Control-W (performs same function as Control-End), choosing Exit from the Exit Menu (by pressing ALT-E, then E), and simply pressing Return without entering any data when the cursor is in the first field of a new record.

Press the Esc key to terminate the data entry process and tell dBASE IV to ignore any additions or changes made to the current record.

Editing Existing Data with the EDIT Command

The EDIT command is used to modify existing records in a database. (The CHANGE command is functionally identical to the EDIT command.) The EDIT command is used most often by experienced users who enter it from the dot prompt as a fast way to make changes to a database. There are reasons why it is usually not wise to use EDIT within a program (these reasons are discussed in Chapter 8). When you enter EDIT, you see a form identical to the form used by the APPEND command. However, instead of displaying a blank set of fields, dBASE IV displays the contents of the current field. Therefore, to effectively use EDIT, you must position the dBASE IV record pointer at the record that is to be edited.

Manipulating the Record Pointer

dBASE IV marks its position in a database with an internal marker called the *record pointer*. When a database is first opened, the record pointer normally points to the first record in the database. The dBASE IV record pointer can be repositioned with the GO command. The syntax for the command is:

```
GO <record number>
GO TOP
GO BOTTOM
```

where the record number desired is entered following the command. As an option, entering GO TOP will cause the record pointer to move to the beginning of the database, while GO BOTTOM will cause the record pointer to move to the end of the database. As an example, to move the record pointer to record number 5 in the mailing list database, the proper command would be:

```
GO 5
```

Once the record pointer is positioned at the desired record, entry of the EDIT command would then cause the record to be displayed within the fill-in form, as shown in Figure 2-4.

Moving the Cursor Within and Between Records

When you edit a record, the cursor keys can be used to move within the record. If the cursor is at the first field in the database, pressing the Up Arrow key will result in the prior record being displayed (unless there is no prior record, in which case pressing the Up Arrow key has no effect). Similarly, if the cursor is at the last field of a record, pressing the Down Arrow key will display the next record; if there are no more, dBASE will display a prompt asking if you want to add new records. The Ins key can be used to switch back and forth between the insert and overwrite modes; in insert mode, all characters typed when the cursor is among existing characters will cause those characters to move to the right, while overwrite mode results in new characters overwriting any existing characters to the right of the cursor on the screen. A complete description of editing keys available when using EDIT or APPEND is shown in Table 2-2.

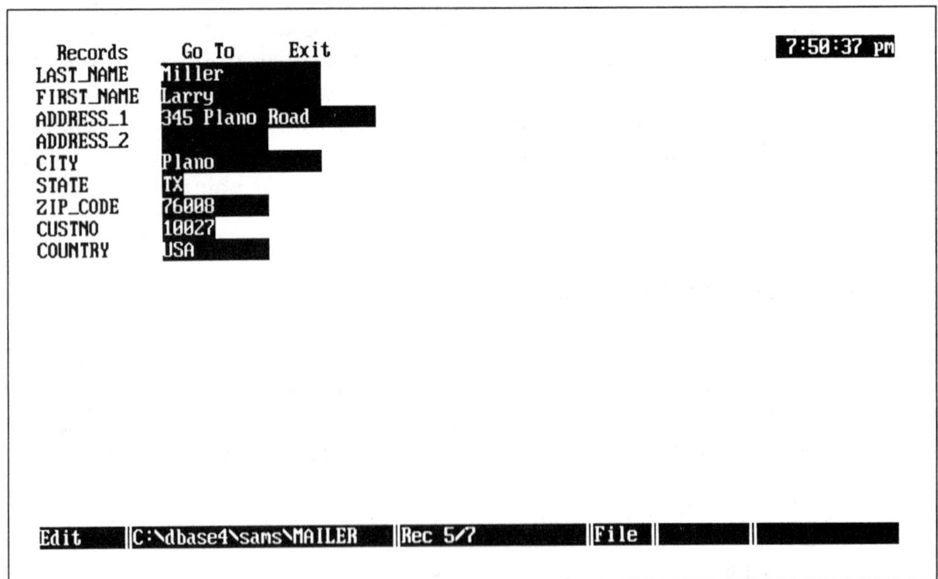

Figure 2-4 Result of Using the EDIT Command

Bookmark

HOWARD W. SAMS & COMPANY

DEAR VALUED CUSTOMER:

Howard W. Sams & Company is dedicated to bringing you timely and authoritative books for your personal and professional library. Our goal is to provide you with excellent technical books written by the most qualified authors. You can assist us in this endeavor by checking the box next to your particular areas of interest.

We appreciate your comments and will use the information to provide you with a more comprehensive selection of titles.

Thank you,

Vice President, Book Publishing
Howard W. Sams & Company

COMPUTER TITLES:

Hardware
- ☐ Apple 140
- ☐ Macintosh 101
- ☐ Commodore 110
- ☐ IBM & Compatibles 114

Business Applications
- ☐ Word Processing J01
- ☐ Data Base J04
- ☐ Spreadsheets J02

Operating Systems
- ☐ MS-DOS K05
- ☐ OS/2 K10
- ☐ CP/M K01
- ☐ UNIX K03

Programming Languages
- ☐ C L03
- ☐ Pascal L05
- ☐ Prolog L12
- ☐ Assembly L01
- ☐ BASIC L02
- ☐ HyperTalk L14

Troubleshooting & Repair
- ☐ Computers S05
- ☐ Peripherals S10

Other
- ☐ Communications/Networking M03
- ☐ AI/Expert Systems T18

ELECTRONICS TITLES:
- ☐ Amateur Radio T01
- ☐ Audio T03
- ☐ Basic Electronics T20
- ☐ Basic Electricity T21
- ☐ Electronics Design T12
- ☐ Electronics Projects T04
- ☐ Satellites T09
- ☐ Instrumentation T05
- ☐ Digital Electronics T11

Troubleshooting & Repair
- ☐ Audio S11
- ☐ Television S04
- ☐ VCR S01
- ☐ Compact Disc S02
- ☐ Automotive S06
- ☐ Microwave Oven S03

Other interests or comments: ______________________________

____

____

Name ______________________________

Title ______________________________

Company ______________________________

Address ______________________________

City ______________________________

State/Zip ______________________________

Daytime Telephone No. ______________________________

A Division of Macmillan, Inc.
4300 West 62nd Street Indianapolis, Indiana 46268

22654

Bookmark

HOWARD W. SAMS
& COMPANY

NO POSTAGE
NECESSARY
IF MAILED
IN THE
UNITED STATES

BUSINESS REPLY CARD

FIRST CLASS PERMIT NO. 1076 INDIANAPOLIS, IND.

POSTAGE WILL BE PAID BY ADDRESSEE

HOWARD W. SAMS & CO.
ATTN: Public Relations Department
P.O. BOX 7092
Indianapolis, IN 46209-9921

Table 2-2 Editing Keys in Full-Screen Modes

Key	Result
Left Arrow	cursor left one character
Right Arrow	cursor right one character
Up Arrow	cursor up one character
Down Arrow	cursor down one character
Control-Left Arrow	cursor left one word
Control-Right Arrow	cursor right one word
Home	cursor to start of field
End	cursor to end of field
PgUp	scroll up page/record
PgDn	scroll down page/record
Ins	switch between insert and overwrite modes
Del	delete character at cursor location
Control-End or Control-W	save record
Esc or Control-Q	exit without saving changes

Opening and Closing Existing Files

Once a dBASE IV database exists, it must be opened before any file operations can be performed on that file. The USE command is used to open an existing file. The syntax for this command is:

```
USE <filename>
```

where <filename> is the name of the database to be opened. The .DBF extension is assumed by dBASE IV. In response to the USE command, dBASE IV will open the database, and the pointer will be placed at the first record in the database. All commands entered following the USE command will perform their desired functions on the database that has been opened with the USE command. For example, to open a database named CLIENTS, the command would be:

```
USE CLIENTS
```

Databases can be closed with a number of commands. The CLOSE DATABASES command will close the database in use. The CLOSE ALL command will close the database and any other files that may be open as a result of other dBASE IV commands. Alternatively, the USE command can be used to close a database. If you don't specify a filename following the USE command, the database in use will be closed without an additional database being opened.

Viewing and Displaying Data

You can review data that has been entered previously using the LIST and DISPLAY commands.

Using LIST

The syntax for the LIST command is:

```
LIST [OFF] [scope] [<field names>] [WHILE <condition>] [FOR <condition>] [<TO PRINT>]
[<TO FILE filename>]
```

Options such as ALL, NEXT X (where X is a number), REST, and record number are collectively known as a *scope*. Specifying a scope is optional with the LIST command. (Scope options are commonly used with many other dBASE IV commands.) When you use a scope, ALL translates to mean all records; NEXT X displays the next number of records specified by the value, X; REST displays all remaining records after the location of the record pointer; and <record number> displays only the record number specified.

The LIST command can be used without specifying the names of desired fields when you want to produce a list of all fields within the database, as shown in the following example:

```
USE MAILER
LIST
```

This gives the following results:

```
Record#  LAST_NAME      FIRST_NAME      ADDRESS_1               ADDRESS_2
CITY         STATE ZIP_CODE     CUSTNO
      1  Jones          Ed              2318 Lake Newport Rd
Reston       VA    22090       10020
      2  Johnson        Larry           2915 Freetown Court
Reston       VA    22091       10021
      3  Jones          Benjamin        3412 Fayetteville St #2B
Durham       NC    27705       10022
      4  Canion         Ron             3 Nice House Lane
Woodlands    TX    74087       10023
      5  Roberts        Clayborne       1415 Buena Vista Ave Apt 5D
Hollywood    CA    90043       10024
      6  Miller         Larry           345 Plano Road
Plano    TX     76020      10027
      7  Smith          William         4343 East Orange Ave
San Jose   CA      94502       10028
```

To produce a list of the contents of the LAST_NAME, ADDRESS_1, CITY, STATE, and ZIP_CODE fields, the following commands could be used:

```
USE MAILER
LIST LAST_NAME, ADDRESS_1, CITY, STATE, ZIP_CODE
```

with these results:

```
Record#  last_name        address_1             city      state zip_code
      1  Jones            2318 Lake Newport Rd Reston    VA    22090
      2  Johnson          2915 Freetown Court  Reston    VA    22091
      3  Jones            3412 Fayetteville St Durham    NC    27705
      4  Canion           3 Nice House Lane    Woodlands TX    74087
      5  Roberts          1415 Buena Vista Ave Hollywood CA    90043
      6  Miller           345 Plano Road       Plano     TX    76020
      7  Smith            4343 East Orange Ave San Jose  CA    94502
```

Using DISPLAY

The DISPLAY command performs a similar function, but in its default mode, DISPLAY shows only chosen records that are selected through the use of a qualifying expression. The syntax for the DISPLAY command is:

```
DISPLAY [scope] [<field names>] [WHILE <condition>] [FOR <condition>] [OFF]
[<TO PRINT>] [<TO FILE filename>]
```

The default use of the command is simply DISPLAY:

```
. go 4
. display
```

This causes the current record to be displayed:

```
Record#  LAST_NAME       FIRST_NAME       ADDRESS_1                ADDRESS_2
CITY         STATE ZIP_CODE   CUSTNO
      4  Canion          Ron              3 Nice House Lane
Woodlands  TX    74087        10023
```

By specifying a scope (ALL, NEXT X where X is a numeric value, or a record number), all records, a group of records in succession, or an individual record can be displayed:

```
. display all last_name, first_name, address_1, city
```

```
Record#  last_name       first_name      address_1            city
      1  Jones           Ed              2318 Lake Newport Rd Reston
      2  Johnson         Larry           2915 Freetown Court  Reston
      3  Jones           Benjamin        3412 Fayetteville St Durham
      4  Canion          Ron             3 Nice House Lane    Woodlands
      5  Roberts         Clayborne       1415 Buena Vista Ave Hollywood
      6  Miller          Larry           345 Plano Road       Plano
      7  Smith           William         4343 East Orange Ave San Jose

.
. display record 3

Record#    LAST_NAME          FIRST_NAME                ADDRESS_1             ADDRESS_2
CITY         STATE ZIP_CODE   CUSTNO
      3    Jones              Benjamin                  3412 Fayetteville St #2B
Durham       NC     27705       10022
```

The FOR option can be used to specify conditions for the records that will be shown with both DISPLAY and LIST, as shown in the following examples:

```
. display all last_name for city = "Reston"
Record#  last_name
      1  Jones
      2  Johnson
. list last_name, address_1 for zip_code > "60000"
Record#  last_name       address_1
      4  Canion          3 Nice House Lane
      5  Roberts         1415 Buena Vista Ave
      6  Miller          345 Plano Road
      7  Smith           4343 East Orange Ave
```

If you add the TO PRINT option to the end of the LIST or DISPLAY command, the results of the command will be printed on the printer *and* displayed on the screen. Adding the TO FILE option routes output to a disk file. There is one difference between the LIST and DISPLAY ALL commands: the DISPLAY ALL command pauses as each screen fills, and you must press a key to continue screen output. The LIST command displays all data without any screen pauses.

Using BROWSE

Another way to display records in dBASE IV is with the BROWSE command. When you enter this command, dBASE IV displays up to 17 records of a database on a screen. While using BROWSE, dBASE IV is in full-screen edit mode, so changes can be made to individual records and fields. Figure 2-5 shows the result of entering BROWSE. Pressing F1 repeatedly while in BROWSE will "toggle"

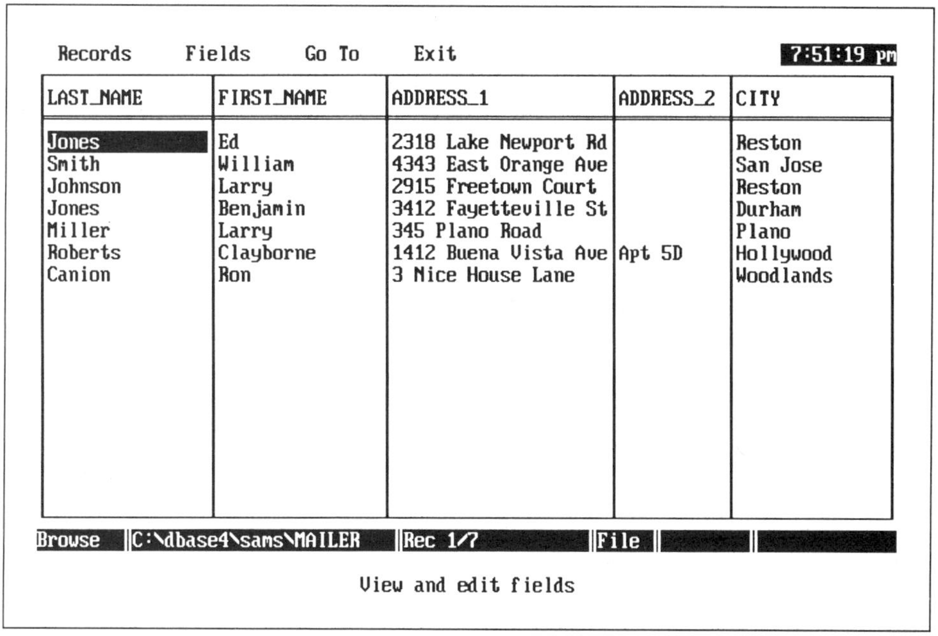

Records Fields Go To Exit 7:51:19 pm

LAST_NAME	FIRST_NAME	ADDRESS_1	ADDRESS_2	CITY
Jones	Ed	2318 Lake Newport Rd		Reston
Smith	William	4343 East Orange Ave		San Jose
Johnson	Larry	2915 Freetown Court		Reston
Jones	Benjamin	3412 Fayetteville St		Durham
Miller	Larry	345 Plano Road		Plano
Roberts	Clayborne	1412 Buena Vista Ave	Apt 5D	Hollywood
Canion	Ron	3 Nice House Lane		Woodlands

Browse C:\dbase4\sams\MAILER Rec 1/7 File

View and edit fields

Figure 2-5 Result of Using the BROWSE Command

(alternately show and hide) a help screen that lists function keys and editing keys you can use with BROWSE.

Pressing Control-End stores any changes you make as you use BROWSE and redisplays the dot prompt, or it then displays a dBASE program. Alternatively, pressing Esc exits the Browse mode without saving any changes.

While in the browse mode, the menu bar at the top of the screen displays menu choices for Records, Fields, Go To, and Exit. Pressing ALT plus the first letter of any menu option opens that menu (for example, ALT-R opens the Records Menu). The Records Menu contains options that directly affect records which are being added or edited.

The Undo Change To Record option of the Records Menu undoes (reverses) the effects of any change made to a record while it is still visible on the screen. The Add New Records option appends a blank record at the end of the database, and displays the cursor in the first field of the new record. The Mark Records For Deletion option lets you mark a record for later deletion, while the Blank Record option erases every field in the current record. The Lock Record option, which applies to users of dBASE IV on a local area network, locks a record so it cannot be modified by other network users until the lock is released. The Follow Record To New Position option works in conjunction with indexes. When this option is turned on, any changes made to the field on which the index is based will cause dBASE IV's record pointer to follow the modified record to its new location based on the index.

The Go To Menu provides methods for control of the record pointer while in the Browse mode. The Top Record and Last Record options of this menu move the record pointer to the first and last records in the database, respectively. (If an index is active, these options move to the first or last records according to the index.) The Record Number option moves to a specific record number, while the Skip option moves the pointer by a specified number of records. The Index Key Search performs a search of a file based on an index expression, while the Forward Search and Backward Search options use the field in which the cursor is located to perform a search for a specific record. (The Index Key Search option is equivalent to the FIND or SEEK commands from the dot prompt. These commands are covered later in this chapter.) The Match Capitalization option tells dBASE whether to consider or ignore differences in case when performing searches.

The Fields Menu provides control over the way fields are displayed when in the browse mode. The Lock Fields On Left option locks a specified number of columns (fields) at the left side of the screen, while remaining columns to the right of the locked ones can be panned with the Tab and Shift-Tab keys. The Blank Field option erases the contents of any field in which the cursor is located. The Freeze Field option restricts editing to a single field, while the Size Field option adjusts the default widths of the columns. Each of these menu options can also be selected through dot prompt commands, as detailed in the following paragraphs.

You can enter BROWSE along with a list of specified fields, in which case only those fields will be available for editing. For example, the command

```
BROWSE FIELDS LAST_NAME, FIRST_NAME, ADDRESS_1, CITY
```

would display only those fields named in the command line for each record. You can specify the FREEZE option to restrict editing to a specific field. As an example, the command,

```
BROWSE FIELDS LAST_NAME, ADDRESS_1, CITY FREEZE LAST_NAME
```

would display only those fields named in the command line. Of those fields, only the LAST_NAME field would be available for editing.

The BROWSE command offers a specific option for locking one or more columns on the screen, while allowing other columns to pan across the screen with the Control-Left Arrow and Control-Right Arrow keys. You can enter BROWSE LOCK <numeric expression>, where <numeric expression> contains a number indicating the number of fields that should be locked at the left side of the screen. As an example, the command,

```
BROWSE LOCK 2
```

creates a display that keeps the first two fields in the database always visible at the left, while the other fields can be panned in and out of view with the combination of the Control and Left or Right Arrow keys.

Use the NOFOLLOW option with indexed files (see the next section, on rearranging a database). After you have edited a key field in an indexed file, BROWSE normally repositions the display to maintain position according to the index. If you want to prevent this from happening, add the NOFOLLOW option to the BROWSE command.

Add the NOAPPEND option to the BROWSE command to prevent users from adding records while in the BROWSE mode. In a similar fashion, the NOEDIT option prevents editing, while the NODELETE option prevents deletions with Control-U. You can deny access to the Menu Bar by including the NOMENU option.

The WINDOW option is a useful one (particularly within your programs) when you want to limit the BROWSE display to a predefined portion of the screen. (You must first use the DEFINE WINDOW command to define the name and screen parameters of the window.) An example appears in the statements shown below:

```
DEFINE WINDOW MyScreen FROM 2,10 TO 12,60
BROWSE WINDOW MyScreen
```

The first statement defines the window "MyScreen" as having screen coordinates from row 2, column 10 to row 12, column 60. The second statement causes the BROWSE display to appear within the predefined window. The WINDOW option can be combined with the other options of the BROWSE command, to provide precise control of BROWSE while in a program. As an example, the statement:

```
BROWSE NOAPPEND NOEDIT NODELETE NOMENU WINDOW MyScreen
```

would present the BROWSE display within the predefined window, while preventing any modifications to the data and denying access to the menu bar.

Rearranging a Database

When the user retrieves data from dBASE IV, the information must often be retrieved in some type of order, such as in alphabetical order by last name, or in order of zip codes. dBASE IV offers two ways to arrange the order of a database: sorting and indexing. Sorting is performed with the SORT command, while indexing is accomplished with the INDEX command. Sorting builds a second database, identical to the first one, with the records arranged (sorted) in a different order. The command syntax for the SORT command is:

```
SORT ON <field name 1> [/A][/C][/D] [,<field name 2> [/A][/C][/D]...][,<field
name 10> [/A][/C][/D]] [ASCENDING][DESCENDING] TO <filename> [scope] [WHILE <condition>]
[FOR <condition>]
```

As indicated by the command syntax, you can sort on one or more fields. The [ASCENDING][DESCENDING] option is used to specify whether the sorted file will be arranged in ascending or descending order. (The default value of dBASE IV is ascending.) The A/D options provide the ability to sort in ascending or descending order on a single field. Character fields, when sorted in alphabetical order, display one trait of dBASE IV that can be annoying: uppercase letters have a higher value than their lowercase counterparts. As a result, records containing character fields will be sorted to list fields in order of A through Z, then a through z. You can solve this problem by using the /C option, which tells dBASE to sort based on "character" order, where uppercase and lowercase letters are treated alike. Another way to solve potential problems caused by the case-sensitive nature of dBASE IV is to use programming functions to cause all character fields to be stored as uppercase. Techniques for doing this will be covered in a later chapter.

If more than one field is named within the SORT command, the database is sorted in priority order according to the named fields. If date fields are chosen as a sort field, the sorted file will be in chronological order. You cannot sort using logical or memo fields. As an example, to sort the MAILER database alphabetically by city and store the sorted output to a file called CITYFILE, you could use the following commands:

```
USE MAILER
SORT ON CITY TO CITYFILE
```

Before the sort the records would look like this:

Record#	last_name	first_name	address_1	city	state
1	Jones	Ed	2318 Lake Newport Rd	Reston	VA
2	Johnson	Larry	2915 Freetown Court	Reston	VA
3	Jones	Benjamin	3412 Fayetteville St	Durham	NC
4	Canion	Ron	3 Nice House Lane	Woodlands	TX
5	Roberts	Clayborne	1415 Buena Vista Ave	Hollywood	CA
6	Miller	Larry	345 Plano Road	Plano	TX
7	Smith	William	4343 East Orange Ave	San Jose	CA

After the sort the records would look like this:

Record#	last_name	first_name	address_1	city	state
1	Jones	Benjamin	3412 Fayetteville St	Durham	NC
2	Roberts	Clayborne	1415 Buena Vista Ave	Hollywood	CA
3	Miller	Larry	345 Plano Road	Plano	TX
4	Jones	Ed	2318 Lake Newport Rd	Reston	VA
5	Johnson	Larry	2915 Freetown Court	Reston	VA
6	Smith	William	4343 East Orange Ave	San Jose	CA
7	Canion	Ron	3 Nice House Lane	Woodlands	TX

To sort the file on a combination of the LAST_NAME and FIRST_NAME fields, with the FIRST_NAME fields arranged in descending order, with the LAST-_NAME field having priority over the FIRST_NAME field, you could use the following commands:

```
USE MAILER
SORT ON LAST_NAME, FIRST_NAME /D TO CITYFILE
```

```
. use mailer
. sort on last_name, first_name /d to cityfile

   100% Sorted          7 Records sorted
```

and following the sort, the records would appear like this:

```
. use cityfile
. list last_name, first_name, address_1, city, state

Record#  last_name        first_name       address_1            city      state
      1  Canion           Ron              3 Nice House Lane    Woodlands TX
      2  Johnson          Larry            2915 Freetown Court  Reston    VA
      3  Jones            Ed               2318 Lake Newport Rd Reston    VA
      4  Jones            Benjamin         3412 Fayetteville St Durham    NC
      5  Miller           Larry            345 Plano Road       Plano     TX
      6  Roberts          Clayborne        1415 Buena Vista Ave Hollywood CA
      7  Smith            William          4343 East Orange Ave San Jose  CA
```

While sorting effectively rearranges the order of a database, it is not the recommended method for doing so. There are three main disadvantages to sorting a database. First, a file as large as the original database is created as a consequence of the sort operation. This wastes disk space and can make sorting larger databases difficult to impossible on a system with large files and limited available disk space. Second, sorting is a relatively slow process (when compared to faster alternatives). And finally, keeping a sorted database in the proper order is difficult. When records are added, new records usually are not in the proper order. Additional sorts must be performed after records have been added or edited to keep the sort order current. For all of these reasons, indexing a database is recommended over sorting.

Indexing a Database

When you use the INDEX command, dBASE IV creates an index file. The index file contains record numbers and a minimum of one field from the corresponding database. The fields contained within the index file are sorted in the desired order, and the record numbers within the index file are used to indicate the desired record number in the corresponding database. In effect, the index file is a virtual index of the database. Although the records within the associated database may not be sorted, once the index is opened, the database will appear to be sorted in the manner of the index. The proper syntax for the INDEX command is:

```
INDEX ON <fieldname 1> [+ <fieldname 2> + <fieldname 3>...] TAG <filename>
[UNIQUE] [DESCENDING]
```

or, alternatively,

```
INDEX ON <fieldname 1> [+ <fieldname 2> + <fieldname 3>...] TO <filename>
[UNIQUE] [DESCENDING]
```

Index files are stored with either an .MDX (multiple index file) or an .NDX extension. Multiple index files can contain multiple index tags; each tag represents a different expression used to provide the index. Index files with the .NDX extension contain index information for a single expression, and are used primarily to provide compatibility with dBASE III and dBASE III Plus, which cannot use multiple index files. The use of the TAG clause or the TO clause determines whether a multiple or an .NDX-style index file will be created. (Using TAG creates the .MDX file, and using TO creates the .NDX file.)

When a database is created, if a Y is placed in any of the index fields within the structure, a multiple index file is created. This file will be given the same name as the database, and it will be opened and updated automatically whenever the database is opened. This index file is also known as the production index file.

Index tags or files can be created from a single field or a combination of fields. As an example, to index the MAILER database on the LAST_NAME and FIRST_NAME fields, you could use the commands:

```
USE MAILER
INDEX ON LAST_NAME + FIRST_NAME TAG NAMES
```

```
. use mailer
. index on last_name + first_name tag names
   100% indexed          7 Records indexed
Record#  last_name       first_name      address_1              city
      4  Canion          Ron             3 Nice House Lane      Woodlands
      2  Johnson         Larry           2915 Freetown Court    Reston
      3  Jones           Benjamin        3412 Fayetteville St   Durham
      1  Jones           Ed              2318 Lake Newport Rd   Reston
      6  Miller          Larry           345 Plano Road         Plano
      5  Roberts         Clayborne       1415 Buena Vista Ave   Hollywood
      7  Smith           William         4343 East Orange Ave   San Jose
```

The resultant index tag, NAMES, contains an index based on LAST_NAME, then FIRST_NAME. Index files can be opened at the same time that a database is opened by specifying the name of the index file along with the name of the database. The syntax for the USE command, when used in this manner, is:

```
USE <database filename> INDEX <index filename>
```

As an example, to open the MAILER database and a corresponding .NDX-style index file called NAMES, the command would be:

```
USE MAILER INDEX NAMES
```

An index file can also be opened independently of the USE command by using the SET INDEX TO command. As an example, to specify an index file named USERS as the active index file, you could enter the command:

```
SET INDEX TO USERS
```

Once an index file is opened, it will be updated automatically when records are added or edited. A manual update of any index file can also be performed at any time by opening the index file and using the REINDEX command. REINDEX will update the index file based on the current contents of the database.

When using multiple index tags in a multiple index file, you can change the tag which is in active use with the SET ORDER command. As an example, if you create three index tags based on last name, city, and customer number with commands like these:

```
USE MAILER
INDEX ON LAST_NAME TAG NAMES
INDEX ON CITY TAG CITIES
INDEX ON CUSTNO TAG CUSTOMERS
```

then CUSTOMERS will be the active index tag, because it was the most recently created tag. You could change the active tag to CITIES by entering the command,

```
SET ORDER TO CITIES
```

and the other tags would remain open (and would therefore be updated when records are added or edited), but the CITIES tag would be the controlling index tag.

dBASE IV allows the simultaneous use of multiple index tags or files. If you need to arrange a database in various ways, such as by last name, by city, or by age, you can use multiple index tags or files to index the database on different fields. Only one tag or file will be active at a time. The database will appear to be sorted in the manner of the active index tag or file. All open index files will be updated each time records are added, edited, or deleted within the database. To open more than one index file, the names of the index files are specified following the USE or SET INDEX TO commands. The index filenames are separated by commas. The first index file to be named will be the active index file. As an example, either of the following commands:

```
USE MAILER INDEX L_NAMES, CITIES, ZIP_CODES
SET INDEX TO L_NAMES, CITIES, ZIP_CODES
```

would open three index files named L_NAMES, CITIES, and ZIP_CODES. In each case, the L_NAMES file would be the active index file. In the case of duplicate .MDX and .NDX filenames, dBASE uses the .MDX file.

Deleting Records

Deleting records is a two-step process with dBASE IV. First, you enter the DELETE command to mark a record or set of records for deletion. Then, you use the PACK command to delete all records that have been marked for deletion.

Using DELETE and RECALL

The syntax of the DELETE command is:

```
DELETE [<scope>] [WHILE <condition>] [FOR <condition>]
```

The command can be used with a scope (ALL, NEXT X, REST), or with a specified record number. If no scope is specified, the current record (wherever the pointer is currently located) will be deleted. As an example, if the record pointer is currently at record #7, then the command,

```
DELETE
```

would cause record 7 to be marked for deletion. The command,

```
DELETE RECORD 2
```

would cause record 2 to be marked for deletion. Deleted records are not physically removed from a file. Instead, an asterisk is stored within a special marker field inside the record. In the following sample database, records 2 and 5 have been deleted with a DELETE command; note the asterisk beside the record number, noting that the record has been marked for deletion.

```
Record#  last_name        first_name       address_1            city
      1  Canion           Ron              3 Nice House Lane    Woodlands
      2 *Johnson          Larry            2915 Freetown Court  Reston
      3  Jones            Ed               2318 Lake Newport Rd Reston
      4  Jones            Benjamin         3412 Fayetteville St Durham
      5 *Miller           Larry            345 Plano Road       Plano
      6  Roberts          Clayborne        1415 Buena Vista Ave Hollywood
      7  Smith            William          4343 East Orange Ave San Jose
```

Deleted records are normally still visible within a database, and they can be "unmarked" from the deleted status with the RECALL command. The RECALL command is used in the same manner as the DELETE command, but with the opposite effect; it removes the deletion marker from the record. The RECALL command uses a syntax that is identical to that of the DELETE command, namely:

```
RECALL [<scope>] [WHILE <condition>] [FOR <condition>]
```

Examples of the use of the RECALL command include:

```
RECALL NEXT 7
RECALL ALL
RECALL NEXT 200 FOR STATUS = "paid"
RECALL ALL FOR LNAME = "Carter" .AND. SALARY <= 7.50
```

Using PACK

The PACK command is used to remove all records marked for deletion from the database. The PACK command also renumbers all remaining records, so that disk space consumed by the database is minimized. If an index file is open at the time the PACK command is used, the index file will be updated. While you can use PACK after you use the DELETE command, it is time-consuming, particularly with large databases. Many dBASE programmers prefer to use PACK infrequently in their applications because it is so time-consuming. You can leave records marked for deletion in the database and make those records appear to have been deleted by using the SET DELETED ON command. A PACK can then be done on a weekly or monthly basis, to recover disk space.

When a user enters the SET DELETED ON command, the records marked for deletion in the sample database are effectively hidden from use by dBASE IV, as shown in this example:

```
. list last_name, first_name, address_1, city
Record# last_name        first_name       address_1            city
      1  Canion          Ron              3 Nice House Lane    Woodlands
      2 *Johnson         Larry            2915 Freetown Court  Reston
      3  Jones           Ed               2318 Lake Newport Rd Reston
      4  Jones           Benjamin         3412 Fayetteville St Durham
      5 *Miller          Larry            345 Plano Road       Plano
      6  Roberts         Clayborne        1415 Buena Vista Ave Hollywood
      7  Smith           William          4343 East Orange Ave San Jose

. set deleted on
. list last_name, first_name, address_1, city
Record# last_name        first_name       address_1            city
      1  Canion          Ron              3 Nice House Lane    Woodlands
      3  Jones           Ed               2318 Lake Newport Rd Reston
      4  Jones           Benjamin         3412 Fayetteville St Durham
```

```
 6 Roberts        Clayborne     1415 Buena Vista Ave Hollywood
 7 Smith          William       4343 East Orange Ave San Jose
```

All records in a database are deleted when you enter DELETE ALL followed by PACK. A faster alternative to empty the entire database is to use the ZAP command. ZAP will delete all records from the active database. Unlike DELETE ALL, the ZAP command provides no way to restore erased records. You could not issue a RECALL ALL command after you had entered a ZAP command. ZAP is a potentially destructive command, so ZAP asks for confirmation first, by displaying the message,

```
ZAP C:FILENAME.DBF? (Y/N)
```

and you must provide appropriate confirmation by entering Y before the database will be emptied of its contents.

Searching for Data

dBASE IV uses four primary commands for searching for specific records: LOCATE, CONTINUE, FIND, and SEEK. The LOCATE command begins a search on any record in a database, and its companion, the CONTINUE command, continues the search if more than one record meets a condition specified by the LOCATE command. The FIND and SEEK commands must be used to search indexed databases; they can perform very fast searches for the first occurrence of specific data contained in an indexed field.

The syntax for the LOCATE command is:

```
LOCATE [<scope>] [WHILE <condition>] [FOR <condition>]
```

The LOCATE command searches all records in the database until the first record meeting the condition specified is found. If no such record is found, the search stops when the dBASE record pointer reaches the end of the database. As an example, to find a part with a description of "bearing" in the PARTNAME field of a database, the command would be:

```
LOCATE FOR PARTNAME = "bearing"
```

The LOCATE command positions the record pointer at the first record in the database that meets the condition specified. This may or may not be the record you want to see. For continuing a search based on a LOCATE command, the CONTINUE command can be used. The CONTINUE command causes the search to resume at the point it ended, continuing to search for the next record meeting the condition originally specified in the LOCATE command. The following commands and records could be displayed as an example of the dBASE IV LOCATE and CONTINUE commands:

```
. locate for city = "Reston"
Record =       1
. display last_name, first_name, address_1, city
Record#  last_name        first_name       address_1            city
      1  Jones            Ed               2318 Lake Newport Rd Reston
. continue
Record =       2
. display last_name, first_name, address_1, city
Record#  last_name        first_name       address_1            city
      2  Johnson          Larry            2915 Freetown Court  Reston
```

LOCATE commands in dBASE IV need not be precise (unless an option known as SET EXACT is turned on)—either of the following commands:

```
LOCATE FOR LAST_NAME = "Johnson"
```

and

```
LOCATE FOR LAST_NAME = "Jo"
```

would find the desired record, assuming it is contained in the database. If a SET EXACT ON command is encountered, dBASE IV will require a precise match, so the second command shown would not find the record if SET EXACT ON were used. The requirements for a precise match can be turned off with the SET EXACT OFF command.

dBASE IV is also case-specific, so that if the command,

```
LOCATE FOR LAST_NAME = "Johnson"
```

were successful in finding the record, then the command,

```
LOCATE FOR LAST_NAME = "johnson"
```

would not be successful. There are conversion functions (discussed in later chapters) that help you restrict entry or storage of data as all uppercase or lowercase.

The FIND and SEEK commands search the database for the first record with an index key that matches the specified character string (in the case of FIND) or expression (in the case of SEEK). The syntax for these commands is:

```
FIND <character string>
SEEK <expression>
```

As an example, if a database is indexed by cities, the command,

```
FIND New
```

would find the first occurrence of a city name beginning with New (whether it be New York, New Orleans, or New Caledonia). The SEEK command performs a similar search, but it is not limited to a character expression. If a character expression is used with SEEK, the character expression must be enclosed in quotes. Examples of the command include:

```
SEEK 920.50
SEEK "Roberts"
```

For both FIND and SEEK, if the search for a match is unsuccessful, the record pointer moves to the end of the file, and the End-of-File function (covered in more detail in Chapter 3) is given a value of True. Your programs can use the End-of-File function to test whether the desired record was found. If the SET NEAR ON command has been used to turn on the SET NEAR capability of dBASE IV, this works somewhat differently. The SET NEAR command, when ON, causes dBASE to place the record pointer at the next record following the record which could not be located with FIND or SEEK. The default value of SET NEAR is OFF.

Global Updates to Records

Large numbers of records can be changed with the UPDATE and REPLACE commands. The REPLACE command uses the syntax,

```
REPLACE [<scope>]<field name 1> WITH <expression> [,<field name 2> WITH <expression>,
...][WHILE <condition>][FOR <condition>][ADDITIVE]
```

The FOR, WHILE, and SCOPE options work as described earlier in the chapter. The ADDITIVE option is used to store data in memo fields from one or more character strings. If the database has no memo fields, this option is ignored. As an example of the use of the REPLACE command, if a user wanted to make an incremental price increase of 4 percent to all records in a sales database containing the word *clothing* in the TYPE field, the following command could be used:

```
REPLACE ALL COST WITH COST + (COST * .04) FOR UPPER(TYPE) = "CLOTHING"
```

The REPLACE command outlined would replace the current contents of the COST field with an amount equal to 104 percent of the cost, for each record that contained the word *clothing* in the TYPE field. In this case, the UPPER function is used to ensure that the replacement is made properly whether the word *clothing* is entered in a field in uppercase or in lowercase letters.

Using MODIFY STRUCTURE

The MODIFY STRUCTURE command is used to change the structure of an existing database. Field names, lengths, types, widths, and inclusion of index tags to the production index can be changed. To change a database structure, open the database with the USE command, then enter the command MODIFY STRUCTURE. The database file structure table will appear. You can type over existing values to make any desired changes to the database structure. Once the changes have been made, press Control-End. If you have changed any field names or field characteristics, dBASE will ask if the data should be copied from all fields of the old file. Once you confirm the changes, the contents of the existing database are copied into the new database. The new database is given the same name as the previous database.

When you change types of fields within the database with MODIFY STRUCTURE, dBASE tries to make use of previous data, making the best assumptions that it can. In some cases, however, data will be lost. If, for example, you change a field from a character field to a memo field, any existing data in the character field will be lost, as the software does not have the capability to perform a mass transfer of the data between character and memo fields. If you change a field from a character field to a date field, dBASE IV will translate the data successfully *only* if the data in the character field was in date format, such as 12/21/82. It will not work for a textual format, such as January 4, 1980.

Files Created by dBASE IV

dBASE IV creates both native and foreign types of files during its use. Native file types are used by dBASE IV, and foreign file types can be directly used by other types of software. Filenames for dBASE files follow DOS conventions for filenames, and extensions are normally one of the default extensions used by dBASE IV for its file types. The extensions supplied can be overridden if you specify a different extension as you enter the command to create the file.

Files Used by dBASE IV

CATALOG (.CAT) Files: dBASE IV offers a catalog feature that can be used to group related database, index, and other file types into a single catalog. A catalog file, normally assigned a .CAT extension, contains the names of the files placed in the catalog. Catalog files are created with the SET CATALOG TO command.

COMMAND (.PRG) Files: Command files are files containing either dBASE IV programs or lists of individual dBASE commands that are executed in a batch mode by dBASE IV. dBASE IV can read and execute command files containing ASCII text that has been created with an external word processor or with the dBASE Editor. dBASE IV can also read and execute encrypted command files that have been created by using the Runtime option to encode an ASCII text command file. Procedure files are a form of command file, used to bundle program subroutines into a single group for increased speed of program execution.

COMPILED (.DBO) Files: Command files which have been compiled by the compiler present in dBASE IV have a .DBO extension. Once a command file has been compiled, dBASE IV will use the compiled (.DBO) file whenever the program is executed. dBASE IV also creates compiled versions of screen format files and report form files, which are assigned the .FMO and .FRO extensions.

DATABASE (.DBF) Files: Database files contain the records for the database, along with the information contained in each field. Memo fields present the one exception: information contained in the memo field is stored in an ancillary file (described later). Database files are created with the CREATE and COPY STRUCTURE commands. Database files can be changed with the MODIFY STRUCTURE command.

DATABASE MEMO (.DBT) Files: Database memo files contain information stored in the memo fields of a database. These files are text files containing the data, along with pointers that are used to link the text with the corresponding record in the database (.DBF) file. Database memo files are automatically created whenever a database that uses memo fields is created.

FORMAT (.FMT) Files: Format files are used to replace the normal full-screen displays that result from full-screen operations like adding records (with APPEND) and editing records (with EDIT) with custom-designed screens. Format files can be created by the Forms Design Screen, which is a part of dBASE IV. Format files can also be created with the dBASE Editor or with any word processor that creates files of ASCII text.

INDEX (.NDX) Files: Index files are files containing selected fields arranged in an order specified by one or more key fields in the corresponding database. Index files allow the use of a dBASE IV database in a logical (alphabetical, numeric, or chronological) order, rather than in the order in which the records were actually entered. Index files can be created with the INDEX ON <key expression> TO <filename> command.

LABEL (.LBL) Files: Label files are used to create mailing labels based on the records contained in a database. Label files are created with the CREATE LABEL command. Existing label files can be changed with the MODIFY LABEL command.

MEMORY (.MEM) Files: Memory files contain memory variables that have been stored for future use. Memory files are created with the SAVE command; they are read from disk back into memory with the RESTORE command. A single memory file can contain up to 500 memory variables.

MULTIPLE INDEX (.MDX) Files: Multiple index files contain index tags which maintain indexes in an order specified by one or more key fields in a corresponding database. Multiple index files can contain up to 47 different index tags. The index tags allow the use of a dBASE IV database in a logical (alpha, numeric, or chronological) order, rather than in the order in which the records were actually entered. Index tags in a multiple index file can be created with the INDEX ON <key expression> TAG <tag name> [TO <.mdx filename>] command.

QUERY (.QBE) Files: Query files contain query specifications that make the database in use appear to have fewer records than are actually contained in the file; only those records meeting the conditions of the query are available to most dBASE IV commands. Query files are created and changed with the CREATE QUERY and MODIFY QUERY commands.

REPORT (.FRM) Files: Report files are used to create reports based on the records contained in a database. Report files are created with the CREATE REPORT command. Existing report files can be changed with the MODIFY REPORT command.

SCREEN (.SCR) Files: Screen files are created by the Forms Design Screen of dBASE IV. Screen files contain the specifications used by the Forms Design Screen to build a custom screen form.

TEXT (.TXT) Files: Various types of text files are created as a method of transferring data between dBASE IV and other software, primarily word processors. Text files that are representations of the records in a database can be created with the COPY command. Text files that record most operations that appear on the screen when a dBASE program is running can be created with the SET ALTERNATE and CLOSE ALTERNATE commands. Two variations of text files are SDF and DELIMITED files; these files contain representations of records in the database, separated by delimiter characters (if DELIMITED is used), or separated into evenly spaced columns (if SDF is used). SDF and DELIMITED files are created with SDF and DELIMITED options of the COPY command.

VIEW (.VUE) Files: View files are files that contain a record of open database files, index files, filter conditions, and relationships between multiple database files. View files are created by dBASE III Plus, but can be used by dBASE IV.

Files Used by Other Software

dBASE II (.DB2) Files: dBASE IV can create database files in dBASE II format. Such files are assigned an extension of .DB2, so they won't be confused with existing dBASE IV database files in the same directory. Before the file can be used in dBASE II, the file must be renamed to a file with a .DBF extension.

DIF (.DIF) Files: Files in DIF format can be created by dBASE IV. Many other software products, including most spreadsheets and database managers, have options for importing DIF files. DIF files are created with the DIF option of the COPY TO command. The files created by this option will be given a .DIF extension, unless a different extension is specified.

Framework II (.FW2) files: Files in Framework II format can be created by dBASE IV. All field types except memo fields can be transferred to Framework II. (Framework III directly reads dBASE IV files, so no conversion is necessary.)

Lotus 1-2-3 (.WKS) Files: dBASE IV can export data from a database in Lotus 1-2-3 worksheet format. While the file will be stored with the .WKS extension (normally used by Lotus 1-2-3 release 1A), it can be directly read by both release 1A and release 2 of Lotus 1-2-3, and by Symphony. WKS files are created with the WKS option of the COPY TO command.

Microsoft (SYLK) Files: dBASE IV can export files that are compatible with most Microsoft products. The files are in Symbolic Link (SYLK) format. Such files can be used by Microsoft Chart, File, and Multiplan. SYLK files are created with the SYLK option of the COPY TO command. The files will not contain an extension, unless you specify one.

PFS:File Files: Files in the format used by PFS:File can be created by dBASE IV. The files will contain the necessary screen formatting and field design information used by PFS:File in a PFS:File database. Files in PFS:File format are created with the EXPORT command. The files will not contain an extension, unless one is specified.

RapidFile (.RPD) files: Files in RapidFile format can be created by dBASE IV. All field types except memo fields can be transferred to RapidFile.

3

Programming Basics

This chapter shows how programs are created and executed under the dBASE IV programming language, and how the software uses expressions, functions, and memory variables.

Programming with dBASE IV is made possible with *command files,* which are files made up of dBASE commands. Any list of instructions or commands that directs the operation of a computer is a *program,* and dBASE programs are simply lists of commands written in the dBASE programming language. This language makes use of the same commands that can be entered manually at the dot prompt. Any series of commands that can be entered from the dot prompt can also be stored in a text file. (The text file can be created by the word processor that is built into dBASE IV or by any word processor that can create text files of ASCII characters.) Command files, or programs, contain dBASE commands. The terms *command file* and *program* are often used interchangeably.

dBASE IV programs can range from a simple list of a few commands to dozens of interrelated files containing hundreds of commands. When multiple files of commands are used to perform various tasks, the collection of files is often referred to as an *application.* As an example, you can design a number of command files to process the various transactions necessary within an accounting system; those command files are referred to as an *accounting application* running under dBASE IV.

Programming in dBASE IV

The dual-mode operation of dBASE IV is what makes programming in dBASE possible. dBASE IV can be used in one of two ways: in an *interactive mode,* in which you enter commands one at a time from the dot prompt or from the Assist (Control Center) Menus; or in a *program mode,* in which you specify the name of a command file. The program mode of dBASE IV is invoked with the DO command. The syntax for this command is:

```
DO <filename>
```

where <filename> is a text file containing the individual dBASE IV commands to be executed. The underlying operation of the software is the same whether you use the interactive mode or the program mode. The only difference is that in the interactive mode, dBASE IV reads commands from the keyboard, while in the program mode, the software reads commands from a disk file. Each command in a command file occupies one or more individual lines. Some programming languages allow more than one command on a single line, but dBASE IV is not one of them.

A line in a dBASE program normally begins with a *command verb,* which is a reserved dBASE word such as DO or INDEX. *Reserved words* are words for use only by dBASE as commands or functions. Such words should therefore not be used as field names or as variable names. (Appendixes A and B describe commands and functions for dBASE IV, which together constitute the reserved words for the software.) The command verb is followed by a *statement,* which can be made up of a number of values or conditions that will control the effect of the operation performed by the command. Lines of a program can start at the left margin, or they can be indented for easier reading. A single command line can consist of more than one line, if each line that makes up the command ends with a semicolon. As an example, the following two lines are read as a single command line when used in a program:

```
? L_NAME + F_NAME + ADDRESS_1 + ADDRESS_2 + CITY + STATE ;
+ ZIP + PHONE
```

Whether joined with semicolons or placed on a single line, complete commands cannot exceed the maximum of 1,024 characters, including spaces.

A Simple Program

As an example of a simple programming task, it might be necessary to enter a series of commands that would open the MAILER database, index the file in alphabetical order by last name, and display the contents of the LAST_NAME, ADDRESS_1, CITY, STATE, and ZIP_CODE fields. From the dot prompt, the commands to perform these tasks could be entered, with the following results:

```
. use mailer
. index on last_name tag names
100% indexed 7 Records indexed

. list last_name, address_1, city, state, zip_code
Record#  last_name      address_1            city       state zip_code
      4  Canion         3 Nice House Lane    Woodlands  TX    74087
      2  Johnson        2915 Freetown Court  Reston     VA    22091
      1  Jones          2318 Lake Newport Rd Reston     VA    22090
```

```
3  Jones         3412 Fayetteville St Durham     NC    27705
6  Miller        345 Plano Road       Plano      TX    76020
5  Roberts       1415 Buena Vista Ave Hollywood  CA    90043
7  Smith         4343 East Orange Ave San Jose   CA    94502
```

An identical set of commands could be stored within a program, named TEST.PRG, as shown in this example:

```
NOTE**TEST.PRG
*This is an example of a command file
USE MAILER
INDEX ON LAST_NAME TAG NAMES
LIST LAST_NAME, ADDRESS_1, CITY, STATE, ZIP_CODE
```

The lines within the program that begin with NOTE, or with an asterisk (*), are comment lines. Comment lines will be ignored by dBASE IV when the program is executed. Comments can be placed on the same line as a program statement if the comment is preceded by a double ampersand (&&). An example of this technique is:

```
INDEX ON LAST_NAME TAG NAMES  && Create index for report
```

Comment lines are helpful (and highly recommended) for documenting the operation of a program. Once the commands are stored in the file, those commands can be executed in sequential order by entering the single command,

```
DO TEST
```

which produces the following result:

```
. do test
100% indexed           7 Records indexed

Record#  LAST_NAME     ADDRESS_1            CITY       STATE ZIP_CODE
      4  Canion        3 Nice House Lane    Woodlands  TX    74087
      2  Johnson       2915 Freetown Court  Reston     VA    22091
      1  Jones         2318 Lake Newport Rd Reston     VA    22090
      3  Jones         3412 Fayetteville St Durham     NC    27705
      6  Miller        345 Plano Road       Plano      TX    76020
      5  Roberts       1415 Buena Vista Ave Hollywood  CA    90043
      7  Smith         4343 East Orange Ave San Jose   CA    94502
```

The Format of a dBASE Program

dBASE IV uses a structured language, but it does not have many of the restrictions that apply to the design of programs in many other structured programming languages. It is not mandatory to follow a specific format when you design dBASE IV programs. However, it is a good idea to do so, as your programs will be easier to read and easier for you or others to debug and change.

The Ideal Program Design

The ideal design of a dBASE IV program, according to Ashton-Tate, follows the format illustrated by this program:

```
***PREAMBLE***********************
* Program..: REPORT1.PRG
* Author...: J.E. JONES ASSOCIATES
* Date.....: 04/06/1988
* Notice...: Copyright (c) 1988, J.E. JONES ASSOCIATES. All Rights Reserved.
* Purpose..: Hybrid prints combo report based on line & column format.
*

***ENVIRONMENT SETUP**************
SET TALK OFF
SET BELL OFF
SET ESCAPE OFF
SET SAFETY OFF
USE SALES
SET ORDER TO NUMBERS

***BODY OF PROGRAM****************
GO TOP
SET PRINT ON
STORE CUSTNUMB TO TEMP
*Set ending customer number for billing
DO WHILE TEMP < 9999 .OR. WHILE .NOT. EOF()
    ?
    ? "    ***Winken, Blinken, & Nod Apparel of  Georgetown***"
    ?
    ? UPPER(CUSTNAME)
    ? "Account number: "
    ?? TEMP
    ?
    ? "  **It is our pleasure to serve you.  Your account status:"
    ?
    ? "============================================================== "
    REPORT FORM SALES FOR CUSTNUMB = TEMP PLAIN NOEJECT TO PRINT
    ? "============================================================== "
    ?
    ? "    --Questions about your account?  Call us at 555-1212.--"
   EJECT
```

```
    *Increment customer number.
    STORE TEMP + 1 TO TEMP
    *find record matching cust. no. to print cust. name.
    LOCATE FOR CUSTNUMB = TEMP
ENDDO

***CLOSING************************
SET PRINT OFF
CLOSE DATABASES
RETURN
```

The Preamble: This section contains comment lines identifying the program's name and author, date the program was created, copyright notice, and purpose of the program. (In a dBASE IV program, comment lines are any lines that begin with the reserved word NOTE or with an asterisk. dBASE IV takes no action on any comment line.)

The Environment Setup: This area contains various dBASE IV SET commands that are used to control certain settings of the operating "environment" for the program, such as what screen colors are used and which disk drives and/or directory will contain related files. *Memory variables,* which are values stored in memory for future use, can also be created by commands within this section.

The Body: This contains the dBASE commands that will perform most of the actual tasks associated with the program. Commands that open various databases, extract information, and communicate with the user are found in this part of the program.

The Closing: This unit of the program contains commands that close database files as needed and return users to a main menu or to the DOS prompt. It can be thought of as a "housekeeping" area of a dBASE program.

Creating a Program

Programs can be created with the dBASE Editor or with a text editor or word processor of your choice. If you use a text editor of your own choosing, it must have the capability to create ASCII text files that do not contain any control characters. Program files are normally assigned the extension .PRG. If you use a different extension, then you must specify the extension as a part of the filename when you run the program with the DO command. To create a program with the dBASE Editor, use MODIFY COMMAND. The syntax for this command is:

```
MODIFY COMMAND <filename>
```

where <filename> is the name of the program file to be created. If no extension is specified, the .PRG extension will be assigned. As an example, entering the command,

```
MODIFY COMMAND TEST
```

will create a file called TEST.PRG and display the dBASE Editor on the screen. After this, you are ready to type commands a line at a time, pressing Return as you complete each line. The Editor in dBASE IV allows up to 1,024 characters on a single line. Text will not wrap, since program commands usually occupy a single line.

You can enter a semicolon at the end of any program line to tell dBASE IV to treat the succeeding line as part of the same line in the program.

Typing errors can be corrected with the cursor, Backspace, and Del keys. Pressing the Ins key will switch back and forth between the insert and overwrite modes of the dBASE Editor. When you use the insert mode, all characters typed will be inserted at the cursor position. If any existing characters occupy the cursor position, these characters will be pushed to the right to make room for the new characters. In the overwrite mode, new characters that are typed will write over any existing characters. Various combinations of control keys can also be used with the dBASE Editor for scrolling the screen, moving the cursor, and for deleting various characters, words, and entire lines. A complete listing of these keys is provided in Table 3-1. Once editing with the dBASE Editor is completed, files can be saved to disk with the Control-End or Control-W key combinations, or by choosing Save Changes and Exit from the Exit Menu. The Esc key can be used to abort an editing process without saving the text.

Using Other Word Processors

The dBASE word processor is a handy tool to have available, but you may prefer your favorite editor. A drawback to the use of another text editor is the need to constantly exit dBASE IV and run that text editor as you create and debug programs. If your computer has sufficient memory, you can overcome that drawback by making your text editor the default text editor that appears when MODIFY COMMAND is used. To do this, you must change the CONFIG.DB file.

The CONFIG.DB file is a configuration file that dBASE IV reads as it is started. The file is normally located in the same hard disk subdirectory that contains the dBASE IV program. The CONFIG.DB file is a normal text file, so it can be changed by the dBASE Editor or by any word processor that will store ASCII text files.

To change the default word processor used by dBASE IV, simply copy the desired word processor into the subdirectory containing dBASE IV, or set a path to the word processor's subdirectory with the DOS PATH command. Then, add a line to the CONFIG.DB file that reads:

```
TEDIT = <name of word processor>
```

Table 3-1 Editing Keys for the dBASE Word Processor

Key	Result
Up Arrow	cursor up one line
Down Arrow	cursor down one line
Left Arrow	cursor left one character
Right Arrow	cursor right one character
Ins	switch between insert and overwrite modes
Del	delete character at cursor
Backspace	delete character to left of cursor
Home	start of line
End	end of line
Control-Left Arrow	cursor left one word
Control-Right Arrow	cursor right one word
Control-Y	delete line
Control-T	delete word from cursor to end
PgUp	scroll up by one screen
PgDn	scroll down by one screen
Control-End	save file to disk
Esc	abort editing; don't save file
ALT-WWR	read file from disk into text at cursor location
ALT-WWW	write file to another filename

As an example, if your preferred text editor is WordStar, and you normally run WordStar by entering WS at the DOS prompt, then the line added to the CONFIG.DB file would read:

```
TEDIT = WS
```

Once this change is made to the CONFIG.DB file, you must quit and restart dBASE IV for the changes to take effect. Your computer must also be equipped with sufficient memory to run both dBASE IV and the text editor simultaneously. Even though dBASE partially unloads from memory when an external word processor is called, a significant portion of dBASE remains in memory. You may have to experiment to determine whether your favorite word processor can be used from within dBASE IV as a program editor. If the word processor is not in the same directory as the dBASE program, you will need to use a PATH command so that dBASE knows where to look for your word processor. You can use the DOS PATH command to specify a path, or you can use the SET PATH TO <pathname> command within dBASE IV.

WARNING: If you use another text editor to create and modify programs, be sure to save the program files as ASCII text, without any special formatting characters in the files. WordStar users can do so by specifying the non-document mode in WordStar when creating the file. Users of Microsoft Word and WordPerfect can choose the "unformatted" option when saving the file to disk. Users of MultiMate and IBM DisplayWrite must use the file conversion utilities supplied with these packages to convert the files to ordinary ASCII text. As a suggestion, the notepad feature present in some memory-resident software such as Borland's Sidekick can also be used as a suitable text editor for creating programs. Sidekick has advantages as a program editor—because it is memory resident, you don't need to stop what you are doing in dBASE to modify the program with Sidekick. And unlike some memory-resident packages, Sidekick is rather well-behaved, and seems to get along with dBASE IV with minimal problems. If you use the Applications Generator in dBASE IV, you may find that SideKick consumes too much memory to be used with dBASE IV. You can minimize this problem by reducing the size of the SideKick notepad. See your SideKick manual for details.

You can keep track of what is in your programs without leaving the dBASE environment by using the dBASE TYPE command. TYPE performs a function similar to the DOS TYPE command—it echoes the contents of a text file on the screen. Enter the command

```
TYPE <filename.prg>
```

to display a program. You can quickly generate a printed listing of the program by adding the TO PRINT option to the TYPE command. As an example, if you enter the command TYPE MAILER.PRG TO PRINT, this would cause the command file, MAILER.PRG, to be displayed on the screen and printed simultaneously.

About Compiling

dBASE IV is the first member of the dBASE line to run programs on a compiled basis, rather than an interpreted basis. (Interpreters translate each line of a program into machine language each time the program is run; compilers translate the entire program into object code once, then run the program using the object code file each time the program is called.) Compilers are faster in executing programs. This is a major reason behind the speed increase of dBASE IV programs over dBASE III and III Plus programs.

When a program is run with the DO command within dBASE, dBASE looks for the filename named in the DO statement, with an extension of .DBO. The .DBO extension refers to an object code file, or a program file which has already been compiled. If the file is found, dBASE runs the program using the compiled code. If the file is not found, dBASE looks for the source code (a file by the named filename with a .PRG extension), and proceeds to compile the source code into an object code (.DBO) file. During this compilation process, dBASE displays the message, "Compiling. . .", near the bottom of the screen. The compiling process slows down the execution time, but only the first time a new or changed program is run. After that, each execution of the program runs significantly faster than the first time since no compiling occurs.

When changes to a program are saved within the dBASE Editor, the editor automatically erases any object code file with the same program name. This causes dBASE to recompile a new version of the object code file, using the changed program source code. If you use your own editor rather than the dBASE Editor to create and modify programs, this can cause a problem: when you run a modified program in dBASE, dBASE will find the older object code (.DBO) file, and run the program without using your changes. You can solve this potential problem in either of two ways. You can erase the .DBO file after making changes to the program. Or, you can enter a SET DEVELOPMENT ON statement at the dot prompt, or add one to the start of your program. The SET DEVELOPMENT ON command tells dBASE to compare the creation dates and times of the source (.PRG) and object code (.DBO) files, as programs are called and executed. Any difference between the creation dates and times will cause dBASE to recompile the object code file.

Operators

Each dBASE IV data type has specific operators that can be used with those data elements. Operators perform various operations on data to produce a value. Mathematic, character string or alphanumeric, logical, and relational operators are all available in the dBASE IV language. Valid operators are described in Table 3-2.

Note that the order, or *precedence,* in which the math operations are performed is first unary, then exponentiation, next multiplication or division, then addition or subtraction. In cases where operators maintain equal precedence (such as multiplication and division), the order of precedence is from left to right. Parentheses can be used within the expression to force a different order. When parentheses are used, dBASE IV calculates from the innermost pair of parentheses and works outwards.

When used with character strings, the plus sign *concatenates,* or combines, strings of characters. As an example, "Mr." + "Smith" equates to the character string, "Mr.Smith".

The order of precedence for logical operators are NOT, then AND, then OR. If different types of operators are used within a single expression, the order of precedence is math and string operators, followed by relational operators, followed by logical operators.

Expressions

Expressions are combinations of fields, memory variables, constants, functions, and/or operators. The only rule governing what may be placed in expressions states that all elements of the expression must be of the same type. You cannot,

Table 3-2 Operators in dBASE IV

Type	Symbol and Meaning
Math (to perform operations with numeric results)	+ and − (unary) signs ^ and ** Exponentiation * Multiplication / Division + Addition − Subtraction () Grouping
Character string	+ Concatenation − Concatenation (strips any trailing spaces)
Relational	= Equal to <> or # Not equal to < Less than > Greater than <= Less than or equal to >= Greater than or equal to $ Substring contained within a string
Logical	.NOT. (Negation or complement) .AND. (Logical AND) .OR. (Logical OR) () grouping

for example, combine numeric elements and character elements within the same expression. Examples of valid expressions include:

```
(SALARY-(TAXES+2.78))
"Ms. " + LAST_NAME
"Robinson"
3.14159
```

The most commonly used expressions in dBASE IV programs are *numeric expressions.* These can consist of numeric memory variables, numeric fields, constants, or any combination of these, linked by any combination of math operators. All of the following are numeric expressions:

```
48
SALARY + 500.50
SALARY * HOURS
((SALARY * HOURS)+2.75)
```

Character expressions are also found throughout dBASE IV programs. *Character expressions* consist of character variables, the contents of character fields, or literal character strings enclosed in quotation marks, usually joined by a plus sign. Examples of character expressions are:

```
"Bob Smith"
FIRST_NAME + LAST_NAME
"Client name is: " + LAST_NAME
```

Memory Variables

dBASE IV allocates an area of memory for the storage of memory variables. *Memory variables* are storage areas set aside to contain data, which can be characters, numbers, dates, or logical (true/false) expressions. Memory variables are designated by assigning a value to a name for the variable.

Memory variable names can consist of a maximum of 10 characters. The first character must be a letter, and memory variables cannot use reserved words (for example, a memory variable named INDEX would be illegal because INDEX is a command verb).

In the dBASE IV programming language, memory variables must be created, or initialized, before they can be used within the program. This is in direct contrast to a programming language like BASIC, where memory variables can be created "on the fly."

Memory variables can be initialized in one of two ways: with the STORE command or as a part of an assignment statement. The syntax of the STORE command is:

```
STORE <expression> TO <variable list>
```

while the syntax of an assignment statement is:

```
<variable> = <expression>
```

The value stored to a memory variable can be a literal value, the contents of a database field, or the contents of another memory variable. For example, to store the word *Robert* to a memory variable called FNAME, either of the following commands could be used:

```
STORE "Robert" TO FNAME
FNAME = "Robert"
```

dBASE IV provides for four types of memory variables: character, numeric, logical, and date. *Character variables* contain strings of characters, which can be composed of a combination of letters, numbers, and punctuation symbols. *Numeric variables* contain numbers, which are recognized as numbers and not as characters by dBASE IV. You can perform calculations on numeric variables. Numbers stored in numeric variables can be whole numbers, or they can be fractional (decimal) numbers. *Date variables* contain dates that follow the dBASE IV date format. *Logical variables* denote a True or False value. Examples of commands for initializing all four types of memory variables are:

```
STORE "PC/XT" TO SYSTYPE
STORE 1344.85 TO SYSCOST
```

```
STORE {12/21/88} TO PURCHDATE
STORE .T. TO SRCONTRACT
```

The first example stores a character string, "PC/XT", to the character variable named SYSTYPE. The second example stores a numeric value, 1344.85, to a numeric variable named SYSCOST. In the third example, curly braces around a string of characters which follow a valid date format store a date value. The last example stores a logical value, True, to the variable SRCONTRACT.

Note that in each case, the type of memory variable (character, numeric, date, or logical) is ascertained by dBASE IV from the manner in which the data is supplied. For example, single or double quotation marks identify data as a character string. The letters T, F, Y, and N surrounded by two periods identify the data as a logical variable. Numbers are assumed to be numeric variables unless the numbers are enclosed in quotation marks. (Curly braces indicate dates.)

Dates represented by strings of characters can be directly stored to a memory variable with the curly braces, or various conversion functions can be used to convert the character data into a date variable. Use the proper syntax when declaring memory variables. You could get into trouble with a command like STORE "1344.85" TO SYSCOST because the quotation marks would tell dBASE IV that the enclosed characters compose a character variable. If you later tried to perform math calculations directly on the variable, dBASE IV would respond with an error message.

Memory Variable Limitations

Specific limitations apply to the use of memory variables. A maximum of 500 memory variables can be declared at any one time. The memory variables in use cannot occupy more than 128,000 characters. (Each character variable uses the number of characters in the string plus two; each numeric or date variable uses nine characters; and each logical variable uses two characters.) These values should be more than enough for all but the most demanding dBASE programs. You can increase the size of the memory available for use by memory variables by placing the MVMAXBLKS and MVBLKSIZE statements in the CONFIG.DB file. To do this, edit the CONFIG.DB file and add two lines of text that read:

```
MVMAXBLKS = <X>
MVBLKSIZE = <Y>
```

where <X> is the maximum number of memory variable blocks available, and <Y> is the number of memory variables stored within each block. The normal default is MVMAXBLKS = 10 and MVBLKSIZE = 50, providing 50 memory variables in each of ten blocks for a total of 500 possible memory variables. Keep in mind that increasing these amounts beyond the default values will use up a corresponding amount of your computer's memory. Every memory variable within a block uses another 64 bytes of your computer's memory. Expanded or extended memory cards can help, as dBASE IV will make use of extra memory beyond the 640K limit.

If the limitations of memory variables start presenting a problem, you can store and retrieve memory variables to and from disk, using the SAVE and RESTORE commands (covered in Chapter 5).

Displaying Memory Variables

To display the contents of memory variables at any time, use the DISPLAY MEMORY and LIST MEMORY commands. The commands perform the same function with one difference: LIST MEMORY will display the contents of all memory variables without pausing, while DISPLAY MEMORY will pause every 24 lines, and you must press a key to display the next 24 lines. Both commands will show the name of the memory variable, its type, the contents, and whether the memory variable is public or private (public versus private memory variables will be discussed in a later chapter).

The results of either of these commands are:

```
. display memory
      User Memory Variables

SRCONTRACT  pub  L  .T.
PURCHDATE   pub  D  12/21/88
SYSCOST     pub  N              1344.85  (1344.850000000000000)
SYSTYPE     pub  C  "PC/XT"

   4 out of 500 memvars defined (and 0 array elements)

      User MEMVAR/RTSYM Memory Usage

  2800 bytes used for 1 memvar blocks (max=10)
   850 bytes used for 1 rtsym blocks (max=10)
     0 bytes used for 0 array element memvars
     5 bytes used for 1 memvar character strings

  3655 bytes total
```

In addition to any memory variables created by dot prompt commands or by a program, the DISPLAY MEMORY command will also show memory variables for printer control within dBASE, and for any windows and menus which have been previously defined.

The ? command can also be used to display the contents of a single memory variable. The syntax of the command, when used in this manner, is:

```
? <variable>
```

As an example, the following command lines produce the results shown:

```
. ? systype
PC/XT
. ? syscost
     1344.85
. ? purchdate
12/21/86
```

Functions

dBASE IV also has 118 functions available for use by the programmer for performing various tasks. Functions can be thought of as special-purpose programs that perform tasks that would otherwise prove difficult or impossible to perform. In dBASE IV, functions are used to convert data from one type to another, to perform specialized math operations, to test for various conditions, and to manipulate data in various ways.

Functions always provide a value, and functions are used either as an expression or within an expression. The common format for a function is:

```
<name of function>[<expression>]
```

As an example, the Square Root (SQRT) function can be combined with an expression (in this case, a given number) to determine the square root of that number:

```
.? SQRT(9)
 3
```

Some functions are not used with an expression. These functions require only the name of the function to operate. An example is the DATE function, which returns the date maintained by the system clock:

```
? DATE()
10/26/88
```

Commonly used functions are described in the following groups of functions. A complete list of functions can be found in Appendix B.

Math Functions

Math functions are used to perform various math operations on a numeric expression. The numeric expression is enclosed in parentheses, following the name of the function. The expression can contain numbers, the contents of numeric fields, or a combination of both. A Math function always produces numeric data, although the data can readily be converted into another type of data with a Conversion function.

EXP: The EXP function provides an exponential value of a numeric expression. The syntax for the EXP function is:

```
EXP(<numeric expression>)
```

Example:

```
? EXP(.5)
1.65
.
```

INT: The INT function converts a numeric expression to an integer. Rounding to a higher number does not occur; instead, all digits to the right of the decimal place are ignored. (To round off numbers, use the ROUND function instead.) The syntax for the INT function is:

```
INT(<numeric expression>)
```

Example:

```
? INT(18.9995)
18

STORE 52.87 TO NUMBER
? INT(NUMBER)
52
```

MIN and MAX: The MIN and MAX functions return the minimum and maximum values, respectively, of two numeric expressions. The syntax for the functions is:

```
MIN(<numeric expression 1>,<numeric expression 2>)
MAX(<numeric expression 1>,<numeric expression 2>)
```

MIN returns the lower of the two expressions, while MAX returns the higher of the two expressions. Often in a program, one expression is the contents of a numeric field, and the other expression is a memory variable that contains some predefined high or low value.

As an example, the following code determines the higher of two expressions. One is a ceiling of repair costs, and the other is an actual figure for repair costs contained within a database.

```
*EXCEEDS.PRG lists ceilings exceeded for building repairs.
INPUT "Enter maximum value for repairs: " TO MAXVAL
USE REPAIRS
LIST COST, MAX(MAXVAL, COST)

. do exceeds
Enter maximum value for repairs: 150.00

Record#      COST MAX(MAXVAL, COST)
      1     56.00            150.00
      2    128.53            150.00
      3     69.90            150.00
      4    218.54            218.54
      5     78.77            150.00
      6    432.95            432.95
      7     45.67            150.00
```

ROUND: The ROUND function rounds off numbers, with a specific number of decimal places retained. The syntax for the ROUND function is:

```
ROUND(<numeric expression>,<number of decimal places>)
```

Example:

```
? ROUND(5.867,2)
5.87

? ROUND(5.867,0)
6
```

Note that if the numeric expression used to specify the number of decimal places is a negative value, the resultant value will be a rounded whole number, as shown in the following example:

```
? ROUND(5.867,-1)
10
```

Each negative value increase by 1 causes a rounding by the next power of 10. For example, −1 will round to the nearest 10, −2 to the nearest 100, −3 to the nearest 1,000, and so on.

SQRT: The SQRT (square root) function calculates the square root of a numeric expression. The numeric expression must be a positive number. The syntax for the SQRT function is:

```
SQRT(<numeric expression>)
```

Example:

```
STORE 25 + 24 TO TEST
? SQRT(TEST)
7
```

Character Functions

Character functions perform various operations on strings of characters: finding subsets of characters within a character string, converting lowercase to uppercase characters and vice versa, removing trailing blanks from a string, and so forth.

Most Character functions consist of the function name followed by a valid character expression.

LTRIM: The LTRIM function removes any leading blanks from a character string. The syntax of the function is:

```
LTRIM(<character expression>)
```

Example:

```
STORE 21 TO NUMBER
? STR(NUMBER)
   21

? LTRIM(STR(NUMBER))
21
```

LOWER: The LOWER function is used to convert uppercase letters to lowercase. The LOWER function has no effect on lowercase letters, numbers, spaces, or punctuation marks. The syntax for the LOWER function is:

```
LOWER(<character expression>)
```

Example:

```
STORE LOWER("SMITH") TO TEST
? TEST
smith
```

UPPER: The UPPER function performs the reverse of the LOWER function; it converts lowercase letters to uppercase. The UPPER function has no effect on uppercase letters, numbers, spaces, or punctuation marks. The syntax for the UPPER function is:

```
UPPER(<character expression>)
```

Example:

```
STORE "rotunda" TO TEST
? UPPER(TEST)
ROTUNDA
```

The LOWER and UPPER functions are useful to force consistency and to overcome problems caused by the case-sensitive nature of dBASE IV. As an example, if a record contains the name "JOHNSON" in a LASTNAME field, and the name is stored as shown (in all uppercase letters), a LOCATE statement using the following syntax would *not* find the record:

```
LOCATE FOR LASTNAME = "johnson"
```

But with a LOWER function used as follows, the name will be found regardless of whether it is stored in the database as lowercase letters, uppercase letters, or a combination of both:

```
LOCATE FOR LOWER(LASTNAME) = "johnson"
```

REPLICATE: The REPLICATE function repeats any character expression a number of times. REPLICATE is useful when used with the CHR function for drawing character graphics. The syntax for the REPLICATE function is:

```
REPLICATE(<character expression>,<numeric expression>)
```

Example:

To draw a series of 40 asterisks on the screen you could enter:

```
? REPLICATE('*',40)
****************************************
```

TRIM: The TRIM function (and its pseudonym, the RTRIM function) strip trailing spaces from a character string. The syntax for the TRIM function is:

```
TRIM(<character expression>)
```

The TRIM function is useful for removing white space between the contents of character fields that are combined as part of an expression, as shown here:

```
USE MAILER
GO 5
? FIRSTNAME + LASTNAME
Larry          Miller
? TRIM(FIRSTNAME) + " " + LASTNAME
Larry Miller
```

SPACE: The SPACE function creates a character string containing a specified number of blank spaces. The SPACE function is useful for initializing memory variables. The syntax for the SPACE function is:

```
SPACE(<numeric expression>)
```

where <numeric expression> translates to a value between 1 and 254.

Example:

```
STORE SPACE(15) TO GAP
? "System" + GAP + "Main" + GAP + "Menu"
System               Main                Menu
```

SUBSTR: SUBSTR is the dBASE IV Substring function. It is used to extract a portion of a character string from a character string. The syntax for the SUBSTR function is:

```
SUBSTR(<character expression>,<starting position>,<number of characters>)
```

Specifying the number of characters is optional. If it is not supplied, the character expression produced by the SUBSTR function will begin with the starting position specified and end with the last character of the character expression.

Example:

```
USE CLIENTS
GO 3
? PHONE
4156893212

STORE SUBSTR(PHONE,1,3) TO AREACODE
```

```
? AREACODE
415
```

Date and Time Functions

Date and Time functions are used to provide character or numeric values for all or parts of valid dBASE dates and times. The time is provided by the system clock. Valid dates can be provided by a dBASE date field or by the system clock.

DATE() and TIME(): The DATE() and TIME() functions provide the current date and time. The value provided by the DATE() function takes the form of a date variable, while the value provided by the TIME() function takes the form of a character variable. dBASE IV does not provide any function for setting the system clock date or time.

Examples:

```
. ? date()
10/26/88
. ? time()
15:48:51
. store date() to today
10/26/88
. store time() to rightnow
15:49:05
. display memory
       User Memory Variables

RIGHTNOW    pub  C  "15:49:05"
TODAY       pub  D  10/26/88

    2 out of 500 memvars defined (and 0 array elements)
```

CDOW: The CDOW function provides the day of the week, in the form of a character expression, from a date expression. The syntax for this function is:

```
CDOW(<date expression>)
```

Example:

```
. store date() to today
 06/01/86
. ? CDOW(TODAY)
 Sunday
```

MONTH, DAY, and YEAR: The MONTH, DAY, and YEAR functions provide a numeric expression equivalent to the month, day, or year, respectively, from a date expression. The syntax for these functions is:

```
MONTH(date expression)
DAY(date expression)
YEAR(date expression)
```

Example:

```
. store {12/22/75} to memdate
12/22/75
. display memory
       User Memory Variables

MEMDATE     pub   D  12/22/75

    1 out of 500 memvars defined (and 0 array elements)

. store month(memdate) to month
           12
. store day(memdate) to day
           22
. store year(memdate) to year
         1975
. display memory
       User Memory Variables

YEAR        pub   N                  1975  (1975.000000000000000)
DAY         pub   N                    22  (22.00000000000000000)
MONTH       pub   N                    12  (12.00000000000000000)
MEMDATE     pub   D  12/22/75
    4 out of 500 memvars defined (and 0 array elements)
```

Conversion Functions

dBASE IV offers a number of Conversion functions that you can use to convert data from one type to another. (The UPPER and LOWER functions can also be considered as Conversion functions; because these functions deal exclusively with character strings, they are listed under the Character functions heading.)

ASC: The ASC function is used to convert a character—or the leftmost character in a character string—into its equivalent ASCII value. The syntax for the ASC function is:

```
ASC(<character expression>)
```

Example:

```
. ? ASC("Nikki")
   78
```

CHR: The CHR function converts a numeric expression containing a valid ASCII value to the equivalent character. The syntax for the CHR function is:

```
CHR(<numeric expression>)
```

Example:

```
.? CHR(78)
 N
```

The CHR function is useful for sending ASCII codes to printers. For example, the code to switch most Epson-compatible printers into compressed printing mode could be sent with the following portion of program code:

```
.SET PRINT ON
 ? CHR(18)
.SET PRINT OFF
```

CMONTH: The CMONTH function converts the month contained within a date value into the character string (March, August, etc.) for the appropriate month. The syntax for the CMONTH function is:

```
CMONTH(<date expression>)
```

Example:

```
 ? DATE()
10/26/88

? CMONTH(DATE())
October
```

CTOD: The CTOD function is the character-to-date Conversion function. CTOD converts a character expression containing a string of characters formatted as a date into a date variable. The default for the format of the characters is MM/DD/YY, but this format can be changed with the SET DATE command. The syntax for the CTOD function is:

```
CTOD(<character expression>)
```

The character string supplied by the expression can vary from 1/1/100 to 12/31/9999.

Example:

```
. STORE CTOD("07/06/74") TO WEDDING
07/06/74

. DISPLAY MEMORY
WEDDING     pub   D  07/06/74
```

To create date variables, it is easier to use the curly braces than the CTOD() function. The CTOD() function is retained primarily to provide compatibility with dBASE III programs, as dBASE III and III Plus could not use the curly braces to create date variables.

DAY: The DAY function returns the numeric day of the month for the day contained within a given date value. The syntax for the DAY function is:

```
DAY(<date expression>)
```

Example:

```
? DATE()
10/26/86

? DAY(DATE())
26
```

DTOC: The DTOC function is the date-to-character Conversion function. DTOC converts a date expression into a string of characters. The format of the characters supplied by DTOC follows the current settings for display of dates, which you can alter with the SET DATE command. The syntax for the DTOC function is:

```
DTOC(<date expression>)
```

Example:

```
. STORE DTOC(WEDDING) TO TEST
07/06/74
.
. ? TEST
```

```
07/06/74

.
. DISPLAY MEMORY
WEDDING     pub  D  07/06/74
TEST        pub  C  "07/06/74"
```

DTOS: The DTOS() function converts a date to a character string in the format of YYYYMMDD. This function is ideal for indexing on a combination of date fields and character fields, to produce indexes that are arranged in true chronological order. As an example, the command:

```
INDEX ON DTOS(HIREDATE) + LASTNAME
```

would create an index based on a combination of the HIREDATE field, and where hire dates are the same, the last name.

DOW: The DOW function returns a number from one to seven. The number provided by DOW corresponds to the day of the week (Sunday being one, Monday being two, and so on, through Saturday, which is equivalent to seven) for the day within a given date value. The syntax for the DOW function is:

```
DOW(<date expression>)
```

Example:

```
? DATE()
10/26/88

? DOW(DATE())
4
```

MONTH: The MONTH function returns a number from 1 to 12, corresponding to the month of the year for the month contained within a given date value. The syntax for the MONTH function is:

```
MONTH(<date expression>)
```

Example:

```
? DATE()
10/26/88

? MONTH(DATE())
10
```

STR: The STR function is used to convert a numeric expression into a character string. The syntax for the STR function is:

```
STR(<numeric expression>,[<length>],[<no. of decimal places>])
```

The default string provided by the STR function will be rounded to an integer and will have a length of 10 characters. As an option, you can change the STR function's settings for the length for the character string and the number of decimal places to be provided. If you specify a length and that length is less than the number of characters to the left of the decimal, the STR function will return asterisks in place of the numbers. If you specify a number of decimal places, and the actual number of decimal places in the numeric expression is greater than the number specified, the expression is rounded off to the specified number of decimal places.

Example:

```
. store str(3.14159,8,2) to pie
    3.14
. display memory
PIE         pub   C  "     3.14"
```

VAL: The VAL function converts strings of numeric characters into numeric expressions. If the character string begins with a non-numeric character that is not a space, the VAL function will provide a value of zero. The syntax for the VAL function is:

```
VAL(<character expression>)
```

Example:

```
. store "1245.864" to first
 1245.864
. store "DB1245.864" to second
 DB1245.864
. ? val(first)
     1245.86
. ? val(second)
          0
```

YEAR: The YEAR function returns a number from 100 to 9999, corresponding to the value of the year contained within a given date value. The syntax for the YEAR function is:

```
YEAR(<date expression>)
```

Example:

```
? DATE()
10/26/88

? YEAR(DATE())
1988

STORE {04/05/2235} TO VULCAN
? YEAR(VULCAN)
2235
```

Specialized Test Functions

Specialized test functions are functions that are used to perform specific tests for various conditions. Such functions can be used to check available disk space, position of the printhead in a printer, record pointer present at the start or end of a file, and so on.

BOF: The BOF function is the Beginning-of-File function. BOF() provides a logical value of true if the record pointer is at the beginning of the database and a logical value of false if the record pointer is not at the beginning of the file. The syntax for the BOF function is:

```
BOF()
```

Example:

```
.USE MAILER
.? BOF()
.F.
.SKIP-1
.? BOF()
.T.
```

COL: The COL function provides the current column location of the cursor. The value provided by the COL function can be stored to a memory variable and used within a program to perform relative addressing (placement of data on the screen, with the position dependent on the current cursor location). For example, to display the contents of a memory variable, QUANTITY, at a position 10 spaces to the right of the current cursor location, this command could be used:

```
@ 8,COL() + 10 SAY QUANTITY
```

DBF: The DBF function provides the name of the currently active database file in the currently selected work area. The syntax for the DBF function is:

```
DBF()
```

Example:

```
USE REALTORS
? DBF()

C:REALTORS.DBF
```

DELETED: The DELETED function indicates records that are marked for deletion. The DELETED function provides a logical True (.T.) value if the current record has been marked for deletion. The syntax for the DELETED function is:

```
DELETED()
```

Example:

```
. use mailer
. delete record 2
      1 record deleted
. delete record 6
      1 record deleted
. display all last_name, city for deleted()

Record#  last_name      city
      2 *Smith          San Jose
      6 *Canion         Woodlands
```

DISKSPACE: The DISKSPACE function provides an integer value indicating the free space, in bytes, on the default disk drive. The DISKSPACE function proves useful in programs that create new files and perform automated backups as a menu option. The syntax for the DISKSPACE function is:

```
DISKSPACE()
```

Example:

```
. set default to c:
. ? diskspace()
  4898816
. set default to A:
```

```
. ? diskspace()
   279552
```

EOF: The EOF function is the End-of-File function. EOF() provides a logical value of True if the record pointer is at the end of the database and a logical value of False if the record pointer is not at the end of the database. The syntax for the EOF function is:

```
EOF()
```

Example:

```
.USE CLIENTS
.? EOF()
.F.
.GO BOTTOM
.? EOF()
.F.
SKIP
.? EOF()
.T.
```

ERROR: The ERROR function provides a value that corresponds to a program error detected during the execution of a dBASE IV program. The ERROR function, along with the MESSAGE function, is useful when you attempt a recovery from an error condition. The use of the ERROR and MESSAGE functions is more fully detailed in Chapter 13, "Debugging Techniques."

FILE: The FILE function checks for the existence of a specified file. This function is useful for preventing errors within a program that attempts to use a database or open an associated file that does not exist. The filename must either be enclosed in quotation marks or identified as a character variable. The file extension, if there is one, must be included as part of the filename. If the file does not reside on the default disk directory, a different directory may be specified as a part of the filename. The syntax for the FILE function is:

```
FILE(<filename>)
```

Example:

```
USE LAWYERS
IF FILE ("LAWINDX.NDX")
   SET INDEX TO LAWINDX
ELSE
```

```
    INDEX ON FIRMNAME TO LAWINDX
ENDIF
```

FOUND: The FOUND() function is used to test for the successful find of a record with a LOCATE, CONTINUE, SEEK, or FIND command. If the command used to search for the record is successful, the FOUND() function provides a logical value of true. Programs written in dBASE IV were limited to using an "IF EOF()" statement to test for a successful find, as shown in this program:

```
USE IFILES INDEX STOCKNO
INPUT "Stock number? " TO SNUMB
SEEK SNUMB
IF EOF()
     ? "No such record!"
     RETURN
ENDIF
```

Programs written in dBASE III Plus or in dBASE IV can accomplish this task with the FOUND() function. The result (and the amount of coding) is the same, but it is more visually evident to a reader of the program what task the function is performing.

Example:

```
USE IFILES INDEX STOCKNO
INPUT "Stock number? " TO SNUMB
SEEK SNUMB
IF .NOT. FOUND()
     ? "No such record!"
     RETURN
ENDIF
```

IIF: The IIF(), or "Immediate IF" function performs a conditional IF test of a logical expression, and returns one of two expressions if the condition is true. The syntax for the IIF() function is:

```
IIF(<logical expression>,<expression 1>,<expression 2>)
```

As an example of the IIF() function, the following line uses IIF() to evaluate whether a company employee is salaried or nonsalaried. If the individual is nonsalaried, a zero is stored to the variable, BENEFITS; if the individual is salaried, an amount equal to 5.7 percent of the salary is stored to the variable, BENEFITS, as shown here:

```
BENEFITS = IIF(SALARIED, .057*SALARY, 0)
```

The IIF() function is faster than the IF . . . ENDIF construction it can replace; it can also be used within reports and label formats.

INKEY: The INKEY() function provides a numeric value representing the ASCII code for the keyboard key most recently pressed. If no key is pressed, INKEY() returns zero as a value. The INKEY() function is useful to monitor the keyboard for responses and to perform actions such as must be taken by a user menu. The following example of program code uses the INKEY function and displays the resultant value provided by INKEY() on the screen.

Example:

```
*Inkey code displayed.
STORE 0 TO KEY
DO WHILE KEY = 0
     STORE INKEY() TO KEY
ENDDO
? "The value of that key is: "
?? KEY
```

ISALPHA: The ISALPHA function evaluates a character expression and provides a logical True value if that expression begins with an alpha character. In dBASE IV, an alpha character is any character between A and Z or a and z.

Example:

```
STORE "TX5400" TO FIRST
STORE "5400TX" TO SECOND

? ISALPHA(FIRST)
.T.

? ISALPHA(SECOND)
.F.
```

ISCOLOR: The ISCOLOR function provides a logical True (.T.) value if dBASE IV is running in color mode and a logical False if dBASE IV is running in monochrome mode. Using the ISCOLOR function, a program can test for the presence of a color environment, and the SET COLOR TO commands can then be used to vary colors as desired. The syntax for the ISCOLOR function is:

```
ISCOLOR()
```

Example:

```
USE CLIENTS
IF ISCOLOR()
   SET COLOR TO W/B, R/G
```

```
ENDIF
CLEAR
DO MENU
```

ISLOWER and ISUPPER: The ISLOWER and ISUPPER functions evaluate character expressions. The ISLOWER function provides a logical True value if the expression begins with a lowercase alpha character. The ISUPPER function provides a logical True if the expression begins with an uppercase alpha character. Both functions will provide a logical False if the first character of the expression is a nonalpha character (any numeral or punctuation symbol).

Example:

```
STORE "little words" TO FIRST
STORE "BIG WORDS" TO SECOND
STORE "10numbers" TO THIRD

? ISUPPER(FIRST)
.F.

? ISUPPER(SECOND)
.T.

? ISUPPER(THIRD)
.F.

? ISLOWER(FIRST)
.T.

? ISLOWER(SECOND)
.F.

? ISLOWER(THIRD)
.F.
```

LUPDATE: The LUPDATE function returns the date that you last updated the database file currently in use by the program. The value provided by LUPDATE is in the form of a date variable. The syntax for the function is:

```
LUPDATE()
```

Example:

```
USE MAILER
STORE LUPDATE() TO LASTDONE

DISPLAY MEMORY

LASTDONE    pub   D  07/09/86
```

MDX, NDX: The MDX and NDX functions provide the name of any open index file in the selected work area. The syntaxes for the MDX and NDX functions are:

```
MDX(<numeric expression>)
NDX(<numeric expression>)
```

where <numeric expression> provides a whole number. The value provided indicates the position, in sequential order, of the index file; as an example, the second index file named would be number 2, the fourth index file named would be number 4, and so on.

Example:

```
. use applican index last, rent, zip
. ? ndx(1)
 C:last.ndx
. ? ndx(2)
 C:rent.ndx
. ? ndx(3)
 C:zip.ndx
```

MESSAGE: The MESSAGE function returns a character string provided as an error message, when dBASE IV detects an error in a program. Both the MESSAGE function and the ERROR function are useful when you attempt a recovery from an error condition. The use of the ERROR and MESSAGE functions are more fully detailed in Chapter 13, "Debugging Techniques."

NDX: See MDX, NDX.

OS: The OS function provides the name and version level of the operating system under which dBASE IV is running. The OS function can prove useful for executing operating system commands from within dBASE IV, when those operating system commands may vary with the level of the operating system. An example is outlined in the following program, which provides an option to format disks. The expression returned by the OS function will be a character expression. The syntax of the OS function is:

```
OS()
```

Example:

```
*FMTDISK.PRG
*Format a disk in 360K format
STORE OS() TO OpSystem
```

```
IF OpSystem = "DOS 2.0" .OR. OpSystem = "DOS 2.1"
   RUN FORMAT A:
ENDIF

IF OpSystem >="DOS 3.0"
   RUN FORMAT A:/4
ENDIF

RETURN
```

PCOL and PROW: The PCOL and PROW functions provide current column and row positions for the printer printhead. Both functions are useful in keeping track of printer positions when writing sophisticated printer routines. The syntax for the functions is:

```
PCOL()
PROW()
```

Example:

```
. ? prow()
   0
. ? pcol()
   0
. set print on
.@ 2,5 SAY "Test of printer."
. set print off
. ? prow()
   2
. ? pcol()
  15
```

READKEY: The READKEY() function provides a value representing the key pressed by the user to exit from a full-screen command such as APPEND or EDIT. The READKEY() function provides one of two possible values: a value between 0 and 36 if no changes were made to the data while in the full-screen mode, or a value between 256 and 292 if changes were made to the data. Using the READKEY function, you can avoid storing records when the user presses the Esc or Control-Q keys to get out of the append or edit modes, while saving the changes if the user pressed Control-End (or its equivalent, Control-W). The example of code that follows uses READKEY() to accomplish this task.

```
*ADDRECS routine adds records; called from Main Menu
APPEND BLANK
READ
*test for user press of Escape or Control-Q.  If so,
```

```
*delete the new record
IF READKEY() = 12
    DELETE
ENDIF
RETURN
*end of ADDRECS.PRG.
```

The values provided by READKEY() in response to keys that can exit from a full-screen mode are shown in Table 3-3.

Table 3-3 READKEY() Values

Keys	Value from READKEY() (no change)	Value from READKEY() (data changed)
Right Arrow or Control-D	1	257
Left Arrow or Control-S	0	256
Up Arrow or Control-E	4	260
Down Arrow or Control-X	5	261
Control-Left Arrow or Control-A	2	258
Control-Right Arrow or Control-F	3	259
PgUp or Control-R	6	262
PgDn or Control-C	7	263
Control-Home or Control-]	33	289
Control-End or Control-W	270	270
Control-PgUp	34	290
Control-PgDn	35	291
Escape or Control-Q	12	12

RECCOUNT: The RECCOUNT function tallies the total number of records in the active database. The function outputs a numeric expression. With dBASE IV, it is no longer necessary to perform the old programmer's trick of opening a file with no index active, entering a GO BOTTOM command, then entering a STORE RECNO() TO <memvar> to find out how many records are in the database. The syntax for the RECCOUNT function is:

```
RECCOUNT()
```

Example:

```
USE C:LAWYERS
? "There are "
```

```
?? RECCOUNT()
?? "records in the database."
```

SOUNDEX: The SOUNDEX() function offers a way to match character strings based on the numeric "Soundex" code. This can be useful for finding an exact match when the user doesn't know the precise spelling of a term. The SOUNDEX function returns a code composed of a letter followed by three numbers, for any character string (or character expression) supplied to the function. The syntax for the SOUNDEX function is:

```
SOUNDEX(<character expression>)
```

The following commands, used to search a database for a last name that "sounds like" *Cannon*, demonstrate the use of the SOUNDEX function.

```
. use mailer

. index on SOUNDEX(last_name) to soundlik
    100% indexed          7 Records indexed

. accept "Last name? " to lname
Last name? Cannon

. findit = SOUNDEX(lname)

. seek findit

. display last_name, first_name, city, state

Record#  last_name       first_name      city            state
      7  Canion          Ron             Woodlands       TX
```

Working with Dates in dBASE IV

The inclusion of a date type for fields, and various date-related functions that interact with date values, have made it much easier to process dates than was possible with earlier versions of dBASE. A big advantage of the date fields used by dBASE IV is that they are stored internally as numeric values. This means you can (to a degree) perform math operations on date values; you can add a number of days to a date, producing another date; or you can subtract a date from another date, providing the number of days between the two dates.

Dates can be displayed in a number of formats, depending on the SET DATE command. However, they are always stored internally as YYYYMMDD, which keeps various operations (like date calculations, and indexing on date fields) chronologically correct. You can create a chronological index based on the contents of a date field by indexing on that field as you would index on any other field. As an example, the command,

```
INDEX ON HIREDATE TO DATES
```

creates an index file based on the contents of the date field, HIREDATE. To index on dates in descending order, use the DESCENDING option of the INDEX command. If you must write a program compatible with earlier versions of dBASE (which cannot directly index in descending order), use a command like:

```
INDEX ON CTOD("01/01/2199") - HIREDATE TO DATES
```

to build an index based on an expression that subtracts the date from some meaningless future date. Such an index file has the characteristics of an index created in descending order, and the TO clause (rather than the TAG clause) in the statement builds an index file compatible with dBASE III or dBASE III Plus.

The display of dates in dBASE IV can take on several formats, depending on the setting of the SET DATE command. The default value is American, which displays dates in a mm/dd/yy format. Another useful choice for formats is ANSI (American National Standards Institute), which displays dates as yy.mm.dd. If you transfer the contents of date fields to another software package using the versatile COPY options of dBASE IV, the other package will probably deal best with dates copied out from ANSI format. The remaining options of the SET DATE command include British and French (both display as dd/mm/yy), Italian (displays as dd-mm-yy), German (displays as dd.mm.yy), Japanese (yy/mm/dd), USA (mm-dd-yy), MDY (mm/dd/yy), DMY (dd/mm/yy), and YMD (yy/mm/dd).

To use the command, enter

```
SET DATE <type>
```

where "type" is one of the eleven acceptable formats—American, ANSI, British, French, German, Italian, Japanese, USA, MDY, DMY, or YMD).

If you need to break the date into character strings, use one of the Date Conversion functions described earlier in this chapter. As an example of the usefulness of these functions, you can combine them with the SET MESSAGE command to place the system date, in character format, at the bottom of the screen. A command like the following:

```
SET MESSAGE TO CDOW(DATE()) + ", " + CMONTH(DATE()) + " " + ;
LTRIM(STR(DAY(DATE()))) + ", " + LTRIM(STR(YEAR(DATE())))
```

would display a message like "Thursday, July 10, 1986" below the Status Bar.

One area that may cause potential problems in a date-intensive application is how you handle dates that stretch into the 21st century. Any @ . . . SAY . . . GETs that you use to edit the contents of a date field will by default assume that you are using dates from the 20th century. Investment databases managed with dBASE IV are encountering problems with this default century, because many bonds have maturity dates in the year 2001 and later. Fortunately, dBASE IV and dBASE III Plus have added the SET CENTURY command, which switches on the full four-digit display of dates. You must include a SET CENTURY ON command if you want to display or edit a year outside of the 20th century.

4

Program Flow in a dBASE IV Program

This chapter covers the use of multiple modules to construct a large dBASE program and how program flow is controlled within the modules.

Modular Program Flow

A well-known rule of programming states that any problem, no matter how large, can be easily solved if it is broken down into smaller, manageable pieces. dBASE IV lends itself to this philosophy by providing commands that enable control within a program to be passed back and forth between smaller parts, or modules, of a dBASE program. Until now, examples of dBASE programs have been fairly simple, with most programs following a straight program flow from beginning to end. In real life, applications are never simple enough to warrant a program flow that runs uninterrupted from start to finish without changing direction.

Most programming languages offer three types of control structures that let the user control the flow of a program, and dBASE is no exception. The different types of control structures are conditional structures, repetitive structures, and branching structures. Control structures are commonly used throughout a dBASE program to provide flexibility for users with different objectives in using the program. With control structures, you can design a program to deal with any one of a number of conditions or to respond to varying user requests.

Branching Controls: DO, RETURN, and RETURN TO MASTER

In a *branching control structure,* one program calls, or executes, another program. A branching structure enables the program to deviate from its normal (sequential) path. Figure 4-1 depicts two program sequences—one that performs no branching and one that does.

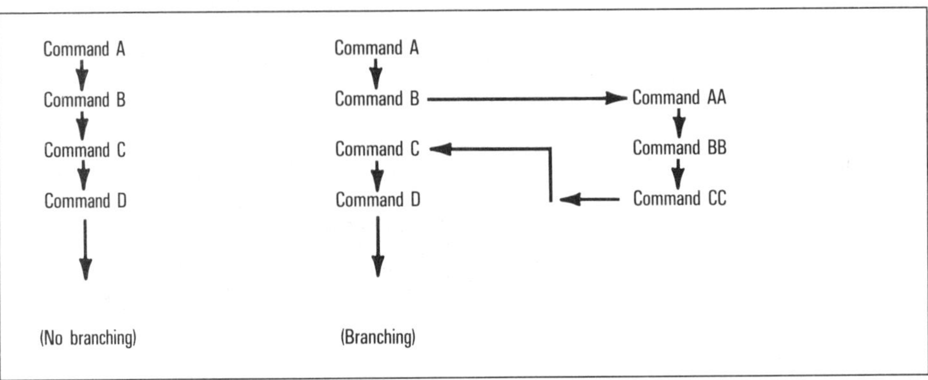

Figure 4-1 Concept of Branching

As described in Chapter 3, you use the DO command to run a dBASE command file (program). However, the DO command can also be used within a program to call (or branch to) another program. Once that program has finished the tasks required of it, control can be passed back to the original (calling) program with the RETURN command. In a sense, it's as if the commands contained within the other program file have become a part of the first program file. This type of program flow is illustrated in the program:

```
MAIN.PRG                    NOFIND.PRG


IF MZIPCODE <> ZIPCODE
     CONTINUE
     IF .NOT. FOUND()
       DO NOFIND            *NOFIND.PRG
                            *Prints a message if person isn't in database
                            CLEAR
                            @7,10 SAY "This person not in database!"
     ENDIF                  @8,10 SAY "Return to menu to enter"
ENDIF                       @9,10 SAY "new names, or to try different"
                            @10,10 SAY "name."
                            WAIT
                            RETURN
```

NOFIND.PRG can be considered to be a subprogram, or module, of the main program. When used within a program, the DO command transfers program control to the first line of the command file named by the DO command. Program control remains in that command file until a RETURN command is encountered (or until the end of the command file is encountered).

When the RETURN command is encountered, program control returns to the line immediately following the DO command that originally called the module, as shown.

The DO command is the only available method for transferring program control to another program module within dBASE IV. The dBASE programming

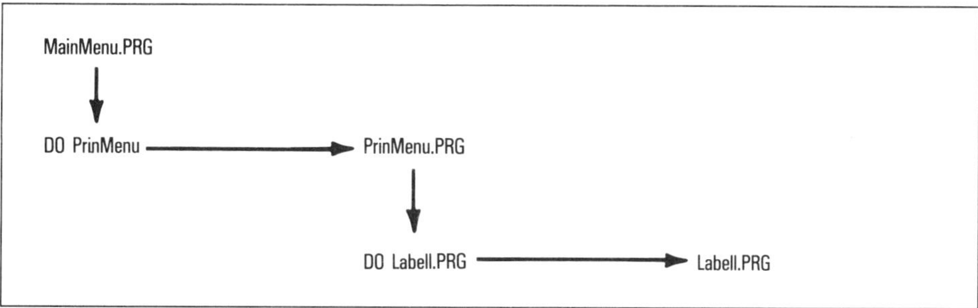

Figure 4-2 Nesting to the Third Level

language encourages structured programming by default; there is no equivalent to the GOTO command present in BASIC and similar unstructured languages. You cannot transfer program control to another part of the same program with the DO command; you can only branch to another module, or subprogram.

Branches to a submodule can be conditional (only occurring when a specified condition is met) or unconditional (always occurring at a given point within the program). The example just given of a branch is conditional; the program, NOFIND.PRG, is run only if the proper zipcode cannot be found in the file.

dBASE IV supports multiple nesting of subroutines, or submodules, within a program. Such nesting takes place when one program uses a DO statement to run another program, which uses a DO statement to run yet another program, and so on. Figure 4-2 illustrates nesting.

In theory, dBASE IV can open submodule after submodule, ad infinitum. However, in practice, dBASE is limited to having a maximum of 99 files (of any type) open at once. Your CONFIG.SYS must contain a FILES = 99 statement to permit dBASE to open the maximum number of files.

In most cases, RETURN is sufficient to end the execution of the submodule. However, a useful option of the RETURN command is RETURN TO MASTER. This option causes program control to be passed to the highest-level module of a program. Complex applications often require programs that are a number of levels deep. In such cases, a user request to return to the Main Menu (assuming the Main Menu is in the highest-level program) can be performed with a RETURN TO MASTER command, as shown in this example:

```
*PRINTER.PRG
DO WHILE .T.
? "Enter choice for desired subreport."
? "1. Summary report"
? "2. Detail report"
? "3. Return to Main Menu"
INPUT TO CHOICE
DO CASE
     CASE CHOICE = 1
```

```
          DO SUMMREPT
          RETURN

     CASE CHOICE = 2
          DO DETAIL
          RETURN

     CASE CHOICE = 3
          RETURN TO MASTER
ENDCASE
```

Effective use of the RETURN TO MASTER command makes it unnecessary for the user to wade through an annoying number of menus in a large application, just to get back to the first menu to choose QUIT. Occasionally, a dBASE programmer who is unfamiliar with RETURN TO MASTER will attempt to perform the same task by calling the highest-level program with another DO command, as shown in the portion of code that follows. Note that in place of RETURN TO MASTER, this (incorrect) version uses the DO command:

```
DO CASE
     CASE CHOICE = 1
          DO SUMMREPT
          RETURN

     CASE CHOICE = 2
          DO DETAIL
          RETURN

     CASE CHOICE = 3
          DO MAINMENU
ENDCASE
```

Don't be tempted to try such an anomaly. This sets up what is known in programming as a *recursive loop,* which means that a program is, in effect, trying to run itself. Seasoned dBASE II veterans may be guilty of this, because dBASE II lets you get away with this trick to a certain number of levels. dBASE IV will *not* let you use recursive programming; you will get "file is already open" error messages if you try it. And Murphy's law of dBASE coding #209 says that if you bury such an option in the 14th level of a massive application, you will forget to test it, and one of your program users will test it for you at the least convenient time!

Conditional Control Within a Program

Conditional controls are used to alter the flow of a program depending on the outcome of an evaluated condition. The most common use of conditional commands in a dBASE program is within the construction of an application's menus. dBASE IV offers two commands for conditional controls: the IF . . . ELSE . . . ENDIF command and the DO CASE command.

Using the IF . . . ENDIF Commands

The IF . . . ENDIF command provides a true/false evaluation of a given condition, enabling dBASE to perform one operation if the condition has a True value and a different operation if the condition's value is False. The syntax for the statement bears a resemblance to English, and in planning a program it helps to think of the statement as following the way in which the syntax is written:

```
IF <condition>
  <commands>
ENDIF
```

or, as an alternate method,

```
IF <condition>
  <commands>
ELSE
  <commands>
ENDIF
```

The IF and ENDIF commands are a matched set, so each IF command sequence must be closed with an ENDIF command. The ELSE command is optional, and can be used to denote an alternative path for program flow. If you omit the ELSE command, then all statements contained within the IF and the ENDIF commands will be carried out, if the condition specified is True. If the condition is not True, program control passes to the first statement following the ENDIF command. In the following example, an IF . . . ENDIF set of commands is used to evaluate whether a printing program will be executed.

```
IF CHOICE = 1
   DO PRINTER
ENDIF
```

In this example, no alternate path is provided; either the condition is True, and the PRINTER program is run, or the condition is False, and program control passes to the command immediately following the ENDIF command. In cases when you want an alternate path, the ELSE statement can be used to specify commands that will be executed if the evaluated condition is False. Consider this example:

```
IF CHOICE = 1
   DO PRINTER1
ELSE
```

```
    DO PRINTER2
ENDIF
```

In this case, if the condition is False (memory variable CHOICE not equal to 1), the command file named PRINTER2 will be run. Simple conditions can be replaced with very complex conditions, when necessary, to form the basis for the desired condition.

Using Immediate IF

With the IIF(), or *Immediate IF,* function you can duplicate an IF . . . ENDIF conditional structure within a single command, so you can use IF conditionals both within a program and from the dot prompt. The syntax for the command is:

```
IIF(<logical expression>,<expression 1>,<expression 2>)
```

It helps to think of the function as actually working something like this:

```
IF <logical expression> IS TRUE THEN,<expression 1> OTHERWISE <expression 2>)
```

As an example, consider the following IF . . . ENDIF construction:

```
IF AGE >= 21
     STORE "Legal drinking age" TO MSTRING
ELSE
     STORE "No alcohol to minors" TO MSTRING
ENDIF
```

Using the Immediate IF function, the entire construction could be accomplished within one line of a program:

```
MSTRING = IIF(AGE >= 21,"Legal drinking age","No alcohol to minors")
```

Use of the Immediate IF function provides two significant benefits. First, it speeds program execution time. Second, it can be used within an expression inside of a report or label form, so your users can produce reports or labels containing different data based on the logical expression provided by the IIF() function.

When you use complex conditions as a part of a program, take care to ensure that the conditional statements you design will achieve the proper results. The following command shows how things can get complicated with complex conditionals.

```
IF SALARY >= 22500
     IF EXEMPTION > 1
          DO TAXCALC1
     ELSE
          DO TAXCALC2
     ENDIF
```

```
ELSE
     IF EXEMPTION > 1
          DO TAXCALC3
     ELSE
          DO TAXCALC4
     ENDIF
ENDIF
```

The most common error when programmers design such conditionals is omission of a closing statement, which sometimes creates bizarre results.

Using DO CASE and ENDCASE

You use the DO CASE and ENDCASE commands when it is necessary to make decisions on any one of several conditions. The syntax for the DO CASE and ENDCASE commands is:

```
DO CASE
  CASE <first condition>
    <commands>
  [CASE <second condition>]
    <commands>
  [CASE <third condition>]
    <commands>
  [CASE <fourth condition>]
    <commands>
  [OTHERWISE]
    <commands>
ENDCASE
```

When dBASE IV encounters a DO CASE command, it begins evaluating the specified condition following each CASE statement, starting with the first one, until the software finds a CASE statement whose condition can be evaluated as True. Once such a statement is found, the commands identified by that statement are carried out. Execution then continues with the next command that follows the ENDCASE command. If no CASE statement in the series evaluates as True, then program control will proceed to the next command following the ENDCASE command, unless you have included the optional OTHERWISE statement. If the OTHERWISE statement is included, commands identified by that statement will be executed if no other CASE statements can be executed.

DO CASE commands are regularly used to design and implement menus, where one choice of a number of possible choices is normally appropriate, as shown in this example:

```
CLEAR
@ 3,10 SAY "P R O D U C T I O N  &  G R A P H I C S  D A T A B A S E"
@  7,26 SAY "1. Add New Records"
```

```
@  8,26 SAY "2. View/Edit Existing Records"
@  9,26 SAY "3. Delete an Existing Record"
@ 10,26 SAY "4. Print Reports"
@ 15,26 SAY "Enter 0 to Exit Program"
STORE 0 TO selectnum
@ 17,33 SAY " Select choice: "
@ 17,50 GET selectnum
READ

DO CASE
  CASE selectnum = 0
    CLEAR ALL
    QUIT

  CASE selectnum = 1
    SET FORMAT TO MYFORM
    APPEND
    STORE ' ' TO wait_subst
    @ 23,0 SAY 'Press any key to continue...' GET wait_subst
    READ

  CASE selectnum = 2
    SET FORMAT TO MYFORM
    DO MyEdit
    STORE ' ' TO wait_subst
    @ 23,0 SAY 'Press any key to continue...' GET wait_subst
    READ

  CASE selectnum = 3
    DO Eraser
    STORE ' ' TO wait_subst
    @ 23,0 SAY 'Press any key to continue...' GET wait_subst
    READ

  CASE selectnum = 4
    DO Reporter
    STORE ' ' TO wait_subst
    @ 23,0 SAY 'Press any key to continue...' GET wait_subst
    READ
ENDCASE
```

In the example, a number entered by the user is stored as a memory variable (SELECTNUM). The CASE statements then compare the contents of the memory variable SELECTNUM to each of the possible alternatives listed between the DO CASE and ENDCASE commands. When a match is found, the statements following that CASE statement are carried out, and the remaining CASE statements in the set are ignored.

Any choices made with a CASE command could also be carried out with multiple IF . . . ENDIF commands, so you may wonder when one approach is preferred over the other. Generally, if more than two pairs of IF . . . ENDIF commands are required, it is better to make use of CASE statements. Consider the following, which shows a simplified menu program using DO CASE, and its equivalent using IF . . . ENDIF commands:

```
? "Enter selection of 1 to 4."
INPUT TO CHOOSY
DO CASE
     CASE CHOOSY = 1
          DO MAKEREC
     CASE CHOOSY = 2
          DO CHANGREC
     CASE CHOOSY = 3
          DO REMOVE
     CASE CHOOSY = 4
          DO PRINTED
     OTHERWISE
          ? "Invalid entry!"
ENDCASE
```

```
? "Enter selection of 1 to 4."
INPUT TO CHOOSY
IF CHOOSY = 1
     DO MAKEREC
ENDIF
IF CHOOSY = 2
     DO CHANGREC
ENDIF
IF CHOOSY = 3
     DO REMOVE
ENDIF
IF CHOOSY = 4
     DO PRINTED
ELSE
     ? "Invalid entry!"
ENDIF
```

Not only are CASE statements easier to read, but they will be executed by the dBASE compiler slightly faster than an equivalent number of IF . . . ENDIF commands.

Repetitive Controls with DO WHILE and ENDDO

Many sequential processes performed by programs require some kind of repetitive, or looping process. Often, sequential processing of records in a database requires that some sort of operation be repeated once for each record in the database. The DO WHILE and ENDDO and the SCAN and ENDSCAN commands provide repetitive, or looping, capability within a dBASE IV program. The syntax for the DO WHILE and ENDDO commands is:

```
DO WHILE <condition>
   <commands>
ENDDO
```

All loops within a dBASE IV program are performed by a DO WHILE . . . ENDDO structure. Most loops are conditional; the loop is terminated when a specified condition changes. Some loops are unconditional. These loops never terminate on their own, but the looping procedure is effectively ended by a branch within the loop that calls another submodule of the program or exits to a calling program.

The process specified by the commands contained between the DO WHILE and ENDDO commands will be repeated until the condition specified as a part of the DO WHILE command is no longer true. Usually, the commands contained within the DO WHILE and ENDDO commands will include a statement that causes a change in the specified condition, resulting in the termination of the repetitive loop. Without such a statement, the loop would repeat endlessly. In this example,

```
DO WHILE .NOT. EOF()
   ? TRIM(FIRSTNAME) + " " + LASTNAME
   ? ADDRESS + CITY + STATE
   ? ZIP
   SKIP
ENDDO
```

the statements between the DO WHILE and ENDDO commands are repeated until the SKIP command causes the record pointer to reach the end of the database (EOF). Once this occurs, the condition specified as a part of the DO WHILE statement (.NOT. EOF()) is no longer true, so the loop terminates, and program control passes to the statement immediately following the ENDDO statement.

The common use of an unconditional (or endless) loop within a dBASE program is when the popular DO WHILE TRUE construction is used—usually to display a prompt or a menu until an appropriate choice is made by the user. Since no condition is specified following the DO WHILE command, a DO WHILE TRUE loop is always true, and the commands contained in the loop are repeated until one of the commands causes an exit, usually by running another module in the program. This use of the DO WHILE command is illustrated in this program:

```
DO WHILE .T.
   ? "Enter 1 for trial report, or 2 for summary report."
   INPUT TO CHOICE
   IF CHOICE = 1
      DO REPORT1
      RETURN
   ENDIF
   IF CHOICE = 2
      DO REPORT2
      RETURN
   ENDIF
   CLEAR
ENDDO
```

The user will be asked to enter a choice for printed reports. If any response other than 1 or 2 is entered, the loop will be repeated, and the user will again be asked to supply a valid choice.

Programmers should keep in mind that the DO WHILE . . . ENDDO loop provided by dBASE is a leading test loop, meaning that the condition to be tested is evaluated at the start of the loop, and if it is not true, the loop is never executed. In some cases, it is desirable to execute a loop once and then test for a condition to determine whether the loop should then terminate or be repeated. In such cases, it may be better to use an endless DO WHILE TRUE loop and use an IF ... ENDIF conditional statement just prior to the end of the loop to determine whether program execution should continue within the loop.

Using LOOP, EXIT to Terminate Loops

A repetitive loop can also be terminated with the LOOP and EXIT commands. The LOOP command causes program flow to return to the DO WHILE command that started the loop, for another test of the condition. LOOP is used to skip any conditional tests that follow the LOOP command, possibly saving some program execution time by immediately returning program control to the start of the DO WHILE loop, as shown in Figure 4-3. The EXIT command, which is considerably more abrupt in its action, causes program flow to leave the DO WHILE loop and continue at the first command following the ENDDO command. Both LOOP and EXIT should be used sparingly, as both commands interrupt the structured flow of a program, making the program logic more difficult to follow and debug. The program flow is illustrated in Figure 4-3.

Using SCAN and ENDSCAN

The SCAN and ENDSCAN commands provide a simpler alternative to the DO WHILE and ENDDO commands. Like DO WHILE and ENDDO, the SCAN and ENDSCAN commands form the basis of a repetitive loop. However, SCAN and ENDSCAN are designed to cycle through records, selecting records for processing which meet a specified condition. All commands between the SCAN

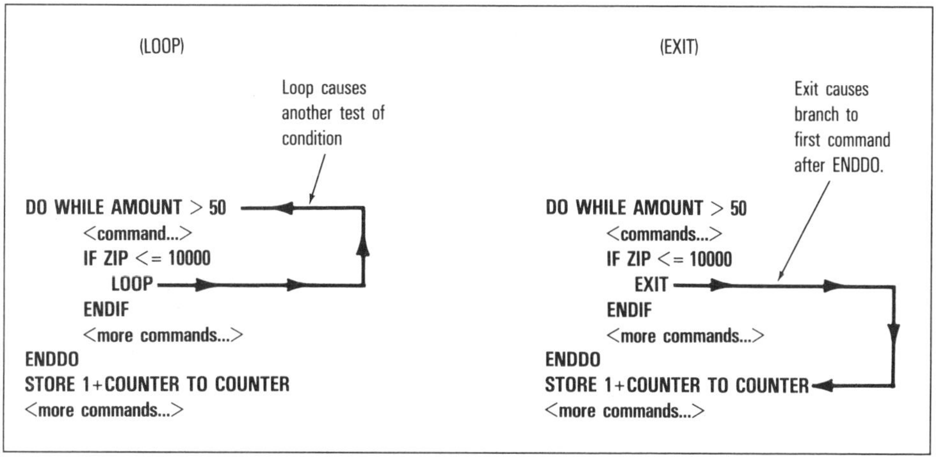

Figure 4-3 Effects of LOOP and EXIT

command and the ENDSCAN command are carried out when the record meets the condition. The syntax for the commands is:

```
SCAN [<scope>] [FOR <condition>] [WHILE <condition>]
      [<commands...>]
ENDSCAN
```

Because the condition can be described as part of the SCAN statement, the SCAN and ENDSCAN commands can often accomplish the same results as the DO WHILE and ENDDO commands, using less program code. Consider the following example, which prints a form letter for each record in a database which has a logical value of "false" in a field called PAID:

```
USE BILLS
SET PRINT ON
DO WHILE .T.
     IF .NOT. PAID
          ? trim(FIRSTNAME), LASTNAME
          ? ADDRESS
          ? trim(CITY), STATE, ZIP
          ?
          ? "Your account is seriously overdue.  Please remit"
          ? "payment of the past due amount immediately."
          EJECT
     ENDIF
     SKIP
ENDDO
SET PRINT OFF
```

When you use DO WHILE and ENDDO, you must add an IF . . . ENDIF conditional to select the desired records. The program shown below can accomplish the same task with SCAN and ENDSCAN:

```
USE BILLS
SET PRINT ON
SCAN FOR .NOT. PAID
          ? trim(FIRSTNAME), LASTNAME
          ? ADDRESS
          ? trim(CITY), STATE, ZIP
          ?
          ? "Your account is seriously overdue.  Please remit"
          ? "payment of the past due amount immediately."
          EJECT
ENDSCAN
SET PRINT OFF
```

The commands falling between the SCAN and ENDSCAN statements are carried out only when the condition named as part of the SCAN statement is true.

Single-Choice Versus Multiple-Choice Logic

The types of conditional commands that are appropriate often depend upon whether the programming task requires a single-choice decision or a multiple-choice decision. Single-choice decisions present a simple task to the programmer; normally, a simple IF . . . ENDIF set of commands will be sufficient to perform the job, as shown:

```
IF CURRSTOCK < 1
    STORE .T. TO OUTSTOCK
ENDIF
```

This type of decision is common in dBASE programs. Multiple-choice decisions, on the other hand, often require planning due to the variety of ways in which the choices can affect the flow of a program. When a multiple-choice decision is evaluated, the result may be to take a single course of action, a number of choices of action, or one course of action for a number of decisions. When a program contains a number of possible choices of which only one choice is to be executed, the CASE . . . ENDCASE commands are usually appropriate, as shown in the portion of the menu program here:

```
DO CASE
   CASE CHOICE = 1
      DO ADDER
   CASE CHOICE = 2
      DO EDITREC
   CASE CHOICE = 3
      DO PRINTREC
ENDCASE
```

In the example, only one course of action will result from the three possible choices. A different approach is needed in programming situations where a number of processes must be performed as a result of satisfying one condition. In such cases, it is usually more effective to use a combination of IF . . . ENDIF commands to test for all required conditions. Consider the following example, in which a value of 2 is entered in response to the user prompt:

```
? "Current inventory level?"
INPUT TO AMOUNT
IF AMOUNT < 10
   STORE AMOUNT TO REORDER
ENDIF
IF AMOUNT < 5
   STORE PARTNO TO XPRESSHIP
ENDIF
IF AMOUNT < 3
   DO NOTIFY
ENDIF
```

In the example, a value of 2 will satisfy all three IF . . . ENDIF conditional tests. Each condition is tested independently of the other conditions.

Still another approach can be taken when a decision must be based on a combination of conditions. One way to handle this task is to nest various IF . . . ENDIF commands within each other. The following example uses this approach to test for matching last names, first names, and zip codes in a mailing list program:

```
IF MLAST = LASTNAME
   IF MFIRST = FIRSTNAME
      IF MZIP = ZIPCODE
         EDIT
      ENDIF
   ENDIF
ENDIF
```

In the example, each condition is evaluated in sequential order. For the second condition to be evaluated, the first must be true, and for the third condition to be evaluated, the second must be true. If any of the conditions test as false, the desired action (execution of the EDIT command) will not be carried out. The same type of logic can be carried out with a single IF . . . ENDIF series of commands and logical functions, as demonstrated here:

```
IF MLAST = LASTNAME .AND. MFIRST = FIRSTNAME .AND. MZIP = ZIPCODE
   EDIT
ENDIF
```

Both examples cause the same analysis to occur within the program. Neither approach is necessarily correct for a given application. The first style is easier for the programmer to understand at a glance. When decisions grow complex (and they will), it becomes visually difficult to follow the logic in a command structured like the one in the second example. When complex logic is required within a program, it often helps to try executing various conditions from the dot prompt. This is an excellent way to discover what will and won't work before you write a complex condition as a part of a program.

Each of the basic control structures can be nested within other control structures, to any level required by the program, as depicted in Figure 4-4. When designing such programs, it often helps to draw lines between the matching statements, to avoid leaving out any of the closing statements.

Terminating Program Execution

Programs can be halted with the CANCEL and QUIT commands. The CANCEL command causes a program to halt, and dBASE IV displays the dot prompt. The QUIT command causes the program to halt, and dBASE IV terminates all op-

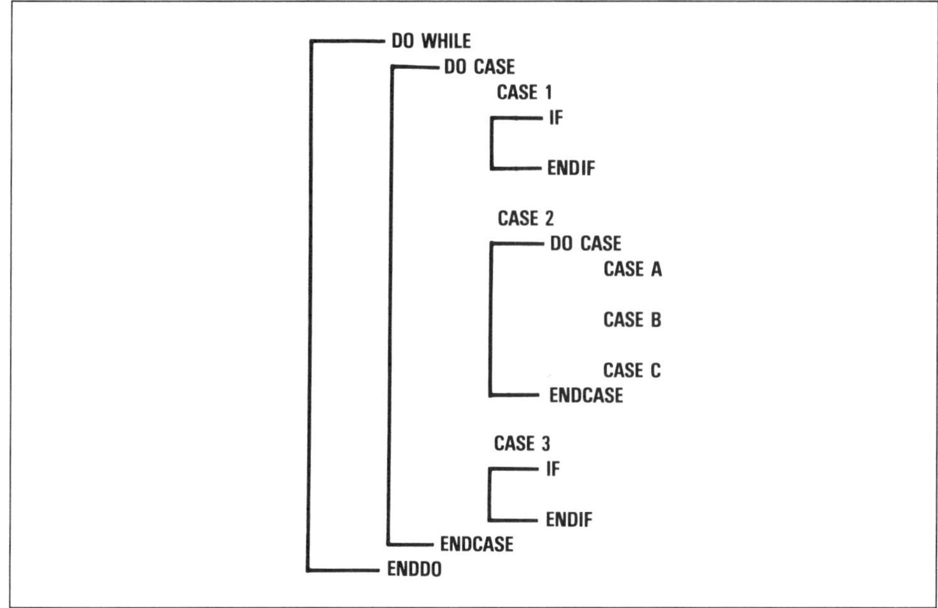

Figure 4-4 Nesting Control Structures

eration, displaying the DOS prompt. It is common to use CANCEL in a dBASE program during the development and testing phase. Before the program is turned over to the users, any CANCEL command should be replaced with a QUIT command that is normally an option from the application's main menu. Users should not be presented with an unexplained dot prompt that will only serve to confuse the inexperienced.

General Hints for Programming Logic

Some of the hints given here may not improve your program's performance, but they will make it easier for you and other programmers to decipher your programs.

First, be sure to use plenty of indentation in all repetitive structures and in decision-making structures. Indentations reveal the very logic structure of your programs, making the logic simple to decipher.

Second, place plenty of comments immediately after the END statements: ENDIF, ENDDO, and ENDCASE. dBASE IV ignores the rest of the line following any of these statements, so it is one of the few places within a program where you can add comments without slowing down the program. Since dBASE IV compiles your programs prior to running them, there will be no speed penalty from the use of indentations or comments. They will be stripped during the compilation process.

Finally, you will gain flexibility by using conditional (IF . . . ENDIF) structures inside of repetitive loops. If you use this technique, you can control repetitions of the loop, based on a wide range of conditions. If you instead resort to the condition that is a part of the loop itself (DO WHILE <condition>), you are more limited as to the number and the variety of conditions which can be used to control the loop.

5

More About Memory Variables

This chapter details how you can store memory variables in disk files for later use by a program and how you can use memory variables to control program flow. Also covered will be the uses of public versus private variables, and the use of arrays.

Memory variables are used for a number of tasks within dBASE IV programs. The most common tasks include (a) storing values the user enters in response to prompts, so that the values can later be acted upon by the program; (b) serving as a "scratchpad" for storing results of expressions, calculations involving functions, and the contents of program counters; (c) storing often-used prompts and messages; and (d) serving as a "validation" area for data that is to be stored in a database file once the user has verified that the information is correct.

Using Memory Variables for Program Control

Memory variables can be used as a part of conditional tests to directly control the execution of a dBASE program. The most common method of controlling program flow is to query the user by means of an on-screen prompt, store the response to a memory variable, and use that memory variable as a part of the decision-making logic within the program. Other common uses of memory variables to control program flow include branching or decision making based upon the result of a calculation involving a number of variables.

Programs can use logical functions (.AND., .OR., and .NOT.) to control program flow; the functions can be used to test the value of logical memory variables. As an example, the contents of a logical field named "NOTPAID" might be used to indicate the status of debts incurred by a customer. As each record in the database is scanned, the contents of the NOTPAID field could be stored to a memory variable named UNPAID. That memory variable could then be used as a part of an expression, to control a DO WHILE loop, as shown in this example:

```
USE BILLFILE
DO WHILE .NOT. EOF()
     STORE NOTPAID TO UNPAID
     DO WHILE UNPAID
          SET PRINT ON
          ? TRIM(FIRSTNAME),LASTNAME
          ? ADDRESS
          ? CITY + STATE + ZIP
          ?
          ? "Your unpaid balance is:"
          ? BALANCE
          EJECT
          SET PRINT OFF
     ENDDO the do-while unpaid
     SKIP
ENDDO the do-while not EOF
```

During each execution of the loop, the logical value present in the database field "NOTPAID" is stored as the memory variable, UNPAID. The DO WHILE UNPAID statement then evaluates whether UNPAID is true or false. If UNPAID is evaluated as true, the statements within the loop are executed, and the customer information is printed on an invoice form. The SKIP command increments the record pointer, and the loop repeats until the end of the file is reached.

Storing Memory Variables to Disk Files

dBASE IV can store any or all memory variables to a disk file. While the software's limit of 500 active memory variables should be sufficient for all but the most demanding applications, you may find yourself writing such a large application that 500 simply is not enough. A better reason for storing memory variables to a disk file is to provide permanent storage for often-used data that is not a part of the database. (When you use QUIT to exit dBASE IV, all memory variables are lost.) As an example, a simple password-protection scheme could maintain a file of passwords as a series of character variables within a disk file. The file could be read for password verification when a user attempts to access the system.

You save memory variables to disk with the SAVE command. The syntax for the command is:

```
SAVE TO <filename> [ALL LIKE/EXCEPT <memory variable name/wildcard>]
```

An example of the SAVE command, in its simplest form, is:

```
SAVE TO BILLMEM
```

By entering this command line, you save all memory variables presently available in memory to a disk file named BILLMEM.MEM. dBASE IV normally assigns an extension of .MEM to any memory variable file, unless a different extension is specified.

If the ALL LIKE/EXCEPT options are included, specific groups of memory variables can be saved to the disk file. Examples for the SAVE command combined with these options are:

```
SAVE ALL EXCEPT <memory variable name/wildcard> TO <filename>
SAVE ALL LIKE <memory variable name/wildcard> TO <filename>
```

To save the memory variables GROSSPAY, GROSSTAX, and GROSSDEDUC to a file named GROSSMEM, you could enter the command:

```
SAVE ALL LIKE GROSS* TO GROSSMEM
```

On the other hand, if you wanted to save only the memory variables with eight-character names, beginning with the letters "GROSS" you could use the following command:

```
SAVE ALL LIKE GROSS??? TO GROSSMEM
```

The EXCEPT option can be used in the same manner as the LIKE option, to exclude specific memory variables from the file. In the following example, all memory variables present except those beginning with the letters "PAY" would be saved to the file named MEMFILE:

```
SAVE ALL EXCEPT PAY* TO MEMFILE
```

You can also choose to specify the name of one memory variable, saving only that variable to a file, as shown:

```
SAVE PROFIT TO PFILE
```

In this example, only the memory variable named "PROFIT" will be stored in the file. Be warned that storing separate memory variables to individual files can consume large amounts of disk space, as each memory variable file normally consumes a minimum of 1,024 bytes, or 2,048 bytes under later versions of DOS, even if only one memory variable is contained in the file.

Restoring Memory Variables from Files

To restore the contents of a memory variable file, use the RESTORE command. The syntax of the command is:

```
RESTORE FROM <filename> [ADDITIVE]
```

An example of the command, in its simplest form, is:

```
RESTORE FROM MEMFILE
```

In this form, the RESTORE command will load all variables contained in the file named MEMFILE.MEM. Any memory variables presently contained in memory will be erased as a result of the RESTORE command. If you wish to keep existing memory variables and add new ones contained in a file, use the ADDITIVE option with the RESTORE command, as shown:

```
RESTORE FROM MEMFILE ADDITIVE
```

If you use the additive option, and a memory variable in the disk file has a name identical to a memory variable present in memory, the memory variable in memory will be overwritten by the memory variable in the disk file.

Deleting Memory Variables

Memory variables can be deleted from memory with the RELEASE command. The syntax for the command is:

```
RELEASE <memory variable list> [ALL [LIKE/EXCEPT <memory variable/wildcard>]]
```

Usage of the RELEASE command is similar to that of the SAVE command, with the ALL, ALL LIKE, and ALL EXCEPT options available to specify which variables should be cleared from memory. Examples of the RELEASE command include:

```
RELEASE GROSSPAY
RELEASE ALL LIKE PAY???
RELEASE ALL EXCEPT NETPAY
RELEASE ALL
```

Useful Commands for Creating Numeric Variables

dBASE IV offers the COUNT, AVERAGE, TOTAL, and SUM commands that can be used for various math operations on a group of records in a database. The COUNT command provides a tally of the number of records in the database that match specified criteria. The syntax for the command is:

```
COUNT [<scope>] [FOR <condition>] [WHILE <condition>] [TO <memory variable>]
```

As an example, to count the number of records containing “NC” or “VA” in the STATE field, and store that count to a variable named MIDEAST, you could enter a COUNT command for these results:

```
. count for state = "NC" .OR. state = "VA" to mideast
     3 records
 display memory
MIDEAST     pub   N          3  (         3.00000000)
```

The AVERAGE command finds the average (mean) value of a specified group of numeric fields or numeric expressions. The syntax for the command is:

```
AVERAGE <expression list> [<scope>] [FOR <condition>]
[WHILE <condition>] [TO <memory variable list>] [TO ARRAY <array name>]
```

As an example, to obtain the average cost for a particular individual, from a database containing a list of building repairs, you could use the AVERAGE command and see these results:

```
. use repair
. average cost for lastname = "Jackson" to jrepair
     3 records averaged
   cost
  94.89

. display memory
JREPAIR      pub   N          94.89  (         94.88666667)
```

The SUM command provides a total of numeric fields or expressions for a group of records in a database. The syntax for the SUM command is:

```
SUM [<expression list>] [<scope>] [FOR <condition>]
[WHILE <condition>] [TO <memory variable list>] [TO ARRAY <array name>]
```

As an example, to add all repair costs in the database and store the result as a memory variable, TOTALS:

```
. use repair
. sum cost to totals
     7 records summed
     cost
   961.70

. display memory
TOTALS       pub   N         961.70  (        961.70000000)
```

The TOTAL command can be used to sum numeric fields in a database and create another database that contains the summary of the totals. The syntax for the TOTAL command is:

```
TOTAL ON <key field> TO <filename> [FIELDS <list of fields>] [FOR <condition>]
[WHILE <condition>]
```

The resultant file generated by the TOTAL command contains summaries of all the numeric fields in the database in use. The database used to generate the summary totals should be sorted or indexed on the desired fields for the groups. Consider the following records, contained in a small database of videotape sales:

```
. use video
. list
Record#  SALEDATE NAME                      QUANTITY
      1  05/21/86 Back to the Future               4
      2  05/21/86 Beverly Hills Cop                2
      3  05/21/86 Gremlins                         2
      4  05/22/86 Gone with the Wind               1
      5  05/22/86 Gremlins                         1
      6  05/23/86 Star Trek III                    2
      7  05/23/86 Back to the Future               3
      8  05/23/86 Casablanca                       1
      9  05/23/86 Witness                          2
     10  05/24/86 Beverly Hills Cop                1
     11  05/24/86 Back to the Future               1
     12  05/24/86 Witness                          2
     13  05/21/86 Beverly Hills Cop                1
     14  05/23/86 Back to the Future               1
     15  05/24/86 Witness                          1
     16  05/23/86 Witness                          1
     17  05/22/86 Gremlins                         3
```

To total the tapes sold and store the contents as individual records in a summary database, the following commands could be used, with the results shown:

```
. use video
. index on name to alpha
   100% indexed          17 Records indexed

. total on name to summary
     17 Record(s) totaled
      7 Records generated

. use summary
. list name, quantity

Record#  name                     quantity
      1  Back to the Future              9
      2  Beverly Hills Cop               4
      3  Casablanca                      1
```

```
4  Gone with the Wind              1
5  Gremlins                        6
6  Star Trek III                   2
7  Witness                         6
```

As a result of the commands, all tapes sold having the same name have been totaled, and the resultant records with the numeric totals have been stored in a new database, named SUMMARY. The TOTAL command may come in handy for certain unusual operations; however, it is usually possible to achieve similar results with less complexity if you use the SUM and COUNT commands.

Public and Private Variables

All dBASE IV memory variables fall into one of two groups: public or private. *Public variables* are variables that are available to all submodules in a given dBASE program. *Private variables* are ones available only within the submodule that created those variables, and within all other modules called by that submodule. dBASE IV memory variables are private by default. dBASE II programmers should note this fundamental difference between dBASE II and dBASE IV; in dBASE II, variables are public to all parts of a program.

To illustrate the problem that can occur as a result of this characteristic of dBASE IV, consider the following programs and the display that results when the programs are run:

```
*MAIN.PRG
SET TALK OFF
INPUT "Enter number of hours worked: " TO HOURS
*run the salary program.
DO SALARY
*calculate the results.
STORE SALARY * HOURS TO GROSSPAY
? "Weekly salary is:"
? GROSSPAY
```

```
*SALARY.PRG
STORE 0.00 TO SALARY
INPUT "Enter salary per hour: " TO SALARY
RETURN
```

```
. do main
Enter number of hours worked: 43.5

Enter salary per hour: 5.75
```

```
Variable not found.
              ?
STORE SALARY * HOURS TO GROSSPAY
Called from - C:main.prg
```

The error reported by dBASE IV emphasizes the fact that the contents of a memory variable created within a submodule of a dBASE IV program cannot be directly passed from that submodule to a higher-level module. The memory variable, SALARY, which was created within the submodule (SALARY.PRG), is released from memory when the RETURN command passes program control back to the MAIN.PRG module. You could save the variable to a disk file and restore it in the higher-level module, but there is a faster way to pass variables from lower- to higher-level modules in a program. The PUBLIC command can be used to declare selected memory variables as public (available to all modules within a program). The syntax for the command is:

```
PUBLIC <list of memory variables>
```

The memory variables must be declared public before a value is assigned to the variables. A syntax error will result if the PUBLIC command is used after the memory variable has been created. By declaring the memory variable SALARY to be a public variable, the flaw in our sample program is solved, with the code and results shown:

```
*MAIN.PRG
SET TALK OFF
INPUT "Enter number of hours worked: " TO HOURS
*run the salary program.
DO SALARY
*calculate the results.
STORE SALARY * HOURS TO GROSSPAY
? "Weekly salary is:"
? GROSSPAY
```

```
*SALARY.PRG
PUBLIC SALARY
STORE 0.00 TO SALARY
INPUT "Enter salary per hour: " TO SALARY
RETURN
```

```
. do main
Enter number of hours worked: 43.5

Enter salary per hour: 5.75
```

```
Weekly salary is:
 250.125
```

Public memory variables are kept in memory when a program ends, so they can be displayed at the dot prompt using the LIST MEMORY or DISPLAY MEMORY commands. This is helpful during program debugging. Also, any memory variables created at the dot prompt are public by default. A common trick during the debugging stage is to create memory variables at the dot prompt and run parts of a program to test the effect on those variables. A common design technique used by many dBASE IV programmers is to initialize, or create, variables that must be used by all parts of the program in the header area of the highest-level module of the program (usually the main menu routine). By doing so, the programmer ensures that the memory variables will take on the characteristics of public variables in that they will be available to all levels of the program, even though they have not explicitly been declared as public.

The PRIVATE command can be used to perform the task opposite to the PUBLIC command. Declaring a variable as private hides that variable from view within any higher-level modules. The syntax of the command is:

```
PRIVATE <list of memory variables> [ALL LIKE/EXCEPT <memory variable/wildcards>]
```

Examples of the use of the PRIVATE command include:

```
PRIVATE AGE, SOCSECNUMB
PRIVATE ALL LIKE MEM???
PRIVATE ALL EXCEPT SALES*
```

Since dBASE IV memory variables are normally private by default, the PRIVATE command is less commonly used than the PUBLIC command. Usually the PRIVATE command is used to permit different values to be stored to the same set of variable names used throughout different modules of a program. Normally, private variables are released at the end of a program or when control is passed to a module at a higher level than the module that created the variables. Private variables can be released ahead of time, with the RELEASE command.

Parameter Passing

Memory variables can be passed from one program to another with less concern for conflicting variable names and declarations of public versus private variables, if you use a programming language feature included in dBASE IV, known as *parameter passing.* You pass parameters with the DO command and its WITH option. The syntax for the command is:

```
DO <program name> [WITH <parameters list>]
```

In the subroutine that is called by the DO statement, you must place a PARAMETERS statement at the start of the file. That statement must list the names of the variables that the parameters passed to the program should be stored under. As an example, the calling program could contain the line,

```
DO SUBPROGA WITH 59, 72, "Williams"
```

and the called program, SUBPROGA, would have a PARAMETERS statement like:

```
PARAMETERS <firstnum>, <secondnum>, <name>
```

The called program would then have available for use three variables: <firstnum> (containing 59), <secondnum> (containing 72), and <name> (containing the character string "Williams"). These variables could then be used by the program as desired. The PARAMETERS line must be the first executable command in the subroutine; only comments can be placed ahead of the PARAMETERS line.

Parameter passing is useful for similar tasks that must be done often throughout different parts of a program. For example, assume your program must be able to tell a user that a search for a record was unsuccessful. In any one of a dozen or so parts of a program, there may be a six or so lines of code that clear the screen and display something like:

```
This last name does not exist in the database!
Return to the main menu to choose a function.
Press a key to continue...
```

In one part of the program, the message may say, "This social security number does not exist." In another part of the program, the message may say, "This stock number does not exist." What it boils down to is that there may be dozens of lines of code in a large program that are being used to place what is essentially the same message on the screen. A far more effective way to do this is to build a submodule that contains the necessary code to place most of the message on the screen, and pass the part of the message that changes to the submodule in the form of a parameter:

```
*Program CANTFIND.PRG
PARAMETER Noun
*Display the 'can't find it' message
CLEAR
? "This " + Noun + " does not exist in the database!"
? "Return to the main menu to choose a function."
WAIT
RETURN
*end of CANTFIND.PRG
```

Then, when the message needs to be displayed, have the calling program run the submodule with something like:

```
DO CANTFIND WITH "Social Security Number"
```

The only hard and fast rule you must follow when it comes to parameter passing is that the number of parameters passed by the calling program must match the number of parameters specified in the PARAMETERS statement of the called program. If the PARAMETERS statement lists 2 variables, the list of parameters in the DO statement must contain 2 (not 1, 3, or 87) variables. Violate this rule, and your program will abruptly crash with an error message.

Normally, when a variable is passed to a called program with parameter passing, that variable is treated like a public variable. Any changes made to the variable by the called program will be made available to the calling program. In most instances, this either (a) is what you desire, or (b) does not matter. In those rare cases where you want the variable in the calling program to remain unchanged by any operations in the subroutine, you can surround the parameters with parentheses, like this:

```
DO PROGA WITH (20)
```

As an example, consider the following programs:

```
*MAIN.PRG
STORE 20 TO DontChange
? "Value is: "
?? DontChange
DO SUBFILE WITH (DontChange)
?
? "Back from subroutine.  The value is now: "
?? DontChange
*end of Main.PRG

*SubFile.PRG
PARAMETERS DontChange
STORE DontChange * 2 TO DontChange
RETURN
*End of subroutine
```

If the program (MAIN) is run as shown, the value of DONTCHANGE at the end of the program is still 20. If the program is run without the parentheses surrounding the variable name in the DO statement, the value of DONTCHANGE at the end of the program is 40, because it has been modified by the subroutine.

Of Memvars, Fields, Verbs, and Precedence

There is a specific precedence that dBASE IV employs to handle memory variables, field names, and command verbs when the same names are used. If there is any confusion about whether a word represents a variable, field name, or command verb, dBASE IV handles the precedence in this order:

1. Command verb
2. Field name
3. Variable name
4. Literal string

Obviously, giving fields and memory variables the same names, or giving a field name the same name as is used by a command verb can get your program into deep trouble. When in doubt, dBASE IV will follow its order of precedence, which may not be precisely what you had in mind. Some violations are flagrantly obvious–you would not name a submodule WHILE.PRG, because the first time you try to call the submodule with DO WHILE, dBASE will complain with a "syntax error" message.

Some problems caused by name conflicts are not so obvious. As an example, consider this database structure:

```
Structure for database: C:crazy.dbf
Number of data records:       2
Date of last update   : 06/29/86
Field  Field Name  Type       Width    Dec
    1  ACCTNO      Numeric        6
    2  INJURYDATE  Date           8
    3  MEMORY      Character    100
    4  CLAIM_AMT   Numeric        8      2
** Total **                     123
```

The database would work, but the first time you tried to show the contents of the field called MEMORY with a LIST MEMORY command, you would get this:

```
          User Memory Variables

    0 out of 500 memvars defined (and 0 array elements)

          User MEMVAR/RTSYM Memory Usage

      0 bytes used for 0 memvar blocks (max=10)
    850 bytes used for 1 rtsym blocks (max=10)
      0 bytes used for 0 array element memvars
```

```
    0 bytes used for 0 memvar character strings

  850 bytes total
```

Curiously enough, if you try to list the contents of the MEMORY field as one field in a fields list, dBASE IV then gives you what you want:

```
. list acctno, injurydate, memory
Record#  acctno injurydate memory
      1  100001 12/12/67   I have a poor memory.

      2  100002 04/30/52   I'll sue the hospital.
```

The results of name conflicts, then, can be inconsistent. It is better to use different names and avoid any possible conflicts. For the same reasons, most dBASE texts advise against naming memory variables with the same names as fields; in a possible conflict, dBASE IV will see the field name and ignore the memory variable name. You can safely use identical names for fields and variables if you use the memory variable prefix (M->) in front of any description of a memory variable, as shown in this example (the database, MAILER, contains a field called LAST_NAME):

```
. store "Test name" to last_name
. use mailer
. go 3

. ? last_name
Johnson

. ? M->last_name
Test name
```

Using Arrays

A major improvement of dBASE IV over earlier versions of dBASE is its support for arrays. An *array* is a group of items of a similar type, arranged in some sort of pattern. Such groups have dimensions: a one-dimensional array is a simple list of a single type of data, while a two-dimensional array is a table of data containing two discrete data types. Following is an example of a small one-dimensional array.

```
MONTH               SALES
============== ==============
January              1010.48
February             1170.50
March                1580.40
April                1490.70
May                  2155.22
June                 2372.18
July                 2090.45
August               2280.76
September            1417.70
October              1112.65
November              878.18
December             1715.90
```

And if the chart were to be extended to cover sales for each month across more than one year, we would have a two-dimensional array. Now, one could store and retrieve all of the data shown in a database file or as a dozen memory variables in a .MEM file. And if you've never worked with arrays, you may be quite content to handle any similar programming needs without using an array. Still, arrays are popular with programmers (most programming languages support arrays), and arrays can be fast at retrieving data.

Each item of data in an array is called an array element. The total number of elements in the array is equal to the number of rows multiplied by the number of columns. (If the array is one-dimensional, it has only one column; two-dimensional arrays have two or more columns.)

Before storing data to an array, you must first initialize it with the DECLARE command. The syntax for the command is

```
DECLARE <array name1> [<number of rows> [,<number of columns>]]
[,<array name2> [<number of rows> [,<number of columns>...]]]
```

For example, to declare a one-dimensional array called SALARIES containing 12 elements, you could use the command,

```
DECLARE SALARIES [12]
```

and to declare a two-dimensional array called MYSALES containing 60 elements in 12 rows by 5 columns, you could use the command

```
DECLARE MYSALES [12,5]
```

All arrays declared from the dot prompt are public values. Arrays declared within a program are normally private, unless you use the PUBLIC ARRAY command to declare a public array. To declare the same array called MYSALES shown above as a public array, you could use the command

```
PUBLIC ARRAY MYSALES [12,5]
```

Once the array has been declared, the STORE command or an assignment statement (=) can be used to store values to elements of the array. When storing the value to the desired array element, refer to that element by the name of the array, followed by the row and column coordinates of the element (put these inside brackets). For example, the statement,

```
STORE 217.45 TO MYSALES [6,4]
```

would store the value of 217.45 to the array element at row 6, column 4. The SCAN ... ENDSCAN or DO WHILE ... ENDDO commands are useful for rapidly storing multiple values from database files to arrays. The data in the arrays can then be used for calculations or other repetitive processing, at speeds faster than would be possible by reading the data directly from the database file each time.

Using Macro Substitution

dBASE IV offers a Macro Substitution feature that can be an invaluable aid during programming. Most dBASE descriptions group it along with the dBASE functions, although it is not a function in the true sense of the term. The dBASE Macro Substitution feature is actually a specialized operation that replaces a memory variable name with the actual contents of the memory variable. It is useful in those instances where dBASE IV would normally interpret what is actually a memory variable name as a literal string of characters. To use Macro Substitution, place an ampersand (&) in front of the memory variable name. Whenever dBASE IV would attempt to use the literal value of the name, the macro will tell dBASE to use the contents of the memory variable in its place.

Sample of Memory Variable Macro

As an example, if you wished to prompt the user for the name of a database file and then use that filename within a statement, the following commands would *not* be successful at this task:

```
? "Enter the name of the file to open."
ACCEPT TO DBNAME
USE DBNAME
```

dBASE IV would interpret "DBNAME" as the actual name of the database file to open, and a "file does not exist" error would likely occur as a result. The use of a macro would correct this flaw:

```
? "Enter the name of the file to open."
ACCEPT TO DBNAME
USE &DBNAME
```

When dBASE IV sees "&DBNAME," it will use the contents of the memory variable DBNAME as the name of the database file to be opened, rather than the literal character string DBNAME.

While a macro takes time to be processed and can often be replaced by some other means of coding, there are times when macros are invaluable aids. Operations on files when filenames are supplied in response to user prompts are one popular example. Consider these examples of a use of a macro:

```
. store "REP*.DBF" TO MYFILES
REP*.DBF
. List files like MYFILES
Database Files     # Records    Last Update     Size

None

4542464 bytes remaining on drive.

. List files like &MYFILES
REPAIRS.DBF          REPAIR.DBF
   1092 bytes in     2 files.
4542464 bytes remaining on drive.

. store "cost" to field1
. store "lastname" to field2



.set fields to &field1, &field2
.set fields on
.list
Record#      COST LASTNAME
      1     26.00 Burr
      2    348.53 Miller
      3     45.90 Darby
      4    245.67 Johnson
      5     87.34 Johnson
      6    565.78 Darby
      7     34.99 Easton
```

dBASE II programs have often used macros to perform a FIND in an indexed database to search for an expression previously stored to a variable. dBASE II programs commonly used code like this:

```
ACCEPT "Enter employee Social Security Number: " TO SEARCHER
FIND &SEARCHER
```

dBASE IV offers the SEEK command, which eliminates such a need for a macro. You can accomplish the same task in dBASE IV, and the program will run faster, if you use this instead:

```
ACCEPT "Enter employee Social Security Number: " TO SEARCHER
SEEK SEARCHER
```

A Warning About Macros and DO WHILE Loops

If you use a macro as a part of the condition for a DO WHILE loop, you should avoid changing the condition that is tested by the loop while control is inside of the loop. Otherwise, problems can occur, as the condition may not be reliably tested by dBASE IV. For example, consider the following portion of a program:

```
USE CLIENTS
STORE CLIENTNAME = "ABC" TO TEST
DO WHILE &TEST = CLIENTCODE
     <commands...>
     STORE CLIENTNAME = "XYZ" TO TEST
     SKIP
ENDDO
<more commands...>
```

The logic of this program appears correct, and in theory it is. But in practice, the compiler within dBASE IV handles DO WHILE loops in a special manner to save on program execution time. The commands in the loop are translated once and executed from memory as many times as necessary. If you change the condition that is represented by the macro, chances are the change won't be properly acted on, and your program may find itself in an endless loop.

6

System Design

This chapter outlines the major steps programmers follow as they design a dBASE IV database application, from planning through program documentation.

Steps in System Design

When you design a complex application, it's essential to follow certain design steps if the application is to remotely resemble what the user actually wanted in the first place. This chapter provides suggestions for proper design of an application in dBASE IV.

Proper application design can be broken down into eight specific steps. These are listed as a guideline for you first, then described in the remainder of the chapter's sections in more detail:

1. Obtain design specification from users (also known as *problem definition*)
2. Define the output requirements
3. Define the input requirements
4. Define the databases
5. Outline the application program
6. Write the program, using top-down design
7. Test and debug the program
8. Document the program for the users

Step 1. Obtain Design Specification from Users

This step can save you more time in recoding than any other step in this process. To different programmers, *design specification* means different things, and this is where you can get into trouble. Some programmers interpret a "design spec" to be a one- or two-line statement, as when an application user requests, "Give us a program to handle our mailing list; here are the categories (fields) we presently use." The programmer goes off and writes what he or she thinks is the ideal program and shows the completed program to the users. After the users have asked for two dozen or so changes to the program, it becomes clear that a more complete design specification should have been requested.

It is unfortunately rare for users to provide a clear design spec from the start. More often than not, you must make an effort to get the users to give you a complete design spec.

In a more complete design specification, each proposed field in each database is reviewed with the user. Are the fields long enough? Are the right types of fields being used? What kinds of data entry screens do the users want to see when entering data? If the program is for a group of users, it makes sense to initially meet with both the person who requested the program and with the users. Effective problem definition is a repetitive process that calls for an initial meeting with the users, then presenting proposed solutions, getting user suggestions, refining those proposed solutions, again meeting with the users, and repeating the process until the users and the programmer are thinking along the same lines.

Step 2. Define the Output Requirements

Starting with the program's output may seem like putting the cart before the horse. But program output is what's important to the users; data entry is just a means to an end. The whole intent in purchasing a database management package is to aid in gathering data that can then be compiled into some sort of report. The desired reports become critical in designing a system. What will the users want out of those reports? How will they want them formatted? What relationships must be drawn between multiple files to produce the desired reports? Often, users are not fully aware of what kinds of reports they can get, or even whether they really want printed reports or on-screen reports (in the form of a "data retrieval" screen that appears in response to a query).

A recommended approach is to take the contents of sample records from the proposed application and use that data to create sample "reports" that will be produced by the proposed system. Since not a single line of code has been committed to paper yet, you'll use something more conventional, like a word processor (or the user's typewriter, if you're desperate) to create sample reports. What's important is to create something that looks like what you think the finished product should represent. More often than not, the users will have something else in mind. And by taking a red pencil to these pseudoreports, you can create more concise plans for the actual reports that will be needed.

Step 3. Define the Input Requirements

Armed with the output requirements, you can proceed to develop, on paper, pseudodata-entry screens that the users will use to enter the data. This will seem like a marginally useful task only to those who haven't developed dBASE applications for a wide range of users. Those who have already know that users will make seemingly nitpicking requests for changes in the layout of the entry screens, and laying them out on paper at first will save much time revising the coding and layout of the entry screens.

Screens should also be designed to minimize possible errors by being clear, straightforward, and as foolproof as possible. (Note the term, "as possible"—for every programmer who thinks he or she has designed a truly foolproof system, there is a novice user lurking in the wings waiting to prove the programmer's assumptions were too great.) But common-sense additions, like clear messages, help screens, and effective error-handling subroutines can do a lot towards minimizing possible problems for users.

This is also the time to think about where all of the data will come from, and whether overall designs of the program can be adjusted to make the data-entry process simpler. If the job is currently being done manually, and the printed forms used to record the information are meeting the needs of the users, then it often makes sense to design entry forms in dBASE that mimic the existing forms.

If data already exists in other, somewhat incompatible sources (such as on magnetic tape or in the form of printed reports from some outmoded time-sharing system no longer in use), don't be too quick to write off such data as unusable for your application. Scanners can read in hard copy, and there is no shortage of firms that will convert computer tapes or 8-inch floppy disks to ASCII text on PC-compatible disks. Certainly your coding work will increase, as import routines must be written to convert such data to acceptable dBASE format. But the potential savings in reduced data-entry time may far exceed your increased programming time.

Step 4. Define the Databases

Once the output and input requirements are firm, the database designs can be laid out. If the first steps in the process have been followed, it should be clear what fields and what databases are needed to support the application. Relationships between multiple files should be determined at this point, and any unnecessary fields that were suggested during the design specification phase should be eliminated. You should also consider what key fields or expressions will work best in organizing the index files to offer fastest search and retrieval times.

Avoid the trap of duplicating unnecessary information in a database file. Instead, use the relational capabilities of dBASE IV to find the needed information within other database files. And finally, it is considered good programming practice to use names that make sense for files, fields, and variables. The reason is that it is easier to track logic with names like ACCOUNTS and HIREDATE than with names like X25 and ABF. Some programmers use the same name for database files as for primary index files. dBASE IV is quite content with this technique, although some dBASE compilers will not accept this naming scheme without problems.

Step 5. Outline the Application Program

Create a diagram showing the design of the main program and the submodules needed to perform the application. Include routines for the reports, labels, error-handling routines, and any help screens. If you are comfortable with computer flowcharts, they can prove useful for this purpose. Having a clear definition of the program structure pinned to a nearby wall helps when you are hours into the coding of a submodule and try to remember where submodule 47 must call submodule 16. Figure 6-1 shows a sample diagram.

Entire textbooks have been written on the benefits of structured design within programming, so such advice needn't be repeated in great detail here. In short, *structured design* emphasizes the use of program modules with simple, clearly defined tasks, and one entry, one exit for each module. The dBASE programming language lends itself to structured programming techniques, and such techniques will make your programs less complex, easier to write, and easier for you (or others) to debug or modify.

During the program design stage, a number of global decisions that will affect the individual parts of the program must be made. If the application is a transaction-based one (such as an inventory or client billing system), different modules must share common files and pass data back and forth within the overall program. Because of such interaction, complex applications can first appear to

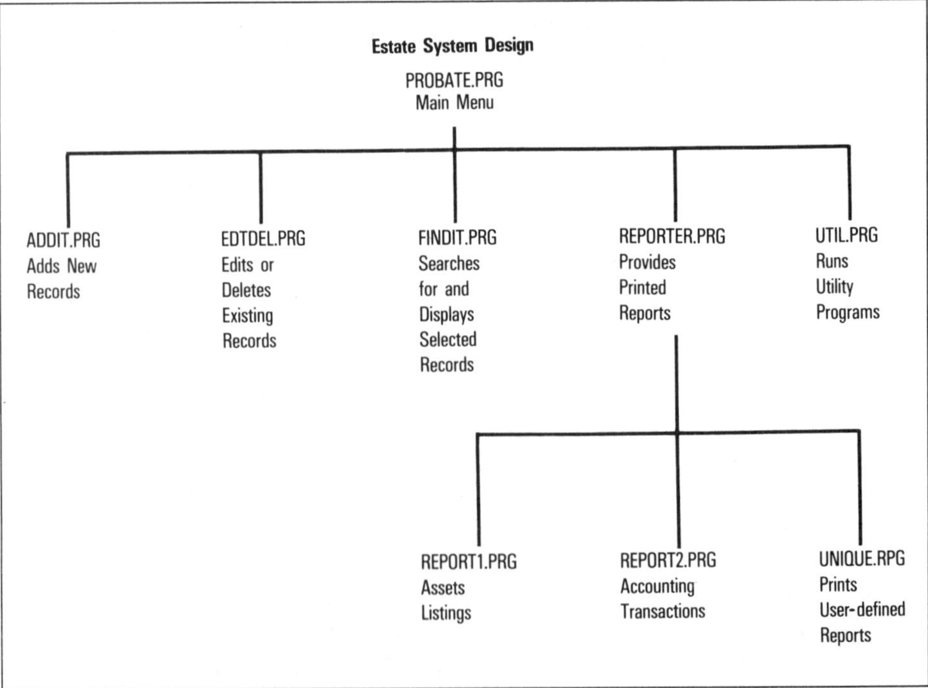

Figure 6-1 Sample Application Outline Chart

be massive tasks. But any large application becomes manageable as a programming task if it is broken down into a series of smaller, modular steps.

Step 6. Write the Program, Using Top-Down Design

Begin the coding of the actual application at the main menu, and work down, coding each respective module independently of most others. (To be precise, *top-down coding* refers to the practice of beginning the program implementation with the overall part of the program that controls program flow throughout the entire system. In most dBASE programs, this is the Main Menu.) If there are any secondary menus that will be called by the Main Menu, these should be designed after the Main Menu has been designed. By coding module by module from the top down, you can test the code as each module is completed.

An advantage of modular design that isn't readily apparent until you've written a few applications is that such modules can serve as part of your library of programming code, to be reused, with appropriate modifications, in future applications. This will drastically reduce the debugging time required for future applications and leave you free to concentrate on improving the application in ways that you have not used before.

It is also a good idea to make use of indentations and comments to clearly define what is going on within the program. You will need this clarity during the program refinement and debugging stage, and comments and indentations can always be removed in the interest of speed of execution once the users are satisfied that the program performs as advertised.

Step 7. Test and Debug the Program

This obvious step of running and debugging the code can be made much easier if you follow step 6. Program code that is written in modular form can be easily debugged a module at a time. When changes are needed, resist the temptation to make multiple major changes without testing the program after each change. If you make five significant changes to the code of a submodule, run the submodule, and it does something wildly different than what you had in mind, it may be difficult to determine which of the five changes resulted in the problem that is now occurring.

One step that all too often is overlooked at this stage is to try to make the program fail, and see if the results won't be too much for the users to handle. Place character data in numeric fields and numeric data in character fields. Press Return alone when data should be entered and choose menu selections that don't exist. Users will do all of these things—and more, and your program should be prepared to deal with these occurrences before its release.

Step 8. Document the Program for the Users

Provide the users with documentation that describes the operation of the program. Include steps clearly detailing what users should do when things don't go as they should. If you are designing a major application, you owe your users clear documentation that includes both a description of how the program works with a "sample" set of data (written at the new user level), and a section that provides a reference guide for more experienced users of the program.

Your documentation does not need to be as exhaustive (or as weighty) as Ashton-Tate's, but most applications deserve more than one or two pages of poorly written text stapled together that provide little more than a description of how to start the program.

High-quality print or electronic documentation includes:

1. a table of contents
2. sections to tell users how to add, edit, and delete records
3. a section describing how to prepare a report with the Report Generator
4. procedures for searching (querying) the database
5. a section describing the use of utilities (backup and file export routines are examples)

You also should include a tutorial section. Well-written tutorials contain examples of each common procedure the system performs or requires (for example, details about how to enter a sample record in the system).

Finally, for more experienced users it's helpful to include a reference section with shorter, one- or two-line explanations of the same tasks. Since these users have experience with the system and simply want a brief explanation of a particular function, you should make the reference section easy-access—an index for printed documentation will minimize users' frustration with locating the information they need.

If your users can benefit from on-line help, a dBASE IV program can provide such an option using the TEXT . . . ENDTEXT commands to display large blocks of explanatory help.

None of the eight steps of system design should be considered more important than the others. System design is a multiple-step process that provides the best results if all of the steps are followed. And adherence to the complete system design process will leave your users with an application that does the job, and that they understand.

7

User Input

This chapter details ways to place data and graphics on the screen in an attractive fashion to request user input, methods for accepting data from users, and ways to make effective use of menus in a dBASE IV program.

Screen Displays

dBASE IV writes to the screen using conventional row-and-column positions *(coordinates)*. The screen is divided into 25 rows of 80 columns. The screen coordinates begin in the upper left corner with row 0, column 0, and end in the lower right corner with row 24, column 79. Figure 7-1 shows the horizontal and vertical coordinates of the screen, as divided by dBASE IV.

The @ . . . SAY command can be used to place data at any screen location. The basic syntax for the command is:

```
@ (<row>,<col>) SAY <expression>
```

If the expression is a character expression, it must be enclosed in quotes. For example, to display the contents of the field LAST_NAME at the screen position of row 5, column 30, the command would be:

```
@ 5,30 SAY LAST_NAME
```

The expression used as a part of the @ . . . SAY command can contain any combination of valid field names, character strings, or numeric data. Functions can also be used with the @ . . . SAY command to provide desired formatting:

```
@ 12,5 SAY "Employee " + NAME + " is " + STR(AGE) + " years old."
```

results in the text,

```
"Employee Bill Smith is 34 years old."
```

displayed beginning at row 12, column 5.

There are a variety of options which can be used with the @ . . . SAY command, and the additional options are detailed in the text that follows. The complete format for the command, when used solely to display data on the screen, is:

```
@ <row>,<column> [[SAY <expression> [PICTURE <clause>]
[FUNCTION <function list>]] [COLOR [<standard> <,enhanced>]]
```

The PICTURE and FUNCTION options, which are described in detail in Chapter 8, can be used to force the displayed data to follow a certain format, such as all capital letters, or numbers displayed in a currency format. The COLOR option can be used to change the colors for the data displayed with the @ . . . SAY command. The syntax for the COLOR option is <std foreground/std background>, <enhanced foreground/enhanced background>, with the usual color codes used within the command. The standard colors change the colors used with the @ . . . SAY options, while the enhanced colors change the colors used with the GET

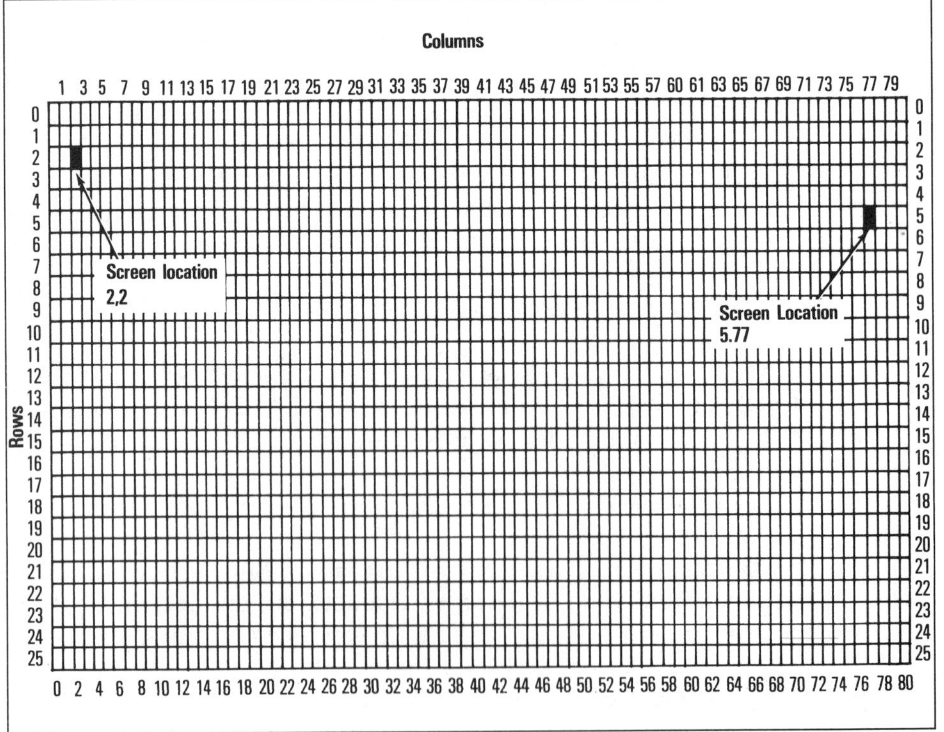

Figure 7-1 Screen Coordinates

option of the @ . . . SAY command, covered later in this chapter. As an example, the command,

```
@ 12,5 SAY "Employee name is: " + LAST_NAME COLOR B/W
```

would display the prompt with a blue foreground and white background.

Using TEXT and ENDTEXT to Write to the Screen

With the TEXT and ENDTEXT commands, you can write large blocks of text to the screen. The format for the TEXT and ENDTEXT commands is:

```
TEXT
<text to appear on screen>
ENDTEXT
```

Any number of lines of text can occupy the space between the TEXT and the ENDTEXT commands; an example of the use of TEXT and ENDTEXT is:

```
DO WHILE .T.
    CLEAR
    @2,0
    TEXT
                ESTATE TRACKING DATABASE SYSTEM

      (A)  Enter New Data to Assets
      (B)  Revise Existing Data in Assets
      (C)  Add New Data to Accounts Received

      (D)  Revise Existing Data in Accounts Received
      (E)  Print Reports
      (F)  FRAMEWORK Export of Client Data

      (G)  Other Utilities (Incl. Client File Maintenance)

      (H)  Use dBASE IV for Other Case Work

      (Q)  QUIT This System and Return to DOS
ENDTEXT
```

The text contained between the TEXT and ENDTEXT commands is displayed on the screen exactly as it appears in the program. The TEXT and ENDTEXT commands offer the advantage of requiring little attention to proper formatting. You needn't be concerned with precise screen locations or with the use of quotation marks around character strings when you use these commands.

On the other hand, there are definite drawbacks to the TEXT and ENDTEXT commands. You cannot include field names or memory variables as a part of the text. Special effects such as highlighting (covered later in the chapter) or a display of the current date and time are difficult or impossible with TEXT and ENDTEXT. The general appearance of a screen in a dBASE program is usually more attractive when well-planned with @ . . . SAY commands than when executed with TEXT and ENDTEXT. And if you are creating menus, dBASE offers commands to create bar and pop-up menus that are a major improvement over menus done with TEXT and ENDTEXT. However, help screens with large blocks of informative text are good candidates for the use of TEXT and ENDTEXT.

Clearing the Screen

The CLEAR command can be used to clear characters from a portion of the screen or the whole screen. The syntax for the CLEAR command is:

```
CLEAR
```

or

```
@<row,column> CLEAR [TO <row,column>]
```

The first CLEAR command line, entered without any screen coordinates, clears the entire screen. The second CLEAR command line clears a rectangular area extending from the first specified location to the second specified location. As an example, the command,

```
@ 5,10 CLEAR
```

clears all areas of the screen to the right of column 10 and below row 5. The command,

```
@ 15,40 CLEAR TO 19,60
```

clears a rectangular area whose upper left corner is located at row 15, column 40, and whose lower right corner is located at row 19, column 60.

The @ . . . FILL command can be used to fill a specific area of the screen with a desired color. The syntax for this command is:

```
@ <row 1>,<column 1> FILL TO <row 2>,<column 2> [COLOR <foreground/background>]
```

where <row1>, <column1> is the location for the upper left corner, and <row2>,<column2> is the location for the lower right corner. The foreground/background coordinates are the standard color codes used by the SET COLOR command. If the color codes are omitted, the @ . . . FILL command clears the screen in the defined area, making it equivalent to the @ . . . CLEAR command.

Getting User Input

User input can be obtained through a combination of commands; the most often used ones are the @ . . . SAY . . . GET and READ, ACCEPT, INPUT, and WAIT commands, and the ON SELECTION command used within menus. The @ command can be used with a number of options to place information or lines on the screen and to clear portions of the screen. The syntax for the @ command, when used solely to place characters on the screen and retrieve user data, is:

```
@ <row,column> [SAY <expression>][GET <variable/field name>]
```

The @ command has other options for formatting that will be covered in detail later. The SAY option is used to display the contents of the expression at the desired location on the screen. The command,

```
@ 12,20 SAY "Enter your password:"
```

would display the prompt indicated at row 12, column 20. The GET option displays a blank fill-in field that is highlighted in reverse video. The GET option can be used alone or in combination with SAY to display a prompt and allow user data entry. After one or more @ . . . GET or @ . . . SAY commands are encountered, a READ command is used to cause dBASE IV to read the values supplied by the user, and store those values to the memory variables or fields specified after the GET. If variables are used with GET, those variables must be initialized prior to the use of GET, or an error message will occur. There are additional options for the @ . . . SAY . . . GET command which let you validate the data entered. These options are covered in Chapter 8.

For example, you can initialize variables and then use a series of @ . . . SAY . . . GET commands, followed by a READ command, to prompt for user data:

```
CLEAR
STORE SPACE(30) TO NAME
STORE 0 TO AGE
STORE 0.00 TO SALARY
@ 5,10 SAY "Name?"
@ 5,20 GET NAME
@ 7,10 SAY "Age?"
@ 7,20 GET AGE
@ 9,10 SAY "Salary?"
@ 9,20 GET SALARY
READ
```

When the commands are encountered, the prompts and blanks in reverse highlight appear on the screen, as illustrated in Figure 7-2.

If field names are used instead of variables, the data entered into the highlighted fill-in fields is stored directly in the database. Such use of @ . . . SAY . . . GET commands is common as a replacement for the less-attractive EDIT and APPEND commands. However, direct entry of user data into databases is considered dangerous by many programmers, for reasons detailed in Chapter 8.

The GET and SAY options of the @ command can be combined on a single line. If you want extra space between the prompts and the data-entry fields, include spaces as a part of the character string following the SAY statement:

```
@ 5,10 SAY "Name?  " GET NAME
@ 7,10 SAY "Age?  " GET AGE
@ 9,10 SAY "Salary?  " GET SALARY
READ
```

If a field or existing variable is too long to fit on a single line when displayed with a GET, it normally wraps around to the next line. This may or may not be attractive; with large fields containing comments of text, the result is usually an unattractive word-wrap that often splits words in two. One way to deal with this is to use scrolling with the FUNCTION clause (described fully in Chapter 8), used with the GET command. With scrolling, you can move the cursor horizontally within the reverse-video blank displayed by the GET. The format for the GET command, when used with this option, is:

```
@ <row, column> GET <field name> FUNCTION "S<width of field>"
```

For example, if a database has a 200-character field called SUMMARY, the following command,

```
@ 8,20 GET SUMMARY FUNCTION "S50"
```

would create a 50-character wide reverse-video "window" into the field beginning at the cursor position indicated. When text is typed into the highlighted area, the text begins scrolling as the end of the window is reached to allow for more text to be displayed. You can also deal with large amounts of text by using windows.

Using Windows for Data Entry

You can place the data entry fields which result from GET statements inside of a window, with the WINDOW option which can be used with GETs. First, define

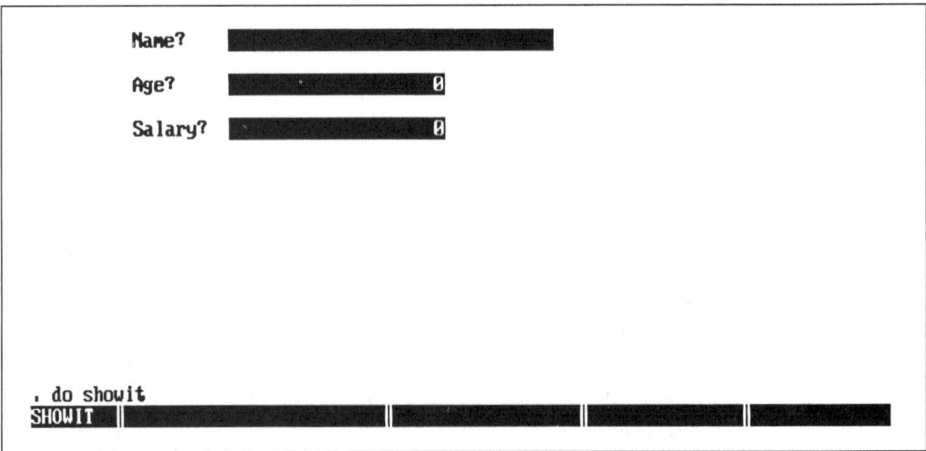

Figure 7-2 Appearance of Fill-In Fields from GETs

the desired window placement and dimensions with the DEFINE WINDOW command. The syntax for the command is:

```
DEFINE WINDOW <window name> FROM <row 1, column 1> TO <row 2, column 2>
[DOUBLE/PANEL/NONE/<border definition string>] [COLOR [<standard>]
[,<enhanced>][,<frame>]]
```

where <window name> is the name given to the window, <row 1, column 1> are the upper left coordinates for the window, and <row 2, column 2> are the lower right coordinates for the window. The DOUBLE/PANEL/BORDER/ <border string definition> options can be used to change the default border for the window, which is a single-line box. As an example, the command,

```
DEFINE WINDOW MyWind FROM 10,5 TO 18,60 DOUBLE
```

defines a window with the upper left corner at row 10, column 5, and the lower right corner at row 18, column 60. The window will be enclosed by a double-line border. After defining the window, activate it when you want to display the window with the ACTIVATE WINDOW command. The syntax for the command is:

```
ACTIVATE WINDOW <window name> / ALL
```

where <window name> is the name of the window defined earlier with the DEFINE WINDOW command. Using the ALL option activates all windows previously defined.

Note that once you've activated the window, any screen operations take place relative to the window, which means that screen coordinates of 0,0 are referenced to the upper left corner of the window, not the entire screen. If you've activated a series of windows with the ALL option of the ACTIVATE WINDOW command, the last window defined is the one which will be in current use. As you use the DEACTIVATE WINDOW command, any multiple windows will close in successive order until the first window that was defined is closed. You can use this effect to present a series of windows, to provide a "layered" or "tiled" look to data entry or help screens.

For simple editing of a large character field, you could define a window with the DEFINE WINDOW command, activate that window with the ACTIVATE WINDOW command, and display the data for the desired fields at desired locations within the window, using coordinates 0,0 as the window's upper left corner as a reference point. Consider the following simple program as an example:

```
USE LITIGATE
INPUT "Enter record number to edit: " TO ANS
GOTO ANS
CLEAR
@ 5,5 SAY "Please enter names of the people involved."
DEFINE WINDOW MYWIND FROM 6,5 TO 18,60
ACTIVATE WINDOW MYWIND
@ 1,1 SAY "Document Number:" GET DOCNUMB
```

```
@ 3,1 GET PERSONS
@ 7,1 SAY "Date of the document: " GET DOCDATE
READ
DEACTIVATE WINDOW MyWind
RETURN
*end of program*
```

After positioning the record pointer to the desired record with the GOTO statement, the DEFINE WINDOW statement is used to define a window which will be used for editing the desired fields. The ACTIVATE WINDOW statement is used to activate the window. The @ . . . SAY . . . GETs then display the desired data inside the window. If a field is too long to fit on a single line within the window, it is automatically wrapped to the next line at the window borders. (Note that you'll still have the problem of words being split at the right edge of long character fields.) The results of the program are shown in Figure 7-3.

After the desired entries or edits are made and Control-End is pressed (or the cursor moves past the last field), the DEACTIVATE WINDOW statement clears the window from the screen. When the window is deactivated, any screen text that was underneath the window prior to its being activated will reappear.

A single window can be used in the same manner to edit the contents of a memo field. Unlike long character fields, memo fields won't break words at the right margin when displayed in a window. Use the WINDOW option along with the name of the memo field within the @ . . . SAY . . . GET command, to display or edit the memo field in a window. The following code demonstrates an example:

```
DEFINE WINDOW MemoBox FROM 8,8 TO 18,65 DOUBLE
@ 7,5 SAY "Comments:" GET COMMENTS WINDOW MemoBox
READ
```

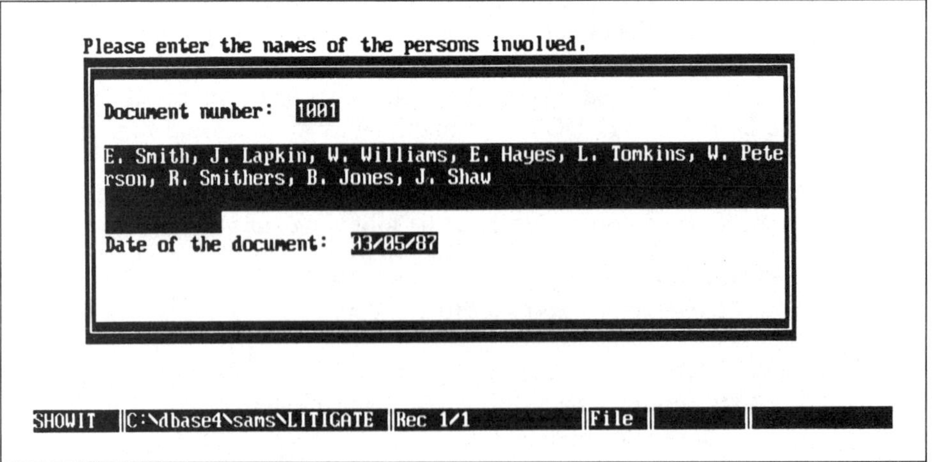

Figure 7-3 Use of Windows

In the example, COMMENTS is the name of a memo field in the database. When using the WINDOW clause of the @ . . . SAY . . . GET command with a memo field, you don't need to activate the window. The single statement,

```
@ 7,5 SAY "Comments:" GET COMMENTS WINDOW MemoBox
```

activates the window. Note that the window will not appear until you press Control-Home to enter the memo field. You can add the OPEN WINDOW <window name> option in place of the WINDOW <window name> option, to specify that the memo field window should open without the user's having to press Control-Home first. In this case, the statement would read as follows:

```
@ 7,5 SAY "Comments:" GET COMMENTS OPEN WINDOW MemoBox
```

and the memo field would open within the window as soon as the corresponding READ command was executed.

Multiple-Page Screens with READ and GETs

Each READ command causes a series of preceding GETs to be read, so you can use multiple READ commands as each screen fills with data. With this technique you can build multiple-page input forms that can be used with large databases, as shown in the following sample program:

```
@ 1,5 SAY "***Membership Data Entry Form***"
@ 3,5 SAY "Member Last Name:" GET L_Name
@ 5,5 SAY "First Name, Middle Init.:" GET  F_Name_M_I
@ 7,5 SAY "Title:" GET TITLE
@ 9,5 SAY "School:" GET SCHOOL
@ 11,5 SAY "School Address:" GET SCHADDR
@ 13,5 SAY "City:" GET CITY
@ 13,40 SAY "State:" GET STATE
@ 13,60 SAY "Zip:" GET ZIPCD
@ 15,5 SAY "School Phone:" GET SCHLPHONE
@ 17,5 SAY "Home Phone:" GET HOMEPHONE
@ 19,5 SAY "Sex:" GET SEX
READ
@ 2, 0 CLEAR
@ 2,5 SAY "Entry date:" GET EDATE
@ 4,5 SAY "Subscription started:" GET DATESTART
@ 6,5 SAY "Expiration Date:" GET EXPDATE
@ 7,5 SAY "Alumni (Y/N)?" GET ALUMNI
@ 7,40 SAY "Associates (Y/N)?" GET ASSOCIATE
@ 9,5 SAY "Honorary member (Y/N)?" GET HONMEMBER
@ 9,40 SAY "Sponsor (Y/N)?" GET SPONSOR
@ 10,5 SAY "Educator (Y/N)?" GET TEACHERS
@ 10,40 SAY "Student (Y/N)?" GET STUDENTS
```

```
READ
CLEAR
```

When the commands shown in the example are encountered, a series of highlighted fields will appear for all entries prior to the first READ statement. That screen remains in place until all entries are made. Once the cursor is moved out of the last field, the next screen appears. When the second screen has appeared, users cannot back up to the first screen with the cursor keys. If you want to provide users with such an option, use READ SAVE in place of the READ command. If you use READ SAVE, the contents of the memory variables named by the GET statements will not be cleared after use, as they normally are with a READ command. You must use the CLEAR GETS command to clear the variables for further use.

Using SET CONFIRM

Normally, the user can move from one entry to the next throughout a screen by simply filling in the screen. In some cases, you may want to force confirmation of an entry before allowing the user to move on to the next entry. In such cases, add a

```
SET CONFIRM ON
```

command to the program. The SET CONFIRM ON command causes dBASE IV to require the user to press Return before the cursor will move to the next entry. The SET CONFIRM OFF command will disable the effect.

Changing Delimiters

If you prefer a more visible marker for the start and end of your entry fields, you can use the SET DELIMITER TO and SET DELIMITER ON commands. These commands will add any characters as starting and ending delimiters. As an example, seasoned dBASE II veterans may prefer to:

```
SET DELIMITER TO "::"
SET DELIMITER ON
```

The delimiters specified must be enclosed in quotes and will appear at the start and end of the entry fields. As another option to alter appearance, you can turn off the reverse highlighting with a SET INTENSITY OFF command.

Using WAIT, ACCEPT, and INPUT

You also can use the WAIT, ACCEPT, and INPUT commands to obtain input from users; these commands are most appropriate when a single-character or one-line response is all that's needed by the program.

The WAIT command causes a pause in program execution and waits for a single key to be pressed. Once the user presses a key, program execution continues. The key pressed can be stored to a character variable for later use by the program. The syntax of the WAIT command is:

```
WAIT[<message>][TO <variable>]
```

The message is optional, and if you use it, be sure to enclose it in quotes. If no message is included, a default message of "Press any key to continue . . ." will appear. This example uses WAIT to indicate when a program can proceed:

```
? "Make sure the printer is turned on, then"
WAIT
SET PRINT ON
LIST L_Name, F_Name_M_I, SCHOOL, CITY, STATE
EJECT
SET PRINT OFF
```

If no message is desired, the default message can be shut off by using a null character variable ("").

Some programmers use WAIT as a way to obtain variables for a choice within menus. This is a matter of style, but keep in mind that somewhat contrary to its name, WAIT does not wait around for user confirmation; the program continues after the first key is pressed. If the user presses the wrong key, there is no opportunity to immediately recover. In most menus, the ON SELECTION statement combined with bar or popup menus is a better choice. These topics are covered later in this chapter.

The ACCEPT command requests input from the user and stores that input as a character string. The user entry is terminated by pressing Return. An optional message can be included as a part of the ACCEPT command; if included, it must be enclosed in quotes. The syntax for the command is:

```
ACCEPT [<message>] TO <variable>
```

It is not necessary for the variable to be initialized before you use ACCEPT. If no variable by the specified name exists, ACCEPT will create a new character variable by the name, and store the entry supplied to that variable. The following example illustrates the use of ACCEPT:

```
.ACCEPT "Enter name:" TO MNAME
  Enter name: Douglas
.ACCEPT "Enter amount:" TO MAMOUNT
  Enter amount: 245

.DISPLAY MEMORY
```

```
MNAME        pub   C  "Douglas"
MAMOUNT      pub   C  "245"
```

If the user simply presses Return in response to ACCEPT, a null ("") will be stored to the character variable. In programs, you can test for the null variable and use it to indicate an exit for a subroutine.

The INPUT command also requests input from the user and stores the data to a memory variable. However, INPUT is a more flexible command in that it does not necessarily store the data as a character variable. INPUT accepts any type of value or expression; even field names or the names of other variables can be entered. When you enter an expression, INPUT will first evaluate the expression, then store the result as the named variable. If a character string is to be supplied to INPUT, it must be enclosed in quotes. Date values can be surrounded by curly braces ({}). An optional message can be included as a part of the INPUT command; if included, it must be enclosed in quotes. The syntax for the command is:

```
INPUT [<message>] TO <variable>
```

Note the following examples of INPUT:

```
. INPUT "Enter name, in quotes: " TO VAR1
Enter name, in quotes: "Johnson"

. INPUT "Enter age: " TO VAR2
Enter age: 22

. INPUT "Enter a valid expression: " TO VAR3
Enter a valid expression: {02/24/52}


. DISPLAY MEMORY
VAR1         pub   C  "Johnson"
VAR2         pub   N            22  (          22.00000000)
VAR3         pub   D  02/24/52
```

If the response provided to INPUT consists entirely of numerals, dBASE IV will assume it to be a numeric variable. This makes INPUT a useful choice in accepting responses for a numbered selection from a menu. Like ACCEPT, the INPUT command does not require the existence of a variable before use. If the user simply presses Return in response to INPUT, the command will have no effect. If the variable named by INPUT already exists, it will remain unchanged. If it does not exist, it will not be created. This could cause an error if you use INPUT in a menu and the user presses Return without entering a value, so you should initialize variables used by INPUT ahead of time if you use INPUT to store menu responses.

The only noticeable disadvantage of the ACCEPT, INPUT, and WAIT commands is the lack of ability to precisely position the prompts on the screen. If aesthetics are important to you, you may prefer to use the ON SELECTION statement, or use @ . . . SAY . . . GET commands for all of your user prompts.

Handling the Esc Key

Since most software standardizes on the Esc (escape) key to terminate various operations, users often reach for Esc when they decide that what your program is attempting to do is not what they really wanted. Normally, dBASE IV terminates program operation if the Esc key is pressed. Then the software displays the "Cancel, Ignore, or Suspend" prompt in a window on the screen. This is not where you want your users to be, so you'll want to handle the Esc key in some other manner.

Earlier versions of dBASE were limited to turning off the response to the Esc key by placing a SET ESCAPE OFF statement within the program. dBASE IV also offers this command, and at the very least, you will want to disable the Esc key. However, if you prefer to provide some sort of message or close files in an orderly way and return to a main menu, you can do so with the ON ESCAPE command. The ON ESCAPE command, placed at or near the start of the program, causes the action specified as part of the ON ESCAPE command to be taken if the user presses Esc. For example, the statement:

```
ON ESCAPE DO ESCPRESS
```

cause the program, ESCPRESS, to be run if the user presses the Esc key. That program can then close any files, or the program can simply display a warning message and continue execution of the prior program. A portion of program code similar to the following could be used:

```
*EscPress handles pressing the Esc key
? CHR(7)
@ 24,0 CLEAR TO 24,78
@ 24,2 SAY "Do NOT attempt to interrupt this operation!"
WAIT
RETURN
```

Using Format Files with APPEND or EDIT

The full-screen dBASE IV commands such as APPEND and EDIT obviously don't present users with the most pleasing entry screen possible. But it's also tedious programming work to include a string of @ . . . SAY . . . GET commands at every needed location in a program that would otherwise use an APPEND or EDIT command. An alternative method is to use format files. *Format files* are text files containing the desired @ . . . SAY . . . GET commands. Format files are assigned an extension of .FMT. Once you have stored the desired @ ... SAY ... GET commands in the format file, you can invoke the use of the file with the SET FORMAT TO <filename> command. As an example, consider the following simple database structure:

Field Name	**Type**
LASTNAME	character
FIRSTNAME	character
ADDRESS	character
CITY	character
STATE	character

If the user opens the database and enters an EDIT command, the standard full-screen editing display appears. For a more visually pleasing screen, you can create a format file that contains the following:

```
*Formfile.fmt for myfile database
@ 5,5 SAY "Last name?  " GET LASTNAME
@ 7,5 SAY "First name? " GET FIRSTNAME
@ 9,5 SAY "Address?    " GET ADDRESS
@ 11,5 SAY "City?  " GET CITY
@ 13,5 SAY "State? " GET STATE
```

When the format file is opened with the SET FORMAT TO command, the display that results uses the fill-in fields and prompts contained in the format file. When you enter the SET FORMAT TO command,

```
.SET FORMAT TO FORMFILE
.EDIT
```

the screen shown in Figure 7-4 is displayed.

Using the Forms Design Screen

You can create format files in any of a number of ways: with your word processor (if it creates ASCII text files), with the dBASE word processor, or with the Forms Design Screen. The Forms Design Screen provides the easiest approach for creating complex screens. The Forms Design Screen is actually the latest incarnation of a utility that has been evolving along with dBASE over the years. dBASE II users knew it as ZIP, and users of dBASE III knew it as either dFORMAT or SED, depending on the version of dBASE III. Users of dBASE III Plus knew this feature as Screen Painter. The Forms Design Screen, however, is more flexible and straightforward than the earlier versions.

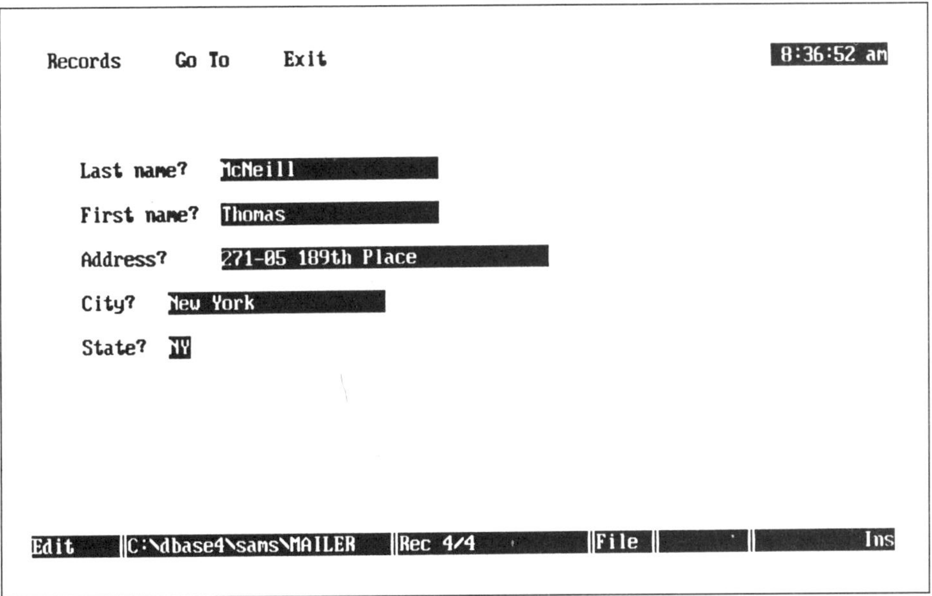

Figure 7-4 Results of Edit

The Forms Design Screen Menus

You run the Forms Design Screen with the CREATE SCREEN <filename> command. When you enter the CREATE SCREEN command, the dot prompt is replaced by a menu-driven system that uses a series of pulldown menus, an example of which appears in Figure 7-5.

The Forms Design Screen offers five menu options: Layout, Fields, Words, Go To, and Exit. Using the Layout Menu, you can select a default design for the form, based on the fields present in the database in use. You can also choose this option to select different database files for use with the form. The Fields Menu offers options for adding, changing, or deleting fields within the form. The Words Menu provides options which affect the display of text within the form, and the Go To and Exit Menus perform tasks similar to those found in the Go To and Exit menus in other parts of dBASE. Once a form has been designed and saved by pressing Control-End or by choosing the Save Changes option of the Exit Menu, the completed form is stored in a format file containing the necessary @ . . . SAY . . . GET commands to place the data on the screen.

The Forms Design Screen

To use the Forms Design Screen, open the desired database file, then enter

```
CREATE SCREEN <filename>
```

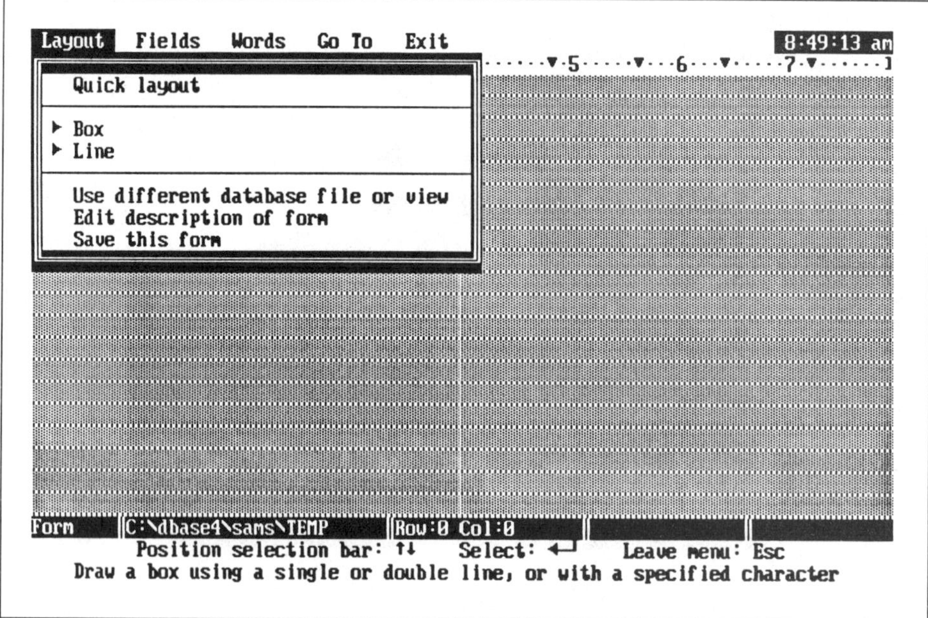

Figure 7-5 Forms Design Screen

where "filename" is the name for the format file. You then place the fields for data entry and editing at the desired locations on the screen. You can quickly place all the fields in a default location at the left margin by choosing the Quick Layout option from the Layout Menu. If you prefer to manually place the fields at the desired locations one by one, you can place the cursor at the desired location for the field, open the Fields Menu with ALT-F, choose Add Field, and select the desired field by name. Figure 7-6 shows the Forms Design Screen after the Quick Layout option of the Layout Menu was used to place all fields in a database onto the work surface.

Within the entire area of the work surface, you can position fields and prompts, and you can add any desired lines or boxes. To move any field, place the cursor in the field and press F6 (Select), then Enter, then F7 (Move). Move the cursor to the new location for the field, and press Enter to place the field. Figure 7-7 shows the results of using this technique to move the fields in the example to different locations on the work surface.

Characters for prompts you want to design can be entered or deleted from any location, using the cursor, Ins, or Del keys. The Ins key toggles in and out of insert mode; the effect is the same as insert mode in other areas of dBASE IV. In the example shown in Figure 7-8, the labels initially provided by the Quick Layout option were deleted, and more attractive names were added next to the new locations for the fields.

You can add lines or boxes to the display by using the Box or Line options from the Layout Menu. Open the Layout Menu with ALT-L, and choose Line or Box, then choose the desired type of line or box (single or double lines are

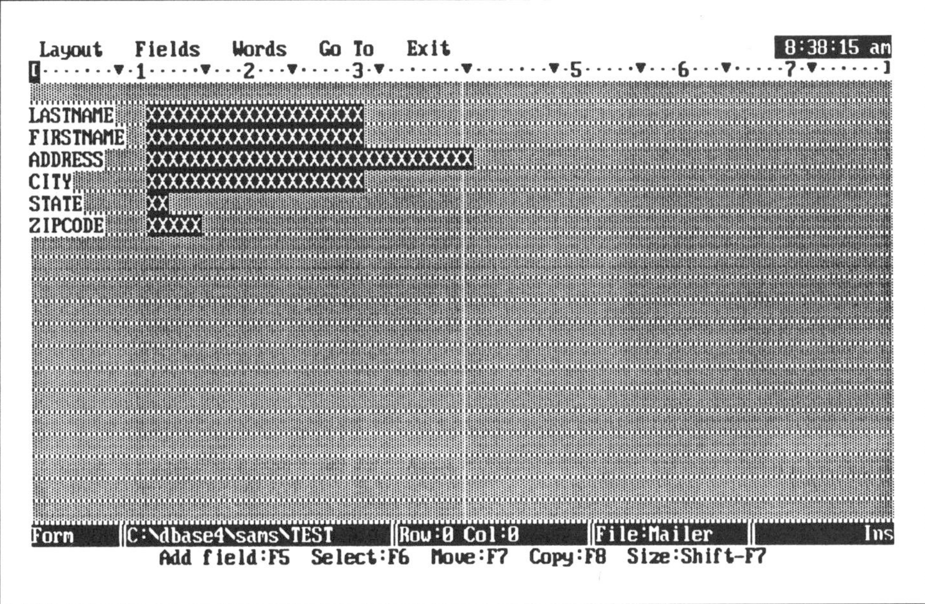

Figure 7-6 Forms Design Screen After Use of Quick Layout Option

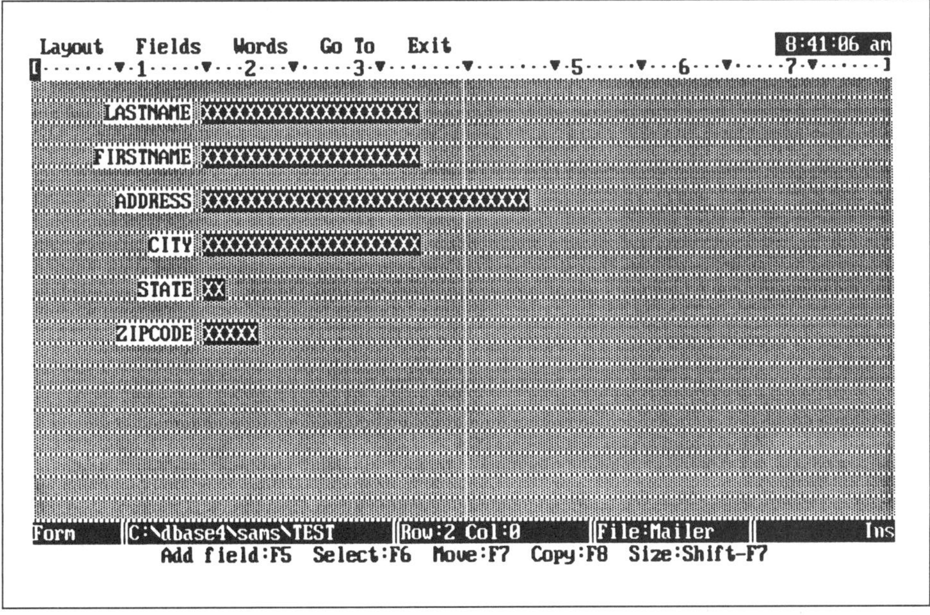

Figure 7-7 New Locations for Fields

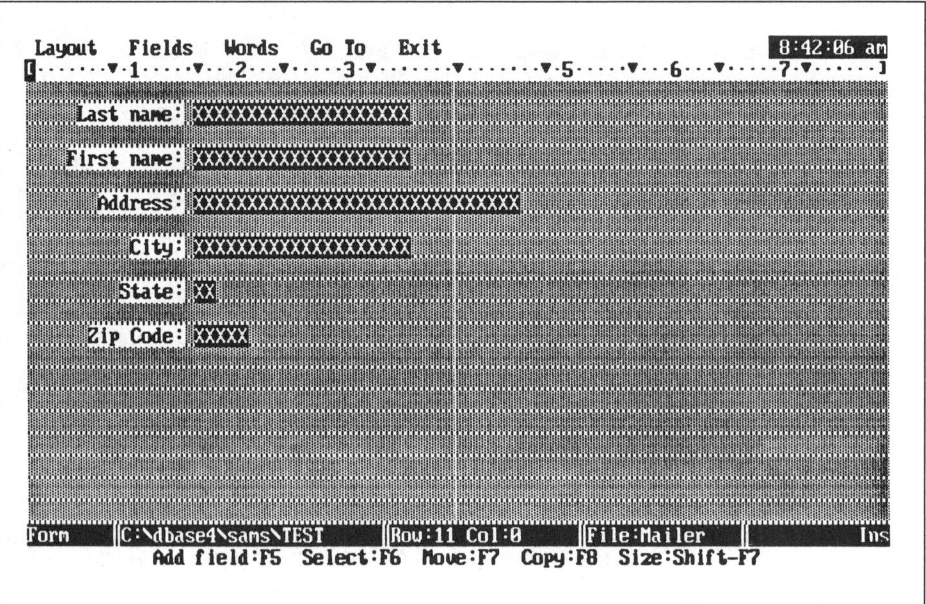

Figure 7-8 New Descriptions for Fields

available) from the next menu to appear. Place the cursor at one end of the line (upper left corner if you are drawing a box) and press Enter; then move the cursor to the other end (lower right corner if you are drawing a box), and press Enter again. Figure 7-9 shows the effect of a double line box drawn from row 2, column 1 to row 14, column 52 in the example.

If you have memo fields in the form, they can be displayed within windows by choosing the Display As Marker/Window option from the Modify Fields menu. Place the cursor in the memo field, and open the Fields Menu with ALT-F; then, choose Modify Fields. From the next menu that appears, choose Display As Marker/Window to change the default style of memo field display from a marker to a window. You will then need to use the Size (Shift-F7) and the Move (F7) keys, along with the cursor keys, to resize and move the memo field window until it is at the desired location on your screen.

Changing the Display Characteristics of a Field

You can change the display characteristics of specific fields by using the Modify Field option of the Fields Menu. A series of template, picture functions, and edit options available from the Modify Field menu option let you alter the way data is displayed or entered, and limit a user's ability to edit specific fields. To use these options, place the cursor in the field you want to modify, then open the Fields Menu with ALT-F, and choose Modify Field. Once you select this option, another menu appears, similar to the example shown in Figure 7-10.

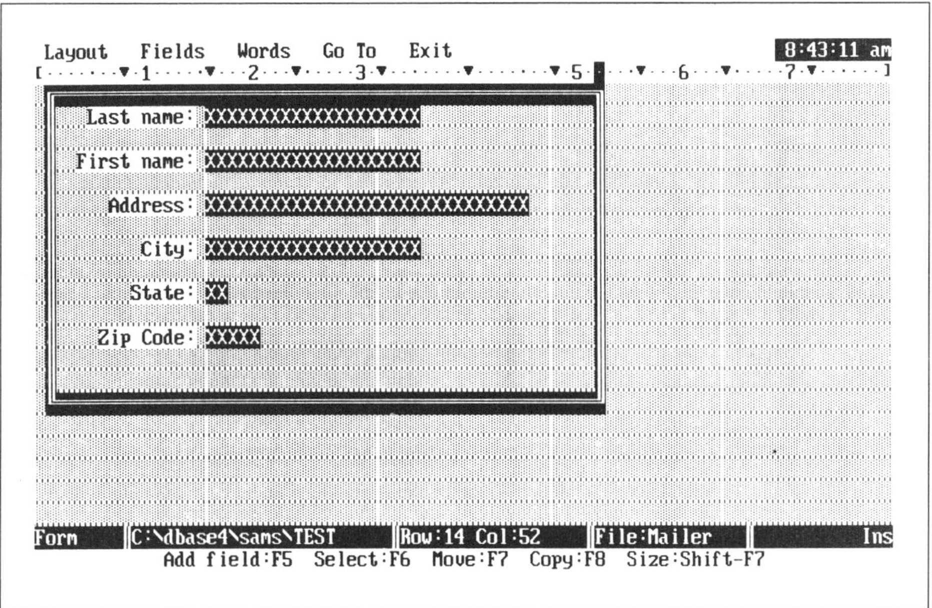

Figure 7-9 Drawing Lines

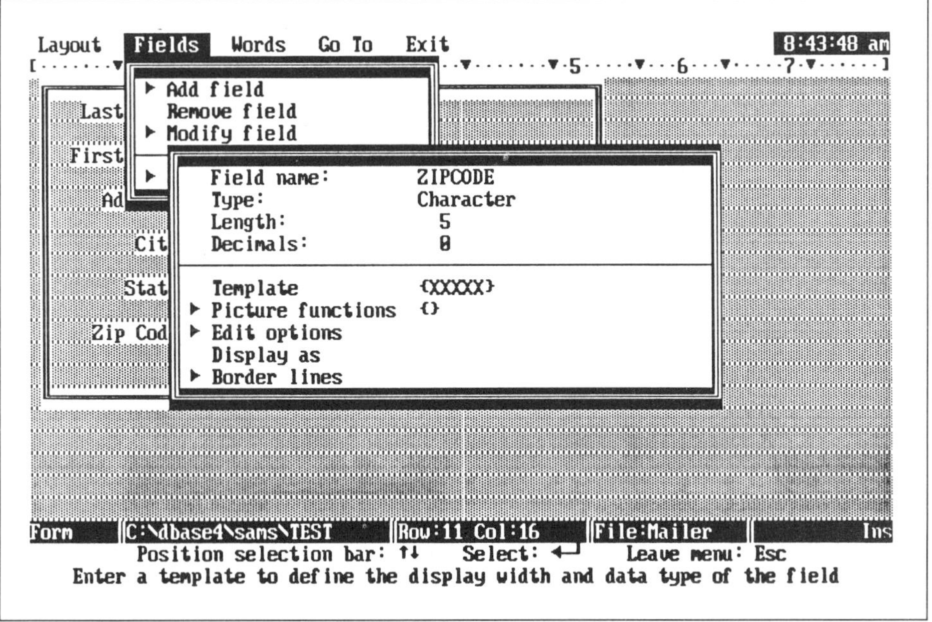

Figure 7-10 Menu Options for Modify Field

The specifications which appear in the top half of the menu box are taken from the database design, and cannot be changed. The lower half of the screen contains the display and editing options which can be changed. What changes can be made will vary, depending on the type of field you are changing. The template and picture functions apply to character, date, numeric, and float fields. These options let you control how the data is displayed and entered; for example, you might want all phone numbers in a phone field to display as (999) 999-9999. Edit Options, which applies to all field types, lets you specify whether the field can be edited, and any minimum and maximum values which will apply to the field. The Messages option lets you set a message which appears at the bottom of the screen when the field is edited. Use the Display As option to change the display for any memo fields to a marker, or to a window. Note that if you manually design format files by typing the @ . . . SAY . . . GET commands in the Editor, you can apply the same types of controls over the display and editing of fields with the PICTURE, FUNCTION, and VALID options of the @ . . . SAY . . . GET commands. These options are covered in more detail in the next chapter.

To save the format file, press Control-End, or choose Save Changes and Exit from the Exit Menu. A file using the filename you specified with CREATE SCREEN, and having a .FMT extension, will be created. (Another file with the same name and a .FMO extension will also be created; this file contains the compiled version of the format file.) The file with the .FMT extension will contain commands similar to the following:

```
*************************************************************
*-- Name....: CLIENTS.FMT
*-- Date....: 10-31-88
*-- Version.: dBASE IV, Format 1.44
*-- Notes...: Format files use "" as delimiters!
*************************************************************
*-- Format file initialization code -----------------------

IF SET("TALK")="ON"
   SET TALK OFF
   lc_talk="ON"
ELSE
   lc_talk="OFF"
ENDIF

*-- This form was created in MONO mode
SET DISPLAY TO MONO

lc_status=SET("STATUS")
*-- SET STATUS was ON when you went into the Forms Designer. IF lc_status = "OFF"
   SET STATUS ON
ENDIF


*-- @ SAY GETS Processing. -------------------------------
```

```
*-- Format Page: 1

@ 0,1 TO 10,43 DOUBLE
@ 2,5 SAY "Last name"
@ 2,15 GET lastname PICTURE "XXXXXXXXXXXXXXXXXXXX"
@ 4,4 SAY "First name"
@ 4,15 GET firstname PICTURE "XXXXXXXXXXXXXXXXXXXX"
@ 6,7 SAY "Address"
@ 6,15 GET address PICTURE "XXXXXXXXXXXXXXXXXXXXXXXXX"
@ 8,9 SAY "City"
@ 8,15 GET city PICTURE "XXXXXXXXXXXXXXX"
@ 8,32 SAY "ST"
@ 8,35 GET state PICTURE "XX"

*-- Format file exit code ------------------------------------


*-- SET STATUS was ON when you went into the Forms Designer.
IF lc_status = "OFF"  && Entered form with status off
  SET STATUS OFF     && Turn STATUS "OFF" on the way out
ENDIF
IF lc_talk="ON"
   SET TALK ON
ENDIF


RELEASE lc_talk,lc_fields,lc_status
*-- EOP: CLIENTS.FMT
```

Format files can be incorporated into dBASE programs in one of two ways. You can use the SET FORMAT TO command along with the APPEND and EDIT commands. Or with a word processor or the dBASE Editor, you can copy the @ . . . SAY . . . GET statements from the format file directly into the program, and then you can use the @ . . . SAY . . . GET commands along with your choice of field names or memory variables. In either case, using the Forms Design Screen is preferable to entering a few dozen @ . . . SAY . . . GET commands by hand.

One advantage offered by dBASE IV over dBASE III is in the use of multiple-page screen forms, when you use format files along with APPEND and EDIT. If you use a SET FORMAT TO command to open a format file, followed by an APPEND or EDIT command, users can use the PgUp and PgDn keys to move between multiple pages of a lengthy data-entry form. Each page of the data-entry form must have an appropriate READ command; if you use the Forms Design Screen to build the form, a READ command will automatically be inserted at the end of each page of a multiple-page screen form. Note that this feature only works with format files when you use the full-screen commands like APPEND and EDIT. This is a mixed blessing, as there are good reasons, covered in the next chapter, for not using APPEND and EDIT within your programs.

The Forms Design Screen normally creates three files for each form designed. One file is assigned an .SCR extension; this file contains the screen layout data used by dBASE IV to construct the form. The second file is the .FMT file, containing the @ . . . SAY . . . GET commands. The third file is the .FMO file, which is a compiled version of the .FMT file. dBASE uses this file when the SET FORMAT TO <filename> is encountered; if it cannot find the file, it recompiles using the file with the .FMT extension. Once you've used the Forms Design Screen to create a format file, you may want to rename the file. If you use the Forms Design Screen again on the same filename, it wili overwrite the existing .FMT file. (You can use the Forms Design Screen on an existing file with the MODIFY SCREEN <filename> command.) Also, if you update the .FMT file manually, no changes are made to the corresponding .SCR file; it will still reflect the original screen design.

Building Effective Menus

The techniques discussed below can be combined with specific menu-building commands in dBASE IV to create effective menus for an application.

Parts of a dBASE IV Application Menu

Most menus for dBASE IV applications are composed of:

- a preamble and environment setup
- a series of DEFINE BAR, DEFINE PAD, or DEFINE POPUP statements, to present custom bar or popup menus
- a series of ON SELECTION statements to obtain the user's response
- a DO CASE/ENDCASE series of options to branch to the appropriate submodule of a program

An example of such a menu is:

```
*MainMenu displays master menu.
*For clients tracking system
*last update 11/01/88
*program copyright (C) 1988, J.E.J.A., Herndon, VA
SET TALK OFF
IF ISCOLOR()
     SET COLOR TO B/W
ENDIF
SET ESCAPE OFF
SET BELL OFF
USE CLIENTS
SET ORDER TO CLIENTS
DEFINE POPUP MyMenu FROM 2,10
```

```
DEFINE BAR 1 OF MyMenu PROMPT "===Choose selection===" SKIP
DEFINE BAR 2 OF MyMenu PROMPT "  Add record"
DEFINE BAR 3 OF MyMenu PROMPT "  Edit record"
DEFINE BAR 4 OF MyMenu PROMPT "  Delete record"
DEFINE BAR 5 OF MyMenu PROMPT "  Print reports"
DEFINE BAR 6 OF MyMenu PROMPT "  Quit"
ON SELECTION POPUP MyMenu DEACTIVATE POPUP
DO WHILE .T.
    ACTIVATE POPUP MyMenu
    DO CASE
     CASE BAR() = 2
     DEACTIVATE POPUP
     DO ADDMENU

     CASE BAR() = 3
     DEACTIVATE POPUP
     DO EDITMENU

     CASE BAR() = 4
     DEACTIVATE POPUP
     DO DELMENU

     CASE BAR() = 5
     DEACTIVATE POPUP
     DO PRINMENU

     CASE BAR() = 6
     QUIT
    ENDCASE
ENDDO
```

dBASE provides menu commands that make it a simple matter to create detailed custom menus. The commands can be used to create bar menus, or popup menus. Bar menus are the type popularized by Lotus 1-2-3, where possible commands appear along a horizontal bar. Popup menus appear in a rectangular box, with a series of choices appearing on different lines within the box. Both types of menus can be combined in dBASE IV to form pulldown menus, where a particular selection from a bar menu causes a popup menu to appear with a list of additional choices. The popup appears to "pull down" from the bar menu, hence the term, "pulldown" menu.

When the bar menu approach alone is used, as in Lotus 1-2-3, the information displayed on much of the screen is not related to the menu; only one or two lines at the top or bottom of the screen contain the menu. The user chooses the desired menu option either by highlighting it with the cursor keys, or by pressing the first letter of the desired menu option. Figure 7-11 shows a typical bar menu. Because dBASE IV menu commands support this type of user interface, it is up to the programmer to try to use different first letters for each of the menu

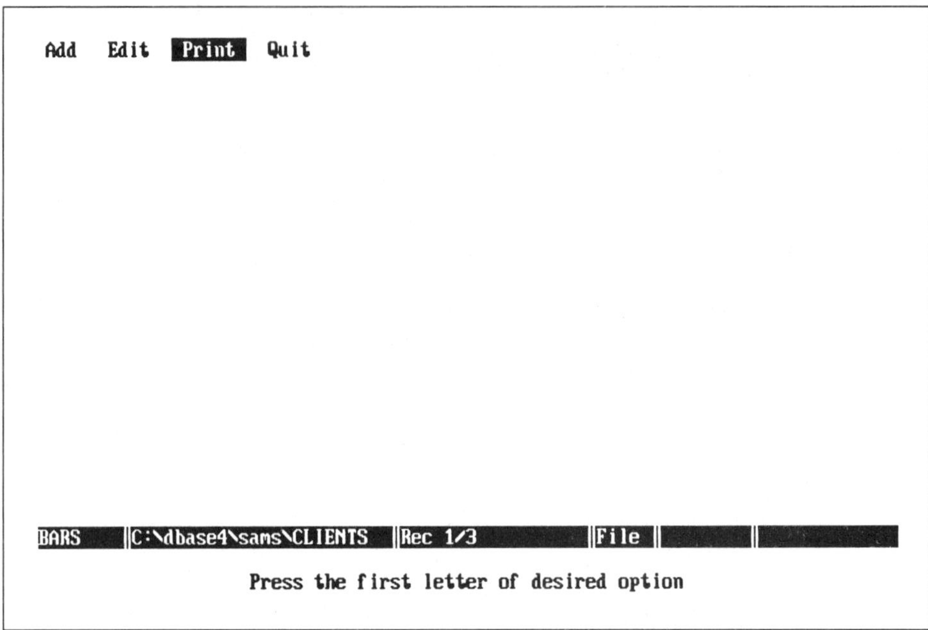

Figure 7-11 Bar Menu

options. If two menu options start with the same first letter, pressing that letter from the menu will always result in the first of the two options being chosen.

When the popup menu approach is used, a list of items appears in a rectangular box framed by a border. Again, the user can select the desired menu choice by moving the cursor to the desired item and pressing Enter, or by pressing the first letter of the desired menu option. Figure 7-12 shows an example of a popup menu.

Pulldown menus can be implemented in dBASE IV programs by combining the bar menu with the popup menu. Figure 7-13 shows an example of a pulldown menu. A major advantage of the pulldown menu approach is that the overall design of the entire system, with all its menu options, is made evident to the user. This advantage has made the pulldown approach to menus quite popular in various software packages; the Control Center in dBASE IV uses a variation of the pulldown menu design.

The commands used to define and display menus in dBASE IV include DEFINE MENU, DEFINE POPUP, DEFINE PAD, DEFINE BAR, ON SELECTION, ACTIVATE MENU, and ACTIVATE POPUP. Once menus have been used and are no longer needed, various commands including DEACTIVATE MENU, DEACTIVATE POPUP, CLEAR MENUS, and CLEAR POPUPS can be used to remove the menus. To define and use a menu, you must follow certain steps, which include naming the menu and the prompts, defining the actions produced by the menu choices, opening and closing the menu, and releasing the menu from memory (if it will not be needed again within the program). The commands used for these steps differ for the type of menu you are using: bar or

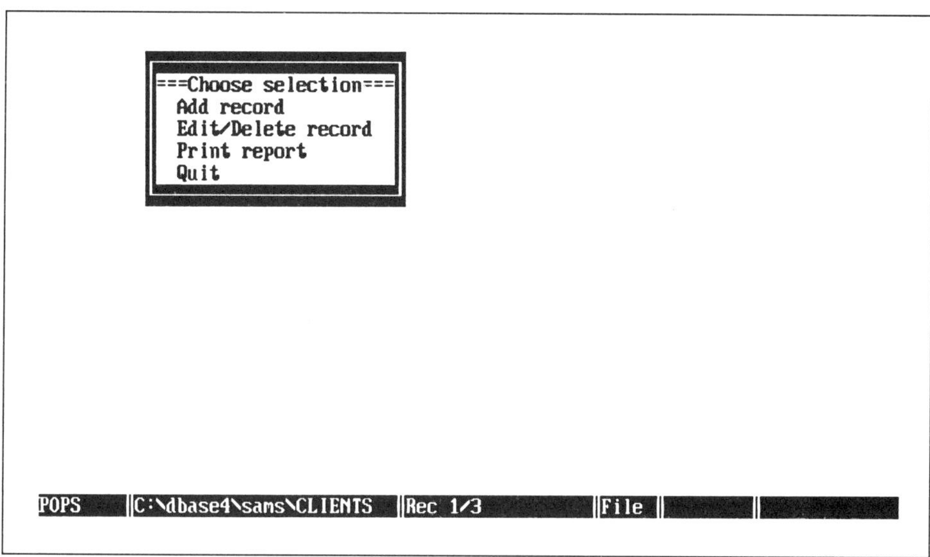

Figure 7-12 Popup Menu

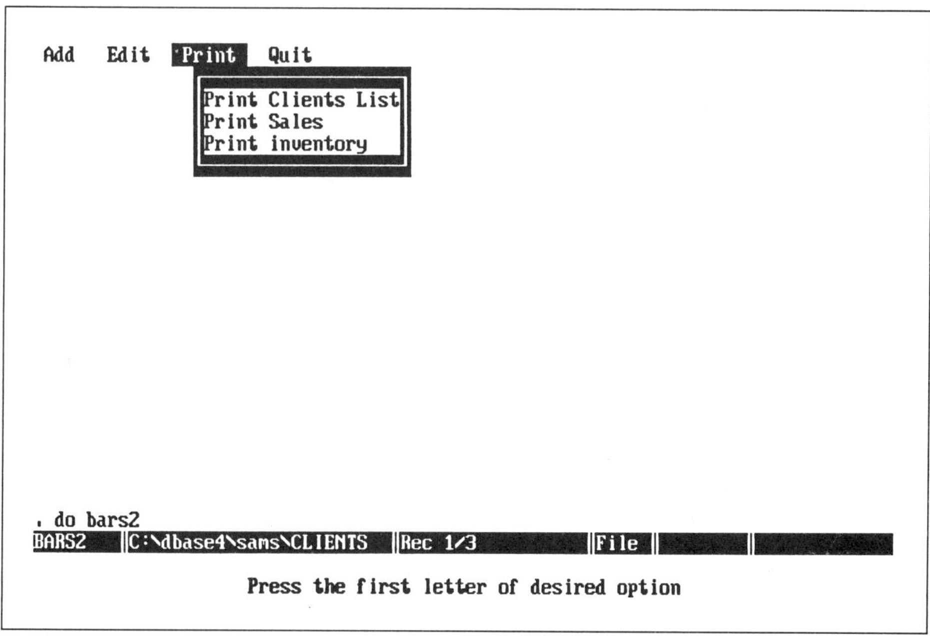

Figure 7-13 Pulldown Menu

popup. The overall steps and the respective commands for each type of menu are shown in Table 7-1.

Implementing a Bar Menu

To implement a bar menu, first define the menu with the DEFINE MENU command, then define the menu choices (called "pads") with the DEFINE PAD command. The syntax for the DEFINE MENU command is:

```
DEFINE MENU <menu name> [MESSAGE <message text>]
```

where <menu name> is the name assigned to the menu, and <message text> is an optional character expression. If the MESSAGE option is used, the message provided appears at the bottom of the screen when the menu is active.

Table 7-1 Menu Commands

Task Desired	Command Used
For Horizontal Bar Menu	
Name the menu	DEFINE MENU
Name the menu prompts	DEFINE PAD
Define the menu actions	ON PAD (or) ON SELECTION PAD
Open the menu	ACTIVATE MENU
Close the menu	DEACTIVATE MENU
Redisplay an inactive menu	SHOW MENU
Release menu from memory	CLEAR MENUS or RELEASE MENUS
For Popup Menu	
Name the menu	DEFINE POPUP
Name the menu prompts	DEFINE BAR
Define the menu actions	ON SELECTION POPUP
Open the menu	ACTIVATE POPUP
Close the menu	DEACTIVATE POPUP
Redisplay an inactive menu	SHOW POPUP
Release menu from memory	CLEAR POPUPS or RELEASE POPUPS

As an example, the statement,

```
DEFINE MENU MyBar MESSAGE "Press the first letter of desired option"
```

would define a bar menu under the name "MyBar". The message enclosed in quotes would appear at the bottom of the screen whenever the menu was displayed with the ACTIVATE MENU or the SHOW MENU command. After defining the menu, the DEFINE PAD command must be used to define the menu choices, or pads. The syntax for the command is:

```
DEFINE PAD <pad name> OF <menu name> PROMPT <character expression>
[AT <row>,<col>] [MESSAGE <message text>]
```

where <pad name> is a name assigned to the pad, <menu name> is the menu name assigned earlier with the DEFINE MENU command, and <character expression> contains the word or words which appear in the menu pad. The AT <row>,<col> clause is optional. If included, it will specify where the pad appears. If omitted, dBASE will place the first pad at the far left side of the menu, and places each successive pad one space to the right of the preceding pad. As an example of both commands (DEFINE MENU and DEFINE PAD) used together, the following could be used to define a horizontal bar menu with four options.

```
DEFINE MENU MyBar MESSAGE "Press the first letter of desired option"
DEFINE PAD Adder OF MyBar PROMPT "Add" AT 2,5
DEFINE PAD Editor OF MyBar PROMPT "Edit" AT 2,20
DEFINE PAD Printer OF MyBar PROMPT "Print" AT 2,35
DEFINE PAD Exit OF MyBar PROMPT "Quit" AT 2,50
```

Once the menu and the pads have been defined, the ON SELECTION PAD command can be used to link the choices (pads) to the desired actions. Those actions can be to execute a command, to call another program or procedure, or to display yet another menu. The syntax of the ON SELECTION PAD command is:

```
ON SELECTION PAD <pad name> OF <menu name> [<command>]
```

where <pad name> is the pad name assigned with the DEFINE PAD command, and <menu name> is the name assigned to the menu. The <command> option lets you specify what the menu action, when chosen, should do. Any other programs or procedures that you use along with the ON SELECTION PAD command can use the PAD() function to determine which pad was chosen from the menu, so the corresponding task can be carried out. As an example of the use of ON SELECTION PAD, the following lines of code would carry out a specific command based on which menu choice was selected.

```
ON SELECTION PAD Adder OF MyMenu APPEND
ON SELECTION PAD Editor OF MyMenu EDIT
```

And the commands described could be combined into a single program like the one shown below, to produce the complete bar menu and respond to the various options. Note that for simplicity's sake, the example responds to the options by directly calling commands, such as APPEND and EDIT. In most applications, the ON SELECTION statements would perform more complex actions, such as calling other procedures or programs, or opening secondary menus.

```
*BARS.PRG displays simple bar menu to add, edit, print data.*
USE CLIENTS
SET ORDER TO CLIENTS
DEFINE MENU MyMenu MESSAGE "Press the first letter of desired option"
```

```
DEFINE PAD Adder OF MyMenu PROMPT "Add"
DEFINE PAD Editor OF MyMenu PROMPT "Edit"
DEFINE PAD Printer OF MyMenu PROMPT "Print"
DEFINE PAD Exit OF MyMenu PROMPT "Quit"
ON SELECTION PAD Adder OF MyMenu APPEND
ON SELECTION PAD Editor OF MyMenu EDIT
ON SELECTION PAD Printer OF MyMenu REPORT FORM MyFile TO PRINT
ON SELECTION PAD Exit OF MyMenu QUIT
ACTIVATE MENU MyMenu
```

To call another menu with any of the pad selections, simply use the ACTIVATE MENU command as the pad action. For example, if the "Print" option in the above menu were to call another menu for choosing a report, that menu could first be defined with the DEFINE MENU command, then the ON SELECTION statement could cause that menu to be displayed, by using a clause like this one:

```
ON SELECTION PAD Printer OF MyMenu ACTIVATE MENU PrintMen
```

and the menu (named "PrintMen" in this case) would then appear on the screen.

Implementing a Popup Menu

The steps for implementing a popup menu are similar. First define the menu with the DEFINE POPUP command, then define the menu choices with the DEFINE BAR command. The syntax for the DEFINE POPUP command is:

```
DEFINE POPUP <popup name> FROM <row1>,<col1> [TO <row2>,<col2>]
[PROMPT FIELD <field name> / PROMPT FILES [LIKE <skeleton>]
/PROMPT STRUCTURE] [MESSAGE <message text>]
```

where <popup name> is the name assigned to the popup menu, and the FROM and TO coordinates define the upper left and lower right corners of the box which encloses the menu. The lower right coordinates are optional; if omitted, dBASE will size the box just large enough to contain the longest prompt. <message text> is an optional character expression. If the MESSAGE option is used, the message provided appears at the bottom of the screen when the menu is active. As an example, the statement,

```
DEFINE POPUP MyMenu MESSAGE "Press the first letter of desired option"
```

would define a popup menu under the name "MyMenu". The message enclosed in quotes would appear at the bottom of the screen whenever the menu was displayed with the ACTIVATE POPUP or the SHOW POPUP command.

The PROMPT FIELD, PROMPT FILES, and PROMPT STRUCTURE options are used when a popup menu is to be used to select from among field names, filenames, or fields in a database structure. If any of these options are used, the DEFINE BAR command cannot be used to select bar options for that menu.

After defining the menu, the DEFINE BAR command should be used to define the menu choices (or "bars"). The syntax for the command is:

```
DEFINE BAR <line number> OF <popup name> PROMPT <character expression>
  [MESSAGE <message text>] [SKIP [FOR <condition>] [NOSPACE]]
```

where <line number> is the number of the line within the popup menu with the first line being line 1, <popup name> is the popup menu name assigned earlier with the DEFINE POPUP command, and <character expression> contains the word or words which appear in the line of the menu. The SKIP option tells dBASE to display that line but not allow it to be selected in the menu, and the FOR option lets you set a condition on which the menu item will be skipped. There is normally a space between the border of the popup and the start of any prompts on the lines; the NOSPACE option omits this space, causing the menu choices to appear flush left against the border of the popup.

As an example of both commands (DEFINE POPUP and DEFINE BAR) used together, the following could be used to define a popup menu with four possible actions and one line which is displayed but cannot be chosen:

```
DEFINE POPUP MyMenu FROM 2,10
DEFINE BAR 1 OF MyMenu PROMPT "===Choose selection===" SKIP
DEFINE BAR 2 OF MyMenu PROMPT "  Add record"
DEFINE BAR 3 OF MyMenu PROMPT "  Edit/Delete record"
DEFINE BAR 4 OF MyMenu PROMPT "  Print report"
DEFINE BAR 5 OF MyMenu PROMPT "  Quit"
```

The first line of the popup menu will display the words, "Choose selection", but the user will only be able to select from one of the four remaining bars to add, edit, print, or quit.

After defining the popup menus and the bar choices, use the ON SELECTION command to link the choices (bars) to the desired actions. The syntax of the ON SELECTION command, when used with popup menus, is:

```
ON SELECTION POPUP <popup name>/ALL [<command>]
```

where <popup name> is the name assigned with the DEFINE POPUP command. The ALL option applies the action to all popup menus. Use the <command> option to specify what the menu action, when chosen, should do. Any other programs or procedures that you use along with the ON SELECTION POPUP command can use the BAR() function to determine which bar was chosen from the menu, so the corresponding task can be carried out. All of the commands described could be combined into a single program like the one shown below, to produce the complete bar menu and respond to the various options.

```
*This is an example of a simple menu and application*
USE CLIENTS
SET ORDER TO CLIENTS
DEFINE POPUP MyMenu FROM 2,10
DEFINE BAR 1 OF MyMenu PROMPT "===Choose selection===" SKIP
```

```
DEFINE BAR 2 OF MyMenu PROMPT "  Add record"
DEFINE BAR 3 OF MyMenu PROMPT "  Edit/Delete record"
DEFINE BAR 4 OF MyMenu PROMPT "  Print report"
DEFINE BAR 5 OF MyMenu PROMPT "  Quit"
ON SELECTION POPUP MyMenu DEACTIVATE POPUP
DO WHILE .T.
ACTIVATE POPUP MyMenu
DO CASE

     CASE BAR() = 2
     DEACTIVATE POPUP
     APPEND

     CASE BAR() = 3
     DEACTIVATE POPUP
     EDIT

     CASE BAR() = 4
     DEACTIVATE POPUP
     WAIT "ready printer, then press a key..."
     REPORT FORM MyFile TO PRINT

     CASE BAR() = 5
     QUIT
ENDCASE
ENDDO
```

Note that the ON SELECTION statement uses a DEACTIVATE POPUP command as the desired action. This is necessary to halt the display of the menu, since the remainder of the program forms a DO WHILE .T. loop which repeats various actions, dependent on which menu choice is selected.

Implementing a Pulldown Menu

Since pulldown menus are nothing more than popup menus which are attached to bar menus, you can combine both types of commands already discussed to form pulldown menus. A modified example of the previous program for displaying a bar menu is shown below, with just two significant differences. First, the ON SELECTION statements for the main menu bar (pads) use ACTIVATE MENU commands to call other popup menus (which were defined at the start of the program). Secondly, the ON PAD command is used near the end of the program in place of the ON SELECTION command. The use of ON PAD is what makes the difference between a popup and a pulldown menu, because true pulldown menus display their options whenever the main menu option is selected. The ON PAD command associates a popup menu with a particular pad of a bar menu. The syntax for the command is:

```
ON PAD <pad name> OF <menu name> [ACTIVATE POPUP <popup name>]
```

and when the command is used, the popup menu named in the command is activated whenever the pad in the horizontal bar menu is selected. This lets you have both the horizontal bar menu and one of the popup menus on the screen at the same time. The program code which produces this effect is shown below. The menu shown earlier in Figure 7-13 is a result of this program.

```
*This is an example of a pulldown menu*
DEFINE MENU MyMenu MESSAGE "Press the first letter of desired option"
DEFINE POPUP AddMenu FROM 1,2
DEFINE POPUP EditMenu FROM 1,8
DEFINE POPUP PrinMenu FROM 1,15
DEFINE BAR 1 OF AddMenu PROMPT "Add to clients file"
DEFINE BAR 2 OF AddMenu PROMPT "Add to sales file"
DEFINE BAR 3 OF AddMenu PROMPT "Add to inventory"
DEFINE BAR 1 OF EditMenu PROMPT "Edit clients file"
DEFINE BAR 2 OF EditMenu PROMPT "Edit sales file"
DEFINE BAR 3 OF EditMenu PROMPT "Edit inventory"
DEFINE BAR 1 OF PrinMenu PROMPT "Print Clients List"
DEFINE BAR 2 OF PrinMenu PROMPT "Print Sales"
DEFINE BAR 3 OF PrinMenu PROMPT "Print inventory"
DEFINE PAD Adder OF MyMenu PROMPT "Add"
DEFINE PAD Editor OF MyMenu PROMPT "Edit"
DEFINE PAD Printer OF MyMenu PROMPT "Print"
DEFINE PAD Exit OF MyMenu PROMPT "Quit"
ON PAD Adder OF MyMenu ACTIVATE POPUP AddMenu
ON PAD Editor OF MyMenu ACTIVATE POPUP EditMenu
ON PAD Printer OF MyMenu ACTIVATE POPUP PrinMenu
ON SELECTION PAD Exit OF MyMenu QUIT
ACTIVATE MENU MyMenu
```

When the main (bar) menu appears, the user can press the left or right arrow keys to highlight the other choices within the horizontal bar. As each choice is highlighted, the respective pulldown menu defined with the DEFINE POPUP and DEFINE BAR commands will appear.

And Those Simpler, Older Ways . . .

For programmers new to the dBASE language, it is worth noting that a simpler form of menu design is a common holdover from dBASE III and dBASE III Plus. Such menus are painted onto the screen with ? commands, or with @ . . . SAY commands. The code used to create such a menu and get responses from a user might resemble the following:

```
*Mainmenu.PRG*
SET TALK OFF
```

```
SET BELL OFF
DO WHILE .T.
     CLEAR
     ?
     ?
     ?
     ? "       ===Secretarial Database Main Menu==="
     ?
     ? "        1. Add new records"
     ? "        2. Edit records"
     ? "        3. Delete records"
     ? "        4. Print Summary Report"
     ? "        5. Other reports"
     ? "        6. Exit system"
     ?
     ?
     INPUT "  Enter selection:" TO CHOICE
     DO CASE

          CASE CHOICE = 1
          DO ADDMENU

          CASE CHOICE = 2
          DO EDITMENU

          CASE CHOICE = 3
          DO DELMENU

          CASE CHOICE = 4
          DO PRINSUMM

          CASE CHOICE = 5
          DO PRINTER

          CASE CHOICE = 6
          QUIT
     ENDCASE
ENDDO
*end of program*
```

Other variations on the same theme placed the menu statements between TEXT and ENDTEXT commands, or used @ . . . SAY commands to position the menu text, and @ . . . SAY . . . GET / READ commands to prompt the user and store a response. Earlier versions of dBASE did not support the bar and popup menu commands, so programmers had little choice. (Bar and popup menus could be simulated in dBASE III programs, but only with fairly convoluted programming techniques.) The simple approach to menus became so entrenched that it still turns up, even in new dBASE IV coding by many programmers. It does not have the visual appeal of the newer dBASE menus, but it is simple, straightfoward, and very easy to code.

Designing Effective Menus

With any menu, some basics of good design should be considered.

1. Menus should have clear headings or prompts that explain precisely what the menu's purpose is. The MESSAGE options of the DEFINE commands can be very useful for this purpose.
2. Menus should be consistent throughout a program; a menu for selecting various reports, for example, should not vary wildly in design from another menu used by the same program for printing mailing labels.
3. Commands should be consistent; don't use ACCEPT commands in some places and WAIT commands for similar functions in other places. The poor user will never know whether he or she is to press Return or just press any key.
4. There should be a limit to the number of options on any single menu. It is better to design tree-structured menus, where one choice leads to another menu with more choices, than to clutter a single menu with a large number of choices.
5. Wording should be concise; overly long descriptions of options can be visually confusing.
6. Above all, there should always be a way out of a menu, in addition to the choices for the options. Few things are as disturbing to a user as being forced to select a choice when what was really wanted was "none of the above."

Special Effects

Beyond these hints for good menu design, you can add special effects to "jazz up" your programs; how far you carry such tricks is limited only by your imagination. The default single line and DOUBLE option of the @ . . . TO command help you design attractive borders. The syntax for these commands is:

```
@ <row>,<column> TO <row>,<column>[DOUBLE]
```

The command draws a solid line between the specified screen coordinates. If the coordinates are on different horizontal and vertical planes, a square or rectangular box is drawn. The default is a single line or box; the DOUBLE option can be added to indicate a double line or box.

Even if you are using popup or bar menus, you may find the single and double line borders useful, for adding emphasis to the menus and to other areas of the screen. Rectangular borders help set off help text or messages containing warnings or other user information. And you can combine a rectangular border with the ACTIVATE MENU command, to display bar menus inside of rectangular borders. The following code provides an example:

```
*BARS.PRG displays simple bar menu to add, edit, print data.*
USE CLIENTS
SET ORDER TO CLIENTS
DEFINE MENU MyMenu MESSAGE "Press the first letter of desired option"
DEFINE PAD Adder OF MyMenu PROMPT "Add" AT 3,5
DEFINE PAD Editor OF MyMenu PROMPT "Edit" AT 3,25
DEFINE PAD Printer OF MyMenu PROMPT "Print" AT 3,45
DEFINE PAD Exit OF MyMenu PROMPT "Quit" AT 3,65
ON SELECTION PAD Adder OF MyMenu APPEND
ON SELECTION PAD Editor OF MyMenu EDIT
ON SELECTION PAD Printer OF MyMenu REPORT FORM MyFile TO PRINT
ON SELECTION PAD Exit OF MyMenu QUIT
@ 2,4 TO 4,71 DOUBLE
ACTIVATE MENU MyMenu
```

In this case, the statement @ 2,4 TO 4,71 DOUBLE displays a double-line box around the bar menu. The coordinates of the box are sized to just cover the placements of the pads in the bar menu, as defined by the DEFINE PAD commands.

Using Graphics

The character graphics that occupy the upper end of the IBM PC's character set can also be placed on the screen. Some word processors let you create these characters by holding the Alt key and entering the code on the numeric keypad, then releasing the Alt key. The dBASE Editor will let you enter graphic characters in this manner.

An alternative is to use the REPLICATE and CHR functions, along with the ASCII value of the desired graphics character, to produce graphic symbols in the program. As an example, the command,

```
@ 6,4 SAY REPLICATE(CHR(178),56)
```

causes 56 repetitions of a graphic character (ASCII 178, which resembles a tiny checkerboard) appearing from column 4 to column 60 of row 6. Try this little program to see the entire graphics portion of the character set en masse:

```
SET TALK OFF
STORE 3 TO ROWNO
STORE 5 TO COLNO
STORE 128 TO COUNT
DO WHILE COUNT < 256
    @ ROWNO, COLNO SAY REPLICATE(CHR(COUNT), COLNO + 50)
```

```
    STORE ROWNO + 1 TO ROWNO
    STORE COLNO + 1 TO COLNO
    STORE COUNT + 1 TO COUNT
    IF ROWNO = 23
      CLEAR
      STORE 3 TO ROWNO
    ENDIF
    IF COLNO = 28
        STORE 5 TO COLNO
    ENDIF
ENDDO
```

Color Highlighting

Liberal use of the COLOR options of the @ . . . SAY . . . GET commands can provide a different display for specific fields. For example, the following portion of a format file causes the lastname entry field to appear in blue characters on a white background, and the firstname field to appear in red characters on a black background. The address is in cyan characters on brown background, the city in black characters on a red background, and the state in green characters on a blue background. A double-line border surrounds the fields, and near the top and bottom of the border, the ASCII characters 176, 177, and 178 are used with the REPLICATE function, to display bars made of checkered character boxes.

```
@ 3,15 TO 13,58 DOUBLE
@ 4,16 SAY REPLICATE(chr(176),42)
@ 5,16 SAY REPLICATE(chr(177),42)
@ 6,19 SAY " LASTNAME"
@ 6,29 GET lastname PICTURE "XXXXXXXXXXXXXXXXXXXX" COLOR b/w,b/w
@ 7,17 SAY "  FIRSTNAME"
@ 7,29 GET firstname PICTURE "XXXXXXXXXXXXXXXXXXXX" COLOR r/n,r/n
@ 8,19 SAY "  ADDRESS"
@ 8,29 GET address PICTURE "XXXXXXXXXXXXXXXXXXXXXXXXX" COLOR bg/gr,bg/gr
@ 9,17 SAY "       CITY"
@ 9,29 GET city PICTURE "XXXXXXXXXXXXXXX" COLOR n/r,n/r
@ 9,46 SAY "STATE"
@ 9,52 GET state PICTURE "XX" COLOR g/b,g/b
@ 10,16 SAY REPLICATE(chr(178),42)
@ 11,16 SAY REPLICATE(chr(177),42)
@ 12,16 SAY REPLICATE(chr(176),42)
```

You can add such color selections for fields when building forms using the Forms Design Screen. Just select the field by placing the cursor in the field, open the Words Menu, and then choose Display from the menu. The display options which appear can be used to select the desired foreground and background colors for the chosen field.

And Sound . . .

If visual prompts aren't enough to catch the attention of some users, it's a simple task to simultaneously ring the PC's "bell" by using the ASCII value for bell (007) within a ? statement. Issuing the command,

```
? CHR(7)
```

will sound the bell. dBASE IV also lets you change the pitch and duration of the tone, an improvement over earlier versions of dBASE. This lets you use a $700 software package to simulate a $29 child's piano, if you enjoy such exercises. Use the command,

```
SET BELL TO <frequency>,<duration>
```

where <frequency> is the desired frequency of the tone as measured in Hertz, and duration is the length in ticks. (Each tick is approximately 0.0549 second.) The frequency can range from 18 to 10,001, and the duration can range from 2 to 20 ticks. The default values are 512 Hertz for the frequency, and 2 ticks for the duration. You could use code similar to the following to play a series of tones and display a message for the user:

```
CLEAR
SET BELL TO 440,8
? CHR(7)
SET BELL TO 880,5
? CHR(7)
SET BELL TO 620,8
? CHR(7)
@ 15, 5 say "Wake up and enter a choice!" GET CHOICE
```

Obviously, it's easy to get carried away with special effects, so a word to the wise about staying within the limits of good taste may be appropriate. The prior example of code is obviously not in great taste. And what looks great on your screen may be an abomination to your printer; most printers can't handle the graphics characters in the IBM graphics set without special programming, so check your printer manual before attempting to include graphic character codes in printed output.

Using Function Keys

You can use the INKEY() function of dBASE IV to test for the value of a key that has been pressed. Using INKEY(), you can structure menus that depend on a specific function key to perform an action. An example of program code offering such a menu is:

```
**MENU.PRG displays menu, uses Function keys for choice
SET TALK OFF
DO WHILE .T.
    CLEAR
    TEXT
            *Main Menu*
       ==================
       |        |        |
       |F1 Add  | F2 Edit|
       |RECORDS|RECORDS  |
       ==================
       |        |        |
       |  F3    |  F4    |
       |BROWSE  | PRINT  |
       ==================
       |                 |
       | F5 Exit         |
       |    System       |
       ==================
        Press a Function Key!
    ENDTEXT
    STORE 0 TO KEY
    DO WHILE KEY = 0
        @ 17,4 SAY TIME()
        @ 18,4 SAY DATE()
        STORE INKEY() TO KEY
    ENDDO

    DO CASE
        CASE KEY = 28
            *F1 was pressed.
            DO ADDIT
        CASE KEY = -1
            *F2 was pressed.
            DO MODIFY
        CASE KEY = -2
            *F3 was pressed.
            BROWSE
        CASE KEY = -3
            *F4 was pressed.
            DO PRINTIT
        CASE KEY = -4
            *F5 was pressed.
            CLEAR
            @5,5 SAY "Remember to perform your BACKUPS!"
            WAIT
            QUIT
```

```
    ENDCASE
ENDDO
*End of MENU.PRG
```

In the example, a continuous loop (DO WHILE KEY = 0) repeats for as long as no key is pressed. As long as the program is in this continuous loop, it takes advantage of this fact to display a running date and time indicator below the display of appropriate function keys. Once a key is pressed, the INKEY() function returns a value. If that value matches one of the CASE statements in the program, the appropriate action is taken; otherwise, the menu repeats its display until an appropriate choice is made.

As long as no key is pressed, the INKEY function returns a zero. The letter keys return their normal ASCII equivalents. Some keys, such as the Alt key, do not return a value unless they are used in combination with another key, and therefore will not provide INKEY() with a value. Some of the more commonly used nonalphanumeric key values provided by the INKEY function are summarized in Table 7-2.

Table 7-2 ASCII Codes Returned by the INKEY() Function

Key	ASCII Code
Home	26
End	2
Up Arrow	5
Down Arrow	24
Left Arrow	19
Right Arrow	4
PgUp	18
PgDn	3
Ins	22
Del	7
F1	28
F2	−1
F3	−2
F4	−3
F5	−4
F6	−5
F7	−6
F8	−7
F9	−8
F10	−9

If you want to find the value returned by INKEY() for some obscure key that isn't listed here (such as Shift-F4), you can run the following program, which will display the INKEY() value for any key you press.

```
*Inkey codes displayed
DO WHILE .T.
     STORE 0 TO KEY
     DO WHILE KEY = 0
          STORE INKEY() TO KEY
     ENDDO
     ? "The value of that key is: "
     ?? KEY
ENDDO
```

Creating Picklists

Using the PROMPT FIELD, PROMPT FILE, or PROMPT STRUCTURE options of the DEFINE POPUP command, you can create point-and-shoot "picklists" based on a list of items in a database field, a list of field names, or a list of filenames. You can use the BAR() function to return the bar number which corresponds to a chosen item. For example, perhaps you have a database containing the names of different cities, and you want to allow a user to fill a city in a data entry field by displaying a list and picking from the list. Assuming a database named DATAFILE containing fields called NAME, ADDRESS, CITY, and STATE, and another database named CITIES with a single field called CITYNAME, the job could be done with a program similar to that shown below. The CITIES database contains a record for each city which is a valid choice for entry into the other database, DATAFILE.

```
SELECT 1
USE DATAFILE
APPEND BLANK
CLEAR
@ 5,5 SAY "    Name? " GET NAME
@ 6,5 SAY "Address? " GET ADDRESS
READ
SELECT 2
USE CITIES
DEFINE POPUP Towns FROM 2,10 PROMPT FIELD Cityname
ON SELECTION POPUP Towns DEACTIVATE POPUP
ACTIVATE POPUP Towns
GOTO BAR()
STORE CITYNAME TO ANSWER
SELECT 1
REPLACE CITY WITH ANSWER
@ 7,15 SAY CITY
@ 8,5 SAY "   State? " GET STATE
READ
<...more commands...>
```

When the program is run, after the user enters the name and address, a popup menu appears with every city in the CITIES file as a possible choice within the menu (Figure 7-14). When the user selects a desired choice from the menu, the name of the city selected is entered into the CITY field of the DATAFILE database with the REPLACE statement. Then the user proceeds to enter the remaining data.

In a similar fashion, you can use PROMPT FILE or PROMPT STRUCTURE with the DEFINE POPUP command. With PROMPT FILE, a list of filenames appears in the popup menu. You can include a file skeleton, to limit the display to a particular type of file. With PROMPT STRUCTURE, a list of fieldnames in the active database structure appears in the popup menu. In any case, use the BAR() function as demonstrated in the above example, to return the selection chosen by the user.

Keeping Track of Time

dBASE IV offers a real-time clock which can be placed at any screen location. The SET CLOCK ON/OFF command is used to display or hide the clock, and the SET CLOCK TO <row,col> is used to place the clock in the desired location. The SET CLOCK TO command is optional; if omitted, the clock will appear in the upper right corner of the screen when the SET CLOCK ON command is encountered. The clock always appears in full-screen operations like BROWSE and EDIT.

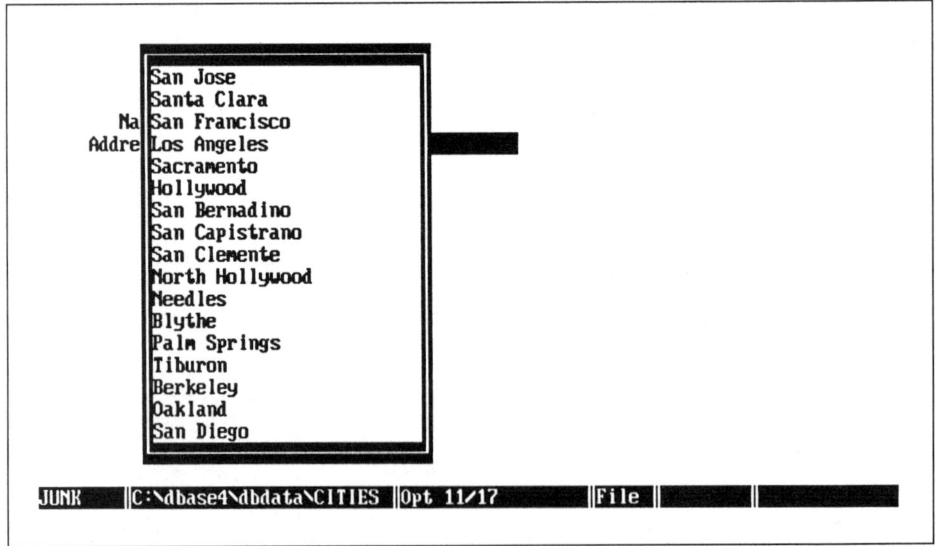

Figure 7-14 Picklist Using Popup Menu

Implementing Help

Help screens are an important (and often underutilized) part of any application. There are a number of ways you can implement help in a dBASE IV application. At the simplest level, help messages can be designed into the various screens and menus of an application. The MESSAGE options of various menu commands can be useful for this, as is the SET MESSAGE TO command, which changes the default message appearing at the bottom of the screen.

A step up from this level are menu options for user-selectable help screens. You can label a menu choice as "Help", and when that menu choice is selected, the screen can be cleared, and TEXT . . . ENDTEXT statements can be used to display more detailed help messages.

While data is being displayed or edited with the @ . . . SAY . . . GET commands, you can offer context-sensitive help, taking advantage of the ON KEY command and dBASE IV's ability to display text within predefined windows. Just prior to the @ . . . SAY . . . GET commands, link the F1 function key to a help routine, with a statement like the following:

```
ON KEY LABEL F1 DO HelpFile
```

and then clear the keyboard buffer of the key pressed with an INKEY() statement after the READ. In the example code shown below, the statement ON KEY LABEL F1 DO HELPFILE causes the HELPFILE.PRG routine to be called if F1 is pressed while the cursor is in the data entry fields. The first executable line in the HELPFILE routine clears the keyboard buffer with INKEY(). Then, the VARREAD() function is used to determine which field the cursor was in when F1 was pressed. (The VARREAD() function returns a character string containing the name of the field the cursor was in when the key was pressed.) Depending on the value provided by the VARREAD() function, the CASE statements act accordingly.

```
ON KEY LABEL F1 DO HELPFILE
CLEAR
@ 5,5 SAY "Company name:" GET NAME
@ 6,5 SAY " Account no.:" GET ACCTNUMB
@ 7,5 SAY "  Order date:" GET ORDERED
@ 8,5 SAY "      Amount:" GET COST
READ
ON KEY
RETURN

*HelpFile.PRG*
STORE INKEY() TO KEYPRESS
DEFINE WINDOW HELPER FROM 8,5 TO 18,75 DOUBLE
ACTIVATE WINDOW HELPER
DO CASE
     CASE VARREAD() = "NAME"
     @ 2,2 SAY "Enter the company name in this field."
```

```
     CASE VARREAD() = "ACCTNUMB"
     @ 2,2 SAY "Enter the five-digit account number for the company."
     @ 3,2 SAY "See your company directory for valid account numbers."
     CASE VARREAD() = "ORDERED"
     @ 2,2 SAY "Enter the date the order was placed in this field."
     CASE VARREAD() = "COST"
     @ 2,2 SAY "Enter the cost of the item.  Do NOT include any"
     @ 3,2 SAY "special discounts authorized by the sales department."
ENDCASE
@ 8,5
WAIT "  --Press a key to exit HELP..."
DEACTIVATE WINDOW HELPER
RETURN
*end of helpfile.prg*
```

Implementing Password Protection

Some applications can benefit from a form of password protection. You can implement a simple form of such protection by storing acceptable passwords in a small database or a file of memory variables. Query the user for a password, and use SET CONSOLE OFF to turn off the screen display as the user enters the password. Then, check the database (or file of memory variables) to see if an acceptable match for the password exists. If no match is found, your program can take appropriate action, as demonstrated in this example:

```
**PASSWORD.PRG, called from main program, checks for valid user
**Uses database called PASSFILE which contains usernames, passwords
**Last update 11/12/88
CLEAR
?
ACCEPT "Enter user name: " TO USER
? "Enter password (not displayed):"
SET CONSOLE OFF
ACCEPT TO PASS
SET CONSOLE ON
USE PASSFILE
LOCATE FOR UPPER(USERNAME) = UPPER(USER)
IF EOF()
     ? "Invalid username!"
     WAIT
     QUIT
ENDIF
IF UPPER(PASSWORD) <> UPPER(PASS)
```

```
    ? "Invalid password!"
    WAIT
    QUIT
ENDIF
*Valid user and password, so run program
CLEAR
DO MAINMENU
*End of PASSWORD.PRG
```

You can use the same technique to add security access levels for different users. A numeric field, called ACCESS, could be added to the password database. Then, different users could be given different access values (such as managers, 4's; supervisors, 3's; users, 2's; and data-entry personnel, 1's). The program could then examine the value of the access value for a given user before granting capabilities to edit or remove records, or to perform other functions.

By security standards, this is a relatively simple scheme, and it should not be depended upon for any application that demands a moderate to high level of security. This type of system could easily be broken by any user with minimal dBASE programming skills.

The security of such a system can be increased somewhat if you use Runtime (supplied with the Developer's Release version of dBASE IV and discussed in Chapter 14) to encode the password database and the program. If still tighter security is an issue, you can use the PROTECT utility, which is accessible by entering PROTECT at the dot prompt. The PROTECT utility can be used to provide encrypted usernames and passwords, and database encryption. Details of the PROTECT utility are in the Network section of the dBASE IV documentation.

8

Adding and Modifying Records Under Program Control

This chapter covers ways to add and edit data within a program. Verification and error trapping of invalid data, filtering of databases to show selected records, deleting records under control of the program, and handling memo fields within a program are all discussed here.

Adding Records

Using APPEND and EDIT to Add or Modify Records

Adding records and editing records within a database file can obviously be performed with the APPEND and EDIT commands, but most dBASE programmers don't use such methods—and for good reason. The main problem with such methods is the increased risk of file damage by leaving files open in the append or edit modes for long periods of time. This increases the likelihood of an unfortunate event (such as a power failure or static) corrupting your database files. Network installations have another problem: APPEND locks the database file, making it unavailable to other users. As a rule, the less time files remain open in an application, the better.

Recommended Method of Adding New Records

For adding records within a database, a better solution than simply using APPEND, particularly with local area networks, is to perform the following steps within the program:

1. Initialize memory variables to hold the data.
2. Query the user for the desired data.
3. Store the data provided by the user to the variables.
4. Perform any necessary validation on the data.

5. When data is validated, store it in the database.

Adding records within a *program* can be done with the APPEND BLANK command, which adds a blank record at the end of the database. Four of the five steps outlined here are used in the following program. (Only validation of data is missing, and more on that topic follows.) The program is designed to add a new item to an inventory file.

```
***INVENT.PRG***
*Adds items to inventory
*Last update 11/01/88
SET TALK OFF
USE MAINFILE INDEX PARTS
*Query user for new part number
CLEAR
STORE 0 TO MPARTNO
@2,30 TO 5,70
@3,40 SAY "Enter part number:"
@4,40 SAY "(press Return to exit)"
@3,59 GET MPARTNO
READ
IF MPARTNO = 0
   CLEAR
   RETURN
ENDIF
SEEK MPARTNO
IF FOUND()
     *Duplicate entry attempted
     @3,40 CLEAR TO 4,69
     @3,40 SAY "Part number already exists!"
     @4,40 SAY "Press a key to return to menu."
     ? CHR(7)
     WAIT""
     CLOSE DATABASES
     RETURN
ENDIF
*Valid new part number
CLOSE DATABASES
STORE SPACE(20) TO MPARTDESC
STORE 0.00 TO MWHOLCOST
STORE 0.00 TO MRETLCOST
STORE 0 TO MQUANTITY
CLEAR
@ 6,  3  TO 18, 50
@ 1,  0  TO 19, 54  DOUBLE
@ 2, 15  SAY "INVENTORY MASTER FILE"
@ 4, 15  SAY "New Item Entry Screen"
```

```
@  7, 12  SAY "Part Number: "
@  7, 26 SAY MPARTNO
@  9, 12  SAY "Description:"
@  9, 25  GET  MPARTDESC
@ 11,  9  SAY "Wholesale Cost:"
@ 11, 25  GET  MWHOLCOST
@ 13, 12  SAY "Retail Cost:"
@ 13, 25  GET  MRETLCOST
@ 15,  7  SAY "Initial Quantity:"
@ 15, 25  GET  MQUANTITY
READ
USE MAINFILE INDEX PARTS
APPEND BLANK
REPLACE PARTNO with MPARTNO, PARTDESC with MPARTDESC
REPLACE WHOLCOST with MWHOLCOST, RETLCOST with MRETLCOST
REPLACE QUANTITY with MQUANTITY
CLOSE DATABASES
RETURN
*End of subroutine
```

The program opens the database file, MAINFILE, and the associated index file. The user is prompted for a new part number, and the response is stored to a variable, MPARTNO. If the value of MPARTNO is zero (meaning the user most likely pressed Return without entering a value), program flow returns to the calling program. If a value is entered, a SEEK command does a fast search on the indexed database for a matching part number. If a match is found, the user is told that the part number already exists, and program execution returns to the calling program. If the part number is new, the database is closed (purely a safety precaution; the less time open, the better), the variables are initialized, and the user supplies the desired data, which is stored to the variables with the GET and READ statements. The database file is opened, APPEND BLANK is used to add a blank record, and a series of REPLACE commands move the contents of the variables into the blank fields. Finally, the database is closed, completing the append operation.

Validating Data

Programs can check for valid data using a number of techniques. One effective technique is to use the PICTURE and RANGE options of the @ . . . SAY . . . GET commands, to restrict the values that will be accepted by the GETS. The syntax for the @ . . . SAY . . . GET command, when used with the PICTURE or RANGE option, is:

```
@<row,column>[[SAY <expression> [PICTURE "<clause>"]
[FUNCTION "<function list>"]] [GET <variable> [[OPEN] WINDOW
<window name>] [PICTURE <clause>] [FUNCTION <function list>]
```

```
[RANGE <low>,<high>] [VALID <condition>] [ERROR <character
expression>]] [WHEN <condition>] [DEFAULT <expression>]
[MESSAGE <character expression>] [COLOR [<standard>][,<enhanced>]]]
```

The PICTURE, FUNCTION, RANGE, VALID, and WHEN clauses provide a wide range of flexibility in validating data. Using PICTURE, you can force data entered to match a specific style, or embed characters automatically within a field. The FUNCTION clause affects all characters entered in a field. The RANGE clause lets you specify a minimum and maximum range for an entry, and the VALID clause lets you define valid responses which the user can enter. Use the WHEN clause to optionally skip the field when a predefined condition is false. (If the condition is true, the cursor will move into the named field, but if the condition is false, the cursor will skip the field and move into the next one.)

The DEFAULT clause is used to specify a default value which automatically appears in the field. If the GET is being used with a database file field (as opposed to a memory variable), the default value is applied only in the case of a new record, when the field would otherwise be blank. If no changes are made to the entry and the Enter key is pressed, the default value gets stored to the variable or field.

Templates

The clauses that follow PICTURE and FUNCTION contain template symbols and/or template functions. *Template symbols* restrict the display or entry of a single character, and one symbol is used to represent each position in the blank. *Functions* affect the entire display for the entry field instead of for single characters. Both the functions and the template symbols for PICTURE are enclosed in quotes. A complete list of functions and templates is provided in Table 8-1.

Common functions used for data validation include the !, A, and 9 functions. The ! function forces data entry to all uppercase letters. The A function restricts entries so they consist of alpha characters (A–Z, a–z) only, and the 9 function restricts entries to numerals only.

The following example uses the ! function to convert all character data to uppercase, reducing the possibility of confusing searches due to some names stored in uppercase and others stored in lowercase:

```
@ 5,6 SAY "Enter name: " GET L_Name FUNCTION '!'
```

For numbers, specific places for digits, decimal points, and asterisks in place of leading zeros can be displayed by means of the following example:

```
@ 10,12 GET AMOUNT PICTURE '*****.99'
```

With this template, leading zeros in the amount will appear as asterisks, and two decimal places will be provided following the decimal point. Only digits will be accepted during data entry; any attempt to enter alpha characters will cause a beep.

In this example,

```
@ 5,5 SAY "Enter last name: " GET L_Name FUNCTION "A"
```

the use of the A function restricts entries to alpha characters only; an attempt to enter a number or a punctuation mark will get no response from dBASE.

You can restrict data entry and visually format the display at the same time by including literal characters within a picture template. Commonly such templates are used with phone numbers, which look best when separated by the

Table 8-1 Picture Templates and Functions

Template	Result
!	Forces letters to uppercase
$	Leading zeros are displayed as dollar signs
*	Leading zeros are displayed as asterisks
.	Identifies a decimal position
,	Identifies a comma, if numbers exist to left of comma
#	Permits digits, blanks, and signs only
9	Permits digits for character data, digits and signs for numeric data
A	Permits letters only
L	Permits logical data (true/false, yes/no) only
N	Permits letters and digits only
X	Permits any characters
Y	Permits logical data as Y or N only
Function	**Result**
!	Forces letters to uppercase
(	Negative numbers will be surrounded by parentheses
^	Numbers displayed in scientific notation
A	Accepts alphabetic characters only
B	Numeric data will be left-justified
C	Letters CR (credit) displayed following positive numbers
D	American date format
E	European date format
I	Centers text
J	Right-justifies text
L	Shows leading zeros
M	Permits list of choices for GET
Sn	Limits display to n characters wide, and scrolls text within field
T	Trims leading and trailing blanks
X	Letters DB (debit) are displayed following negative numbers
Z	Zeros displayed as blanks

customary hyphens or spaces and parentheses around the area codes. In this example,

```
@ 14,20 SAY "Home Phone? " GET H_Phone PICTURE "(999)-999-9999"
```

the parentheses and hyphens are not template symbols; therefore, dBASE IV interprets these characters to be literals and includes them in the display created by the GET. The user need only enter the actual 10 digits of the phone number, and the entry will fall into place within the parentheses and hyphens automatically added by the software. If you use literals, the database field that eventually receives the data must be long enough for the data and the literals. In the example just given, a 14-character database field would be needed to store the 10-digit phone number.

If you are using logical fields, the Y template allows the entry of the letters Y or N only, and lowercase entries of these letters will be converted to uppercase.

The M function is useful when you want to limit possible responses to a predefined list. The clause uses the format,

```
FUNCTION "M <list of possible choices>"
```

where "list of possible choices" are the valid choices, separated by commas. As an example, a field named "LOCATION" in a personnel database might have responses of "San Jose", "Tiburon", or "Berkeley" as acceptable responses. You could validate the field's entry for one of the possible responses with a command like the following:

```
@ 5,5 SAY "Location?" GET LOCATION FUNCTION "M San Jose,Tiburon,Berkeley"
```

A significant advantage of this function is that the first choice named in the list automatically appears in the field as the default value, and you can press the spacebar until the desired value appears. You can also press the first letter of the desired choice. If there is more than one item in the list which begins with the same letter, pressing that letter again will display successive choices in the list that begin with the letter.

Selective Editing of Fields

With the WHEN clause, you can tell dBASE to skip past a field during data entry if a specific condition isn't met. As the user moves the cursor into the field, any condition specified after the WHEN clause is evaluated by dBASE. If the condition is true, the cursor moves into the field, and editing is permitted. If the condition is false, the cursor moves past the field, and into the next field. An example appears below in the case of a personnel database, with a logical field for "MARRIED", and a character field for the name of the spouse ("SPOUSE"):

```
@ 5,5 SAY "Married? Y/N:" GET MARRIED PICTURE "Y"
@ 7,5 SAY "Spouse's name:" GET SPOUSE WHEN MARRIED
```

```
@ 9,5 SAY "Dependents?" GET DEPENDENTS
READ
```

If the logical value of false ("N") is entered into the MARRIED field, the next field, SPOUSE, will be skipped by the cursor.

Using VALID

The VALID clause is a powerful option of the @ . . . SAY . . . GET command which lets you accept data meeting certain criteria, while rejecting data that falls outside that criteria. One common use of VALID is to test for acceptable characters in response to a user prompt, as is demonstrated in the following example:

```
STORE " " TO Chooser
@ 5,10 SAY "(A)ll records or (S)elected ones?"
@ 6,10 SAY "Enter (A), (S), or (C) to CANCEL report."
@ 6,52 GET Chooser FUNCTION "!" VALID Chooser $ "ASC"
READ
```

The VALID Chooser $ "ASC" portion of the statement uses the substring function ($) along with the VALID clause to limit possible entries to A, S, or C. Any other entry will not be accepted in the fill-in field, and an "invalid entry" message appears at the bottom of the screen. If you would like the error message to be more descriptive, add the ERROR clause, followed by your own message (in quotes). In this example, the command might be:

```
@ 6,52 GET Chooser FUNCTION "!" VALID Chooser $ "ASC";
   ERROR "Please enter A, S, or C!"
```

You can combine other functions with VALID to further define your control over entries. Consider a part number field, in a database where all part numbers use any letter other than N as the third character in a seven-character part number:

```
STORE SPACE(7) TO NEWPART
@ 5,15 SAY "Part number?" GET NEWPART FUNCTION "!";
   VALID .NOT. LEFT(NEWPART,3) $ "N"
```

In this case, the .NOT. LEFT(NEWPART,3) $ "N" portion of the statement uses the LEFT function to return the third character in the variable, NEWPART. The substring ($) function compares this to the character "N", and the .NOT. operand tells VALID not to accept an "N" in the defined position.

The VALID clause is also useful for checking the validity of filenames, to ensure that the user doesn't enter a forbidden character, as shown in this example:

```
STORE SPACE(8) TO MFILE
@ 5,5 SAY "Name of report form file to use? (no extension)"
@ 6,5 GET MFILE VALID .NOT. SUBSTR(MFILE,1,8) $ " .,!@#$%^&*_=+"
READ
IF FILE(&MFILE)
```

```
    *file exists, so use it...
    WAIT "Ready printer, press a key..."
    REPORT FORM &MFILE TO PRINT
ENDIF
```

And one of VALID's most powerful abilities is to perform validity checks by referencing another database file. For example, you may want to make sure a part number exists before you accept that part number in a database of orders received. Gone are the days when you had to jump to the other database, manually perform a search, initialize a variable to indicate the success (or failure) of the search, and jump back to the orders database. All of this can now be accomplished with a single VALID clause. Once the files and indexes are open, just use the VALID clause, along with an Immediate IF function and the new SEEK function, to search for a matching entry in the other database. The syntax for the VALID clause, when used in this manner, would be:

```
VALID IIF(SEEK(MVAR,ALIAS),.T.,.F.)
```

where MVAR is the memory variable containing the term you are searching for in the index, and ALIAS is the filename or alias name for the indexed file that is open in another work area. Alias must be surrounded by quotes. For example:

```
SELECT 2
USE PARTS INDEX PARTS
*this file is indexed on the part number field.
SELECT 1
USE ORDERS
APPEND BLANK
@ 5,5 SAY "Part number to ship?"
@ 5,25 GET PNUMB VALID IIF(SEEK(PNUMB,"PARTS"),.T.,.F.);
   ERROR "There is no such part number in the parts file!"
```

The IIF(SEEK(PNUMB,"PARTS"),.T.,.F.) portion of the statement uses the Immediate IF (IIF) function to return a logical value of TRUE if the SEEK finds the record in the parts database, and a logical value of FALSE if the SEEK does not find the record in the parts database. The PARTNO field in the parts database is pointed to with the alias name ("PARTS"). Whenever the expression evaluated by VALID returns a logical value of FALSE, the data is not accepted, and the error message appears at the bottom of the screen. The section later in this chapter under the subheading Using Data Dictionaries contains additional examples of the use of VALID to cross-check against the contents of other database files.

While PICTURE functions and templates can't perform all necessary validation for you, they can provide a needed hand in preventing data entry errors.

Using RANGE

The RANGE option of the @ ... SAY ... GET command can also be used during the data validation process to limit entries to an acceptable range of data.

RANGE works with numeric data, and with dates. The syntax for the RANGE option is:

```
@<row,column> GET <variable> [RANGE <lower limit>,<upper limit>]
```

For example, to restrict the entry of zip codes to the State of California, you could enter:

```
@ 12,2 GET ZIPCODE RANGE 90000,99999
```

To restrict a single end of the range, include the comma and specify the value for the desired end. For example,

```
@ 15,9 GET HOURLYPAY RANGE 2.70,
```

sets a minimum of 2.70 for the salary, with no maximum. The command,

```
@ 15,9 GET HOURLYPAY RANGE ,20.05
```

sets no minimum for the salary and a maximum of 20.05. To use RANGE with dates, enclose the dates in curly braces. As an example, the following command:

```
@15,5 GET HIREDATE RANGE {05/15/83},{06/01/86}
```

restricts entries to valid dates that fall between 5/15/83 and 6/1/86. The command,

```
@15,5 GET HIREDATE RANGE {05/15/83}, DATE()
```

restricts entries to valid dates that fall between 5/15/83 and the current date maintained in the system clock. Obviously, such a scheme means that the PC's clock must be correct. If the system clock defaults to the "01/01/80" date because it was not properly set, users of such a program might find it impossible to enter what would otherwise be an acceptable date. Or worse yet, if the system clock date were less than the date specified within the curly braces, the program would crash with a "syntax error" when the RANGE portion of the statement attempted to use a lower range that is actually higher in value than the upper range.

Testing for Blank Records

Data-entry modules of a program should include a test for a blank record, so that a successive APPEND BLANK command does not accidentally add a blank record to the database. One way to do this is to use the TRIM function to trim trailing spaces from the variables used to store the data, then use the LEN function to see if the length supplied by TRIM is zero. Following the READ statement that reads the GET functions, you could have a portion of code like this:

```
*Add the record
DO WHILE .T.
    CLEAR
```

```
        @ 6,10 SAY "Name? " GET MEMNAME
        @ 7,10 SAY "Age? " GET MEMAGE
        @ 8,10 SAY "I.D. Number? " GET MEMID
        READ
        IF LEN(TRIM(MEMNAME)) = 0
             *Apparent blank record
             STORE "Y" TO ABORT
             ? CHR(7)
             @ 24,1 SAY "**Entry MUST be made in NAME FIELD! "
             @ 24,35 SAY "Abort new record addition? (Y/N): "
             @ 24,70 GET ABORT $"YNyn"
             READ
             IF UPPER(ABORT) = "N"
                  LOOP
             ENDIF
             RETURN
        ENDIF
        *Not blank, so add the record
        USE MYFILE INDEX NAMES
        APPEND BLANK
        REPLACE NAME WITH MEMNAME, AGE WITH MEMAGE, IDNUM WITH MEMID
        CLOSE DATABASES
        CLEAR
        ACCEPT "  --Add another? (Y/N): " TO ANS
        IF UPPER(ANS) = "N"
             RETURN
        ENDIF
ENDDO
```

In this case, if the memory variable used to store the last name contains zero characters when evaluated by the LEN and TRIM functions, an appropriate error message will be displayed at the bottom of the screen. The user will be given the option of exiting (in which case the APPEND BLANK statement is never executed) or of looping back to the start of the DO WHILE loop to repeat the data entry process.

Testing for Possible Duplicates During Data Entry

Some programmers also prefer their programs to check for possible duplicate entries in the database before accepting an additional record in customer lists or mailing lists. When the application does not offer a unique field to index on, you can often get close enough results by indexing on a combination of fields, such as with these commands:

```
USE MAILER
INDEX ON UPPER(LAST_NAME) + UPPER(FIRST_NAME) + ZIP_CODE TO COMBO
```

These statements create an index file that contains fairly unique data, and the use of the UPPER function avoids later problems with the case significance of dBASE IV. Before it adds records, the program can first perform a SEEK to see if any records exist with a similar subset of data in the index. Once any possible duplicates are found, they can be displayed, and the user can then be asked if the new record is to be added nevertheless. The following code uses this approach, with an index file created with the commands just listed:

```
*This is TEST.PRG
*Routine adds new records and tests for duplicate records
SET TALK OFF
SET PROCEDURE TO TEST
CLEAR
STORE SPACE(15) TO M_LAST
STORE SPACE(15) TO M_FIRST
STORE SPACE(20) TO M_ADD1
STORE SPACE(10) TO M_ADD2
STORE SPACE(10) TO M_CITY
STORE SPACE(2) TO M_STATE
STORE SPACE(10) TO M_ZIP
STORE 0 TO M_CUSTNO
STORE SPACE(10) TO M_COUNTRY
@ 5,6 SAY "Last name: " GET M_LAST
@ 6,5 SAY "First name: " GET M_FIRST
@ 7,1 SAY "Address Line 1: " GET M_ADD1
@ 8,1 SAY "Address Line 2: " GET M_ADD2
@ 9,11 SAY "City: " GET M_CITY
@ 10,10 SAY "State: " GET M_STATE
@ 11,7 SAY "Zip Code: " GET M_ZIP
@ 12,8 SAY "Country: " GET M_COUNTRY
@ 14,1 SAY "Customer number: " GET M_CUSTNO
READ
STORE M_LAST + M_FIRST + M_ZIP TO FINDIT
STORE UPPER(FINDIT) TO FINDIT
USE MAILER
SET INDEX TO COMBO
SEEK FINDIT
IF .NOT. FOUND()
    *No similar record, so proceed with addition
    DO ADDIT
    RETURN
ENDIF
CLEAR
? "Similar records currently in the database are as follows:"
?
DISPLAY LAST_NAME, ADDRESS_1 WHILE ;
UPPER(LAST_NAME + FIRST_NAME + ZIP_CODE) =  FINDIT
```

```
?
ACCEPT "  --Add new record anyway? (Y/N): " TO ANS
IF UPPER(ANS) = "Y"
   CLEAR
   DO ADDIT
ENDIF
RETURN
**
Procedure AddIt
APPEND BLANK
REPLACE LAST_NAME WITH M_LAST, FIRST_NAME WITH M_FIRST
REPLACE ADDRESS_1 WITH M_ADD1, ADDRESS_2 WITH M_ADD2
REPLACE CITY WITH M_CITY, STATE WITH M_STATE, ZIP_CODE WITH M_ZIP
REPLACE CUSTNO WITH M_CUSTNO, COUNTRY WITH M_COUNTRY
CLOSE DATABASES
RETURN
```

This is one way to guard against duplicate entries in a database, and there are others. An equally common technique is to not slow down the data-entry process, but to instead weed duplicates out of the database at a later time by writing code that searches for and deletes duplicate records, or by providing printer routines from a utility menu that print out suspected duplicates for operator verification.

Using SOUNDEX to Check for Duplicates

One problem with using ordinary indexes to check for duplicate names is that misspellings or different spellings of names are often missed. For example, a mailing list might contain entries for Therman Smith and Thermon Smith, when both entries happen to be the same address. Only one name is correct, but the different spellings of the first name caused an accidental duplicate in the database.

A solution to this common problem involves the use of SOUNDEX, an algorithm that assigns each letter in a word a numeric value. The numeric values of the letters are used to build a string of numbers which identify the word by sound. Similar-sounding words such as "they're," "there," and "their" have the same SOUNDEX code.

Earlier versions of dBASE could perform SOUNDEX translations with complex programming. dBASE IV provides the SOUNDEX() function, which makes the use of SOUNDEX a simple affair. The syntax for the function is:

```
SOUNDEX(<character expression>)
```

and the function returns a four-character code, using the following algorithm:

1. The first character in the string becomes the first character in the SOUNDEX code.
2. All occurrences (after the first character) of the letters *A, E, H, I, O, U, W*, and *Y* are dropped.

3. Remaining letters are assigned the following numbers:

B,F,P,V	1
C,G,J,K,Q,S,X,Z	2
D,T	3
L	4
M,N	5
R	6

4. When two or more letters are the same, all but the first letter in the group of letters are dropped.

The code returned by the SOUNDEX() function will always be in the form of CNNN, where C is a letter and N is a digit. All digits after the third are dropped. If the algorithm produces a code with less than three digits, trailing zeroes are added to produce three digits.

The SOUNDEX code can be used to build an index. Similar-sounding words will then have the same code in the index. Assuming the presence of a field called LASTNAME, the index could be built with commands like the following:

```
USE MAILER
INDEX ON SOUNDEX(LASTNAME) TAG SOUNDS
```

Once the index exists, a routine designed to show all names similar to a given name might resemble the following:

```
STORE SPACE(20) TO LNAME
@ 5,5 SAY "Last name?" GET LNAME
READ
FINDIT = SOUNDEX(LNAME)
SEEK FINDIT
IF .NOT. FOUND()
     CLEAR
     WAIT "No similar names found.  Press any key."
     RETURN
ENDIF
CLEAR
? " Similar sounding names are as follows:"
DISPLAY ALL LASTNAME, FIRSTNAME WHILE ;
    SOUNDEX(LASTNAME) = SOUNDEX(LNAME)
WAIT
```

In a similar way, you could use the SOUNDEX() function as a part of your search routines, to find records for editing. This may be the best way to find records for editing if your users are notorious for misspelling names during data entry.

Using Data Dictionaries for Validation of Data

Data dictionaries can be used to guard against incorrect data entry. A prime example is in many sales applications, where the master file often contains a sales rep ID number, a client ID number, and a sales category. Data to be entered into the sales transaction file can be verified against the master file. By checking to see if the data entered exists in another file, incorrect data can often be caught and rejected before it gets into the database.

Consider the following portion of a program for entering sales transactions:

```
*Romella's Hair Care
*Sales Transaction Program
*Last update 11/01/88
SET TALK OFF
ON ESCAPE RETURN
SELECT 2
USE EMPLOYEE
SET ORDER TO IDNUMB
SELECT 3
USE CLIENTS
SET ORDER TO CUSTNO
SELECT 1
CLEAR
STORE "  " TO M_EMPID
STORE "   " TO M_CLIENTID
STORE "A" TO M_SALESCAT
STORE 0.00 TO AMOUNT
@ 5,10 SAY "Enter sales rep ID number:" GET M_EMPID PICTURE "99";
    VALID IIF(SEEK(M_EMPID,"EMPLOYEE"),.T.,.F.);
    ERROR "There is no employee with that sales rep ID!"
@ 6,10 SAY "Enter customer number:" GET M_CLIENTID PICTURE "999";
    VALID IIF(SEEK(M_CLIENTID,"CLIENTS"),.T.,.F.);
    ERROR "No such client in the client files!"
@ 7,10 SAY "Enter category:" GET M_SALESCAT FUNCTION "!";
   VALID M_SALESCAT $ "ABCDEFG" ERROR "Valid codes are ABCDEFG"
@ 9,10 SAY "Enter amount of the sale:" GET AMOUNT
READ
SET ESCAPE OFF
USE SALES
APPEND BLANK
REPLACE EMPID WITH M_EMPID
REPLACE CLIENTID WITH M_CLIENTID
REPLACE SALESCAT WITH M_SALESCAT
REPLACE SALEAMT WITH AMOUNT
CLEAR
SET ESCAPE ON
WAIT "Record added.  Press a key to get back to menu..."
RETURN
```

In the example, valid customer numbers and employee numbers are stored in two databases that serve as dictionaries. The entries supplied for the customer number (CLIENTID) and the salesrep ID number (IDNUMB) are checked against the valid numbers contained in the dictionaries, with the use of the IIF and SEEK functions along with the VALID clause. If the matching values are not found, an error message is displayed, with the use of the ERROR clause of the @ . . . SAY . . . GET command.

If a record of additions to a database is important for security purposes, you can resort to the use of an *audit file* that will keep track of all entries made by the user. The audit file can be a secondary database, similar in structure to the main database, but with a field added for the name of the user. From the same menu used to add or edit records, you can prompt for the user's name and store that name in a field in the audit file. You may also want to store the date of the change and the value of certain fields before the changes were made in the audit file. If any question arises at a later time about the validity of the data in the master files, you can print the contents of the audit file to provide a record of the users' changes.

Editing and Deleting Records Under Program Control

Programs for editing and deleting records are usually quite similar to programs used for adding data, with one significant difference. In place of an APPEND BLANK to add a new record, a search routine is used to find the desired record to edit or delete. An acceptable series of steps for editing a record would be:

1. Query the user for the search term used to find the desired record.
2. Store the search term to a variable.
3. Use FIND, SEEK, or LOCATE to find the record.
4. Store the values contained in the fields of the record to variables.
5. Display the contents of the variables.
6. If the record is to be edited, allow editing with @ . . . SAY . . . GET commands. If it is to be deleted, ask for confirmation of the deletion.
7. If the record was edited, move the contents of the variables back to the database fields with REPLACE commands. If the record is to be deleted, use DELETE to mark the record for deletion.
8. Close the files.

Finding the desired record is always easier if the file is indexed on a unique field (such as an employee ID number, part number, or social security number). In such cases, you can use FIND or SEEK to perform a fast search of the indexed field. If there is no unique field, FIND or SEEK can still be used, but since only the first occurrence will be found, your program may need to display a succession of records following the found record until the desired one is verified by the user. If the database is not indexed, you must resort to the LOCATE command, which operates at a snail's pace compared to FIND and SEEK. This alone is a good reason for indexing the database.

The following command file is used to find a record and edit that record; its design is adapted from the program used to add data, described earlier.

```
***EDITINV.PRG***
*Edits items in inventory
*Last update 04/15/86
SET TALK OFF
USE MAINFILE INDEX PARTS
*Query user for part number to edit
CLEAR
STORE 0 TO MPARTNO
@2,30 TO 5,70
@3,40 SAY "Enter part number:"
@4,40 SAY "(press Return to exit)"
@3,59 GET MPARTNO
READ
IF MPARTNO = 0
   CLEAR
   RETURN
ENDIF
SEEK MPARTNO
IF .NOT. FOUND()
     *No such P/N found
     @3,40 CLEAR TO 4,69
     @3,40 SAY "No such part number!"
     @4,40 SAY "Press a key to return to menu."
     ? CHR(7)
     WAIT""
     CLOSE DATABASES
     RETURN
ENDIF
*Valid part number
STORE PARTDESC TO MPARTDESC
STORE WHOLCOST TO MWHOLCOST
STORE RETLCOST TO MRETLCOST
STORE QUANTITY TO MQUANTITY
CLEAR
@  6,  3  TO 18, 50
@  1,  0  TO 19, 54  DOUBLE
@  2, 15  SAY "INVENTORY MASTER FILE"
@  4, 15  SAY "Editing Screen"
@  7, 12  SAY "Part Number: "
@  7, 26  SAY MPARTNO
@  9, 12  SAY "Description:"
@  9, 25  GET  MPARTDESC
@ 11,  9  SAY "Wholesale Cost:"
@ 11, 25  GET  MWHOLCOST
```

```
@ 13, 12  SAY "Retail Cost:"
@ 13, 25  GET  MRETLCOST
@ 15,  7  SAY "Initial Quantity:"
@ 15, 25  GET  MQUANTITY
READ
REPLACE PARTDESC with MPARTDESC, QUANTITY with MQUANTITY
REPLACE WHOLCOST with MWHOLCOST, RETLCOST with MRETLCOST
CLOSE DATABASES
RETURN
*End of subroutine
```

A similar program can be used to delete records under control of the program. In place of the @ . . . SAY . . . GETS for editing, use @ . . . SAY commands to display the data and ask for confirmation of the deletion. Once confirmation is provided, you can use the DELETE command, as illustrated in this program excerpt:

```
STORE .T. TO ANSWER
@ 20,5 SAY "Delete this record? " GET ANSWER PICTURE  'Y'
READ
IF ANSWER
     DELETE
ENDIF
```

Of course, these methods of finding records to edit or to delete work with a simple case: the database has a field that contains a unique entry for each record in the database. In this case, it is the part number for the inventory item. Databases that keep track of people often use social security numbers for this purpose; if they are not available, some sort of unique account number can be chosen. If at all possible, find something that is unique about each record and use that item as an indexed key to perform searches. If you are building an application, and the users have not specified a unique field for the database specification, strongly suggest one. It will save you much coding (and users' time) if the program can perform searches on a unique, indexed field.

Nevertheless, there will be times when an application doesn't have a unique field, or it has one, but the user can't recall John Smith's social security number, so the user wants to search on something a lot more generic than a social security number. The user recalls that the person's last name is Smith, so the user wants to search for Smith (despite the fact that there are 157 "Smiths" in the database). The LOCATE and CONTINUE commands will spring to mind only if you've never used them in a sizable database. Use them once, and you are likely to abandon them for life because they're so slow. As an example, for a 6000 record mailing list, a LOCATE command took 18 seconds to find the desired record (and this was on an AT-compatible, running in high-speed mode). Try it on a plain-vanilla 4.77-mHz PC compatible, and your users will take one coffee break for each record that's edited.

A workable alternative is to index the file on the field that will be searched, use FIND or SEEK to find the first record in a group of records, and then display the records and let the user pick the record to edit. Perhaps you want to display records one by one using @ . . . SAY commands to display each possible match, until the record that's desired is found.

An alternative is to list to the screen all records in the group, along with their respective record numbers. The user can then be prompted for a record number to edit. The following program uses the first technique, showing all records in a group of records that have the same client number. The records are displayed one by one for possible editing:

```
**EDCASH.PRG edits records in A/R (Cash) database
**Last update 11/01/88
SET TALK OFF
CLEAR
STORE 9999 TO MCLIENT
@5,5 SAY "Enter client code: " GET MCLIENT
READ
USE CASH INDEX CASH
SEEK MCLIENT
IF .NOT. FOUND()
    CLOSE DATABASES
    @7,5 SAY "No such client code in Accounts Rec. files!"
    ? CHR(7)
    WAIT "  -Press a key to return to previous menu."
    RETURN
ENDIF

DO WHILE CLIENTCODE = MCLIENT
     STORE "N" TO ANS
     CLEAR
     STORE PAYOR TO MPAYOR
     STORE CHECKNUMB TO MCHECK
     STORE AMOUNT TO MAMOUNT
     STORE DESCRIPT TO MDESCRIPT
     @ 4,5 SAY "===Verification Screen==="
     @ 5,7 SAY "Client ID: "
     @ 5,19 SAY MCLIENT
     @ 6,5 SAY "Name of payor: "
     @ 6,21 SAY MPAYOR
     @ 7,5 SAY "Check Number: "
     @ 7,20 SAY MCHECK
     @ 8,5 SAY "Amount: "
     @ 8,15 SAY MAMOUNT
     @ 9,5 SAY "Description: "
     @ 9,19 SAY MDESCRIPT
     @ 12,5 SAY "**Is this the desired record? (Y/N): "
     GET ANS
     READ
```

```
          IF UPPER(ANS) = "Y"
               CLEAR
               @ 4,5 SAY "===Editing Screen==="
               @ 5,5 SAY "Client ID:      " GET MCLIENT
               @ 6,5 SAY "Name of payor: " GET MPAYOR
               @ 7,5 SAY "Check Number:  " GET MCHECK
               @ 8,5 SAY "Amount:         " GET MAMOUNT
               @ 12,5 SAY "Description:  " GET MDESCRIPT
               READ
               REPLACE PAYOR WITH MPAYOR, CHECKNUMB WITH MCHECK
               REPLACE AMOUNT WITH MAMOUNT, DESCRIPT WITH MDESCRIPT
               CLOSE DATABASES
               RETURN
          ELSE
               SKIP
          ENDIF
ENDDO
CLEAR
@ 5,5 SAY "No more records with that client ID in the database."
@ 6,5 SAY "Press any key to return to Main Menu."
WAIT ""
RETURN
*End of EDCASH.PRG
```

The example uses a database that is indexed on a key field (client ID numbers), and a SEEK command locates the first in a series of records containing that client ID number. A DO WHILE loop then uses a series of @ . . . SAY commands to display (but not yet allow editing) of variables. The user is queried whether the displayed record is the one to be edited. If the user answers with Y for Yes, a series of @ . . . SAY . . . GETS allow editing of the variables, and the READ and REPLACE statements move the variable contents into the database. If the user enters N in response to the query, a SKIP moves the record pointer to the next record in indexed order, and that record is displayed (as long as the client ID still matches the one originally supplied). Once all records matching that client code have been viewed, the DO WHILE loop ends, and an error message indicates that no further records for that client are available for editing.

Using BROWSE for Data Entry and Editing

There was a time when dBASE programmers shared a near-universal disdain for using BROWSE in end-user applications. The BROWSE mode certainly provided a quick and dirty way for programmers to add and edit data during testing. But providing end users with access to BROWSE within a program was another matter entirely. The lack of editing controls and the ability to write changes directly to the database file with no validation made BROWSE a dangerous command in the hands of a novice user.

dBASE IV has added options that let the programmer exercise tight control over the capabilities of BROWSE. With the new options, this command is worth a close look. In editing applications, using BROWSE within a predefined window can provide "point-and-shoot" access to a particular record in a database file. You can allow editing but no adding or deleting; allow adding and editing but no deleting; or allow viewing of records only. And, you can display a table of records with BROWSE and leave the table visible on a portion of the screen, while showing fields of a particular record on another part of the screen.

For example, perhaps you would like to provide "point-and-shoot" access to finding a record to edit. The user should be able to enter part or all of a last name, and view a table of records in the vicinity of the name that was entered. Once the user highlights the desired record in the table and presses ESCAPE, the record should appear within a full-screen form, ready for editing. Assuming a database of customers indexed on the LAST_NAME field, the job could be done using code like the following:

```
*Edits by using browse display and on-screen form.*
SET TALK OFF
CLEAR
STORE SPACE(20) TO LNAME
SET NEAR ON
@ 5,5 SAY "Enter all or part of the last name:" GET LNAME
READ
SEEK LNAME
CLEAR
DEFINE WINDOW Browser FROM 10,5 TO 20,70 DOUBLE COLOR W/B
DEFINE WINDOW Editor FROM 1,1 TO 9,75 DOUBLE COLOR G/B
@ 8,10 SAY "Highlight the desired record to edit, then press ESC."
BROWSE LOCK 1 NOAPPEND NOEDIT NODELETE NOCLEAR NOMENU WINDOW Browser
ACTIVATE WINDOW Editor
@ 0,5 SAY " Last name:" GET LAST_NAME COLOR N/R
@ 1,5 SAY "First name:" GET FIRST_NAME COLOR N/R
@ 2,5 SAY " Address 1:" GET ADDRESS_1 COLOR N/R
@ 3,5 SAY " Address 2:" GET ADDRESS_2 COLOR N/R
@ 4,5 SAY "      City:" GET CITY COLOR N/R
@ 4,40 SAY "State:" GET STATE FUNCTION "!" COLOR N/R
@ 4,52 SAY "ZIP Code:" GET ZIP_CODE PICTURE "99999-9999" COLOR N/R
@ 6,5 SAY "Control-End when done." COLOR B/W
READ
CLEAR
DEACTIVATE WINDOW ALL
SET NEAR OFF
RETURN
*end of editing program.*
```

The SET NEAR ON command is used to let dBASE position the record pointer at or near the closest record to the desired entry, so if a precise match isn't found, the user will be in the general area of the desired record. Two windows are then defined—one for the BROWSE display, and another for the full-screen editing of the record. The BROWSE command with the options named results in a display of the records in the window, but the user cannot make any modifications to the records shown in the table. Once the user highlights the desired record and presses ESCAPE, the record appears in the upper half of the screen for full-screen editing, as shown in Figure 8-1.

If you want to provide capabilities for entering but not deleting data while in BROWSE, specify the NODELETE option along with the BROWSE command within your programs. To limit the user to adding one (and only one) record, you could use commands like these:

```
APPEND BLANK
BROWSE NOMENU NOAPPEND NODELETE
```

and this would allow the user to add a single record in the Browse mode, without performing any other functions. If you wanted to place no limit on the number of records that could be added, but still limit deletions or other uses of the Browse Menu, you could use the command,

```
BROWSE NOMENU NODELETE
```

to accomplish the task.

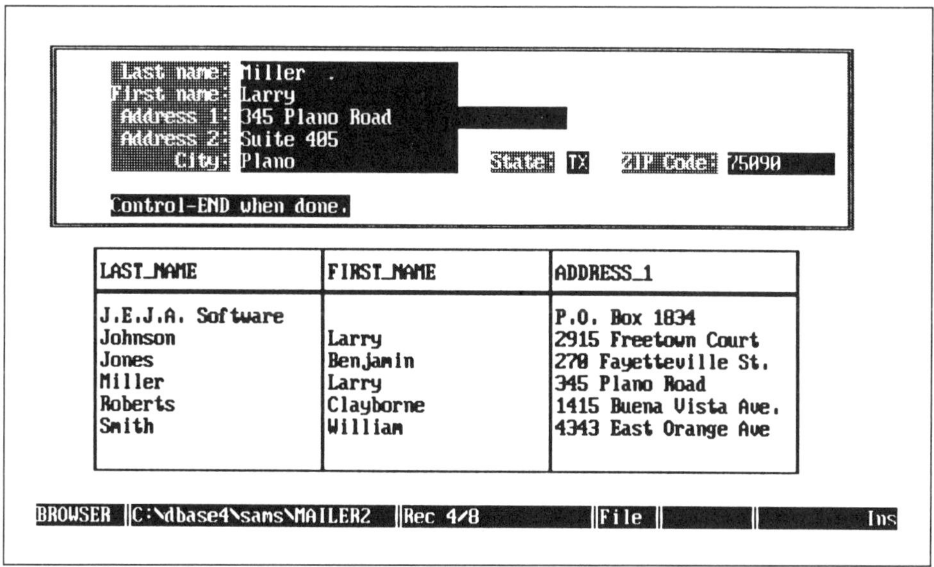

Figure 8-1 Simultaneous Display of BROWSE Table and Edit Fields

Using Filters

The SET FILTER Command

dBASE IV accepts filters, which can be used to control precisely what data can be displayed or edited by dBASE. The use of such filters results in a specified condition applied to the database in use, making it appear that the database contains fewer records than it actually has. Filters are implemented with the SET FILTER command. Use of SET FILTER is a viable alternative to the DO WHILE loop described previously; SET FILTER will be slower than an indexed database using DO WHILE, but there are times when SET FILTER presents the best alternative. The syntax for the command is:

```
SET FILTER TO <condition> <FILE/ <query filename>
```

The QUERY FILE option is used if a menu-driven feature of dBASE IV, called Query-By-Example, is used to build a file containing a filter. Use of the Query-By-Example is discussed shortly; however, for many programmers' needs, it is easier to build conditions by specifying the desired condition within the command. As an example, the command,

```
SET FILTER TO CLIENTCODE = 4792
```

restricts all output from the database to only those records containing the value 4792 in the CLIENTCODE field. Once a filter has been set with the SET FILTER command, the appropriate commands can be used to display and edit the filtered records. Some additional examples of the SET FILTER command include:

```
SET FILTER TO HIREDATE =< {09/01/86} .AND. UPPER(TITLE) = "MANAGER"

SET FILTER TO ((CITY = "LAS VEGAS" .OR. CITY = "RENO") .AND. INCOME =< 45000)

SET FILTER TO EVENTDATE = {07/14/84} .AND. "weapon" $ SUMMARY
```

(The last example uses the text string search capability of dBASE IV to include only those records whose SUMMARY fields contain the word *weapon* in the middle of a string of text.)

The SET FILTER command affects all visible database records, not just those commands you use to edit records. When you enter a SET FILTER command, program commands used to list data, print reports, or view records such as @ . . . SAY commands, as well as any uses of EDIT and BROWSE, will only view those records that meet the filter condition.

Using the Query Menu to Build a Filter File

The SET FILTER TO FILE <query filename> command is used when a filter file has been created with the Query Design Screen. The Query Design Screen provides a menu-assisted way for dBASE IV users to enter filter conditions similar to those described. The Query Design Screen is opened by entering the command,

```
CREATE QUERY <filename>
```

where <filename> is the name of the query file to be created. All query files are normally stored with a .QBE extension, unless you specify otherwise. When you enter the command, the Query Design Screen shown in Figure 8-2 is displayed.

The upper portion of the screen contains the File Skeleton, a visual model of the database files used to build the query. Filenames from the active database are displayed in this area. (If no database is active when the CREATE QUERY command is entered, this area will initially appear blank.) Queries can be based on multiple database files; when this is the case, the fields from multiple files will appear in successive rows of the File Skeleton.

The bottom of the Query Design Screen contains the View Skeleton, a visual model of the fields which will be contained in the view that results from the query. Movement around the Query Design Screen can be accomplished with the cursor, Tab, and Shift-Tab keys. The F3 (Previous) and F4 (Next) keys are used to move between the File Skeleton and the View Skeleton. The Home and End keys can also be used to move to the far left and far right sides of a skeleton.

Building the desired query is basically a matter of selecting the desired fields and adding them to the View Skeleton, and entering any conditions that will limit the records made accessible to the query. In the first step of the two-step process, you must select the desired fields, and add them to the View Skeleton.

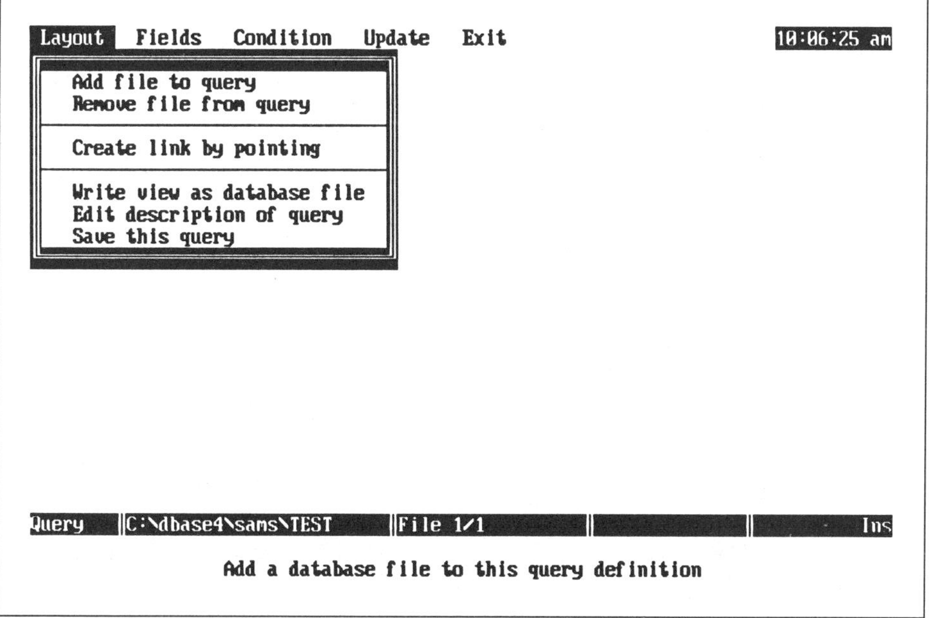

Figure 8-2 Query Design Screen

To do this, either add each desired field from the File Skeleton to the View Skeleton by moving the cursor to the field and pressing F5; or, place the cursor at the far left of the File Skeleton (under the filename) by pressing Home, then press F5 to add all the fields to the View Skeleton. You can then move the cursor down to the View Skeleton with F4, and remove any unwanted fields by placing the cursor in that field and pressing F5. Figure 8-3 shows a query containing a File Skeleton for the "MAILER" database. Because the database file was open when the query was created, all fields in the database appear as part of the File Skeleton. In the example, the LAST_NAME, FIRST_NAME, ADDRESS_1, and ADDRESS_2 fields were added to the View Skeleton by moving the cursor to each of the fields, and pressing F5.

The second step in building the query is to enter any desired expression in the fields of the File Skeleton. The expressions are used to select the desired records. As an example, the expression,

```
STATE = "TX"
```

would cause the query to limit all records to those with "TX" in the STATE field. Any valid dBASE expression can be used as a part of the query. To enter a long expression and see the expression as it is entered, press F9 (Zoom). Figure 8-4 shows a query which selects records from the database where the city is "Lakeland" and the state is "FL".

"AND" logic within queries can be implemented by entering the various conditions in the different columns, as shown in the above example (CITY is Lakeland "AND" STATE is FL). To implement "OR" logic in a query, simply

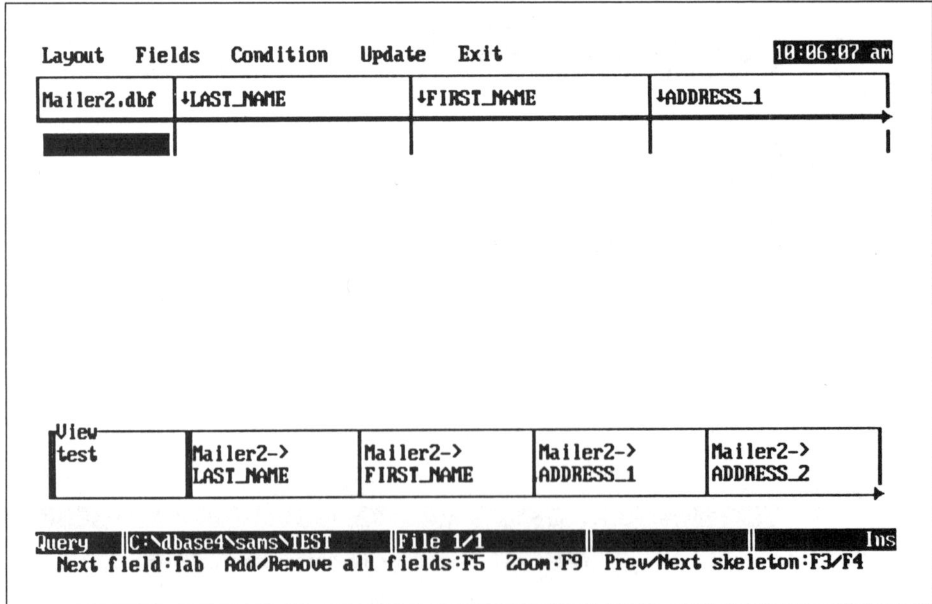

Figure 8-3 Query Design Screen with File, View Skeletons

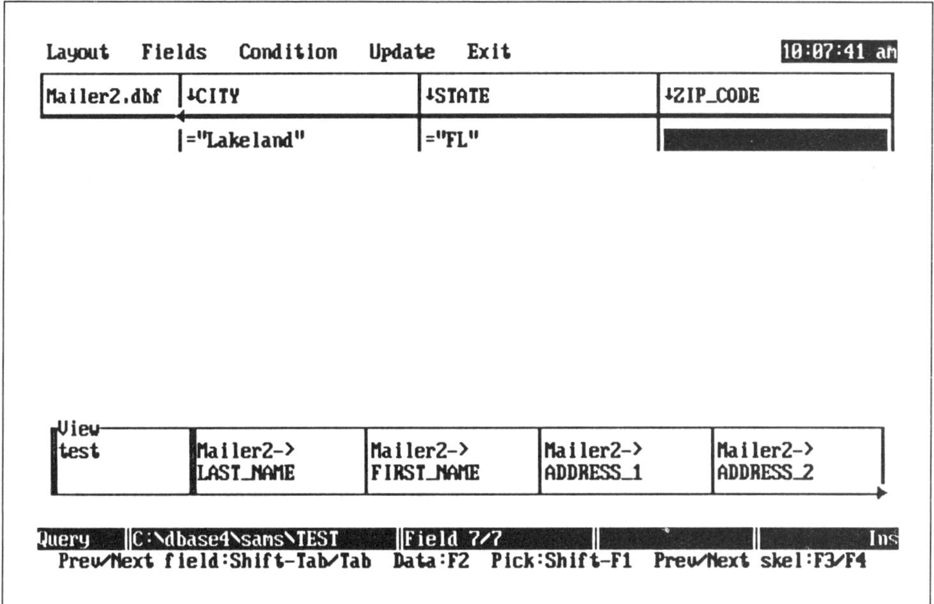

Figure 8-4 Sample Query

use multiple lines in the File Skeleton, by using the down arrow key to move the cursor down. Enter additional conditions on the successive lines of the File Skeleton. Each line then contains separate conditions which, if met, will satisfy the query. As an example, Figure 8-5 shows a query which will select records if the state field contains "FL" OR "TX" OR "CA".

Once the query is completed, it can be saved by pressing Control-End, or by choosing Save Changes and Exit from the Exit Menu. The saved query can be applied from the dot prompt, or within a program, with the SET FILTER TO FILE <query filename> command.

Query Operators and Symbols

The operators and symbols shown in Table 8-2 are valid within a query expression.

In addition to the above, the standard DOS wildcards of asterisk (*) for any number of characters, and question mark (?) for any single character, may be used in a query expression. As an example, the expression,

```
="A*s"
```

would qualify all entries beginning with the letter *A* and ending with the letter *s*.

The Query Design Screen Menu Options

When designing a query, various menu options are accessible which aid in constructing the query. As in all menu-driven parts of dBASE IV, the menus may

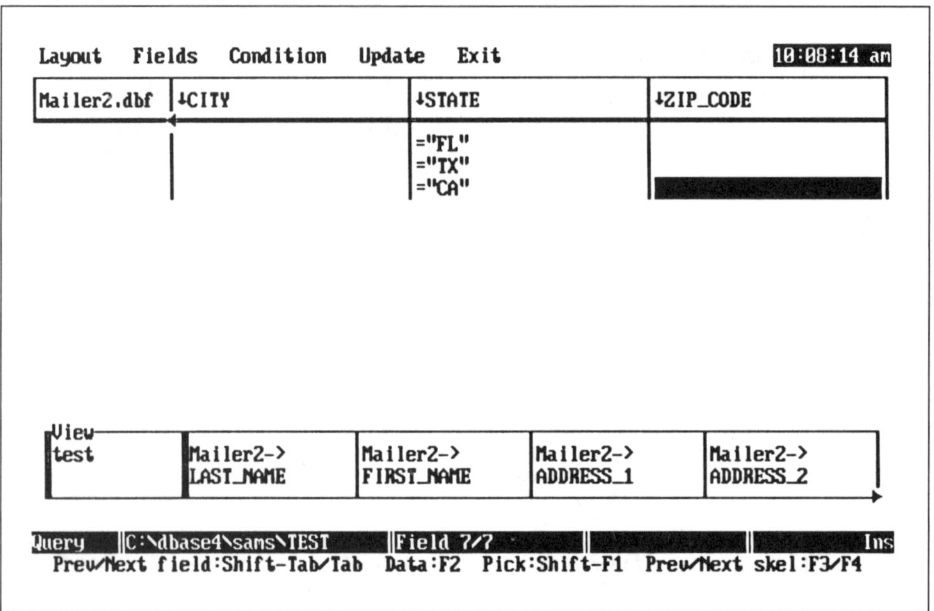

Figure 8-5 Sample Query Using OR Logic

be accessed with F10, or by pressing ALT plus the first letter of the menu name. Figure 8-6 shows the Layout Menu.

Use the Add File To Query option to add a database file to the File Skeleton. The Remove File From Query option has the opposite effect; it removes a file from the File Skeleton. The Create Link By Pointing option lets you link multiple files by drawing a relation. (More details on relational links can be found in Chapter 10.)

Use the Write View As Database File option to build another database with selected records based on the conditions in the query. The Edit Description option lets you add or edit a one-line description which appears if the query is accessed from the Control Center (Assist) menus. The Save This Query option saves all changes while remaining within the Query Design Screen.

The Fields Menu, shown in Figure 8-7, is used to add, edit, and remove fields used in the view, or to reorder the database based on specific fields.

Use the Add Field To View and Remove Field From View options to add or remove fields from the View Skeleton. (You can also use the F5 key for the same purpose. Place the cursor in a field of the File Skeleton and press F5 to add it to the view, or place the cursor in a field of the View Skeleton, and press F5 to remove it from the view.)

The Edit Field Name option is used to change the name of a field shown in the view (the change applies only to the view, and the actual fieldname in the database file is not affected). The Sort On This Field option causes dBASE to sort the database to another file when the query is performed. Use the Include

Table 8-2 Valid Query Operators and Symbols

Operator or Symbol	Meaning
+	Addition
−	Subtraction
*	Multiplication
/	Division
=	Equals
<	Less than
>	Greater than
<=	Less than or equal to
>=	Greater than or equal to
$	Contains
like	Pattern matching for characters
sounds like	Similar to in sound
avg	Average of numeric value
max	Maximum of numeric values
min	Minimum of numeric values
sum	Sum of numeric values
cnt	Count (number) of values
date()	Matches today's date

Indexes option to tell dBASE to apply an index (created previously) to the records shown by the query.

Figure 8-8 shows the Condition Menu, which is used to add, delete, or show *condition boxes*. Condition boxes are simply an alternate way of entering query conditions; instead of placing the conditions in the columns of the File Skeleton, they may be placed on individual rows of a condition box. If users are more familiar with the Query Menu used by dBASE III Plus, they may be more comfortable with the use of condition boxes than with the use of the skeletons. In Figure 8-8, the condition box displayed in the lower right corner of the Query Screen is equivalent to the query entered into the File Skeleton in Figure 8-4, where all records from Lakeland, FL would be chosen.

Queries can also be designed as Update Queries, which will update (or perform global replacements) on a database file. The options in the Update Menu, shown in Figure 8-9, are used to design Update Queries. Use the Perform The Update option to apply the instructions in the query and begin updating the records in the active database file. Use the Specify Update operation to define how the records will be updated once the query is performed. The Exit Menu options are similar to Exit Menus used throughout dBASE IV. This menu contains options for saving the query, or for abandoning the query without saving any changes.

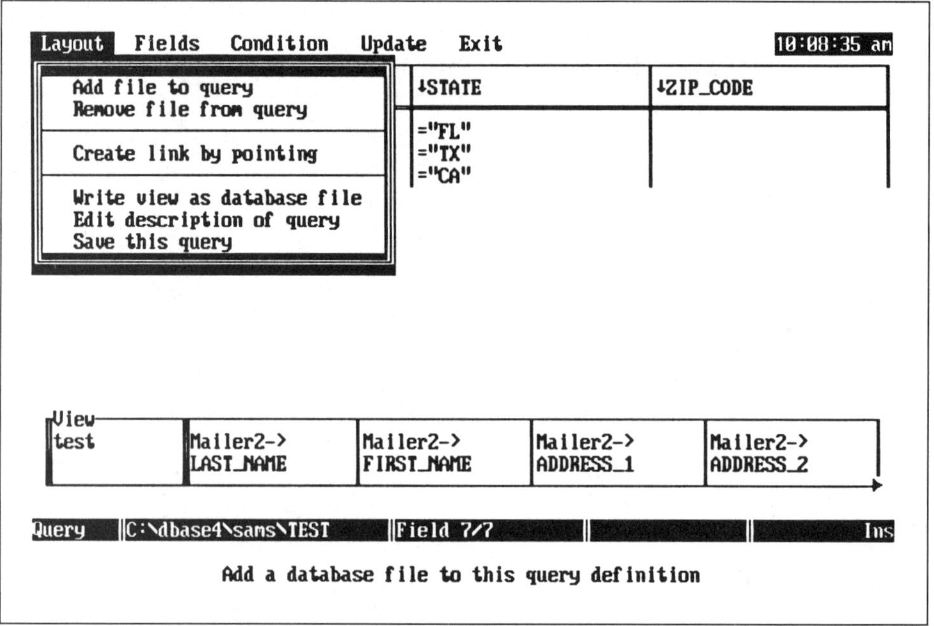

Figure 8-6 Layout Menu

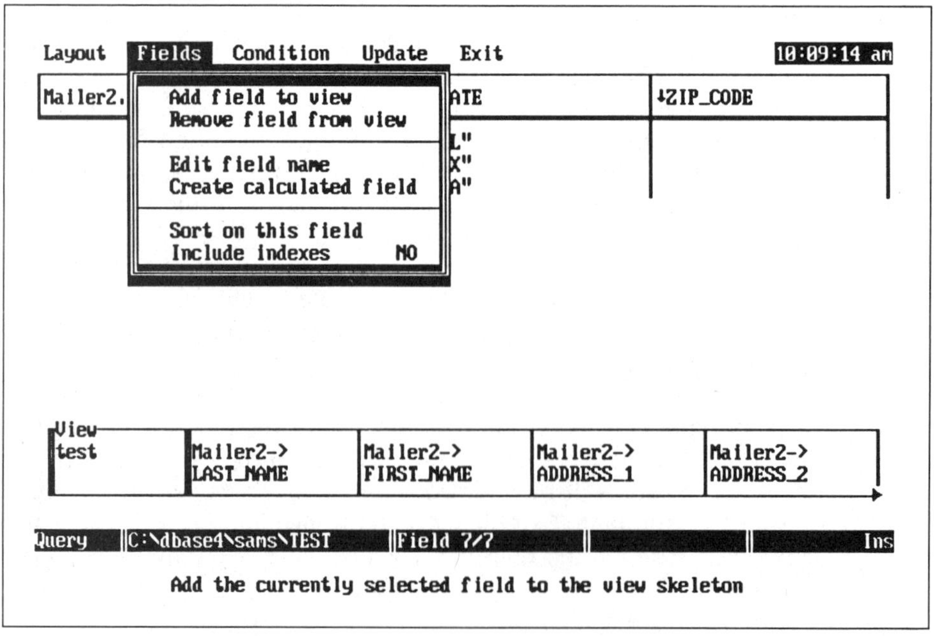

Figure 8-7 Fields Menu

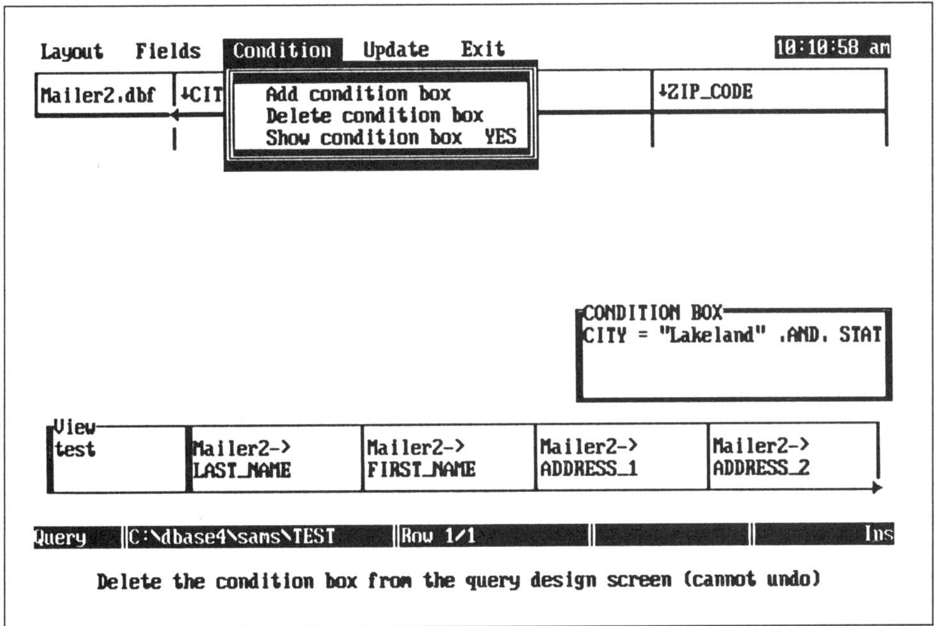

Figure 8-8 Condition Menu

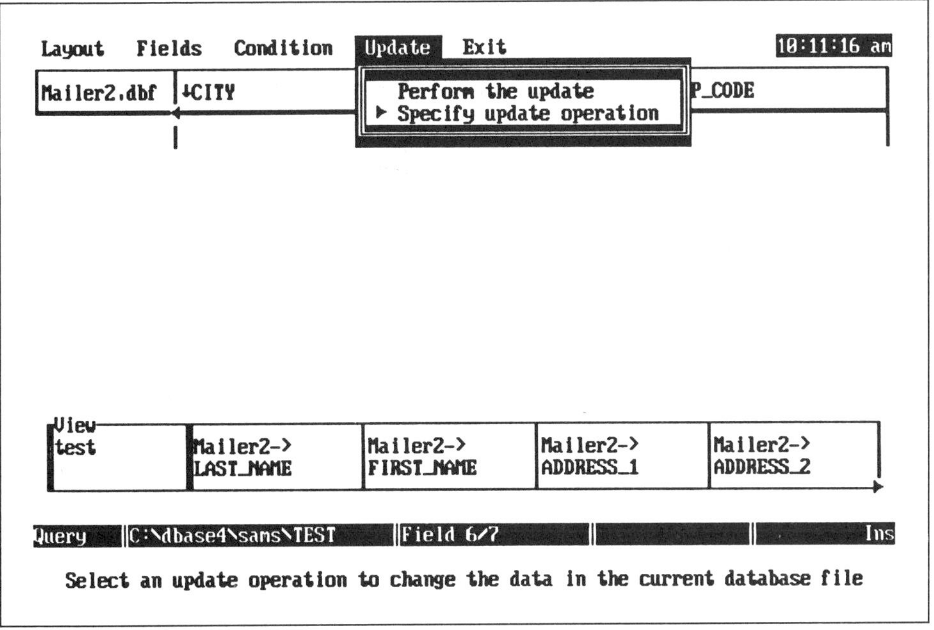

Figure 8-9 Update Menu

Update Menu

Since all of the choices from the Query Design Screen can be implemented with program commands such as SET FILTER TO, it is natural to ask why the Query-By-Example system implemented in dBASE IV would be of interest to programmers. Other than ease of use (which is not necessarily a requirement among programmers), using the Query Design Screen has one significant advantage over manually coding the filter expression: end-user flexibility. You can offer the Query Design Screen as a menu option within your programs. This allows computer-savvy users the option of creating their own custom filters by choosing a menu selection that implements a CREATE QUERY <filename> command.

For example, menu choices for creating and using custom filters could be implemented by CASE statements of a menu, as shown in this example of program code:

```
**Custom filter program
**Last update 11/12/88
DO WHILE .T.
CLEAR
@ 6,5 SAY "============================================== "
@ 8,5 SAY "    1.   Choose an existing filter."
@ 9,5 SAY "    2.   Create a new filter using Query Menu."
@10,5 SAY "    3.   Return to Main Menu."
@12,5 SAY "============================================== "
STORE 1 TO FILT
INPUT "   Enter a selection (1-3): " TO FILT
CLEAR
DO CASE
CASE FILT = 1
          DISPLAY FILES LIKE *.QBE
          ?
          ? "Enter name of query file (DO NOT INCLUDE EXTENSION!)"
          ACCEPT TO QNAME
          STORE QNAME + ".QBE" TO QNAME
          SET FILTER TO FILE &QNAME
     CASE FILT = 2
          CLEAR
          ACCEPT "Enter name for Query file (NO EXTENSION):" TO QNAME
          CREATE QUERY &QNAME
     CASE FILT = 3
          RETURN TO MASTER
ENDCASE
ENDDO
```

WARNING: The current record will not always be checked right after implementing a SET FILTER command. Depending on how your programs are structured, this may result in a record being included in a display or edit routine of records, even though it does not meet the filter condition. The simple solution to this problem is to issue a GO TOP to move the record pointer right after a SET FILTER command.

To Pack, or Not to Pack?

Should you pack deleted records following a series of deletions, or should you leave the records hidden but still in the database with the SET DELETED ON command? A dozen programmers will give a dozen different answers to this question. It's largely a matter of programming style (and of how regularly your client deletes records and then asks you to resurrect them out of thin air). An alternative is to copy the deleted records out to a temporary database, then do a PACK. As an example, the following commands would do this, along with some housekeeping to get rid of the temporary file when done:

```
SET DELETED OFF
COPY ALL FOR DELETED() TO TEMPFILE
PACK
USE KILLFILE
APPEND FROM TEMPFILE
CLOSE DATABASES
ERASE TEMPFILE.DBF
```

If a recall of old records ever proves necessary, the records can be manually copied back from the file of deleted records (in this case, KILLFILE.DBF). The file of deleted records could be purged every few months if things run smoothly.

Dealing with Memo Fields

A major improvement in dBASE IV over earlier versions of dBASE is its ability to work with memo fields as a normal part of the @ . . . SAY . . . GET statements used when adding and editing records. The default display of the memo field when used with the GET is the memo marker, in which the word, "MEMO" appears in a small entry field at the location specified by the GET. As an example, using a memo field called "REVIEW", with the following statement:

```
@ 16,10 SAY "Review comments?" GET REVIEW
```

the memo marker (a reverse-video entry field containing the word "MEMO") appears after the text defined with the SAY clause. When the cursor moves into the memo marker, the user must press Control-Home to view or edit the memo field text. Once Control-Home is pressed, the text of the memo field appears within the dBASE Editor, and any additions or edits can be made. The changes can then be saved with Control-End, or by choosing Save Changes and Exit from the Editor's Exit Menu. Once this is done the cursor reappears in the memo marker, and the user can proceed to the next field.

As an option, you can show the contents of the memo field in a window, by defining the window and then using the WINDOW clause along with the @ ... SAY ... GET command. As an example, the following statements:

```
DEFINE WINDOW ForNotes FROM 10,5 TO 18,60
@ 9,5 SAY "Review comments?" GET REVIEW WINDOW ForNotes
READ
```

would cause the contents of the memo field to appear in the window from row 10, column 5 to row 18, column 60. The same cursor movement, insert, and delete keys can be used in the window as in the Editor. Control-Home and Control-End are still used to enter and exit the window. To make an entry into the editing mode mandatory, add the OPEN clause ahead of the WINDOW clause in the statement.

Dealing with Large Databases: The Masterbase and Childbase Concept

Powerful database software like dBASE IV lends itself to implementing massive projects. You may find yourself dealing with files that are so large that opening them on a regular basis for data entry gets to be a cause for real worry. An alternative is to perform data entry in a smaller, identical copy of the larger database, and update the larger database *(masterbase)* based on the contents of the smaller database *(childbase).* This is a favorite tactic among developers of accounting systems, which normally maintain up to a month's worth of transactions "posted" to a master file at the end of the month. For this reason, systems built around masterbases and childbases are often referred to as *transaction-based processing systems.*

The following section of program code uses this type of design for data entry into a legal assets tracking system:

```
**ADDCASH.PRG adds records to A/R (CASHIN) database
**Last update 11/12/88
USE CASHIN INDEX CASHIN
CLEAR
@5,5 SAY "...preparing entry database; please wait."
COPY STRUCTURE TO TEMP
USE TEMP
STORE "Y" TO ANS
DO WHILE UPPER(ANS) = "Y"
    APPEND BLANK
    CLEAR
    **At-says courtesy of format file
     @  1, 24  SAY "Accounts Received Data Screen"
```

```
    @  4,  4  SAY "Client ID:"
    @  4, 15  GET  CLIENTCODE
    @  4, 33  SAY "Date Received:"
    @  4, 48  GET  DATERECD
    @  6,  4  SAY "Payor:"
    @  6, 10  GET  CASHPAYOR
    @  9,  4  SAY "Type:"
    @  9, 10  GET  CASHTYPE
    @  9, 24  SAY "Issue Date:"
    @  9, 36  GET  CISSUEDAT
    @  9, 48  SAY "Amount:"
    @  9, 56  GET  CASHAMT  PICTURE "99,999,999.99"
    @ 12, 13  SAY "Record Date:"
    @ 12, 26  GET  CRECORDAT
    @  0,  0  TO 18, 79    DOUBLE
    **
    READ
    CLEAR
    @24,5 CLEAR
    @5,5 SAY "Add another record for this client? (Y/N): " GET ANS
    READ
    IF CLIENTCODE = 0
        DELETE
    ENDIF
ENDDO
*Move temporary records into master file
@7,5 SAY "Please wait...updating master file..."
SET ESCAPE OFF
USE CASHIN INDEX CASHIN
APPEND FROM TEMP
CLOSE DATABASES
DELETE FILE TEMP.DBF
RETURN
*End of ADDCASH.PRG
```

When the program is run, the master database file structure is copied out to a temporary file. An APPEND BLANK and a series of @ ... SAY ... GET commands then fill in records in the temporary file. At the end of each record, the operator is queried to see if more records are to be added. Once all desired records have been added, the temporary file is closed, and the master file is opened. All records from the temporary file are then copied back to the master file, after which time the temporary file is deleted to save disk space. If you use this technique and you aren't using SET ESCAPE OFF to disable the Esc key throughout your programs, include a SET ESCAPE OFF statement prior to using APPEND FROM to move the records back to the master files. If SET ESCAPE is not OFF, and the user presses the Esc key in the middle of an update, some new records will probably be lost, as the next time the user attempts to add records, a new temporary file will overwrite the old one. It might help prevent disaster if you include a message warning the user to stay away from the keyboard while the update process is taking place.

The same program concept can be used to edit records, although things get more complex. You can selectively copy a group of records from a large database to a smaller one, and then you can delete those records from the larger database. With SET DELETED set to ON, the deleted records won't be seen in normal database operations. Edit the desired records in the smaller database, and when the editing is complete, copy the edited records back to the larger database, and zap or erase the smaller database. The following program shows this approach:

```
**EDSTOCK.PRG edits records in Corporate Stocks database
**Last update 11/12/88
SET ESCAPE OFF
CLEAR
STORE 9999.999 TO MCLIENT
@5,5 SAY "Enter client code: " GET MCLIENT
READ
USE STOCKS INDEX STOCKS
*See if this client code exists
SEEK MCLIENT
IF EOF()
    CLOSE DATABASES
    @7,5 SAY "No such client entry in Corporate Stocks files!"
    ? CHR(7)
    WAIT "  -Press a key to return to previous menu."
    RETURN
ENDIF
*Valid client code, so create childbase for editing
@7,5 SAY "...building temporary file for this client;  please wait."
COPY STRUCTURE TO TEMP
*Move all records with this client number into temporary file
COPY TO TEMP WHILE CLIENTCODE = MCLIENT
*Now delete from masterbase the records that were copied to temp. file
SEEK MCLIENT
DO WHILE .NOT. EOF() .AND. CLIENTCODE = MCLIENT
    DELETE
    SKIP
ENDDO
*Switch to childbase for editing
USE TEMP
SET FORMAT TO STOCKS
EDIT
CLEAR
@7,5 SAY "Please wait... updating master file..."
*Copy edited records back to masterbase
USE STOCKS INDEX STOCKS
```

```
APPEND FROM TEMP
CLOSE DATABASES
*Get rid of temporary file
DELETE FILE TEMP.DBF
RETURN
*End of EDSTOCK.PRG
```

To avoid slowing things down with this approach, index the large database on the field used to define the group of records to be copied to the smaller database. Use FIND or SEEK to locate the first applicable record in that group, then use a COPY TO <filename> WHILE <condition> statement to copy the records to the smaller database. For editing records, this approach is worthwhile if your database is truly mammoth in size.

One possible problem area will crop up if you have a hardware failure in the midst of an editing process. Even a simple loss of power that leaves the system intact may leave users baffled when a number of changes made during the editing process don't appear in the database after the system is restarted. While dBASE IV offers the BEGIN TRANSACTION, END TRANSACTION, and ROLLBACK commands to maintain a transaction log, performing a ROLLBACK after a power failure would just restore the database to its original state before the data entry began. This may not be precisely what you had in mind. A possible remedy is to include a file recovery option, accessed from a utilities menu, that will open the temporary files and append the contents to the master files. On the positive side, it is better to damage or trash a small temporary database than to wipe out the one that contains 10,000 records.

The masterbase/childbase approach works well with large files, but it has one potential drawback even if your hardware never goes down. With the masterbase/childbase system, the data contained in the master database does not always reflect reality. If a data entry person has been adding records for six hours, the master file may not contain any of those records unless the data entry person terminates the data entry process, causing the program to proceed with the process of updating the master files. At most sites, this is not a problem. On a local area network, this becomes a problem of monstrous proportions, unless you use file locking to prevent updates to the master database while the child database is being updated.

One more benefit of using the masterbase/childbase method of adding or editing records is that you can safely use the APPEND or EDIT commands, along with an appropriate format file to clean up the screen display. Most programmers prefer leaving a temporary—rather than the master—database open for longer periods of time.

Use Common Modules for Appending and Editing

Much of the code used in submodules for adding and editing records shares similarities. You can capitalize on these similarities and save yourself coding time if you further break down the modules into smaller modules for placing data on the screen with @ . . . SAYs, getting and reading the data with GETs and READs, and moving data around with REPLACE commands. The examples shown earlier in the chapter for adding and editing records under program control could be rewritten to use this approach, with resulting code like these samples:

```
***INVENT.PRG***
*Adds items to inventory; updated to use submodules
*Last update 11/12/88
SET TALK OFF
USE MAINFILE INDEX PARTS
*Query user for new part number
CLEAR
STORE 0 TO MPARTNO
@2,30 TO 5,70
@3,40 SAY "Enter part number:"
@4,40 SAY "(press RETURN to exit)"
@3,59 GET MPARTNO
READ
IF MPARTNO = 0
   CLEAR
   RETURN
ENDIF
SEEK MPARTNO
IF FOUND()
     *Duplicate entry attempted
     @3,40 CLEAR TO 4,69
     @3,40 SAY "Part number already exists!"
     @4,40 SAY "Press a key to return to menu."
     ? CHR(7)
     WAIT""
     CLOSE DATABASES
     RETURN
ENDIF
*Valid new part number
CLOSE DATABASES
DO MAKEVARS
DO DISPLAY
READ
USE MAINFILE INDEX PARTS
APPEND BLANK
DO FILLER
CLOSE DATABASES
RETURN
*End of subroutine

*MAKEVARS.PRG
*Creates memory variables for adding records
```

```
PUBLIC MPARTDESC, MWHOLCOST, MRETLCOST, MQUANTITY
STORE SPACE(20) TO MPARTDESC
STORE 0.00 TO MWHOLCOST
STORE 0.00 TO MRETLCOST
STORE 0 TO MQUANTITY
RETURN

*DISPLAY.PRG
*Displays screen format
CLEAR
@  6,  3  TO 18, 50
@  1,  0  TO 19, 54  DOUBLE
@  2, 15  SAY "INVENTORY MASTER FILE"
@  4, 15  SAY "New Item Entry Screen"
@  7, 12  SAY "Part Number: "
@  7, 26 SAY MPARTNO
@  9, 12  SAY "Description:"
@  9, 25  GET  MPARTDESC
@ 11,  9  SAY "Wholesale Cost:"
@ 11, 25  GET  MWHOLCOST
@ 13, 12  SAY "Retail Cost:"
@ 13, 25  GET  MRETLCOST
@ 15,  7  SAY "Initial Quantity:"
@ 15, 25  GET  MQUANTITY
RETURN

*FILLER.PRG
*Moves contents of memory variables to database file
REPLACE PARTNO with MPARTNO, PARTDESC with MPARTDESC
REPLACE WHOLCOST with MWHOLCOST, RETLCOST with MRETLCOST
REPLACE QUANTITY with MQUANTITY
RETURN
```

In cases where the same code must be used in the editing and deleting subroutines, the common modules for replacing variables, displaying screen data, and other such operations could be called from the appropriate program.

9

User Output

This chapter presents ways to produce reports, using a combination of the dBASE IV Report Generator and programming techniques. The chapter also covers techniques for dealing with nonstandard reports and for controlling print devices.

Reports are a vital function of any database application, and there are a number of ways to produce reports within a dBASE IV program. The simplest way to produce a report is to use a LIST command to list fields and/or memory variables, such as in this example:

```
LIST L_Name, Cust_ID, Unit_Cost, Quantity, (Unit_Cost*Quantity) TO PRINT
```

Such a straightforward technique will print out a simple columnar report, and little else. If the data doesn't fill a single page and no special formatting is needed, this will generally suffice. Any report of a more complex nature may be a candidate for the dBASE IV Report Generator.

Introduction to the dBASE IV Report Generator

The Report Generator can be used to quickly produce detailed reports without spending a lot of time coding a report program. A companion utility built into dBASE IV is the Label Generator; it provides a similar way to quickly create mailing labels. Reports created with the Report Generator can include totals and subtotals with names, custom headings, appropriate margins, and page breaks. For reports of selected records, commands can be used to indicate what databases a report created with the Report Generator must use, and what selective conditions apply when printing the report.

A Sample of Report Generator Capabilities

The following shows two sample reports produced with the Report Generator. The first uses a columnar layout, while the second uses a line-oriented (or "form") layout.

```
Page No.    1
11/06/88
LAST_NAME        FIRST_NAME       ADDRESS_1              ADDRESS_2

Jones            Ed               2318 Lake Newport Rd
Smith            William          4343 East Orange Ave
Johnson          Larry            2915 Freetown Court
Jones            Benjamin         3412 Fayetteville St  Apt 2B
Miller           Larry            345 Plano Road
Roberts          Clayborne        1415 Buena Vista Ave  Apt 5D
Canion           Ron              3 Nice House Lane
```

The second sample report follows.

```
Page No.    1
11/06/88

LAST_NAME   Jones
FIRST_NAME  Ed
ADDRESS_1   2318 Lake Newport Rd
ADDRESS_2
CITY        Reston
STATE       VA
ZIP_CODE    22090
CUSTNO      10020
COUNTRY     USA

LAST_NAME   Smith
FIRST_NAME  William
ADDRESS_1   4343 East Orange Ave
ADDRESS_2
CITY        San Jose
STATE       CA
ZIP_CODE    94502
CUSTNO      10021
COUNTRY     USA

LAST_NAME   Johnson
FIRST_NAME  Larry
ADDRESS_1   2915 Freetown Court
ADDRESS_2
CITY        Reston
STATE       VA
ZIP_CODE    22091
```

```
CUSTNO      10023
COUNTRY     USA

LAST_NAME   Jones
FIRST_NAME  Benjamin
ADDRESS_1   3412 Fayetteville St
ADDRESS_2   Apt 2B
CITY        Durham
STATE       NC
ZIP_CODE    27705
CUSTNO      10026
COUNTRY     USA

LAST_NAME   Miller
FIRST_NAME  Larry
ADDRESS_1   345 Plano Road
ADDRESS_2
CITY        Plano
STATE       TX
ZIP_CODE    76020
CUSTNO      10027
COUNTRY     USA
```

The Report Generator provided by dBASE IV is a major advance over the report generators in earlier versions of dBASE. Many programmers have avoided the report generators in dBASE III and dBASE III Plus due to their limitations, preferring to code reports mostly or entirely by hand. If you have avoided the report generator prior to dBASE IV because of its limitations, the dBASE IV Report Generator is worth another look. Reports based on an infinite number of subgroups are now possible, as are line-oriented reports, flexible headings and footings, and very specific controls of printer settings. Perhaps the best feature from the programmer's point of view is that the Report Generator creates a dBASE program which can then be run to produce the report. The program code can be merged into a larger application, and modified as desired by the programmer.

Using the Report Generator

To run the Report Generator, enter the command

```
CREATE REPORT <filename> or MODIFY REPORT <filename>
```

Both commands perform the same action, that of creating or modifying an existing report. If the report by the name <filename> exists, it will be modified; otherwise, a new report is created. The <filename> can be omitted, in which case you will be prompted for a filename when saving the report.

When you enter the CREATE REPORT or MODIFY REPORT command, the Report Design Screen appears (Figure 9-1). The Menu Bar displays seven

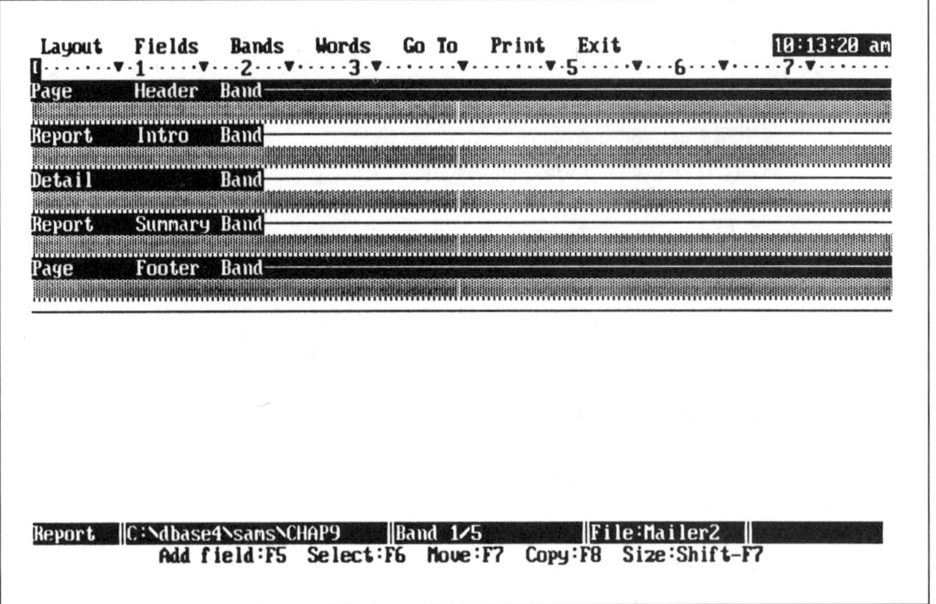

Figure 9-1 Report Design Screen

possible menu options: Layout, Fields, Bands, Words, Go To, Print, and Exit. As with other menus in dBASE, these menus can be accessed with ALT plus the first letter of the menu name, or by pressing F10 and using the cursor keys. The ESC key can be used to close a menu without making a selection.

When at the Report Design Screen, the screen shows the Report Specification, which contains several areas of the report broken up into horizontal bands. The contents of the bands control what appears in the report when it is run (with the REPORT FORM command). Figure 9-2 highlights the possible bands within a Report Specification.

Information contained within the Page Header Band will appear once for every page of the report, at the top of the page. In a similar fashion, the Page Footer Band contains information that appears at the bottom of every page. Typically, items such as title headings, page numbers, and the date as specified by the system clock are placed in the Page Header and Page Footer Bands.

The Report Intro Band contains any information that is to appear once at the start of the report. This can include but is not limited to specialized headings. Paragraphs of text can also be placed in this area as an explanation to data contained in a report.

Group Bands are optional bands which specify a level of grouping for the data which appears in the report. As an example, a report of customers could be grouped by state, and within each state group, by city. There is no limit to the number of possible group levels in a report.

The Detail Band contains the actual data that will appear within the report. Labels for fields and field masks, which represent the actual fields, are typically

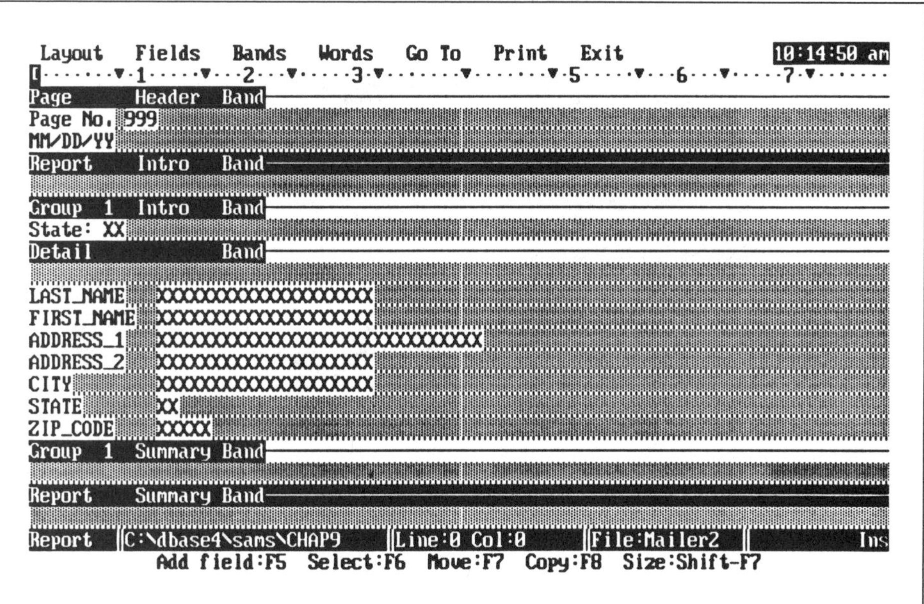

Figure 9-2 Bands of the Report Specification

placed in this area. The data may be placed in a tabular (or columnar) format, in a line-oriented format (where different fields appear on successive lines), or using a combination of the two.

The Report Summary Band contains any information which is to appear once at the end of the report. Typically, numeric totals appear in this area.

Creating Default Reports with the Quick Layouts Option

The Quick Layouts option of the Layout Menu can be used to quickly create one of three default report types: column layout, form layout, or MailMerge. The Column Layout option arranges all fields in the database file or view currently in use in a columnar format. Users of earlier versions of dBASE will find this format similar to the report formats provided by the report generators in those products. In the example shown in Figure 9-3, the MAILER database was opened and the report generator started, then the Quick Layouts option of the Layout Menu was selected, followed by the Column Layout choice. As seen in the figure, this default places a standard page number and date in the Page Header Band, along with labels that are the same as the field names in the database file (or view). In the Detail Band appear the field masks representing the actual data in the fields. The first sample report shown at the start of the chapter was produced by saving this default layout, and running the report with the REPORT FORM command.

Using the same database and choosing the Form Layout option after the Quick Layouts option of the Layout Menu is selected results in the default form

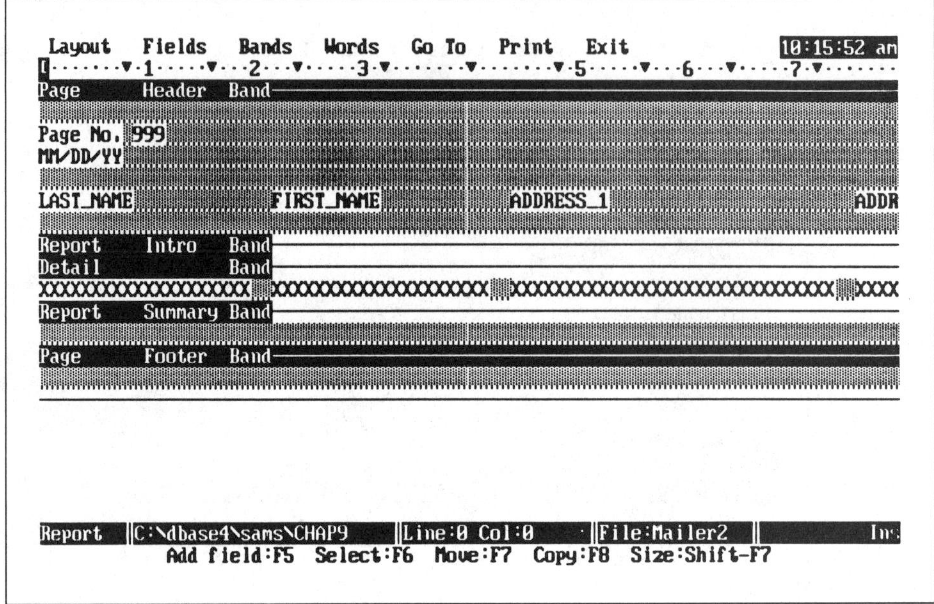

Figure 9-3 Default Columnar Report

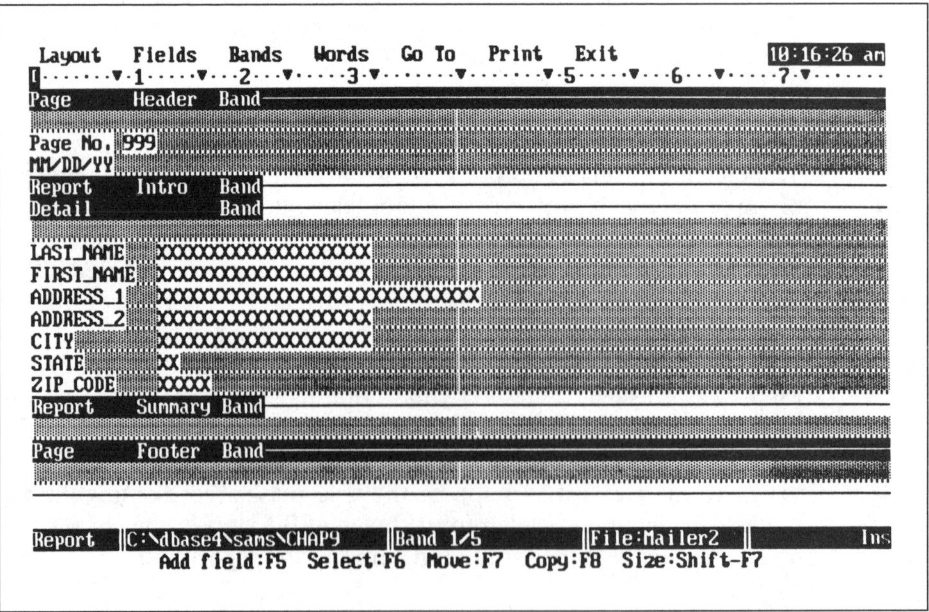

Figure 9-4 Default Form Layout

report shown in Figure 9-4. With this line-oriented style of report, each field in the database (or view) appears on a separate line, preceded by a label which is the same as the field name. The Header Band will contain a standard Page number and date. The second sample report shown at the start of the chapter was produced by saving this default layout, and running the report with the REPORT FORM command.

The default MailMerge layout, shown in Figure 9-5, differs from the other default reports in that it does not automatically insert any fields into the bands; also, all bands are automatically closed as shown in the figure, with the exception of the detail band. The MailMerge layout is designed to accommodate form letters produced as a report. Paragraphs of "boilerplate text" are typed into the detail band, and the word-wrap option of the Editor is automatically turned on. Fields from the active database may be inserted into any location in the boilerplate text, using the options within the Fields Menu.

With all three default options, the report specifications provided can serve as starting points for your report. They can be immediately saved with no further changes (although to save the MailMerge type with no modifications would make little sense, since no default fields or text is inserted). You also have the flexibility to make changes to the default designs, using the various menu options to add bands for further grouping; to add, move, or remove fields; and to add descriptive text or additional headings. You can also choose to design the report entirely from a blank report specification. Instead of choosing a default layout, you can manually add desired headings, fields, labels, and other items to the report.

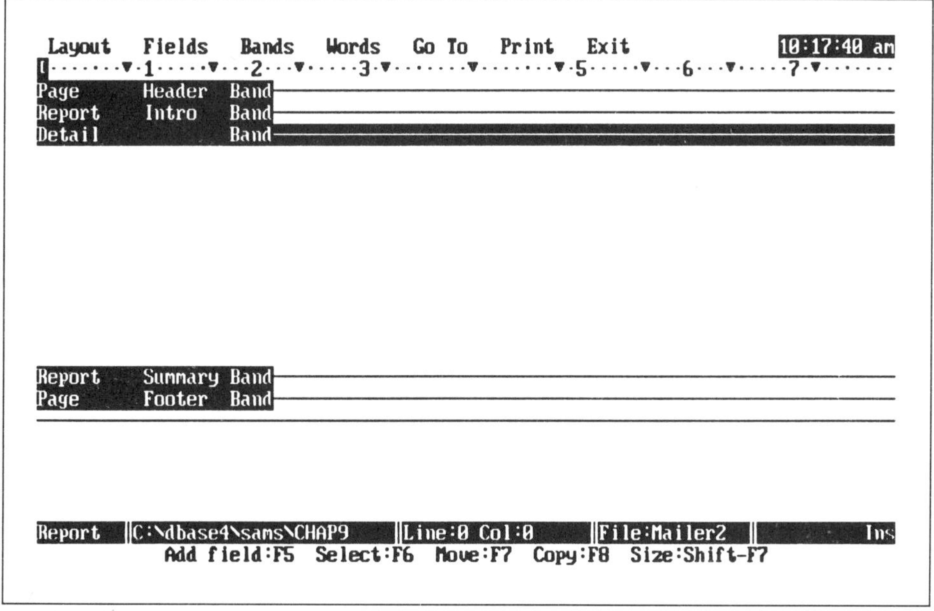

Figure 9-5 Default MailMerge Layout

Designing the Report

Whether you choose to modify a default report format or start with a blank report specification, you can make changes to the design of the report using the menu options provided to add, rearrange, or remove fields; set field display characteristics; change the style of print fonts; and make other changes desired. To add text in the form of headings, field names, or other descriptive labels, simply place the cursor at the desired location and type the desired text. With columnar reports, field labels are usually entered in the Report Intro Band aligned above the actual fields (in the Detail Bands). The field labels then print once at the start of the report. The report shown in Figure 9-3 follows this format, with the field labels in the Report Intro Band, aligned directly above the fields in the Detail Band.

With Form (line-oriented) reports, field labels are usually entered alongside the fields, in the Detail Bands. This causes the field label to appear along with the data for each record printed in the report. The report shown in Figure 9-4 follows this format, with the field labels appearing alongside the fields.

You can add blank lines to a band by pressing Enter while in the Insert mode, or by using the Add Line option of the Words Menu. To add a field to the report, place the cursor at the desired location, and choose Add Field from the Fields Menu; then, choose the desired field from the list of fields which appears. If you want to design relational reports which access data from more than one database, first construct a relational view using the CREATE QUERY command, or use a combination of SET RELATION and SET FIELDS (as outlined in Chapter 10) to make the fields from multiple files available to the report generator. Then use the CREATE REPORT command to begin designing the report. All fields specified in the query or with the use of the SET FIELDS command will be available when designing the report.

In addition to the fields in the active database file or view, the report generator also lets you add calculated fields, summary fields (for numeric summaries of numeric fields), and predefined fields (such as date, time, record number, or page number) to a report. If you choose to create a calculated field for use in the report, you can then enter an expression that uses other fields (usually numeric) to produce the value which appears in the calculated field. For example, a calculated field called "SALESTAX" could multiply a value in a database field, COST, by a given amount (.06) to produce a figure representing the sales tax on an item. While calculated fields are not stored in the database, they do appear in the report.

The Immediate IF function, IIF(), can be used as part of the expression in a calculated field to produce one form of output if a condition proves true, and another form of output if the condition evaluates as false. For example, the following expression entered as the basis for a calculated field,

```
IIF (PAID, "Thanks for your payment","Amount is PAST DUE!")
```

would cause the report to evaluate the contents of the logical field, PAID, for each record encountered. If the field contained the value of true, the first message would appear at the location of the calculated field within the report. If the field contained the value of false, the second message would appear at the field's location in the report.

Another useful function in calculated fields is the TRANSFORM() function. The TRANSFORM() function causes the data to be displayed in a special format, similar to the PICTURE clauses of @ . . . SAY . . . GET commands. The TRANSFORM() function can be placed in the expression used to construct a calculated field. For example, a database field called GROSSAMT might contain a dollar value, 4562.38. In a report, this is how such a value would appear. However, if in place of the database field, you were to create a calculated field and use the following expression to define the contents of that field,

```
TRANSFORM(GROSSAMT,"$9,999.99")
```

the resultant amount in the report would always appear with the dollar sign and the commas specified.

Once the needed fields have been placed at the desired locations in the Detail Band and any necessary headers or titles have been added to the Page Header, Report Intro, Report Summary, or Page Footer Bands, the report can be saved with Control-End, and run from the dot prompt or within a program with the REPORT FORM command. If the report is to provide data broken down into groups, use the options of the Bands Menu to add the necessary groups. (The section below discusses this in greater detail.)

About the Report Design Screen Menus

Figure 9-6 shows the Layout Menu, used to control the basic layout of the report.

As mentioned, the Quick Layout option lets you select one of three possible default layouts for the design of the report. The Box and Line options are used to add boxes or lines to a report (your printer must support the IBM Extended Character Graphics Set to correctly print these items). The Use Different Database File Or View option is used to change the database (or view) being used to build the report. The Edit Description option lets you add or change a one-line description which appears when the report name is highlighted in the Control Center (Assist) menus. The Save This Report option is used to save changes to the design of a report while remaining at the Report Design Screen.

The Fields Menu, shown in Figure 9-7, is used to add, modify, or remove fields within the report.

The Add Field option, when chosen, displays a list of all fields available in the database file or view currently in use. The field that is selected from the list then appears in the form of a field mask at the cursor location. Fields are usually added to a desired location in the Detail Band, although on occasion you may want to place selected fields elsewhere. When grouping, for example, the field used to specify the group is often placed in the Group Band, so that the contents of that field will appear in the report once each time the group changes.

Use the Remove Field option to remove an existing field from the report specification. The Modify Field option is used to change the display characteristics of a field; this option provides access to picture template and function options

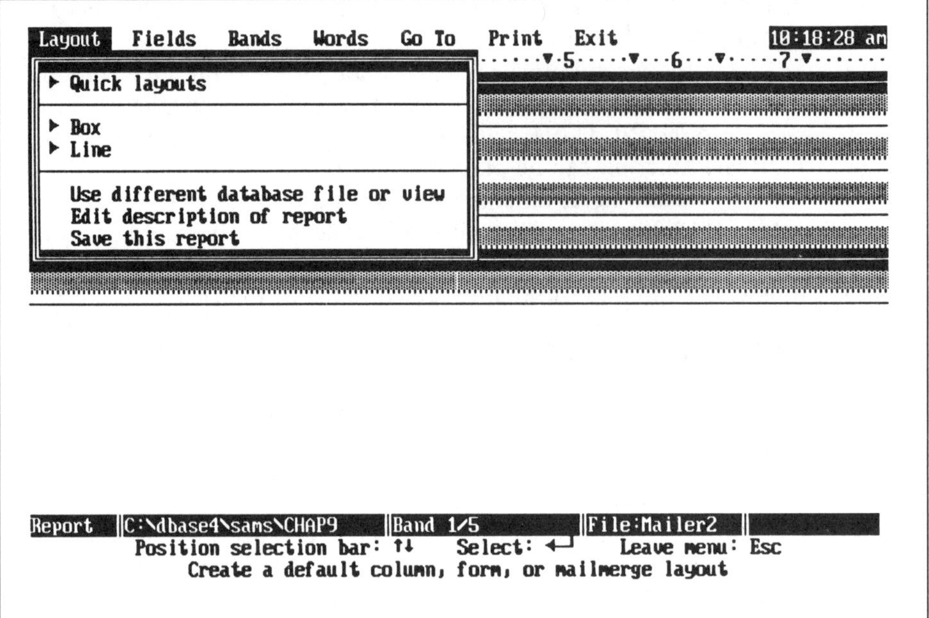

Figure 9-6 Layout Menu

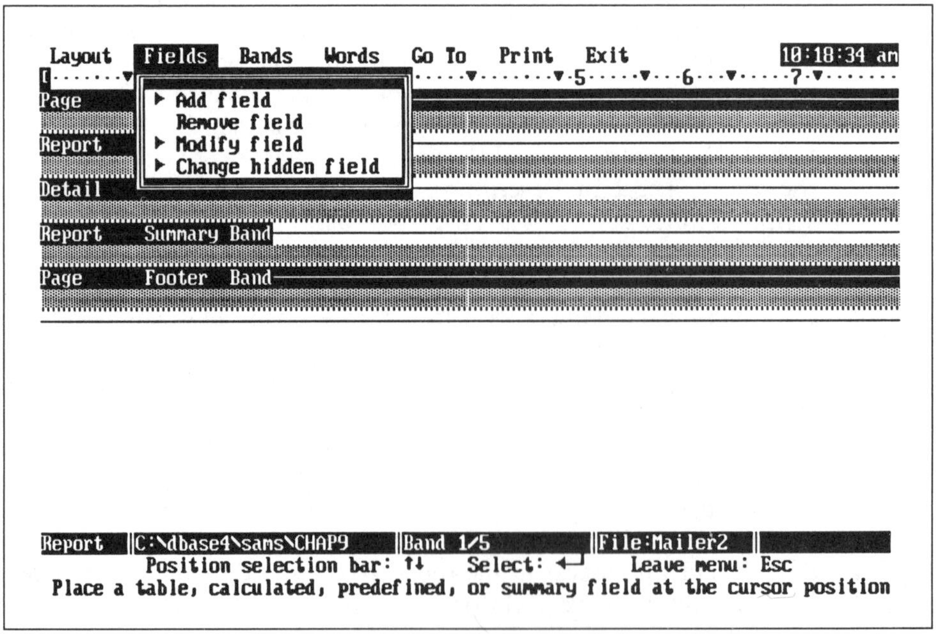

Layout Fields Bands Words Go To Print Exit 10:18:34 am
Page
Report
Detail
Add field
Remove field
Modify field
Change hidden field
Report Summary Band
Page Footer Band
Report C:\dbase4\sams\CHAP9 Band 1/5 File:Mailer2
Position selection bar: ↑↓ Select: ↵ Leave menu: Esc
Place a table, calculated, predefined, or summary field at the cursor position

Figure 9-7 Fields Menu

that will control a field's format when printed. The Change Hidden Field option is used to change the characteristics of hidden fields. (Hidden fields are calculated fields or summary fields placed on a report purely for making calculations.)

The Bands Menu, shown in Figure 9-8, is used to add group bands to the report, and to specify other characteristics for the existing bands.

Use the Add A Group Band option to add a new band for grouping at the cursor location. The Remove Group option is used to remove an existing group band, while the Modify Group option lets you change the definitions for existing group bands. The Group Intro On Each Page option is used to tell dBASE to print a group introduction at the top of a new page whenever the group detail extends past the prior page.

Use the Open All Bands option to open all bands in a report. (Only open bands will print in a report.) Use the Begin Band On New Page option to start a new page each time the contents of the chosen band start printing. The Word Wrap Band option is used to automatically word-wrap text and margins at the right margin when printing. When the MailMerge style of default report is selected, this option is turned on.

The Text Pitch For Band and Quality Print For Band options can be used to specify which text pitch is desired (pica, elite, or condensed), and whether quality print is on or off. Note that your printer must support these options, and the correct printer driver must be installed along with dBASE IV for these options to work correctly. The Spacing Of Lines option is used to change the line spacing within a given band of the report. Possible choices here are default (same as the rest of the report), single, double, or triple.

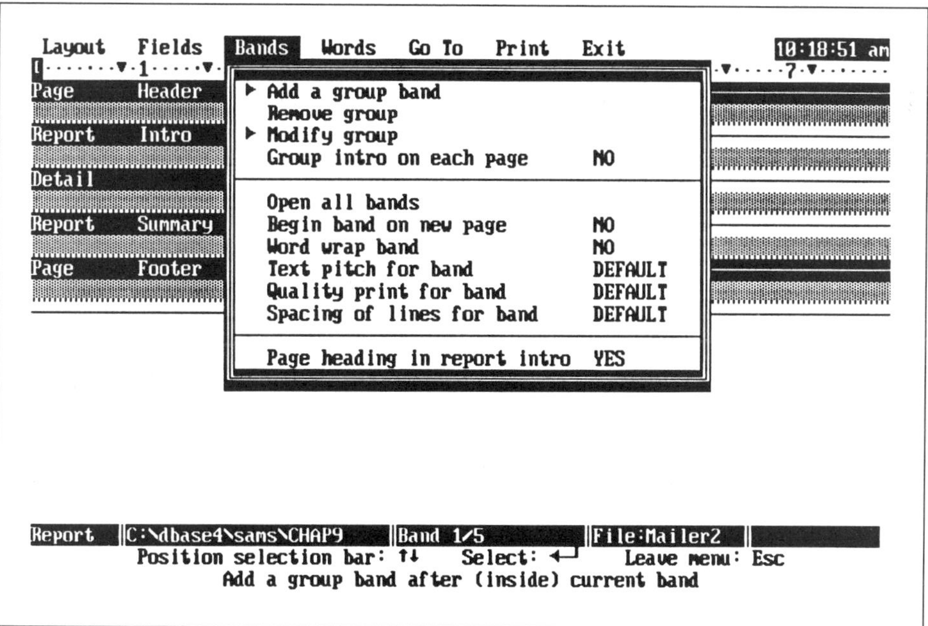

Figure 9-8 Bands Menu

When groups are used, the report begins a new group (or breakpoint) each time the basis of the group expression changes. Groups are optional within a report; if you use them, you must sort or index the database on the field or expression used as the basis for the group.

For example, if a report is grouped on the basis of the ZIPCODE field within a database, the report will contain a breakpoint, with any included subtotals of numeric fields or expressions, each time the contents of the ZIPCODE field changes. The fieldname or expression to be used for the breakpoint can be entered into the "Field Value" or "Expression Value" options which appear when the Add A Group Band option is selected from the Bands Menu. While many reports require the entry of a field name, grouping can also be controlled by entering any valid dBASE IV expression. For example, entering

```
STATE
```

in the Field Value entry causes the report to break on groups of states, and the file should be sorted or indexed on the STATE field before running the report. On the other hand, entering

```
STATE + DTOS(PURCHDAT)
```

in the Expression Value entry would cause the report to break whenever a combined index based on a state and a purchase date (PURCHDAT) field changes in value. For such a report to work properly, the appropriate index tag or file must be created in advance of using the report. For this example, something like:

```
INDEX ON STATE + DTOS(PURCHDATE) TAG STATDAYS
```

would be sufficient.

You can also choose to base a group on a number of records, by choosing Record Count from the submenu which appears after choosing the Add A Group Band option of the Bands Menu. Enter an integer to specify that the report should divide the data into groups of records; for example, you might want to keep 20 records together on a single page, and force a new group every 20 records. Once you select the desired type of grouping, the report generator inserts a new Intro Band and a new Summary Band for the group. Note that a Group Band cannot be placed inside of a Detail Band; you must move the cursor outside of the Detail Band before you can select the Add A Group Band option from the Bands Menu.

After the group bands have been added, you may want to place fields in the Intro Bands or Summary Bands for the groups. Figure 9-9 shows a report for the MAILER database with a group band for the STATE field, and within each state group, another group band for the CITY field. In each case, the field has been placed in the Group Intro Band so that the name of the new state (or city) will appear when the group changes. Summary fields using the COUNT option have also been added to the Summary Bands for the groups, so a record count of the records within each group will be printed at the end of the group.

If you desire any sort of a heading to appear at the start of each group, type that heading in the Intro Band for the group. If you want a new page to begin

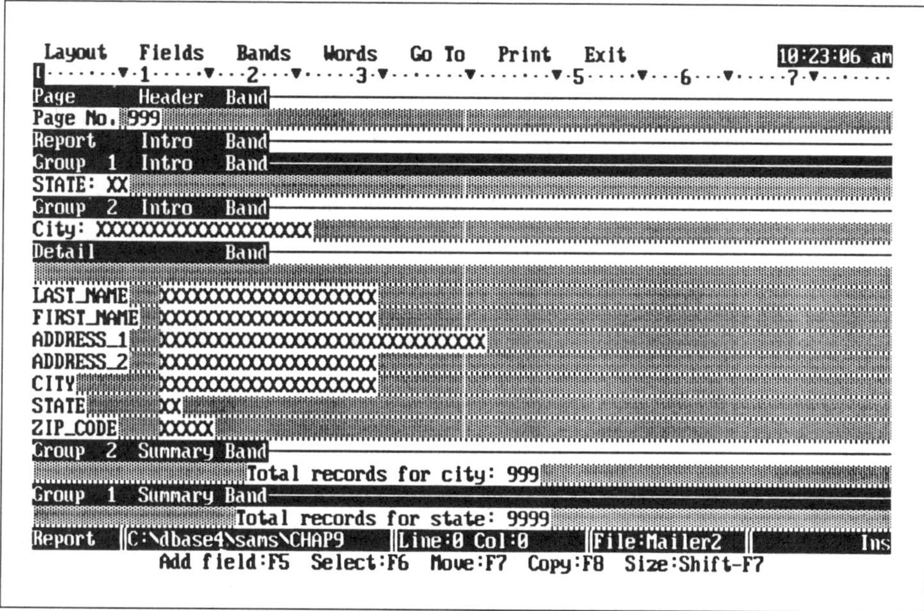

Figure 9-9 Sample Report with Two Levels of Grouping

each time the group changes, first place the cursor in the group band. Then choose the Begin Band On New Page option of the Bands Menu, and press Enter until the option changes from "NO" to "YES."

The Words Menu, shown in Figure 9-10, provides options which affect the style, display, and positioning of the words in the report.

Use the Style option to change the style of selected text. Available choices here are normal, bold, underline, italic, raised (superscript), and lowered (subscript). (The Display option is used when designing screen forms, and is not available when designing a report.) The Position option is used to set the alignment of selected text as left-aligned, right-aligned, or centered. Use the Modify Ruler option to change the margins and tab settings of the ruler line, and use the Hide Ruler option to hide the ruler when creating the report.

The Enable Automatic Indent option will be available only when in word-wrap mode. This option lets you use spaces or tabs as an indentation setting for paragraphs of text typed in the detail band of a report.

Use the Add Line and Remove Line options to add or remove a line in the report. If the Remove line option is used and the line in which the cursor is located contains any fields, they will be removed along with the line. (Any remaining text underneath moves up by one line.) The Write/Read Text File option can be used to write selected text out to a file, or to read a text file into the cursor location. This option can be useful when building form letters with the MailMerge style of layout; a form letter created with a word processor and stored as ASCII text could be read into the report specification using this option.

The Go To Menu, shown in Figure 9-11, is used to move the cursor to a specific line (row) of the report, or to a specific search term.

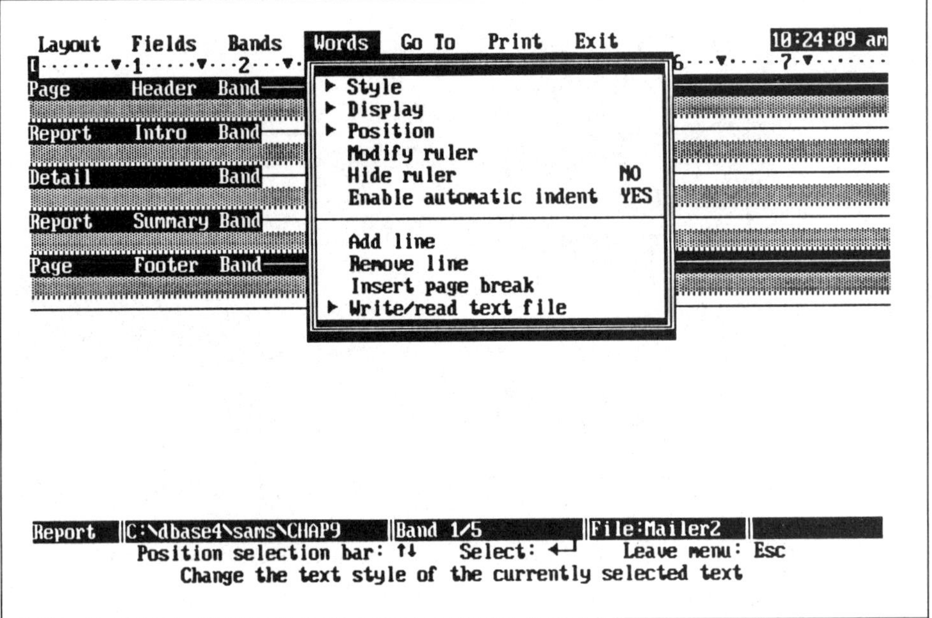

Figure 9-10 Words Menu

```
Layout   Fields   Bands   Words   Go To   Print   Exit          10:24:23 am
Page     Header  Band
Report   Intro   Band        Go to line number        {0}
Detail           Band        Forward search           {}
Report   Summary Band        Backward search          {}
Page     Footer  Band        Replace                  {}
                             Match capitalization     NO

Report  C:\dbase4\sams\CHAP9   Band 1/5   File:Mailer2
     Position selection bar: ↑↓   Select: ←┘   Leave menu: Esc
                      Move to the specified line
```

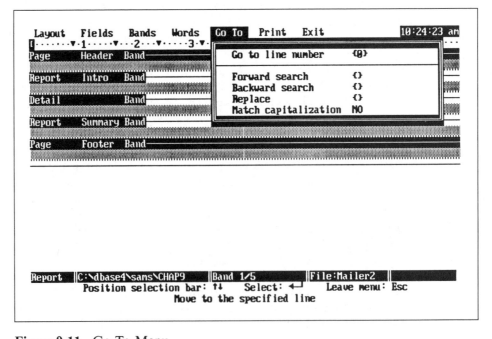

Figure 9-11 Go To Menu

The Forward Search, Backward Search, and Replace options let you search for a specific string of text, or perform a search-and-replace operation on a string of text. (These options may be useful with pages of boilerplate text in form letters, but will have little use elsewhere when designing reports.) The Match Capitalization option is used along with the search options to tell dBASE whether or not to ignore case when searching for a string of text. When the option is set to YES, the case of the search term must match the case of any text which is to be found.

The Print Menu, shown in Figure 9-12, provides printing options which can be used while designing the report.

The Begin Printing option starts printing of the report. This can be useful for testing the design of a report before saving the report and exiting the Report Generator. The Eject Page Now option sends a page eject (form feed) code to the default print device. The View Report On Screen option displays the report on the screen, with a screen pause at the end of each screen full of data.

The next two options, Use Print Form and Save Settings To Print Form, let you work with previously defined print settings. Once other options in the Print Menu such as Destination, Output Options, and Page Dimensions have been redefined, all the settings can be saved to a print form using the Save Settings To Print Form option. Once the settings are saved to disk, the report may be run with those same settings by selecting the Use Print Form option of the Print Menu, and entering the name that the settings were previously saved under.

The Destination option is used to redirect the default output of a report. The report may be sent to the printer, or to a DOS file. If the DOS File option is chosen, the file produced may contain printer initialization strings unless the

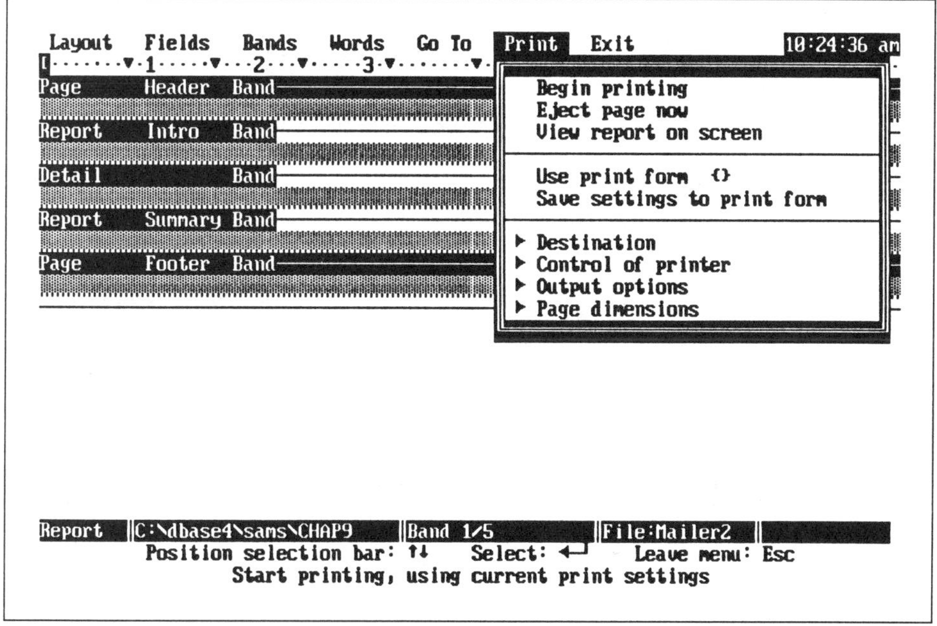

Figure 9-12 Print Menu

printer model option is changed to "GENERIC" when the Destination option is selected.

The Control Of Printer option, when chosen, displays another menu for various printer control options (Figure 9-13).

The Text Pitch option lets you select the pitch among default, pica, elite, and condensed. The Quality Print option selects quality (or "emphasized") printing. Use the New Page option to specify whether a page eject is sent before the report starts, after the report ends, both before and after, or not at all. The Wait Between Pages option may be used to specify whether the printer should pause between each page (This is useful with manually fed daisywheel printers). The Advance Page Using option lets you specify whether form feeds or line feeds will be used to advance the paper to the start of a new page. Form feeds are faster, but a few older printers do not support form feeds.

The Starting Control Codes and Ending Control Codes can be used to specify whether control codes should be sent to the printer at the start or end of the report. To send escape codes as ASCII values, enter the ASCII values in curly {} braces. (See your printer manual for the specific ASCII codes for your printer.)

The Output Options choice from the Print Menu provides another menu with four selections: Begin On Page, End After Page, First Page Number, and Number of Copies. Use the Begin On Page and End After Page choices to specify the starting and ending pages of the report when a portion of the report is desired. The First Page Number option is used to change the page number printed on the

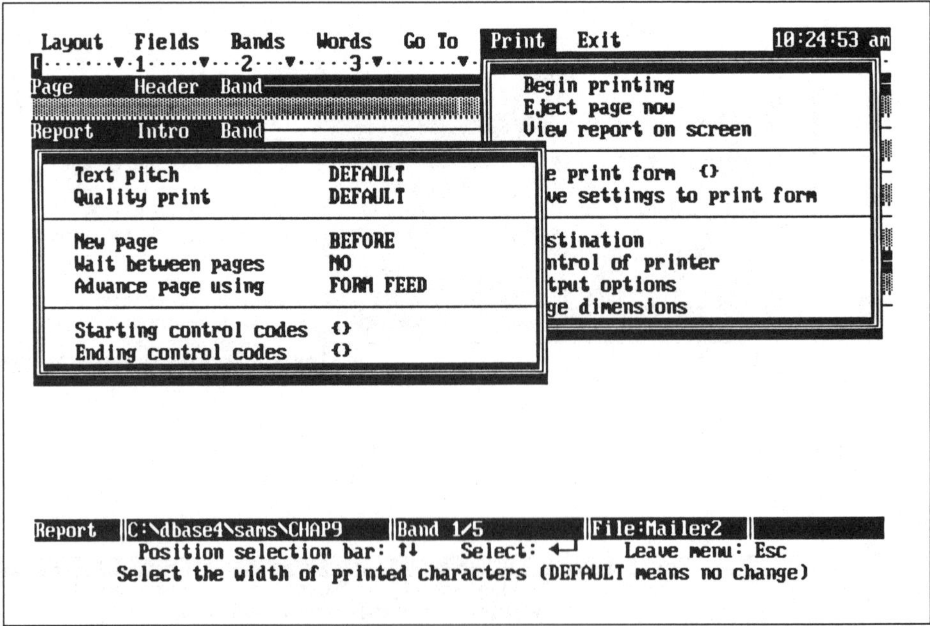

Figure 9-13 Control Of Printer Submenu

first page of the report to something other than the default of 1. The number of copies option lets you specify more than one printed copy for the report.

The Page Dimensions choice from the Print Menu provides a menu with three selections: Length of Page, Offset From Left, and Spacing of Lines. Use the Length of Page option to change the page length from the default value of 66. The Offset From Left option is used to change the left offset (margin) from the default of zero. And the Spacing Of Lines option is used to designate the overall report's spacing as single, double, or triple.

The Exit Menu performs the same tasks as elsewhere in dBASE IV, with the Save Changes And Exit option of this menu used to save the report and exit the Report Generator.

Files Produced by the Report Generator

Saved reports are stored in two files. Both files have the same filename (the name originally assigned to the report), but they have different extensions. One file is saved with a .FRM extension. This file contains the information dBASE uses to lay out and produce the report. The second file has an .FRG extension. This file is of major interest to programmers, as it contains the dBASE source code that will, when run at the dot prompt, also produce the report. If you prefer tight control over all the code in your application, you can choose to copy the .FRG file into your program, and modify it as desired. (If you don't intend to modify the code, you will use up fewer lines of space in your program by simply calling the report with a REPORT FORM command.) As an example of the code produced by the Report Generator, the following listing was produced by a report saved using the default columnar format in the Report Generator. To keep things simple, no extra headings or levels of additional grouping exist in this report.

Listing 9-1: Sample .FRG Code Produced by Default Report Selection

```
* Program............: C:\DBASE4\SAMS\MAILER.FRG
* Date...............: 11-06-88
* Versions...........: dBASE IV, Report 1
*
* Notes:
* ------
* Prior to running this procedure with the DO command
* it is necessary to use LOCATE because the CONTINUE
* statement is in the main loop.
*
*-- Parameters
PARAMETERS gl_noeject, gl_plain, gl_summary, gc_heading, gc_extra
** The first three parameters are of type Logical.
** The fourth parameter is a string.
PRIVATE _peject
```

```
*-- Test for End of file
IF EOF()
   RETURN
ENDIF

IF _plength < 9
   SET DEVICE TO SCREEN
   DEFINE WINDOW gw_report FROM 7,17 TO 11,62 DOUBLE
   ACTIVATE WINDOW gw_report
   @ 0,1 SAY "Increase the page length for this report."
   @ 2,1 SAY "Press a key ..."
   x=INKEY(0)
   DEACTIVATE WINDOW gw_report
   RELEASE WINDOW gw_report
   RETURN
ENDIF

*-- NOEJECT parameter
IF gl_noeject
   IF _peject="BEFORE"
      _peject="NONE"
   ENDIF
   IF _peject="BOTH"
      _peject="AFTER"
   ENDIF
ENDIF

*-- Set-up environment
ON ESCAPE DO prnabort
IF SET("TALK")="ON"
   SET TALK OFF
   gc_talk="ON"
ELSE
   gc_talk="OFF"
ENDIF
gc_exact=SET("EXACT")
gc_space=SET("SPACE")
SET EXACT ON
SET SPACE OFF
gc_time=TIME()      && system time for predefined field
gd_date=DATE()      && system date  "    "    "    "
gl_continu=.F.      && indicates that continue happened in the page break
gl_fandl=.F.        && first and last record flag
gn_level=0          && current band being processed
gn_page=_pageno     && capture page number for multiple copies
gn_length=LEN(gc_heading)  && store length of the HEADING
gl_prntflg=.T.      && Continue printing flag
```

```
gl_widow=.T.        && flag for checking widow bands
*-- records to position to for multiple copies
gn_record1=0
gn_record2=0
gn_record3=0
gn_record4=0
gn_record5=0
gn_record6=0
gn_record7=0
gn_record8=0
gn_record9=0
gn_record0=0
*-- record prior to continue
gn_prevue1=0
gn_prevue2=0
gn_prevue3=0
gn_prevue4=0
gn_prevue5=0
gn_prevue6=0
gn_prevue7=0
gn_prevue8=0
gn_prevue9=0
gn_prevue0=0

DO Getrecs
DO Initrecs

*-- Print Report

PRINTJOB

*-- Initialize summary variables.
r_msum1=0

_plineno=0          && set lines to zero
_pageno=gn_page     && set page number for multiple copies
DO Toprecs          && position to top record in the view

*-- Set up procedure for page break
IF _pspacing > 1
   gn_atline=_plength - (_pspacing + 1)
ELSE
   gn_atline=_plength - 2
ENDIF
IF gl_plain
   ON PAGE AT LINE gn_atline EJECT PAGE
ELSE
   ON PAGE AT LINE gn_atline DO Pgfoot
ENDIF
```

```
DO Pghead

*-- File Loop
DO WHILE IIF(FOUND(),.T.,Twotimes()) .AND. .NOT. EOF() .AND. gl_prntflg
*-- Detail lines
   IF .NOT. gl_summary
      DO Detail
   ENDIF
   IF .NOT. gl_continu
      DO Upd_Vars
      CONTINUE
   ELSE
      gl_continu=.F.
   ENDIF
ENDDO

ll_eof=EOF()
IF gl_prntflg
   DO Rsumm
   IF _plineno < gn_atline
      EJECT PAGE
   ENDIF
ELSE
   DO Rsumm
   IF ll_eof
      GO BOTTOM
      SKIP +1
   ENDIF
   SET EXACT &gc_exact.
   SET SPACE &gc_space.
   SET TALK &gc_talk.
   ON ESCAPE
   ON PAGE
   RETURN
ENDIF

IF ll_eof
   GO BOTTOM
   SKIP +1
ENDIF
ON PAGE
gl_fandl=.F.  && reset first and last record checking

ENDPRINTJOB

SET EXACT &gc_exact.
SET SPACE &gc_space.
```

```
SET TALK &gc_talk.
ON ESCAPE
RETURN
* EOP: C:\DBASE4\SAMS\MAILER.FRG

PROCEDURE Upd_Vars
*-- Summary calculation - Sum
r_msum1=r_msum1+CUSTNO
RETURN
* EOP: Upd_Vars

PROCEDURE Getrecs
gn_prevue1=IIF(.NOT. EOF(1),RECNO(1),0)
gn_prevue2=IIF(.NOT. EOF(2),RECNO(2),0)
gn_prevue3=IIF(.NOT. EOF(3),RECNO(3),0)
gn_prevue4=IIF(.NOT. EOF(4),RECNO(4),0)
gn_prevue5=IIF(.NOT. EOF(5),RECNO(5),0)
gn_prevue6=IIF(.NOT. EOF(6),RECNO(6),0)
gn_prevue7=IIF(.NOT. EOF(7),RECNO(7),0)
gn_prevue8=IIF(.NOT. EOF(8),RECNO(8),0)
gn_prevue9=IIF(.NOT. EOF(9),RECNO(9),0)
gn_prevue0=IIF(.NOT. EOF(10),RECNO(10),0)
RETURN
* EOP: Getrecs

PROCEDURE prnabort
gl_prntflg=.F.
RETURN
* EOP: prnabort

PROCEDURE Pghead
PRIVATE _wrap
IF _wrap
   _wrap = .F.
ENDIF
?
IF .NOT. gl_plain
   ?? "Page No." AT 0,
   ?? _pageno PICTURE "999" AT 9
ENDIF
*-- Print HEADING parameter ie. REPORT FORM <name> HEADING <expC>
IF .NOT. gl_plain .AND. gn_length > 0
   ?? " "
   ?? gc_heading FUNCTION "I;V"+;
   LTRIM(STR(_rmargin-_lmargin-(_pcolno*2)))
ENDIF
?
IF .NOT. gl_plain
   ?? gd_date AT 0
ENDIF
?
```

```
?
?? "LAST_NAME" AT 0,
?? "FIRST_NAME" AT 17,
?? "ADDRESS_1" AT 34,
?? "ADDRESS_2" AT 56,
?? "CITY" AT 68,
?? "STATE" AT 85,
?? "ZIP_CODE" AT 92,
?? "CUSTNO" AT 104,
?? "COUNTRY" AT 112
?
?
RETURN
* EOP: Pghead

PROCEDURE Detail
PRIVATE _wrap
IF _wrap
   _wrap = .F.
ENDIF
?? LAST_NAME FUNCTION "T" PICTURE "XXXXXXXXXXXXXXX" AT 0,
?? FIRST_NAME FUNCTION "T" PICTURE "XXXXXXXXXXXXXXX" AT 17,
?? ADDRESS_1 FUNCTION "T" PICTURE "XXXXXXXXXXXXXXXXXXXX" AT 34,
?? ADDRESS_2 FUNCTION "T" PICTURE "XXXXXXXXXX" AT 56,
?? CITY FUNCTION "T" PICTURE "XXXXXXXXXXXXXXX" AT 68,
?? STATE FUNCTION "T" PICTURE "XX" AT 85,
?? ZIP_CODE FUNCTION "T" PICTURE "XXXXXXXXXX" AT 92,
?? CUSTNO PICTURE "99999" AT 104,
?? COUNTRY FUNCTION "T" PICTURE "XXXXXXXXXX" AT 112
?
RETURN
* EOP: Detail

PROCEDURE Rsumm
PRIVATE _wrap
IF _wrap
   _wrap = .F.
ENDIF
?? r_msum1 PICTURE "99999" AT 104
?
RETURN
* EOP: Rsumm

PROCEDURE Pgfoot
PRIVATE _box
gl_widow=.F.
?
```

```
IF .NOT. gl_plain
PRIVATE _wrap
IF _wrap
   _wrap = .F.
ENDIF
ENDIF
EJECT PAGE
*-- is the page number greater than the ending page
IF _pageno > _pepage
   GOTO BOTTOM
   SKIP
   gn_level=0
ENDIF
*-- if there is not a group break in progress
IF gn_level < 3 .AND. .NOT. EOF()
   DO Upd_Vars
   CONTINUE
   gl_continu=.T.
ENDIF
IF .NOT. EOF()
   IF .NOT. gl_plain .AND. gl_fandl
      DO Pghead
   ENDIF
ENDIF
RETURN
* EOP: Pgfoot

*-- Due to the fact that positioning is done with GOTO gn_record
*-- to handle multiple copies, the FOUND() function will return
*-- false the first time, so this UDF returns true and after the
*-- last record is found, this UDF will also need to return false.
FUNCTION Twotimes
gl_fandl=.NOT. gl_fandl
RETURN gl_fandl
* EOUDF: Twotimes

PROCEDURE Toprecs
IF gn_record1 <> 0
   GOTO gn_record1 IN (1)
ENDIF
IF gn_record2 <> 0
   GOTO gn_record2 IN (2)
ENDIF
IF gn_record3 <> 0
   GOTO gn_record3 IN (3)
ENDIF
IF gn_record4 <> 0
```

```
   GOTO gn_record4 IN (4)
ENDIF
IF gn_record5 <> 0
   GOTO gn_record5 IN (5)
ENDIF
IF gn_record6 <> 0
   GOTO gn_record6 IN (6)
ENDIF
IF gn_record7 <> 0
   GOTO gn_record7 IN (7)
ENDIF
IF gn_record8 <> 0
   GOTO gn_record8 IN (8)
ENDIF
IF gn_record9 <> 0
   GOTO gn_record9 IN (9)
ENDIF
IF gn_record0 <> 0
   GOTO gn_record0 IN (10)
ENDIF
RETURN
* EOP: Toprecs

PROCEDURE Initrecs
gn_record1=gn_prevue1
gn_record2=gn_prevue2
gn_record3=gn_prevue3
gn_record4=gn_prevue4
gn_record5=gn_prevue5
gn_record6=gn_prevue6
gn_record7=gn_prevue7
gn_record8=gn_prevue8
gn_record9=gn_prevue9
gn_record0=gn_prevue0
RETURN
* EOP: Initrecs
```

The code produced by the Report Generator is highly proceduralized, making it easier to modify to meet any unusual needs you may have. Note the Page Head procedure and the Detail Procedure, which control the printing of the page heading and the contents of the detail band. Since many changes to existing reports involve the headings and the contents of the detail area, you can make quick changes to the program code in these areas as you desire. However, there is much to be said for the ease of simply making changes when at the Report Design Screen of the Report Generator, and copying the program code produced by the modified report into your application.

The REPORT FORM Command

Completed reports are run with the REPORT FORM command, which offers a number of flexible options. The syntax for the command is:

```
REPORT FORM <filename> [<scope>][WHILE <condition>][FOR <condition>][PLAIN]
<character expression> [HEADING][NOEJECT][TO PRINT/TO FILE <filename>][SUMMARY]
```

For example, the command,

```
REPORT FORM MYFILE
```

displays the specified report, with no conditions, on the screen. The command,

```
REPORT FORM MYFILE NEXT 30 FOR L_NAME = "Smith" PLAIN TO PRINT
```

processes only the next 30 records in the database for the report. The FOR L_NAME = "Smith" would further refine the report contents to specified records, where "Smith" appears in the L_NAME field. The PLAIN option would drop the page numbers and date normally printed in a report, and the TO PRINT option would print, as well as display, the report. The PLAIN option drops the system clock date and page numbers, while the HEADING option, followed by a character expression, prints that heading at the top of each page. (This is in addition to any heading that you may have specified within the report design.) The NOEJECT option cancels the form feed that normally occurs when the TO PRINT option (which routes output to the printer) is used. The TO FILE option can store the output to a text file. The text file will be assigned a .TXT extension, unless you specify a different extension. The SUMMARY option cancels the normal display or printing of detail lines within a report; if you include SUMMARY, only totals and subtotals will appear.

If you do not want screen output while a report is printed, you can disable the screen with the SET CONSOLE OFF command. Remember, though, to turn the screen back on after processing with a SET CONSOLE ON command!

If you have designed the report using a relational query or the SET RELATION and SET FIELDS commands to take advantage of multiple databases open in different work areas, you must set up the work areas and identify the relationships between files before using the REPORT FORM command. This step must be taken each time the report is run. Programming steps for a report designed to simultaneously use two databases, CUSTOMER and ORDERS, might resemble the following:

```
SELECT 1
USE CUSTOMER INDEX ACCTNUMB
SELECT 2
USE SALES INDEX ACCTNUMB
SET RELATION TO ACCTNUMB INTO CUSTOMER
SET FIELDS TO CUSTNUMB, CUSTNAME, ACCOUNT, BALANCE, COST
REPORT FORM SALES TO PRINT
```

Again, if these commands are unfamiliar, Chapter 10 will provide a more detailed explanation. Veterans of dBASE II will find these command lines familiar; dBASE II used "SELECT PRIMARY" and "SELECT SECONDARY" to set up two files simultaneously in multiple work areas. However, the dBASE II Report Generator did not directly support the use of multiple files.

Setting Conditions for Reports Within a Program

Most reports require selective processing of some sort; rarely does a user want a report of every scrap of data contained in a database. The more common request is for reports of specific names, or ranges of zip codes, or last month's sales, or whatever. A variety of conditional commands can be combined with the REPORT FORM command to create reports that are selective subsets of all the data in the database.

Probably the most common use of conditionals with a report is specifying the condition along with the REPORT FORM command. As an example, if a car dealer wanted a report listing all customers who purchased subcompacts in 1989, you could create the report using a command like this one:

```
REPORT FORM SALES FOR TYPE = UPPER(SUBCOMPACT) .AND. YEARSALE = 1989 TO PRINT
```

Depending on how the database is structured (and how large it is), you might or might not want to use this method. With a large database, dBASE IV will spend inordinate amounts of time in what is, in effect, a slow sequential search as it qualifies each record. In a large database, it would be better to index the database and use the WHILE option, as shown with these commands:

```
INDEX ON TYPE + STR(YEARSALE) TO MODELS89
SEEK "SUBCOMPACT1989"
REPORT FORM SALES WHILE TYPE = UPPER(SUBCOMPACT) .AND. YEARSALE = 1989 TO PRINT
```

Since the WHILE condition processes records until the specified condition is no longer met, dBASE IV will start at the first appropriate record and then *batch process* that group of records. Since the records are indexed, the chosen records will fall into a contiguous group, making the WHILE option an effective one. You can include such commands as a result of menu options to give users an ability to process records meeting selected conditions.

Note that you can use the FOR and WHILE options at the same time with dBASE IV. Earlier versions of dBASE limited you to the use of one or the other, but not both at the same time. If the FOR and WHILE conditions are used within the same program statement, the WHILE condition takes precedence over the FOR condition.

Using SET FILTER for Reports

The SET FILTER command can also be used to provide users with choices of conditions that apply to data printed with a report. As an example, the command,

```
SET FILTER TO TYPE = UPPER(SUBCOMPACT)
```

would, in the case of our car dealer, restrict all data printed within the report to records containing the word *subcompact* in the TYPE field. Once a filter has been set with the SET FILTER command, the appropriate report can be printed with the REPORT FORM command.

The beauty of using SET FILTER along with your report options is that you can offer users various menu options that call up different filters and then print the same report. With this technique, users can print reports based on selected conditions, and you don't have to program your way around the conditions by opening and closing multiple index files to match a string of WHILE conditions. For example, a user may want a report for a specific group of names or cities or states or a range of zip codes. You can use CASE choices within a menu to create a string of SET FILTER commands that activates specific filters for each menu selection. The following program shows such an approach:

```
**Reporter program
**Sets filter, then prints report
**Last update 11/12/88
CLEAR
@ 5,5 SAY "Enter filter condition, if any, for report."
@ 6,5 SAY "============================================ "
@ 8,5 SAY "    1.   All Members (no filter in effect.)"
@ 9,5 SAY "    2.   By Last Name"
@10,5 SAY "    3.   By School or Business Name"
@11,5 SAY "    4.   By State"
@12,5 SAY "    5.   Range of Zip Codes"
@14,5 SAY "============================================ "
STORE 1 TO SIFTIT
INPUT "  Enter a selection (1-5): " TO SIFTIT
CLEAR
DO CASE
     CASE SIFTIT = 1
          SET FILTER TO
          *No filter used
     CASE SIFTIT = 2
          STORE SPACE(15) TO ML_NAME
          @5,5 SAY "Last name: " GET ML_NAME
          READ
          STORE UPPER(ML_NAME) TO SIFTERS
          SET FILTER TO UPPER(L_NAME) = SIFTERS
     CASE SIFTIT = 3
          STORE SPACE(25) TO MSCHOOLBUS
          @5,5 SAY "School or Business Name: " GET MSCHOOLBUS
          READ
          STORE UPPER(MSCHOOLBUS) TO SIFTERS
          SET FILTER TO UPPER(SCHOOL_BUS) = SIFTERS
```

```
        CASE SIFTIT = 4
            STORE SPACE(2) TO MSTATE
            @5,5 SAY "State: " GET MSTATE
            READ
            STORE UPPER(MSTATE) TO SIFTERS
            SET FILTER TO UPPER(STATE) = SIFTERS
        CASE SIFTIT = 5
            STORE SPACE(10) TO MZIPSTART
            STORE SPACE(10) TO MZIPEND
            @5,5 SAY "Enter starting Zip Code: " GET MZIPSTART
            @7,5 SAY "Enter ending Zip Code: " GET MZIPEND
            @10,5 SAY "(enter same codes for a single zip code.)"
            READ
            SET FILTER TO ZIP > MZIPSTART .AND. ZIP < MZIPEND
ENDCASE
CLEAR
? "Turn on your printer and press any key when ready,"
? "or press C to cancel this report request."
WAIT "" TO PRINTANS
IF UPPER(PRINTANS) = "C"
    RETURN
ENDIF
*Print the report
GO TOP
REPORT FORM MEMBERS TO PRINT
*Clear any filter
SET FILTER TO
*Back to the program that called this one
RETURN
```

In the example, each set of commands following a CASE gets a user response, stores the response to a variable, and uses that variable to set an appropriate filter for the database. If your program runs multiple reports and mailing labels, you may decide to build a filter routine similar to this one as a submodule that is called by the other report- and label-generating modules. If you use this approach, be sure to declare the variables used in the filter submodule as public variables, or the filters will be lost when you pass program control back to the calling program. Also be sure to turn off any filters with a SET FILTER TO command (with no condition specified) after printing the reports; otherwise, users will get thoroughly confused when they discover large numbers of records to be "missing" from the database.

The disadvantage to the use of SET FILTER is that it can be terribly slow when used with large, indexed database files. This may not become an apparent problem until your users start complaining about the length of time that SET FILTER takes when a particular menu selection or selective report is chosen. Because the SET FILTER command qualifies each record in the database starting from record 1 and proceeding to the last record, having an index open drastically slows the process by forcing dBASE to jump all over the index while checking records in sequential order. If you are generating reports based on selective records from large files and you still want to use SET FILTER, you may want to consider this alternate approach. Turn off the indexes with a SET ORDER TO 0 command; then set the filter with the SET FILTER command, and copy the selected records out to a temporary file with commands like,

```
GO TOP
COPY TO TEMPFILE
```

Then open the temporary file, build an index to control the desired order in which the records should be printed, and produce the report with the REPORT FORM command or with your program code. If the temporary file is just a small subset of the large file, performance will be greatly improved when compared to the time needed to set a filter across the large file with the indexes active.

Writing Reports Under Program Control

While the Report Generator can produce all but the most unusual types of reports, some programmers may prefer to code reports manually (perhaps because old habits die hard). Various commands can be used to code reports. As an example, Table 9-1 describes the structure of a legal depositions database. The portion of program code shows an example used to print a line-oriented report based on that legal database:

```
**REPORT1.PRG
**Prints deposition summaries by person named
CLEAR
ACCEPT "Name of person involved in deposition?" TO MPERSONS
STORE UPPER(MPERSONS) TO MPERSONS
USE LEGAL
STORE 1 TO PAGECOUNT
STORE 0 TO LINECOUNT
SET FILTER TO UPPER(PERSONS) = MPERSONS
SET PRINT ON
?
? "  ***Deposition Summaries for witness: " +  MPERSONS
? "======================================================== "
?
DO WHILE .NOT. EOF()
     ? "Document number: "
     ?? DOCUMENT
     ? "Date of document: "
     ?? DOCUDATE
     ? "Source of document: " + DOCSOURCE
     ? "Summary: " + SUMMARY
```

```
    ? "***********************************************"
    STORE 6 + LINECOUNT TO LINECOUNT
    IF LINECOUNT > 54
        STORE 0 TO LINECOUNT
        STORE 1 + PAGECOUNT TO PAGECOUNT
        EJECT
        ? "                                          -Page  #"
        ?? PAGECOUNT
        ? "  ***Deposition Summaries for witness: "  + MPERSONS
        ? "================================================= "
        ?
    ENDIF
ENDDO
? "***End of deposition report.***"
SET PRINT OFF
EJECT
RETURN
*End of print routine
```

In this program the ? and ?? commands are used to print the data. Page breaks are handled with a counter (STORE 6 + LINECOUNT TO LINECOUNT), which increments by 6 for each record printed. Once the value of the variable, LINECOUNT, indicates that the total number of lines printed is greater than the desired number of 54 lines per page, an EJECT command causes a form feed to be sent to the printer, and the next page starts.

Table 9-1 Database Structure for LEGAL.DBF

Field Name	Type
DOCUMENT	numeric/6
DOCDATE	date
DOCSOURCE	character/10
PERSONS	character/50
SUMMARY	character/254

Printing Data

Two methods can be used for printing data. They are SET PRINT ON, combined with the ? and ?? commands, or SET DEVICE TO PRINT, combined with the @ . . . SAY commands. The ? and ?? commands will print a line at a time. The line will print at the next available printer position unless that AT clause is used to specify a desired column position for the data. The ? command prints a carriage return and linefeed to position the printhead at the left margin of the next line, then prints the contents of the expression. The ?? command prints the contents of the expression on the same line as the current printer location and does not index the printer. If @ . . . SAY commands are used, the SET DEVICE TO PRINT command will cause all results of the @ . . . SAY commands to be routed to the printer instead of to the screen.

Using @ . . . SAY commands gives you more direct control over where the data will be printed; the row and column locations translate to the appropriate printhead row and column locations. (With the AT clause of the ? command, you can specify the column, but you can't specify the row.) When you use this route, exercise care not to send the printer a row location that is lower in value than the previous row location. Such a command will cause a form feed to be sent, ejecting the previous page. dBASE IV cannot make your printer perform reverse indexing with an @ . . . SAY command, even if the printer is actually capable of such feats (as are some daisy wheel printers).

For example, if you print the contents of a variable at printer location 9,15 and then try to print the next variable at location 8,50, the printer will eject the page and align the new page so the printhead is at position 8,50.

Recommended Method of Report Design from a Program

A general outline you can follow to design a report that operates entirely under program control might be as follows:

1. Open any desired index files and set any desired filters.
2. Initialize variables for a line counter and page counter.
3. Use SET PRINT ON or SET DEVICE TO PRINT to route output to the printer.
4. Print any desired report headings.
5. Start a scan of the database with a DO WHILE loop.
6. Print the selected contents of a record.
7. After printing a record, check the value of the line and page counters. Perform a form feed and print new headings and page numbers when necessary.
8. SKIP to the next record and repeat the contents of the DO WHILE loop.
9. When the desired records have been printed, turn off printer output with SET PRINT OFF or SET DEVICE TO SCREEN. Clear any filters that were in effect.

As an example of a more complex report than the one shown earlier, the report below makes use of the SET DEVICE TO PRINT command, combined with @ . . . SAY commands, to place the data at the desired printer locations.

```
*BenPrt.PRG is for benefits report to printer.*
GO TOP
CLEAR
```

```
@ 5,5 SAY "Printing... please wait..."
STORE 10 TO LINES
STORE 1 TO PAGES
SET DEVICE TO PRINT
@ 1,5 SAY "Page No." + LTRIM(STR(PAGES))
@ 2,5 SAY DATE()
@ 3,31 SAY "The Personnel Director"
@ 4,34 SAY "Benefits Report"
@ 6,5 SAY REPLICATE("=",70)
@ 7,5 SAY "Name          Health Plan   Date of   Amount 1   Amount 2    Comment"
@ 8,5 SAY "                                   Plan"
DO WHILE .NOT. EOF()
     @ LINES,  5 SAY LASTNAME
     @ LINES, 20 SAY BPLAN1
     @ LINES, 31 SAY BDATE1
     @ LINES, 40 SAY BFAMOUNT1
     @ LINES, 50 SAY BSAMOUNT1
     @ LINES, 60 SAY BCOMMENT1
     STORE LINES + 1 TO LINES
     @ LINES,  5 SAY FIRSTNAME
     @ LINES, 20 SAY BPLAN2
     @ LINES, 31 SAY BDATE2
     @ LINES, 40 SAY BFAMOUNT2
     @ LINES, 50 SAY BSAMOUNT2
     @ LINES, 60 SAY BCOMMENT
     STORE LINES + 1 TO LINES
     @ LINES, 20 SAY BPLAN3
     @ LINES, 31 SAY BDATE3
     @ LINES, 40 SAY BFAMOUNT3
     @ LINES, 50 SAY BSAMOUNT3
     @ LINES, 60 SAY BCOMMENT3
     STORE LINES + 1 TO LINES
     @ LINES, 20 SAY BPLAN4
     @ LINES, 31 SAY BDATE4
     @ LINES, 40 SAY BFAMOUNT4
     @ LINES, 50 SAY BSAMOUNT4
     @ LINES, 60 SAY BCOMMENT4
     STORE LINES + 3 TO LINES
     IF LINES > 50
       EJECT
       STORE PAGES + 1 TO PAGES
       STORE 10 TO LINES
       @ 1,5 SAY "Page No." + LTRIM(STR(PAGES))
       @ 2,5 SAY DATE()
       @ 3,31 SAY "The Personnel Director"
       @ 4,34 SAY "Benefits Report"
       @ 6,5 SAY REPLICATE("=",70)
       @ 7,5 SAY "Name     Health Plan  Date of  Amount 1 Amount 2  Comment"
       @ 8,5 SAY "                              Plan"
```

```
    ENDIF
    SKIP
ENDDO
IF LINES > 10
   EJECT
ENDIF
SET DEVICE TO SCREEN
RETURN
```

This report also makes use of a popular report-coding technique known as relative cursor addressing. A memory variable named LINES is used to contain the row position of the printer. Data is then printed at the desired location on each row with a statement like,

```
@ LINES, 20 SAY BPLAN1
```

and when the data for an entire row has been printed, the variable is incremented for the next line with the statement,

```
STORE LINES + 1 TO LINES
```

and a successive series of @ . . . SAY statements prints the data for the next line. This continues throughout the DO WHILE loop, until all of the data has been printed. The results of this particular report, containing 22 fields in a columnar arrangement of five columns, resemble the following:

```
                           The Personnel Director
                              Benefits Report

Name             Health       Date of   Amount 1 Amount 2 Comment
                   Plan          Plan

Doe              BCBS         01/01/84 230               Std option
Jane             Kaiser P.    07/22/86 212               no dental
                                / /
                                / /
Doe              CIGNA #2     01/01/85 210               monthly
John                            / /                      contrib.
                                / /
                                / /
Smith            Kaiser P.    01/01/87 210
Susan                           / /
                                / /
                                / /
```

A Problem Area: The Case of the Missing Last Line

When you write reports using program code, you will occasionally find that the last line of a report does not print on the printer until your program begins another printing operation. When the second printing operation begins, the last line of the first printing operation prints along with the first lines of the second printing operation. (Many laser printers carry this problem a step further by not printing the final page of a report until another print operation begins.) This problem is caused by the buffers in some printers, which are not cleared unless a printer eject code or a carriage return and linefeed code is received. To get around this problem, issue an EJECT command or send a carriage return and linefeed with a

```
? CHR(13) + CHR(10)
```

statement.

Combined Reports

When you build a report through programming, you must handle headings, page breaks, totals and subtotals, and any spacing between lines and columns. An alternate method that, in some instances, can save time and effort is to use both methods by creating a combined report. Combined reports use a combination of programming and report formats. To create such reports, use the NOEJECT option of the REPORT FORM command. You can use the ? and ??, or @ . . . SAY commands, prior to or after the REPORT FORM command, to print line-oriented data, complex math calculations, or text that, for one reason or another, you don't want to handle with the Report Generator.

For example, consider a database of sales purchases. A line-oriented format is needed to display the customer name, customer number, and sales messages; then, a columnar report that shows sales purchases follows. Each customer must receive a separate page, which calls for a page eject each time the customer number changes. Table 9-2 shows the structure of such a database, named SALES.DBF. Following is an example of the program code used to handle the task:

```
*Report prints invoices based on line and column format
*Last update 11/12/88
SET TALK OFF
SET SAFETY OFF
USE SALES
INDEX ON CUSTNUMB TO NUMBERS
GO TOP
SET PRINT ON
STORE CUSTNUMB TO TEMP
*Set ending customer number for billing
DO WHILE TEMP < 1004
```

```
    ?
    ? "    ***Winken, Blinken, & Nod Apparel of Georgetown***"
    ?
    ? UPPER(CUSTNAME)
    ? "Account number: "
    ?? TEMP
    ?
    ? "  **It is our pleasure to serve you.  Your account status:"
    ?
    ? "=============================================================== "
    *Report form command creates columnar portion of report
    REPORT FORM SALES FOR CUSTNUMB = TEMP PLAIN NOEJECT TO PRINT
    ? "=============================================================== "
    ?
    ? "  --Questions about your account?  Call us at 555-1212.--"
    EJECT
    *Increment customer number
    STORE TEMP + 1 TO TEMP
    *Find record matching cust. no. to print cust. name
    LOCATE FOR CUSTNUMB = TEMP
ENDDO
SET PRINT OFF
```

A printed invoice from the SALES.DBF report program looks like:

```
***Winken, Blinken, & Nod Apparel of Georgetown***

Y. SHARI MCCOY        Account number:       1002

  **It is our pleasure to serve you.  Your account status:

===============================================================

        Stock      Quantity   Description                  Total
        Number                                              Cost


        C34377            1 BMW racing jacket               95.90
        F12166            1 sunglasses                      27.90
        L45780            3 sunscreen lotion                23.55
       *** Total ***
                                                           147.35

===============================================================

   --Questions about your account?  Call us at 555-1212.--
```

Table 9-2 Database Structure for SALES.DBF

Field Name	Type
CUSTNAME	character/20
CUSTNUMB	numeric/4/0
ITEMCODE	character/6
QUANTITY	numeric/3/0
DESC	character/20
UNITCOST	numeric/7/2

Creating Mailing Labels

The dBASE IV CREATE LABEL command builds forms for mailing labels. The CREATE LABEL command brings up a series of menus, similar to those of the Report Generator, to create labels of varying sizes. Nine standard label sizes can be chosen from a menu, or you can enter dimensions of your own choosing. The syntax for the command is:

```
CREATE LABEL <filename>
```

The MODIFY LABEL command is equivalent to the CREATE LABEL command. If the label does not exist, either command will create a new label; if the label exists, either command can be used to modify the existing label. When you enter either command, the Label Design Screen shown in Figure 9-14 appears. Operationally, the Label Design Screen is similar to the Report Design Screen used by the Report Generator. Seven menus appear at the top of the screen: Layout, Dimensions, Fields, Words, Go To, Print, and Exit. The Fields, Words, Go To, Print, and Exit Menus perform the same tasks as at the Report Design Screen; see the earlier portion of this chapter for a description of these menu options. The Layout Menu provides three options: Use Different Database File or View, Edit Description of Label Design, and Save This Label Design.

Use the first option of the Layout Menu, Use Different Database File or View, to change the active database file (or view) being used to design the mailing label. The Edit Description option lets you add or edit a one-line description of the label. (This description appears when the label name is highlighted at the Control Center menus.) The Save This Label Design option is used to save changes and continue working at the Label Design Screen.

The Dimensions Menu, shown in Figure 9-15, is used to change the dimensions of the mailing label.

When the Predefined Size option of this menu is selected, another menu appears with nine possible label sizes. The available sizes are (in inches):

1. 15/16 x 3 1/2 x 1
2. 15/16 x 3 1/2 x 2

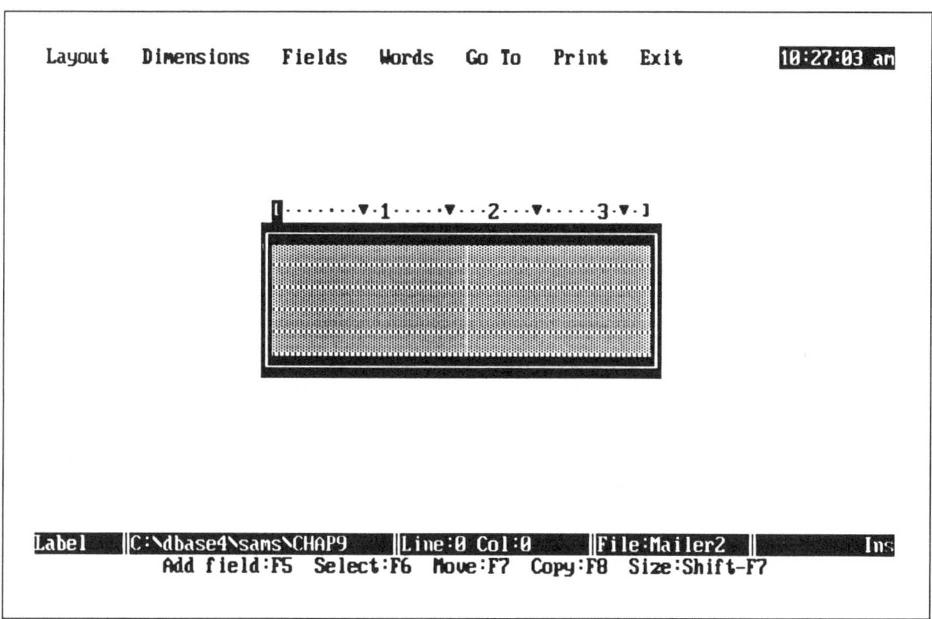

Figure 9-14 Label Design Screen

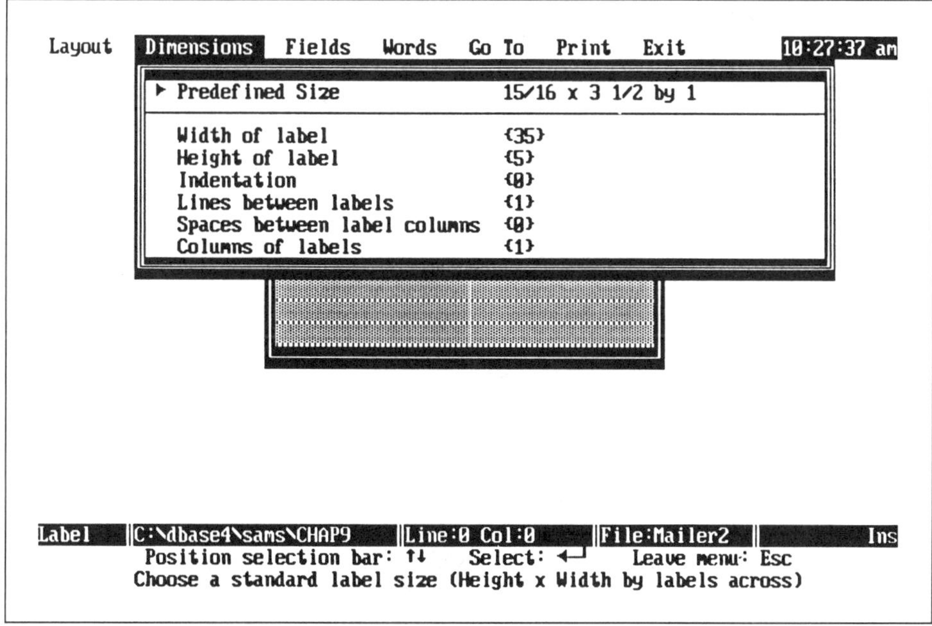

Figure 9-15 Dimensions Menu

3. 15/16 x 3 1/2 x 3
4. 11/12 x 3 1/2 x 3 (Cheshire)
5. 1 7/16 x 5 x 1
6. 3 5/8 x 6 1/2 envelope (#7)
7. 4 1/8 x 9 7/8 envelope (#10)
8. Rolodex (3 x 5)
9. Rolodex (2 1/4 x 4)

The first number indicates the label height, and the second indicates the label width. If a third value appears, it indicates the number of labels across a page. If a predefined size is chosen, appropriate sizes for that type of label are automatically entered in the remaining menu options of the Dimensions Menu. As an alternative method to label design, you can forgo the predefined sizes, and manually enter the desired values in the various options of the Dimensions Menu.

Once the label size has been established, the desired fields can be placed in the label with the Add Field, Remove Field, and Modify Field options of the Fields Menu. To add a field, place the cursor at the desired location, and choose Add Field from the Fields Menu; then, select the desired field from the list of fields which appears. As with reports, you can add fields from the active database file or view, or you can add calculated fields or predefined fields. (You cannot add summary fields, but to do so with labels would make little sense, since there are no groups to summarize.)

You can include a variable as part of an expression in a calculated field; this can be useful for placing messages on a label that may change on a regular basis. (Note that you should create the variable in memory with a STORE or an assignment command before you try to create the label.) As an example, your program might create a character expression called PHRASE; the calculated field using the expression in the label could contain an advertising message that is to appear at the bottom of each label. If the mailing labels are to contain the contents of that variable in a calculated field, first create the variable, then use the CREATE LABEL command, such as follows:

```
STORE "Big sale in progress!" TO PHRASE
CREATE LABEL FLYERS
```

You can then include the variable, PHRASE, as a part of the label without incurring the wrath of a dBASE IV "variable not found" error message. Of course, another way to handle this need is to simply type the text directly into the label. But then, every time the phrase changes, you must change the label design again. By storing the phrase to a variable, you need only initialize the variable in memory before running the label.

When placing two fields on the same line of a label (such as is commonly done with a first name, followed by the last name), separate the fields with a SPACE (typed by pressing the spacebar). This is important because it allows the default "trim" function of character fields to take effect, so that the last name appears one space after the first name, with extra blanks trimmed. If the fields are separated by moving the cursor over rather than by using the spacebar, the trim function will have no effect, and the result may be an unattractive gap between the two fields. Figure 9-16 shows a completed label design.

As with reports, labels may be previewed before saving, with the View Labels On Screen option of the Print Menu. When the creation of the label is complete, save the label with Control-End, or use the Save Changes and Exit option of the Exit Menu. When you save a label, two files are saved. One has an extension of .LBL, and it contains the layout of the label and is used by dBASE to produce the labels. The other file has a .LBG extension, and it contains the dBASE program code that, when run, will also produce the label. As with reports source code, you can copy the .LBG program code into your applications and modify it as you may desire.

Once created, labels can be produced with the LABEL FORM command. The syntax of the command is:

```
LABEL FORM <filename>/?[<scope>][WHILE <condition>][FOR <condition>][SAMPLE][TO
PRINT/TO FILE <filename>]
```

If the user wants an index order for the labels, an index file should be created or opened prior to using the LABEL FORM command. As with the REPORT FORM command, labels can be limited to a subset of records from within the database by using the WHILE or FOR options, or by setting a database filter with the SET FILTER command. The SAMPLE option produces a sample label (actually a series of asterisks) that helps in aligning the labels in the printer. The TO FILE

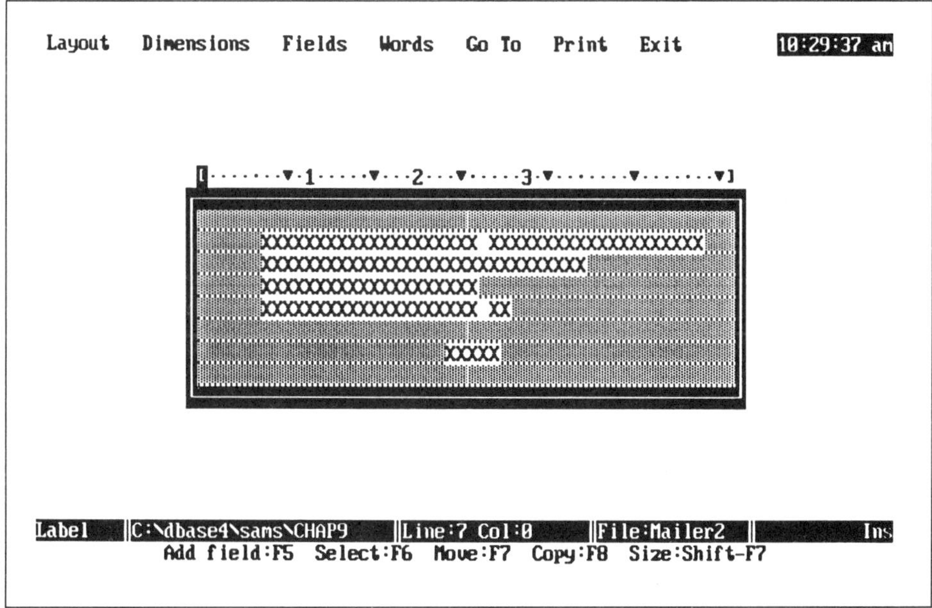

Figure 9-16 Completed Label

option writes the output to a text file. The text file will be given a .TXT extension, unless a different extension is specified. The ? option can be used in place of a filename, in which case a picklist of available label forms appears. The user can then choose the desired label from the list.

Printer Controls

dBASE IV assumes that your printer is connected to the default DOS list device—normally, LPT1. If this is not the case, you must redirect printer output to the appropriate printer port. This can be done with the DOS MODE command or with the SET PRINTER command within dBASE. The syntax for the SET PRINTER command is:

```
SET PRINTER TO LPT1/LPT2/COM1/COM2
```

The default device is LPT1. If multiple printers are used with an application, this command can be used to select the appropriate printer for a particular job. The addition of this handy command makes it possible to switch between a letter-quality and a dot-matrix printer from within the program, with code like this:

```
TEXT
===========================

Choose a Printer.

  *Enter 1 for dot-matrix.

  *Enter 2 for daisy-wheel.

===========================
ENDTEXT
INPUT "Your choice? " TO PRCHOOSE
IF PRCHOOSE = 1
     SET PRINTER TO LPT1
ELSE
     SET PRINTER TO LPT2
ENDIF
<rest of commands...>
```

Note that the colon required to follow the LPT1 or LPT2 designations in DOS is not needed when using the SET PRINTER command in dBASE IV. If you must change the baud rates and parity settings for a serial printer, you can use the DOS MODE command first to make the necessary changes. Then you can redirect output to the serial printer port, such as with the following commands from within dBASE IV:

```
RUN MODE COM1: = 1200,E,7,1
RUN MODE LPT1: = COM1:
```

For this use of MODE to be successful, the file MODE.COM must be contained in the same subdirectory as is dBASE, or MODE must be accessible through a PATH command in DOS.

Special Printer Effects

dBASE IV controls many printer defaults with the use of certain system memory variables. The system memory variables appear when you enter the LIST MEMORY or DISPLAY MEMORY commands from the dot prompt. The listing below shows an example of the system memory variables displayed with the LIST MEMORY command:

```
          Print System Memory Variables
_BOX        pub  L  .T.
_TABS       pub  C  ""
_PCOLNO     pub  N                   21  (21.00000000000000000)
_PLINENO    pub  N                   22  (22.00000000000000000)
_PAGENO     pub  N                    1  (1.000000000000000000)
_ALIGNMENT  pub  C  "LEFT"
_INDENT     pub  N                    0  (0.000000000000000000)
_RMARGIN    pub  N                   80  (80.00000000000000000)
_LMARGIN    pub  N                    0  (0.000000000000000000)
_WRAP       pub  L  .F.
_PLOFFSET   pub  N                    0  (0.000000000000000000)
_PLENGTH    pub  N                   66  (66.00000000000000000)
_PCOPIES    pub  N                    1  (1.000000000000000000)
_PSPACING   pub  N                    1  (1.000000000000000000)
_PEPAGE     pub  N                32767  (32767.00000000000000)
_PBPAGE     pub  N                    1  (1.000000000000000000)
_PECODE     pub  C  ""
_PSCODE     pub  C  ""
_PADVANCE   pub  C  "FORMFEED"
_PWAIT      pub  L  .F.
_PEJECT     pub  C  "BEFORE"
_PQUALITY   pub  L  .F.
_PPITCH     pub  C  "DEFAULT"
_PDRIVER    pub  C  "Generic.PR2"
_PFORM      pub  C  ""
```

All system memory variables that begin with _p are used to control print settings. Many of these variables can be recognized by their similarities with the various options of the Print Menu in dBASE. The printer variables affect settings such as page length, page offset, number of copies printed in a report, and line spacing.

When dBASE is started, the system memory variables are initialized to their default values. You can change these values in your programs by storing different values to the variables. (The variables will also be changed if the user selects related options from the Print Menus while inside dBASE.) The values that you can use are defined in the following list.

_PCOLNO: Repositions the printhead at the specified cursor location before any text is printed.

_PLINENO: Repositions the printhead at the specified line number before any text is printed.

_PAGENO: Defines the page number to begin numbering a report with, if something other than 1 is needed. Use an integer from 1 to 32,767.

_PLENGTH: Defines the page length of the printed page. Default is 66; use 84 for U.S. legal (14-inch) paper.

_PCOPIES: Defines the number of copies printed of a report. Default is 1.

_PSPACING: Defines the overall line spacing for a report. Default is 1, possible options are 1, 2, or 3.

_PLOFFSET: Defines the offset from the left edge where printing begins. Use an integer value.

_PSCODE: Defines starting control or escape codes to be sent to printer at the start of a report.

_PECODE: Defines ending control or escape codes to be sent to printer at the end of a report.

_PBPAGE: Defines first desired page in a report, if the entire report is not to be printed.

_PEPAGE: Defines last desired page in a report, if the entire report is not to be printed.

_PADVANCE: Contains character string of "FORMFEED" or "LINEFEED" which determines whether page advances are done with formfeeds or linefeeds.

_PWAIT: Contains logical "false" if printer should not pause between pages, or logical true if printer should pause between pages.

_PEJECT: Contains character string of "BEFORE" (if formfeed should occur before report), "AFTER" (if formfeed should occur after report), "BOTH" (if formfeed should occur before and after report), or "NONE" (if no formfeeds are needed).

_PQUALITY: Contains logical "false" if normal print quality is desired, or logical "true" if emphasized print quality is desired.

_PPITCH: Contains character string which determines the print typestyle. Possible options are "DEFAULT", "PICA", "ELITE", or "COMPRESSED."

_PDRIVER: Contains character string with the name of the installed printer driver.

_PFORM: Contains character string with the name of the stored print form to be used.

If you use the dBASE IV Report Generator to build many or all of your reports, you may prefer to select the various settings from the menus while at the Report Design Screen, then save the settings to a Print Form with the "Save Settings To Print Form" option of the Print Menu. You can then change to those same settings from any location in the program with a statement like,

```
_PFORM = "PrFile"
```

where "PrFile" is the name of the Print Form you saved while at the Report Design Screen. This is often much faster than using the individual variables to change the different settings, particularly if you've already created the report and the print form file. Note that you do not have to be using a stored report form to make use of a Print Form file; you can use a Print Form file with a report you've designed using program code, and the settings you have stored in the Print Form file will take effect.

Special print capabilities for reports (such as bold, compressed, and emphasized print) can also be invoked by sending the appropriate printer control characters to the printer with the ? command, in combination with the CHR() function. Most printers respond to an Esc control character followed by an appropriate control character that indicates the desired print style (bold, compressed, and so on). The Esc control character can be sent to the printer by using ? CHR(27) within a dBASE program. If the printer is compatible with Epson printer codes, the commands listed in Table 9-3 will cause the printer result listed, once the Esc code has been sent.

You can store the escape code along with the desired printer code as part of a variable, then send the contents of the variable to the printer each time a special effect is needed. For example, with Epson printers the following commands would create variables that would store on and off values for emphasized, compressed, and italics print:

```
STORE CHR(27) + CHR(4) TO ITALICSON
STORE CHR(27) + CHR(5) TO ITALICSOFF
STORE CHR(27) + CHR(15) TO COMPRESSED
```

```
STORE CHR(27) + CHR(18) TO NOCOMPRESS
STORE CHR(27) + CHR(45) TO EMPHASIZON
STORE CHR(27) + CHR(46) TO EMPHASIZOF
```

Table 9-3 Print Commands for Epson-Compatible Printers

Command	Result
? CHR(4)	italics on
? CHR(5)	italics off
? CHR(15)	compressed print on
? CHR(18)	compressed print off
? CHR(47)	double strike on
? CHR(48)	double strike off
? CHR(45)	emphasized on
? CHR(46)	emphasized off
? CHR(27)	printer reset

Then, each time you wanted to change a printer mode, you could use that variable as part of a PRINT statement, such as with:

```
SET PRINT ON
? ITALICSON
SET PRINT OFF
REPORT FORM MINE TO PRINT
SET PRINT ON
? ITALICSOFF
SET PRINT OFF
```

If you are using different types of printers with varying special codes, you can store each set of variables to a different memory variable file and restore the contents of that file when you use that particular printer. By using the same names for the variables, your programs can use special effects for a range of printers, without requiring any changes in the program code.

10

Managing the Database

This chapter discusses the use of various commands that affect the data in a database and the relationships between multiple databases that can be used at once.

Further honing of data used by your programs is possible with some specialized dBASE commands: SET EXACT and SET UNIQUE. The SET EXACT command determines how two character strings will be compared by dBASE IV. The syntax for the command is:

```
SET EXACT OFF/ON
```

and the default value is OFF, meaning dBASE IV does not attempt to match strings character for literal character. As an example, if a database contains an entry of "Simon, Jr." in the NAME field, any of the following commands would find the record:

```
LIST FOR NAME = "Simon"
LIST FOR NAME = "Simon, Jr."
LIST FOR NAME = "Sim"
```

To dBASE IV, "Sim" = "Simon, Jr.", even though this is clearly not the case. This anomaly can be remedied with the SET EXACT command. When you use SET EXACT, dBASE IV searches for a precise match among character strings being compared, down to the last space or punctuation symbol. There are times when a precise match is desired, and times when it isn't. If SET EXACT is ON, searches for character data must be precise to obtain results. On the other hand, SET EXACT can be useful for finding duplicate records that differ slightly.

Duplicate records are a bane of mailing systems. How many times have you received two or more flyers from the same firm, because you are in someone's database more than once? The SET UNIQUE command, used along with a database that is indexed on a unique key field, can be used to avoid duplicate records. In effect, SET UNIQUE is used to filter duplicate records from an index file. When you SET UNIQUE ON and then index the file, the resultant index will contain only unique records (or records that have unique entries in the key field).

The duplicate records may still be in the database, but as long as the index file is used, the duplicates will be hidden from use in the program, because they will not be in the index file.

To illustrate this concept with an example, assume a database contains the following five records, of which the second and third are accidental duplicates of the first:

```
Record# LNAME          FNAME            ACCTNO
      1 McCoy          Y. Shari           1014
      2 McCoy          Yvonne Shari       1014
      3 McCoy          Yvonne S.          1014
      4 Laufer         B.                 1015
      5 Randell        Susan              1016
```

If you entered the following commands, a new index file containing no duplicate account numbers would be created, with the results shown:

```
. set unique on
. index on acctno to accounts
   100% indexed            3 Records indexed

. list
Record# LNAME          FNAME            ACCTNO
      1 McCoy          Y. Shari           1014
      4 Laufer         B.                 1015
      5 Randell        Susan              1016
```

Whenever a duplicate account number is encountered during the indexing process, dBASE IV keeps the first unique record found intact and omits any additional records with the same entry in the key field from the resultant index file.

Using Relational Capabilities

A major (and underused) strength of dBASE IV is its *relational* feature—the ability to draw a relationship between more than one open database. dBASE IV can have up to 10 database files open at once. Each open file is held in a separate work area. By default, the work areas are numbered from 1 through 10. Work areas can be given *alias* names that are more descriptive than the numbers 1 to 10. If no alias is assigned, each area will assume an alias that is the same as the name of the database file after one is opened in that work area.

Selection of Work Areas

When you initially open a database, dBASE IV opens the file in work area 1 unless told otherwise. Work areas are chosen with the SELECT command, the syntax of which is:

```
SELECT <work area number>[<ALIAS>alias name]
```

Once the SELECT command is used to choose a work area, the desired database is opened. As an example, to open 2 database files (such as CLIENTS and LAWYERS) in work areas 1 and 2, these commands would be appropriate:

```
SELECT 1
USE CLIENTS
SELECT 2
USE LAWYERS
```

Once you've opened a number of files, any file can be made the active file by selecting that work area, either by its number or by the alias name. For example,

```
SELECT 2
```

will make the LAWYERS database active, while the command

```
SELECT CLIENTS
```

will make the CLIENTS database the active one. The active database is the database that will be directly affected by dBASE commands, such as APPEND, LIST, and LOCATE. If you want an alias other than the default alias, assign one by including the alias name with the SELECT command:

```
SELECT 1 ALIAS WEALTHY
USE CLIENTS
*CLIENTS.DBF is now the active file
SELECT 2
USE LAWYERS
*LAWYERS.DBF is now the active file
SELECT WEALTHY
*CLIENTS.DBF is now the active file
```

The use of multiple work areas lets you keep one database in active use (or in the foreground, so to speak), while other open database files remain accessible in the background. A different record pointer is maintained in a separate location in each database. So, if your program were to use a file in work area 2, make changes to record 5, move to work area 1, display record 92, and move back to work area 2, the record pointer for that database would still be at record 5.

Advantages of Using Multiple Work Areas

If you've never used multiple files in a dBASE application, you're probably thinking, "There must be a good reason for all of this," and you're right. Many applications are difficult to impossible to deal with unless you use multiple files. As an example, consider the database structure for clothing sales shown in Table 10-1.

Table 10-1 Structure of the CLOTHING SALES Database

Field Name	Type
CUSTACCT	Numeric
CUSTNAME	Character
CUSTADDR	Character
CUSTCITY	Character
CUSTSTATE	Character
CUSTZIP	Character
DESCRIPT	Character
STOCKNO	Numeric
PRICE	Numeric

Such a database would work, but it would be terribly inefficient. If the same customer buys five suits, that customer's name and address must be duplicated in five different records. It would be far more efficient to open two databases, with structures like those shown in Table 10-2. What's needed for this scheme to work effectively is a key field that contains items common to both databases. In this example, the CUSTACCT field is the key field. In an application that uses multiple files, the SELECT command can be used to switch between the files, and the necessary commands can be used to extract data from the files for simultaneous use by the program. The following program illustrates such use of multiple databases:

```
**Program prints names, city, state, and sales desc. from 2 files
SELECT 1
USE CUSTOMER
SELECT 2
USE SALES
DO WHILE .NOT. EOF()
     STORE CUSTACCT TO MATCH
     SELECT CUSTOMER
     LOCATE FOR CUSTACCT = MATCH
     ? CUSTACCT
     ?? "   " + CUSTNAME + "   " +  CUSTCITY + "   " + CUSTSTATE + "   "
     SELECT SALES
     ?? DESCRIPT + "   "
```

```
    ?? STOCKNO
    ?? " "
    ?? PRICE
    SKIP
ENDDO
*End of program
```

Table 10-2 Structure of CUSTOMER and SALES Databases

Field Name	Type
CUSTOMER Database	
CUSTACCT	Numeric
CUSTNAME	Character
CUSTADDR	Character
CUSTCITY	Character
CUSTSTATE	Character
CUSTZIP	Character
SALES Database	
CUSTACCT	Numeric
DESCRIPT	Character
STOCKNO	Numeric
PRICE	Numeric

Those of you who will complain, "But this program doesn't draw any relations," are quite observant, and more on that topic shortly. The program opens the CUSTOMER database in work area 1 and the SALES database in work area 2. The value contained within the CUSTACCT field of the SALES database is stored as a variable, MATCH. Data from the second database is to be displayed in the first columns of the report, so SELECT CUSTOMER opens the database, and a LOCATE command finds the record in the customer database that contains the same account number. The desired data in the fields of the CUSTOMER database is displayed. A SELECT SALES statement then switches back to the SALES database in work area 2, and appropriate data from the fields of the SALES database is displayed. Finally, a SKIP command indexes the record pointer, and the ENDDO command ends the loop, which repeats until all records in the SALES database have been displayed. The output from the report looks like this:

```
1002 Leopold, Alvin  Queens  NY Hayes Smartcom software      4540 190.50
1002 Leopold, Alvin  Queens  NY Prog. Ref. Guide to dBASE 3+ 3009  18.95
1001 Jones, Judie    Reston  VA Ultimate ROM Chip, Mod 100   2523 179.90
1004 Sweeney, Eileen Salem   NJ MS-DOS Version 4.0           5117 249.95
1003 Richards, Jim   Raleigh NC MS-DOS Version 4.0           5117 249.95
1003 Richards, Jim   Raleigh NC dUTIL III Software           2085 209.90
```

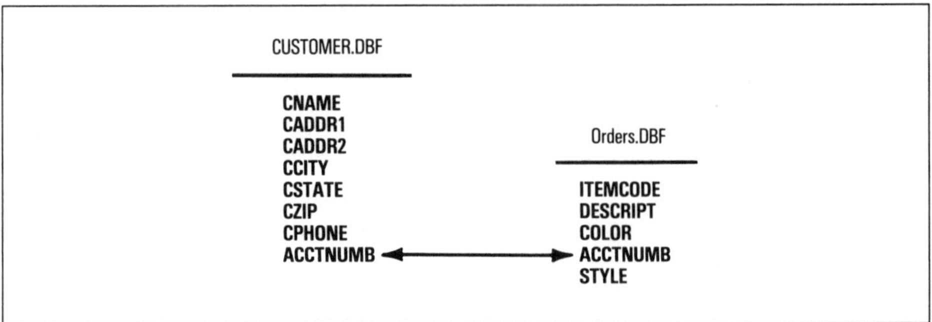

Figure 10-1 Common Database Fields Between CUSTOMER and ORDERS Database Necessary to Use SET RELATION

A Better Way to Use Relational Features—SET RELATION

The process just described is not the only way to access data from more than one database at a time, and it is usually not the best way. This is the way it was done with dBASE II, because dBASE II programmers had no other options. A major drawback to this approach is that it is difficult to impossible to use it along with the stored reports or formats created with the Report Generator or the LABEL FORM command.

The SET RELATION command works with the stored report and label formats, and it is faster and less tedious than using program code to scan for matching key fields. SET RELATION draws a relationship between a key field that is common to two or more databases (Figure 10-1). The syntax for the SET RELATION command is:

```
SET RELATION TO <expression> INTO <alias>
```

If, for example, our CUSTOMER file is open in work area 1 and our ORDERS file is open in work area 2, the SET RELATION command can be used to link the common field, ACCTNUMB, so that whenever the record pointer is moved to a record in the ORDERS file, the record pointer in the CUSTOMER file will be moved to the record containing the same account number. You must have indexed the file in the second work area on the field or expression you plan to use to link the files before you use the SET RELATION command. The following example shows the effects of the SET RELATION command:

```
.SELECT 1
.USE CUSTOMER
.SET INDEX TO ACCOUNTS
.SELECT 2
.USE SALES
.SET RELATION TO CUSTACCT INTO CUSTOMER
```

```
.GO 3
.DISPLAY

Record#  CUSTACCT DESCRIPT                         STOCKNO  PRICE
      3      1001 Ultimate ROM Chip for Mod 100     2523 179.90

.SELECT CUSTOMER
.DISPLAY CUSTNAME, CUSTACCT

Record#  CUSTNAME        CUSTACCT
      1  Jones, Judie        1001

.SELECT SALES
.GO 5
.DISPLAY

Record#  CUSTACCT DESCRIPT                         STOCKNO  PRICE
      5      1003 MS-DOS Version 4.0                5117 249.95

.SELECT CUSTOMER
.DISPLAY CUSTNAME, CUSTACCT

Record#  CUSTNAME        CUSTACCT
      3  Richards, Jim       1003
```

A program for listing the records from both databases, written to take advantage of SET RELATION, could look like this:

```
**Program prints names, city, state, and sales desc. from 2 files
**Set relation command used for added speed
SELECT 1
USE CUSTOMER INDEX ACCOUNTS
SELECT 2
USE SALES INDEX STOCKS
SET RELATION TO CUSTACCT INTO CUSTOMER
SELECT CUSTOMER
GO TOP
DO WHILE .NOT. EOF()
     ? CUSTACCT
     ?? "   " + CUSTNAME + "   " + CUSTCITY + "   " + CUSTSTATE + "   "
     SELECT SALES
     ?? DESCRIPT + "   "
     ?? STOCKNO
     ?? "   "
```

```
    ?? PRICE
    SELECT CUSTOMER
    SKIP
ENDDO
*End of program
```

When your program uses multiple files, you can specify fields from different files within a command by giving the alias name for the work area, then an alias marker (->), then the name of the field. For example, the expression,

```
CUSTOMER->CUSTCITY
```

would refer to the CUSTCITY field in the customer database, even if it is in a different work area than the selected area.

Consider the following program, and the results:

```
SELECT 1
USE CUSTOMER
INDEX ON CUSTACCT TO ACCOUNTS
SELECT 2
USE SALES
SET RELATION TO CUSTACCT INTO CUSTOMER
LIST DESCRIPT, STOCKNO, PRICE, CUSTOMER->CUSTNAME, CUSTOMER->CUSTCITY
```

```
Hayes Smartcom software        4540 190.50 Leopold, Alvin    Queens
Prog. Ref. Guide to dBASE 3+   3009  18.95 Leopold, Alvin    Queens
Ultimate ROM Chip for Mod 100  2523 179.90 Jones, Judie      Reston
MS-DOS Version 4.0             5117 249.95 Sweeney, Eileen   Salem
MS-DOS Version 4.0             5117 249.95 Richards, Jim     Raleigh
dUTIL III Software             2085 209.90 Richards, Jim     Raleigh
```

In the example, the LIST command is listing data simultaneously from two databases. Because the CUSTNAME and CUSTCITY fields are not contained within the active database, they must be identified with an alias name—in this case, CUSTOMER. Once a relation has been established with the SET RELATION command, alias names can then be used to indicate any field within the related databases. Alias names can also be used within expressions inside calculated fields used in the Report Generator and the Label Generator.

For example, in the case of our SALES and CUSTOMER databases, a columnar report containing customer name, account number, description, stock number, and price may be desired. The customer name and account number fields are contained within the CUSTOMER database, while the account number, description, stock number, and price fields are contained within the SALES database.

The four fields in the active database, CUSTACCT, DESCRIPT, STOCKNO, and PRICE, could be selected from the fields list when designing the report. Since the fifth field, CUSTNAME, is not in the active file but is in the related file open in the other work area, it will not appear in the picklist of fields when you are designing a report or a label. However, the field can be referenced in a report, by using the fieldname along with the alias and pointer (->) symbol in the expression which forms a calculated field. In the example report, a calculated field was created, and the following expression was entered as the basis for the calculated field:

```
CUSTOMER->CUSTNAME
```

The calculated field was then used as the field in the "customer name" column of the report.

Once the report form has been created, use the SET RELATION and SELECT commands within the program to open the desired files and draw the relation between the files; then, use the REPORT FORM command to run the report. A sample program is listed here, providing the report shown:

```
SELECT 1
USE CUSTOMER INDEX ACCOUNTS
SELECT 2
USE SALES
SET RELATION TO CUSTACCT INTO CUSTOMER
REPORT FORM RELATE TO PRINT
```

```
Page No.     1
11/12/88
                      Relational Report
                        Uses Data From
                      Sales and Customer
                          Databases

Account Customer Name   Item Description                Stock    Cost
Number                                                  Number

   1002 Leopold, Alvin  Hayes Smartcom software          4540  190.50
   1002 Leopold, Alvin  Prog. Ref. Guide to dBASE 3+     3009   18.95
   1001 Jones, Judie    Ultimate ROM Chip for Mod 100    2523  179.90
   1004 Sweeney, Eileen MS-DOS Version 4.0               5117  249.95
   1003 Richards, Jim   MS-DOS Version 4.0               5117  249.95
   1003 Richards, Jim   dUTIL III Software               2085  209.90

*** Total ***
                                                              1099.20
```

Notes about SET RELATION

The SET RELATION command is not limited to two files; you can link a number of databases, as long as a common key field exists between any two linked databases. As an example, a customer file might be linked to a sales file by the customer account number; the sales file might be linked to a detailed inventory file by item stock number; and the inventory file might be linked to a file of pricing histories for each item, also by stock number.

You can also have multiple relations per work area. Also, SET RELATION works best when you have matching contents in all of the records in the linked files. If the linked file does not contain an entry matching the key field of the active file, the record pointer of the linked file will be positioned at the end of the file.

If you are programming an application and the possibility of not finding a corresponding record exists, you may want to test for an end-of-file condition with an IF .NOT. FOUND() statement in an appropriate location of the program. Existing relations may be cleared by using the SET RELATION TO command without specifying any file; you can also use the CLEAR ALL and CLOSE DATABASES commands to clear a relation. Keep in mind that the SET RELATION command takes priority over the SET DELETED ON and SET FILTER commands. Data contained in the related database will be accessible, even if the records have been hidden by means of a filter or marked for deletion. You won't have this problem in the active database (the one you are setting the relation from); in that work area, the SET FILTER and SET DELETED commands will operate in a normal manner.

Using SET FIELDS

The SET FIELDS command is a powerful command in dBASE IV. You use it to create a group of fields from any number of open databases. Once the group of fields has been identified with SET FIELDS, dBASE IV will use only those fields as a part of your program commands (LIST, DISPLAY, and so on). You describe a list of affected fields with the SET FIELDS TO command and turn on or off the limitations of SET FIELDS with the ON or OFF options. The syntax for the commands is:

```
SET FIELDS TO [<list of fields>][ALL]
SET FIELDS OFF/ON
```

For example, all of the fields in the CUSTOMER and SALES databases could be placed in a group of fields with the following commands:

```
SET FIELDS TO CUSTACCT, CUSTNAME, CUSTADDR, CUSTCITY, CUSTSTATE, CUSTZIP, SALES->
DESCRIPT, SALES->STOCKNO, SALES->PRICE

SET FIELDS ON
```

Once the group of fields exists and you have told the system to use the fields list with a SET FIELDS ON statement, you can use the desired commands within your program to access the data in the databases, as shown in the example:

```
LIST CUSTNAME, CUSTCITY, STOCKNO, PRICE
```

```
Record# CUSTNAME         CUSTCITY   STOCKNO  PRICE
      1 Leopold, Alvin   Queens        4540 190.50
      2 Leopold, Alvin   Queens        3009  18.95
      3 Jones, Judie     Reston        2523 179.90
      4 Sweeney, Eileen  Salem         5117 249.95
      5 Richards, Jim    Raleigh       5117 249.95
      6 Richards, Jim    Raleigh       2085 209.90
```

While the fields named following the LIST command exist in separate databases, the LIST command needs no alias names to access the fields, because the alias names have already been provided with the SET FIELDS command. The SET FIELDS command offers the same advantage for the dBASE Report Generator or LABEL FORM command, so you can use it to create reports and mailing labels. This eliminates the need for using calculated fields to refer to fields in related files. Once a field has been declared with SET FIELDS, it appears in the picklist when you are designing reports or labels.

SET FIELDS is an additive command; you can add more fields to the group while leaving fields within the group intact by using another SET FIELDS command. The CLEAR FIELDS command can be used to remove all fields from a group of fields. One unpleasant trap you can encounter with SET FIELDS: if you use the SET FIELDS ON command before specifying a list of fields with the SET FIELDS TO command, all database fields will be hidden from view.

Using CREATE VIEW

dBASE IV also offers a way for you to "view" a file that can save you some time in programming. View files can be created with the CREATE VIEW FROM ENVIRONMENT command. A view file can be thought of as a record of all open database files, index files, format files, and relationships between linked files. View files are given an extension of .VUE. The view files created with the CREATE VIEW FROM ENVIRONMENT command are fully compatible with dBASE III Plus, which can use view files (but cannot use the query files created at the Query Design Screen).

Once a view file has been created, it can be specified with the SET VIEW TO <filename> command. By creating a view file and repeatedly using the SET VIEW command, you can avoid repeatedly selecting work areas and relations, since all of this information is stored in the view file. Consider this example:

```
SELECT 1
USE CUSTOMER
INDEX ON CUSTACCT TO ACCOUNTS
SELECT 2
USE SALES
INDEX ON STOCKNO TO STOCKS
SET RELATION TO CUSTACCT INTO CUSTOMER
SET FORMAT TO FORMFILE
CREATE VIEW MYSALES FROM ENVIRONMENT
DISPLAY STATUS
```

```
Select area:  1, Database in Use: C:CUSTOMER.DBF   Alias: CUSTOMER
    Master index file:  C:ACCOUNTS.NDX  Key: CUSTACCT

Currently Selected Database:
Select area:  2, Database in Use: C:SALES.DBF   Alias: SALES
    Master index file:  C:STOCKS.NDX  Key: STOCKNO
    Format file: C:FORMFILE.FMT
Related into: CUSTOMER
Relation: CUSTACCT

File search path:   Default disk drive: C:
Print destination:  PRN:
Margin =      0
Refresh count = 0
Reprocess count = 0
Number of files open = 9
Current work area =    2

Press any key to continue...
```

The work areas, open files, and relation listed by the DISPLAY STATUS command are all contained within the view file, MYSALES.VIEW. If you enter a CLEAR ALL command, the files are closed and the relation is cleared, as shown in the example:

```
.CLEAR ALL
.DISPLAY STATUS

File search path:   Default disk drive: C:
Print destination:  PRN:
Margin =      0
Refresh count = 0
Reprocess count = 0
```

```
Number of files open = 5
Current work area =    1

Press any key to continue...
```

Now that the view file exists, it can be used to open the files, work areas, and relations with a single SET VIEW command, as shown:

```
.SET VIEW TO MYSALES
.DISPLAY STATUS

Select area:  1, Database in Use: C:CUSTOMER.DBF    Alias: CUSTOMER
    Master index file:  C:ACCOUNTS.NDX  Key: CUSTACCT
Currently Selected Database:
Select area:  2, Database in Use: C:SALES.DBF    Alias: SALES
    Master index file:  C:STOCKS.NDX  Key: STOCKNO
         Format file: C:FORMFILE.FMT
    Related into: CUSTOMER
    Relation: CUSTACCT

File search path:   Default disk drive: C:
Print destination:  PRN:
Margin =      0
Refresh count = 0
Reprocess count = 0
Number of files open = 9
Current work area =    2

Press any key to continue...
```

In dBASE IV, relationships between files can also be created by defining a relational link within a query. The query can then be activated within a program with the SET FILTER TO FILE <query filename> command. Entering the command CREATE QUERY <filename> reveals the Query Design Screen, as detailed previously in Chapter 8. To build queries of a relational nature, add a File Skeleton from each desired database file to the view by choosing the Add File To Query Option of the Layout Menu. To link the files, place the same example variable in the matching fields of the File Skeleton. This can be done by manually typing an identical variable in the matching fields of the File Skeletons, or by choosing the Create Link By Pointing Option from the Layout Menu. In the example shown in Figure 10-2, the File Skeletons for the SALES and the CUSTOMER databases described earlier were first added to the Query Design Screen, using the Add File To Query option of the Layout Menu. Next, the cursor was moved to the CUSTACCT field, since this field needed to be linked between the files. (It does not matter which File Skeleton you place the cursor in first, when linking the two.)

After placing the cursor in one of the CUSTACCT fields, choose the Create Link By Pointing option from the Layout Menu. This causes an example variable

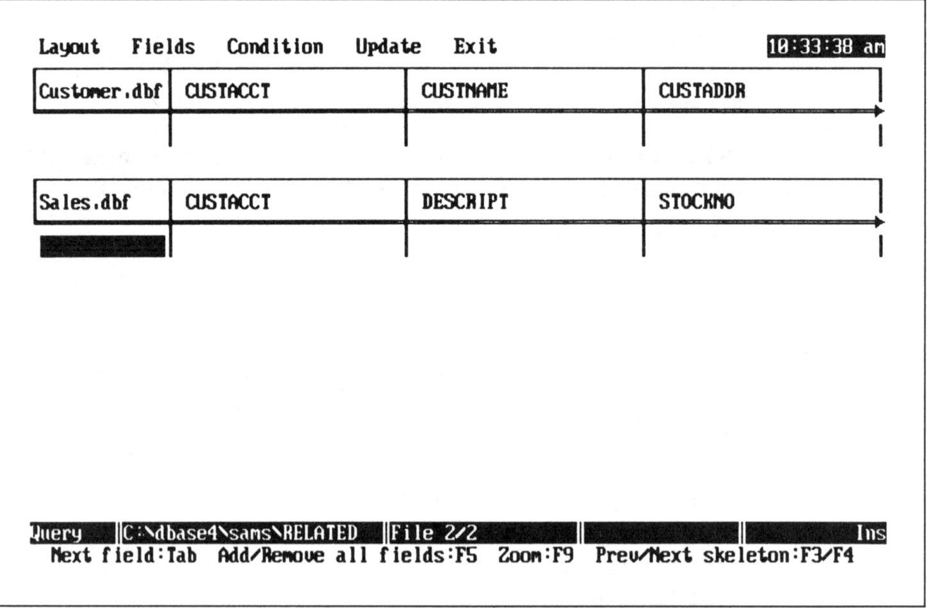

Figure 10-2 New Query with File Skeletons for CUSTOMER, SALES Database Files

to automatically appear in the field of the File Skeleton, and the message at the bottom of the screen reads,

```
Cursor to another file and press Enter
```

The cursor is then moved to the matching field, CUSTACCT, in the other File Skeleton (the F3 and F4 function keys can be used to move between the File Skeletons). Once Enter is pressed, the matching example variable is automatically entered into the field of the second File Skeleton.

All that remains is to add the desired fields to the View Skeleton with F5. Then the query can be saved with Control-End, or by choosing Save Changes and Exit from the Exit Menu. Figure 10-3 shows the completed query.

If you want to limit the records to a specific group, you can also use the Condition Box, or you can enter expressions within the columns of the query (as described in Chapter 8) to qualify records processed by the query. Choosing the Include Indexes option of the Fields Menu tells dBASE to include any index expressions as part of the File Skeletons. After the file has been saved, use the SET FILTER TO FILE <query filename> command within a program to apply the relationships and conditions within the query to your database files.

For programmers, there is no notable advantage in using the Query Design Screen over using the CREATE VIEW FROM ENVIRONMENT command; whichever method strikes your fancy is perfectly acceptable. In a program, you can save some coding effort by using the CREATE VIEW FROM ENVIRON-

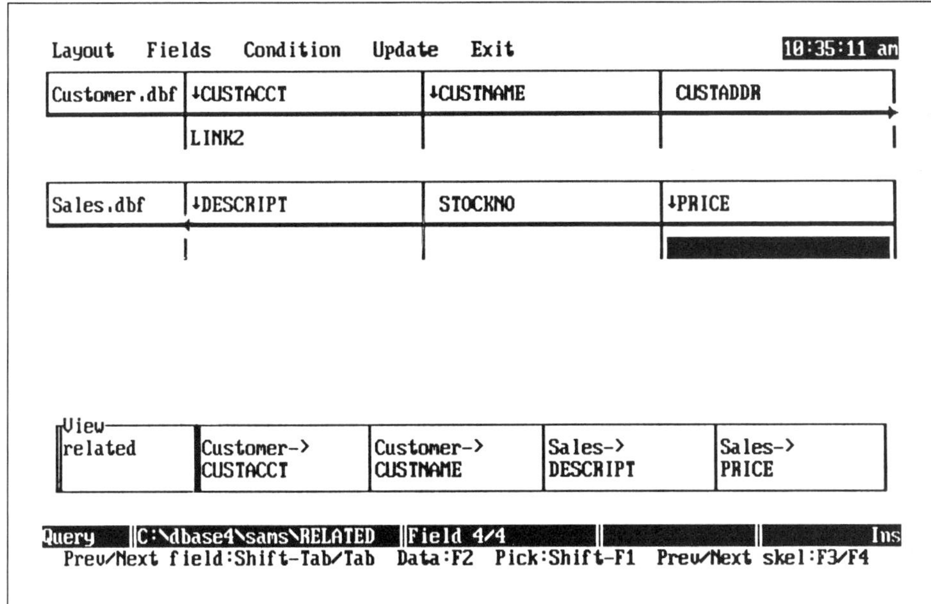

Figure 10-3 Completed Query

MENT and SET VIEW commands—in place of repetitive SELECT, USE, SET RELATION, and SET FIELDS commands—when you want to open and close files for transaction-based processing.

About Catalogs

dBASE IV also offers a Catalogs feature, a system of grouping often-used files together in a group of files known as a *catalog.* A catalog is actually a modified database that contains the names of all files that are to be included in that catalog. Once a catalog is opened, only the files in the catalog are visible by the Control Center Menus. Catalogs can contain multiple database and index files, screen format files, view files, query files, or a combination of these files. Catalogs are of minimal interest to the programmer, as their prime purpose is to offer novice users a way to display only those files that they are interested in using through the Control Center Menus.

To create or use a catalog, enter the command,

```
SET CATALOG TO <filename>
```

where <filename> is the name of the catalog to be created. If the catalog exists, it will be opened; if not, a new catalog will be created. Catalogs are stored with .CAT file extensions, unless a different extension is specified with the filename. When you create a new catalog, dBASE IV will prompt for a descriptive title for the catalog, which can be any character string up to 80 characters long. Once the catalog has been created, any dBASE commands that normally open files (CREATE, USE, SET INDEX, SET FILTER, SET VIEW, and so on) will add those files to the catalog. Thereafter, each time you open the catalog, the Control Center Menus will only display those files that are present in the catalog. An open catalog can be closed by entering the SET CATALOG TO command without specifying the name of a catalog.

Changing a Database Structure Under Program Control

Changing the structure of a database while under program control is a task that calls for two specialized dBASE IV commands: COPY STRUCTURE EXTENDED and CREATE FROM.

The task is a simple one from the dot prompt: the user simply opens the database, enters MODIFY STRUCTURE, plugs in the new field definitions, and saves the modified database. Existing records are copied over, and *voila*—the database is ready for further use.

If you want to provide program users with this capability, it calls for some fancy footwork with existing files, macros, and two lesser-known commands. The COPY STRUCTURE EXTENDED command is a special version of the COPY STRUCTURE command. COPY STRUCTURE EXTENDED always creates a new database with five fields, named FIELD_NAME, FIELD_TYPE, FIELD_LEN, FIELD_DEC, and FIELD_IDX. These fields contain the field names, data types, widths, decimal places (if any) describing the fields contained in the original database, and a "Y/N" indicating the presence of an index tag in the production .MDX index file.

For example, consider the use of the COPY STRUCTURE EXTENDED with the MAILER database:

```
.USE MAILER
.LIST STRUCTURE

Structure for database: C:MAILER.DBF
Number of data records:       7
Date of last update   : 06/28/86
Field  Field Name  Type       Width    Dec
    1  LAST_NAME   Character     15
    2  FIRST_NAME  Character     15
    3  ADDRESS_1   Character     20
    4  ADDRESS_2   Character     10
    5  CITY        Character     10
    6  STATE       Character      2
    7  ZIP_CODE    Character     10
    8  CUSTNO      Numeric        5
```

```
   9  COUNTRY      Character      10
** Total **                       98


.COPY TO datafile STRUCTURE EXTENDED

.USE DATAFILE
.LIST STRUCTURE
```

```
Structure for database: C:DATAFILE.DBF
Number of data records:        9
Date of last update   : 11/06/88
Field  Field Name  Type       Width    Dec    Index
    1  FIELD_NAME  Character     10               N
    2  FIELD_TYPE  Character      1               N
    3  FIELD_LEN   Numeric        3               N
    4  FIELD_DEC   Numeric        3               N
    5  FIELD_IDX   Character      1               N
** Total **                      19


. LIST

Record#  FIELD_NAME FIELD_TYPE FIELD_LEN FIELD_DEC FIELD_IDX
      1  LAST_NAME  C                 15         0 N
      2  FIRST_NAME C                 15         0 N
      3  ADDRESS_1  C                 20         0 N
      4  ADDRESS_2  C                 10         0 N
      5  CITY       C                 15         0 N
      6  STATE      C                  2         0 N
      7  ZIP_CODE   C                 10         0 N
      8  CUSTNO     N                  5         0 N
      9  COUNTRY    C                 10         0 N
```

Each record in the database created with the COPY STRUCTURE EXTENDED command contains one record for each corresponding field in the original database; in effect, COPY STRUCTURE EXTENDED creates a database that is a facsimile of the design of any database file.

Without the CREATE FROM command, the newly created database would be of little practical use. CREATE FROM is designed to build a new database without requiring any design specifications from the user. In place of the specifications normally supplied by the user in an interactive mode, the CREATE FROM command gets its specifications from a database that has been created with the COPY STRUCTURE EXTENDED command. The CREATE FROM command creates a new database, with fields based on the contents of the database created with COPY STRUCTURE EXTENDED.

So, to change the structure of that database, all you need to do is to add or edit records in the database created with COPY STRUCTURE, before using the CREATE FROM command to build the new database. Again, consider the mailing list example:

```
. USE DATAFILE
. APPEND BLANK
. REPLACE field_name WITH "PHONE"
      1 record replaced
. REPLACE field_type WITH "C"
      1 record replaced
. REPLACE field_len WITH 12
      1 record replaced
. REPLACE field_dec WITH 0
      1 record replaced
. REPLACE field_idx WITH "N"
      1 record replaced

. LIST
Record#  FIELD_NAME FIELD_TYPE FIELD_LEN FIELD_DEC FIELD_IDX
      1  LAST_NAME  C                 15         0 N
      2  FIRST_NAME C                 15         0 N
      3  ADDRESS_1  C                 20         0 N
      4  ADDRESS_2  C                 10         0 N
      5  CITY       C                 10         0 N
      6  STATE      C                  2         0 N
      7  ZIP_CODE   C                 10         0 N
      8  CUSTNO     N                  5         0 N
      9  COUNTRY    C                 10         0 N
     10  PHONE      C                 12         0 N
```

Using the REPLACE command, the tenth record (added with APPEND BLANK) has been filled with the data describing the new field to be added to the existing database. The CREATE FROM command can now be used to create the new database file:

```
. CLOSE DATABASES
. CREATE NEWFILE FROM DATAFILE

. APPEND FROM MAILER
      7 records added
```

```
. REPLACE ALL PHONE WITH "000-000-0000"
      7 records replaced

. USE NEWFILE
. LIST LAST_NAME, CITY, STATE, PHONE
Record#  LAST_NAME        CITY       STATE PHONE
      1  Jones            Reston     VA    000-000-0000
      2  Smith            San Jose   CA    000-000-0000
      3  Johnson          Reston     VA    000-000-0000
      4  Jones            Durham     NC    000-000-0000
      5  Miller           Plano      TX    000-000-0000
      6  Canion           Woodlands  TX    000-000-0000
      7  Roberts          Hollywood  CA    000-000-0000
```

Since all of these commands can be used within a program, it is a relatively simple matter to provide users with a way of creating new databases or modifying existing databases. The program module shown is one example:

```
*ADDFIELD.PRG adds a new field to any database
*Last update 11/06/88
SET SAFETY OFF
SET TALK OFF
CLEAR
DISPLAY FILES LIKE *.DBF
?
?"Enter name of database to add field to."
?"(**Do NOT include the .DBF extension.**)"
?
ACCEPT TO FNAME
STORE FNAME + ".DBF" TO FNAME
IF .NOT. FILE("&FNAME")
     ? "No such database on this disk!"
     WAIT
     RETURN
ENDIF
USE &FNAME
COPY TO TEMPFILE STRUCTURE EXTENDED
CLOSE DATABASES
CLEAR
ACCEPT "Enter new name for field: " TO Newname
ACCEPT "Enter field type; C, N, L, D, or M: " TO Newtype
INPUT "Enter length of field: " TO Newlength
INPUT "Enter decimal places (enter zero if none used): " TO Newdec
ACCEPT "Index? Y/N:" TO Newidx
USE TEMPFILE
APPEND BLANK
REPLACE field_name WITH Newname
```

```
REPLACE field_type WITH Newtype
REPLACE field_len WITH Newlength
REPLACE field_idx WITH Newidx
IF UPPER(field_type) = "N"
     REPLACE field_dec WITH Newdec
ENDIF
CLOSE DATABASES
CREATE NEWFILE FROM TEMPFILE
APPEND FROM &FNAME
CLOSE DATABASES
DELETE FILE &FNAME
RENAME NEWFILE.DBF TO &FNAME
CLEAR
? "Requested field has been added to database."
WAIT
RETURN
*End of ADDFIELD.PRG
```

If you plan to provide such capability within a program, be prepared to deal with a Pandora's box of other complications. If the program must then work on the database with @ . . . SAY . . . GET commands or with format files for adding and editing data, you must provide a way for the program to deal with the new fields.

11

File Management

This chapter gives details about dBASE commands and functions useful in managing various files. It also describes techniques you can use to restore damaged database files.

dBASE IV offers programmers a number of file manipulation operations. Using such operations often eliminates the need to exit dBASE to perform some routine DOS function, such as copying or erasing files. And when it becomes necessary to return to DOS (to run a program, for example), this can be done from within dBASE IV with the RUN command.

Using COPY

The COPY command is a multipurpose command you use to copy database files or other types of files to any available drive. The command comes in two forms: the COPY command, which works on open database files, and the COPY FILE command, which works with any type of file (the file must be closed). The COPY command copies part or all of a database file to another file. With various options, it can provide compatible files that can be used with Lotus 1-2-3, Multiplan, and many other software packages. The syntax for the COPY command is:

```
COPY TO <filename> [<scope>] [FIELDS <field list>] [FOR <condition>] [WHILE
<condition>] [TYPE <file type>]
```

A database must be open before you can use the COPY command. With no options specified, the COPY command produces an identical copy of the database, with the new name (specified in <filename>) assigned to the file. The scope and the FOR and WHILE options can be used as with other dBASE commands, to limit the number of records that will be copied to the resultant file. The FIELDS option specifies a list of fields to include in the file. If no list is specified, all fields are included. As an example, the command

```
COPY TO NEWFILE NEXT 300 FIELDS L_NAME, F_NAME_M_I, AGE, SOCSEC FOR AGE > 17
```

copies the L_NAME, F_NAME_M_I, AGE, and SOCSEC fields from the database currently in use to a new database named NEWFILE.DBF. Only those records containing an age greater than 17 will be copied to the file.

If records in the original file have been marked for deletion and SET DELETED is ON, the marked records will not be copied to the new file. If SET DELETED is OFF, the marked records will be copied, and they will remain marked for deletion in the new file.

Copying Foreign Files

The COPY command can also be used to copy the contents of a database into *foreign files,* that is, files you intend to export from dBASE IV for use with other software. When you use COPY in this fashion, a TYPE option must be added at the end of the COPY command. The TYPE option tells dBASE IV which file format to use in writing the foreign file. The TYPE options include

DELIMITED
SDF
DIF
SYLK (Multiplan file format)
WKS (Lotus 1-2-3 format)
DBASE II
RPD (Rapid File file format)
FW2 (Framework II file format)
DBMEMO3 (dBASE III and III Plus with memo fields)

As an example of the use of the TYPE option, the following command will create a spreadsheet file that can be used by Lotus 1-2-3:

```
COPY TO OUTFILE FIELDS L_NAME, F_NAME_M_I, AGE, SALARY, TAXRATE TYPE WKS
```

Delimited Format

Files that use the DELIMITED option contain data with fields separated by a specific character or characters (usually a comma). Each record occupies an individual line, and the line always ends with a carriage return and linefeed. Within the record, each field is separated from the next field with a comma. Each character field is normally enclosed in quotation marks, and trailing blanks are stripped. The default separator of quotation marks can be changed by adding a WITH <delimiter> option to the TYPE specification. As an example, consider the MAILER database used in various parts of this text. (The structure for that database appears in Figure 2-2 on page 11.) The command

```
USE MAILER
COPY TO FILEA DELIMITED
```

copies a dBASE file to a new file with the following format:

```
"Jones","Ed","2318 Lake Newport Rd","","Reston","VA","22090",23245,""
"Smith","William","4343 East Orange Ave","Apt 4A","San Jose","CA","95402",""
"Johnson","Larry","2915 Freetown Court","","Reston","VA","22091",23299,""
"Jones","Benjamin","3412 Fayetteville St","#2B","Durham","NC","27705",23248,""
"Miller","Larry","345 Plano Road","Suite 405","Plano","TX","76020",30310,""
"Canion","Ron","3 Nice House Lane","","Woodlands","TX","74087",18145,""
"Roberts","Clay","1415 Buena Vista Ave","Apt 5D","Hollywood","CA","90043",""
```

In contrast, the following command,

```
USE MAILER
COPY TO FILEB DELIMITED WITH #
```

creates the following file:

```
#Jones#,#Ed#,#2318 Lake Newport Rd#,##,#Reston#,#VA#,#22090#,23245,##
#Smith#,#William#,#4343 East Orange Ave#,#Apt 4A#,#San Jose#,#CA#,#95404#,#
#Johnson#,#Larry#,#2915 Freetown Court#,##,#Reston#,#VA#,#22090#,23299,##
#Jones#,#Benjamin#,#3412 Fayetteville St#,##2B#,#Durham#,#NC#,#27705#,23248,##
#Miller#,#Larry#,#345 Plano Road#,#Suite 405#,#Plano#,#TX#,#75090#,30310,##
#Canion#,#Ron#,#3 Nice House Lane#,##,#Woodlands#,#TX#,#74087#,18145,##
#Roberts#,#Clay#,#1415 Buena Vista Ave#,#Apt 5D#,#Hollywood#,#CA#,#90043,##
#Jones#,#Benjamin#,#1514 Alston Ave#,##,#Durham#,#NC#,#27705#,0,##
```

Date values in a database that is exported to a delimited format are represented by an eight-digit number. The first four digits indicate the year, the fifth and sixth digits indicate the month, and the seventh and eighth digits indicate the day. Memo fields will not be copied out to a delimited file. If there are any memo fields in the database, they will be dropped during the copying process and will not exist in the newly created file. A number of other software packages, including most PC-based database managers, can import files in delimited format.

SDF Files

SDF files store data in columnar fields, with an equal number of spaces between the start of each successive field. Each record represented by a line in an SDF file is of equal length, and each line always ends with a carriage return and linefeed. Spaces are used to pad the field contents, when necessary, so that the length of each record is identical. SDF files are useful for transferring data to spreadsheets that don't accept the DIF, WKS, or SYLK file formats. The following commands create the SDF file that follows:

```
USE SALES
```

```
COPY TO FILEC SDF FIELDS CUSTNAME, ITEMCODE, QUANTITY, DESC
    7 records copied

TYPE FILEC.TXT

Larry Johnson       N34675  3 men's dress shirts
Larry Johnson       C56578  2 cologne
Yvonne McCoy        C34377  1 BMW racing jacket
Yvonne McCoy        F12166  1 sunglasses
Yvonne McCoy        L45780  3 sunscreen lotion
Bruce Laufer        C45488  1 men's sweater
Bruce Laufer        B54591  2 men's scarf
```

As with delimited files, SDF files do not contain the contents of a memo field. Date fields are represented by an eight-digit number, with the first four digits being the year, next two digits being the month, and last two digits being the day.

DIF, SYLK, FW2, RPD, and WKS Files

DIF, SYLK, FW2, RPD, and WKS files are files containing data within a proprietary format that can be read by many other programs. The DIF file internally resembles delimited files. DIF was developed as an aid in transferring data from first-generation PC spreadsheet software, and it is a popular format, used for file transfer by many PC software packages. SYLK is used by Microsoft for a number of the Microsoft application packages, including Multiplan, Chart, and File. Other Ashton-Tate products use the RPD and FW2 file formats; RPD is the RapidFile file manager format, and FW2 files are used by Framework II. (Framework III can directly read and write dBASE files, so no conversion is necessary.) The WKS format is used by Lotus 1-2-3 and by Symphony. Due to the popularity of Lotus 1-2-3, a number of other software packages can also work with files in WKS format.

Table 11-1 shows the suggested file types for creating files that can be read by many popular software packages.

DIF, SYLK, RPD, and WKS files will not contain the contents of a memo field. Date fields are represented by an eight-digit number, with the first four digits being the year, next two digits being the month, and last two digits being the day.

Two special cases are noteworthy if your program needs to provide file export capabilities. The first is with Framework or Framework II. Framework, by Ashton-Tate, can directly read a dBASE IV database. While you can use the FW2-type option to write a Framework II file, you can also choose to leave the file in dBASE format and read it into Framework. Both Framework and Framework II can read files in dBASE III/IV format; Framework III added the capability to write files in dBASE III/IV format. Framework can even convert the memo

Table 11-1 File Types for Software Exchange

Software Package	Type
Lotus 1-2-3	WKS
Microsoft Excel	WKS
Microsoft Multiplan	SYLK
Microsoft Chart	SYLK
Microsoft File	SYLK
R:Base 5000, System V, for DOS	DIF or DELIMITED
Supercalc 2	SDF
Supercalc 3 or 4	WKS
WordPerfect	DELIMITED
WordStar (MailMerge)	DELIMITED

fields in a dBASE database to character fields in the Framework database. So if your database uses memo fields, be sure to copy the .DBT file into the Framework subdirectory before trying to open the database when in Framework. Memory limits the size of the database Framework can work with. Unlike dBASE IV, all versions of Framework store the entire database in available memory.

If your program is to provide export capabilities to Framework I, II, or III, you will probably want to filter the database in some way so that the copied files for use in Framework contain a subset of the records from the entire database. (As an option, such filtering can also be done within Framework, if the user is familiar with the filter commands necessary within Framework to filter the incoming records.)

The second special case is in exporting data to PFS:File. dBASE IV offers the IMPORT and EXPORT commands, to transfer data to and from PFS:File databases. The syntax for these commands is:

```
EXPORT TO <filename> TYPE PFS
IMPORT FROM <filename> TYPE PFS
```

The EXPORT command will create a PFS:File database with the same filename as the dBASE IV database in use. The IMPORT command creates a new dBASE IV database, with the same name as the existing PFS:File database. The IMPORT process from PFS type files is relatively clean, because dBASE IV analyzes the database structure and data-entry form design for the PFS:File database. dBASE IV then duplicates that design, so you do not need to work with trying to design databases to receive data from PFS:File.

Using APPEND FROM

dBASE IV also provides a method to import files of the eight named types (DELIMITED, SDF, DIF, SYLK, WKS, WK1, RPD, and FW2). The APPEND FROM command can use the same TYPE options as are specified with the COPY TO command. One new type, WK1, is also available with the APPEND FROM command. This type supports Lotus 1-2-3, Release 2. The syntax for the command is:

```
APPEND FROM <filename> [FOR <condition>][TYPE <file type>]
```

If you are using the DELIMITED or SDF TYPE options, and no extension is specified as a part of the filename, dBASE IV assumes that the filename has an extension of .TXT. You therefore may need to specify the filename when using the SDF or DELIMITED options of APPEND FROM. As an example of APPEND FROM, the command

```
APPEND FROM LOTUSFL1 TYPE WK1
```

would read in a file created by Lotus 1-2-3, Release 2, and append the contents of the file to the database currently in use. Note that when using APPEND FROM to read in foreign files, the data structure must match that of the database that is to receive the data. With some applications, you may find it necessary to create a temporary database to hold the data imported from the foreign file. You can later transfer data from the temporary database into other databases on a selective basis.

Importing and Exporting the Contents of Memo Fields

dBASE IV offers two new commands, APPEND MEMO and COPY MEMO, which can be used to import and export the contents of memo fields. The APPEND MEMO command writes the contents of a memo field out to a text file, while the COPY MEMO command reads a text file into a memo field. The syntax for the APPEND MEMO command is:

```
APPEND MEMO <memo field name> FROM <filename> [OVERWRITE]
```

where <memo field name> contains the name of the memo field, and <filename> is the name of the file containing the text to be added to the memo field. An extension of .TXT is assumed for the text file; if the extension is different, it must be included with the filename. Text from the file is normally added to the memo field after any existing data in the memo field. If the OVERWRITE option is used, the text read in from the file will overwrite any existing text in the memo field.

The syntax for the COPY MEMO command, used to copy the contents of the memo field to a file, is:

```
COPY MEMO <memo field name> TO <filename> [ADDITIVE]
```

where <memo field name> contains the name of the memo field, and <filename> is the name of the text file to be written. An extension of .TXT is assigned to the text file; if a different extension is desired, it must be included with the filename. If a file by the name specified already exists, it is normally overwritten by the COPY MEMO command. The ADDITIVE option may be specified, in which case the memo field text is added to the end of any existing file.

Since the APPEND MEMO and the COPY MEMO commands work with the current record in the active database, it is up to your program to position the record pointer at the desired record. If you are exporting the memo field contents from a group of records, you can use the COPY MEMO command within a DO WHILE or a SCAN . . . ENDSCAN loop. Include the ADDITIVE option so that the exported file gets each successive memo field's contents added to the end of the file. An example of a program which copies the contents of a memo field to a text file appears below:

```
CLEAR
SET ALTERNATE TO WPFILE.TXT
SET ALTERNATE ON
? "Memo fields from litigation file.   Date: 11/8/88"
? "================================================= "
?
CLOSE ALTERNATE
USE LITIGATE
DO WHILE .NOT. EOF()
     COPY MEMO COMMENTS TO WPFILE.TXT ADDITIVE
     SKIP
ENDDO
```

The SET ALTERNATE commands are used to initially create the file, as well as to add a header. When the ADDITIVE option is used with COPY MEMO, the named file must exist prior to the use of the COPY MEMO command, or dBASE will display an error message. The results of the above program appear in the form of ASCII text, as shown below:

```
Memo fields from litigation file. 11/8/88
=================================================
This may be the smoking gun we need. Phillips said that Jones promised him that he
would pay Phillips $300,000 to keep his mouth shut about the impending takeover.
Conversation took place in a bar on Wisconsin Avenue.
At this point the entire transaction began to unravel. First time that Phillips said
that he was considering retaining counsel and filing suit to block the takeover.
This is beginning to sound like a plot from The Bold And The Beautiful. Smith said
if Phillips didn't stay away from his spouse, he (Smith) would resort to draconian
measures.
To further complicate matters, Jones claims to have hard evidence the president's
daughter has been laundering profits from her illegal exotic bird business through
the company.
```

The text file produced may then be imported into most word processors, using the Read ASCII File commands (see your word processor manual for details).

Using COPY FILE

The COPY FILE command copies any type of file. It can be used as an alternate way to copy a database file, but the file must be closed. You cannot set any specifying conditions regarding the contents of the file; the COPY FILE command copies the entire file. The syntax for the COPY FILE command is:

```
COPY FILE <source file.ext> TO <destination file.ext>
```

Both filenames must include the filename and extension, if one has been used. Also, a drive designator and path should be included if a drive and path other than the default ones are desired.

An obvious use for the COPY FILE and COPY commands is to provide a means of automated backup within a program. The following program, for example, backs up a large database to floppy disks by copying portions of the database file to each floppy.

```
**Backup program
**Copies database in 500 record chunks to floppy backup
**Last update 11/13/88
CLEAR
? "This menu option backs up your database."
? "Insert backup disk #1 in drive A, then..."
WAIT
USE MASTER
COPY NEXT 500 TO A:MBACKUP1
IF EOF()
     RETURN
ENDIF
? "Insert backup disk #2 in drive A, then..."
WAIT
COPY NEXT 500 TO A:MBACKUP2
IF EOF()
     RETURN
ENDIF
? "Insert backup disk #3 in drive A, then..."
WAIT
COPY NEXT 500 TO A:MBACKUP3
IF EOF()
     RETURN
ENDIF
? "Insert backup disk #4 in drive A, then..."
WAIT
COPY NEXT 500 TO A:MBACKUP4
IF EOF()
     RETURN
ENDIF
```

```
*Got this far, so must be more than 2000 records
? "Your database has grown in size past the full capabilities"
? "of this backup program.  Contact the DP department as soon"
? "as possible for a modification to this program."
WAIT
RETURN
**End of BACKUP.PRG
```

This method of performing backup from within a program requires no additional software (other than blank floppy disks for the storage of the backup files). Its drawback is that it can be slow, particularly with databases that have a large number of fields. A faster option, which requires the addition of the BACKUP.COM file from the DOS disk, is demonstrated in the following program code. This portion of the program uses the RUN command to execute DOS BACKUP.

```
**BACKUP program using DOS
**Last update 11/13/88
CLEAR
CLOSE DATABASES
? "This menu option backs up your database."
? "You will need sufficient FORMATTED floppy disks to proceed."
?
ACCEPT "Would you like to format disks first? (Y/N): " TO ANS
*Change to DOS subdirectory
RUN CD\DOS
IF UPPER(ANS) = Y
     RUN FORMAT A:
ENDIF
RUN BACKUP C:\DBASE\MYFILE.DBF A: /S
CLEAR
? "Backup process complete.  Remove disk from drive A."
WAIT
RETURN
**End of BACKUP.PRG
```

Using ERASE and RENAME

With the ERASE and RENAME commands, you can erase and rename files from within a dBASE program. The syntax for these commands is:

```
ERASE <filename>
```

```
RENAME <old filename> TO <new filename.ext>
```

Both commands require the addition of the extension, if one exists. Also include a drive designator and path, if you want to use ones other than the defaults.

Unlike the DOS ERASE command, the DOS asterisk (*) wildcard cannot be used with ERASE. If this capability is needed in a program, you can use the actual DOS ERASE command, by running that DOS function from within dBASE with the RUN command.

Using the RUN Command

With the RUN command, you execute another program or a DOS command from within dBASE IV. When you use RUN, dBASE builds a DOS *shell* and exits to DOS, transferring control to the program or the DOS command. When the program or command has completed its operations, control is returned to dBASE IV. The syntax for the RUN command is:

```
RUN <command> or
! <command>
```

The specified command must be either a valid resident DOS command (ERASE, DIR, and so on), batch file, or an executable DOS file (with an extension of .COM or .EXE). Also, your computer must contain a minimum of 17K of free memory past the minimal amount needed by dBASE to operate (around 540K), along with the amount of memory (if any) required by the program you are trying to run. dBASE IV will display an "insufficient memory" error message if you do not have enough memory to run the desired program.

Parameters normally used by the program you are running can be passed from within dBASE IV. For example, if you were to include this command in a dBASE IV program:

```
RUN FORMAT A:/S
```

the DOS FORMAT command (assuming it is present in the default directory or available through a DOS path) would be run, with the parameters A: and /S being passed to the format command. Once the desired disks have been formatted and the user answers No to the "Format another?" prompt, control passes back to dBASE IV, and the dBASE program containing the RUN statement continues execution.

Fair Warning . . .

Programs that take over portions of memory (including all memory-resident programs like SideKick, Ready!, and Metro) should not be loaded from within dBASE IV with the RUN command. Such programs will often overwrite portions of memory that dBASE IV has stored its overlay files in, with the result that the system locks up, requiring a reboot or a power-down. If you must have them, memory-resident programs should be loaded before loading dBASE IV. Since dBASE IV requires nearly 640K of installed RAM to operate, any memory-resident programs you use should consume relatively little memory, or should be capable of using extended or expanded memory.

Using DIR or DISPLAY FILE

The DIR command, like the DOS command of the same name, provides a listing of files. If you use this command without any DOS wildcard options, DIR shows dBASE database files. The syntax for the command is:

```
DIR [<drive:>][<path>][<skeleton>]
```

The DIR command normally shows the filenames, database file sizes, number of records in the files, and date of last updates in the display, as shown in the example:

```
. dir

Database Files    # Records    Last Update     Size
REPAIRS.DBF               7    06/08/86         396
LAWYERS.DBF              98    06/04/86       21062
DOCTORS.DBF              57    03/16/86        8733
SALES.DBF                 7    06/09/86         660
REALTORS.DBF             15    03/16/86        2409
RENTS.DBF                14    05/08/86        2751
MAILER.DBF                7    06/02/86        1008
LAWMAIL.DBF             346    03/29/86       81478
MASTER.DBF                9    04/05/86        1869
EEI.DBF                   3    04/06/86        2560
CLIENTS.DBF               6    06/04/86         938
MAINFILE.DBF              3    06/04/86         317

 124181 bytes in     12 files.
5812224 bytes remaining on drive.
```

If other types of files are to be displayed, use appropriate DOS wildcards (or skeleton) to indicate the type of files. When you use a skeleton, a simple columnar list (of up to four columns) containing only filenames will appear, as shown in this example:

```
. dir *.NDX

NAMES.NDX          NAMES2.NDX          NUMBERS.NDX          LAWINDX.NDX
```

```
    11776 bytes in      4 files.
  5812224 bytes remaining on drive.
```

The DISPLAY FILE command can be used as an alternative to the DIR command (both commands perform the same function). However, the DISPLAY FILE command can concurrently direct output to the printer by using a TO PRINT option. The syntax for the DISPLAY FILE command is:

```
DISPLAY FILE [LIKE <skeleton>][TO PRINT]
```

The DIR or DISPLAY FILE command can be useful within a program for displaying files of a given type and then letting the user pick a filename to be opened or acted upon by the program. The following portion of program code uses this approach to allow a mailing label program to use any number of dBASE-III style (.NDX) index files:

```
**Label printer
**Last update 11/19/88
CLEAR
DISPLAY FILE LIKE *.NDX
?
?
? "Enter the name of the index file."
? "(*Do NOT include the period and NDX!*)"
ACCEPT "Enter index filename: " TO DEXER
STORE DEXER + ".NDX" TO DEXER
*Use macro function to set index by character variable
SET INDEX TO &DEXER
CLEAR
? CHR(7)
@ 5,5 SAY "Make sure your printer is turned on and LABELS are installed."
@ 6,5 SAY "Then press Return (or press C to cancel)."
WAIT "" TO PCHOICE
IF UPPER(PCHOICE) = "C"
     RETURN
ENDIF
LABEL FORM LABEL1 SAMPLE TO PRINT
RETURN
```

Repairing Damaged Database Files

A somber saying claims that there are only two kinds of computer users in this world: those who have lost data, and those who will. dBASE IV is a complex database management system, and as with any complex system, there is always a possibility that data in a file will be damaged or lost. As a developer, you can minimize the chances of data loss by performing good housekeeping techniques

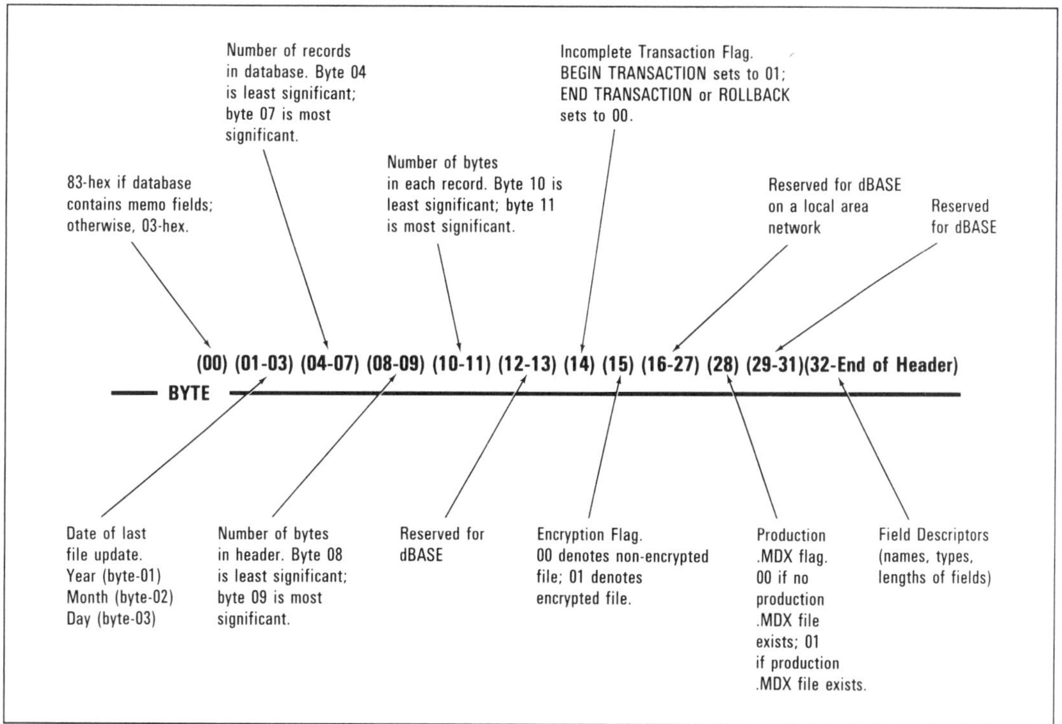

Figure 11-1 dBASE Header Structure

(such as opening files only when necessary and closing files as soon as possible, and including good backup routines in your programs). However, it helps to understand a little more than the average dBASE user about how dBASE IV stores data in a database file. Such knowledge may come in handy if one of your application files gets unexplainably damaged, and contrary to your dire warnings, the users haven't performed a backup in two months.

A dBASE IV database file consists of a file header, the file data (in the form of individual records), and an end-of-file marker (ASCII decimal-26 or hex-1A). The contents of the memo fields are another matter entirely; these are stored in a separate file with a .DBT extension. The memo field in the database (.DBF) file contains a pointer used to find the text in the associated .DBT file. The file header contains the date of the last file update, the number of records present in

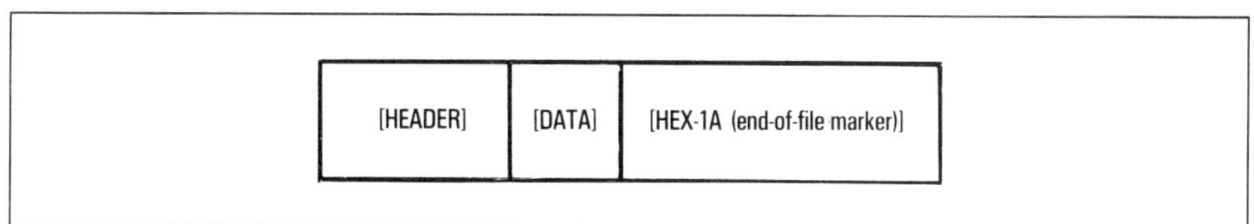

Figure 11-2 Database Structure

Table 11-2 Field Descriptor Design

Byte	Contains
0–10	Field name in ASCII (zero-filled)
11	Field type in ASCII (C=character, D=date, F=float, N=Numeric, L=logical, M=Memo)
12–15	Reserved by dBASE
16	Field length in binary
17	Field decimal count in binary
18–19	Reserved by dBASE
20	ID of work area
21–31	Reserved by dBASE

the file, a rather cryptic description of the database structure known as the Field Descriptor, and other information needed by dBASE IV. For the technically knowledgeable (or mildly curious), the design of a dBASE IV header is shown in Figure 11-1. Figure 11-2 illustrates the structure of the entire database. The design of the Field Descriptor, which occupies the end of the header, is detailed in Table 11-2.

The contents of the fields are packed into records that are not delimited or separated with any special characters. Each record begins with one byte that contains a space (ASCII decimal 32, or 20 hex) if the record is not deleted, and an asterisk (ASCII decimal 42, or 2A hex) if it is deleted.

As evident from the description in Figure 11-1, dBASE keeps a count of the number of records in a database by means of various hex codes stored in the file header. If the header is damaged or destroyed, you have run up against the more serious type of damage that can occur. This damage masks some of the records so dBASE IV shows fewer records in the file than are actually present, or worse yet, the software will refuse to open the file and will instead display the heart-stopping error message,

```
NOT a dBASE DATABASE
```

when your program attempts to use the file. If the header has been damaged, any repair attempt requires a program that lets you edit the data contained in the header; this cannot be done from within dBASE. If you are familiar with the DOS DEBUG utility, you can use it to change the contents of the header. (See your DOS manual for more instructions about DEBUG.) If the file is relatively small, you can use a good program editor (such as PCWrite, a "shareware" product available on bulletin boards) to edit the header in a word processing mode.

In either case, make backup copies of the damaged file before you attempt to perform any repairs. Once you have made a backup copy, you can attempt to manually calculate the proper hex values and rebuild the header to the point where dBASE IV will recognize it as a valid database header. If dBASE IV manages to open a file with a damaged header, the record count within the file should be immediately suspect. Because the record count is the last part of a header that is updated just before the file is closed, any system crash that occurs while a file is open will probably leave the header with an incorrect record count. You should use the COPY command to immediately create a new file, copying the records out to that file, with commands like:

```
USE <damaged>
COPY TO <goodfile>
```

When the COPY command has completed copying valid records out to the new file, it will update the record count in the header of the new file with an accurate figure. The old file can then be deleted, and the new file substituted in its place.

Good Header, Bad Data

More common among trashed dBASE files is a file that contains a valid header, but damaged data. Your program performs an EDIT function, and the display for some of the records is garbled. When you list the fields, you get something that looks like this:

```
LNAME       FNAME       ADDRESS             CITY          STATE ZIP
Hobbs       Kerie       1607 Valencia Way   Reston        VA    22090
Hoffman     Carol       1569 Trails Edge Ln Reston        VA    22091
Hoffman     Carol^!        1569 Trails Edge L n ResHogan        Debra
982 Gr anby Court  Ste rling        VA22070     Hummer      Annette
   1528 Sca ndia Circle Lee sburg        VA22075     Hunt    John W.
   1604 Sto we Road     Her ndon         VA22070     Hutcheson   Charles
```

For reasons unknown, random extra data has been introduced to your data file, or a portion of existing data has been deleted, resulting in a corruption of the database. The contents of the fields appear to straddle the field limits, and it appears that rekeying the data is the only way to proceed. Before resorting to such a drastic solution, try restoring the file first. Copy the file to another temporary file and use that file for the attempt at database repair.

First, open the temporary file and search for the first damaged record. Delete that record and the record prior to it (in many cases, the record prior to the first record that appears damaged is the one that's causing the problem). Then, pack the database. These simple steps may (or may not) repair the damage.

If the problem still exists, you must resort to a program other than dBASE IV that will let you directly edit the database file. Do *NOT* attempt to bring a database file into the dBASE Editor. Bizarre results may occur, and your system may lock up. Use DEBUG or a program editor to find the damaged record, then insert or remove hex 20 (blank spaces) as needed until the data aligns properly within the fields of dBASE IV. You can probably manage to do this by deleting characters that don't appear to belong and/or inserting spaces in the faulty record on a trial-and-error basis. Go in and out of the browse mode in dBASE IV to check on the progress until the data appears to fill the fields properly.

Random End-of-File Marker

Another type of damage you may encounter occasionally is an extra end-of-file marker (hex value 1A) that has been placed somewhere in the database file. This commonly occurs when the user exits abnormally from dBASE—perhaps the user rebooted the system before dBASE had a chance to properly close the file.

Extra end-of-file markers cause dBASE IV to behave in an interesting and baffling manner. The telltale signs are as follows: you enter LIST STRUCTURE, and dBASE tells you that there are 198 records in the database. (Your user says that she remembers having that many records just before the power failure occurred, so you assume this to be correct.) You enter a LIST command, and dBASE shows you everything up to record number 82, then redisplays the dot prompt. The BROWSE command gives you bizarre results, sometimes displaying an "end of file encountered" message (this is a strong hint as to what's wrong!), sometimes displaying most of the records, and sometimes displaying all of the records in a normal fashion. Your report and label-generating programs process as though nothing exists above record 82. If you enter GO 84 to move to record number 84, and then enter a LIST NEXT 200, dBASE IV then shows you the remaining records in the database.

What has happened is this: somehow an extra end-of-file character occupies a space at or near the end of record number 82. This problem can be corrected without leaving dBASE (although if you are fluent with DEBUG or with your program editor, by all means use that route). Use the COPY command to copy the records prior to the end-of-file character to a temporary file, something like:

```
USE CLIENTS
COPY TO TEMP1
```

Then go to the record following the false end-of-file marker and copy the remaining records to another database, such as by entering:

```
GO 84
COPY NEXT 9999 TO TEMP2
```

Then, use the first temporary file and copy the records from the second file into the first with:

```
USE TEMP1
APPEND FROM TEMP2
```

Finally, delete your damaged file and rename your temporary file to the name of the damaged file. At the most, you might lose one record with this approach.

If you can't stand the thought of losing a single record, you will have to resort to using your program editor or DEBUG to repair the damage. Find the extra end-of-file marker and replace it with a space.

There are also programs available from third-party vendors which attempt to repair damaged dBASE database files. In many cases these programs are successful, and in any case, once you've made a copy of the damaged file, you have nothing (but your time) to lose by trying. One popular program of this nature is dSALVAGE from Comtech Publishing (P.O. Box 456, Pittsford, NY 14534). The program can rebuild damaged headers, remove unwanted end-of-file markers, and realign offset data. If you support other dBASE users who may or may not be making backups when they should, a program like this one may save you considerable stress someday.

Index Files

When a database has been damaged, all associated index files become immediately suspect. Any index files should be re-created from scratch before the application is used again. Don't use REINDEX, as it is possible that the structure of the index file has also been damaged.

The Case of the Missing Memo File

One problem that's less serious than dBASE IV indicates is that of a missing (or accidentally erased) memo file. When dBASE IV loads a database file, it examines the first byte of the header. If that byte contains hex 83, indicating the presence of memo fields, dBASE IV will display an error message indicating that the memo file cannot be found. dBASE also asks for confirmation to create an empty memo file to replace the last one. When you select YES from the confirmation box, an empty memo file will be created to replace the missing one.

The best time to think about recovering from the effects of damaged files is *before* such damage occurs. Assume the worst will happen and take steps to provide recovery from system crashes. If your users don't remember to make routine backups, a forceful reminder using the RUN command to run DOS BACKUP upon program exit is a great help (sooner or later, they will have to exit from the Main Menu). If your application doesn't require a daily backup procedure, use the date conversion functions so that the program forces a backup every Thursday, or every 10th and 20th of the month, or some similar schedule.

If money is no object when it comes to data security, recommend good surge protection, high-speed tape backup, and an uninterruptible power supply. Don't wait until the users call frantically pleading for help to decide how you'll go about the business of crash recovery.

12

Managing Your Environment

To make your programs run more effectively, there are some parameters that you can change for maximum efficiency. These parameters fall into three areas: those set within DOS, those read by dBASE upon start-up, and those that are included in the program itself (often in the environment area at the start of the main program).

Managing DOS

Too many dBASE programmers assume that all of the work of making a program efficient falls under the realm of dBASE coding, and DOS does little more than support the running of dBASE. The dBASE manual hints that DOS has more to offer, as it suggests the creation (or modification) of a CONFIG.SYS file before you start any serious use of dBASE IV. The Installation program also automatically creates a CONFIG.SYS file with a FILES = 20 statement, unless you override the creation of this file with a specific menu option during the installation. The CONFIG.SYS file is vital to improving the performance of DOS with dBASE when your programs run, as it lets you allocate varying amounts of space for two important DOS items: files and buffers.

Juggling Open Files

With DOS you can open a specific number of files. The default, if no CONFIG.SYS is in use, is 6 files. That sounds like plenty, but for most applications it is actually very limiting. The suggestions in the dBASE manual indicate a FILES = 20 statement in the CONFIG.SYS file will provide sufficient working space. Sometimes, 20 turns out to be not enough, depending on the complexity of your programs, and you may be forced to rewrite your programs to use fewer files.

Here's why: DOS uses 5 files just to manage the keyboard, screen, disk drive I/O, and error handling. dBASE IV uses at least 2 more, in loading the main program dBASE.EXE and one or more various overlay files used by dBASE. So you use 7 files just to get the program started. Run a dBASE command file, and that makes the total 8. If the command file opens a database, an associated index file, and a format file, you now have 11 files open. Open another work area, with another database and associated index file, and you are up to 13. Then you start calling other command files as subroutines, and opening view files, and it doesn't take long to run into the DOS wall of insufficient file space. When you do, you will get the error message,

```
Too Many Files Are Open
```

and you will have to exit dBASE and change the CONFIG.SYS file to allocate more file space (or rewrite your program to use fewer files simultaneously). Some early versions of DOS are limited to a maximum of 20 files, so you may not be able to get any more file space from DOS.

On the other hand, in some cases, 99 files may be too many; if the PC running your application has minimal memory (640K with no expanded or extended memory, for example), or if your users have a liking for piling all sorts of memory-resident packages into RAM, the performance of dBASE may suffer noticeably if you open too many files.

If memory is no object, by all means open as many files as DOS will let you get away with; if memory is tight, rewrite your programs to make better use of fewer files open at once. dBASE IV supports up to 99 files open, but your CONFIG.SYS file must support the desired value.

How Many Buffers Are Enough?

In a similar fashion, you can increase or decrease the number of buffers available for use by DOS and by dBASE. The default CONFIG.SYS suggested in the Ashton-Tate documentation is 15 of these. *Buffers* are areas of memory set aside by DOS to speed I/O tasks between the PC's CPU and various external devices (such as keyboards and disk drives). Buffers are used to temporarily store data that may be read from and written to disk. Adding buffers can increase the speed of operation to a point, because data that is still in the buffers is used without additional disk access. The more buffers, the more data that is available in memory for dBASE IV to use without going back to disk. The default value for buffers (if you don't use a CONFIG.SYS file) is 2; the maximum is 99.

One's first thought of "The more buffers, the better" may sound appealing until you see what effect opening large numbers of buffers has on available memory space. Consider the results of running the DOS CHKDSK command after booting a PC, equipped with 512K, with the following CONFIG.SYS file:

```
FILES = 20
BUFFERS = 24

C>
```

```
C>chkdsk
Volume STARFIRE    created Feb 3, 1986 8:19p

 21309440 bytes total disk space
    94208 bytes in 10 hidden files
   102400 bytes in 33 directories
 17321984 bytes in 1634 user files
    30720 bytes in bad sectors
  3760128 bytes available on disk

   524288 bytes total memory
   475328 bytes free
```

And compare the memory bytes free value with this CONFIG.SYS file, loaded on the same machine:

```
FILES = 20
BUFFERS = 80
```

```
C>
C>chkdsk
Volume STARFIRE    created Feb 3, 1986 8:19p

 21309440 bytes total disk space
    94208 bytes in 10 hidden files
   102400 bytes in 33 directories
 17321984 bytes in 1634 user files
    30720 bytes in bad sectors
  3760128 bytes available on disk

   524288 bytes total memory
   445760 bytes free
```

You run into the same constraints with buffers as with files: in theory, a large number would be nice, but there are practical limits as to what can be done within the confines of the PC's memory. You reach a point of diminishing returns, because DOS reduces the size of available RAM by 528 bytes for each buffer that is opened. In machines with limited memory, a juggling act may be necessary to find an acceptable value for the BUFFERS statement. In a system with no expanded or extended memory, it is possible to run out of memory if enough buffers are open and if dBASE is working with multiple database files. dBASE IV is fairly stingy about memory usage as it works with database files, but some RAM is eaten up simply to keep each file open.

As an example, opening a database with 1000 records of 14 fields each (and a total of 210 characters per record) used just over 1K of RAM on an AT clone.

On a machine with sufficient memory, dBASE IV seems to work best when the number of available buffers is between 20 and 30. If speed is paramount to your application, you may want to perform some speed tests, while varying the size of the buffers (the machine must be rebooted after each change to the CONFIG.SYS file for the change to take effect).

Using CONFIG.DB

Upon start-up, dBASE IV reads the contents of the CONFIG.DB file. This text file can contain any one of a number of parameters that customize the operation of dBASE IV. The settings for function keys, available memory variable space, SET commands that use ON/OFF options, and more, can be controlled by the contents of the CONFIG.DB file.

Sample CONFIG.DB File

Like CONFIG.SYS, the CONFIG.DB file is a text file, containing a line of text for each environmental parameter. A sample CONFIG.DB file might look like:

```
*
*dBASE IV Configuration File
*Wednesday September 28, 1988
*
COLOR OF NORMAL      = W+/B
COLOR OF HIGHLIGHT   = GR+/BG
COLOR OF MESSAGES    = W/N
COLOR OF TITLES      = W/B
COLOR OF BOX         = GR+/BG
COLOR OF INFORMATION = B/W
COLOR OF FIELDS      = N/BG
COMMAND              = ASSIST
DISPLAY              = COLOR
PDRIVER              = HPLAS100.PR2
PRINTER 1            = HPLAS100.PR2 NAME "Hewlett-Packard LaserJet
                       100 dpi graphics mod" DEVICE LPT1
PRINTER 2            = FX80_1.PR2 NAME "Epson RX-80
                       Low resolution graphs" DEVICE LPT1
SQLDATABASE          = SAMPLES
SQLHOME              = C:\DBASE4\SQLHOME
STATUS               = ON
```

The following parameters can be set by means of the CONFIG.DB file:

ALTERNATE = <filename>

AUTOSAVE = OFF/ON

BELL = OFF/ON

BELL = frequency,duration

BLOCKSIZE = <1 to 128>

BORDER = single/double/panel/none/border-definition string

CARRY = OFF/ON

CATALOG = <filename>

CENTURY = OFF/ON

CLOCK = ON/OFF

CLOCK = row/column

COLOR = ON/OFF

COLOR = <letters specifying foreground, background, border colors>

COMMAND = <dBASE command and accompanying arguments>

CONFIRM = OFF/ON

CONSOLE = ON/OFF

CURRENCY = <expC>

CURRENCY = LEFT/RIGHT

DATE = american/ansi/british/french/german/italian/japan/usa/mdy/dmy/ymd

DEBUG = OFF/ON

DECIMALS = <0 to 14>

DEFAULT = <drive identifier>

DELETED = OFF/ON

DELIMITER = OFF/ON

DELIMITER = <delimiter characters>

DESIGN = OFF/ON

DEVELOPMENT = OFF/ON

DEVICE = <PRINT, SCREEN>, or FILE <filename>

DISPLAY = MONO/COLOR/EGA25/EGA43/MONO43/MONO50/VGA25/VGA50

ECHO = OFF/ON

ENCRYPTION = ON/OFF

ESCAPE = OFF/ON

EXACT = OFF/ON

EXCLUSIVE = ON/OFF

F<2–10> = <expression for function key>

HEADINGS = OFF/ON

HELP = OFF/ON

HISTORY = ON/OFF

HISTORY = <0 to 16000>
HOURS = 12/24
INSTRUCT = OFF/ON
INTENSITY = OFF/ON
LOCK = OFF/ON
MARGIN = <1 to 254>
MEMOWIDTH = <0 to 250>
NEAR = ON/OFF
ODOMETER = <1 to 200>
PATH = <pathname>
POINT = <character expression>
PRECISION = <0 to 20>
PRINTER = ON/OFF
PRINTER = LPT1/LPT2/LPT3/COM1/COM2
PROMPT = <prompt string>
REFRESH = <0 to 3600>
REPROCESS = <1 to 32000>
SAFETY = OFF/ON
SCOREBOARD = OFF/ON
SEPARATOR = <character expression>
SPACE = OFF/ON
SQL = OFF/ON
STATUS = OFF/ON
STEP = OFF/ON
TALK = OFF/ON
TEDIT = <external text editor for use with MODIFY COMMAND>
TRAP = ON/OFF
TYPEAHEAD = <0 to 32,000>
UNIQUE = OFF/ON
WP = <external text editor for editing memo fields>

Values Changed Only with the CONFIG.DB File

Most values that can be changed through the use of CONFIG.DB can also be changed by using commands within a dBASE IV program (such as the SET commands). The following are exceptions, which can only be changed through the use of the CONFIG.DB file.

COMMAND: This identifies a dBASE command to be carried out upon start-up of dBASE IV. Normally it is used to name a program that will run when dBASE IV is initially loaded.

PROMPT: This specifies the prompt used by dBASE IV. The default is the dot (.) prompt.

TEDIT: With this entry you specify an external word processor that appears when MODIFY COMMAND is used. Note that use of a word processor requires additional memory above the approximately 540K of free RAM required by dBASE.

WP: This entry specifies an external word processor that appears when memo fields are edited. Note that use of a word processor requires additional memory above the approximately 540K of free RAM required by dBASE.

Also note that to use the TEDIT and WP specifications, you must have COMMAND.COM in the same directory that was used to start the PC. If you boot up with a floppy disk that may be changed later, you should use the DOS SET COMSPEC command to tell dBASE where it can find a copy of COMMAND.COM. For example, if COMMAND.COM is in a directory named DOS that is on drive C, the following line in your AUTOEXEC.BAT file would suffice:

```
SET COMSPEC = C:\DOS\COMMAND.COM
```

One warning about CONFIG.DB applies: the CONFIG.DB file must be contained in the same directory as the dBASE program, or the contents of the file will not be read on start-up of dBASE.

Using SET Commands

Various SET commands can also be placed throughout the program (often in the environment area, near the beginning of the program), to control certain behavior of dBASE when it is running the program.

Common SET Commands

A complete description of all SET commands can be found in Appendix A; those SET commands commonly used to control the environment include the following. (This list is for information; it is *not* a syntax listing.)

SET BELL <frequency,duration>: This command sets the frequency and duration of the bell.

SET BELL ON/OFF: This command turns the bell on or off when the cursor reaches the end of a field or variable or when an invalid data type is supplied.

SET BLOCKSIZE TO <n>: Use this command to set the block size used with memo fields. Note that only the size of 1 is compatible with dBASE III/III Plus database files.

SET BORDER TO SINGLE/DOUBLE/PANEL/NONE/<border definition string>: Use this command to redefine the default border.

SET CARRY ON/OFF: This command copies or does not copy the contents of a previous record into a new record created with APPEND BLANK or INSERT BLANK.

SET CATALOG ON/OFF: This command updates or does not update an open catalog as new files are created or opened.

SET CATALOG TO: This command identifies a catalog for use by dBASE IV.

SET CLOCK ON/OFF: This command displays (or hides) the system clock.

SET CLOCK TO <row,column>: This command places the clock in a location other than the default (upper right corner) location.

SET COLOR ON/OFF, SET COLOR TO: Use these commands to select color choices for color monitor displays.

SET DATE american/ansi/british/french/german/italian/japan /usa/mdy/dmy/ ymd: This command sets the default display for dates.

SET DEFAULT TO: With this command you choose the default disk drive.

SET DEVELOPMENT ON/OFF: This command turns on (or off) the date-and-time checking of .PRG and .OBJ files when run with the DO command. If SET DEVELOPMENT is ON and the file creation dates and times do not match, the file is recompiled.

SET DISPLAY TO MONO/COLOR/EGA25/EGA43/MONO43/MONO50/ VGA25/VGA50: Use this command to set the display type and number of lines displayed.

SET ESCAPE ON/OFF: This command enables or disables the Esc key's ability to interrupt a dBASE program.

SET FORMAT TO: This command selects a format file for use with full-screen commands.

SET FUNCTION <value> TO: Use this command when you want to program the function keys.

SET HELP ON/OFF: This command enables or disables the "do you want some help?" message.

SET HOURS 12/24: Use this command to set the default display of hours to either 12 or 24-hour (military) format.

SET INSTRUCT ON/OFF: Use this command to enable (or disable) the display of information boxes.

SET INTENSITY ON/OFF: This command enables or disables reverse video display of full-screen operations.

SET MESSAGE TO: Use this command to create a custom message that appears at the bottom of the screen.

SET PATH TO: This command identifies a DOS path for dBASE to search if files are not found in the default directory. Note that the SET PATH command has been known to be unreliable in early versions of dBASE IV. You may want to use the DOS PATH command directly within a RUN statement instead.

SET PRINTER: With this command you choose the DOS device to use for printed output.

SET PRINTER ON/OFF: Use this command to direct all output not formatted with @ . . . SAY commands to the printer.

SET PRINTER TO: Use this command to redirect the printer output to a logical device.

SET SAFETY ON/OFF: This command determines whether dBASE will prompt for confirmation before overwriting existing files.

SET STATUS ON/OFF: This command determines whether the Status Bar displays at the bottom of the screen.

SET TALK ON/OFF: This command enables or disables the display of various responses to dBASE commands during program execution.

Programming the Function Keys with SET

One SET command, effectively used, can save so much data-entry time that it is worth talking about in greater detail. The SET FUNCTION command lets you set the output from any of 29 programmable function keys (F2 through F10, Shift-F1 through Shift-F10, and Control-F1 through Control-F10) to a string of text of your choice, including carriage returns. The F1 key is always set to HELP and cannot be reprogrammed.

The syntax for the command is:

```
SET FUNCTION <numeric expression> TO <character expression>
```

The numeric expression evaluates to a number from 2 to 30, indicating which function key should be reprogrammed. The numbers 2 through 10 apply to unshifted function keys. The numbers 11 through 20 apply to shifted function keys. The numbers 21 through 30 apply to combinations of the Control key and the function keys. A semicolon at the end of the character expression indicates that a carriage return should follow the character string indicated. As an example, the command,

```
SET FUNCTION 8 TO "Clear All;Use Sales;Set Index to Accounts;"
```

enters all three commands whenever the F8 function key is pressed. If the keys have not been reprogrammed, the default values of the function keys are:

Key	Function	Key	Function
F1	Help	F6	Display status
F2	Assist	F7	Display memory
F3	List	F8	Display
F4	Dir	F9	Append
F5	Display structure	F10	Edit

By reprogramming the function keys to match often-used character strings, you can make life much easier for the data-entry operators using the system. A series of commands like:

```
SET FUNCTION 2 TO "Los Angeles"
SET FUNCTION 3 TO "Irvine"
SET FUNCTION 4 TO "Santa Ana"
SET FUNCTION 5 TO "Culver City"
SET FUNCTION 6 TO "Torrance"
SET FUNCTION 7 TO "El Segundo"
SET FUNCTION 8 TO "Hollywood"
SET FUNCTION 9 TO "North Hollywood"
```

could be saved in a subroutine, to be loaded into memory and executed as a part of a menu option. When filling in GETS in a data-entry screen, operators can repeatedly press F2 instead of being forced to type the longer string, "Los Angeles," each time.

Calculating Disk Space

dBASE IV offers some useful functions that you can use in programs to track whether sufficient disk space exists to perform various operations. The DISK-

SPACE() function returns a numeric value equivalent to the number of free bytes available on the default drive. The RECCOUNT() function provides the number of records in a database, while the RECSIZE() function provides the number of bytes used by a single record. Multiplying the values provided by RECCOUNT() and RECSIZE() will give you a value that is almost the size of the database. What's missing is the size of the database header; this can be calculated with the following formula:

Header Size (bytes) = (no. of fields in database * 32) + 34

If a database in use has 12 fields, the following commands would provide the size of such a database:

```
STORE (12 * 32) + 34 TO <headsize>
STORE RECCOUNT() * RECSIZE() TO <datasize>
STORE HeadSize + DataSize TO <filesize>
? "This file size, in bytes, is: "
?? Filesize
```

Programs that perform operations that may use large amounts of disk space (such as file exports, sorts, or building large indexes) can use these techniques—along with the DISKSPACE() function—to determine if sufficient room exists on the default drive before performing the desired operation, as shown:

```
STORE (12 * 32) + 34 TO HeadSize
STORE RECCOUNT() * RECSIZE() TO DataSize
STORE HeadSize + DataSize TO FileSize
IF DISKSPACE() < FileSize * 2
    ? "Cannot perform copy operation."
    ? "Insufficient disk space.  Remove some files first."
    WAIT
    RETURN
ENDIF
COPY TO RBASEFIL.TXT DELIMITED
<more commands...>
```

Giving Your Users More Than One Application

As long as Ashton-Tate has provided all of the fancy features for running programs under DOS, changing paths, and providing menus through ASSIST, it often makes sense to provide users with menu selections to perform tasks other than the one your primary application has to offer. Users should never be forced to quit your system and load a PFS:File disk to examine their personal database of investments or wine collections; after all, dBASE IV is a database manager, no matter how obscure the application may seem.

You can provide users the ability to safely work with simple databases of their own design by using the RUN command to change directories, and switching on the Control Center with the ASSIST command. The user then performs whatever operations he or she desires in the different subdirectory (so the user doesn't accidentally trash any of your application's files). Through the Control Center, users can create files, add and edit records, build their own simple reports—in short, most things that novice users would want to do within dBASE IV. Once the user presses Esc to exit the Control Center, program control is safely returned to your Main Menu. The following portion of code is from a Main Menu that provides that option:

```
CASE BAR = 5
   *Change directories; enter assist mode
   CLEAR
   RUN CD\USERS
   @5,5 SAY "To exit to DOS when done, choose EXIT TO DOS from the"
   @7,5 SAY "Exit Menu.  Or to return to Main Menu, press Esc key"
   @8,5 SAY "from within dBASE Control Center Menus, then choose YES."
   ?
   ?
   ?
   WAIT
   CLEAR ALL
   ASSIST
   CLEAR ALL
   RUN CD\dBASE

   CASE BAR() = 6
   <more commands...>
```

In response to a menu bar from a Main Menu, this portion of code uses the RUN command to access the DOS CD\ command for changing subdirectories. This is purely a safety precaution, so that users can't gain access to application files in the application subdirectory. If the users try to exit to a dot prompt by pressing Esc, program control brings them back to the application's Main Menu.

Assuming you have plenty of extended or expanded memory, you can use a similar approach of changing subdirectories to run other programs, reducing any need for the users to exit your application just to type a two-page memo with their word processing software. The Main Menu code that follows offers word processing and spreadsheet choices, by running the appropriate packages (WordPerfect and Lotus 1-2-3) from within dBASE.

```
**This is ESTATE.PRG**
**Last update 11/07/88
SET DEFAULT TO C:\dBASE
SET DELETED ON
SET ESCAPE OFF
SET TALK OFF
DO WHILE .T.
   CLEAR
```

```
    @2,0
    TEXT
             ESTATE PLANNING DATABASE SYSTEM

      (A)  Use Estate Tracking Assets System
      (B)  Use Accounts Receivable System
      (C)  Use Accounts Payable System
      (D)  Print Reports
      (E)  Other Utilities (includes Client File Maintenance)
      (F)  Use dBASE IV for other tasks
      (G)  Run WordPerfect
      (H)  Run Lotus 1-2-3

      (Q)  QUIT This System and Return to DOS
ENDTEXT
@1,2 TO 16,60 DOUBLE
@18,0
ACCEPT "     Enter selection? " TO CHOOSE
STORE UPPER(CHOOSE) TO CHOOSE
DO CASE
    CASE CHOOSE = 'A'
        DO EstMenu
    CASE CHOOSE = 'B'
        DO CashIn
    CASE CHOOSE = 'C'
        DO CashOut
    CASE CHOOSE = 'D'
        DO Reporter
    CASE CHOOSE = 'E'
        DO Utility
    CASE CHOOSE = 'F'
        *Change directories; enter ASSIST mode
        CLEAR
        RUN CD\USERS
        SET PATH TO C:\dBASE
        @5,5 SAY "To exit to DOS when done, choose EXIT TO DOS from the"
        @7,5 SAY "Exit Menu.  Or to return to Estate System, press Esc key"
        @8,5 SAY "from within dBASE Control Center Menus, then choose YES."
        ?
        ?
        ?
        WAIT
        CLEAR ALL
        ASSIST
        CLEAR ALL
        RUN CD\dBASE
    CASE CHOOSE = 'G'
```

```
        *Change directories; run WordPerfect
        CLEAR
        CLEAR ALL
        RUN CD\PERFECT
        WP
        RUN CD\dBASE
    CASE CHOOSE = 'H'
        *Change directories; run Lotus 1-2-3
        CLEAR
        CLEAR ALL
        RUN CD\LOTUS
        LOTUS
        RUN CD\dBASE
    CASE CHOOSE = 'Q'
        QUIT
    OTHERWISE
        ? CHR(7)
        ? "***INVALID SELECTION!***"
        WAIT
    ENDCASE
ENDDO
```

Such a scheme has the one drawback of demanding excessive amounts of memory, as portions of the dBASE code remain in memory while the other software (and a copy of the DOS COMMAND.COM shell) get loaded into another portion of memory. You cannot use this trick without additional memory above the 640K base RAM. And you may need to experiment with your software to see whether it can be run from within dBASE. Some packages, like Ashton-Tate's Framework, hog so much memory that running them from within dBASE just isn't possible.

13

Debugging Techniques

This chapter outlines various strategies for debugging programs, along with techniques for preventing bugs while you design the application and techniques that enable a program to handle bugs without your assistance.

If you write programs of any complexity (and if you didn't, you wouldn't be reading this book), you will encounter bugs. All programmers face bugs in their code from time to time; it's a sign of imperfection, and nobody's perfect. dBASE IV has a number of tools to aid in the eternal hunt for bugs in program code. These tools are the ON ERROR, RESUME, SET DEBUG, SET DOHISTORY, SET ECHO, SET HISTORY, SET STEP, and SUSPEND commands. Some other commands that were not intended solely for debugging but are nevertheless useful in this task are the SET ALTERNATE and SET TALK commands. dBASE IV also provides a powerful debugger which can be used to monitor program execution and trap errors.

Using SUSPEND and RESUME

When an error serious enough to halt program execution occurs, dBASE IV displays a dialog box containing the following choices:

```
Cancel, Ignore, Suspend
```

This is a major improvement over earlier versions of dBASE, which simply gave you the choice of halting the program or attempting to continue. Of the three choices, Cancel and Suspend will both halt the program, but with very different results. Cancel will halt the program, close all open program files, and clear all variables from memory. Suspend, on the other hand, will leave the program files open and leave all memory variables intact. Suspend is also designed to be used with the RESUME command, which restarts program execution at the point of interruption.

If faults in the program logic are causing your errors, you can use the Suspend option, and then use DISPLAY MEMORY or LIST MEMORY TO PRINT to examine the contents of the variables for possible clues to the problem. Once you have finished poking around the dBASE memory from the dot prompt, you can use the RESUME command to attempt to continue execution of the program. Entering RESUME will cause a program to continue execution at the place in the file where the error interrupted the program.

An effective debugging technique is to use Suspend, next use STORE commands to change the contents of various memory variables, then try using RESUME and seeing what the results are with the new variables in use by the program.

Using HISTORY and SET HISTORY

Another aid to correcting program flaws in dBASE IV is the availability of a History feature, which is kept in memory. The History area keeps track of the last 20 commands entered from the dot prompt. The HISTORY feature is useful for retrying commands from the dot prompt, and changing the options in the command line until the command has the desired results. You can display the contents of History by pressing the Up Arrow key to move forward in the History area, and the Down Arrow key to move in reverse through History.

You can also use the DISPLAY HISTORY or LIST HISTORY commands to show the entire contents of History at a glance. These commands can be combined with a TO PRINT option, to print the contents of HISTORY at the printer.

If a review of the last 20 commands isn't enough to track down your error, you can increase the size of the memory set aside for History with the SET HISTORY command. For example, the command

```
SET HISTORY TO 50
```

will tell dBASE IV to retain the last 50 commands executed in the History area.

Besides its usefulness in debugging programs, the History feature is useful for correcting typos at the dot prompt. Probably one of the few things that dBASE II users regretted giving up when the advance to dBASE III was made was the ability to correct typos with the "correct and retry" message of dBASE II. The more recent versions of dBASE have given us back that capability with History, and with the EDIT choice, which automatically appears when a syntax error is detected. You may be entering a long filter condition, and you enter one wrong character, as in this example:

```
SET FILTER TP NAMES > "M" .AND. NAMES < "Williams"
```

and when you press Return, you get the dreaded "syntax error" message. Choose EDIT from the dialog box, and the command is displayed again. You can move the cursor to the incorrect character, correct the typo with the Ins and Del keys, and press Return again. The corrected command will be re-entered.

Using SET STEP, SET ECHO, and SET DEBUG

When you find it necessary to call out the really heavy artillery to shoot down troublesome bugs, try the SET STEP, SET ECHO, and SET DEBUG commands. Entering SET STEP ON will cause dBASE IV to execute the program in a single-step mode. After each line of the program is executed, the message,

```
Press SPACE to step, S to suspend, or Esc to cancel...
```

appears on the screen. You can choose to continue the program (by pressing the Spacebar), or suspend the program, examine the variables, and resume the single-step operation with RESUME, or you can press the Esc key and halt the program's execution.

Entering SET ECHO ON will display each line of the program on the screen as that line is executed. With SET ECHO turned on, you can read the program statements along with the results. This may become visually confusing, so the SET DEBUG command can be used to send the output of SET ECHO to the printer. If you enter SET DEBUG ON, any output normally displayed by SET ECHO is routed to the printer instead.

Note that if SET DEBUG and SET ECHO are both ON, the output from any error messages, as well as from the SET TALK command, is not sent to the printer.

Using SET TALK

The SET TALK command can also display the results of various processing operations within a program. Normally, programs turn off TALK with a SET TALK OFF command at the start of the program. When you are debugging, it may help to see the results of calculations and processing operations on various files, so you may want to include a SET TALK ON command in an appropriate location.

Using SET ALTERNATE

The SET ALTERNATE commands can be very useful for troubleshooting a large program, particularly if the errors seem to be occurring when the users are on the scene and you aren't. Name a file with the SET ALTERNATE TO <filename>

command, then open that file with the SET ALTERNATE ON command. Once the file is open, all data that is displayed on the screen, with the exception of full-screen commands like BROWSE and EDIT, will also be stored in the file named in the SET ALTERNATE command. At some point, you must close the file with a CLOSE ALTERNATE command. The file will be assigned a .TXT extension, unless another extension is specified. If you have plenty of space on the hard disk, you can open a file with SET ALTERNATE and leave that file open for a day of use. Then close the file and examine its contents for possible indications of user techniques that are giving your program grief.

Using SET TRAP

The SET TRAP command can be used to automatically start the program debugger, which is detailed in the following paragraphs. Use the SET TRAP ON command, near the start of a program or at the dot prompt, to tell dBASE to display the debugger whenever a program error occurs. You can then use the features of the debugger to find and correct the cause of the error. If SET TRAP is ON and you press the ESC key while a program is running, the debugger will also be invoked. The default value of SET TRAP is OFF.

Using the Debugger

dBASE IV provides a powerful debugger which can be used to further isolate the source of program errors. The debugger can be started in a number of ways. From the dot prompt, enter DEBUG [<filename>], where <filename> is an optional name for the program which is to be run with the debugger active. If <filename> is omitted, the debugger will be started without any program active. The debugger can also be started by choosing Debug Program from the Exit Menu of the Editor. You can add the WITH parameter at the end of the DEBUG <filename> statement, to pass parameters just as can be done with the DO command. The parameters passed to the program can contain any valid dBASE expressions.

Once you enter the debugger, a help screen appears over the debugger windows. Pressing F1 hides the help screen, revealing all of the debugger, as shown in Figure 13-1. (You can repeatedly hide and display the Help Screen with F1.)

The debugger is composed of four windows. The Debugger Window, which is the active window when the debugger is entered, appears at the bottom of the screen. The Debugger Window contains the database filename, name of the active index file, name of the active program or procedure file, the currently selected work area, and the line number of the program. Note that the line number is referenced by the start of the program or procedure file you are using, and not the start of an individual procedure in a procedure file.

The various debugger commands are issued while the cursor is at the ACTION prompt in the Debugger Window. When in any of the other windows, pressing ESC returns you to the ACTION prompt in the Debugger Window.

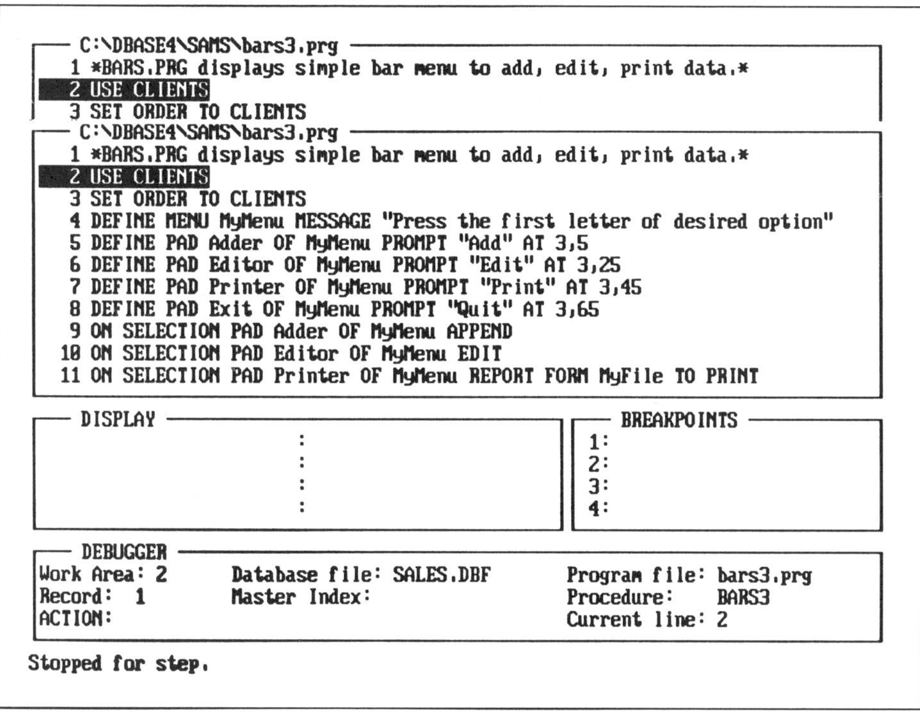
C:\DBASE4\SAMS\bars3.prg
1 *BARS.PRG displays simple bar menu to add, edit, print data.*
2 USE CLIENTS
3 SET ORDER TO CLIENTS
C:\DBASE4\SAMS\bars3.prg
1 *BARS.PRG displays simple bar menu to add, edit, print data.*
2 USE CLIENTS
3 SET ORDER TO CLIENTS
4 DEFINE MENU MyMenu MESSAGE "Press the first letter of desired option"
5 DEFINE PAD Adder OF MyMenu PROMPT "Add" AT 3,5
6 DEFINE PAD Editor OF MyMenu PROMPT "Edit" AT 3,25
7 DEFINE PAD Printer OF MyMenu PROMPT "Print" AT 3,45
8 DEFINE PAD Exit OF MyMenu PROMPT "Quit" AT 3,65
9 ON SELECTION PAD Adder OF MyMenu APPEND
10 ON SELECTION PAD Editor OF MyMenu EDIT
11 ON SELECTION PAD Printer OF MyMenu REPORT FORM MyFile TO PRINT
DISPLAY
BREAKPOINTS
1:
2:
3:
4:
DEBUGGER
Work Area: 2
Database file: SALES.DBF
Program file: bars3.prg
Record: 1
Master Index:
Procedure: BARS3
ACTION:
Current line: 2
Stopped for step.

Figure 13-1 Debugger Screen

At the top of the screen appears the Edit Window. To enter it, press E while at the ACTION prompt in the Debugger Window. The Edit Window will contain the program or procedure you are currently running. Use the Edit Window to modify the program code while in the debugger. Once your changes are completed, you can save them with Control-End. Note that you must then exit the debugger and rerun the program (so it will be recompiled) before the changes will take effect.

The Breakpoint Window is visible at the right side of the screen, directly above the Debugger Window. (Breakpoints are conditions which, when encountered during program execution, will halt the program and display the debugger.) To enter, press B while at the ACTION prompt in the Debugger Window. Use this window to enter breakpoints. You can enter up to ten at a time. When the program is run, the breakpoints you've entered are evaluated after each line of code is processed. If any of the breakpoint conditions evaluates as true, the program halts and the debugger appears. The message "breakpoint" will appear on the message line, along with the breakpoint line number which caused the program interruption.

The Display Window appears at the left of the Breakpoint Window. To enter it, press D while at the ACTION prompt in the Debugger Window. The Display Window shows the status of the program environment as the program executes. You can enter expressions in the left side of the Display Window. As each line of code is executed, the debugger evaluates the expression, and displays the results in the right side of the Display Window. Any valid dBASE expression may be entered in the left side of the Display Window. Note that you only need to enter the expression itself; you do not need to add a ? command prior to the expression.

Debugger Commands

While at the ACTION prompt in the Debugger Window, you can enter any one of a number of commands, either to enter one of the other windows, or to perform other actions. Table 13-1 shows the valid debugger commands.

A common use for the debugger when tracing elusive bugs is to step through the program one line at a time. You can press Enter repeatedly at the ACTION prompt to step through a program. As you do so, the current line of the program will be highlighted in the Edit Window. At the ACTION prompt, you can also enter a number *n* followed by the S command (such as 5S) to tell the debugger to run the trace while halting every *n* occurrences. For example, if you enter 5S, the debugger will step through the program, halting once every five lines. The N command can be used to accomplish the same task, but the program will halt only while at the current program level or at higher levels. Any procedures or programs called from the current level will execute, but the S or N commands will have no effect until program control returns to the current level.

Another useful command is the R command, which tells the debugger to run the program until an error occurs. Any errors will halt the program and cause the debugger screen to appear. You can then use the features of the debugger to find and correct the cause of the error.

Table 13-1 Debugger Commands at the ACTION Prompt

B	Enter Breakpoint Window
D	Enter Display Window
E	Enter Edit Window (edit program file)
L	Start program execution at line number specified
[n]N	Step through program *n* steps at a time (but only at current or higher level)
P	Display trace of calling procedure or program
Q	Quit debugger
R	Run program until error or debugger interrupt occurs
[n]S	Step through program *n* steps at a time
X	Exit to dot prompt
Enter	Perform next step
Esc	Open Debugger Window
F1	Toggle Debugger Help On/Off
F9	Toggle between debugger and user display (what the user would see as the program is running)

Getting Out . . .

You can enter X at the ACTION prompt to suspend the debugger, and return to the dot prompt. This leaves the debugger in the suspended mode of operation; entering RESUME at the dot prompt will return you to the debugger. If you wish to terminate the use of the debugger completely, use the Q command at the ACTION prompt.

Using ON ERROR

dBASE IV has an ON ERROR command that can perform another command or transfer control to a submodule if a program error occurs. Until this feature came along, program errors left users with any one of a number of unfriendly messages on the screen. Now, you can use the ON ERROR command to provide a friendlier alternative if your program encounters an error. The syntax for the command is:

```
ON ERROR <command>
```

An ON ERROR command should be placed near the beginning of the program, before any errors are likely to occur. If an error occurs in the program, the command specified will be carried out. In most cases, the command will be a DO command that runs another program, such as in the example,

```
ON ERROR DO WARNING
```

In this case, the command file, WARNING.PRG, will be executed if an error occurs. That command file may contain something as simple as an error message informing the user that a problem has occurred, or it may contain procedures for handling the error. The ERROR() function can be used along with the ON ERROR command. The ERROR() function displays a numeric value that corresponds to the type of error that occurred. The MESSAGE() function can also be used to display the dBASE error message that defines the type of error you've encountered.

The most comprehensive use of ON ERROR—along with the ERROR() function—is to run an *error-trapping routine,* which is a section of programming code that is designed to deal with program errors. If you include such a section of code in your program, the program may be able to recover from errors without your assistance (a nice touch when the program bombs and you are not in the office). Even when the program cannot automatically recover from an error condition, the use of ON ERROR will present users with a less confusing set of error messages.

The following program makes use of the ON ERROR command and the ERROR function to deal with program errors:

```
**MASTER.PRG
**Uses MASTER database; displays Main Menu
```

```
**Last update 11/08/88
ON ERROR DO PANIC WITH ERROR()
<commands...>

**PANIC.PRG
**Error-handling routine
PARAMETERS Errorcode
*Interpret the code
CLEAR
DO CASE

    CASE Errorcode = 1
        ? "I can't find that file on the disk.  Contact the"
        ? "DP department immediately."
        WAIT
        QUIT

    CASE Errorcode = 41
        ? "The memo field file is not accessible to dBASE."
        ? "Use the QUIT option and contact DP Tech Support immediately."
        WAIT
        RETURN TO MASTER

    CASE Errorcode = 56
        ? "The disk is full.  Return to the Main Menu, quit this"
        ? "system, erase some files from the disk, then try again."
        CLOSE DATABASES
        WAIT
        RETURN TO MASTER

    CASE Errorcode = 125
        ? "A NOT READY error code has been received from the printer."
        ? "Please take corrective action and press a key to continue."
        WAIT
        RETRY

ENDCASE
*Errorcode unknown, so call for help!
? "An uncorrectable error has occurred.  The error code is: "
?? ERRORCODE
?
? "Contact DP Tech Support and report this error code."
WAIT
SET ALTERNATE TO ERRNOTES
SET ALTERNATE ON
SET CONSOLE OFF
? "Error is: "
```

```
?? Errorcode
LIST MEMORY
LIST STATUS
SET CONSOLE ON
CLOSE ALTERNATE
QUIT
```

In the example, the ON ERROR statement at the start of the program causes the error-trapping submodule (PANIC.PRG) to be run if an error occurs. Parameter passing is used to pass the value obtained by the ERROR() function to the submodule, PANIC.PRG. If an error occurs, the "PARAMETERS Errorcode" statement at the beginning of PANIC.PRG causes the value provided by the ERROR() function to be stored to a numeric variable, ERRORCODE. The CASE statements then act on that value, and appropriate user error messages are displayed. If the error code is a code that the program cannot deal with, a message to that effect is displayed, and the program opens an alternate file to store the status of the variables and files, as an aid to the programmer. Then the QUIT command closes all files and exits back to DOS.

Note that operating-system level errors (no disk in drive, lack of printer handshaking, error reading the data file, and so on) cannot be handled from within dBASE. These must be dealt with through the operating system.

Avoiding the Bugs

Some general techniques will help you avoid bugs while you're still designing the program. Bugs are caused either by syntax errors or by errors in the program logic. Syntax errors are easier to spot, since these are a direct result of typos, missing spaces, or improper use of the dBASE programming language. Logic errors can be far more difficult to detect, as they often don't interrupt the program; they may just cause the program to do something that's totally different than what you had in mind.

Types of Bugs

The most common program bugs include the following:

Mismatched Data Types: You cannot interchange different data types (such as a numeric variable and a character field) within the same expression. If you do so, the common "Data type mismatch" error message will be displayed.

Syntax Errors in Variable Names, Field Names, or Commands: dBASE IV will provide a "syntax error" or "unrecognized command verb" message if commands or options for commands are misspelled. If variable names or field names are misspelled, you will get a "variable not found" message.

Where you can really get into trouble is if the field name or variable name is misspelled, and the misspelling matches a different field name or variable. Then you have a logic problem on your hands, as your program tries to work with the wrong data. The best safeguard against this flaw is to give fields and memory variables names that are distinctively different.

Improper Construction of Matching Statements: Each IF command must be followed by an ENDIF command; each TEXT requires an ENDTEXT; each DO CASE requires an ENDCASE; each SCAN requires an ENDSCAN; and each DO WHILE command must have a matching ENDDO command. When such commands are nested to multiple levels, it is easy to leave out a closing command and cause problems that are hard to track down. It is also common to find program bugs caused by nesting control structures incorrectly, as shown in the following example:

```
DO WHILE .T.
IF COUNTER < 5
<commands...>
ENDDO
ENDIF
```

The ENDIF statement being placed after the ENDDO statement causes an overlapping control structure. Such a use of nested commands in dBASE is improper and will cause bugs that are often particularly difficult to track down, because they will not always occur upon execution of the line of code that is actually causing the problem.

Missing Punctuation (Periods, Commas, Colons and Semicolons, and Character Delimiters Such as Quotation Marks): dBASE will almost always display a "syntax error" message when you omit punctuation. On rare occasions, the error will slip by dBASE's error checking, producing possibly bizarre results.

Memory Variables Not Initialized at Point of Program Execution: An attempt to use a variable that has not been created with a STORE or assignment (=) statement will cause a rather obvious "variable not found" error. A more subtle version of the same error will crop up if you don't declare variables PUBLIC, transfer control to a higher-level subroutine, and attempt to use that variable.

Debugging the Modular Program

Finally, consider one more plug for the merits of modular system design. Debugging is an area where modular design comes in quite handy. Small modules are far easier to debug than is one large program. It can be argued that no single module should contain more than two letter-sized pages of dBASE commands. If the program is any larger than that, it probably belongs in more than one module. If your programs comprise modules sufficiently small in size, you can effectively debug by running each module independently of the others. If the error proves to be a baffling one, you can always rewrite the entire submodule, which is a less intimidating thought if the module is small to begin with.

Don't Ignore the Possibility of a dBASE Bug . . .

If the statement, "All complex programs have bugs" is assumed to be true, and the statement "dBASE IV is a complex program" is assumed to be true, then the resultant Boolean conclusion is rather obvious. If you feel that you've hit your head against a wall for long enough, pick up the phone and call Ashton-Tate technical support (and have your software's serial number handy). It's not inconceivable that a bug in dBASE is causing problems in your program. Have pity on the support staff, however, and only resort to this when you are as sure as possible that your program code isn't causing the problem.

Programming Aids

If you are programming or plan to program extensively in dBASE, you or your company may find it worthwhile to invest in various programming aids offered by third-party companies. There are a number of such packages currently on the market. Some of the more popular ones are described in this section.

CLEAR+

This programming tool helps programmers understand complex dBASE code. CLEAR+ produces high-resolution flow charts and tree charts, and lets you simulate a program's execution by means of on-screen or printed diagrams. In essence, the program takes your dBASE programs and procedure files, and converts them into flowchart-style diagrams. CLEAR+ uses virtual-memory techniques to draw diagrams of unlimited size. The program is fully compatible with dBASE IV, and supports the SQL mode of dBASE IV programming. User-defined functions (UDFs) are also supported. The program can save files in .PIC and .PCX formats, for export to paint programs or to desktop publishing programs. The visual diagrams provided by CLEAR+ (or a program like this one) can be extremely helpful when you are faced with deciphering a complex dBASE program which was written by someone else. CLEAR+ is available from Clear Software, 637 Washington St., Brookline, MA 02146.

SCAN-A-LYZER

This is a programming aid which creates charts and documented listings of programs. With SCAN-A-LYZER, you can build tree charts of entire systems; program listings with line numbers and control-structure matching with connecting lines; reformatting and reindenting of control structures like SCAN . . . ENDSCAN and IF . . . ENDIF; and cross-reference tables of all program variables.

The line-draw capabilities of the program support both dot-matrix and laser printers. SCAN-A-LYZER also provides design listings on dBASE design objects, such as report forms, label forms, databases, indexes, and view files, directly from DOS. This lets you show index keys, database structures, and the like, without having to load dBASE. SCAN-A-LYZER is available from Tech III, 255 W. 5th, San Pedro, CA 90731.

BRIEF

BRIEF is a programmer's editor. You can edit programs with BRIEF, as you can the editor present in dBASE IV, but you can also perform other tasks not possible with the standard dBASE Editor. BRIEF provides a full "undo" capability and can work with multiple files. BRIEF also provides keyboard macros, and lets you reconfigure your keyboard, if desired. BRIEF supports EGA and large-screen displays. When combined with another offering by the same company called dBRIEF, the program can also paint data-entry screens and generate the resulting dBASE code. BRIEF is supplied in both a standard and a small version, with the small version taking up just 57K of RAM. The small version can be named as the alternate editor using the TEDIT specification in the CONFIG.DB file, even in a machine with just 640K of RAM. BRIEF is available from Solution Systems, 541 Main St., Suite 410Y, Weymouth, MA 02190.

Documentor

The Documentor is a program which generates technical documentation for dBASE applications. The program details the logic flow, mechanics, structures, and elements of each program or procedure in an application. The Documentor produces a variety of forms of output, including action diagrams, hierarchy charts, variable concordance reports, database file and index file reports, and the like. In addition to supporting dBASE IV, the Documentor also supports two dBASE-compatible compilers, Quicksilver and Clipper. Documentor is available from WallSoft Systems, 233 Broadway, New York, NY 10279.

Step IVWard

Users of the three most popular dBASE-compatible languages (Clipper, Quicksilver, and FoxBASE+) should consider the use of Step IVWard, a conversion utility offered by Ashton-Tate. Clipper, Quicksilver, and FoxBASE+ all provide programming languages which are compatible in most ways with dBASE IV. However, each of these dBASE-compatible languages provides extensions to the language in the form of different programming commands and functions. As a result, programs originally written in Clipper, Quicksilver, or FoxBASE+ often will not run under dBASE IV without major modifications.

Step IVWard is a utility which greatly reduces the changes you must make to a Clipper, Quicksilver, or FoxBASE+ program to run that program under dBASE IV. Step IVWard reads in a program written in one of the dBASE-compatible languages, and produces an output file designed to run under dBASE IV. In most cases, Step IVWard is able to convert commands specific to the other language into equivalent commands that are compatible with dBASE IV. When a command in the other program has no direct equivalent in dBASE IV, Step IVWard will change the offending line of code into a comment line in the output file indicating the source of the incompatibility. Step IVWard also summarizes all error and warning messages in a file called WARNING.TXT. This file contains the name(s) of the program(s), the line numbers where the incompatibilities arose, and the messages generated by Step IVWard.

A Warning About Step IVWard

Warning: Step IVWard is designed to work with the source code, or uncompiled program code, written in the dBASE-compatible language. Step IVWard cannot convert a program already compiled under Clipper, Quicksilver, or FoxBASE+.

Installation

Installation of Step IVWard is straightforward. The program is not copy-protected, and comes on a single disk. The contents of the disk can be copied into a separate subdirectory, and then the DOS PATH command can be used to set a path to that directory. Or, you can simply copy the contents of the disk into the same subdirectory that contains your source code files. Finally, enter STEP at the DOS prompt to start the program. Once the program loads, the Step IVWard menus, shown in Figure 13-2, appear.

About the Step IVWard Menus

Step IVWard uses menus which are operationally similar to those in the Control Center portion of dBASE IV. The menu bar contains five choices: Setup, Options, Print, Translate, and Exit. The Setup Menu is visible in Figure 13-2.

Use the Input Filename choice to enter the name of the input, or source, program to be translated. Use the Output Filename choice to enter a name for the output file which is to be created. By default, Step IVWard will give the output file the same name as the input file, and will rename the input file to a file with an extension of .ORG. If you want to prevent this from happening and retain the input file under the original name, use the Output Filename option to specify a different name for the output file. Also, note that if you do not include any filename under the output name, no output file will be created; instead, the output will be directed only to the screen or printer.

The Programmer's Name option is used to add a comment line of up to 40 spaces at the start of the programs created by Step IVWard. Finally, use the Copyright Notice option to add a comment line containing copyright information of your choosing.

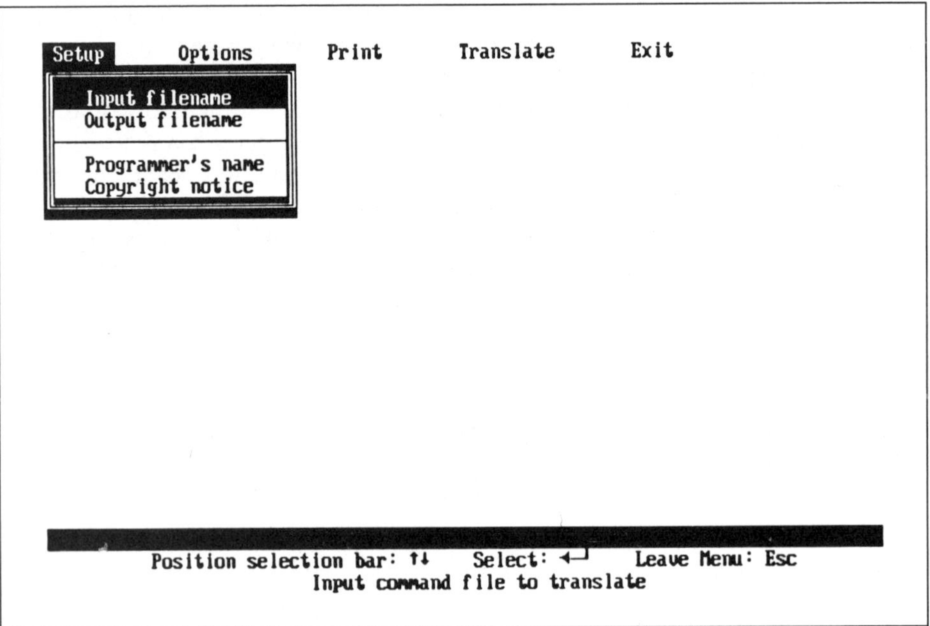

Figure 13-2 Step IVWard Menus

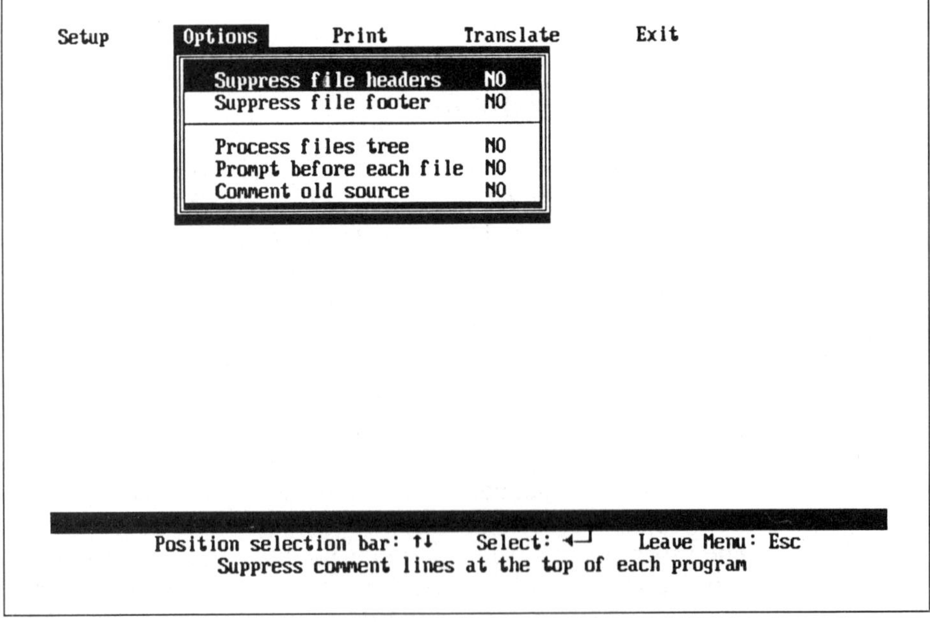

Figure 13-3 Options Menu

The Options Menu (Figure 13-3) contains various choices which control processing of the conversion.

The first two choices, Supress File Header and Supress File Footer, are used to turn off the normal inclusion of header and footer comments in the converted program. Step IVWard normally places headers and footers composed of comment lines at the start and end of programs. If you prefer to omit these comments, set either of these options to Yes.

The Process Files Tree option, when set to Yes, tells Step IVWard to process all programs called by your main program. Note that the default setting for this option is No, meaning Step IVWard will only convert the program you named with the Input Filename option of the Setup Menu. In most cases, you will want to change the Process Files Tree option to Yes, so that the main program and all other programs called by that program will be converted.

The Prompt Before Each File option, when set to Yes, tells Step IVWard to ask you before translating each file. The default setting for this option is No.

The Comment Old Source option, when turned to Yes, tells Step IVWard to insert your old source code into the new program in the form of comments. This can make debugging easier, although it also makes for an output program that is twice the length of your input file.

The Print Menu, shown in Figure 13-4, contains various options which control printing during the code conversion.

The first option, Printer, is used to specify whether messages detailing the conversion process should be directed to the printer, or to the screen. If the option

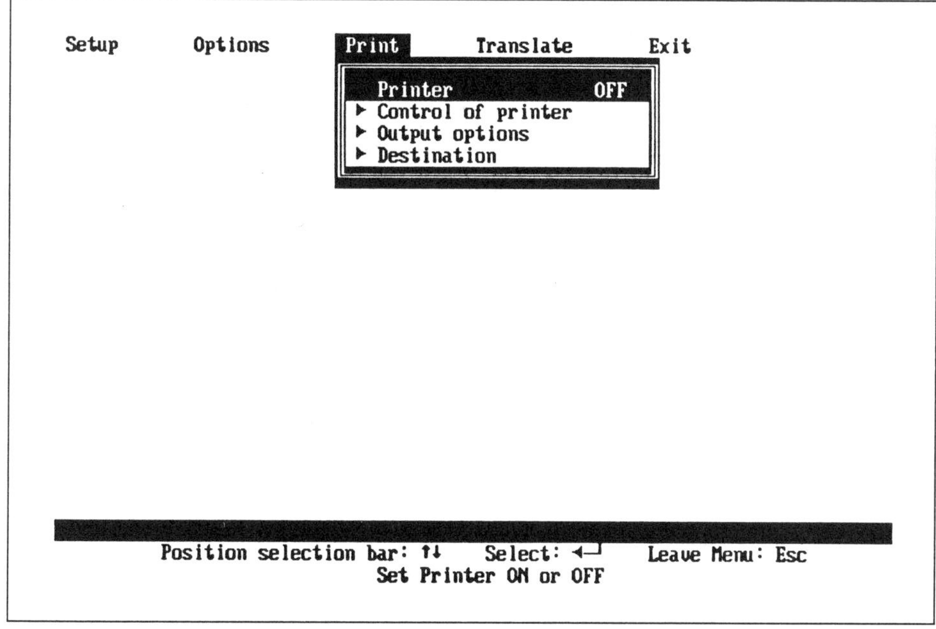

Figure 13-4 Print Menu

is set to ON, this output is routed to the printer. In its default setting of OFF, the output is routed to the screen.

The Control Of Printer option, when selected, displays the submenu shown in Figure 13-5. This submenu lets you select IBM Graphics compatible or Hewlett-Packard LaserJet compatible printers. You can also set Condensed Print or Double Strike ON or OFF, and you can enter any desired control codes for condensed print, double-strike print, or for starting and ending control codes. The last two options, Eject Before Printing and Eject After Printing, let you force page ejects before or after printing occurs. The default for both these options is OFF.

The Output Options, when selected from the Print Menu, also displays a submenu. This submenu contains five choices: Page Headings, Width Of Page, Include Banner, Length Of Page, and Left Tab Margin. The Page Headings option, when set to ON, places page headings at the top of each page. Use Width Of Page to set the page width to a numeric value, up to 255 characters (the default is 80). The Include Banner option, when set to ON, adds a banner composed of asterisks at the top of each program listing. The Length Of Page option lets you set the number of lines per page (the default is 60). Finally, use the Left Tab Margin setting to change the left margin of the printout (the default is 0).

The Destination option of the Print Menu contains two choices when selected: Write To, and Name Of DOS FIle. The Write To option is a multiple-choice toggle which can specify PRINTER or FILE. If you choose FILE, use the Name Of DOS File option to specify a name for the DOS file which will contain the output that would normally go to the printer.

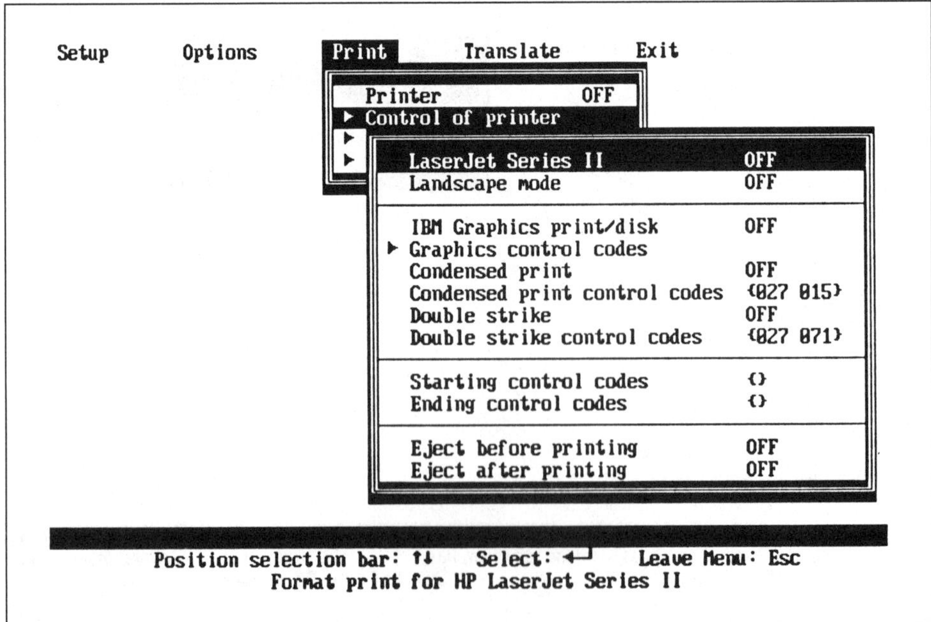

Figure 13-5 Control Of Printer Submenu

The Translate Menu, shown in Figure 13-6, contains various choices which control the code conversion process.

The Begin Translation option tells Step IVWard to start the code conversion. The Language To Convert From option is used to specify the language of the source code (Clipper, Quicksilver, or FoxBASE+). The Supress Display During Translation option tells Step IVWard to supress the normal screen display of the converted code.

The Exit Menu of Step IVWard contains just two choices: Abandon Settings And Exit, and Save Settings And Exit. If you choose Abandon Settings And Exit, you are returned to DOS without any menu selections saved. Choosing Save Settings And Exit saves your menu settings for future use.

Using Step IVWard

Using Step IVWard is a fairly straightforward process, in spite of the large number of menu options. In most cases, you perform the following steps to translate your application:

1. Choose Input Filename from the Setup Menu.
2. Enter the filename of the source file.
3. Choose Output Filename from the Setup Menu.

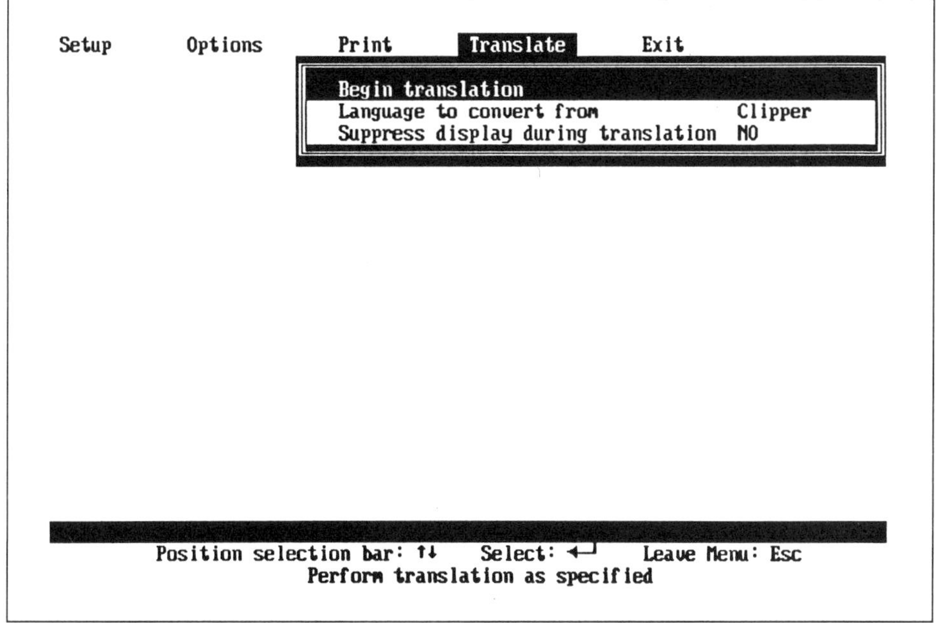

Figure 13-6 Translate Menu

4. Enter the desired filename for the output file, or accept the default (same name as the input file, in which case the input file gets renamed).
5. Set Process Files Tree from the Options Menu to Yes.
6. Choose Select Language To Convert From from the Translate Menu.
7. Choose the desired source language (Clipper, Quicksilver, or FoxBASE+).
8. Choose Begin Translation from the Translate Menu.

You can vary your precise steps to suit specific conditions. For example, if you only wanted to convert one module within a complete application, you could set the Process Files Tree option to No. In any case, once you choose Begin Translation, the code is converted to dBASE IV, and the output simultaneously appears on the screen or is routed to the printer (unless you set the Suppress Display During Translation option to Yes).

Running Step IVWard from DOS

You can also run Step IVWard directly from the DOS prompt, without using the menus, by including optional parameters (or "switches") after the word STEP. To do so, enter STEP, followed by the source filename, the language parameter, and any of the optional parameters shown in Table 13-2. The language parameters are /C for Clipper, /F for FoxBASE+, and /Q for Quicksilver.

The source filename and one of the three language parameters are mandatory; the other parameters are optional. As an example, you could convert a Clipper source code file named STAFF.PRG to dBASE IV code with the following DOS command:

```
STEP STAFF.PRG /C
```

Table 13-2 Optional Parameters

Parameter	Meaning
/S2	Output filename
/S3	Programmer's name
/S4	Copyright notice
/O1	Suppress file headers
/O2	Suppress file footers
/O3	Process files tree
/O4	Prompt before each file
/O5	Comment old source code
/P1	Printer
/T1	Suppress display during translation

and you can also include optional drive identifiers or pathnames in the command, as shown in the following example:

```
STEP C:\PERSONS\STAFF.PRG /C
```

You can also include the optional parameters, in any order you desire. As an example, the following command converts a FoxBASE+ source file called ACCOUNTS.PRG. An output filename of ACCTS4.PRG is specified, a copyright notice is included, the process files tree option is turned on, and the display is suppressed during code translation.

```
STEP ACCOUNTS.PRG /F /03 /T1 /S2 ACCTS4.PRG /S4 JEJA Software, Inc.
```

Finally, a tip: since Step IVWard is not copy-protected, it makes sense to copy the contents of the entire program into the directory which contains your Clipper, Quicksilver, or FoxBASE+ application. The code conversion will be considerably faster when Step IVWard does not need to perform its work through various DOS PATH settings.

A Sample of Code Converted with Step IVWard

The following code is an example of the conversion of a typical Clipper program into dBASE IV, using Step IVWard.

Listing 13-1: Sample Conversion from a Clipper Program to dBASE IV, Using Step IVWard

```
***Filters.PRG Sets standard filters for Employee database.***
*Last update 09/25/87*
PUBLIC SIFTERS, SIFTERS1, SIFTERS2
@  2,2 CLEAR TO 18,78
@  2,2 TO 18,78 DOUBLE
@  3,5 SAY "Select filter condition, if any, for report."
@  4,3 TO 4,77 DOUBLE
@  6,10 PROMPT [1. All Employees (no filter in effect) ]
@  7,10 PROMPT [2. By Status                           ]
@  8,10 PROMPT [3. By Department                       ]
@  9,10 PROMPT [4. By Job Title                        ]
@ 10,10 PROMPT [5. By Sex                              ]
@ 11,10 PROMPT [6. By Race                             ]
@ 12,10 PROMPT [7. Within A Salary Range               ]
@ 13,10 PROMPT [8. Use A Custom Filter                 ]
```

```
@ 17,10 Say [Highlight choice with arrow keys, press Return]
MENU TO SIFTIT
@  2,2 CLEAR TO 18,78
@  2,2 TO 18,78 DOUBLE
DO CASE
     CASE SIFTIT = 1
          SET FILTER TO
          *no filter used.
     CASE SIFTIT = 2
          STORE SPACE(15) TO M_STATUS
          @ 5,5 SAY "Status: " GET M_STATUS
          READ
          STORE UPPER(M_STATUS) TO SIFTERS
          SET FILTER TO UPPER(STATUS) = SIFTERS
     CASE SIFTIT = 3
          STORE SPACE(30) TO M_WORKGRP
          @ 5,5 SAY "Department: " GET M_WORKGRP
          READ
          STORE UPPER(M_WORKGRP) TO SIFTERS
          SET FILTER TO UPPER(WORKGROUP) = SIFTERS
     CASE SIFTIT = 4
          STORE SPACE(30) TO M_JOBTIT
          @ 5,5 SAY "Job Title: " GET M_JOBTIT
          READ
          STORE UPPER(M_JOBTIT) TO SIFTERS
          SET FILTER TO UPPER(JOBTITLE) = SIFTERS
     CASE SIFTIT = 5
          STORE SPACE(1) TO M_SEX
          @ 5,5 SAY "Sex: " GET M_SEX
          READ
          STORE UPPER(M_SEX) TO SIFTERS
          SET FILTER TO UPPER(SEX) = SIFTERS
     CASE SIFTIT = 6
          STORE SPACE(1) TO M_RACE
          @ 5,5 SAY "Race: " GET M_RACE
          READ
          STORE UPPER(M_RACE) TO SIFTERS
          SET FILTER TO UPPER(RACE) = SIFTERS
     CASE SIFTIT = 7
          STORE 0.00 TO M_SALLOW
          STORE 1.00 TO M_SALHIGH
          @ 5,5 SAY " Low end of salary range: " GET M_SALLOW
          @ 6,5 SAY "High end of salary range: " GET M_SALHIGH
          READ
          STORE M_SALLOW TO SIFTERS1
          STORE M_SALHIGH TO SIFTERS2
          SET FILTER TO SRATE1 >= SIFTERS1 .AND. SRATE1 <= SIFTERS2
     CASE SIFTIT = 8
```

```
          CLEAR
          DO CUSTOM
ENDCASE
*check for valid records.
GO TOP
IF EOF()
     CLEAR
     ? CHR(7)
     @ 5,5 SAY "***WARNING: No records satisfy the filter clause"
     @ 6,5 SAY "that you specified. Press C to CANCEL the report."
     @ 8,5
     SET FILTER TO
     GO TOP
     RETURN
ENDIF
*back to program that called this one.
CLEAR
RETURN
*End of Filters.PRG.
```

The resulting output from Step IVWard follows:

Listing 13-2: Output in dBASE IV Resulting from Conversion of Clipper Program Using Step IVWard

```
* Converted to dBASE IV by Step IVWard 1.0 1/4/89 6:11 PM
* FILE NAME: FILTERS.PRG
* BY: Edward Jones
* NOTICE: J.E.J.A. Software, Inc.
***Filters.PRG Sets standard filters for Employee database.***
*Last update 09/25/87*
PUBLIC SIFTERS, SIFTERS1, SIFTERS2
@  2,2 CLEAR TO 18,78
@  2,2 TO 18,78 DOUBLE
@  3,5 SAY "Select filter condition, if any, for report."
@  4,3 TO 4,77 DOUBLE
DEFINE POPUP POPUP1 FROM 6, 10
DEFINE BAR 1 OF POPUP1 PROMPT [1. All Employees (no filter in effect) ]
DEFINE BAR 2 OF POPUP1 PROMPT [2. By Status                           ]
DEFINE BAR 3 OF POPUP1 PROMPT [3. By Department                       ]
DEFINE BAR 4 OF POPUP1 PROMPT [4. By Job Title                        ]
DEFINE BAR 5 OF POPUP1 PROMPT [5. By Sex                              ]
DEFINE BAR 6 OF POPUP1 PROMPT [6. By Race                             ]
DEFINE BAR 7 OF POPUP1 PROMPT [7. Within A Salary Range               ]
DEFINE BAR 8 OF POPUP1 PROMPT [8. Use A Custom Filter                 ]
@ 17,10 Say [Highlight choice with arrow keys, press Return]
*:: MENU TO SIFTIT
```

```
*ll Warning: statement converted, but behavior different under dBASE IV
s4_popbar = 0
ON SELECTION POPUP POPUP1 DO POP_SEL
ACTIVATE POPUP POPUP1
STORE s4_popbar TO SIFTIT
@  2,2 CLEAR TO 18,78
@  2,2 TO 18,78 DOUBLE
DO CASE
CASE SIFTIT = 1
   SET FILTER TO
   *no filter used.
CASE SIFTIT = 2
   STORE SPACE(15) TO M_STATUS
   @ 5,5 SAY "Status: " GET M_STATUS
   READ
   STORE UPPER(M_STATUS) TO SIFTERS
   SET FILTER TO UPPER(STATUS) = SIFTERS
CASE SIFTIT = 3
   STORE SPACE(30) TO M_WORKGRP
   @ 5,5 SAY "Department: " GET M_WORKGRP
   READ
   STORE UPPER(M_WORKGRP) TO SIFTERS
   SET FILTER TO UPPER(WORKGROUP) = SIFTERS
CASE SIFTIT = 4
   STORE SPACE(30) TO M_JOBTIT
   @ 5,5 SAY "Job Title: " GET M_JOBTIT
   READ
   STORE UPPER(M_JOBTIT) TO SIFTERS
   SET FILTER TO UPPER(JOBTITLE) = SIFTERS
CASE SIFTIT = 5
   STORE SPACE(1) TO M_SEX
   @ 5,5 SAY "Sex: " GET M_SEX
   READ
   STORE UPPER(M_SEX) TO SIFTERS
   SET FILTER TO UPPER(SEX) = SIFTERS
CASE SIFTIT = 6
   STORE SPACE(1) TO M_RACE
   @ 5,5 SAY "Race: " GET M_RACE
   READ
   STORE UPPER(M_RACE) TO SIFTERS
   SET FILTER TO UPPER(RACE) = SIFTERS
CASE SIFTIT = 7
   STORE 0.00 TO M_SALLOW
   STORE 1.00 TO M_SALHIGH
   @ 5,5 SAY " Low end of salary range: " GET M_SALLOW
   @ 6,5 SAY "High end of salary range: " GET M_SALHIGH
   READ
   STORE M_SALLOW TO SIFTERS1
```

```
   STORE M_SALHIGH TO SIFTERS2
   SET FILTER TO SRATE1 >= SIFTERS1 .AND. SRATE1 <= SIFTERS2
CASE SIFTIT = 8
   CLEAR
   DO CUSTOM
ENDCASE
*check for valid records.
GO TOP
IF EOF()
   CLEAR
   ? CHR(7)
   @ 5,5 SAY "***WARNING: No records satisfy the filter clause"
   @ 6,5 SAY "that you specified. Press C to CANCEL the report."
   @ 8,5
   SET FILTER TO
   GO TOP
   RETURN
ENDIF
*back to program that called this one.
CLEAR
RETURN
*End of Filters.PRG.
*:: Line(s) below inserted by Step IVWard
PROCEDURE POP_SEL
s4_popbar = BAR()
DEACTIVATE POPUP
RETURN
* Converted to dBASE IV by Step IVWard 1.0 1/4/89 6:11 PM
```

Note the extensive use of comments and the conversion from Clipper's PROMPT . . . MENU method of menu bar selections into appropriate popup menu commands within dBASE IV. Also, comment lines (preceded by asterisks) clearly show where Step IVWard has made additions or changes to the original code.

In most cases, Step IVWard will not perform a complete conversion for you. But it will typically handle 80 to 90 percent of the work involved in converting an application from Clipper, Quicksilver, or FoxBASE+ to dBASE IV. After the conversion is complete, you can use your editor's search commands to search for comment lines indicating possible difficulties in conversion; you can then analyze the logic used and make the appropriate changes manually.

14

Faster Program Execution

This chapter details hints for increasing the execution speed of your programs, including the use of Runtime (provided with the Developer's Edition of dBASE IV), and true compilers like Clipper and dBIII Compiler.

Using Procedure Files

dBASE IV supports the use of *procedure files,* which are files containing subroutines to be used by the main program. Up to 1,170 subroutines, or procedures, can be stored in a single procedure file. (dBASE IV can access only 1 procedure file at a time.) Procedures are identified by enclosing each group of program code between a PROCEDURE <name> statement and a RETURN statement. By including a series of small command files in a single procedure file, dBASE can quickly execute the contents of the command files without opening and closing multiple files. The design of a procedure file is shown in Figure 14-1.

Procedures are contained within an individual procedure file. Since the procedures are in a separate procedure file, the name of the procedure file must be identified in the program with a SET PROCEDURE TO <procedure filename> command. What follows is an example of a procedure file, used to choose reports and labels within a program:

```
**REPORTER.PRG chooses reports or labels
**Calls procedures in PRINTREP.PRG
SET PROCEDURE TO PRINTREP
DO WHILE .T.
     TEXT
     Enter 1 for Sales Report.
     Enter 2 for Client Billing Report.
     Enter 3 for mailing labels.
     Enter 4 to set range of zip codes for labels.
     Enter 5 to return to Main Menu.
     ENDTEXT
```

```
     INPUT " Your choice? " TO SELECT
     DO CASE
          CASE SELECT = 1
               DO SALESREP
          CASE SELECT = 2
               DO CLIBILL
          CASE SELECT = 3
               DO LABELS
          CASE SELECT = 4
               DO SIFTER
          CASE SELECT = 5
               RETURN
     ENDCASE
ENDDO
*End of REPORTER.PRG

**PRINTREP.PRG is procedure file for use with REPORTER
**
PROCEDURE SALESREP
WAIT "Turn on printer, and press a key."
REPORT FORM SALESREP TO PRINT
RETURN
**
PROCEDURE CLIBILL
WAIT "Turn on printer, install WIDE paper, and press a key."
REPORT FORM CLIBILL TO PRINT
RETURN
**
PROCEDURE LABELS
WAIT "Turn on printer, install mailing labels, and press a key."
LABEL FORM LABELS TO PRINT SAMPLE
RETURN
**
PROCEDURE SIFTER
PUBLIC ZIP1, ZIP2
ACCEPT "Enter starting zip code: " TO ZIP1
ACCEPT "Enter ending zip code: " TO ZIP2
SET FILTER TO ZIP >= ZIP1 .AND. ZIP =< ZIP2
RETURN
*End of procedure file
```

Procedures can be stand-alone in their functions, or they can pass data among themselves and other programs by means of parameter passing. Procedures save a great deal of time, as dBASE IV does not have to go to disk each time a subroutine that is a part of a procedure file must be executed. When the SET PROCEDURE TO <procedure filename> command is encountered in your program, dBASE IV reads the entire procedure file into memory. From that point on, whenever the program encounters a DO command, dBASE IV first attempts to find a procedure by that name within the procedure file. If it cannot find the procedure, it then looks for a command file by that name on the disk.

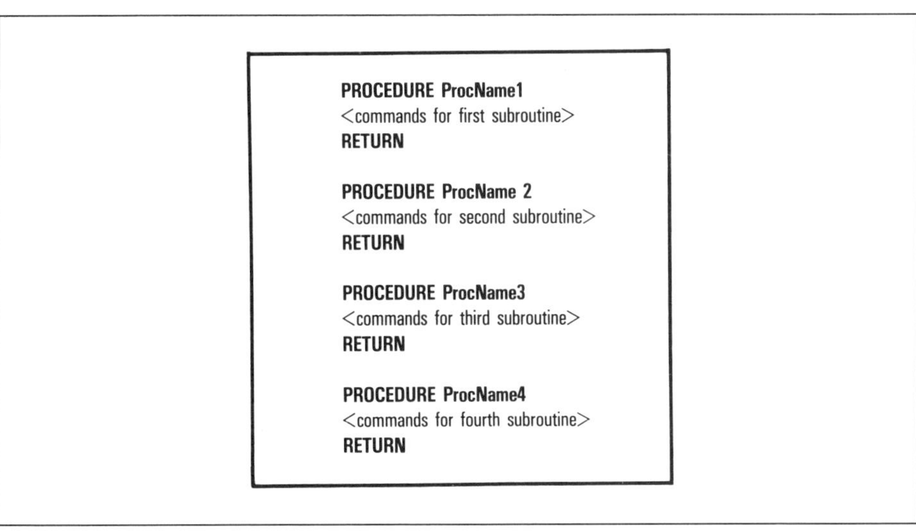
PROCEDURE ProcName1
<commands for first subroutine>
RETURN
PROCEDURE ProcName 2
<commands for second subroutine>
RETURN
PROCEDURE ProcName3
<commands for third subroutine>
RETURN
PROCEDURE ProcName4
<commands for fourth subroutine>
RETURN

Figure 14-1 Procedure File Design

A maximum of 1,170 procedures can be contained in any 1 procedure file; however, this maximum may be further limited by your computers' available memory. You can also resort to multiple SET PROCEDURE TO commands to open various procedure files applicable to different parts of the program. Procedure files offer the greatest speed increase if you use them to accomplish tasks that must be done often by your program. Rarely done jobs (like reindexing the index files or maintenance PACKs) are best left contained in an individual program file.

Using Abbreviated Commands

dBASE IV supports the use of four-letter word abbreviations, using the first four letters of any dBASE command in place of the entire command word. APPEND BLANK can be written as APPE BLAN, DISPLAY can be written as DISP, and so on. Shortening all dBASE commands in your programs to their four-letter equivalents won't speed program execution time, since the dBASE compiler converts the source code to "tokenized" object code. However, initial entry of the four-letter variants of commands can be less time-consuming.

Using User-Defined Functions (UDFs)

dBASE IV also supports the use of User-Defined Functions (UDFs). While UDFs may not directly speed the actual execution of your program, they can make a major difference in development time, by making it easier for you to store common tasks which can be called on from various parts of your application. In a way, they are like procedures, in that you can build them for a desired purpose, and call them from a part of your program. And in a way they are like dBASE IV's other functions, in that you can pass them values, and they return a value. User-defined functions pick up where the standard functions in dBASE leave off; when you need a function that doesn't exist to perform a task that may be specific to your application, you can create a user-defined function to handle that task. You then call on the function as you would any other dBASE function.

UDFs are placed in a procedure file along with your procedures, and they begin with the FUNCTION command. The UDFs contain the commands and the list of parameters needed to return the desired value. The design of a typical UDF resembles the following:

```
FUNCTION <UDF name>
PARAMETERS <parameter list>

     <...commands...>

RETURN(<value or variable>)
```

As an example, perhaps you often want to include the printed form of a date in reports (such as "April 30, 1988"). The DATE() function won't provide what you need, as it returns a date in one of the valid dBASE date formats (such as "04/30/88"). You could define a function within a procedure file like the following:

```
FUNCTION Daywords
PARAMETERS Thedate
DateOut = CMONTH(Thedate) + " " + LTRIM(STR(DAY(Thedate))) + ;
", " + LTRIM(STR(YEAR(Thedate)))
RETURN DateOut
```

And at any location in the program, you could call the function with a command statement like:

```
? Daywords(DATE())
```

and the function would return a text string representing the date passed to the function, such as "April 30, 1988."

Often, UDFs will return a value of true or false, depending on how a condition is evaluated by the UDF. And you can use UDFs along with VALID clauses of the @ . . . SAY . . . GET commands, to validate data according to a specific need. An example of both these techniques appears in the UDF shown below:

```
FUNCTION StateOK
PARAMETERS States
IF UPPER(states) $ "AK AL AR AZ CA CO CT DC DE FL GA HI IA ID IL + ;
  IN KA KY LA MA MD ME MI MN MO MS MT NB NC ND NH NJ NM NV NY OH + ;
```

```
  OK OR PA RI SC SD TN TX UT VA VT WA WI WV WY"
     RETURN .T.
ENDIF
RETURN .F.
```

And a portion of a program might prompt the user for the name of a state, as shown in the line of code below:

```
STORE SPACE(2) TO ANSWER
@ 5,5 SAY "State? " GET ANSWER VALID StateOK(answer)
READ
```

When the user responds with a two-letter code for a state, the VALID clause will call the user-defined function, StateOK(). The function returns a logical true if the user's entry matches one of the two-letter codes contained within the IF . . . ENDIF statement in the function.

RAM Disks to Speed Execution

If the PC running the application has lots of memory your program won't need, you may be able to significantly cut program execution time by creating a RAM disk and using it for program or temporary data storage. The wealth of commands for changing drives and paths, and copying and erasing files from within dBASE IV make this a very workable approach. If you are using DOS Version 3.0 or above, you can use VDISK (contained on your DOS disk) to build a RAM disk in extra memory. If you don't have DOS 3.0, you can get VDISK from most PC users' groups. Most multipurpose expansion boards for the PC also come with RAM disk software.

A nice approach, if the company will spring for the few hundred in hardware costs, is to install an expanded memory board, such as Intel's Above Board, and designate the 2Mb of expanded memory as one giant RAM disk. Then, write your application so that when the application is first started, the database and index files are copied to the RAM disk. Work with the files in RAM, and when the user exits the application, copy the updated files back to the original data disk, preferably a hard disk.

If you take this route, you may want to include an option on the Main Menu that lets users copy the latest file back out to the hard disk at any time. Many users get understandably nervous about leaving their edits in RAM for extensive periods of time.

Printing to Disk

This common technique won't speed up your program's execution one iota (it may actually slow things down a bit). But users will *think* the program's speed has been improved drastically if you use the technique of printing reports and labels to disk. The perception of speed comes from performing the report process when users are not using the machine–the middle of the night is an ideal time to process lengthy reports. Filter conditions and DO WHILE loops take time to evaluate and process data, and such tasks can be done in an unattended mode.

Once the necessary reports have been printed to disk, the resultant disk files can be printed (the next morning, for instance) by using either the dBASE or the DOS COPY command to copy the disk file to the print device (usually LPT1). Users who must then wait for a printer to complete its tasks won't have to also wait for dBASE to perform detailed evaluations of conditions necessary to produce the reports.

About Runtime

If you are using the Developer's Release version of dBASE IV, you can use Runtime to speed execution of code and to distribute stand-alone applications. As a secondary benefit, by removing the source code from your applications, you make it impossible for others to view the contents of your programs.

Why Runtime?

The main advantage of Runtime is that it lets you distribute stand-alone applications. Your end users will not need to purchase dBASE IV to run applications compiled with Runtime. You will need to provide assorted Runtime files which are needed to run the compiled object code produced from your applications' .PRG files. The Runtime files you will need are provided on disks contained in the Developer's Release version of dBASE IV.

What You Will Need

Runtime consists of the Runtime files and two utilities, BUILD and DBlink. Here are the Runtime files, which must be included with each application you distribute:

Runtime.EXE
Runtime1.OVL
Runtime2.OVL
Runtime3.OVL
Runtime4.OVL
dBASE1.RES
Protect.OVL

The Protect.OVL file is needed only if your application makes use of access levels on a local area network (see Chapter 15 for details).

The utility files, which are used to build the application but should not be given to the end users, are:

Build.COM

Buildx.EXE

Buildx.RES

Dblink.EXE

Dblink.RES

All of the above files, along with the source code and other objects (databases, indexes, reports, etc.) used by your application should be present in a subdirectory before using Runtime.

Using Runtime

Once you have copied the above files and your application into a subdirectory, enter BUILD at the DOS prompt to start the process. The Build Utility is used to compile and link your programs for use with the Runtime compiler. While the DBlink utility does the actual linking of the separate modules in your application, the Build Utility automatically compiles any programs which haven't been compiled, and calls the DBlink utility when necessary; hence, you need only use Build to do the entire job.

Once you enter BUILD and the program loads, the Build Menu appears. The Build Menu resembles the menus used inside of dBASE, with three menus: Build, Options, and Exit (Figure 14-2).

The Build Menu contains four options: Compile, Link, Output Destination, and Perform BUILD. Select the Compile option to enter the name of the main module of your application.

The Link option can be set to Yes or No, to tell Build to automatically invoke DBlink to link separate modules in your application into a single module. The default value for this option is Yes.

The Output Destination option can be used to tell Build to place the output files in another directory or on another drive. If you leave this option blank, the output files get stored in the current directory.

The Perform BUILD option is used after all other options have been set, to proceed with the compiling and linking of the application. Once you choose Perform BUILD, the Build utility will output a fully compiled and linked application, ready for use with the Runtime files. When all the application files and the Runtime files have been copied to the end user's disk, the user can then type:

```
RUNTIME <appname>
```

where <appname> is the name of your application's main module, to run the application.

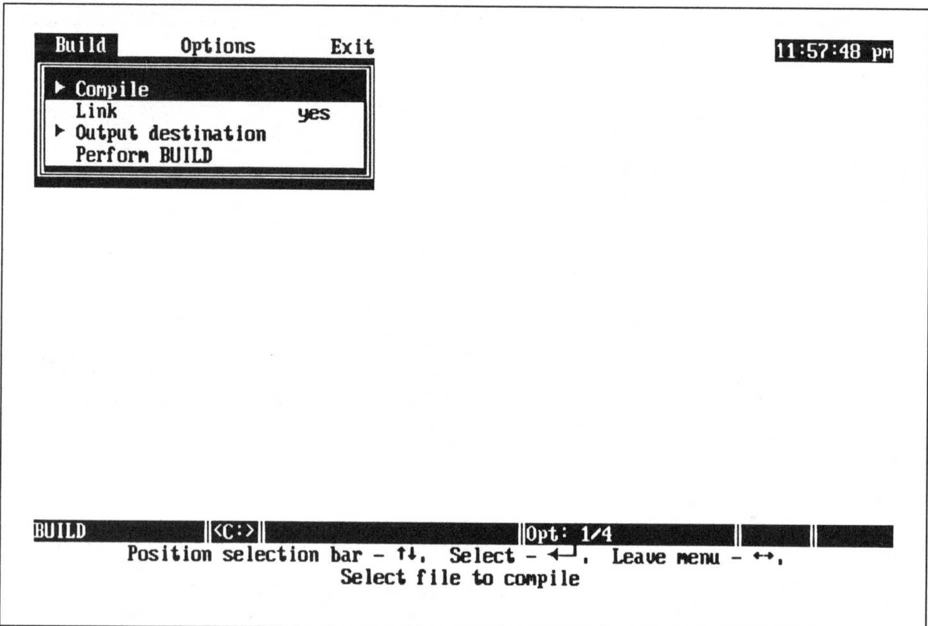

Figure 14-2 Build Menu

The output provided by the Build utility will be in the form of a single .DBO file if you set the "Link" option in the Build Menu to Yes. If you set the Link option to No, the output from Build will be in the form of separate .DBO files for every program (source code) file in your original application.

The Options Menu Choices

While in Build, the Options Menu can be used to change certain default parameters for Build. Figure 14-3 shows the Options Menu within Build.

The Search For New Functions option lets you tell Build to search for user-defined functions (UDFs) which may have name conflicts with reserved words in dBASE IV. Your source code might contain user-defined functions with names that are the same as command verbs in dBASE IV. This is a particularly common problem with UDFs that were developed in dBASE-compatible languages outside of dBASE IV. dBASE IV considers such UDFs as duplicates of existing commands, and does not execute them, so any program containing such UDFs will not work properly. Changing the Search For New Functions option to Yes tells Build to watch for possible suspect functions. If any functions that duplicate dBASE reserved words are found during the compiling process, appropriate warning messages will appear.

The Accept Only Runtime Commands option tells dBASE to display an error message if an illegal command appears in your source code as it is being compiled for Runtime. (Some valid dBASE commands, such as ASSIST and

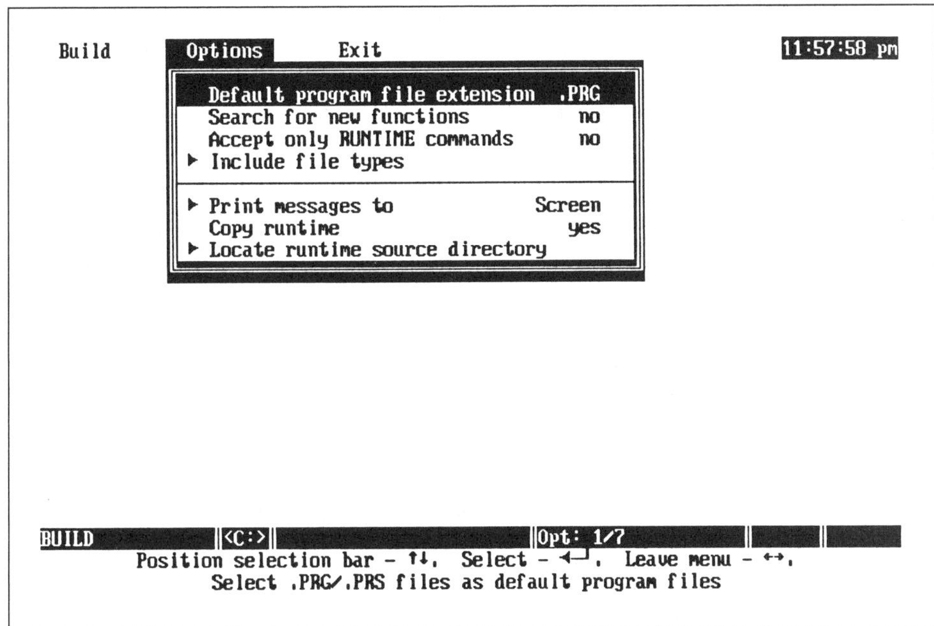

Figure 14-3 Options Menu

MODIFY STRUCTURE, cannot be used in Runtime. A complete list of illegal commands can be found near the end of this section.) The default for this option is Yes.

The Include File Types option causes a list of all dBASE IV file types to be displayed, along with a yes/no option for each file. You can use this option to select which files will be included in the copy operation that copies the finished files to the destination disk or directory. Note that this option does not change the compiling and linking process; it only changes the number of files copied. The option comes in handy when you have made a minor change to one or two modules of a complex application, and you only want to copy the object files from those specific modules, rather than the entire application, to the destination disk or directory.

The Print Messages To option is used to change the default destination for any messages displayed during the Build process. The messages normally appear on the screen, but you can choose to direct any messages to the printer, or to a file.

The Copy Single User Runtime option lets you tell the Build utility to copy the single-user Runtime files to the destination disk or directory, along with the compiled application. Note that there is no option in Build for copying the multi-user version of Runtime to a destination disk or directory. If you need the multi-user version of Runtime, you must manually install the multi-user version of Runtime on the network file server (see the Installation Manual of your Developer's Release package for details).

The Locate Runtime Source Directory option lets you enter a drive name and path for the location of the single-user Runtime files. Use this option if you want to use the option described in the above paragraph, and if the Runtime files are located in a directory other than the default directory.

Notes and Warnings

Some commands, valid in dBASE IV, are illegal in Runtime and must be avoided in your programs. These commands include the following:

ASSIST
COMPILE
CREATE or MODIFY FILE
CREATE or MODIFY LABEL
CREATE or MODIFY REPORT
CREATE or MODIFY QUERY
CREATE or MODIFY SCREEN
CREATE or MODIFY VIEW
HELP
HISTORY
Macro (&) substitution of command verbs
SET (with no options; menu-driven version)
SET DEBUG
SET ECHO
SET HISTORY
SET INSTRUCT
SET SQL
SET STEP
SET TRAP
SUSPEND

You can produce applications with Runtime that will operate on a dual-floppy system. In such cases, the programs contained on your three master Runtime disks are grouped so that Disk 1 is removed after the program loads, and Disk 2 stays in the drive along with your application. The routines on Disk 3 are used less frequently; the system will prompt for Disk 3 if it is needed.

If desired, you can manually use DBlink from the DOS prompt to link already-compiled applications. If you use DBlink outside of Build, you are responsible for making sure that all the programs have already been compiled by dBASE IV (Build does this automatically when necessary). You must also manually perform the tasks otherwise handled by the menu options within Build, such as automatic copying of Runtime files to a destination disk. At the DOS prompt, enter the command:

```
DBLINK <filename>
```

where <filename> is the name of the already-compiled version of your main module. DBlink will proceed to link all compiled programs and procedures called by your main module into a single compiled (.DBO) file. You can add the /L option at the end of the command, in which case a text file containing a list of all files linked will also be created. The text file will have the same name as the source file, but with a .TXT extension.

If you are setting the Build destination as another directory, the directory must exist prior to the use of Build. If you are setting the destination as a floppy drive, the disk in the drive should be formatted before using Build.

Using Compilers

If you are serious about developing fast applications in dBASE code, seriously consider purchasing a true compiler. *Compilers* are programming tools that create program files which are compiled. Although dBASE IV uses a compiler, it is not a true compiler in the absolute sense of the term. The compiler present in the standard version of dBASE IV is more accurately called a "tokenizer," as it converts the source mode into "tokens" of object code. The object code executes much faster than the interpreted code processed by earlier versions of dBASE, but the object code still requires dBASE IV to run. A true compiler, on the other hand, converts the source code into a free-standing program with an .EXE or .COM extension; the program can then be run directly from DOS.

How Compilers Process Code and Errors

Compilers operate quite differently than interpreters, acting on the entire program at once instead of a line at a time. Any errors that occur will still be reported by the compiler; however, the compiler will not halt due to an error, but will continue the compilation process until the entire program has been compiled.

When a compiler reads your program, it converts your program *(source code)* into an intermediate file, called *object code.* The object code is then "linked" by a linker. The linker provides access to any runtime program routines that will be needed by the program. These runtime routines are designed by the makers of the compiler, and are supplied with the compiler. The linking process produces a freestanding program (with a .COM or .EXE extension), which can then be run without the use of dBASE IV. You run the program by entering the program name at the DOS prompt like any other program, and the program runs at a faster speed because no reading and checking of tokenized code is occurring.

Compilers designed to handle dBASE program code offer two major advantages: increased program execution speed and the ability to develop stand-alone programs that can be distributed without the expense of a dBASE IV package for each user of the program. There are always two sides to a coin, and you will encounter some disadvantages. Compilers do not support all dBASE IV commands, so it will usually be necessary to make changes to your programs before they will compile and run without error.

Brands of dBASE IV Compilers

At the time of this writing, there are numerous compilers announced or available to the dBASE IV user. These include The Professional Compiler; Clipper, from Nantucket Software; and Quicksilver, from Wordtech Systems. Which works best for your application is a subject of great debate among fans of each. Because Clipper is (at the time of this writing) outselling the others on a wide basis, this chapter describes Clipper in depth.

An important note for programmers who must deal with local area networks: Nantucket and Wordtech Systems support the networking commands and functions present in dBASE IV within their compiler offerings. There are some older versions of the compilers still in use that do not support networks. If you use a compiler, make sure you use a version that supports networks.

Professional Compiler

It is rumored that a compiler called Professional Compiler will be available for owners of Developer's Release version of dBASE IV, versions 1.0 and 1.1. It is expected that when version 1.1 is released, the compiler will be available to purchasers of it as well as to those who have purchased version 1.0. A reputed advantage of this compiler is its high level of compatibility with dBASE IV commands. Other compilers may or may not support some of the dBASE commands which are new to dBASE IV, such as the menu-design commands and functions.

Clipper Compiler

Clipper software comes in the form of a manual and two disks, one containing the compiler, and the other containing the linker. The manual assumes that you have a good working knowledge of dBASE IV programming—if you're looking for a programmer's tutorial, you won't find it in the Clipper documentation.

Running Clipper is a straightforward process. After copying your dBASE IV program (.PRG) and database files onto a disk or into a subdirectory, you insert the Clipper compiler disk into drive A and enter a command similar to:

```
A:CLIPPER C:<program filename>
```

Clipper then compiles the file, indicating its progress by displaying the line number of the program it is working on. Any errors encountered during the compilation process will be reported on the screen. The errors flash by so fast that if there are many of them, it is impossible to read all the messages. You can direct the output of Clipper's error messages to an error message file by adding the greater-than sign, followed by a filename for the error file, as shown in this example:

```
A:CLIPPER C:MYFILE > ERRORS1
```

Once the program has finished, you (usually) go back into dBASE IV or your preferred programming editor to make any necessary changes to the code that caused the errors. You then rerun the compiler on the program file and hope that no errors occur. You don't need to worry about the location of procedures or command files that are called by other command files—if your program uses dBASE commands to call other programs or procedures, Clipper will access and compile the procedures and subroutines as necessary.

When the compiler has produced a debugged object code (.OBJ) file, you are ready to link the file to produce the freestanding program. You insert the Clipper Linker disk in drive A and run the linker with a command like this:

```
A:PLINK86 FILE C:MYFILE C:PROGRAM
```

When you enter this command, a copyright message will appear, and the linker program will access your disk drives for what seems like an interminably long time. When it is finally finished, you'll see a message indicating that an .EXE file bearing the name of your program has been created. This file will take up a good deal (well over 100K) of disk space, as the runtime libraries that Clipper must include to make your program freestanding are not small in size.

In entering filenames for use with the compiler and the linker, you can include pathnames, and you can omit both the pathnames and the disk drive identifiers if the programs and the linker all reside in the same directory on the same disk.

Most errors that are reported by the compiler are a direct result of commands and programming techniques that are valid in dBASE, but forbidden in Clipper. Some dBASE IV commands are not supported by Clipper, and some others are supported in different ways. None of the interactive commands are supported; these include

APPEND
ASSIST
BROWSE
CHANGE
EDIT
HELP

MODIFY COMMAND

SET

Initially, nonsupport of APPEND and EDIT may sound like a serious flaw, but if you consider the danger of allowing users direct use of such commands, you realize that you aren't giving up much when you don't use APPEND and EDIT. Clipper supports APPEND BLANK, which can be used along with variables to add records. The same use of variables is recommended for editing records, using @ . . . SAY . . . GETs and REPLACE commands in place of the EDIT command.

Clipper also does not support the CREATE LABEL, CREATE REPORT, MODIFY LABEL, MODIFY REPORT, or MODIFY STRUCTURE command. (Report form files and label form files created with dBASE III Plus can be used by Clipper, and Clipper does support the REPORT FORM and LABEL FORM commands.) Clipper also provides a utility disk with its own report- and label-building utilities, which are similar in design to those provided by dBASE III Plus.

The CREATE command is supported, but it operates differently, calling for some minor programming tricks if you want to give users of your programs the option of creating new database files.

Finally, many dBASE IV commands that can be used without specifying a list of fields must have a fields list included when used in Clipper. These commands include AVERAGE, DISPLAY, LIST, and SUM.

In return for making you think differently about some things as you design a program that will eventually be compiled, Clipper offers a number of enhancements that, to date, are not possible with dBASE. One significant improvement is in the number of fields that can be in a database; Clipper supports up to 1,024 fields. (Obviously, once you go past 256, you must use Clipper to create the database, as dBASE IV will not create a database with more than 256 fields.) Clipper also supports up to 64,000 active memory variables, a number far above the dBASE limit. Up to 250 open files are supported, a relief for programmers who have witnessed the dreaded "too many files are open" error message once too often.

Assembler and C language programmers will appreciate the CALL command, which calls routines outside of the Clipper environment. And Clipper can establish multiple relations out of a single work area.

Finally, the SAVE SCREEN and RESTORE SCREEN commands can temporarily overwrite a screen (for example, with a help screen) and later redraw that screen with a single command.

One minor drawback to taking full advantage of Clipper's enhanced features is that your Clipper programs will no longer run under dBASE IV, which means that you must use Clipper for all further testing and debugging.

Quicksilver

Quicksilver is a popular compiler offered by WordTech Systems, Inc. The compiler supports dBASE database and .NDX-style index files, although at the time of this writing, multiple index (.MDX) files are not supported. As with Clipper, you use Quicksilver to compile the source code (.PRG programs and procedure files) into object code. You then use a linker (supplied with Quicksilver) to produce the executable .EXE files which will run your application from the DOS level. Quicksilver includes its own debugger, along with a performance optimizer to further speed execution of the compiled program. Quicksilver also provides a number of advanced commands for management of windows, although these are different in syntax than the windowing commands implemented in dBASE IV.

15

Programming for Network Users

This chapter explains programming tools and techniques for writing programs in a network environment. The chapter assumes the installation of the multi-user version of dBASE IV on a network.

Introduction to dBASE on a Network

dBASE IV can be installed either in single-user or in multi-user mode. When installed in the multi-user mode, dBASE is normally installed on a file server connected to the network. As of this writing, dBASE is compatible with the Novell S/Net network, the 3Com 3+ network, and the IBM Token Ring network, and with any networks that are 100% NETBIOS compatible with the above. The standard version of dBASE allows network access by one user at a time. The Developer's Release version allows access by up to three users. Additional users can be granted access by purchasing dBASE IV LAN Packs. Each LAN Pack allows access for five additional users.

In addition to the commands and functions present in the single-user versions of dBASE IV, the multi-user version of dBASE offers commands and functions that you use to lock and unlock records and files. dBASE also provides PROTECT, a security system that limits network access to dBASE by maintaining a file of authorized user-names and passwords.

Programming Concerns for a Network

This chapter assumes that dBASE is installed on the network, and that your prime concern is how to effectively program within a network environment. *Database integrity* is the major issue to deal with when you write programs for use on a network. Database integrity is endangered when the program is not designed to deal with multiple users, and two or more users attempt a record modification or a global update to a database file at the same time. At best, one user overwrites another's changes. At worst, the network operating system crashes, bringing the entire network down and possibly damaging the database file in the process.

A second common problem with database software on a network is the potential problem of *file deadlock,* also known as a "deadly embrace." A file deadlock can result if two programs contend for the same files, and the error-trapping routine causes an unconditional retry of the file access. To guard against the potential problems that can arise in a multiple-user environment, dBASE IV offers the programmer manual file and record-locking facilities, automatic file and record locking, and a means of designating whether files will be available for shared or for private use.

Also useful when operating on a network are the LIST and DISPLAY STATUS commands, which now indicate the status of file and record locks, and the LIST USERS command, which shows all users logged onto dBASE on the network.

File Attribute Modes

Database files can be opened in one of two attribute modes: exclusive or shared. When a file is opened in *exclusive mode,* no other network user can access that file until the file is closed, or the attribute is in some way changed from exclusive to shared. If the file is opened in *shared mode,* any number of network users can gain access to the file. Exclusive use of a file is granted on a first-come, first-served basis. The default attribute for a database file is exclusive; dBASE will open any database file in exclusive mode unless told otherwise by your programs, or by entering SET EXCLUSIVE OFF at the dot prompt.

Most other types of files opened by dBASE will also be opened in exclusive mode by default. Table 15-1 lists whether the default mode of a type of file is exclusive or shared, but a simple way to remember without referring to a table is this: if the command results in a file being written to (such as the COPY TO, INDEX, or any command that begins with the reserved words CREATE or MODIFY), it is opened exclusive by default. If the command results in the file being read from but not written to (such as with REPORT FORM, LABEL FORM, SET FORMAT TO, or SET PROCEDURE TO), it is opened on a shared basis by default. This rule applies to all types of files directly used by dBASE.

The default value for index and the associated memo field files is always the same as it is for the database associated with those files. Also, the USE command is described in the table as opening files in exclusive mode. This is true only when SET EXCLUSIVE is set to ON.

Lock Commands and Functions

As the programmer, it is up to you to determine what should and should not be locked by the program. Once you have made that decision, dBASE offers locksmiths' tools, comprising three commands and three functions. The commands

Table 15-1 Status of Open Files

Command	Type of File	Default Attribute
APPEND FROM	.DBF (database)	SHARED
CREATE LABEL	.LBL (label)	EXCLUSIVE
CREATE	.DBF (database)	EXCLUSIVE
CREATE QUERY	.QRY (query)	EXCLUSIVE
CREATE REPORT	.FRM (report form)	EXCLUSIVE
CREATE VIEW	.VUE (view)	EXCLUSIVE
COPY STRUCTURE	.DBF (database)	EXCLUSIVE
COPY TO	.DBF (database)	EXCLUSIVE
DO	.PRG (program)	SHARED
INDEX	.MDX or .NDX (index)	EXCLUSIVE
JOIN TO	.DBF (database)	EXCLUSIVE
LABEL FORM	.LBL (label)	SHARED
MODIFY COMMAND	.PRG (program)	EXCLUSIVE
MODIFY LABEL	.LBL (label)	EXCLUSIVE
MODIFY QUERY	.QBE (query)	EXCLUSIVE
MODIFY REPORT	.FRM (report form)	EXCLUSIVE
MODIFY STRUCTURE	.DBF (database)	EXCLUSIVE
MODIFY VIEW	.VUE (view)	EXCLUSIVE
QUERY	.QBE (query)	SHARED
RESTORE	.MEM (mem. var.)	SHARED
REPORT FORM	.FRM (report form)	SHARED
SAVE	.MEM (mem. var.)	EXCLUSIVE
SET ALTERNATE TO	.TXT (alternate)	EXCLUSIVE
SET CATALOG TO	.CAT (catalog)	SHARED
SET FILTER TO FILE	.QBE (query)	SHARED
SET FORMAT TO	.FMT (format)	SHARED
SET INDEX TO	.MDX or .NDX (index)	EXCLUSIVE*
SET PROCEDURE TO	.PRG (program)	SHARED
SET VIEW TO	.VUE (view)	SHARED
SORT TO	.DBF (database)	EXCLUSIVE
TOTAL TO	.DBF (database)	EXCLUSIVE
UPDATE FROM	.DBF (database)	SHARED
USE	.DBF (database)	EXCLUSIVE*

*Default is EXCLUSIVE when SET EXCLUSIVE is ON.

are SET EXCLUSIVE, USE EXCLUSIVE, and UNLOCK. The functions are LOCK(), FLOCK(), and RLOCK().

As mentioned earlier, SET EXCLUSIVE, with the ON or OFF options, causes all files opened following the SET EXCLUSIVE command to be opened on an exclusive or shared basis. If the program is to offer shared access, you will want to include a SET EXCLUSIVE OFF command at the start of the program. If you prefer to lock the files, use SET EXCLUSIVE ON. As an alternate to SET EXCLUSIVE ON, you can use the USE EXCLUSIVE <filename> command to open a database. This variation of USE will open the named file in the exclusive mode.

The locking functions, LOCK(), FLOCK(), and RLOCK(), provide the ability to test for the presence of a file or record lock and to lock the file or record at the same time. In this respect, these functions differ from all other functions in dBASE IV. Where other functions simply return a value, the locking functions return a True or False value and perform an action. If the file or record is not previously locked, the locking function will place a lock on the file or record. The FLOCK() function tests for file locking, while the RLOCK() function and its synonym, LOCK(), test for record locking. The functions can be used in the interactive mode or from within a program. In the interactive mode, you can enter:

```
? FLOCK()
```

or

```
? RLOCK()
```

If the file or record was unlocked prior to the command, dBASE will respond with True (.T.), indicating a successful lock. Enter a LIST or DISPLAY STATUS command to show the file or record to be locked, as in this example:

```
. ? flock()
.T.
. display status

Currently Selected Database:
Select area:  1, Database in Use: E:\DBASE\MAILER.DBF    Alias: MAILER
Production  MDX file:  E:\DBASE\MAILER.MDX
           Index TAG:     LAST_NAME  Key: LAST_NAME
           Index TAG:     NAMES  Key: LAST_NAME
           Lock list: database  locked


Alternate file: E:\DBASE\INSERT40
File search path:
Default disk drive: E:
```

```
Print destination:  PRN:
Margin =      0
Refresh count =     0
Reprocess count =     0
Number of files open =     6
Current work area =     1

ALTERNATE  - ON    DELIMITERS - OFF   FULLPATH   - OFF   SAFETY     - ON
AUTOSAVE   - OFF   DESIGN     - ON    HEADING    - ON    SCOREBOARD - ON
BELL       - ON    DEVELOP    - ON    HELP       - ON    SPACE      - ON
CARRY      - OFF   DEVICE     - SCRN  HISTORY    - ON    SQL        - OFF
Press any key to continue...
```

If either function returns a logical False, the record or file in question has been locked by another user.

Within a program, you can use the locking functions as part of a conditional statement that tests for a lock and performs the desired operation if the lock is successful. An example of such use is:

```
**CHANGEIT.PRG locks, edits record
**Last update 11/09/88
CLEAR
INPUT "Enter stock number of record to be edited." TO MNUMB
USE INVFILES INDEX STOCKNO
SEEK MNUMB
IF EOF()
     ? "Sorry...no such stock number."
     WAIT
     RETURN
ENDIF
CLEAR
*Found the record, so test for a previous lock, and
*if not already locked, lock the record
IF RLOCK()
    STORE DESCRIPT TO MDESCRIPT
    STORE UNITCOST TO MUNITCOST
    STORE QUANTITY TO MQUANTITY
    @ 5,5 SAY "Item description: " GET MDESCRIPT
    @ 7,5 SAY "Unit cost: " GET MUNITCOST PICTURE "99999.99"
    @ 9,5 SAY "Quantity: " GET MQUANTITY PICTURE "999"
    READ
    REPLACE DESCRIPT WITH MDESCRIPT
    REPLACE UNITCOST WITH MUNITCOST, QUANTITY WITH MQUANTITY
    CLOSE DATABASES
    RETURN
ELSE
    ? CHR(7)
    @ 5,5 SAY "Sorry...another network user is updating that record."
```

```
    @ 7,5 SAY "Try your request again later."
    WAIT
ENDIF
**End of CHANGEIT.PRG
```

The program tests for the value returned by the RLOCK() function with the IF ... ELSE ... ENDIF statements. If RLOCK() returns a value of true, the temporary variables are created, and the @ ... SAY ... GET commands followed by the REPLACE commands allow editing of the record. If the record is already locked, control passes to the ELSE statement, which advises the user that the record is not presently available for editing.

Using UNLOCK

The UNLOCK command is used to unlock a previously locked record or file. The syntax for the command is:

```
UNLOCK [ALL]
```

If you don't specify the ALL option, UNLOCK will remove the last lock implemented in the active work area. If you include the ALL option, UNLOCK will remove all locks in all work areas. The following example shows the effects of the UNLOCK command:

```
. display status

Currently Selected Database:
Select area:  1, Database in Use: E:\DBASE\MAILER.DBF   Alias: MAILER
Production  MDX file:  E:\DBASE\MAILER.MDX
           Index TAG:     LAST_NAME  Key: LAST_NAME
           Index TAG:     NAMES  Key: LAST_NAME
           Lock list:       3,      5,      6  locked


Alternate file: E:\DBASE\INSERT41
File search path:
Default disk drive: E:
Print destination:  PRN:
Margin =     0
Refresh count =    0
Reprocess count =    0
Number of files open =    6
Current work area =    1

ALTERNATE   - ON    DELIMITERS - OFF   FULLPATH   - OFF   SAFETY     - ON
```

```
AUTOSAVE    - OFF   DESIGN      - ON    HEADING     - ON    SCOREBOARD - ON
BELL        - ON    DEVELOP     - ON    HELP        - ON    SPACE      - ON
CARRY       - OFF   DEVICE      - SCRN  HISTORY     - ON    SQL        - OFF
Press any key to continue...
*** INTERRUPTED ***

. unlock all
. display status

Currently Selected Database:
Select area:  1, Database in Use: E:\DBASE\MAILER.DBF   Alias: MAILER
Production  MDX file:  E:\DBASE\MAILER.MDX
           Index TAG:     LAST_NAME  Key: LAST_NAME
           Index TAG:     NAMES  Key: LAST_NAME
           Lock list:

Alternate file: E:\DBASE\INSERT41
File search path:
Default disk drive: E:
Print destination:  PRN:
Margin =      0
Refresh count =     0
Reprocess count =     0
Number of files open =    6
Current work area =    1

ALTERNATE   - ON    DELIMITERS - OFF   FULLPATH    - OFF   SAFETY     - ON
AUTOSAVE    - OFF   DESIGN     - ON    HEADING     - ON    SCOREBOARD - ON
BELL        - ON    DEVELOP    - ON    HELP        - ON    SPACE      - ON
CARRY       - OFF   DEVICE     - SCRN  HISTORY     - ON    SQL        - OFF
CATALOG     - OFF   ECHO       - OFF   INSTRUCT    - ON    STATUS     - OFF
Press any key to continue...
```

As a general rule, your programs will be most efficient on a network if you lock records when individual updates must be performed and lock files only when global updates (such as a REINDEX command) are performed. Also, an important point to note is that any access granted by locking commands and functions in a program can be overridden by the network operating system software or by the read/write attributes set with the PROTECT option within dBASE. If, for example, you use a network command or the PROTECT utility to designate a file as read-only, users will not be able to update the file, regardless of whether the file is locked or not.

In addition to programming control of locking functions, certain dBASE commands automatically place a lock on the file before these commands can take effect. The commands that perform a mandatory file lock are:

APPEND FROM

AVERAGE

CALCULATE
COPY
COPY STRUCTURE
COUNT
DELETE <scope>
INDEX
JOIN
LABEL
PROTECT
RECALL <scope>
REPLACE <scope>
REPORT
SORT
SUM
TOTAL
UPDATE

This brings up the question of what happens to your program's execution if the record or file cannot be locked (because another user has already placed a lock on the file or record). If this occurs, dBASE reports that the record or file has been locked by another. This will happen often on a network with any number of users sharing files, so error trapping to handle expected locking failures within your programs is a necessity.

Handling Failures to Lock with Error Trapping

Your error-trapping routines (covered in detail in Chapter 13) must include commands to handle locking failures if you offer shared access to files within a program. The ERROR() function will provide values that indicate the failure of a file-lock or record-lock attempt. In the error-handling routine, include an IF . . . ENDIF or CASE statement that detects an error value of 109 ("locked record error") and the error values of 108 ("locked file error").

Your program should also test for a possible error code of 148, which indicates a network server busy condition caused by the network operating system software. Such use of error trapping is shown in this example:

```
**ERRTRAP.PRG
**Error-trapping routine for INVENT.PRG on a Novell network
**Last update 06/17/86
DO CASE
```

```
    CASE ERROR() = 108 .OR. ERROR() = 109 .OR. ERROR = 158
        ? "The file or record is currently in use by another user."
        ACCEPT "Shall I continue trying to access it? (Y/N): " TO ANS
         IF UPPER(ANS) = "Y"
            CLEAR
            ? "...retrying access..."
            STORE 1 TO COUNT
            DO WHILE COUNT < 100
                STORE 1 + COUNT TO COUNT
            ENDDO
            RETRY
        ENDIF
        *User wants no retry, so give up and back out
        CLOSE DATABASES
        RETURN TO MASTER
    CASE ERROR() = 148
        ? "Getting a NET SERVER BUSY message from the file server."
        ? "...Please try again later."
        WAIT
        RETURN TO MASTER
    CASE ERROR() = 1
        ? "Cannot find the file.  Contact Network Administrator."
        CLEAR ALL
        WAIT
        QUIT
    CASE ERROR() = 20 .OR. ERROR() = 26
        ? "The index seems to be missing a record.  Please wait,"
        ? "while I repair the index."
        SET TALK ON
        INDEX ON STOCKNO TAG STOCKNO
        SET TALK OFF
        RETRY
    OTHERWISE
        ? "A serious error has occurred.  Please record the following"
        ? "message, and contact the DP Department."
        ?
        ? MESSAGE()
        WAIT
        SET ALTERNATE TO ERRORS
        SET ALTERNATE ON
        DISPLAY MEMORY
        DISPLAY STATUS
        CLOSE ALTERNATE
        QUIT
ENDCASE
*End of file ERRTRAP.PRG
```

Precisely how you handle the error is a matter of programming style. Some programmers prefer to tell the user to try the operation again later and pass control back to a higher-level module in the program. Other programmers prefer to start a timing loop and retry the operation at the end of the loop. If your thoughts lean toward the second method, include the RETRY command, or use SET REPROCESS (covered in the following section). RETRY causes program control to return to the program that called the error-trapping routine, at the same line of the program that caused the error. This is different than the RETURN command, which will pass control back to the program that called the error-trapping routine, but which starts execution at the line following the one that called the program.

Using RETRY, you can repeat the access attempt on the file or the record indefinitely, or until the user indicates that he or she is tired of waiting for the record or file to become available. The error-trapping program listed previously uses a timing loop along with an optional abort of the RETRY operation. The option is chosen when the user decides whether to make repeated tries for access or return to the calling program without accessing the file.

Performing Automated Retries

You can use the SET REPROCESS command to perform automated retries of a record lock or file lock attempt. The syntax for this command is:

```
SET REPROCESS TO <n>
```

where <n> is a numeric value from 1 to 32,000. The default for SET REPROCESS is zero, meaning dBASE immediately reports an error condition if the lock cannot be placed. By entering the SET REPROCESS TO <n> command, you tell dBASE to retry any locking attempt by the specified number of times before the error condition is reported. Note that you can also enter any negative number as the value, in which case dBASE will retry the attempt on an infinite basis.

Using Transaction Processing

dBASE IV provides a transaction processing facility, which maintains a transaction log of all changes made to a database. This transaction log can, if needed, be used to restore the database to its original condition before an update operation was started. This capability can be used in either the single-user mode or the multi-user mode of dBASE IV. It is described in this chapter because transaction processing is commonly done with networked database applications.

dBASE IV supports transaction processing with three commands. They are BEGIN TRANSACTION, END TRANSACTION, and ROLLBACK. The BEGIN TRANSACTION command tells dBASE IV to open a transaction file, and begin keeping a record of all changes made to the active database in the transaction file. This process continues until dBASE encounters an END TRANSACTION command. The END TRANSACTION command closes the transaction file, and deletes it.

If something goes wrong before an END TRANSACTION command is encountered, the ROLLBACK command can be used to restore the database to its original state, at the time the BEGIN TRANSACTION command was originally encountered. Typically, you would use BEGIN TRANSACTION and END TRANSACTION when performing a series of updates on a database file. And the ROLLBACK command can be instituted automatically if desired, as part of an error-trapping condition. The following code shows an example of an update procedure with an automated rollback:

```
STORE 0.00 TO INCREASE
@ 5,5 SAY "Amount of salary increase for all workers? "
@ 6,5 GET INCREASE PICTURE "9.99"
READ
USE STAFF
ON ERROR DO PROBLEMS
BEGIN TRANSACTION
     REPLACE ALL SALARY WITH SALARY + INCREASE
END TRANSACTION


ON ERROR
<...more commands...>


PROCEDURE PROBLEMS
CLEAR
STORE "N" TO ANSWER
@ 5,5 SAY "WARNING! Error encountered during update."
@ 7,5 SAY "Retry update? Y/N:" GET ANSWER PICTURE "!"
READ
IF ANSWER = "Y"
     RETRY
ELSE
     ROLLBACK
ENDIF
RETURN
```

Whenever a rollback is performed (either manually or within your programs), all changes made to the database, including deletions, will be undone up to the time the BEGIN TRANSACTION command took effect. The transaction processing facilities of dBASE IV can prove useful anytime an event occurs which makes you suspect the accuracy of your databases; the event could be a hardware malfunction, a power failure, or a failure to obtain use of a specific record or file.

Three functions which may also prove useful when you are using the transaction processing commands are ROLLBACK(), ISMARKED(), and COM-

PLETED(). The ROLLBACK() function lets you test for the successful completion of a ROLLBACK command. After using the ROLLBACK command, the ROLLBACK() function should return a value of true, indicating a successful rollback. A value of false after a ROLLBACK command may indicate a serious problem, such as a corrupted data file, or a hardware malfunction.

The ISMARKED() function lets you test to see whether someone already has a transaction log open on a database. If another user is updating a database and a BEGIN TRANSACTION command has already been applied to the database, the ISMARKED() function will return a logical value of true.

The COMPLETED() function lets you test for successful completion of a transaction. After the BEGIN TRANSACTION command is encountered, the COMPLETED() function returns a logical value of false. Once the END TRANSACTION command has purged the transaction file, the COMPLETED() function wil return a logical value of true.

Testing for a Network

If you are writing programs which may or may not be used on a network (and you can't be sure which is the case), you may find the NETWORK() function useful in your programs. You can use this function to test for the presence of a network. When in the multi-user mode, NETWORK() returns a logical value of true; in a single-user mode, NETWORK() returns a logical value of false. Portions of programs could be written to run in either environment, as shown in the example below:

```
IF NETWORK()
     SET REPROCESS TO 20
     SET REFRESH TO 5
     SET TALK OFF
     SET BELL OFF
ELSE
     SET TALK OFF
     SET BELL OFF
ENDIF
```

Avoiding Deadly Embrace

As mentioned before, a condition to watch for with multiple files on a network is the deadly embrace (file deadlock). A deadly embrace occurs when programs in use by two users contend for two or more of the same database files, and they become locked in an endless loop, each user's program waiting for the other program to unlock a desired file. Consider this example:

```
SET EXCLUSIVE OFF
ON ERROR DO ERRTRAP
SELECT 1
USE CUSTOMER
? FLOCK()
SELECT 2
USE SALES
? FLOCK()
SELECT 1
DO MAINMENU
<more commands...>
```

```
SET EXCLUSIVE OFF
ON ERROR DO ERRTRAP
SELECT 1
USE CUSTOMER
? FLOCK()
SELECT 2
USE SALES
? FLOCK()
SELECT 1
DO MAINMENU
<more commands...>
```

```
*ERRTRAP.PRG
IF ERROR() = 158
     *File locked, so try again
     RETRY
ENDIF

IF ERROR() = 1
     <more commands...>
```

If one user's program happens to start an instant in time behind the other user's program, a deadly embrace can occur. The first user's program selects work area 2 and locks SALES at the same time the second user's program comes along and locks CUSTOMER in work area 1. The first user's program tries to SELECT 1, but the CUSTOMER database is locked by the second user, so an error condition occurs. The second user's program tries in vain to open SALES, which is locked by the first user, and another error condition results. The error-trapping routine is causing a RETRY on notification of a locking failure, so both programs will retry the access to the files, with neither program gaining full control of both files. The result is that both users are caught in an endless loop, with no clear way out.

To avoid this possibility, include a time limit on any RETRY attempts and don't place an unconditional RETRY for file or record locks in the error-trapping routine. At the very least, give the user an option to break the retry process if things seem to be taking too long.

Automatic Record Locking

If your programs use the full-screen EDIT command, it will not be necessary for the program to lock records before they can be viewed. In a network environment, the EDIT command will automatically lock the current record. An automatic lock placed on a record with Edit will be automatically released if the user moves to another record with the arrow keys or the PgUp or PgDn keys, or if the user leaves the edit mode with the Esc or Control-End keys. If the user attempts to edit a record that is already locked, dBASE displays the message,

```
Record is in use by another
```

which indicates that a previous lock on the record exists. The user can press the Spacebar to retry the locking attempt or press Esc to abort the editing operation.

Other Network-Specific Commands

Other dBASE IV commands can prove useful with a network. These are DISPLAY STATUS, LIST STATUS, DISPLAY USERS, LIST USERS, and SET PRINTER. (One additional command, SET ENCRYPTION, will be covered shortly.)

The DISPLAY STATUS and LIST STATUS commands perform the same functions as in the single-user version of dBASE IV (display of the default drives and paths, database names, work area numbers and alias names, index filenames, open relations, and index keys for the index files). In addition to the information displayed by these commands, the status of any active file locks or record locks is included. Status of the locks appears along with the information identifying the filenames, work areas, and alias names, as shown in the following example:

```
. display status

Currently Selected Database:
Select area:  1, Database in Use: E:\DBASE\MAILER.DBF   Alias: MAILER
Production   MDX file:  E:\DBASE\MAILER.MDX
          Index TAG:     LAST_NAME  Key: LAST_NAME
          Index TAG:     NAMES  Key: LAST_NAME
          Lock list:       2,      4  locked


Alternate file: E:\DBASE\INSERT42
File search path:
Default disk drive: E:
Print destination:  PRN:
Margin =     0
Refresh count =    0
Reprocess count =    0
Number of files open =    6
Current work area =    1
```

```
ALTERNATE  - ON    DELIMITERS - OFF   FULLPATH   - OFF   SAFETY     - ON
AUTOSAVE   - OFF   DESIGN     - ON    HEADING    - ON    SCOREBOARD - ON
BELL       - ON    DEVELOP    - ON    HELP       - ON    SPACE      - ON
CARRY      - OFF   DEVICE     - SCRN  HISTORY    - ON    SQL        - OFF
Press any key to continue...
CATALOG    - OFF   ECHO       - OFF   INSTRUCT   - ON    STATUS     - OFF
CENTURY    - OFF   ENCRYPTION - ON    INTENSITY  - ON    STEP       - OFF
CONFIRM    - OFF   ESCAPE     - ON    LOCK       - ON    TALK       - ON
CONSOLE    - ON    EXACT      - OFF   NEAR       - OFF   TITLE      - ON
DEBUG      - OFF   EXCLUSIVE  - OFF   PAUSE      - OFF   TRAP       - OFF
DELETED    - OFF   FIELDS     - OFF   PRINT      - OFF   UNIQUE     - OFF

Programmable function keys:
F2        - assist;
F3        - list;
F4        - dir;
F5        - display structure;
F6        - display status;
F7        - display memory;
F8        - display;
F9        - append;
F10       - edit;
CTRL-F1  -
CTRL-F2  -
CTRL-F3  -
CTRL-F4  -
CTRL-F5  -
CTRL-F6  -
Press any key to continue...
CTRL-F7  -
CTRL-F8  -
CTRL-F9  -
CTRL-F10 -
SHIFT-F1 -
SHIFT-F2 -
SHIFT-F3 -
SHIFT-F4 -
SHIFT-F5 -
SHIFT-F6 -
SHIFT-F7 -
SHIFT-F8 -
SHIFT-F9 -
```

Both DISPLAY STATUS and LIST STATUS can make use of the TO PRINT option in the network environment. The output will be directed to the default printer (LPT1), unless you have changed the default printer status with a network operating system command or with the dBASE SET PRINTER command.

The DISPLAY USERS and LIST USERS commands show all workstations on the network that are currently using dBASE; an example of the use of the command is shown. The name shown by the command will be the user name assigned by the network operating system software. The greater than (>) symbol points to the currently logged user.

```
. list users

  Computer name
  -------------
 > ED
   ROBERTO
   MARY
   KAREN
   CARL
```

The SET PRINTER command provides a means for redirecting printer output to another printer on the network. Print output can be sent to the local printer attached to the workstation, to another printer attached to another workstation, or to a server. To send printer output to a printer other than the one attached to that workstation, the syntax for the command is:

```
SET PRINTER TO \\<computer name>\<printer name> = <destination>
```

where <computer name> is the workstation name assigned under the network software and <printer name> is the network assigned printer name. The <destination> designation is LPT1, LPT2, or LPT3, as appropriate with the particular setup.

To redirect printer output back to the local printer (the one attached to that workstation), the command is:

```
SET PRINTER TO LPT1/LPT2/LPT3
```

By default, the assigned printer is the shared printer on the network (often attached to the file server). Users of Novell networks can enter a shorter command for choosing the default printer, which is:

```
SET PRINTER TO \\SPOOLER
```

If you must access a serial printer (often a messy business), you can use the dBASE RUN command to run MODE from DOS, and then use the SET PRINTER command, as shown in this example:

```
*DIABLO.PRG sets up Diablo 630 in accounting for line report
RUN MODE COM1:1200,N,8,1
SET PRINTER TO \\USER5\PRINTER=COM1
? "To print report,"
WAIT
REPORT FORM ACCOUNTS TO PRINT
EJECT
*Redirect print output back to shared laser
RUN MODE LPT1:
SET PRINTER TO \\SPOOLER
RETURN
*End of program DIABLO.PRG
```

Note that if you want to redirect output to a local printer and you are running Novell Netware, you must use the Novell SPOOL command before starting dBASE (see the Netware documentation for details). Also note that when spooling under Netware to a shared printer, the queuing of data to the printer does not actually begin until the SET PRINTER command is executed within dBASE.

The SET REFRESH command sets the interval for the updating of the screen display when the user is in a full-screen mode such as EDIT or BROWSE. Each time the screen is updated, any changes made by other users will appear. The syntax for the command is:

```
SET REFRESH TO <n>
```

where <N> is a numeric value from 1 to 3600. The value represents the time, measured in seconds, between the screen updates. If the command is not used, dBASE defaults to an interval value of zero.

The CONVERT command converts a database file used under the single-user version of dBASE IV for use on a network. When the CONVERT command is used with a database file, a new field named _DBASELOCK is added to the file. The new field is a character field, with a default width of eight characters. The new field is used by the SET REFRESH command, and by the CHANGE() and LKSYS() functions which test to see if a record has been changed, and to see who has locked a record. The existence of the new field also makes it possible for the EDIT and BROWSE modes to detect changes by other users.

The syntax for the command is:

```
CONVERT [TO number]
```

where the [TO number] clause is optional, and determines the length of the new field. The desired database should be opened; then the CONVERT command is entered. If the TO option is omitted, dBASE adds a 16-character field. This provides enough space for dBASE to keep track of the needed network data, plus 8 characters for a user name. (This user name is returned by the LKSYS() function to tell your program who has locked a record.) If a value is entered with the TO option of the CONVERT command, the value must be between 8 and 24. A value of 8 allows dBASE to store needed network information, but leaves no room for a user name, and any use of the LKSYS() function will return a null string. A value of 24 will leave room for a user name of up to 16 characters.

Moving Your Single-User Applications to a Network

dBASE IV's automatic file and record locking do much toward making it easy to bring an application previously written for a single-user environment onto a network. The performance of the application under multiple users will improve if you take full advantage of selective locking; however, you can perform a few minimal steps to quickly get an application "up and running" on a network. Once the application is network-ready, you can then concentrate on ways to improve the performance by implementing selective locking functions and error routines. The following steps can be considered as the least you should do when moving an application to a network.

- At or near the start of the program, add a SET EXCLUSIVE OFF statement. Without this statement, dBASE will default to exclusive mode, and your network users will be very upset when only one user can access the database at a time.
- Add a SET REPROCESS TO <n> statement, so that dBASE does not immediately present a user with an error message every time an attempt is made to access a locked record. The number provided should not be so high that users get tired of waiting to gain access to the locked record or file.
- If there are any locations in the program where you prefer not to have the automatic record locking of dBASE in effect, add a SET LOCK OFF statement at that location in the program. Be sure to restore the automatic locking capability when necessary with SET LOCK ON.

Implementing Security Functions Within a Program

dBASE IV offers PROTECT, a menu-driven utility used to assign usernames, passwords, and access levels to each user of dBASE on the network. The use of PROTECT is optional on the part of any Network Administrator (the person who manages the network). If PROTECT is not used, all users can use dBASE, and all users will have an access level of 1. Through a series of menu options within the PROTECT command, various users can be assigned access levels ranging from 1 (the most access) through 8 (the least access). If PROTECT is used, you can make use of the ACCESS() function and the LOGOUT command to control security within your dBASE programs.

To run the PROTECT utility, enter PROTECT at the dot prompt. The utility uses a series of menus similar to the other menus used from the Assist mode of dBASE to set security and file access levels. The network portion of the dBASE documentation details the use of the PROTECT utility.

The ACCESS() function displays a value between 1 and 8, indicating the access level of the user who is running your program. The precise value provided by the ACCESS() function does not correspond to any preconceived "powers of access" granted by dBASE; the Network Administrator, and the programmer, can determine what the numbers actually represent. In one application, you may decide to provide any user having an access level of 7 or lower the ability to revise any database. In another application, you may decide that only users with access levels of 1 or 2 can change database files.

By including the ACCESS() function in your program menus, you can control which facilities are available to users, as shown in the following example:

```
TEXT
***
(Menu displayed here...)
***
ENDTEXT
INPUT " -Your selection? " TO CHOICE
DO CASE
     CASE CHOICE = 1
          IF ACCESS() > 5
               ? "Access denied!"
               WAIT
               RETURN
          ENDIF
          DO ADDRECS
     CASE CHOICE = 2
          IF ACCESS() > 3
               ? "Access denied!"
               WAIT
               RETURN
          ENDIF
          DO UPDATE
     <rest of commands...>
```

The LOGOUT command can force a user out of a protected dBASE network environment. (LOGOUT has an effect only if the PROTECT utility has been used by the Network Administrator to assign names and passwords to users.) When dBASE IV encounters a LOGOUT command, all databases and associated files are closed, and the user is presented with the dBASE Log-In Screen. The Log-In Screen asks for the username, group name, and password; these items must be supplied before the user can again use dBASE.

Taking our prior example a step further, you could add a LOGOUT command that kicks the user out of the system after an attempt to use a procedure for which he or she has no authorized access, as shown in this portion of code:

```
INPUT " -Your selection? " TO CHOICE
DO CASE
     CASE CHOICE = 1
          IF ACCESS() > 5
               ? CHR(7)
```

```
            @5,5 SAY "Security Violation!  Re-enter"
            @7,5 SAY "your password at the prompt."
            WAIT
            LOGOUT
        ENDIF
        DO ADDER
    <rest of commands...>
```

If nothing else, forcing users out of the system in response to improper access attempts will cut down on users' habits of trying system menus that they do not have security approval for.

File Encryption

As a security feature, dBASE IV has the ability to encrypt database files. Original encryption of a database file is performed through the use of the PROTECT utility, by setting file access privileges from the Files Menu of the PROTECT Utility. Once a database has been encrypted, users must have authorized access levels—as set by the PROTECT utility—to open the file. dBASE keeps track of users as they log onto the network and automatically determines if a user has clearance to open an encrypted database.

How does all of this affect you as the programmer? Not much, unless you also happen to be the Network Administrator, in which case you should at the very least learn the use of the PROTECT utility. As a programmer, your only significant concern regarding the area of encryption is to decide whether you want new files that are created by your programs to maintain the same encryption levels that have been placed on the existing file by the Network Administrator.

If you use the COPY command to copy part or all of an encrypted file to another file, the new file will also be encrypted unless you turn off encryption with the SET ENCRYPTION OFF command. There are times when you will want to turn off encryption, such as when you are copying files for use in a single-user dBASE IV environment. (The default value for SET ENCRYPTION is ON.) If any of the TYPE options (WKS, DELIMITED, SDF, SYLK, and so on) are used with the COPY command, SET ENCRYPTION must be turned off prior to the use of the COPY command.

For example, you might want to include a program option that creates a Lotus 1-2-3 compatible file, based on the contents of an encrypted database. You could check a user's access level; if the access level is the proper value, your program could then turn off encryption with SET ENCRYPTION OFF, followed by the appropriate COPY command, as displayed in this example:

```
**EXPORTIT.PRG builds files for use in Lotus 1-2-3.
CLEAR
IF ACCESS() > 2
    ? "You do not have security approval to create this file."
    WAIT
```

```
    RETURN TO MASTER
ENDIF
ACCEPT "Enter name for Lotus file to create (no extension): " TO LNAME
IF FILE("&LNAME.WKS")
    CLEAR
    ? "A worksheet named " + LNAME + ".WKS already exists!"
    ACCEPT "Overwrite this file? (Y/N): " TO ANS
    IF UPPER(ANS) < > "Y"
        RETURN
    ENDIF
    ? "Creating Lotus 1-2-3 file.  Please wait..."
    SET ENCRYPTION OFF
    STORE LNAME + ".WKS" TO LNAME
    COPY TO &LNAME TYPE WKS
    SET ENCRYPTION ON
    ? "File has been created."
    WAIT
ENDIF
RETURN
*end of EXPORTIT.PRG.
```

Some points to remember on the subject of encrypted files: once an index file is used along with an encrypted database, dBASE automatically encrypts the index file. To create a decrypted version of the index, you must SET ENCRYPTION OFF, copy the database to an unencrypted file, and use that file to build a new index. You must also create an unencrypted version of a database before using MODIFY STRUCTURE to change the file design.

If maintaining security is an important aspect of an application, you may want to delete all of the .PRG files after the application has been completely compiled by the dBASE compiler. If the source code for programs is left available, any user with a reasonable degree of computer savvy could wreak pure havoc by changing the tests for access levels that you build into your programs. You could find yourself locked out of your own application, an embarrassing thought if your job is to implement a supposedly "secure" system!

16

The Old and the New

This chapter describes the changes necessary for programmers who have worked with earlier versions of dBASE. dBASE II users must make considerable alterations to programs developed under that software and must convert database files before they can be used with dBASE IV. dBASE III and dBASE III Plus programmers can use their database files and programs without modifications, but in many instances can streamline parts of those programs and enhance the user interface by using added commands and functions included in dBASE.

What's Changed

dBASE II users face a number of changes, although much remains familiar. Notably, database files use a different header than is used by dBASE II files, and the other associated dBASE II files (index files, report form files) are not compatible with dBASE IV. A utility provided with dBASE IV, called dCONVERT, provides help with the conversion of most types of dBASE II files into dBASE IV format. All dBASE III and dBASE III Plus files are fully compatible with dBASE IV, and no changes are mandatory.

dBASE II programmers face three tasks in converting programs to operate under dBASE IV. They are:

1. The conversion of necessary database and associated files
2. The conversion of programs to use different functions and commands
3. Any necessary modifications needed to programs due to differences in some ways that dBASE IV operates

dBASE III and III Plus users face considerably less work, as programs written in dBASE III and dBASE III Plus will run unchanged. Beyond what's required to convert programs, give some thought to what changes are not *mandatory,* but that would improve the performance or appearance of the program. A dBASE II program that has been run through dCONVERT is not necessarily an efficient program, as it will not take advantage of the added features of dBASE IV. A common example is in the use of multiple files. dBASE II allowed just two files to be open at any one time. Programs that had to routinely work with three or more databases performed a juggling act: they opened and closed files, and they passed data back and forth through memory variables. dBASE IV will perform the same juggling act if asked, but runs much faster if your program opens all the needed files at once.

Using dCONVERT

For dBASE II users, Ashton-Tate provides a dCONVERT conversion utility on one of the system disks. The program is actually the same dCONVERT utility that was provided with dBASE III and dBASE III Plus. Since dBASE III files are directly readable in dBASE IV, you can use this same utility to convert files from dBASE II to dBASE IV. dCONVERT is stored on the System Disk #9. It's a fully executable program that runs directly from DOS. Copy the program, DCONVERT.EXE, from the System Disk #9 to the disk or subdirectory containing the dBASE II programs you want to convert, then load the utility from the DOS prompt by entering

```
DCONVERT
```

The dCONVERT Menu shown in Figure 16-1 is displayed.

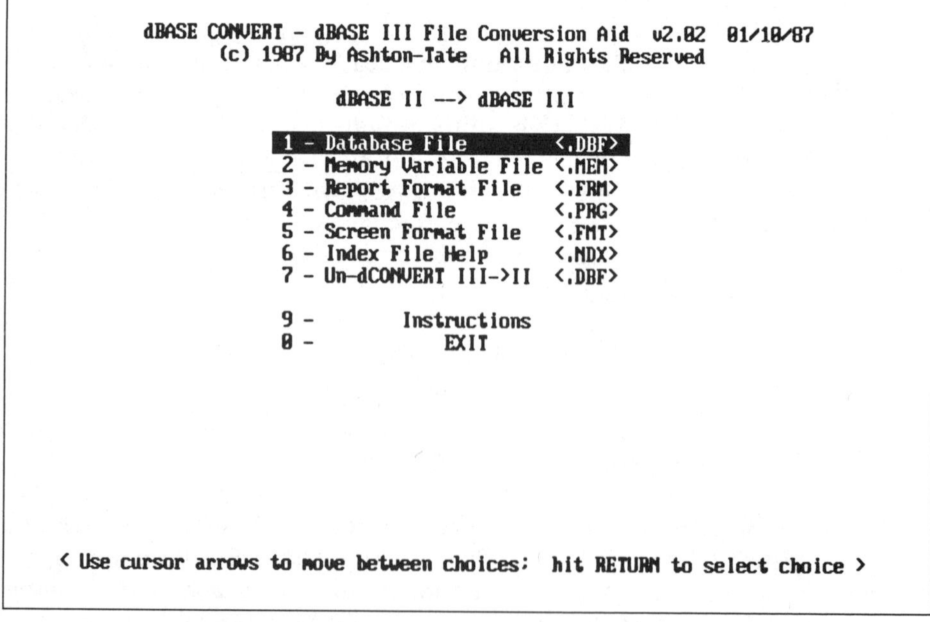

Figure 16-1 dCONVERT Menu

What dCONVERT Does

dCONVERT converts five types of files and offers help with the sixth type (index files) by creating small command files that you can then use inside of dBASE IV to create the desired index file. You make selections from the dCONVERT Menu either by selecting the number or moving the highlight to the option with the cursor keys and pressing Return. Once you have specified a file type, dCONVERT lists the files of that type contained in the default directory. Then it prompts you for the names of files to be converted.

As files are converted, dCONVERT displays a row of periods on the screen to indicate its progress. At the completion of the conversion, dCONVERT renames your original dBASE II files by changing the last letter of the extension to a B (dBASE II database files become .DBB, command files become .PRB, and so on). The converted dBASE IV files have the proper extensions. Only index files are not actually converted by dCONVERT; instead, dCONVERT builds a command file having the same name as the index file and an extension of .NDX.

To build the required index file, you must load dBASE IV, open the associated database, and from the dot prompt, enter DO <filename>.NDX, where "filename" is the name of the "converted" index file created by dCONVERT. The command file created by dCONVERT will then build the needed index file. Many programmers find it a simpler matter to just open the converted database and create the needed index files from scratch.

Using dCONVERT from DOS

dCONVERT can also be run directly from DOS, bypassing the dCONVERT Menu. To use the utility in this manner, at the DOS prompt enter:

```
DCONVERT A:<filename.ext> B:
```

where A represents the drive containing the input files, and B represents the drive that is to contain the converted files. You can use wildcards with this approach, to convert a series of files at once. For example, entering

```
DCONVERT A:*.PRG C:\DBASE
```

would convert all command files on the disk in drive A and store the converted files in the DBASE subdirectory on drive C.

The database, report form, screen format, and memory variable files converted by dCONVERT can be used by dBASE IV with no further attention. The command files are another matter. Due to significant syntax differences between dBASE II and dBASE IV, converted dBASE II programs will probably not run properly under dBASE IV. dCONVERT handles all the syntax conversions that it can deal with, but you must analyze some operations and handle them manually. When dCONVERT encounters a change in syntax it cannot handle (such as a dBASE II command that has no direct dBASE IV equivalent), it turns that line of code into a comment, starting with an asterisk and two exclamation points.

Immediately following the conversion of dBASE II programs, you can print out the files and look for such comments, then decide how to deal with the dBASE II commands that are no longer valid.

Changing Your dBASE II Programs

The first step in modification of a dBASE II program so that it will run effectively under dBASE IV is running dCONVERT. The next step is to deal with what dCONVERT won't handle for you—those problems are discussed in greater detail here. The most significant problem areas are:

1. dBASE II commands that have no dBASE IV equivalent
2. dBASE II commands that operate differently in dBASE IV
3. Testing for location of the record pointer after a FIND
4. Handling macro (&) operations

The Record Pointer

One of the thorniest areas in conversion of dBASE II programs to dBASE IV format is in dealing with the record pointer as your program manipulates the database. dBASE II and dBASE IV handle indications of the location of the record pointer in significantly different ways. In dBASE II, the # function indicates the position of the record pointer. dBASE IV uses the RECNO() function for this purpose. Since dBASE II used the # as both the record pointer function *and* as a substitute for the not-equals operator (<>), it isn't just a matter of replacing all occurrences of the # symbol in a dBASE II program with the RECNO() function.

dCONVERT tries to analyze the parts of the statement surrounding the # symbol in a dBASE II program, and dCONVERT will usually manage to make the correct conversion to either the RECNO () function or the not-equals operator. But in some cases, the correct conversion may not be made, and you will have to make the necessary changes.

In dBASE II, the indication for beginning of file was a record number equal to zero. dBASE IV uses the BOF() function, which provides a logical True if the record pointer reaches the beginning of the database. Any dBASE II programs that used sequential positioning of the record pointer, along with a #=0 statement to test for beginning of file, must be rewritten. This is necessary because the #= 0 test in dBASE II is also used to indicate an unsuccessful FIND operation. If your dBASE II program generates the commands,

```
STORE "Johnson" TO LNAME
FIND &LNAME
```

and the search for a matching record is unsuccessful, a test for the location of the record pointer will yield the following:

```
? #
0
```

dCONVERT cannot be sure about whether your dBASE II program logic is using the #=0 statement to test for unsuccessful find or to test for the beginning of file. Therefore, dCONVERT will include a warning comment in your program at any location of the #=0 statement, and you must analyze the program's logic and make the required changes.

Macros

Macros are another potential problem area. When a program has been converted, it is best to print out copies of both the dBASE II and dBASE IV versions, then examine them side by side. Be suspicious of *all* macros in a dBASE II program. Some may not be needed with dBASE IV, and some may cause your program to crash. Replace any FIND & macros with SEEK (dCONVERT will not do this for you). Whenever possible, replace dBASE II macros entirely with dBASE IV functions that can perform the same tasks with less delay in program execution time.

Memory Variables

Memory variables in subroutines present another area that will require your attention. In dBASE II, all memory variables are global by default. Since a program is converted by dCONVERT as just another command file, any subroutine memory variables that must be accessed by higher-level routines will need to have PUBLIC declarations included in the program.

Tests for Blank Spaces

In dBASE II, when a user presses Return in response to a GET blank or an ACCEPT, INPUT, or WAIT statement, a blank space is returned. In dBASE IV, pressing the Return key generates a null, which is not the same as a blank space. If your programs test for blank spaces in response to pressing Return, the programs must be changed to match the responses provided by dBASE IV.

Nonequivalent Commands

Certain commands available in dBASE II have no equivalent in dBASE IV. These are commands that are no longer necessary because dBASE performs the function differently, or DOS doesn't need those commands. The commands that have been removed, and suggested replacements for them, include the following.

QUIT TO: This is used in dBASE II to quit dBASE and run a program. The RUN command accomplishes the same function while allowing the user to return to dBASE IV.

READ NOUPDATE: This dBASE II command performs a read and leaves the GETS intact. Use the SAVE option of the READ command instead.

REMARK: In dBASE II this command places text on the screen, one line at a time. Use @ . . . SAY commands instead.

RESET: This command was used with the CP/M operating system to reset disk controller circuits after changing floppy disks. It is not needed by DOS.

SET COLON ON: dBASE II uses this command to turn on the display of colons as a full-screen field delimiter. Use SET DELIMITERS TO and SET DELIMITERS ON instead.

SET DATE TO: This is used in dBASE II to set a date figure that could appear in reports, but it is not updated by the computer's clock (if any clock is present). Under DOS, use the PC's system clock (which can be reset with a RUN command) and use the dBASE DATE() function to retrieve the date.

SET EJECT ON/OFF: In dBASE II this command determines whether a page eject will occur at the end of a report. Page eject options in dBASE IV can be set from within the report format.

SET HEADING ON/OFF: This command is used in dBASE II to set a heading for a report. In dBASE IV, report headings can be specified within the report design.

Program Changes That Are Made Automatically

Program changes that are handled automatically by dCONVERT include the following:

- SELECT PRIMARY and SELECT SECONDARY, used to choose between two possible work areas, are converted to SELECT 1 and SELECT 2.
- The record number function, RECNO(), is changed from # to RECNO().
- The test for a deleted record is changed from * to DELETED.
- The AT, SUBSTR, RANK, and UPPER functions are changed from @ to AT(), $ to SUBSTR(), RANK to ASC(), and ! to UPPER().
- The Beginning-of-File and End-of-File functions are changed from BOF and EOF to BOF() and EOF().

- The USING option of the @ . . . SAY command in dBASE II will be replaced with the PICTURE clause of the @ . . . SAY command.
- Logical variables are converted to .T. and .F., which differ from their storage in dBASE II, where their logical values are T and F. If you use T, F, Y, or N as memory variable names in your dBASE II programs, you can get into trouble, as dCONVERT will usually convert such names into logical variables. The best approach is to change such variable names while you are still using dBASE II, make sure the changed program runs under dBASE II, and then use dCONVERT to convert the program.
- Various dBASE II commands will be replaced by dCONVERT with equivalent dBASE IV commands. These include CLEAR (now CLEAR ALL), ERASE (now CLEAR), and DISPLAY FILE (now DIR). The dBASE II DELETE FILE command can still be used, or its synonym, ERASE, can be used.

Changing Your dBASE III/dBASE III Plus Programs

The above isn't a misprint. As mentioned, you can get away with no changes to your dBASE III or dBASE III Plus programs, but there are a number of benefits to be gained from making some changes. These areas should be considered when taking programs from either version of dBASE III to dBASE IV:

Menus: A more standardized user interface can be implemented by using the DEFINE BAR, DEFINE PAD, DEFINE POPUP, and ON SELECTION commands to present bar, popup, or pulldown menus. User familiarity is another possible benefit, as users of other software packages are likely to be familiar with bar or popup menus.

Data Entry: Data entry errors can be greatly reduced by taking advantage of the VALID option combined with the @ . . . SAY . . . GET command. If the entry screens contain large numbers of fields, it may be faster to paint new screens containing validation settings with the CREATE SCREEN command, then copy the resultant @ . . . SAY . . . GET commands from the .FMT file.

Windows: Use windows for specialized browsing and editing, displays of lists, and editing of memo fields. Not only can the appearance be eye-catching, but it also harmonizes with the look of the menus done with the dBASE IV menu commands.

Reports: Often applications don't provide everything users want in reports, simply because it can be such an enormous task to code different reports for every format the users desire. Let dBASE do most of the coding work, by designing the reports with the Report Generator.

A Note About Backwards Compatibility and Memo Fields

Note that dBASE III and dBASE III Plus will not be able to read the contents of memo fields in database files created with dBASE IV. Use the DBMEMO3 type option of the COPY TO command to create database files with memo fields that are compatible with dBASE III and dBASE III Plus.

17

Program Generators

This chapter highlights the use of *program generators,* or programs that profess to write other dBASE programs. There are a number of such tools on the market; this chapter examines two such packages, one of which is supplied with dBASE IV. They are the dBASE IV Applications Generator, and GENIFER, by Bytel.

Introduction to Program Generators

The computer program that can be given the command,

```
DO WHAT I WANT
CALL ME WHEN DONE
```

and that merrily churns out code while you lounge in the hammock is, as of this writing, still a dream. Developers have tried to give us something close to this concept with program generators, and there is no shortage of such tools in the dBASE world. All of these products have their limitations, but some of them may actually save you time by generating relatively bug-free code that can then be further modified to suit your particular need.

The Applications Generator, supplied with dBASE IV by Ashton-Tate, is free if you have dBASE IV, so it is worth trying. The other programs on the market warrant this advice: try to obtain a low-cost demo disk on any package you are considering before investing in a program generator. Like humans, program generators have different styles of writing code. You may like the style of a program generator, and then again, you may not. Many programmers feel that they must spend so much time modifying the code produced by a program generator that it is not worth their while to bother with such tools. Other programmers, in a rush to meet deadline on a project, have been thankful for the core of code that a good program generator could produce. You'll have to decide for yourself.

dBASE IV Applications Generator

The dBASE IV Applications Generator is well worth investigating, for two reasons: it is powerful, and assuming you've obtained dBASE IV, it is free. Users of dBASE III Plus can rest assured that the Applications Generator provided with dBASE IV is a major improvement over the extremely limited applications generator that was a part of dBASE III Plus. The dBASE IV Applications Generator lets you build complete applications or parts of applications (such as individual menus). Even if you prefer to maintain tight control over your program code, the Applications Generator can save significant amounts of coding time by building applications which you can then modify as desired.

Steps Involved in Building the Application

When building an application with the Applications Generator, typically you perform a sequence of design steps which result in the completed application. Those steps are as follows:

1. Start the Applications Generator, with the CREATE APPLICATION/ MODIFY APPLICATION command, or from the Control Center menus.
2. Open the Design Menu, and choose the desired object to design (such as a menu).
3. From the object menu which appears (Menu Menu, Application Menu, List Menu, or Batch Menu) assign the desired attributes to the object.
4. Repeat steps 2 and 3 for all needed objects in the application.
5. Using the Item Menu, specify the action for each item within each design object.
6. At the Generate Menu, select the desired template (MENU.GEN for program code, or DOCUMENT.GEN for documentation).
7. At the Generate Menu, choose Begin Generating to generate the application.
8. At the Exit Menu, choose Save Changes And Exit to save the changes and leave the Applications Generator.

Starting the Applications Generator

The Applications Generator can be started by entering the command, CREATE APPLICATION <application name>, or MODIFY APPLICATION <application name>. With either command, the results are the same. If an application by that name already exists, entering CREATE APPLICATION or MODIFY APPLICATION will start the Applications Generator, and load the existing application. If no application exists by that name, entering CREATE APPLICATION or

MODIFY APPLICATION will tell the Applications Generator to begin designing a new application. The Applications Generator can also be accessed from the Control Center menus, by choosing the CREATE option of the APPLICATIONS menu.

Once the command has been entered, the Application Definition screen appears (Figure 17-1). Use the Application Definition screen to enter initial parameters about the application.

In the Application Name box, you can enter a name for the application. The name must follow DOS file-naming conventions, as it will be saved to a file with the .APP extension. In the Description box, you can enter a one-line description of the application. This description appears when the application is highlighted by name in the Control Center menus.

In the Main Menu Type box, you can press the spacebar to select between bar, popup, or batch for a main menu type. In the Main Menu Name box, you must enter a name which will be assigned to the main menu. In the Database/View box, enter the name of the primary database file or view used by the application. (Applications are not limited to using only one database file; choices from another menu which appears later can be used to temporarily override the choice of primary database file.)

The Set Index To and Order boxes can be used to enter a controlling index for the database file named above, and to enter any order to use with the index files. With both these entries, as with the Database/View entry, you can press Shift-F1 and pick an entry from a list of available files in the current directory.

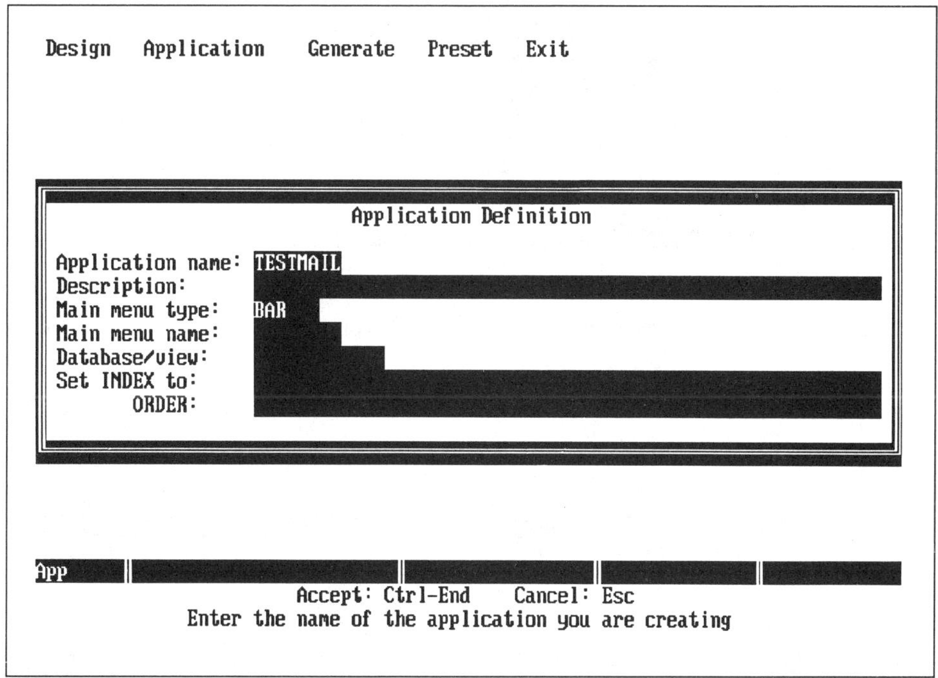

Figure 17-1 Application Definition Screen

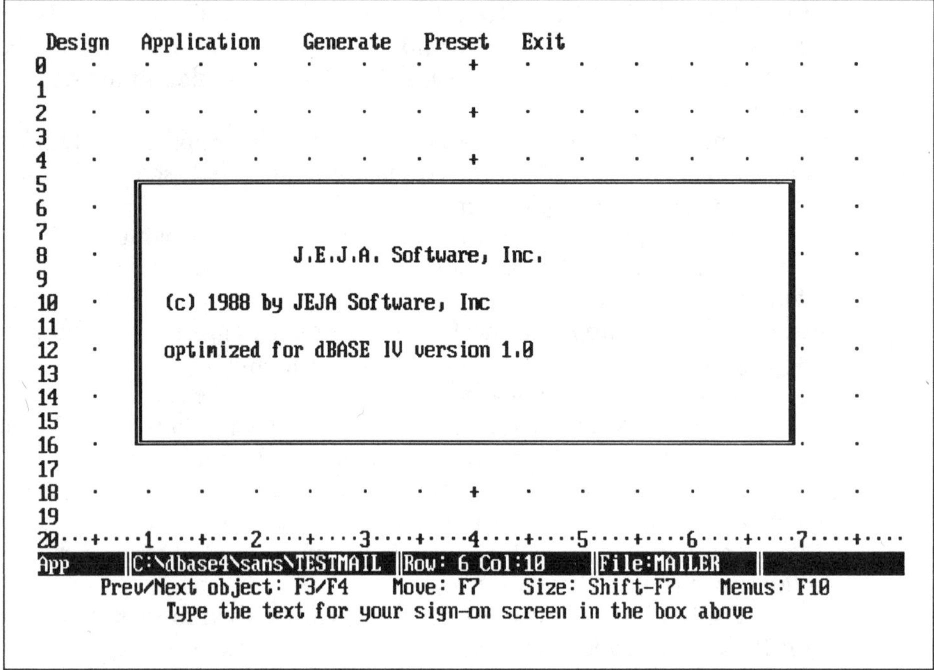

Figure 17-2 Application Object

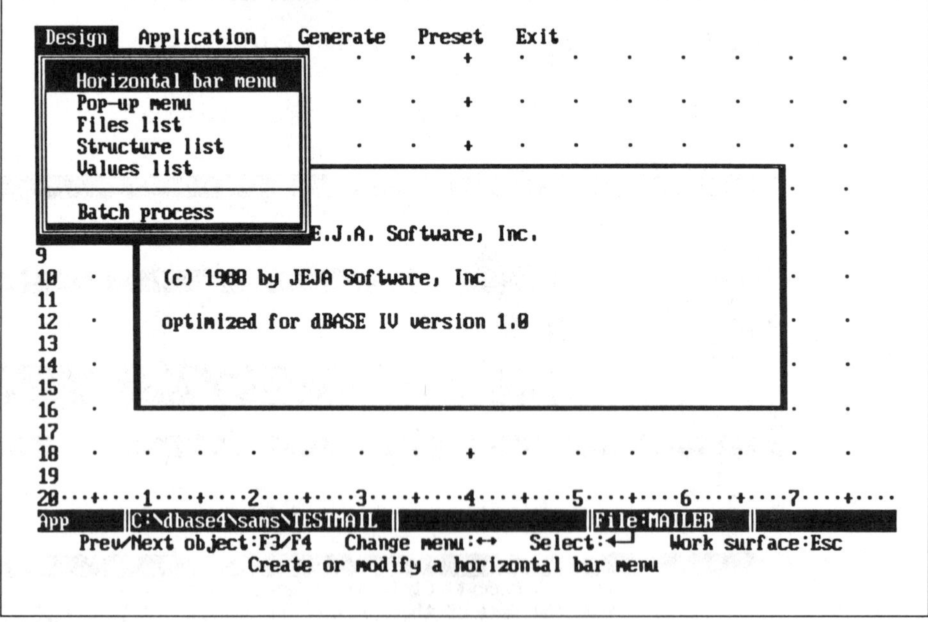

Figure 17-3 Design Menu

Once the data has been entered in the Application Definition screen and Control-End has been pressed, the Application Object appears on the screen, and the five menu options of the Applications Generator are now accessible (Figure 17-2).

The Application Object remains on the desktop as you are designing an application, although it can be moved or reduced in size. The Application Object can also serve as a sign-on banner which appears when the application starts; the text contained within the object can be replaced by any text you desire. To move the Application Object, use F7 (Move); to change its size, use Shift-F7 (Size). You can press Control-Y repeatedly to delete the standard text in the Application Object and replace it with text of your own choosing. Choosing the Display Sign-On Banner option from the Application Menu tells dBASE to use the Application Object as a sign-on banner when the application starts.

After making any desired changes to the Application Object, you are ready to begin designing your application, using the various options of the menus which appear at the top of the screen. Figure 17-3 shows the Design Menu; it is used to design objects used within the application.

Use the Horizontal Bar Menu option to create a bar menu (a menu that is laid out horizontally across the screen). The Popup Menu option creates a popup (rectangular) menu. Popup menus that you create in the Applications Generator can be combined with bar menus to form pulldown menus.

The Files List option is used to design a list of files to choose from. The Structure List option lets you tell the application to display a list of fields in the

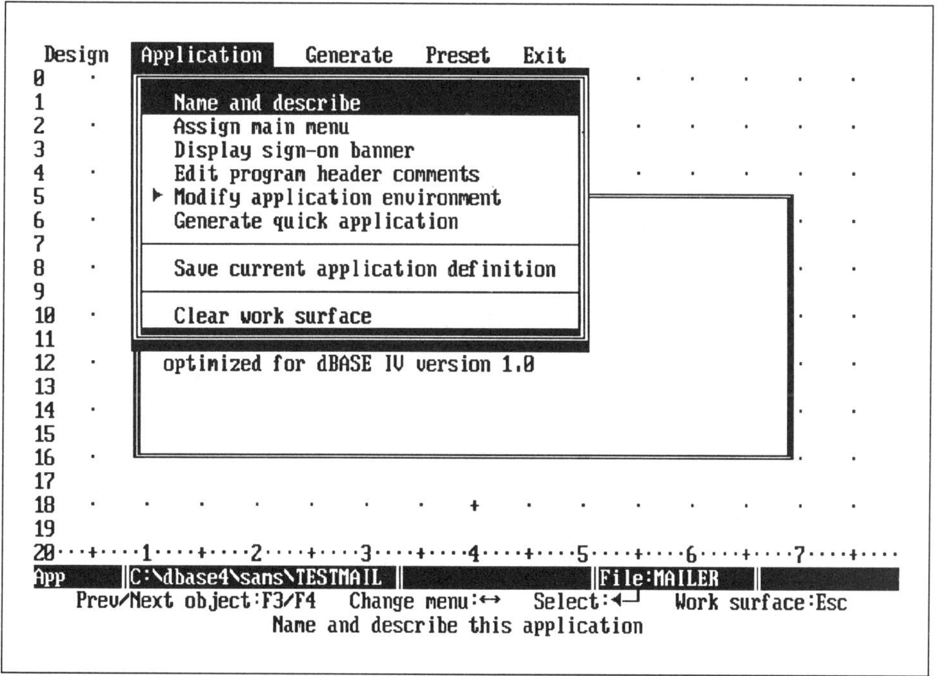

Figure 17-4 Application Menu

current database file or view. The Values List option lets you present a list of values from a specific database field. Finally, use the Batch Process option to create or modify a batch process (or, a list of actions which will be performed in sequential order).

Figure 17-4 shows the Application Menu. Use the Application Menu to specify the various attributes for your application. These attributes include options such as the use of the Application Object as a sign-on banner, and the name and description of the application.

Use the Name And Describe choice to add or edit the name and description of the application. (This is the same name and description entered when initially defining the application; these menu options just provide a way of changing them after you've left the Application Definition screen.)

Use the Assign Main Menu option to assign a menu you have designed (with the Design Menu) as the main menu of the application. When this option is selected, a two-line prompt appears on the screen. In the first line, you can press the spacebar to select one of the three menu types (bar, popup, and batch). In the second line, you enter the name of the main menu.

The Display Sign-On Banner option is used to tell the Applications Generator to display the Application Object as a sign-on banner when the application is started. Use the Edit Program Header Comments option to change the default comment which appears in the Application Object.

Choosing Modify Application Environment results in the display of another menu (Figure 17-5).

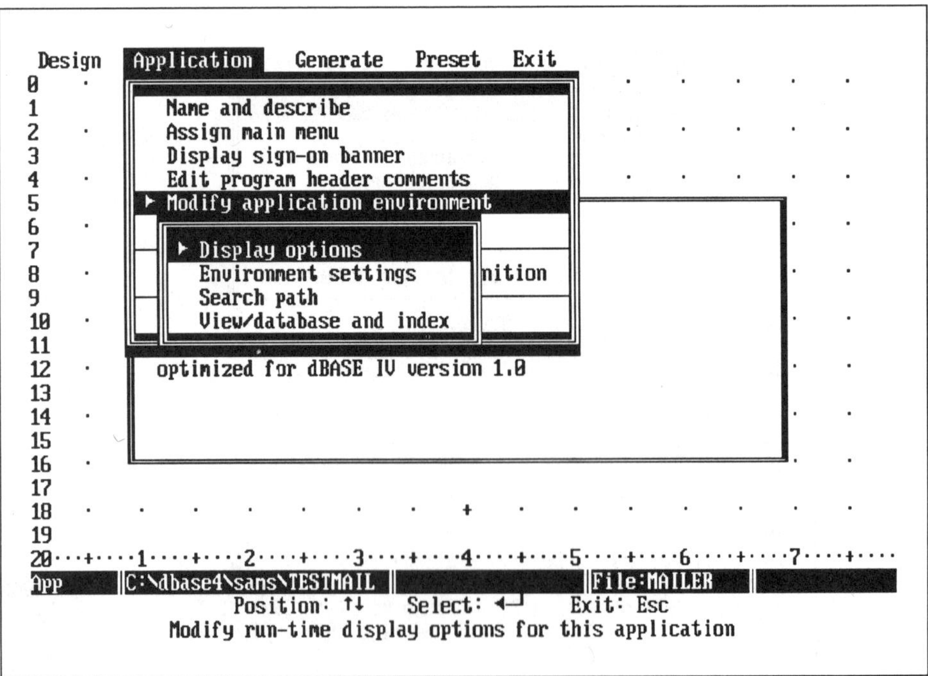

Figure 17-5 Modify Application Environment Submenu

Use the Display Options choice of this menu to change the default colors and borders used in the application. Use the Environment Settings to change environmental variables, such as whether the bell is on or off, and whether the Esc key is ignored or not. The Search Path lets you define a search path for the application, and the View Database And Index option lets you select or change the default database file or view used by the application.

The Generate Quick Application option tells the Applications Generator to generate a simple application for adding, editing, and reporting of records. When this menu option is chosen, an entry screen appears, as shown in Figure 17-6.

In the appropriate blanks, the name of the database file, report format file, screen format file, and label format file can be entered. The Set Index To and Order entries can contain data on the index files and the desired order (if any) used within the index. An optional application author and menu heading can be entered at the bottom of the screen. Once these items have been entered, Control-End is pressed, and dBASE displays a menu asking if the quick application should be generated. Choosing Yes from the menu starts the generation of the quick application.

The final two options of the Application Menu, Save Current Application Definition and Clear Work Surface, let you save an application definition and continue working, or clear the desktop and continue working with the application.

The Generate Menu, shown in Figure 17-7, contains options which affect the generation of the actual code of the application.

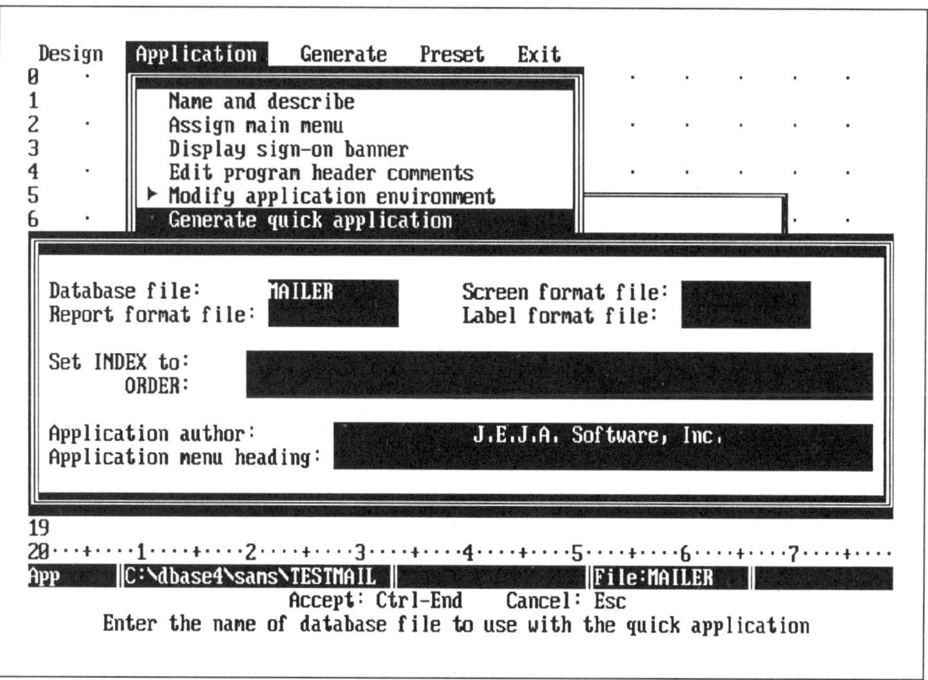

Figure 17-6 Entry Screen for Generating Quick Application

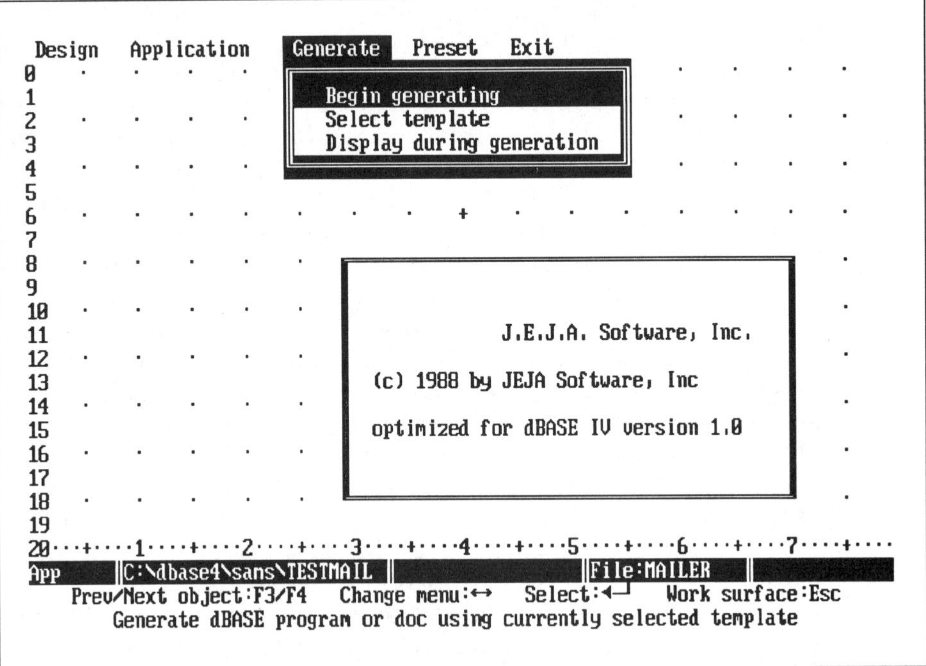

Figure 17-7 Generate Menu

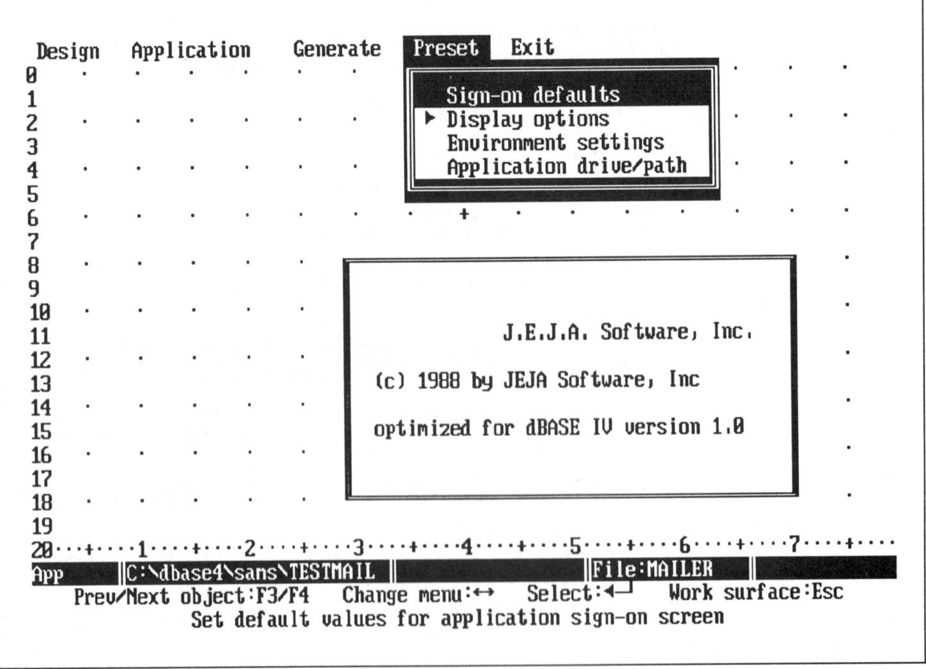

Figure 17-8 Preset Menu

Use the Begin Generating option to tell the Applications Generator to begin generating the code for the selected object. If the Application Object is selected when Begin Generating is chosen, code will be generated for an entire application, including any menus and corresponding actions you have detailed through the use of the Item Menu options. If an object other than the Application Object (such as a menu) is highlighted when you select Begin Generating, code will be generated for that specific object.

The Select Template option lets you choose a different template to be used in generating the code of the application. Three templates—DOCUMENT.GEN, MENU.GEN, and QUICKAPP.GEN—are provided with dBASE IV. The default choice is MENU.GEN unless you choose to create a quick application, in which case the Applications Generator automatically selects QUICKAPP.GEN as the template used to generate the application. If DOCUMENT.GEN is chosen, the Applications Generator generates technical documentation for the application. If you have the Developer's Release version of dBASE IV, you can modify the templates, or build templates of your own design which will control the style of applications produced by the Applications Generator. See your Developer's Release documentation for details.

The Display During Generation option causes the code to be displayed on the screen as it is generated. This can be entertaining, but it slows the process of code generation slightly.

The options in the Preset Menu, shown in Figure 17-8, let you change various system defaults, such as path names and display options.

The Sign-On Defaults choice can be used to change the default message which appears in the Application Object when you begin building a new application. The Display Options choice is used to change the border style of objects, and the standard and enhanced screen colors of text, message boxes, titles, and entry fields. The Environment Settings option is used to change various SET values, such as the bell, century display, and whether the Esc key is ignored. Finally, the Application Drive/Path option lets you change the default drive and path for the application files.

The Exit Menu is like all Exit menus within dBASE IV, with choices for saving the changes and leaving the Applications Generator, or for exiting the Applications Generator without saving any changes.

Designing the Main Menu for the Application

The nature of the Applications Generator encourages top-down design, where the main menu of an application is designed first, and secondary menu items and actions resulting from the menu choices follow the main menu design. To design your main menu, open the Design Menu, and choose Horizontal Bar Menu or Popup Menu. When you make your selection, a list box first appears, containing any menus of the chosen type (bar or popup) which already exist, along with a Create option. Select the Create option, and a dialog box appears asking for the name of the menu, an optional description, and a message line prompt (Figure 17-9).

```
Design  Application   Generate   Preset   Exit
 Horizontal bar menu
 Pop-up menu

Name:
Description:

Message line prompt:

12
13                          (c) 1988 by JEJA Software, Inc
14
15                          optimized for dBASE IV version 1.0
16
17
18
19
20···+····1····+····2····+····3····+····4····+····5····+····6····+····7····+····
App   C:\dbase4\sans\TESTMAIL                 File:MAILER
                     Accept: Ctrl-End    Cancel: Esc
                    Enter the name of this pop-up menu
```

Figure 17-9 Dialog Box for New Menu

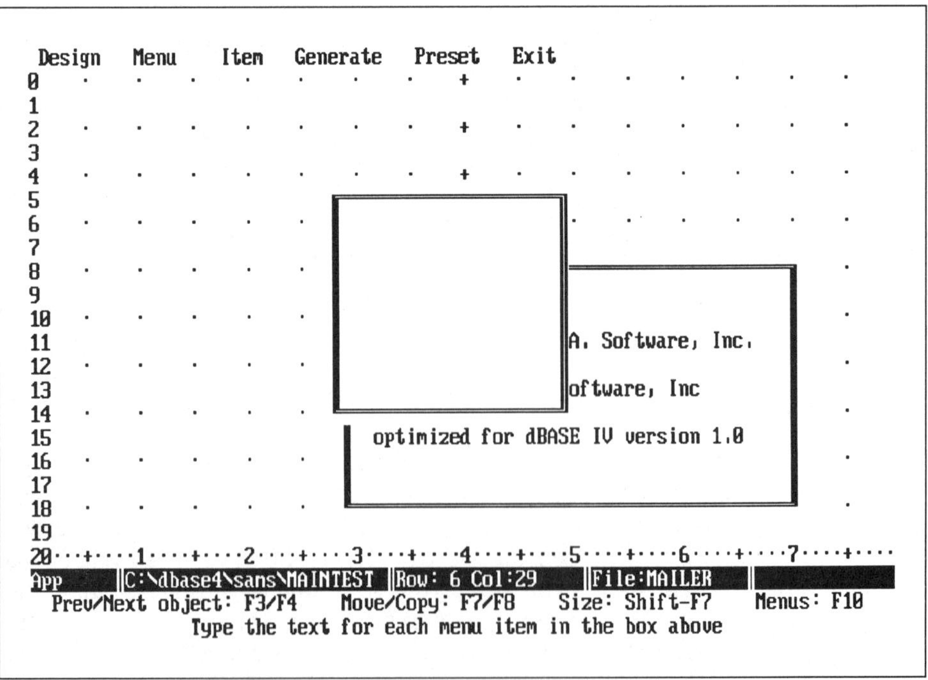

Figure 17-10 New Menu

In the Name field, you enter the name of your application's main menu. You can enter an optional description in the Description field. In the Message Line Prompt field, enter a one-line message. When the application runs, this message appears on the message line (at the bottom of the screen) whenever the main menu is visible, unless another message choice that you make for one of the menu options overrides this message.

After you enter the information described above in the dialog box and press Control-End, the new menu appears on the screen, as shown in the example in Figure 17-10. You can use the Move (F7) and Size (Shift-F7) keys to move or resize the menu. You type your desired menu options on each line of the menu; pressing Enter moves the cursor to the next line of the menu.

Once the main menu (or any other menu) is on the screen, two new menus appear at the top of the screen; the Menu Menu, and the Item Menu. The options within the Menu Menu let you change various attributes for the menu you are currently designing. The Item Menu options are used to change the attributes for the selected menu items; you use this menu to assign the actual actions performed within the application, such as a record appearing within an on-screen form when a menu choice for editing records is selected. Figure 17-11 shows the Menu Menu.

Use the Name And Describe option of the Menu Menu to change the menu name and its description. The Override Assigned Database Or View option is used if you want to use a database or view other than the default database or view whenever the menu you are designing is active. The Write Help Text option

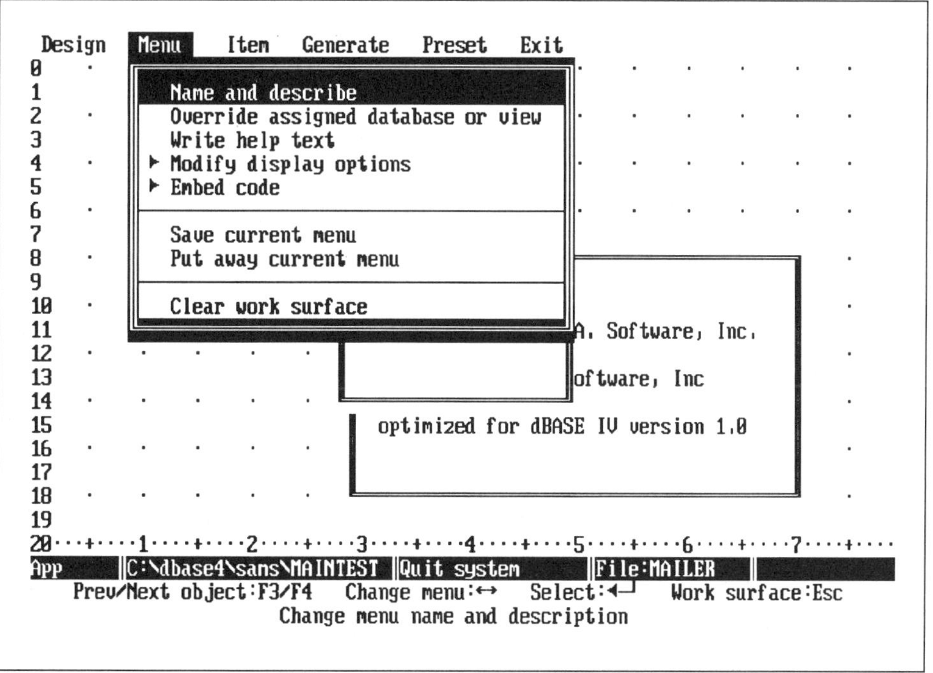

Figure 17-11 Menu Menu

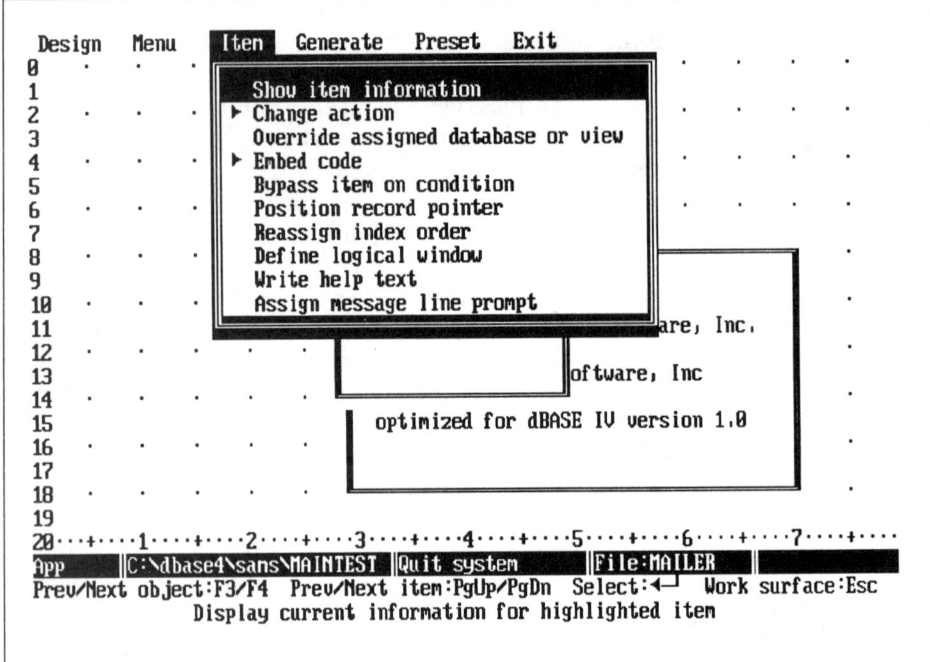

Figure 17-12 Item Menu

displays an editing window in which you can enter a full screen of help text. The help text will then be accessible when the menu is on the screen while the application is running.

Use the Modify Display Options to change the border style, or the standard or enhanced screen colors for the menu. The Embed Code option lets you add custom dBASE code of your own design; the code can be executed either before the menu appears, or after the menu is deactivated. The Save Current Menu option saves the changes to the menu while leaving the menu on the screen, while the Put Away Current Menu saves the changes and clears the menu from the screen. The Clear Work Surface option will clear the work surface, and let you continue designing the application.

Figure 17-12 shows the Item Menu, used to specify actions and attributes for the menu items. The Item Menu is of major importance when designing applications, as it is here that you control what the application does in response to the various menu choices you define.

Choosing the first option, Show Item Information, will display a dialog box containing the name of the object (menu), the item currently selected within the menu, the current database or view, any active index, and the current action to be taken when the item is selected from the menu. Figure 17-13 shows a sample dialog box which appears when Show Item Information is selected.

The Change Action option of the Item Menu is used to assign the desired action to the currently selected menu item. For example, you may have a menu

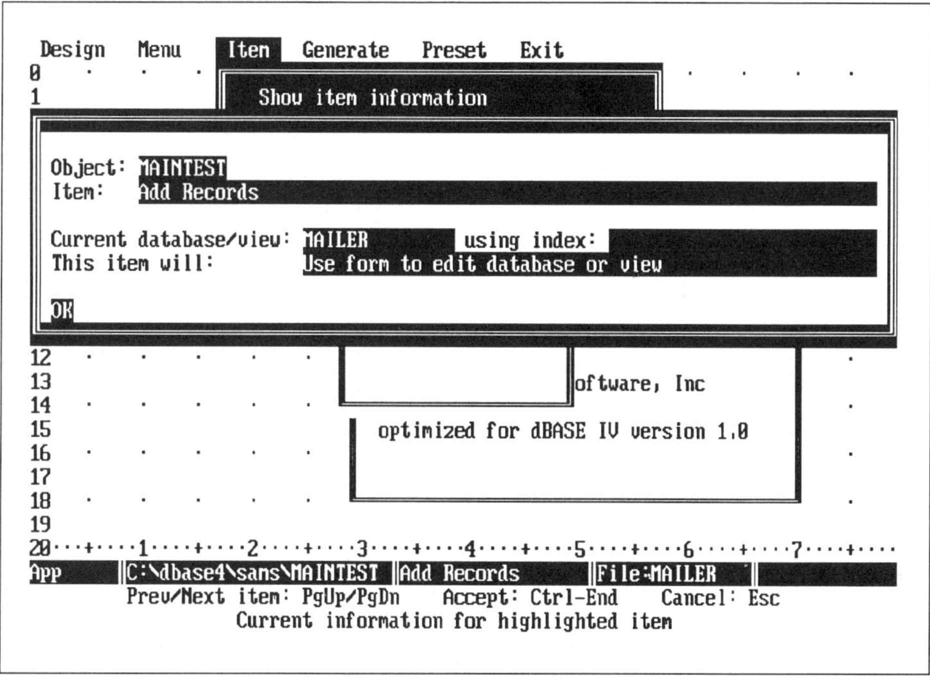

Figure 17-13 Show Item Information Dialog Box

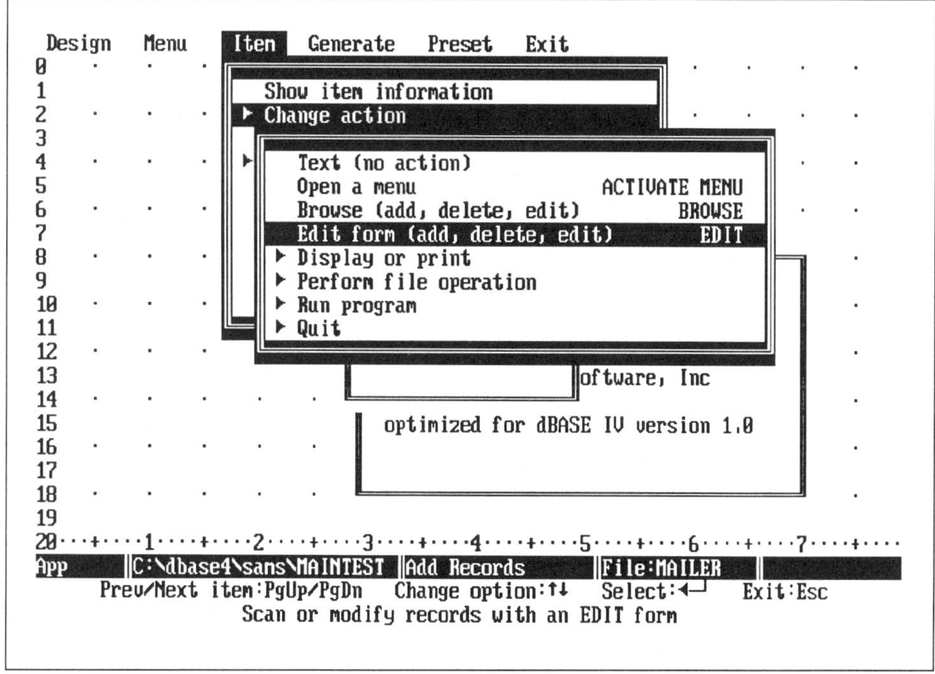

Figure 17-14 Change Action Submenu

choice defined as "Edit Records." Using Change Action, you could tell the Applications Generator to use a particular database, and enter the Browse mode whenever that menu option is chosen by the user. Selecting the Change Action option causes another menu, shown in Figure 17-14, to appear on the screen.

The first option, Text, is provided as a way of displaying user information; no action is taken by a menu choice if this option is assigned. The Open A Menu option causes the menu choice to open a secondary menu. (You must proceed to define the secondary menu and the respective actions for its choices.)

The Browse and Edit Form options are used to enter the Browse or the Edit modes, respectively. When you choose Browse, a dialog box opens with various options you can enter to control the browse process, as shown in Figure 17-15.

In the Fields entry, you can specify an optional list of fields; if you do so, only those fields will appear in the Browse display. The Filter entry may be used to specify a filter condition which will limit the records available for Browse. You can also specify a number of fields which should lock at the left side, a maximum column width, a field which should be frozen for editing, and the name of a format file whose display characteristics should apply to the Browse display. The options in the bottom half of the dialog box let you limit the user's ability to add, edit, or delete records, and control options such as compressed display and access to the Browse Menu.

If you choose Edit Form from the menu which appears when Change Action is selected, a similar dialog box appears for control of various editing options, as shown in Figure 17-16.

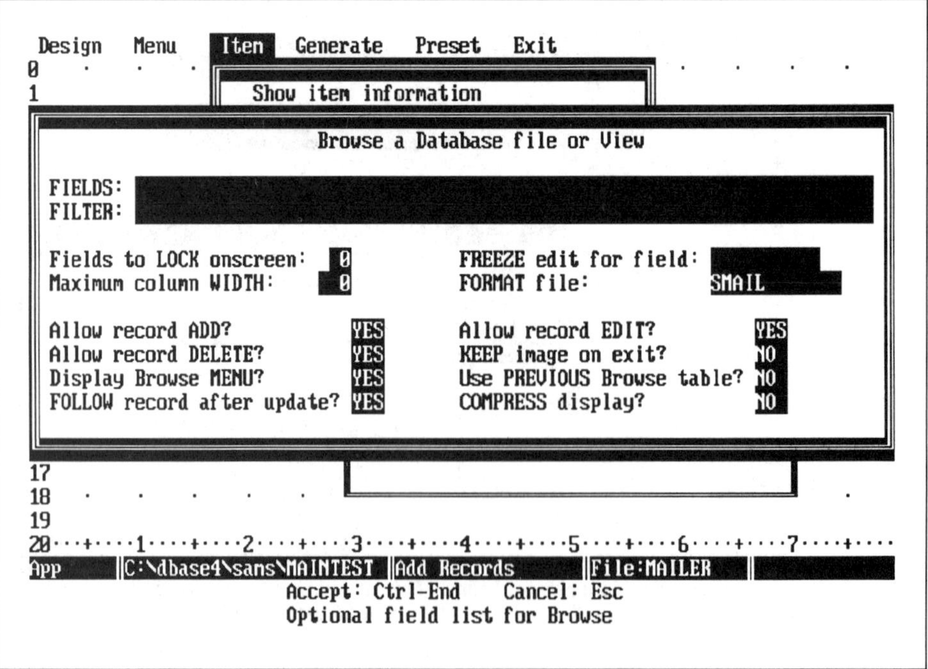

Figure 17-15 Dialog Box for Browse

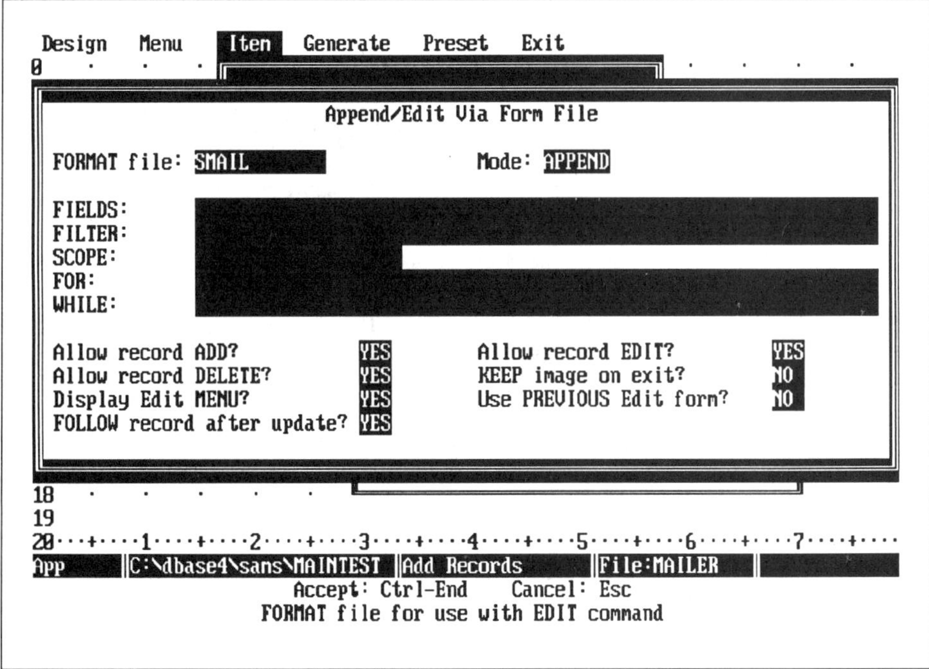

Figure 17-16 Dialog Box for Edit Form

Use the Format File entry to name a format file which should be used during the editing process. In the Mode entry, you can press the spacebar to choose between APPEND and EDIT. In the Fields entry, you can specify an optional list of fields; if you do so, only those fields will appear in the Edit display. The Filter entry may be used to specify a filter condition which will limit the records available for editing. You can further control the records available for editing by adding a scope, or a FOR or WHILE condition in the available Scope, For, and While entry fields. The options in the bottom half of the dialog box let you limit the user's ability to add, edit, or delete records, and control options such as access to the Edit Menu.

Choosing Display or Print from the Change Action submenu causes yet another menu to be displayed, with three choices: Report, Labels, or Display/List. Choosing Report lets you select a stored report form, to be used to produce a report. In a similar fashion, you can choose Labels to select a stored label form for printing of mailing labels. The Display/List option will use the DISPLAY or LIST command to list the contents of a database or view.

Choosing Perform File Operation from the Change Action submenu results in the File Operations Menu, shown in Figure 17-17, appearing on the screen.

Use the various options in this menu to perform file operations, such as global replacements, marking or unmarking records, deleting marked records, sorting or indexing, and importing or exporting files.

Choosing Run Program from the Change Action submenu reveals another menu, with choices for calling another dBASE program, executing a batch process

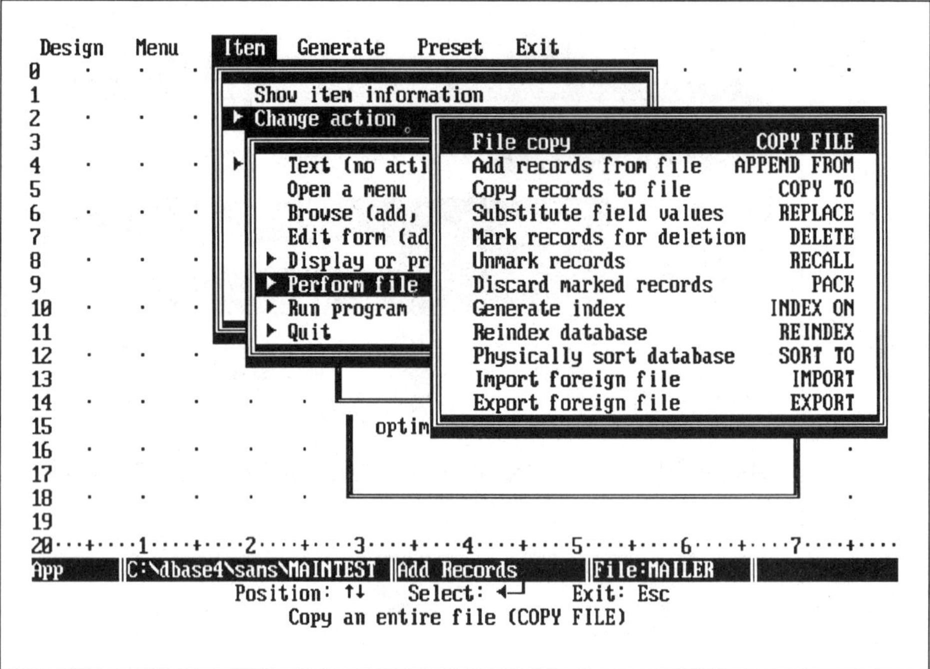

Figure 17-17 File Operations Menu

defined within the Applications Generator, inserting dBASE code, running a DOS program, running a binary program, or playing a stored macro.

The next choice on the Item Menu, Override Assigned Database or View, is used when you need a particular menu item to use a different database or view before another action is carried out. You can use this option along with a different option for the same menu item. For example, you could choose Override Assigned Database or View and name a new database file for a particular menu item, then pick Change Action, then Browse for the same menu item. When you select Override Assigned Database or View from the Item Menu, the dialog box shown in Figure 17-18 appears.

In the upper half of the dialog box appear the database or view name, index name, and index order currently assigned to the menu item. In the center field labeled "For this item you may use values," you can press the spacebar to change between one of three choices: Above, Below, or In Effect At Run Time. By changing this entry from Above to Below and then entering a new database or view name, index name, and order name in the entry boxes at the bottom half of the dialog, you cause the application to switch to that database or view, along with the corresponding index, whenever the menu choice you are defining is selected. Choosing In Effect At Run Time tells dBASE to continue to use the database or view and index that are currently active.

The Embed Code option of the Item Menu is used to add custom dBASE code of your choosing. The code will be executed either before or after the action

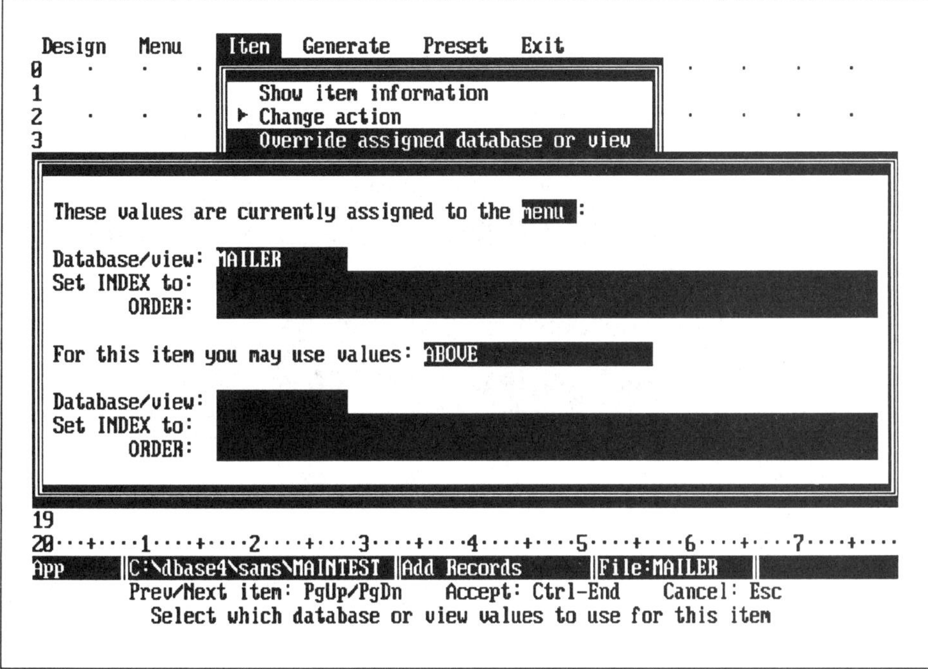

Figure 17-18 Dialog Box for Override Assigned Database Or View

assigned to the item is carried out, depending on your choice of Before or After when Embed Code is first selected. When you select the item and respond to another prompt by choosing Before or After, a full-screen editing window appears. You can enter up to 22 lines of program code which will be executed.

The Bypass Item On Condition option lets you enter a condition which, if true, will cause the menu item to be skipped.

The Position Record Pointer option is used to position the record pointer in response to a menu choice by the user. When you choose this option, the dialog box shown in Figure 17-19 appears.

You can choose to display a positioning menu at run time (and the user chooses the desired menu option when the application is running), or you can use one of the other options in the dialog box to position the record pointer. These options—Seek, Go To, Locate, For, and While—work in the same manner as they do at the dot prompt.

Use the Reassign Index Order option to change the order of the index currently in use. The Define Logical Window option is used to define a window in which the assigned action will be carried out. The Write Help Text option displays an editing window in which you can enter help text that will be accessible when the menu option is selected by the user. Finally, the Assign Message Line Prompt option lets you assign a one-line message to the menu item; this message will appear on the message line (at the bottom of the screen) whenever the menu item is highlighted within the menu.

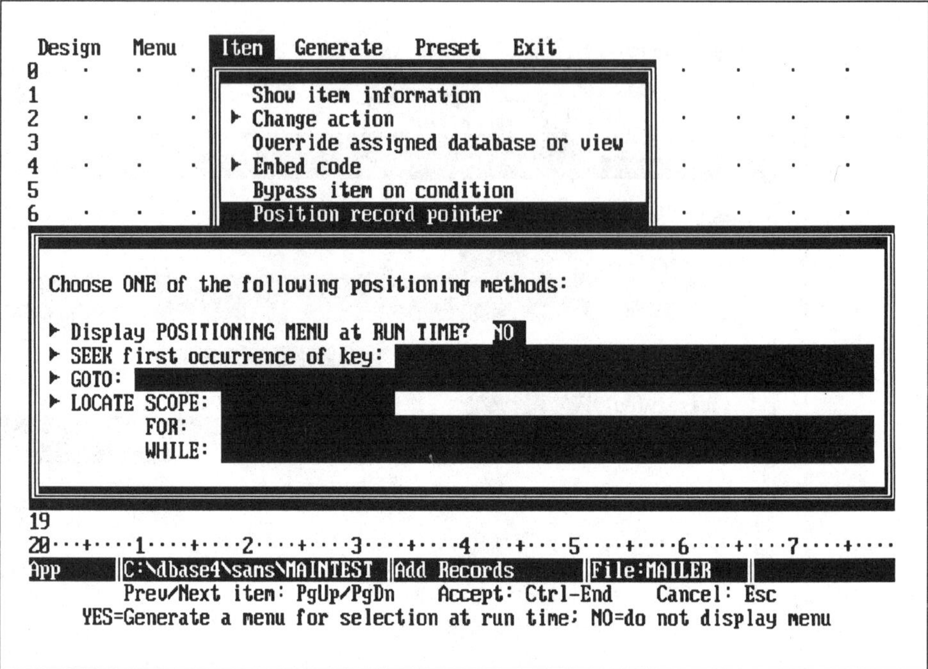

Figure 17-19 Position Record Pointer Dialog Box

The Design Process for a Sample Application

Typically, the database files, index files, reports, screen forms, and labels which will be used within an application are created before the application is defined with the Applications Generator. Once the needed objects have been designed, the Applications Generator can then be used to design the menus, and specify the menu actions which result in the code for the entire application.

Consider the mailing list database defined in Chapter 3, and assume that a simple screen form, report form, and label form all exist for that database. The screen form has been named SMAIL, the report form RMAIL, and the label form LMAIL. The database has been indexed on the last name field in the production (.MDX) index file; the index tag is called NAMES. The following steps result in a simple application, with menu options for adding records through a screen form, editing or deleting records while in a Browse mode, and printing reports or mailing labels.

After starting the Applications Generator, enter the application name, description, main menu type and name, database view, index, and order into the Application Definition screen which initially appears when a new application is defined. In this example, the completed Application Definition resembles the example shown in Figure 17-20.

Next, enter the desired sign-on text in the Application Object, and choose Display Sign-On Banner from the Application Menu, to tell the Applications

```
Design   Application   Generate   Preset   Exit

                      Application Definition

Application name: TESTAPP
Description:      Mailing list application
Main menu type:   POP-UP
Main menu name:   MAILS
Database/view:    MAILER
Set INDEX to:
         ORDER:   NAMES

App
                 Accept: Ctrl-End    Cancel: Esc
      Enter the name of the controlling index (to determine ORDER)
```

Figure 17-20 Completed Application Definition Screen

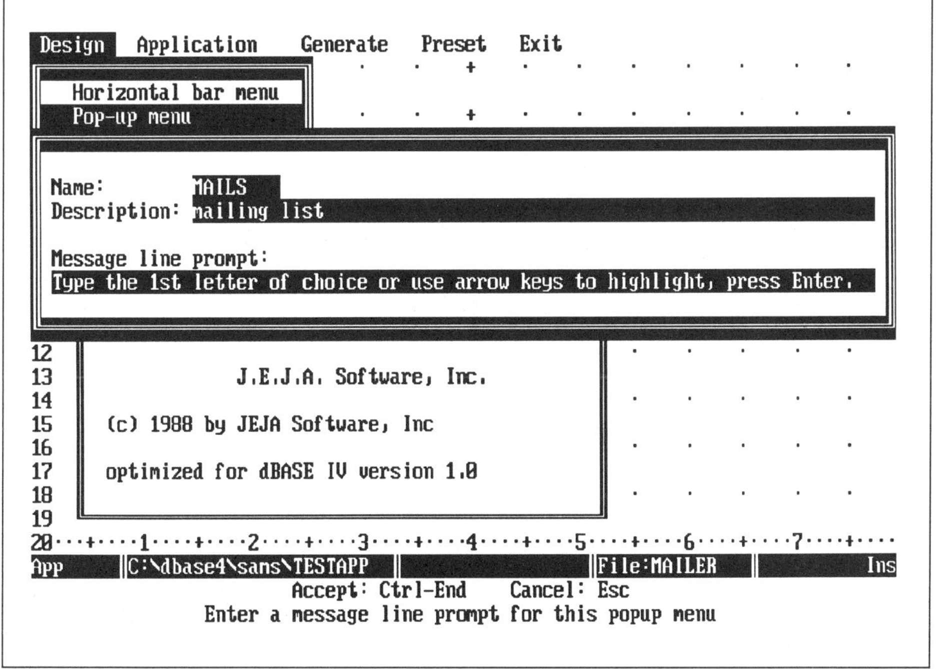

Figure 17-21 Dialog Box for New Popup Menu

Generator to display the contents of the Application Object as a sign-on banner upon program execution. With these preliminaries done, the next step is to design the main menu, and begin defining the menu actions for each of the items within the main menu.

After opening the Design Menu, select the Popup Menu option. From the List Box which next appears, choose the Create option. This causes the dialog box shown in Figure 17-21 to appear.

Next, enter the data shown in the figure into the fields of the dialog box; the main menu name is the same as was defined in the original Application Definition Screen which appeared at the start of the application. After you save the data with Control-End, the new blank menu appears. Enter the desired menu options onto the successive lines of the new menu; when complete, the menu resembles the example shown in Figure 17-22.

The first menu item, Add Records, is now highlighted within the new menu. Open the Item Menu, and choose Change Action from the menu. To enable the adding of records when this menu choice is selected, choose Edit Form from the next menu to appear; this causes the Append/Edit Dialog Box to be displayed. In this case, the desired mode is the Append mode, and the adding of records is to take place through an on-screen form (SMAIL.FMT) designed previously. As a result, the Append/Edit Dialog Box, when filled in with the desired options, resembles the example shown in Figure 17-23.

The Edit/Delete option is next highlighted at the new menu, and again, open the Item Menu and select Change Action. From the Change Action submenu

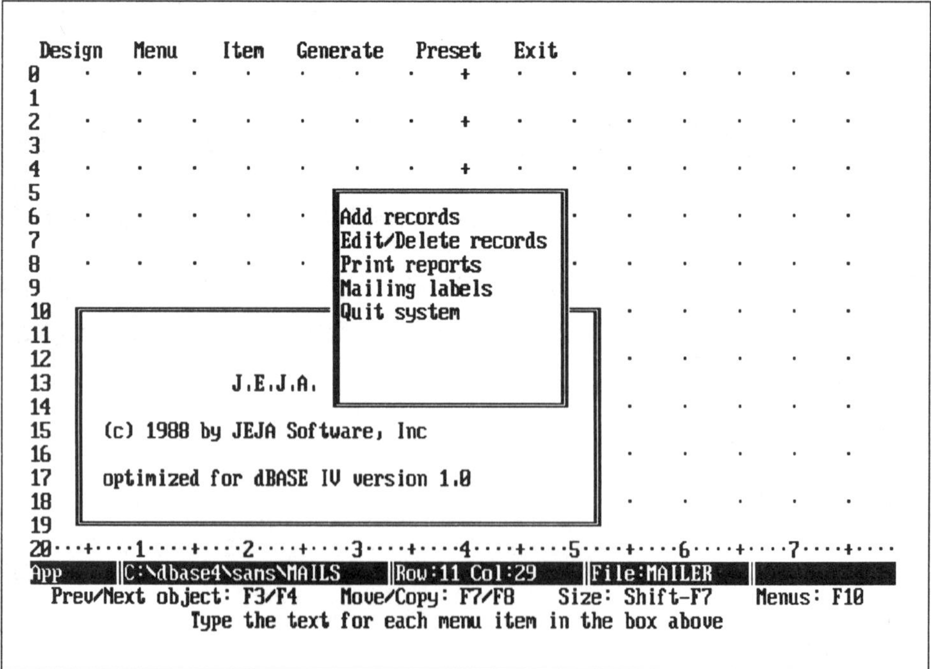

Figure 17-22 Completed Menu

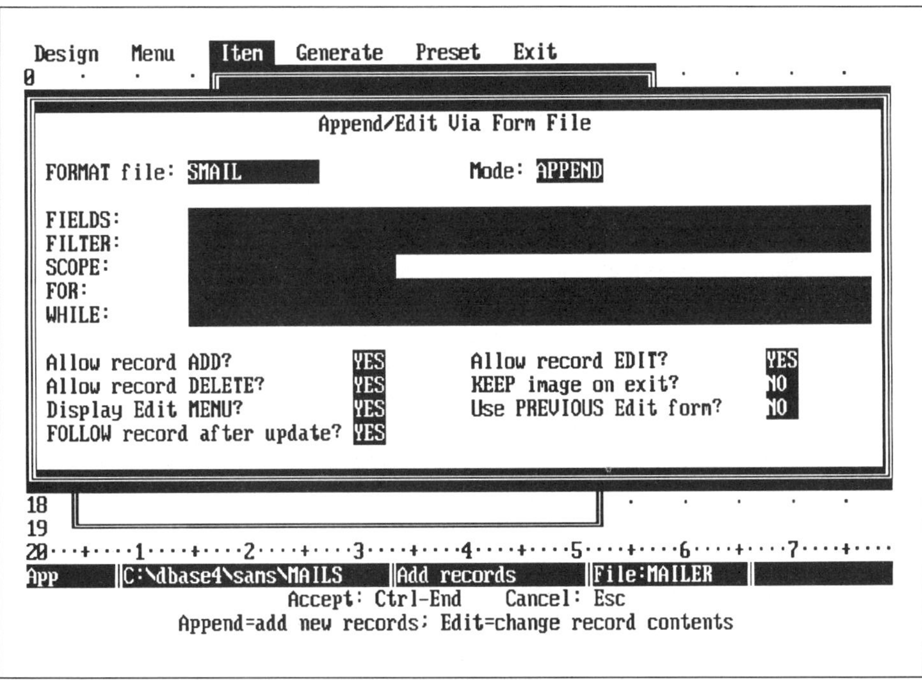

Figure 17-23 Completed Append/Edit Dialog Box

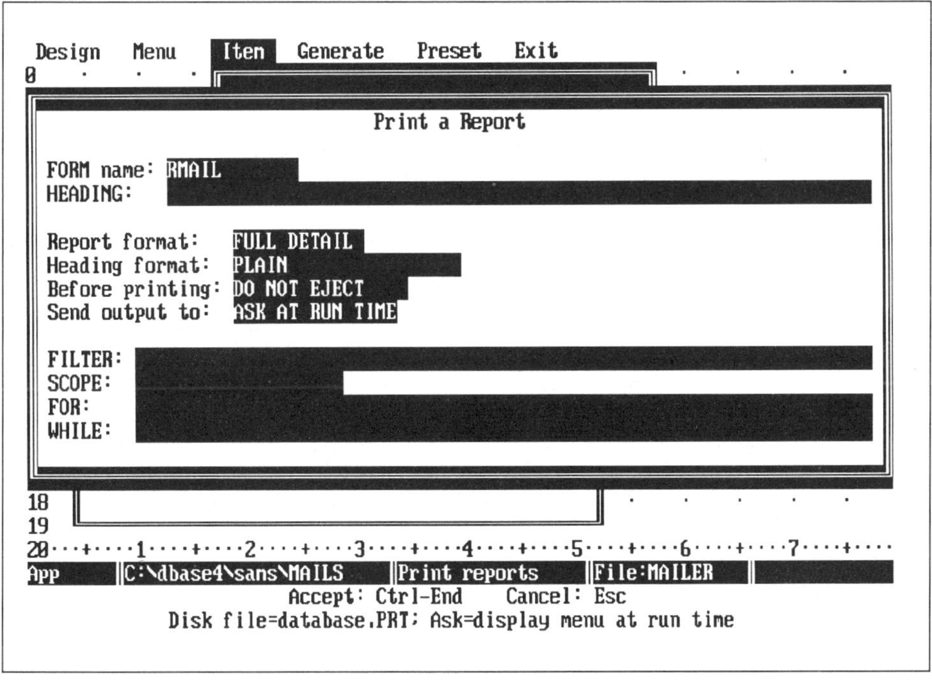

Figure 17-24 Report Form Dialog Box

which appears, choose Browse. In this case, no adding of records is to be permitted, so in the dialog box which appears after Browse is selected, set the "Allow Record ADD" option to "NO."

Next, highlight the Print Reports option at the new menu. Open the Item Menu, and select Change Action from the menu. From the submenu which next appears, choose Display Or Print, followed by Report Form. Fill in the dialog box which appears as shown in the example in Figure 17-24. Note the selection of the Ask At Run Time option (made by pressing the spacebar) in the Send Output To entry; this useful option causes a menu choice for printing a report to display a popup choice box with user options for printer, screen, or disk file.

Next, highlight the Mailing Labels option at the new menu. Open the Item Menu, and select Change Action. From the submenu which next appears, choose Display Or Print, followed by Label Form. Then fill in the dialog box which appears as shown in the example in Figure 17-25.

Finally, highlight the Quit System option within the new menu. Open the Item Menu, and select Change Action; from the submenu which appears, choose the Quit option. Then open the Menu Menu and select Put Away Current Menu. Doing so leaves only the Application Object on the screen.

To complete the application, open the Generate Menu and select Begin Generating. The Applications Generator proceeds to generate the entire application, returning to the menus when done. At that point, use the Save Changes option of the Exit Menu (or the Control-End key combination) to save the completed application, and exit the Applications Generator.

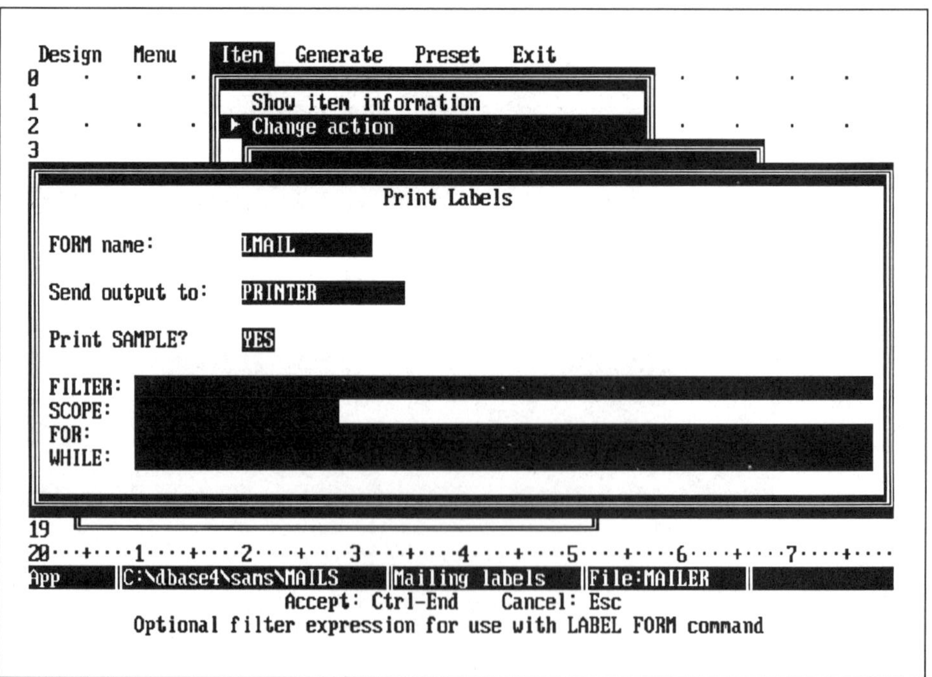

Figure 17-25 Label Form Dialog Box

Once the application is complete, a program file (with the same name as your application and a .PRG extension) contains the source code generated by the Applications Generator. The code generated by the Applications Generator is heavily proceduralized, and the final procedure will always contain the code that generates the main menu.

Using Other Common Menu Options

Many of the Applications Generator menu options (particularly those found on the Item Menu) can be used in different ways to add flexibility to the resulting application. Some common tasks you can perform when designing applications are detailed below.

Creating a Submenu of a Higher-Level Menu

Often one menu option should lead to a secondary menu containing additional choices. For example, a main menu choice for printing might need to display a secondary menu containing four print options for different reports and labels. One way to do this is to design a popup menu, then use the Item Menu to assign the popup menu name as the desired action for the menu item in the higher-level menu. First, open the Design Menu; then select Popup Menu to begin creating the secondary menu. Choose the Create option from the picklist of available menus which appears. The next dialog box to appear asks for a name and description for the new menu. In this example, PRINTER is entered as a name for the menu.

Once you have entered the menu name and any desired description and message line prompts, the new menu appears on the screen. Then enter the desired menu choices into the secondary menu, as illustrated in Figure 17-26.

Next, highlight each item in the new menu in succession, and choose Change Action from the Item Menu. From the Change Action submenu which appears, select Display Or Print, and enter an appropriate report form or label form in the dialog box for each of the desired menu choices.

Finally, you must link the new menu to the higher-level, or calling, menu. Open the Menu Menu and use the Put Away Current Menu option to put away the new secondary menu. Select the main menu as the current object. This is done by choosing Popup or Horizontal Menu from the Design Menu, and selecting the main menu by name (if it is not already on the screen), or by using the F3 or F4 key to select the main menu (if it is already on the screen). Highlight the Print choice within the main menu, since this is the choice that must call the secondary menu. Open the Item Menu and select Change Action. From the Change Action submenu, choose Open A Menu. The final step is to enter the secondary menu name and menu type in the dialog box which appears. These steps can be repeated for as many multiple menus and levels of menus as are necessary in an application.

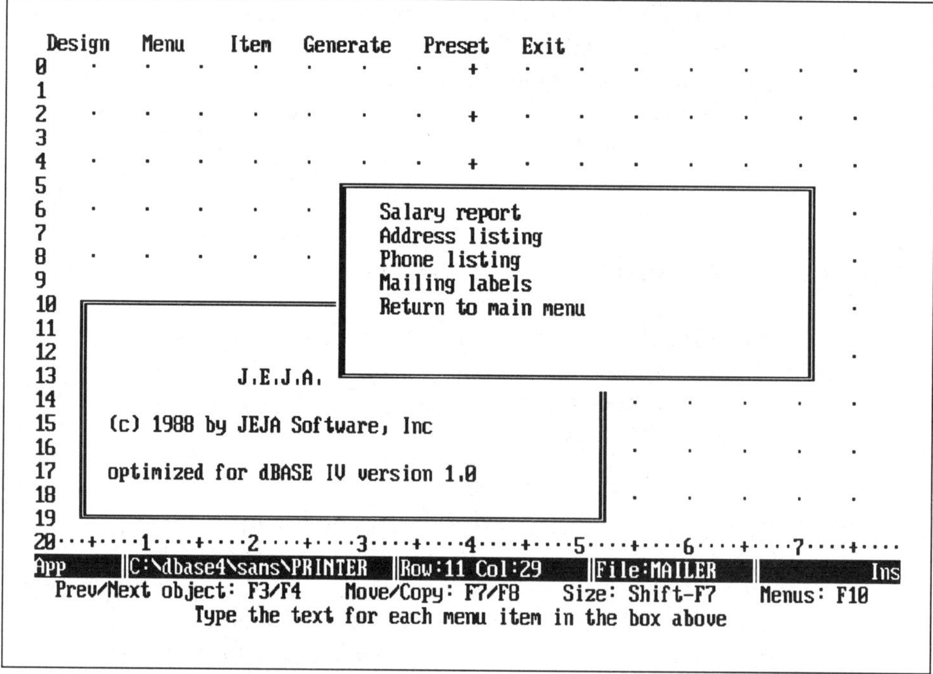

Figure 17-26 New Print Menu

Using Embedded Code to Locate a Record

The Embed Code option of the Item Menu can prove useful for adding custom routines that allow record positioning before editing data. For example, perhaps a database is indexed on a combination of last name and first name, and you want to prompt the user for an index key before displaying data in a data entry form. From the Item Menu, Change Action has already been used to define the Edit choice on the menu as Edit Form. So, when the Edit choice is made from the menu, an on-screen form appears, and the user is placed in Edit mode, with the menu bar at the top of the screen. However, in this case, you don't want the user left at the first record in the file; instead, you want to place the user directly at the desired record using program code. You could highlight your existing Edit option in the menu of the application, then open the Item Menu, and choose Embed Code. The next prompt asks whether the embedded code is to be executed before or after the assigned action. The user needs to be prompted for the desired index key before the record can be found, so Before would be the desired response to the prompt. After you make this entry, a full screen appears with room for up to 22 lines of dBASE code. In this example, a program similar to the following would suffice:

```
CLEAR
STORE SPACE(20) TO m_last, m_first
@ 5,5 SAY " Last name?" GET m_last
```

```
@ 6,5 SAY "First name?" GET m_first
READ
   Findit = m_last + m_first
SEEK Findit
IF .NOT. FOUND()
   CLEAR
   WAIT "No such record in database! Press a key."
RETURN
ENDIF
CLEAR
```

And when the application runs and the Edit option is selected from the menu, the embedded code would result in the user's being prompted for the index key before the application enters the Edit mode.

Defining Logical Windows

You can improve user interface by using windows throughout your applications built with the Applications Generator. Any action that you could define within a window with ordinary dBASE code—edit or browse operations, or lists of data—can also be enclosed in windows using menu options of the Applications Generator. To do this, simply choose Define Logical Window from the Item Menu while you are assigning the action for that particular item. When you choose Define Logical Window from the Item Menu, the dialog box shown in Figure 17-27 appears.

In the Window Name field, enter a name for the window. In the Display Border As field, you can choose Single, Double, or Panel, or you can use a border character as a custom border. You can also enter color codes for the desired colors for the window. Finally, enter the coordinates for the upper left corner and the lower right corner of the window. Once you have entered all the options, press Control-End to close the dialog box, and proceed to define the action for that item (if you haven't already done so). When the assigned action takes place as the application runs, it will occur within the window parameters you have defined.

Generating Technical Documentation

If you make use of the Applications Generator, take advantage of its ability to clearly document the design of the code. After the application has been completely designed, get into the Applications Generator and open the Generate Menu, then choose Select Template. In the dialog box that appears, enter DOCUMENT.GEN. This will tell the Applications Generator to use the Document template rather than the Menu or the Quickapp templates. Next, choose Begin Generating from the Generate Menu. The Applications Generator will proceed to generate technical documentation based on the design of your application; the documentation will be stored in a text file with the same name as your application, but with a

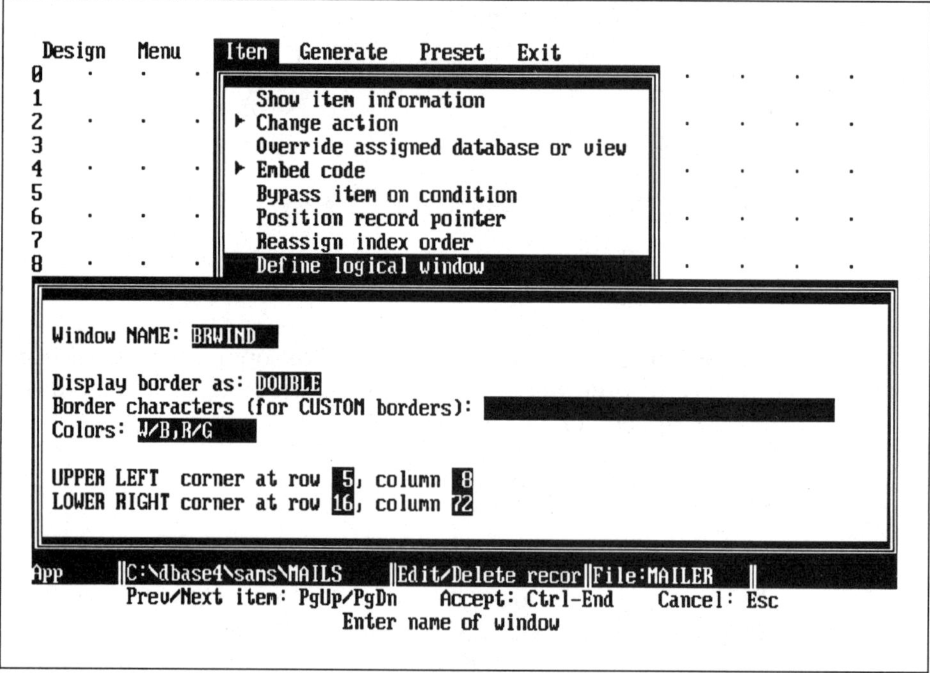

Figure 17-27 Windows Dialog Box

.DOC extension. Below is an example of technical documentation, generated by the Applications Generator for the sample application described above.

Listing 17.1: Sample Technical Documentation Produced by the Applications Generator

```
Page: 1  Date: 11-19-88

Application Documentation for System: MAILER.PRG

Application Author:              J.E.J.A. Software, Inc.
Copyright Notice..:  (c) 1988 by JEJA Software, Inc.
dBASE Version.....:  optimized for dBASE IV version 1.0


Display Application Sign-On Banner: Yes

Screen Image:
   0         10        20        30        40        50        60        70
  >....+....|....+....|....+....|....+....|....+....|....+....|....+....|....+.
00:
01:
```

```
02:
03:
04:
05:        ============================================================
06:        "                                                          "
07:        "                                                          "
08:        "              J.E.J.A. Software, Inc.                     "
09:        "                                                          "
10:        "  (c) 1988 by JEJA Software, Inc.                         "
11:        "                                                          "
12:        "  optimized for dBASE IV version 1.0                      "
13:        "                                                          "
14:        "                                                          "
15:        "                                                          "
16:        ============================================================
17:
18:
19:
20:
21:
22:
23:
24:
  >.....+....|....+....|....+....|....+....|....+....|....+....|....+..

Main Menu to Open after Sign-On: MAILS.POP

Sets for Application:
---------------------
  Bell          ON
  Carry         OFF
  Century       OFF
  Confirm       OFF
  Delimiters    OFF
  Display Size  25 lines
  Drive
  Escape        ON
  Path
  Safety        ON

Starting Colors for Application:
--------------------------------
 Color Settings:
   Text              : W+/B
   Heading           : W/B
   Highlight         : GR+/BG
```

```
Page: 2  Date: 11-19-88  2:46p

   Box            : GR+/BG
   Messages       : W+/N
   Information    : B/W
   Fields         : N/BG

Database/View: MAILER.DBF
Index Order: NAMES

===========================================================================

Menu/Picklist definitions follow:
---------------------------------


Page: 3  Date: 11-19-88

Layout Report for Popup Menu: MAILS
-----------------------------------

Screen Image:
   0         10        20        30        40        50        60        70
>....+....|....+....|....+....|....+....|....+....|....+....|....+....|....+.
00:
01:
02:
03:
04:
05:                           ======================
06:                           "Add Records          "
07:                           "Edit/Delete Records  "
08:                           "Print Reports        "
09:                           "Mailing Labels       "
10:                           "Quit System          "
11:                           "                     "
12:                           "                     "
13:                           "                     "
14:                           ======================
15:
16:
17:
18:
19:
20:
21:
22:
```

```
23:
24:
  >.....+....!....+....!....+....!....+....!....+....!....+....!....+.

Setup for MAILS follows:

------------------------


 Description: mailing list
 Message Line Prompt for Menu: Choose selection, press Enter.

Colors for Menu/Picklist:
-------------------------
 Color Settings:
   Text           : W+/B
   Heading        : W/B
   Highlight      : GR+/BG
   Box            : GR+/BG
   Messages       : W+/N
   Information    : B/W
   Fields         : N/BG

Bar actions for Menu MAILS follow:

----------------------------------
Bar: 1
 Prompt: Add Records
 Action: APPEND
 Format File: smail.fmt


 Page: 4  Date: 11-19-88  2:46p

----------------------------------------------------------------------


Bar: 2
 Prompt: Edit/Delete Records
 Action: Browse File
 Command Options:
  NOAPPEND

----------------------------------------------------------------------


Bar: 3
 Prompt: Print Reports
 Action: Run Report Form RMAIL.frm
 Command Options:
```

```
 NOEJECT
Print Mode: Ask User at Runtime

----------------------------------------------------------------------

Bar: 4
 Prompt: Mailing Labels
 Action: Run Label Form LMAIL.lbl
 Command Options:
  SAMPLE
 Print Mode: Send to Default Printer

----------------------------------------------------------------------

Bar: 5
 Prompt: Quit System
 Action: Return to calling program

---------------------------------------------------------------


End of Application Documentation
```

GENIFER

Among the more recent offerings in the area of program generators for dBASE IV is GENIFER, from Bytel Corp. of Berkeley, California. If you are serious about putting program generators to best use, GENIFER deserves close examination. GENIFER is a comprehensive program generator that supports the use of multiple database files and also supports dBASE-compatible programming environments like Clipper and Quicksilver.

GENIFER can produce code for detailed reports with up to nine levels of breakpoints, in a variety of line-oriented or column-oriented formats. Applications produced by GENIFER can validate entry data using data dictionaries, picture and range functions, or a list of acceptable values that you select. The code also uses a consistent user interface for data screens, making use of a Lotus-style menu selection for various options. And numerous sorting and filter choices are provided within the applications created by GENIFER.

Usage

Building an application using GENIFER is a three-step process. During the first step, you enter database specifications (field names and types, picture templates and ranges, aliases for multiple files, and validation criteria). The second step involves defining menus, screens, and reports. The final step is the actual generation of the program code. It takes some time to learn enough about the program to put its power to good use; there are a number of screens in GENIFER for performing various tasks involved in creating an application, and you will need to be familiar with each of the screens. However, once you are familiar with the program, you can generate complex applications in a very short period of time.

GENIFER uses your word processor to design screens, so you are not forced to learn another word processor for screen design. As a quick test of GENIFER's style of coding, a database using a file with the following fields was created, and the necessary definitions supplied to the program. The following code was produced just for the submodule for adding records (other submodules for editing records and printing reports produced equally detailed code):

Listing 17.2: Sample Code Produced by GENIFER

```
* PROGRAM: ADDIT.PRG

* Description:  Add Sales Records
* Author:       E. Jones with GENIFER 1.0
* Contains copyright (c)1986 material licensed from Bytel Corp.
* Date:         07/13/86    Time: 09:42

* MAINTENANCE OPTIONS:
  * Duplic. keys: yes
  * Modify key:   yes
  * Auto add:     yes
  * Partial key:  no
  * Comments:     yes
  * Help screens: no

PROCEDURE ADDIT

* FILES
  * Sales Records
  database1 = 'SALES'
  index_fil1 = 'SALES'

* VARIABLES
  * Key in database SALES
    custacct = 0
  * Fields in database SALES
    descript = ''
    stockno = 0
    price = 0

  * Flags
    abort_rec = .F.
    dupl_rec = .F.
```

```
    empty = .F.
    files_ok = .T.
    del_rec = .F.
    valid_rec = .T.
    show_all = .T.
    filter_on1 = .F.
    set_filter = .F.
  * Others
    key1 = 'str(m->custacct,4,0)'
    index1 = 'str(custacct,4,0)'
    null_key1 = '   0'
    comp_key1 = 'trim(str(m->custacct,4,0))'

    list1 = 'custacct,descript,stockno,price'
    pack1 = .F.
    choice = ''
    option = ''
    filter1 = ''
    scr_num = 1
    num = '1'
    max_screen = 1
    record_no = 0

* ENVIRONMENT
  set exact off
  set heading off
  set bell off
  set deleted on

* SCREEN
  do disp_scr

* OPEN FILES
  do chk_fils
  if .not. files_ok
    return
  endif
  index_str = index_fil1
  select 1
  use &database1 index &index_str
  select sales
  record_no = recno()
  * Database is empty if eof() = .T.
  empty = eof()
  if empty
    do disp_msg with 'Database empty'
```

```
    option = 'A'
  endif

* PROCESSING LOOP
  do while scr_num >= 1
    record_no = recno()
    * Preserve option if in add mode
    if .not. (option = 'A' .and. scr_num = max_screen)
      do disp_rec
      option = 'M'
    endif
    do get_optn with 'Ret/Beg/End/Next/Prev/Skip/Modify/Add/Copy/' + ;
                     'Del/List/Filt/Tally/Quit','RBENPSMACDLFTQ',option

    do case
    * Add
      case option = 'A'
        do add
    * Beginning
      case option = 'B'
        go top
    * Copy
      case option = 'C'
        do add
    * Delete
      case option = 'D'
        do delete
    * End
      case option = 'E'
        go bottom
    * Filter
      case option = 'F'
        do filter
    * List
      case option = 'L'
        do list with list&num
        show_all = .T.
        do disp_scr
        go record_no
    * Modify
      case option = 'M'
        do modify
    * Next
      case option = 'N'
        skip
        if eof()
          skip -1
```

```
          do disp_msg with 'Last record'
        endif
    * Previous
      case option = 'P'
        skip -1
        if bof()
          skip
          skip -1
          do disp_msg with 'First record'
        endif
    * Retrieve
      case option = 'R'
        do retrieve
    * Skip
      case option = 'S'
        do skip
    * Tally
      case option = 'T'
        do tally
    endcase

  * Quit
    if option = 'Q'
      scr_num = scr_num - 1
      num = str(scr_num,1)
      if scr_num <> 0
        select &num
        empty = .F.
        show_all = .T.
        do disp_scr
      endif
    endif
  enddo (while scr_num >= 1)

  if del_rec
    do pack_all
  endif
  close databases
return

* PROCEDURES (listed alphabetically)

Procedure Add
* Add a new record (if option = 'A') or copy the current
* record (if option = 'C')
  if option = 'A'
    do init_key
```

```
    do init_fld
  endif
  * The following "get record" loop can be exited either when a valid
  * record is entered (valid_rec = .T.), or when entry is aborted by
  * (1) blank key, (2) duplicate key (if not allowed), or (3) abort
  * request from the validation procedure (if called)
  abort_rec = .F.
  valid_rec = .F.
  do while .not. (valid_rec .or. abort_rec)
    do get_key
    do get_flds
    read
    comp_key = comp_key&num
    if null_key&num = &comp_key
      * Blank key
      abort_rec = .T.
    else
      do val_rec
    endif (null_key = comp_key)
  enddo (while .not. (valid_rec .or. abort_rec))
  if valid_rec
    do save_rec with .T.
  else
    * Break out of "Add" if record invalid
    if empty
      option = 'Q'
    else
      option = 'M'
      if .not. dupl_rec
        go record_no
      endif
    endif (empty)
  endif (valid_rec)
return

Procedure Chk_fils
* Set files_ok to .F. and display a message if a file is missing;
* create an index file if one does not exist
  close databases
  file_num = 1
  do while file_num <= max_screen .and. files_ok
    seq = str(file_num,1)
    if .not. file (database&seq + '.dbf')
      do disp_msg with 'File ' + database&seq + ' not found'
      files_ok = .F.
    endif
    if files_ok .and. .not. file (index_fil&seq + '.ndx')
```

```
      @ 23,00
      @ 23,00 say 'Indexing'
      db = database&seq
      ind = index_fil&seq
      use &db
      ind_key = index&seq
      index on &ind_key to &ind
      use
    endif
    file_num = file_num + 1
  enddo (while file_num <= max_screen .and. files_ok)
  @ 23,00
  @ 24,00
return

Procedure Clr_flds
* Clear screen field areas
  @  8,23 say space (30)
  @ 10,20 say space (4)
  @ 12,21 say space (6)
return

Procedure Delete
* Delete current record upon user approval
  choice = 'N'
  do get_optn with 'Delete (Y/N)','YN',choice
  if choice = 'Y'
    delete
    * Reposition to the next record
    skip
    * If last record deleted, go to beginning of database
    if eof()
      go top
    endif
    if eof() .and. filter_on&num
      * If no records left in filter, remove the filter
      filt_str = filter&num
      set filter to &filt_str
      filter_on&num = .F.
      @ 0,0 say space(9)
      go top
    endif (eof() .and. filter_on&num)
    if eof()
      * Quit if last record deleted and database becomes empty
      option = 'Q'
    endif
    del_rec = .T.
```

```
    pack&num = .T.
  endif (choice = 'Y')
return

Procedure Disp_msg
parameters message
* Display "message" + '...' at line 23; wait for entry of any key
  @ 23,00
  @ 22,79
  wait message + '...'
return

Procedure Disp_rec
* Load fields from database and display record
  do load_var
  do get_key
  do get_flds
  clear gets
  show_all = .F.
return

Procedure Disp_scr
* Display stationary part of screen
  clear
  @  3,15 say 'Add Sales Records'
  @  6,10 say 'Customer Account:'
  @  8,10 say 'Description:'
  @ 10,10 say 'Stock No.:'
  @ 12,10 say 'Unit Cost:'
  if filter_on&num
    @ 0,0 say 'FILTER ON'
  else
    @ 0,0 say space(9)
  endif
return

Procedure Filter
* Set filter on database
  choice = 'Y'
  do get_optn with 'Set Filter (Yes/No/Cancel)','YNC',choice
  if choice = 'Y'
    set_filter = .T.
    do init_key
    do init_fld
    do get_key
    do get_flds
    read
```

```
    filt_str = ''
    if m->custacct <> 0
      custacct = str(m->custacct,4,0)
      filt_str = filt_str + 'custacct = &custacct .and.'
    endif
    if '' <> trim(m->descript)
      filt_str = filt_str + 'descript = trim("&descript") .and.'
    endif
    if m->stockno <> 0
      stockno = str(m->stockno,4,0)
      filt_str = filt_str + 'stockno = &stockno .and.'
    endif
    if m->price <> 0
      price = str(m->price,6,2)
      filt_str = filt_str + 'price = &price .and.'
    endif
    if '' = trim(filt_str)
      filt_str = filter&num
      set filter to &filt_str
      filter_on&num = .F.
    else
      if '' <> trim(filter&num)
        filt_str = filter&num + '.and.' + filt_str
      endif
      filt_str = substr(filt_str,1,len(filt_str)-6)
      set filter to &filt_str
      go top
      filter_on&num = .not. eof()
      if .not. filter_on&num
        do disp_msg with 'No records match the filter'
        filt_str = filter&num
        set filter to &filt_str
        go record_no
      endif
    endif ('' = trim(filt_str))
  endif (choice = 'Y')
  if choice = 'C'
    filt_str = filter&num
    set filter to &filt_str
    filter_on&num = .F.
  endif (choice = 'C')
  if filter_on&num
    @ 0,0 say 'FILTER ON'
  else
    @ 0,0 say space(9)
  endif
```

```
  set_filter = .F.
return

Procedure Get_flds
* Get field variables
  @  8,23 get m->descript picture '@!'
  @ 10,20 get m->stockno
  @ 12,21 get m->price picture '999.99'
return

Procedure Get_key
* Get key variables
  @  6,28 get m->custacct picture '9999'
return

Procedure Get_optn
parameters message, choices, choice
* Display the string "message" on line 23; get a character
* (defaulted to "choice"), validate it against "choices", and
* return in "choice" (must be a memory variable, not literal).
* If choice = 'A' display choice without accepting it
  @ 23,00 say message + '? '
  @ 23,len(message)+3
  char = ' '
  do while .not. char $ choices
    char = choice
    @ 23,len(message) + 2 get char picture '!'
    if choice <> 'A'
      read
    else
      clear gets
    endif
  enddo (while .not. char $ choices)
  choice = char
return

Procedure Init_fld
* Clear field variables
  descript = space(30)
  stockno = 0
  price = 0.00
return

Procedure Init_key
* Clear key variables
  custacct = 1001
  if set_filter
```

```
    custacct = 0
  endif
return

Procedure List
parameters list_items
* List records beginning from current record
  do while .T.
    clear
    display off next 20 &list_items
    if eof()
      do disp_msg with 'OK'
      exit
    endif
    choice = 'Y'
    do get_optn with 'More','YN',choice
    if choice = 'N'
      exit
    endif
  enddo (while .T.)
return

Procedure Load_var
* Copy fields from database record to memory variables
  custacct = custacct
  descript = descript
  stockno = stockno
  price = price
return

Procedure Modify
* Modify current record
* The following "get record" loop is exited when either (1) a valid record
* is entered (valid_rec = .T.), or (2) entry is aborted by a duplicate
* key (when not allowed), or a request from the validation procedure
  valid_rec = .F.
  abort_rec = .F.
  do while .not. (valid_rec .or. abort_rec)
    do get_key
    do get_flds
    read
    comp_key = comp_key&num
    if null_key&num = &comp_key
      abort_rec = .T.
    else
      do val_rec
    endif (null_key = comp_key)
```

```
  enddo (while .not. (valid_rec .or. abort_rec))
  if valid_rec
    do save_rec with .F.
  else
  endif (valid_rec)
return

Procedure Pack_all
* Pack deleted records with user confirmation
  choice = 'N'
  do get_optn with 'Pack all deleted records (Y/N)','YN',choice
  if choice = 'Y'
    @ 23,00
    @ 23,00 say 'Packing, please wait'
    do while scr_num < max_screen
      scr_num = scr_num + 1
      num = str(scr_num,1)
      if pack&num
        select &num
        pack
      endif
    enddo (while scr_num < max_screen)
  endif
return

Procedure Repl_rec
* Replace database fields with memory variables
  replace custacct with m->custacct
  replace descript with m->descript
  replace stockno with m->stockno
  replace price with m->price
return

Procedure Retrieve
* Accept key and seek record; if not found reposition to record_no
  do clr_flds
  do init_key
  do get_key
  read
  comp_key = comp_key&num
  if null_key&num = &comp_key
    * Blank key
    return
  endif
  key = key&num
  seek &key
  if eof()
```

```
    do disp_msg with 'Not found'
    go record_no
  endif
return

Procedure Save_rec
parameters new_rec
* If new_rec: append record currently in memory to database;
* if .not. new_rec: replace database record record_no with memory fields
  choice = 'Y'
  do get_optn with 'Save (Y/N)','YN',choice
  if choice = 'Y'
    if new_rec
      append blank
    endif
    do repl_rec
    empty = .F.
    if filter_on&num
      * Check to see if record matches filter
      record_no = recno()
      skip
      skip -1
      if recno() <> record_no
        go top
        if eof()
          * Remove filter
          filt_str = filter&num
          set filter to &filt_str
          filter_on&num = .F.
          @ 0,10 say space(9)
          go record_no
        endif
      endif
    endif (filter_on&num)
  else
    if .not. empty
      go record_no
    endif
  endif (choice = 'Y')
return

Procedure Skip
* Move forward/backward several records
  skip_no = 0
  @ 23,70 say '  Recs' get skip_no picture '@Z 999'
  read
  skip skip_no
```

```
  if eof()
    skip -1
    do disp_rec
    do disp_msg with 'Last Record'
  endif
  if bof()
    skip
    skip -1
    do disp_rec
    do disp_msg with 'First record'
  endif
return

Procedure Tally
* Count and display number of records in database
  @ 23,00
  @ 23,00 say 'Counting, please wait'
  count to number_
  do disp_msg with 'Count: ' + str (m->number_,6) + ' records'
  go record_no
return

Procedure Val_rec
* Set valid_rec to .F. if a field doesn't pass validation test;
* set abort_rec to .T. or .F., depending on user's response
  valid_rec = .T.
  if m->custacct < 1001 .or. m->custacct > 9000
    valid_rec = .F.
    do disp_msg with chr(7) + "Invalid Customer Number!"
  endif
  if m->price < 1.00 .or. m->price > 999.99
    valid_rec = .F.
    do disp_msg with chr(7) + "Amount falls outside OK range."
  endif
  abort_rec = .F.
  if .not. valid_rec
    choice = 'Y'
    do get_optn with 'Invalid entries.  Correct (Y/N)', 'YN', choice
    if choice = 'N'
      abort_rec = .T.
    endif
  endif (.not. valid_rec)
return

* EOF ADDIT.PRG
```

An analysis of the code reveals several techniques evident in GENIFER's style of coding. The code is heavily proceduralized, and procedures are listed alphabetically to make them easier to find. Common tasks—displaying screen prompts and graphics, replacing memory variables, moving the record pointer, and performing data validation—are stored in the procedures and used repeatedly for maximum efficiency. And this code resulted from a simple example; the more complex the application, the more complex the resultant code. Test applications that used multiple files, multiple reports with complex breakpoints, and multiple methods of validating files resulted in code that spanned dozens of pages.

Limitations

On the minus side, code produced by GENIFER can be complex and therefore harder to modify, particularly for less-experienced programmers. Also, GENIFER can be quite useful if you use dBASE-compatibles like Clipper. But if you stick purely with dBASE IV, you may find the dBASE IV Applications Generator to be comparable in power and flexibility to GENIFER. And GENIFER is also fairly expensive, priced at the time of this writing at around $400.

18

dBASE IV SQL

dBASE IV provides a SQL mode of operation, under which dBASE uses commands compatible with SQL (Structured Query Language), a data management standard for mainframe computers. Release 1.0 of dBASE IV does not have the ability to directly access mainframe data through SQL commands. At the time of this writing, Release 1.1 is scheduled to support mainframe data access through the Ashton-Tate/Microsoft SQL Server. Whether you need direct access to mainframe data or not, you can take advantage of SQL compatibility by using existing SQL programs written for other SQL systems. Such programs are likely to require some level of modification before they will run in dBASE IV, because programs written in dBASE SQL are a mixture of dBASE and SQL commands.

A significant advantage of SQL for existing SQL users is added familiarity. If you are already familiar with SQL, you may prefer to write programs in the SQL mode of dBASE IV. This chapter assumes some familiarity with SQL, but for those who have not worked with SQL before, a brief overview follows.

Differences in Terminology

In dBASE, database files are used to contain sets of data. In SQL, a database is a collection of one or more tables. The tables contain the actual data used by the application. Tables are made up of rows of data, with each row containing columns of data items. The fields in dBASE are analogous to columns in SQL, and the records in dBASE are analogous to rows in SQL. SQL also utilizes views, which are virtual tables made up of selected rows and columns from one or more actual tables. As information stored in the actual tables changes, the view is updated. Finally, SQL makes use of catalogs (these are different from dBASE catalogs), which are special tables that maintain a description of the SQL database and its contents.

Entering Interactive SQL Mode

To enter SQL mode from the dot prompt, use the SET SQL ON statement. When the statement is entered, the prompt changes from a period alone to a period preceded by the letters, SQL. You can exit the interactive SQL mode by entering SET SQL OFF at the dot prompt.

Once in SQL mode, you can enter SQL statements in one of two ways. They can be entered on a single line, which can be up to 1,024 characters long. Or, you can open an editing window by pressing Control-Home. With the editing window open, you can enter SQL statements on more than one line. At the end of the statement, add a semicolon, and press Control-End to close the editing window and execute the command. All SQL statements entered in the interactive mode of SQL must end with a semicolon.

Creating Databases and Tables

The differences between native dBASE and SQL mode begin to appear at the very start of a database design project. Before creating the tables which will hold the data you must define the database with the CREATE DATABASE command. The syntax for the command is:

```
CREATE DATABASE [<path>] <database name>;
```

As with all dBASE SQL commands, the command ends in a semicolon. The <database name> is the name assigned to the database. The name must follow DOS file-naming conventions, because dBASE creates a new subdirectory by the same name. The path is optional and can include a drive identifier. As an example, the command,

```
CREATE DATABASE sales;
```

would cause dBASE to create a new DOS directory named SALES within the current directory, along with a set of SQL catalog tables which will be automatically maintained by dBASE whenever the new database is used.

Once a database exists, it must be made active before any tables can be added or manipulated within that database. To make a database the active database, use the START DATABASE command. The syntax for the command is:

```
START DATABASE <database name>;
```

and entering a command like:

```
START DATABASE sales;
```

would make the SALES database the active database. You can use the STOP DATABASE <database name> command to make an active SQL database inactive, and the SHOW DATABASE <database name> command to display a list of all SQL databases in the current directory.

Once the database has been defined and made active, tables can be created for data storage. Use the CREATE TABLE command to create new tables. The syntax for the command is:

```
CREATE TABLE <table name>
(<column name> <data type> <width>
[,<column name> <data type> <width>...]);
```

where <table name> is the name for the new table. Again, DOS file naming conventions must be followed, as dBASE creates a database file for every table you define. The <column name> is the name for each column in the table, <data type> is an acceptable data type, and <width> is the column width, in the case of CHAR, DECIMAL, FLOAT, or NUMERIC type columns. (The other types have a predefined width, so no width needs to be specified.) The column name can be any name of up to ten characters, with no spaces. The data type can be any of the types shown in Table 18-1.

As an example, you could create a SQL table for storing data on company personnel with a command like the following:

```
CREATE TABLE employed
(soc_sec CHAR(11),
last_name CHAR(15),
first_name CHAR(15),
salary DECIMAL(6,2),
exemptions SMALLINT);
```

and as with all SQL statements in dBASE IV, you can enter a statement on multiple lines by pressing Control-Home to open an editing window. After entering the statement, press Control-End to close the window.

dBASE IV provides a close match to the IBM SQL mainframe offerings, as far as valid column types are concerned. As shown in the table, dBASE provides character, decimal, floating, integer, small integer, and numeric types. dBASE IV also supports date and logical column types, with the same characteristics as date and logical fields in native dBASE. (The date and logical types are not supported by most mainframe versions of SQL.) Note that memo fields are not supported in dBASE SQL.

In SQL, you can modify the structure of an existing table with the ALTER TABLE command. The syntax of this command is:

```
ALTER TABLE <table name>
ADD (<column name> <data type> <width>
[,<column name> <data type> <width>,. . .]);
```

where <column name> is the name of the column to be added, and <data type> and <width> define the type and width of the column. Note that you cannot

Table 18-1 Acceptable dBASE SQL Data Types

Data Type	Description
CHAR(n)	Stores a character string, with the maximum length defined by (n). Character strings must be surrounded by quotes. Values can be stored as character variables, as string constants, or from character columns in other tables.
DATE	Stores a date. Dates can be stored from date variables, from character strings in date format converted with the CTOD() function, or from date columns in other tables.
DECIMAL(a,b)	Stores a number of up to (a) digits (including the sign), with (b) decimal places.
FLOAT(a,b)	Stores a floating number of up to (a) digits (including the sign and the decimal point), with (b) decimal places. Constants entered can be expressed in scientific (exponential) form.
INTEGER	Stores an integer value of up to 11 digits, including the sign. Values can range from −9,999,999,999 to 99,999,999,999.
LOGICAL	Stores a logical (true/false) value. Values can be entered as logical memory variables, or as constants .T., .t., .F., .f., .Y., .y., .N., or .n..
NUMERIC(a,b)	Stores a number of up to (a) total digits (including the sign and decimal point) with (b) decimal places. Allowable values for (a) are 1 to 20, and allowable values for (b) are 0 to 18. (b) cannot be greater than (a)−2.
SMALLINT	Stores an integer value of up to six digits, including the sign. Values can range from −99,999 to 999,999.

remove columns with this command; columns can only be added, and they are placed at the end of the existing table.

Using CREATE SYNONYM

The CREATE SYNONYM command can be used to provide an alternate name (or alias) for a table or a view. The syntax for the command is:

```
CREATE SYNONYM <synonym name> FOR <table or view name>;
```

and once the synonym has been defined, it can be used in any SQL command in place of the appropriate table or view name.

Creating Indexes

To build indexes on any columns in a SQL table, use the CREATE INDEX command. The syntax for the command is:

```
CREATE [UNIQUE] INDEX <index name> ON <table name>
(<column name> [[ASC]/DESC]
[,<column name> [[ASC]/DESC],. . .]);
```

where [UNIQUE] is an optional clause which denotes a unique index key, much like the UNIQUE clause used with the INDEX command in native dBASE; <index name> is the name for the new index; and <table name> is the name of the table containing the column(s) to index. Use [<column name> [[ASC]/DESC],. . .] to define the name of the column to build the index on, and whether it should be in ascending (ASC) or descending (DESC) order. If the order clause is omitted, the index is built in ascending order. Separate each column designation by a comma, and surround the list of columns by parentheses. As an example, you could index the table created in the earlier example on a combination of last and first names by using the following command:

```
CREATE INDEX names ON employed (last_name, first_name);
```

The contents of columns used to create the index are stored as tags in a multiple index file. When you start a database in SQL mode, dBASE automatically opens the tables and any associated indexes as necessary, and updates the indexes during all successive operations.

Using the DROP Command

Various options of the DROP command can be used to delete objects from a SQL database. The DROP TABLE <table name> command will delete an entire table from the database. The dBASE IV database file used to store information for the named table is deleted, as are all index files for that table. Also, all references to the table in the master catalog for the SQL database are purged.

The DROP INDEX <index name> command will delete an index from the database. And DROP DATABASE <database name> will delete the entire SQL database, including all tables and indexes associated with that database.

Manipulating Data

Once the table exists, SQL offers various ways to add data. The standard SQL method for insertion of rows into a table is with the INSERT command. Data can be added in an interactive mode, or data can be added from another table having the same structure as the table receiving the data.

Inserting Data

The syntax for the INSERT command is:

```
INSERT INTO <table name> [(column list)] VALUES (<values list>);
```

where <table name> is the name of the table receiving the data; [(column list)] is an optional list of columns; and (<values list>) contains the values to be inserted into the new row of the table. The column list needs to be specified only if the values in the values list do not match the order of the columns in the receiving table. As an example of the use of the INSERT command, the following statement would insert a record for an employee into the table defined earlier:

```
INSERT INTO employed
VALUES("094-56-7890","Smith","Cheryl",452.80,2);
```

or, you might have a smaller table with the same structure called TEMP, used by a data-entry operator to store data on new employees. You could append the rows of the smaller table into the larger one with a command like:

```
INSERT INTO employed SELECT FROM temp;
```

and the contents of the TEMP table would be inserted into the EMPLOYED table. In this example, the use of the SELECT command with no qualifiers results in the addition of all records in the TEMP table. You can add rows selectively by including conditions with SELECT, as shown in the examples below:

```
INSERT INTO employed SELECT FROM temp WHERE salary > 650;
```

which limits rows added to those with an amount greater than $650.00 in the SALARY column. You could make a similar qualification with commands like these:

```
INSERT INTO employed SELECT FROM temp WHERE last_name = "Smith" AND first_name = "
Lynn";
```

Note that when in the SQL mode of dBASE, it is not necessary to add periods around the AND and OR qualifiers.

Updating and Deleting Rows

The UPDATE command is used in SQL to update one or more rows of a table. The syntax for this command is:

```
UPDATE <table name>
SET <column name> = <expression>
[,<column name> = <expression>. . .]
[<WHERE condition>];
```

As an example, a command like the following might be used to update a selected row of a table:

```
UPDATE PERSONS SET SALARY = 580.55
WHERE last_name = "Smith" AND first_name = "Cheryl";
```

By broadening the scope of the optional WHERE clause, global updates can be performed on the rows of a table. An example appears in the following command:

```
UPDATE PERSONS SET SALARY = SALARY + .85
WHERE HIREDAY > {01/01/86};
```

which causes an increase in the salaries of all employees with a hire date later than 01/01/86.

Rows may be deleted with the DELETE command, which uses the following syntax:

```
DELETE FROM <table name> [WHERE <condition>];
```

and as an example, a command like the following:

```
DELETE FROM PERSONS
WHERE last_name = "Smith" AND first_name = "Cheryl";
```

would result in the deletion of the named row.

Using LOAD DATA and UNLOAD DATA

You can also load data into a SQL table with the LOAD DATA command, designed to load data from files with non-dBASE file formats. The syntax for this command is:

```
LOAD DATA FROM [path] <filename> INTO TABLE <table name>
[TYPE SDF/DIF/WKS/FW2/RPD/DBASEII/SYLK/DELIMITED
[WITH BLANK] [WITH <delimiter>]];
```

where [path] is an optional path name, <filename> is the name of the foreign file, <table name> is the name of the table receiving the data, and TYPE is one of the acceptable foreign file types. (See Chapter 16 for descriptions of the file types.) Any data is inserted at the end of the receiving table. You cannot specify conditions when loading data from a foreign file, but you can load the data into a temporary SQL table, then specify conditions while using INSERT to move rows from the temporary table into a permanent table. For example, the following command might be used to load data into the personnel table from a Lotus 1-2-3 spreadsheet named PERSONS:

```
LOAD DATA FROM c:\lotus\persons INTO TABLE employed TYPE WKS;
```

The UNLOAD DATA command performs a similar function in the reverse direction, copying data from a SQL table into a foreign file. The syntax for this command is:

```
UNLOAD DATA TO [path] <filename> FROM TABLE <table name>
[TYPE SDF/DIF/WKS/FW2/RPD/DBASEII/SYLK/DELIMITED
[WITH BLANK] [WITH <delimiter>]];
```

and the options are the same as with the LOAD DATA command.

Using SELECT to Perform Queries

A major advantage of SQL is its ability to perform complex queries using the SELECT command. Consider what may appear to be a simple example. You have two tables. One contains employee names and employee ID numbers. The other table contains a column for employee ID numbers, along with a column for week ending dates (called WEEKEND) and another column for hours worked (called HOURS). You need a list containing the name of every employee who worked during the week ending 4/2/88. The needed data resides in two tables; the table containing the hours has employee ID numbers but no corresponding names. The table containing employee names has no record of the week ending dates. To handle such a query, you need to draw a relational link between multiple tables. If you were using the native mode of dBASE IV, one way to do this in a program would resort to code like the following:

```
SELECT 1
USE EMPLOYED
INDEX ON EMPID TO PEOPLE
SELECT 2
USE TIMES
INDEX ON WEEKEND TO DATES
SET RELATION TO EMPID INTO PERSONS
SET FILTER TO WEEKEND = {04/02/88}
GO TOP
DO WHILE .NOT. EOF()
    DISPLAY A->LASTNAME, A->FIRSTNAME, HOURS, WEEKEND
SKIP
    ENDDO
```

On the other hand, you could do the same job with a single SQL statement like the following:

```
SELECT persons.lastname, persons.firstname, times.hours,
times.weekend FROM persons, times WHERE weekend = {04/02/88};
```

And all SQL SELECT commands will make use of a similar syntax. The SELECT command can be used alone or as a part of other SQL statements to retrieve, insert, update, and delete data. In its simplest form, the SELECT command uses this syntax:

```
SELECT <column names> FROM <table name>;
```

and the result is a display of all values in the columns listed, from the specified table. An asterisk can be used as a wildcard, as in the case of the example:

```
SELECT * FROM persons;
```

which would provide a listing of all columns from all rows. You can add various clauses to specify the data you desire, and in what order it should appear. Add the WHERE clause to apply selection criteria to the desired data. The syntax for the SELECT command with a WHERE clause added is:

```
SELECT <column names> FROM <table names> WHERE <condition is true>;
```

For example, the command,

```
SELECT lastname, firstname, salary FROM persons WHERE salary > 800
AND lastname = "Johnson";
```

would display all records with employees named "Johnson" who are earning more than $800 each pay period.

In SQL, data retrieval commands are structured into three distinct parts, which together comprise the SELECT statement. These are:

SELECT	lists the columns that are to be displayed (or stored in another table) as a result
FROM	names the tables providing the data
WHERE	specifies optional conditions for row selection. These conditions can apply to a single table, or to more than one table.

You can also combine the common algebraic expressions (AND, OR, and NOT) with the WHERE clause, to build complex SELECT statements. As an example, a command like the following:

```
SELECT model, cost, quantity, partno FROM hardware
WHERE ((model = "IBM" AND cost < 2800) OR
(model = "Zenith" AND cost < 2800)) ;
```

would retrieve a listing of all computers in the inventory bearing the names specified, provided the price amount is less than $2,800.

The SELECT command also offers the aggregate functions of SUM, COUNT, MINIMUM, MAXIMUM, and AVERAGE. You can structure a command like:

```
SELECT * SUM cost FROM hardware;
```

to obtain a cumulative figure representing the total of all values in the cost columns of the particular table. To find the number of employees, you could use a command like:

```
SELECT * COUNT lastname FROM persons
```

Data retrieved by SELECT normally appears in the same order as was originally entered into the table. To retrieve the data in a specific order, add the ORDER BY clause to the SELECT command. The syntax for the command then becomes:

```
SELECT <column names> FROM <table names>
WHERE <condition is true>
ORDER BY <columns to sort on>;
```

and when using the ORDER BY clause, you name the columns which will determine the sort order. For example, to sort the names in alphabetical order, you could use commands like the following example.

```
SELECT * FROM persons ORDER BY lastname, firstname;
```

If you plan to retrieve data regularly in a particular order, building an index in that order will speed data retrieval.

The Benefits of SQL Views

Using SQL commands, you can create a virtual table, that is, a table based upon certain rows and columns in existing tables. This virtual table is commonly known as a view, and it provides an effective method of retrieving data in a relational fashion. The major reason for using views is to make it easier for end users to perform relational queries. Multiple tables arranged in a relational fashion have always been difficult for novices to handle. With the capability to build views, you can define a virtual table as a part of the database. Doing so will ease the complexity of relational queries. In SQL, you define a view with the CREATE VIEW command. The command uses the following syntax:

```
CREATE VIEW <view name> <columns in the view>
AS SELECT <select statement>
FROM <table names>
WHERE <condition is true>;
```

For example, to create a relational view which combines data from two tables named SALES and STOCK, you could use a command like:

```
CREATE VIEW SOLD (saledate, price, quantity)
AS SELECT sales.saledate, stock.price, sales.quantity
FROM sales, stock
WHERE sales.stockno = stock.stockno;
```

and once the definition of the view is added to the database, the virtual table created by the view can be used for queries or reports, just as any other table can be used. The virtual table that makes up the view does not exist as a separate actual table of raw data; rather, it is constructed on demand by dBASE IV whenever a user or a program statement issues a command calling for the retrieval of relational data. The concept of a view offers a significant advantage over alternate methods of creating relational data by combining tables (as is done with the JOIN command). The big savings come in disk space, as a virtual table does not duplicate the data unnecessarily.

Using DBDEFINE

The DBDEFINE command is provided to aid in converting your non-SQL dBASE databases to use as tables in a SQL database. The command adds catalog entries in the SQL master catalog for the database files (tables) and any associated indexes. The syntax for the DBDEFINE command is:

```
DBDEFINE [<database file name>];
```

where the [<database file name>] is optional. If no filename is specified, all dBASE IV database files in the current directory will be updated for use as SQL tables in the active database. Before using the DBDEFINE command, you must first enter SQL mode, and start a database with the START DATABASE command. Then use DBDEFINE to convert the dBASE IV database files to tables in the active (SQL) database.

Using Embedded SQL

You can include SQL commands within your dBASE programs. SQL commands within programs and procedures are also referred to as the *embedded mode* of SQL. Whenever you include SQL statements in your program code, the program files must have a .PRS extension rather than the .PRG extension. When dBASE IV runs a program file with the .PRS extension, it automatically switches into SQL mode. While you are in the embedded SQL mode, you can use all the SQL commands to create databases and tables, start databases, insert data into tables, and retrieve data with SELECT statements.

In dBASE SQL programs and procedures, you use most of the same dBASE commands that are used in the native mode of dBASE to handle tasks like getting user responses, moving data between memory variables, printing reports, and building menus. What may be obvious is that many, but not all, dBASE commands can be used while in the SQL mode of operation. When dBASE enters SQL mode, either with a SET SQL ON statement, or by executing a program file with a .PRS extension, approximately 100 native dBASE commands are rendered invalid. The most obvious examples are those commands which open and close database files, and select work areas. In a set-oriented language like SQL, database files are opened automatically as needed in response to the data manipulation commands as they are entered. Any dBASE commands or functions which manipulate the record pointer, or which open files or select work areas (such as SKIP, USE, or SELECT 2) are invalid in SQL mode.

Programs will contain a mixture of native dBASE and SQL statements. Procedure files can be used in SQL mode. You can call a program file with a .PRS extension (SQL mode) from a program file with a .PRG extension (native dBASE mode), and vice versa. This lets you switch in and out of SQL mode as needed in an application.

You can include memory variables within SQL statements that use the embedded SQL commands. Memory variables are commonly used when in SQL mode to store user data in new rows, and to transfer data from existing rows in tables. You can also use memory variables to transfer data between dBASE programs written in SQL mode, and dBASE programs written in native dBASE.

Functions can also be used within SQL statements. Note, however, that you cannot use user-defined functions (UDFs) within a SQL program.

A Note About Open Work Areas and Your Programs

While you cannot manipulate work areas when in SQL mode, dBASE IV nevertheless uses work areas to manage the tables utilized by your program. Each table that you refer to in a SELECT statement requires one work area. Also, each open cursor named in the OPEN CURSOR command used for data retrieval requires a work area. Even if you switch out of SQL mode between programs, the work areas remain in use until you switch back into SQL mode and use the STOP DATABASE command. Each GROUP BY or ORDER BY clause of a SELECT statement requires an additional work area, and additional work areas may be opened for temporary files if you use BEGIN TRANSACTION and END TRANSACTION in your programs. Keep these points in mind to avoid opening so many files that you encounter an error due to the limit of ten work areas within dBASE.

Embedded Data Definition Statements

All of the SQL data definition commands described earlier in this chapter can be embedded in SQL programs. Together, they can be used to define tables and indexes, update tables, and delete unneeded objects. The data definition statements include the following:

CREATE TABLE	Creates new table
ALTER TABLE	Adds columns to a table
DROP TABLE	Deletes a table
CREATE VIEW	Creates view based on one or more tables
DROP VIEW	Deletes a view
CREATE SYNONYM	Creates alternate name for a table or view
DROP SYNONYM	Deletes a synonym
CREATE INDEX	Builds an index based on columns of a table
DROP INDEX	Deletes an index

Embedded SELECT Statements

The flexibility of the SELECT statement makes it one of the most-used commands in embedded SQL. You can use SELECT statements in programs to list data from a table or view, to transfer data between memory variables and rows of a table, to delete specific rows of a table, or to update specific columns of a row. As an example, consider the task of displaying a list, within a window, of all the employees who work in the Shipping department, with the list arranged in alphabetical order by last name. The following two examples show first how such a task could be done in native dBASE, then how the task could be done in SQL mode.

Listing 18.1: Sample Task Done in Native dBASE Code

```
DEFINE WINDOW Staffers FROM 5, 5 TO 15, 75
ACTIVATE WINDOW Staffers
USE EMPLOYED
INDEX ON LASTNAME TAG NAMES
CLEAR
DISPLAY ALL LASTNAME, FIRSTNAME, DEPARTMENT, SALARY ;
FOR DEPARTMENT = "SHIPPING"
WAIT "Press a key to continue. . ."
DEACTIVATE WINDOW
```

Listing 18.2: Sample Task Done in SQL Mode

```
DEFINE WINDOW Staffers FROM 5, 5 TO 15, 75
ACTIVATE WINDOW Staffers
CLEAR
SELECT LASTNAME, FIRSTNAME, DEPARTMENT, SALARY FROM STAFF
WHERE DEPARTMENT = "SHIPPING"
ORDER BY LASTNAME;
WAIT "Press a key to continue. . ."
DEACTIVATE WINDOW
```

As in the native mode of dBASE, you can use memory variables as part of the clauses in the SELECT statements, to select data based on the responses to user prompts. The following code is a brief example:

```
STORE 0 TO LOWSAL
STORE 20 TO HISAL
@ 5, 5 SAY "Low salary?" GET LOWSAL PICTURE "99.99"
@ 6, 5 SAY "High salary?" GET HISAL PICTURE "99.99"
READ
SELECT LASTNAME, FIRSTNAME, DEPARTMENT, SALARY FROM STAFF
WHERE SALARY >= LOWSAL AND SALARY <= HISAL;
```

Adding Rows with Embedded INSERT Commands

You can add new data to a table by using embedded INSERT commands. A common way to do this is first to initialize a series of memory variables for storage of the new data, then to use @. . .SAY. . .GET commands to prompt the user and fill in the new memory variables with the user responses. Then, use the INSERT command, and include the list of memory variables in the VALUES clause, in an order that matches the order of columns in the table. The code which follows demonstrates the use of INSERT under program control to add new rows to a table.

```
*routine for adding new rows.
DO WHILE .T.
   m_socsec = "000-00-0000"
   m_last = SPACE(20)
   m_first = SPACE(20)
   m_salary = 5.50
   m_hired = DATE()
   CLEAR
   @ 3, 5 SAY "Enter new record. Press PgDn when done."
   @ 5, 5 SAY " Soc. Sec:" GET m_socsec
   @ 6, 5 SAY " Last name:" GET m_last
   @ 7, 5 SAY "First name:" GET m_first
   @ 9, 5 SAY "  Salary:" GET m_salary
   @ 9,40 SAY "Date hired:" GET m_hired
   READ
   *check for blank entry.*
   IF m_socsec = "000-00-0000"
       RETURN
   ENDIF
   *proceed to add new row.*
   INSERT INTO PERSONS
   VALUES (m_socsec, m_last, m_first, m_salary, m_hired);
   CLEAR
   ANSWER = "N"
   @ 12, 10 SAY "Add another? Y/N:" GET ANSWER PICTURE "!"
   READ
   IF ANSWER = "N"
       RETURN
   ENDIF
ENDDO
```

Updating Tables with DECLARE, OPEN, FETCH, and CLOSE

To transfer data from rows of a SQL table to memory variables, you use the DECLARE, OPEN, FETCH, and CLOSE commands. In SQL, a "cursor" is used to return column values from chosen rows. The cursor operates on a single row at a time, and is similar in operation to the record pointer in native dBASE. The major difference between positioning the record pointer in native dBASE and using the cursor in SQL is that in SQL the cursor points at a row in a result table. The result table is a temporary table created as a result of a SELECT statement in SQL. The four commands named below are all used to control the cursor and manipulate data using the cursor.

DECLARE <cursor name> CURSOR FOR <select statement>: Used to define the cursor. The SELECT statement identifies the rows that will appear in the result table. <cursor name> is then assigned as the name of the result table.

OPEN <cursor name>: Executes the SELECT statement defined with the DECLARE command, creating the result table. The cursor is placed ahead of the first row of the result table. If the result table is empty, the cursor is placed at the end of the file.

FETCH <cursor name> INTO <memory variable list>: Moves the cursor to the next selected row of the result table, then copies the column values to the named memory variables.

CLOSE <cursor name:> Closes the cursor, releasing the work area for further use. If you later open the same cursor, the SELECT statement associated with that cursor is executed again, creating a new result table.

These SQL commands can be used to manipulate data, often for the purpose of updating rows within a table. The general sequence of events for updating tables is as follows:

```
DECLARE cursor FOR (select statement to obtain data to update)
FROM table name WHERE conditions
FOR UPDATE OF list of columns to update;
OPEN cursor;
FETCH cursor INTO (memory variables);
   (. . .dBASE commands to manipulate data. . .)
UPDATE table name
SET columns = memory variables
WHERE CURRENT OF cursor;
CLOSE cursor;
```

The key to updating a selected row of a table is the use of the UPDATE . . . WHERE CURRENT OF statement. This variant of the UPDATE command lets you update the row pointed to by the cursor. The syntax for this version of the UPDATE command is:

```
UPDATE <table name>
SET <columns to desired values>
WHERE CURRENT OF <cursor name>;
```

and the following portion of code shows an example of such use of the UPDATE command, to edit a row of a table while under program control.

```
*routine for editing rows.
CLEAR
m_socsec = "000-00-0000"
@ 5, 5 SAY "Social sec no of employee?"
@ 6, 5 GET m_socsec PICTURE "999-99-9999"
READ
    DECLARE Findit CURSOR FOR
SELECT soc_sec, last_name, first_name, salary, exemptions
FROM PERSONS
WHERE SOC_SEC = m_socsec
FOR UPDATE OF soc_sec, last_name, first_name, salary, exemptions;
OPEN Findit;
FETCH Findit INTO m_socsec, m_last, m_first, m_salary, m_exempt;
CLEAR
@ 3, 5 SAY "Edit record. Press Control-END when done."
@ 5, 5 SAY " Soc. Sec:" GET m_socsec
@ 7, 5 SAY " Last name:" GET m_last
@ 9, 5 SAY "First name:" GET m_first
@ 11,5 SAY "  Salary:" GET m_salary
@ 13,5 SAY "Exemptions:" GET m_exempt
READ
UPDATE PERSONS
SET SOC_SEC = m_socsec, LAST_NAME = m_last, FIRST_NAME = m_first,
SALARY = m_salary, EXEMPTIONS = m_exempt
WHERE CURRENT OF Findit;
CLOSE Findit;
CLEAR
RETURN
*end of program*
```

Deleting Rows

In a similar fashion, you can delete rows under program control by using the WHERE CURRENT OF clause with a DELETE command. Declare the cursor, open the cursor, and use FETCH (if necessary) to place the values in the columns into memory variables, so the values can be displayed for user verification before the row is deleted. Then use the syntax,

```
DELETE FROM <table name> WHERE CURRENT OF <cursor name>;
```

to delete the current row from the table. The program code which follows deletes a selected row in this manner.

```
*routine for deleting rows.
```

```
m_socsec = "000-00-0000"
@ 5, 5 SAY "Social sec no to delete?"
@ 6, 5 GET m_socsec PICTURE "999-99-9999"
READ
DECLARE Findit CURSOR FOR
SELECT soc_sec, last_name, first_name, salary, exemptions
FROM PERSONS
WHERE SOC_SEC = m_socsec
FOR UPDATE OF soc_sec, last_name, first_name, salary, exemptions;
OPEN Findit;
FETCH Findit INTO m_socsec, m_last, m_first, m_salary, m_exempt;
CLEAR
@ 5, 5 SAY " Soc. Sec:" + m_socsec
@ 7, 5 SAY " Last name:" + m_last
@ 9, 5 SAY "First name:" + m_first
@ 11,5 SAY "  Salary:"
@ 11,17 SAY m_salary
@ 13,5 SAY "Exemptions:"
@ 13,17 SAY m_exempt
ANSWER = "N"
@ 15, 10 SAY "DELETE this employee? Y/N:" GET ANSWER PICTURE "!"
READ
IF ANSWER = "Y"
     DELETE FROM PERSONS
     WHERE CURRENT OF Findit;
ENDIF
CLOSE Findit;
CLEAR
RETURN
*end of program*
```

Using Error-Handling Variables

Two variables which you may find useful while manipulating data within SQL are the SQLCNT and SQLCODE variables. These are special system variables, created by dBASE while it is operating in SQL mode. The SQLCNT variable will contain a numeric value which indicates the number of rows affected by the last SQL operation. The SQLCODE variable contains one of three possible values, depending on the results of the last SQL operation. The possible values of SQLCODE and their meanings are:

- 0 Successful completion of SQL command
- 1 Execution error occurred, or user had insufficient access rights to perform the operation
- 100 Operation returned no rows (no rows in the table met the specified conditions, or a FETCH was attempted beyond the last row of the result table)

In addition to these variables, you can also use the error codes returned by error conditions within your dBASE SQL programs. Error trapping routines such as the ones described in Chapter 13 can test for values provided by the errors, and appropriate responses can be taken within your program.

Reporting Needs

Simple reporting needs in SQL mode can be accomplished with a combination of the SET PRINT ON/OFF statement and the SELECT statement. Entering SET PRINT ON, followed by a SELECT statement with the appropriate clauses, results in the list of desired data being routed to the printer as well as the screen. For any reporting needs more demanding than this, you must resort to creating a report using program code, as detailed in Chapter 9. You cannot use the REPORT FORM command to produce a stored report while in SQL mode, as the REPORT FORM command is not allowed within SQL. A viable alternative is to exit the SQL mode, open the database file that contains the SQL table with a USE command, and produce a report with the REPORT FORM command.

19

Complete Database Systems

This chapter contains sample applications for tracking sales data and for managing a mailing list. The sales application centers around a transaction file, which contains records with customer ID numbers, sales rep ID numbers, product ID numbers, quantity of items sold, and dates of the sales. Three databases support the transaction file: a customer file, containing customer data; a product file, containing inventory data; and a sales rep file, containing sales rep data.

Sales Tracking System

As new sales transactions are added into the transaction file, data validation is performed using entries contained within the other files. For primary reports, the SET RELATION command is used to link the transaction file with the appropriate secondary file; then, SET FIELDS makes fields available from the linked files, and stored report formats are processed to produce reports. Secondary databases are accessed through a file maintenance menu. This menu has options for adding and editing records, and for printing simple reports containing the contents of those databases. (See the system design in Figure 19-1.) The four databases used by the sales tracking system are:

```
Structure for database: C:TRANSACT.DBF
Number of data records:       15
Date of last update   : 07/13/86
Field  Field Name  Type       Width    Dec
    1  CUSTID      Numeric        4
    2  REPID       Numeric        2
    3  PRODUCTID   Numeric        4
    4  QUANTITY    Numeric        5
    5  SALEDATE    Date           8
    6  UNITCOST    Numeric        9      2
** Total **                      33
```

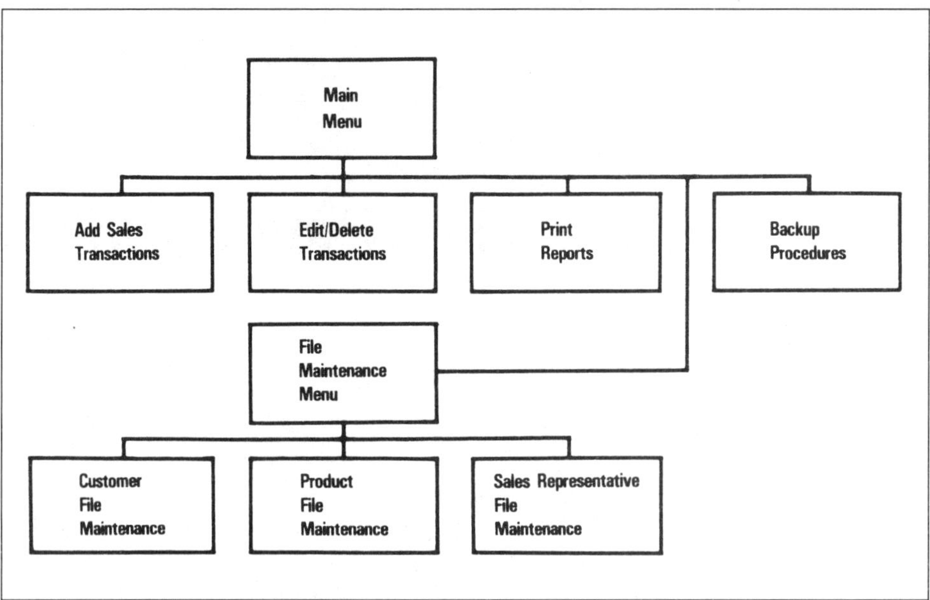

Figure 19-1 Sales Tracking System Design

```
Structure for database: C:CUSTOM.DBF
Number of data records:        5
Date of last update   : 07/12/86

Field  Field Name  Type       Width    Dec
    1  CUSTID      Numeric        4
    2  CNAME       Character     40
    3  CADDRESS    Character     40
    4  CCITY       Character     20
    5  CSTATE      Character      2
    6  CZIP        Character     10
    7  CPHONE      Character     12
** Total **                     129


Structure for database: C:PRODUCT.DBF
Number of data records:        4
Date of last update   : 07/12/86

Field  Field Name  Type       Width    Dec
    1  PRODUCTID   Numeric        4
    2  DESCRIPT    Character     40
    3  PRODCOST    Numeric        9      2
```

```
    4  SUPPLIERID  Character     30
** Total **                      84


Structure for database: C:SALESREP.DBF
Number of data records:       6
Date of last update   : 07/12/86
Field  Field Name  Type        Width    Dec
    1  REPID       Numeric         2
    2  REPL_NAME   Character      20
    3  REPF_NAME   Character      20
    4  COMMISSION  Numeric         2
** Total **                       45
```

After the programmer creates the databases, accompanying index files for each database are generated. For TRANSACT.DBF, the CUSTID field would be used as the key to create TRANSACT.NDX. The programmer would index on the REPID field to SREP.NDX and on the PRODUCTID field to PRODID.NDX.

For CUSTOM.DBF, the CUSTID field would be indexed to CUSTOM.NDX. For PRODUCT.DBF, the programmer would index on the PRODUCTID field to PRODUCT.NDX. For SALESREP.DBF, the key field for the index file would be the REPID field to SALESREP.NDX.

The programs that form the application follow:

Listing 19.1: Programs for Sales Tracking System

```
* Program..: SALES.PRG
* Author...: E. JONES, J.E. Jones Associates
* Date.....: 07/12/86
* Notes....: Main Menu calls first level of subroutines
SET SAFETY OFF
SET TALK OFF
SET BELL OFF
SET STATUS ON
SET DELETED ON
SET ESCAPE OFF
SET CONFIRM ON
ON ERROR DO PANIC WITH ERROR()

DO WHILE .T.

   * ---Display menu options, centered on the screen
   *    Draw menu border and print heading
   CLEAR
   @ 2,0 TO 15,79 DOUBLE
   @ 3,16 SAY [S A L E S   T R A N S A C T I O N   S Y S T E M]
   @ 4,1 TO 4,78 DOUBLE
```

```
* ---Display detail lines
@  7,26 SAY [1. Add Sales Transactions]
@  8,26 SAY [2. Edit/Delete Transactions]
@  9,26 SAY [3. File Maintenance]
@ 10,26 SAY [4. Print Sales Reports]
@ 11,26 SAY [5. Backup Procedures]
@ 13,26 SAY '0. EXIT'
STORE 0 TO selectnum
@ 15,33 SAY " select      "
@ 15,42 GET selectnum PICTURE "9" RANGE 0,5
READ

DO CASE
   CASE selectnum = 0
      QUIT

   CASE selectnum = 1
      DO ADDSALE
      SET CONFIRM OFF
      STORE ' ' TO wait_subst
      @ 23,0 SAY 'Press any key to continue...' GET wait_subst
      READ
      SET CONFIRM ON

   CASE selectnum = 2
      DO EDITSALE
      SET CONFIRM OFF
      STORE ' ' TO wait_subst
      CLEAR
      ? CHR(7)
      @ 12,5 SAY 'No more transactions for that customer/salesrep.'
      @ 23,0 SAY 'Press any key to continue...' GET wait_subst
      READ
      SET CONFIRM ON

   CASE selectnum = 3
      DO MAINTAIN
      SET CONFIRM OFF
      STORE ' ' TO wait_subst
      @ 23,0 SAY 'Press any key to continue...' GET wait_subst
      READ
      SET CONFIRM ON

   CASE selectnum = 4
      DO SREPORT
      SET CONFIRM OFF
      STORE ' ' TO wait_subst
```

```
         @ 23,0 SAY 'Press any key to continue...' GET wait_subst
         READ
         SET CONFIRM ON

      CASE selectnum = 5
         CLEAR
         ? "Get your formatted backup disks ready, then"
         WAIT
         RUN CD\DOS
         RUN BACKUP C:\DBASE\*.DBF A:
         RUN CD\DBASE
         SET CONFIRM OFF
         STORE ' ' TO wait_subst
         @ 23,0 SAY 'Press any key to continue...' GET wait_subst
         READ
         SET CONFIRM ON
ENDCASE

ENDDO
RETURN
*End of SALES.PRG


* Program..: ADDSALE.PRG adds new sales transactions
* Date.....: 07/12/86
* Notes....: **
SET BELL OFF
SET TALK OFF
STORE .F. TO INVALID
*Query user for customer, salesrep, product numbers
CLEAR
STORE 9999 TO MCUSTID
STORE 99 TO MREPID
STORE 9999 TO MPRODID
@2,20 TO 8,60
@3,25 SAY "Enter Customer Number:  " GET MCUSTID
@4,25 SAY "Enter Sales Rep Number: " GET MREPID
@5,25 SAY "Enter Product Number:   " GET MPRODID
@7,27 SAY "(press RETURN 3 times to exit)"
READ
IF MCUSTID = 9999 .AND. MREPID = 99 .AND. MPRODID = 9999
   CLEAR
   RETURN
ENDIF
*Validate customer, salesrep, product numbers
CLEAR
@ 5,5 SAY "Verifying data...please wait..."
```

```
USE PRODUCT INDEX PRODUCT
SEEK MPRODID
IF EOF()
    CLOSE DATABASES
    STORE .T. TO INVALID
    CLEAR
    ? CHR(7)
    @ 7,5 SAY "Invalid Product Number!"
ENDIF
*Store other display info to memvars
IF .NOT. INVALID
    STORE DESCRIPT TO MDescrip
    STORE PRODCOST TO MCost
ENDIF
USE CUSTOM INDEX CUSTOM
SEEK MCUSTID
IF EOF()
    CLOSE DATABASES
    STORE .T. TO INVALID
    CLEAR
    ? CHR(7)
    @ 8,5 SAY "Invalid Customer Number!"
ENDIF
*Store other display info to memvars
IF .NOT. INVALID
    STORE CNAME TO MCustname
    USE SALESREP INDEX SALESREP
ENDIF
USE SALESREP INDEX SALESREP
SEEK MREPID
IF EOF()
    CLOSE DATABASES
    STORE .T. TO INVALID
    CLEAR
    ? CHR(7)
    @ 9,5 SAY "Invalid Sales Rep Number!"
ENDIF
*Store other display info to memvars
IF .NOT. INVALID
    STORE REPL_NAME TO MSalesrep
    STORE COMMISSION TO MSalescomm
ENDIF
IF INVALID
    *Nice place to add ways to list the valid codes
    @ 10,5 SAY "Use File Maintenance for list of valid numbers."
    RETURN
ENDIF
```

```
*Valid numbers, so...
CLOSE DATABASES
STORE DATE() TO MSALEDATE
STORE 0 TO MQUANTITY
CLEAR
@  1,  1  TO 18, 79 DOUBLE
@  2, 30  SAY "SALES TRANSACTION FILE"
@  4, 27  SAY "New Transaction Entry Screen"
@  7, 2   SAY "Customer Number: "
@  7, 22  SAY MCUSTID PICTURE "9999"
@  7, 28  SAY "Customer: "
@  7, 38  SAY MCustname
@  9, 2   SAY "Product Number:"
@  9, 21  SAY  MPRODID PICTURE "9999"
@  9, 28  SAY "Product Cost: "
@  9, 44  SAY  MCost PICTURE "99,999.99"
@ 10, 2   SAY "Product Description: "
@ 10, 23  SAY  MDescrip
@ 12, 9   SAY "Sales Rep:"
@ 12, 20  SAY  MREPID PICTURE "9999"
@ 12, 28  SAY  "Sales Rep Name:"
@ 12, 44  SAY  MSalesrep
@ 14, 9   SAY "Quantity Sold:"
@ 14, 23  GET  MQUANTITY PICTURE "99999"
@ 16,  9  SAY "Date of Sale:"
@ 16, 23  GET  MSALEDATE
READ
USE TRANSACT INDEX TRANSACT, SREP, PRODID
*Test for no data entry before adding record
IF MQUANTITY <> 0
    APPEND BLANK
    REPLACE CUSTID with MCUSTID, REPID with MREPID
    REPLACE PRODUCTID with MPRODID, SALEDATE with MSALEDATE
    REPLACE QUANTITY with MQUANTITY, UNITCOST with MCOST
ENDIF
CLOSE DATABASES
RETURN
*End of subroutine
```

```
* Program..: EDITSALE.PRG edits records in transaction files
* Date.....: 07/12/86
* Notes....: **
SET BELL OFF
SET TALK OFF
STORE .F. TO INVALID
*Query user for customer, salesrep numbers
```

```
CLEAR
STORE 9999 TO MCUSTID
STORE 99 TO MREPID
@2,20 TO 7,60
@3,25 SAY "Enter Customer Number:  " GET MCUSTID
@4,25 SAY "Enter Sales Rep Number: " GET MREPID
@6,27 SAY "(press RETURN 2 times to exit)"
READ
IF MCUSTID = 9999 .AND. MREPID = 99
    CLEAR
    RETURN
ENDIF
*Validate customer, salesrep numbers
CLEAR
@ 5,5 SAY "Verifying data...please wait..."
USE CUSTOM INDEX CUSTOM
SEEK MCUSTID
IF EOF()
    CLOSE DATABASES
    STORE .T. TO INVALID
    CLEAR
    ? CHR(7)
    @ 8,5 SAY "Invalid Customer Number!"
    WAIT
ENDIF
*Store other display info to memvars
IF .NOT. INVALID
    STORE CNAME TO MCustname
ENDIF
USE SALESREP INDEX SALESREP
SEEK MREPID
IF EOF()
    CLOSE DATABASES
    STORE .T. TO INVALID
    CLEAR
    ? CHR(7)
    @ 9,5 SAY "Invalid Sales Rep Number!"
ENDIF
*Store other display info to memvars
IF .NOT. INVALID
    STORE REPL_NAME TO MSalesrep
    STORE COMMISSION TO MSalescomm
ENDIF
IF INVALID
    *Nice place to add ways to list the valid codes
    @ 10,5 SAY "Use File Maintenance for list of valid numbers."
    WAIT
```

```
    RETURN
ENDIF
*Valid numbers, so...
USE TRANSACT INDEX TRANSACT, SREP, PRODID
SET FILTER TO REPID = MREPID
SEEK MCUSTID
DO WHILE CUSTID = MCUSTID
    STORE "N" TO ANS
    CLEAR
    STORE PRODUCTID TO MPROD
    STORE QUANTITY TO MQUANTITY
    STORE SALEDATE TO MSALEDATE
    STORE UNITCOST TO MCOST
    @  1,  1  TO 20, 79 DOUBLE
    @  2, 30  SAY "SALES TRANSACTION FILE"
    @  3, 30  SAY "Edit Transaction Screen"
    @  5, 20  SAY "Use PgDn key to see next record for this category."
    @  7, 2   SAY "Customer Number: "
    @  7, 22  SAY MCUSTID PICTURE "9999"
    @  7, 28  SAY "Customer: "
    @  7, 38  SAY MCustname
    @  9, 2   SAY "Product Number:"
    @  9, 21  SAY  PRODUCTID PICTURE "9999"
    @  9, 28  SAY "Unit Sale Cost: "
    @  9, 44  SAY  MCOST PICTURE "99,999.99"
    @ 12,  9  SAY "Sales Rep:"
    @ 12, 20  SAY  MREPID PICTURE "9999"
    @ 12, 28  SAY  "Sales Rep Name:"
    @ 12, 44  SAY  MSalesrep
    @ 14, 9   SAY "Quantity Sold:"
    @ 14, 23  GET  MQUANTITY PICTURE "99999"
    @ 14, 35  SAY "Enter ZERO to VOID this record!"
    @ 16,  9  SAY "Date of Sale:"
    @ 16, 23  GET  MSALEDATE
    @ 18, 10  SAY "To maintain validity of data, only DATE and QUANTITY fields"
    @ 19, 10  SAY "can be changed.  Delete & re-enter record for other changes."
    READ
    *Test for instruction to delete
    IF MQUANTITY = 0
        DELETE
        CLOSE DATABASES
        RETURN
    ENDIF
    REPLACE SALEDATE with MSALEDATE
    REPLACE QUANTITY with MQUANTITY
    SKIP
ENDDO
```

```
**
CLOSE DATABASES
RETURN
*End of EDITSALE.PRG


* Program..: SREPORT.PRG
* Date.....: 07/15/86
* Notes....: Calls report programs

DO WHILE .T.

    * ----Display menu options, centered on the screen
    *    Draw menu border and print heading
    CLEAR
    @ 2,0 TO 14,79 DOUBLE
    @ 3,28 SAY [S A L E S   R E P O R T S]
    @ 4,1 TO 4,78 DOUBLE
    * ---Display detail lines
    @  7,26 SAY [1. Print Customer Activity Report]
    @  8,26 SAY [2. Print Sales Rep Activity Report]
    @ 12,26 SAY '0. Return to Main Menu'
    STORE 0 TO selectnum
    @ 14,33 SAY " select     "
    @ 14,42 GET selectnum PICTURE "9" RANGE 0,2
    READ

    DO CASE
       CASE selectnum = 0
          SET BELL ON
          CLEAR ALL
          RETURN

       CASE selectnum = 1
          DO REPORT1
          STORE ' ' TO wait_subst
          @ 23,0 SAY 'Press any key to continue...' GET wait_subst
          READ

       CASE selectnum = 2
          DO REPORT2
          STORE ' ' TO wait_subst
          @ 23,0 SAY 'Press any key to continue...' GET wait_subst
         READ

    ENDCASE
```

```
ENDDO T
RETURN
* End of SREPORT.PRG


* Program..: REPORT1.PRG
* Date.....: 07/12/86
* Notes....: Prints relational report of customer transactions
SELECT 2
USE CUSTOM INDEX CUSTOM ALIAS CS
SELECT 1
USE TRANSACT INDEX TRANSACT
SET RELATION TO CUSTID INTO CS
SET FIELDS TO CUSTID, REPID, UNITCOST, PRODUCTID, QUANTITY
SET FIELDS TO SALEDATE, CS->CNAME, CS->CCITY, CS->CSTATE
SET FIELDS ON
CLEAR
ACCEPT "(S)creen or (P)rinter? " TO ANS
IF UPPER(ANS) = "P"
   REPORT FORM CUSTOM TO PRINT
ELSE
   REPORT FORM CUSTOM
ENDIF
CLOSE DATABASES
RETURN
* End of REPORT1.PRG


* Program..: REPORT2.PRG
* Date.....: 07/15/86
* Notes....: Prints relational report by sales rep.
SELECT 2
USE TRANSACT INDEX SREP ALIAS TR
SELECT 1
USE SALESREP INDEX SALESREP
SET RELATION TO REPID INTO TR
SET FIELDS TO REPID, REPL_NAME, REPF_NAME, COMMISSION
SET FIELDS TO TR->CUSTID, TR->PRODUCTID, TR->QUANTITY, TR->UNITCOST
SET FIELDS ON
CLEAR
ACCEPT "(S)creen or (P)rinter? " TO ANS
IF UPPER(ANS) = "P"
   REPORT FORM SALESREP TO PRINT
ELSE
   REPORT FORM SALESREP
ENDIF
CLOSE DATABASES
```

```
RETURN
* End of REPORT2.PRG


* Program..: MAINTAIN.PRG
* Date.....: 07/12/86
* Notes....: Calls file maintenance programs

DO WHILE .T.

    * ---Display menu options, centered on the screen
    *    Draw menu border and print heading
    CLEAR
    @ 2,0 TO 14,79 DOUBLE
    @ 3,24 SAY [F I L E   M A I N T E N A N C E]
    @ 4,1 TO 4,78 DOUBLE
    * ---Display detail lines
    @  7,26 SAY [1. Maintain Customer Files]
    @  8,26 SAY [2. Maintain Product Files]
    @  9,26 SAY [3. Maintain Sales Rep Files]
    @ 12,26 SAY '0. Return to Main Menu'
    STORE 0 TO selectnum
    @ 14,33 SAY " select     "
    @ 14,42 GET selectnum PICTURE "9" RANGE 0,3
    READ

    DO CASE
       CASE selectnum = 0
          SET BELL ON
          CLEAR ALL
          RETURN

       CASE selectnum = 1
          DO CFMAINT
          STORE ' ' TO wait_subst
          @ 23,0 SAY 'Press any key to continue...' GET wait_subst
          READ

       CASE selectnum = 2
          DO PFMAINT
          STORE ' ' TO wait_subst
          @ 23,0 SAY 'Press any key to continue...' GET wait_subst
          READ

       CASE selectnum = 3
          DO SRMAINT
          STORE ' ' TO wait_subst
```

```
        @ 23,0 SAY 'Press any key to continue...' GET wait_subst
        READ

    ENDCASE

ENDDO T
RETURN
* End of MAINTAIN.PRG


* Program..: CFMAINT.PRG
* Date.....: 07/12/86
* Notes....: Customer File Maintenance Menu
SET CONFIRM OFF
DO WHILE .T.

    * ---Display menu options, centered on the screen
    *    Draw menu border and print heading
    CLEAR
    @ 2,0 TO 13,79 DOUBLE
    @ 3,16 SAY [C U S T O M E R   F I L E   M A I N T E N A N C E]
    @ 4,1 TO 4,78 DOUBLE
    * ---Display detail lines
    @  7,25 SAY [1. Add Customers]
    @  8,25 SAY [2. Edit Customers]
    @  9,25 SAY [3. Print or Display Customer List]
    @ 11,25 SAY '0. Return to Prior Menu'
    STORE 0 TO selectnum
    @ 13,33 SAY " select     "
    @ 13,42 GET selectnum PICTURE "9" RANGE 0,3
    READ

    DO CASE
      CASE selectnum = 0
        CLEAR ALL
        RETURN

      CASE selectnum = 1
        DO ADDCUST
        STORE ' ' TO wait_subst
        @ 23,0 SAY 'Press any key to continue...' GET wait_subst
        READ

      CASE selectnum = 2
        DO EDITCUST
        STORE ' ' TO wait_subst
```

```
            @ 23,0 SAY 'Press any key to continue...' GET wait_subst
            READ

         CASE selectnum = 3
            DO REPTCUST
            STORE ' ' TO wait_subst
            @ 23,0 SAY 'Press any key to continue...' GET wait_subst
            READ
      ENDCASE

ENDDO
RETURN
* End of CFMAINT.PRG



* Program..: PFMAINT.PRG
* Date.....: 07/12/86
* Notes....: Product File Maintenance Menu
SET CONFIRM OFF
DO WHILE .T.

   * ---Display menu options, centered on the screen
   *    Draw menu border and print heading
   CLEAR
   @ 2, 0 TO 13,79 DOUBLE
   @ 3,16 SAY [P R O D U C T   F I L E   M A I N T E N A N C E]
   @ 4,1 TO 4,78 DOUBLE
   * ---Display detail lines
   @  7,25 SAY [1. Add Inventory Items]
   @  8,25 SAY [2. Edit Inventory Items]
   @  9,25 SAY [3. Print or Display Inventory List]
   @ 11,25 SAY '0. Return to Prior Menu'
   STORE 0 TO selectnum
   @ 13,33 SAY " select     "
   @ 13,42 GET selectnum PICTURE "9" RANGE 0,3
   READ

   DO CASE
      CASE selectnum = 0
         CLEAR ALL
         RETURN

      CASE selectnum = 1
         DO ADDPROD
         STORE ' ' TO wait_subst
```

```
            @ 23,0 SAY 'Press any key to continue...' GET wait_subst
            READ

         CASE selectnum = 2
            DO EDITPROD
            STORE ' ' TO wait_subst
            @ 23,0 SAY 'Press any key to continue...' GET wait_subst
            READ

         CASE selectnum = 3
            DO REPTPROD
            STORE ' ' TO wait_subst
            @ 23,0 SAY 'Press any key to continue...' GET wait_subst
            READ
      ENDCASE

ENDDO
RETURN
* End of PFMAINT.PRG



* Program..: SRMAINT.PRG
* Date.....: 07/12/86
* Notes....: Sales Rep Maintenance Menu
SET CONFIRM OFF
DO WHILE .T.

    * ---Display menu options, centered on the screen
    *    Draw menu border and print heading
    CLEAR
    @ 2, 0 TO 13,79 DOUBLE
    @ 3,13 SAY [S A L E S   R E P   F I L E   M A I N T E N A N C E]
    @ 4,1 TO 4,78 DOUBLE
    * ---Display detail lines
    @  7,25 SAY [1. Add New Sales Representatives]
    @  8,25 SAY [2. Edit/Remove Sales Reps from Files]
    @  9,25 SAY [3. Print or Display Sales Staff List]
    @ 11,25 SAY '0. Return to Prior Menu'
    STORE 0 TO selectnum
    @ 13,33 SAY " select     "
    @ 13,42 GET selectnum PICTURE "9" RANGE 0,3
    READ

    DO CASE
       CASE selectnum = 0
```

```
            CLEAR ALL
            RETURN

         CASE selectnum = 1
            DO ADDSREP
            STORE ' ' TO wait_subst
            @ 23,0 SAY 'Press any key to continue...' GET wait_subst
            READ

         CASE selectnum = 2
            DO EDITSREP
            STORE ' ' TO wait_subst
            @ 23,0 SAY 'Press any key to continue...' GET wait_subst
            READ

         CASE selectnum = 3
            DO REPTSREP
            STORE ' ' TO wait_subst
            @ 23,0 SAY 'Press any key to continue...' GET wait_subst
            READ
      ENDCASE

ENDDO
RETURN
* End of SRMAINT.PRG


* Program..: ADDCUST.PRG
* Date.....: 07/12/86
* Notes....: Adds new customers to customer file
**
USE CUSTOM
*Assign new customer number first
GO BOTTOM
STORE RECNO() TO Tempnumb
STORE Tempnumb + 1000 TO MCUSTID
STORE SPACE(40) TO MCNAME
STORE SPACE(40) TO MCADDRESS
STORE SPACE(20) TO MCCITY
STORE SPACE(2) TO MCSTATE
STORE SPACE(10) TO MCZIP
STORE SPACE(12) TO MCPHONE
CLEAR
*Display memvars and get data
@  2, 21  SAY "Customer File Maintenance Screen"
@  4,  8  SAY "Customer ID:"
@  4, 22  SAY  MCUSTID PICTURE "9999"
```

```
@  4, 31  SAY "(Enter BLANK Cust. Name to VOID this entry.)"
@  6,  7  SAY "Customer Name:"
@  6, 23  GET  MCNAME
@  7, 14  SAY "Address:"
@  7, 23  GET  MCADDRESS
@  8, 14  SAY "City:"
@  8, 23  GET  MCCITY
@  9, 14  SAY "State:"
@  9, 23  GET  MCSTATE
@ 10, 14  SAY "Zip:"
@ 10, 23  GET  MCZIP  PICTURE "99999-9999"
@ 11, 14  SAY "Phone:"
@ 11, 23  GET  MCPHONE  PICTURE "999-999-9999"
@ 13,  7  SAY "Fill all fields or use Control-End to save additions & changes."
@  1,  1  TO 14, 76    DOUBLE
READ
IF LEN(TRIM(MCNAME)) > 0
    USE CUSTOM INDEX CUSTOM
    APPEND BLANK
    REPLACE CUSTID WITH MCUSTID, CNAME WITH MCNAME
    REPLACE CADDRESS WITH MCADDRESS, CCITY WITH MCCITY
    REPLACE CSTATE WITH MCSTATE, CZIP WITH MCZIP
    REPLACE CPHONE WITH MCPHONE
    CLOSE DATABASES
ENDIF
RETURN
*End of ADDCUST.PRG
```

```
* Program..: EDITCUST.PRG
* Date.....: 07/12/86
* Notes....: Edits records in customer file
**
SET TALK OFF
CLEAR
STORE 9999 TO MCUSTID
@5,5 SAY "Enter customer number: " GET MCUSTID
READ
USE CUSTOM INDEX CUSTOM
SEEK MCUSTID
IF EOF()
    CLOSE DATABASES
    @7,5 SAY "No such customer number in customer files!"
    ? CHR(7)
    RETURN
ENDIF
STORE CNAME TO MCNAME
```

```
STORE CADDRESS TO MCADDRESS
STORE CCITY TO MCCITY
STORE CSTATE TO MCSTATE
STORE CZIP TO MCZIP
STORE CPHONE TO MCPHONE
CLEAR
*Display memvars and get data
@  2, 21  SAY "Customer File Maintenance Screen"
@  4,  8  SAY "Customer ID:"
@  4, 22  SAY  MCUSTID PICTURE "9999"
@  4, 30  SAY "Enter BLANK name to DELETE this record."
@  6,  7  SAY "Customer Name:"
@  6, 23  GET  MCNAME
@  7, 14  SAY "Address:"
@  7, 23  GET  MCADDRESS
@  8, 14  SAY "City:"
@  8, 23  GET  MCCITY
@  9, 14  SAY "State:"
@  9, 23  GET  MCSTATE
@ 10, 14  SAY "Zip:"
@ 10, 23  GET  MCZIP  PICTURE "99999-9999"
@ 11, 14  SAY "Phone:"
@ 11, 23  GET  MCPHONE  PICTURE "999-999-9999"
@ 13,  7  SAY "Fill all fields or use Control-End to save additions & changes."
@  1,  1  TO 14, 76 DOUBLE
READ
IF LEN(TRIM(MCNAME)) = 0
    DELETE
    RETURN
ENDIF
REPLACE CUSTID WITH MCUSTID, CNAME WITH MCNAME
REPLACE CADDRESS WITH MCADDRESS, CCITY WITH MCCITY
REPLACE CSTATE WITH MCSTATE, CZIP WITH MCZIP
REPLACE CPHONE WITH MCPHONE
CLOSE DATABASES
ENDIF
RETURN
*End of EDITCUST.PRG


* Program..: REPTCUST.PRG
* Date.....: 07/12/86
* Notes....: Columnar report for customer file
* Replace the following code, as desired, with reports
* created with the Report Generator for nicer formatting
**
USE CUSTOM INDEX CUSTOM
```

```
CLEAR
@ 5,0
ACCEPT "Print report in alphabetical order? (Y/N): " TO ANS
IF UPPER(ANS) = "Y"
    ? "Indexing...please wait..."
    INDEX ON CNAME + CZIP TO ALPHA
ENDIF
CLEAR
@ 5,0
ACCEPT "(S)creen or (P)rinter? " TO ANS
IF UPPER(ANS) = "P"
    SET PRINT ON
ENDIF
CLEAR
GO TOP
*Replace display with appropriate Report Form command
DISPLAY ALL CUSTID, CNAME, CCITY, CSTATE OFF
IF UPPER(ANS) = "P"
    SET PRINT OFF
ENDIF
CLOSE DATABASES
RETURN
*End of REPTCUST.PRG

* Program..: ADDPROD.PRG
* Date.....: 07/12/86
* Notes....: Adds new items to product inventory file
**
USE PRODUCT
*Assign new stock number first
GO BOTTOM
STORE RECNO() TO Tempnumb
STORE Tempnumb + 1000 TO MPRODID
STORE SPACE(40) TO MDESCRIPT
STORE 0 TO MPRODCOST
STORE SPACE(30) TO MSUPPLIER
CLEAR
*Display memvars and get data
@  2, 25  SAY "Product Data Screen"
@  4,  5  SAY "Product ID:"
@  4, 19  SAY  MPRODID
@  7,  5  SAY "Description:"
@  7, 18  GET  MDESCRIPT
@  9,  5  SAY "Unit Cost:"
@  9, 18  GET  MPRODCOST  PICTURE "99,999.99"
@ 11,  5  SAY "Supplier:"
@ 11, 18  GET  MSUPPLIER
```

```
@ 13,  2  SAY "Fill all fields or use Control-End to save additions & changes."
@  1,  1  TO 14, 71 DOUBLE
READ
IF LEN(TRIM(MDESCRIPT)) > 0
    USE PRODUCT INDEX PRODUCT
    APPEND BLANK
    REPLACE PRODUCTID WITH MPRODID, DESCRIPT WITH MDESCRIPT
    REPLACE PRODCOST WITH MPRODCOST, SUPPLIERID WITH MSUPPLIER
    CLOSE DATABASES
ENDIF
RETURN
*End of ADDPROD.PRG


* Program..: EDITPROD.PRG
* Date.....: 07/12/86
* Notes....: Edits records in products file
**
SET TALK OFF
CLEAR
STORE 9999 TO MPRODID
@5,5 SAY "Enter product number: " GET MPRODID
READ
USE PRODUCT INDEX PRODUCT
SEEK MPRODID
IF EOF()
    CLOSE DATABASES
    @7,5 SAY "No such product number in inventory files!"
    ? CHR(7)
    RETURN
ENDIF
STORE DESCRIPT TO MDESCRIPT
STORE PRODCOST TO MPRODCOST
STORE SUPPLIERID TO MSUPPLIER
CLEAR
*Display memvars and get data
@  2, 30  SAY "Product Data Screen"
@  4,  5  SAY "Product ID:"
@  4, 19  SAY  MPRODID
@  4, 30  SAY  "(Enter BLANK description to delete record.)"
@  7,  5  SAY "Description:"
@  7, 18  GET  MDESCRIPT
@  9,  5  SAY "Unit Cost:"
@  9, 18  GET  MPRODCOST  PICTURE "99,999.99"
@ 11,  5  SAY "Supplier:"
@ 11, 18  GET  MSUPPLIER
@ 13,  2  SAY "Fill all fields or use Control-End to save additions & changes."
```

```
@ 1,  1 TO 14, 78 DOUBLE
READ
IF LEN(TRIM(MDESCRIPT)) = 0
    DELETE
    RETURN
ENDIF
REPLACE PRODUCTID WITH MPRODID, DESCRIPT WITH MDESCRIPT
REPLACE PRODCOST WITH MPRODCOST, SUPPLIERID WITH MSUPPLIER
CLOSE DATABASES
ENDIF
RETURN
*End of EDITPROD.PRG


* Program..: REPTPROD.PRG
* Date.....: 07/12/86
* Notes....: Columnar report for product inventory file
* Replace the following code, as desired, with reports
* created with the Report Generator for nicer formatting
**
USE PRODUCT INDEX PRODUCT
CLEAR
@ 5,0
ACCEPT "Print report in alphabetical order? (Y/N): " TO ANS
IF UPPER(ANS) = "Y"
    ? "Indexing...please wait..."
    INDEX ON DESCRIPT TO ALPHA
ENDIF
CLEAR
@ 5,0
ACCEPT "(S)creen or (P)rinter? " TO ANS
IF UPPER(ANS) = "P"
    SET PRINT ON
ENDIF
CLEAR
GO TOP
*Replace display with appropriate Report Form command
DISPLAY ALL PRODUCTID, DESCRIPT, PRODCOST OFF
IF UPPER(ANS) = "P"
    SET PRINT OFF
ENDIF
CLOSE DATABASES
RETURN
*End of REPTPROD.PRG


* Program..: ADDSREP.PRG
```

```
* Date.....: 07/12/86
* Notes....: Adds new sales reps to staff file
**
USE SALESREP
*Assign new employee number first
GO BOTTOM
STORE RECNO() TO Tempnumb
STORE Tempnumb + 10 TO MREPID
STORE SPACE(20) TO MREPLNAME
STORE SPACE(20) TO MREPFNAME
STORE 10 TO MCOMMISS
CLEAR
*Display memvars and get data
@  2, 17  SAY "Sales Representative Data Screen"
@  4,  9  SAY "Sales Rep ID Number:"
@  4, 30  GET  MREPID
@  6,  9  SAY "Last Name:"
@  6, 21  GET  MREPLNAME
@  7, 21  SAY "(Enter BLANK last name to void record.)"
@  9,  9  SAY "First Name:"
@  9, 21  GET  MREPFNAME
@ 11,  9  SAY "Commission Rate:"
@ 11, 26  GET  MCOMMISS  RANGE 10, 25
@ 12, 10  SAY "(in percent)"
@ 14,  3  SAY "Fill all fields or use Control-End to save additions & changes."
@  1,  1  TO 15, 71 DOUBLE
READ
IF LEN(TRIM(MREPLNAME)) > 0
    USE SALESREP INDEX SALESREP
    APPEND BLANK
    REPLACE REPID WITH MREPID, REPL_NAME WITH MREPLNAME
    REPLACE REPF_NAME WITH MREPFNAME, COMMISSION WITH MCOMMISS
    CLOSE DATABASES
ENDIF
RETURN
*End of ADDSREP.PRG
```

```
* Program..: EDITSREP.PRG
* Date.....: 07/12/86
* Notes....: Edits records in staff file
**
SET TALK OFF
CLEAR
STORE 99 TO MREPID
@5,5 SAY "Enter Sales Rep ID Number: " GET MREPID
READ
```

```
USE SALESREP INDEX SALESREP
SEEK MREPID
IF EOF()
    CLOSE DATABASES
    @7,5 SAY "No such employee number currently on staff!"
    ? CHR(7)
    RETURN
ENDIF
STORE REPL_NAME TO MREPLNAME
STORE REPF_NAME TO MREPFNAME
STORE COMMISSION TO MCOMMISS
CLEAR
*Display memvars and get data
@  2, 17  SAY "Sales Representative Data Screen"
@  4,  9  SAY "Sales Rep ID Number:"
@  4, 30  GET  MREPID
@  6,  9  SAY "Last Name:"
@  6, 21  GET  MREPLNAME
@  7, 21  SAY "(Enter BLANK last name to delete employee.)"
@  9,  9  SAY "First Name:"
@  9, 21  GET  MREPFNAME
@ 11,  9  SAY "Commission Rate:"
@ 11, 26  GET  MCOMMISS  RANGE 10, 25
@ 12, 10  SAY "(in percent)"
@ 14,  3  SAY "Fill all fields or use Control-End to save additions & changes."
@  1,  1  TO 15, 71 DOUBLE
READ
IF LEN(TRIM(MREPLNAME)) = 0
    DELETE
    RETURN
ENDIF
REPLACE REPID WITH MREPID, REPL_NAME WITH MREPLNAME
REPLACE REPF_NAME WITH MREPFNAME, COMMISSION WITH MCOMMISS
CLOSE DATABASES
ENDIF
RETURN
*End of EDITSREP.PRG


* Program..: REPTSREP.PRG
* Date.....: 07/12/86
* Notes....: Columnar report for staff file
* Replace the following code, as desired, with reports
* created with the Report Generator for nicer formatting
**
USE SALESREP INDEX SALESREP
CLEAR
```

```
@ 5,0
ACCEPT "Print report in alphabetical order? (Y/N): " TO ANS
IF UPPER(ANS) = "Y"
    ? "Indexing...please wait..."
    INDEX ON REPL_NAME + REPF_NAME TO ALPHA
ENDIF
CLEAR
@ 5,0
ACCEPT "(S)creen or (P)rinter? " TO ANS
IF UPPER(ANS) = "P"
    SET PRINT ON
ENDIF
CLEAR
GO TOP
*Replace display with appropriate Report Form command
DISPLAY ALL REPID, REPL_NAME, REPF_NAME, COMMISSION OFF
IF UPPER(ANS) = "P"
    SET PRINT OFF
ENDIF
CLOSE DATABASES
RETURN
*End of REPTSREP.PRG
```

```
**PANIC.PRG
**Error-handling routine
PARAMETERS Errorcode
CLEAR
DO CASE
    CASE Errorcode = 1
        ? "File not found.  Contact DP Department immediately."
        WAIT
        RETRY

    CASE Errorcode = 56
        ? "Your disk is full.  Erase some files and redo operation."
        CLOSE DATABASES
        WAIT
        RETURN TO MASTER

    CASE Errorcode = 125
        ? "Printer NOT READY.  Correct problem and press a key."
        WAIT
        RETRY
```

```
ENDCASE
*Errorcode unknown, so call for help!
? "An uncorrectable error has occurred.  The error code is: "
?? Errorcode
? "Error message is: "
?? MESSAGE()
WAIT
QUIT
*End of PANIC.PRG
```

Mailing Label System

In using a slightly different approach for comparison's sake, the mailing list system makes heavy use of subroutines for common tasks, such as displaying screens and error messages, and replacing field contents with variables. The programs use a single database (MAILER.DBF), with two index files (indexed on last names and on zip codes). Two programs are provided to print mailing labels and a line-oriented report.

The code that produces the labels and the report could be significantly shortened if you make use of the Report Generator or Label Form command instead. The design of the mailing label system is illustrated in Figure 19-2.

The database used by the mailing label system is structured as follows:

```
Structure for database: C:MAILER.DBF
Number of data records:       8
Date of last update    : 07/15/86
Field  Field Name  Type       Width    Dec
    1  LAST_NAME   Character     15
    2  FIRST_NAME  Character     15
    3  ADDRESS_1   Character     20
    4  ADDRESS_2   Character     10
    5  CITY        Character     10
    6  STATE       Character      2
    7  ZIP_CODE    Character     10
    8  CUSTNO      Numeric        5
    9  COUNTRY     Character     10
** Total **                      98
```

An index file need not be created in advance; the program will search for an appropriate index file and build one if the index cannot be found. The programs that form the application are found in Listing 19.2.

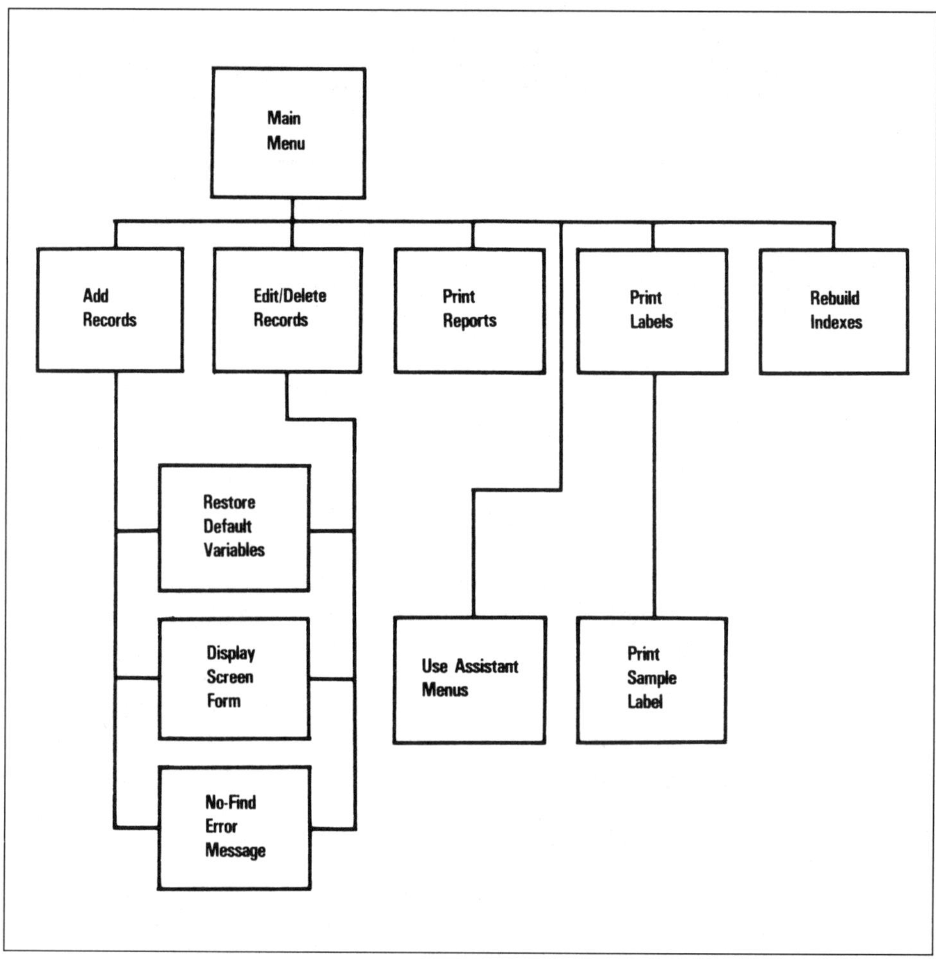

Figure 19-2 Mailing Label System Design

Listing 19.2: Programs for Mailing Label System

```
** MAILER.PRG
** -Main Menu for Mailing List System
** Last update 07/15/86
SET SAFETY OFF
SET ESCAPE OFF
SET TALK OFF
SET EXACT OFF
SET DELETED ON
ON ERROR DO PANIC WITH ERROR()
USE MAILER
*Build index files if not present
IF .NOT. FILE("NAMES.NDX")
```

```
    ? "Please wait...building index."
   INDEX ON LAST_NAME TO NAMES
   INDEX ON ZIP_CODE TO ZIPS
ENDIF
DO while .T.
   STORE ' ' TO SELECT
   SET MESSAGE TO "Date: " + DTOC(DATE())
   CLEAR
   *Display the menu
   @ 3,3 SAY "Press a letter key corresponding to the desired entry:"
   @ 5,10 SAY "A      To Add New Entries"
   @ 7,10 SAY "C      To Change or Delete Existing Entries"
   @ 9,10 SAY "I      To Index Database by Name or by Zip Code"
   @ 11,10 SAY "L      To Print Mailing Labels"
   @ 13,10 SAY "R      To Produce Reports"
   @ 15,10 SAY "D      To Use dBASE IV with Assistant"
   @ 17,10 SAY "Q      To Quit"
   @ 1,1 TO 19,70 DOUBLE
   @ 1,15 SAY [ M A I L I N G   L I S T   S Y S T E M ]
   *Prompt for choice, store it, and select command file
   @ 20,22 SAY 'PLEASE ENTER YOUR CHOICE: '
   @ 18,50 CLEAR TO 21,60
   @ 18,50 TO 21,60 DOUBLE
   @ 20,55 GET SELECT
   READ
   DO CASE
      CASE UPPER(SELECT)='A'
         DO ADD
      CASE UPPER(SELECT)='C'
         DO EDIT
      CASE UPPER(SELECT)='R'
         DO REPORT
      CASE UPPER(SELECT)='I'
         DO RESORT
      CASE UPPER(SELECT)='L'
         DO LABEL
      CASE UPPER(SELECT)='Q'
         RELEASE ALL
         CLOSE DATABASES
         QUIT
      CASE UPPER(SELECT)='D'
         RELEASE ALL
         CLOSE DATABASES
         ASSIST
   ENDCASE
ENDDO
```

```
** ADD.PRG ** Used to add new records to MAILER database
USE MAILER INDEX NAMES, ZIPS
STORE .T. TO DECIDE
DO WHILE DECIDE
   DO DEFAULTS
   CLEAR
   DO FORM
   RESTORE FROM FAULTS
   @ 24,2 SAY 'ADD AS MANY AS YOU WISH; WHEN DONE ENTER BLANKS FOR ALL ENTRIES'
   READ
   * Test to see if finished
   IF LEN(TRIM(MLASTNAME)) > 0
      APPEND BLANK
      * Put screen data into file
      REPLACE LAST_NAME WITH UPPER(MLASTNAME)
      REPLACE FIRST_NAME WITH UPPER(MFIRSTNAME)
      REPLACE ADDRESS_1 WITH UPPER(MADDRESS1)
      REPLACE ADDRESS_2 WITH UPPER(MADDRESS2)
      REPLACE CITY WITH UPPER(MCITY)
      REPLACE STATE WITH UPPER(MSTATE)
      REPLACE ZIP_CODE WITH MZIPCODE
      REPLACE CUSTNO WITH MCUSTNO
      * Release input fields
      RELEASE ALL EXCEPT DECIDE
   ELSE
      STORE .F. TO DECIDE
   ENDIF
ENDDO
RELEASE DECIDE
CLOSE DATABASES
RETURN
```

```
** EDIT PROGRAM
** Used to change or delete records
CLEAR
STORE SPACE(25) TO LNAME
STORE SPACE(10) TO ZCODE
@2,5 SAY "Enter the following information for the desired record."
@4,10 SAY "Enter last name:  " GET LNAME
@6,12 SAY "Enter zip code: " GET ZCODE
READ
*Begin the search routine
STORE "N" TO SELECT2
USE MAILER
SET INDEX TO NAMES, ZIPS
SET FILTER TO ZIP_CODE = ZCODE
STORE UPPER(LNAME) TO LNAME
FIND &LNAME
IF EOF()
```

```
    DO NOFIND
    RETURN
ENDIF
*Lastname, zipcodes match, so verify
DO WHILE LAST_NAME = LNAME
   CLEAR
   @4,10 SAY "Lastname: " + LAST_NAME
   @5,8 SAY "First name: " + FIRST_NAME
   @6,9 SAY "Address 1: " + ADDRESS_1
   @7,9 SAY "Address 2: " + ADDRESS_2
   @8,14 SAY "City: " + CITY
   @9,13 SAY "State: " + STATE
   @10,15 SAY "Zip: " + ZIP_CODE
   @15,5 SAY "Is this the correct record?" GET SELECT2
   READ
   IF UPPER(SELECT2)="Y"
      CLEAR
      @10,10 SAY "[C]hange or [D]elete record?"
      @11,10 SAY "...enter C or D then press RETURN to confirm!"
      @12,0
      ACCEPT TO CHOICE2
      IF UPPER(CHOICE2)="D"
        DELETE
        @ 14,0
        ACCEPT "   Recover disk space now? (Y/N): " TO CHOICE2
        IF UPPER(CHOICE2) = "Y"
             ? "...please wait...packing database..."
             PACK
        ENDIF
        RETURN
      ENDIF
      CLEAR
      @3,10 SAY "Last name: " GET LAST_NAME
      @4,8 SAY "First name: " GET FIRST_NAME
      @5,9 SAY "Address 1: " GET ADDRESS_1
      @6,9 SAY "Address 2: " GET ADDRESS_2
      @7,14 SAY "City: " GET CITY
      @8,13 SAY "State: " GET STATE
      @9,15 SAY "Zip: " GET ZIP_CODE
      @10,11 SAY "Cust. No.: " GET CUSTNO
      @15,2 SAY "Enter necessary changes.  Use arrow keys to edit."
      READ
      RETURN
   ENDIF
   SKIP
   IF EOF()
      DO NOFIND
```

```
      RETURN
   ENDIF
ENDDO
*Not found in WHILE scope, so...
DO NOFIND
RETURN


**DEFAULTS.PRG
** Builds default variables
STORE SPACE(25) TO MFIRSTNAME
STORE SPACE(25) TO MLASTNAME
STORE SPACE(30) TO MADDRESS1
STORE SPACE(30) TO MADDRESS2
STORE SPACE(25) TO MCITY
STORE SPACE(2) TO MSTATE
STORE SPACE(10) TO MZIPCODE
STORE 9999 TO MCUSTNO
SAVE TO FAULTS
RETURN


**FORM.PRG
**Screen format for mailing list system
RESTORE FROM FAULTS
@ 3,0 TO 21,60 DOUBLE
@ 6,2 SAY 'Last Name-'
@ 6,16 GET MLASTNAME
@ 8,2 SAY 'First Name-'
@ 8,16 GET MFIRSTNAME
@ 10,2 SAY 'Address Line 1-'
@ 10,19 GET MADDRESS1
@ 12,2 SAY 'Address Line 2-'
@ 12,19 GET MADDRESS2
@ 14,2 SAY 'City-'
@ 14,9 GET MCITY
@ 16,2 SAY 'State-'
@ 16,9 GET MSTATE
@ 18,2 SAY 'Zip-'
@ 18,9 GET MZIPCODE PICTURE '99999-9999'
@ 20,2 SAY 'Customer Number-'
@ 20,20 GET MCUSTNO PICTURE '9999'
SAVE TO FAULTS
RETURN
```

```
** LABEL.PRG
** Prints one-across mailing labels
** Could be replaced with Label Form of your design
** for greater printing flexibility
USE MAILER
CLEAR
@5,5 SAY "Turn on printer, then"
WAIT
CLEAR
@5,5 SAY "Print labels in (N) Name order or (Z) Zip Code order?"
@6,5 SAY "Enter N or Z now."
WAIT " " TO RESPONSE
IF UPPER(RESPONSE) = "N"
    SET INDEX TO NAMES
ENDIF
IF UPPER(RESPONSE) = "Z"
    SET INDEX TO ZIPS
ENDIF
CLEAR
@5,5 SAY "Shall I print an alignment pattern? (Y/N)"
WAIT " " TO PATTERN
IF UPPER(PATTERN) = "Y"
    DO PRINPATT
ENDIF
*As option, replace next 16 lines with Label Form (name) Sample to Print
SET PRINT ON
DO WHILE .NOT. EOF()
          *Loop prints one label per record
          ? TRIM(FIRST_NAME) + " " + LAST_NAME
          ? ADDRESS_1
          ? ADDRESS_2
          ? TRIM(CITY) + " " + STATE + " " + ZIP_CODE
          ? "                      "
          ?? CUSTNO
          ?
          ?
          ?
          * Add a ques. mark for each space needed for nonstandard labels
          SKIP
ENDDO
SET PRINT OFF
CLEAR
@5,5 SAY "Total records printed: "
@5,30 SAY RECCOUNT()
@7,10 SAY "To return to the menu,"
@10,0
```

```
WAIT
RETURN


**NOFIND.PRG
** Error message for person not found
CLEAR
@6,5 TO 10,50 DOUBLE
@7,10 SAY "This person isn't in the mailing list."
@8,10 SAY "Return to the menu to add new names, or"
@9,10 SAY "to try a different name. "
@16,0
WAIT
RETURN


**RESORT.PRG
** Reindexes the database
USE MAILER
CLEAR
@5,5 SAY "Please wait while I reindex the database by names."
SET TALK ON
INDEX ON LAST_NAME TO NAMES
CLEAR
@5,5 SAY "Please wait while I reindex the database by zip codes."
INDEX ON ZIP_CODE TO ZIPS
SET TALK OFF
RETURN


**REPORT.PRG
** Print reports of the MAILER database
** Replace this program with custom REPORT FORMAT of your choice
USE MAILER INDEX NAMES
CLEAR
? "Turn on printer, then"
WAIT
CLEAR
*As option, replace next 15 lines with Report Form (name) to Print
SET PRINT ON
DO WHILE .NOT. EOF()
    ? "Customer number: " + STR(CUSTNO)
    ? "Customer name: "
    ?? LAST_NAME + " " + FIRST_NAME
    ? "Address: " + ADDRESS_1 + ADDRESS_2
    ? "City: " + CITY
    ? "State: " + STATE
```

```
    ?? "  Zip code: " + ZIP_CODE
    ? "============================================================"
    ?
    SKIP
ENDDO
? CHR(7)
SET PRINT OFF
WAIT
RETURN



**PRINPATT.PRG
** Prints an alignment pattern; called from LABEL.PRG
** This program not needed if you use Label Form in LABEL.PRG
STORE .T. TO AGAIN
DO WHILE AGAIN
    CLEAR
    @5,5 SAY "Set up printer and align labels, then "
    WAIT
    SET PRINT ON
    ? "=====NAME================ "
    ? "=====ADDRESS LINE 1======"
    ? "=====ADDRESS LINE 2======"
    ? "=====CITY, STATE, ZIP===="
    ? "======================Cust. No.=="
    ?
    ?
    ?
    SET PRINT OFF
    CLEAR
    @5,5 SAY "Print another alignment pattern? (Y/N)"
    WAIT " " TO DECIDE
    IF UPPER(DECIDE) = "N"
        STORE .F. TO AGAIN
    ENDIF
    STORE "Y" TO DECIDE
ENDDO
RETURN



**PANIC.PRG
**Error-handling routine
PARAMETERS Errorcode
CLEAR
DO CASE
    CASE Errorcode = 1
        ? "File not found.  Contact DP Department immediately."
```

```
        WAIT
        RETRY

    CASE Errorcode = 56
        ? "Your disk is full.  Erase some files and redo operation."
        CLOSE DATABASES
        WAIT
        RETURN TO MASTER

    CASE Errorcode = 125
        ? "Printer NOT READY.  Correct problem and press a key."
        WAIT
        RETRY

ENDCASE
*Errorcode unknown, so call for help!
? "An uncorrectable error has occurred.  The error code is: "
?? Errorcode
? "Error message is: "
?? MESSAGE()
WAIT
QUIT
*End of PANIC.PRG
```

A

dBASE IV Command Summary

This appendix summarizes the commonly used dBASE IV commands. After each command's name its purpose is detailed. Then the proper syntax for entering the command is shown, followed by an example of the command's use. For a similar summary of the dBASE IV functions, see Appendix B.

?, ??: The question mark shows the contents of a dBASE IV expression. A single question mark displays the contents of the expression after a carriage return and linefeed. A double question mark displays the expression appearing on the same line as the present cursor location. Use PICTURE, FUNCTION, and STYLE options to customize the format of displayed data. Use AT to place data at a precise location. The syntax for these commands is:

```
? <expression> [PICTURE "clause"] [FUNCTION "function list"] [AT expN] [STYLE font]
?? <expression> [PICTURE "clause"] [FUNCTION "function list"] [AT expN] [STYLE font]
```

Example:

```
? (5 * SALES) + 27
?? AMOUNT2
```

???: This command sends the characters specified by the expression to the printer, without changing the current row or column cursor locations. Control codes can be specified as part of the expression by enclosing them in curly {} braces. The syntax for this command is:

```
??? <expC>
```

Example:

```
??? "{015}"
```

@ (for drawing or clearing line or box): The @ command draws a single or double line or box between the specified coordinates. If the coordinates share the same horizontal and vertical planes, a horizontal or vertical line is drawn; if not, a box is drawn. CLEAR erases characters below and to the right of the coordinates. The syntax for this command is:

```
@ <row,col> [CLEAR] TO <row,col> [DOUBLE]
```

Examples:

```
@ 5,1 TO 50,4
```

This command draws a single-line box.

```
@ 7,1 TO 7,45 DOUBLE
```

Entering this command line draws a double line.

@ (for cursor movement): Moves the cursor to a given screen location, specified by the row and column coordinates given following the @ symbol. The SAY option shows the contents of the specified expression on screen. The GET option displays data on the screen in reverse video (or "full-screen edit") mode. The PICTURE and FUNCTION options are used with templates, to control the display of data (with SAY), or to specify the types of data that can be entered (with GET). The RANGE option is used to limit data retrieved with GET to a specific range of entries. Use VALID to specify a valid list of acceptable entries. Use ERROR to specify an optional error message displayed if the VALID condition is not met. Use COLOR to specify standard or enhanced color codes. The syntax for this command is:

```
@ <row,col> [SAY <expression> [PICTURE <clause>]] [GET <variable>[PICTURE <clause>
[FUNCTION <function list>] [RANGE <lower value>,<upper value>]/[CLEAR]]
[VALID <condition>] [ERROR expC] [COLOR standard/enhanced]
```

Example:

```
@ 15,5 SAY "Enter your password: " GET PW PICTURE "AAAAA"
```

@. . .FILL: This command changes the screen colors within the defined area. <color attribute> is X/Y, where X is the foreground color code and Y is the background color code. If the COLOR option is omitted, dBASE clears the screen within the defined area. The syntax for this command is:

```
@ <row1>,<col1> FILL TO <row2>,<col2> [COLOR <color attribute>]
```

Example:

```
@ 7,5 FILL TO 12,60 COLOR B/W
```

ACCEPT: This command displays a prompt and stores a character string as a memory variable. If an optional character string is included, it will be displayed as a prompt. The value provided in response to ACCEPT will be stored as a character variable. The syntax for this command is:

```
ACCEPT [<character string>] TO <memvar>
```

Example:

```
ACCEPT "Month of bond maturity? " TO XMONTH
```

ACTIVATE MENU: ACTIVATE MENU activates a predefined menu and displays the menu on the screen. If PAD is specified, the highlight appears at the named pad; otherwise, the first pad in the menu is highlighted. The syntax for this command is:

```
ACTIVATE MENU <menu name> [PAD <pad name>]
```

Example:

```
ACTIVATE MENU Main PAD Edit Records
```

ACTIVATE POPUP: ACTIVATE POPUP activates a predefined Pop Up Menu, and displays that Pop Up Menu on the screen. The syntax is:

```
ACTIVATE POPUP <popup name>
```

Example:

```
ACTIVATE POPUP Sales
```

ACTIVATE SCREEN: ACTIVATE SCREEN provides a full screen display of the contents of a predefined window. The syntax is:

```
ACTIVATE SCREEN
```

Example:

```
ACTIVATE SCREEN
```

ACTIVATE WINDOW: ACTIVATE WINDOW activates a window (the window must have been previously defined in memory). After the ACTIVATE WINDOW command is executed, all screen output appears in the window. If the ALL clause is used, all windows currently defined in memory are displayed in the order in which they were defined. The syntax for this command is:

```
ACTIVATE WINDOW <window name list>/ALL
```

Example:

```
ACTIVATE WINDOW Lister
```

APPEND: Adds a record to the end of a database and enters the full-screen editing mode. If you include the BLANK option with APPEND, it adds a blank record to the end of the database, and dBASE does not go into the full-screen editing mode. The syntax for this command is:

```
APPEND [BLANK]
```

Example:

```
USE SALES
APPEND
```

APPEND FROM: Copies records from another file to a database. The FOR and WHILE <condition> options can be used to specify conditions that must apply before records are copied. The various TYPE options import non-dBASE IV files. The syntax for this command is:

```
APPEND FROM <filename> [WHILE <condition>] [FOR <condition>] [TYPE
SDF/DELIMITED/WKS/SYLK/DIF/FW2/RPD/WK1/DBASEII]
```

Examples:

```
APPEND FROM SALES FOR GROSSAMT > 5000
APPEND FROM LOTUS2.WR1 TYPE WKS
```

APPEND FROM ARRAY: APPEND FROM ARRAY appends records to a database file from the named array. The values in each row of the array are transferred to a corresponding new record in a database file. The first column in the array is stored in the first field, the second column in the array is stored in the second field, and so on. If there are more columns in the array than there are fields in the database, extra columns are ignored. If there are more fields in the database than there are columns in the array, the extra fields are empty. The optional FOR clause defines a condition which must be met before data in the array will be added to the new record. The array must exist (see DECLARE) before you can use the APPEND FROM ARRAY command. The syntax for this command is:

```
APPEND FROM ARRAY <array name> FOR <condition>
```

Example:

```
APPEND FROM ARRAY SalesFigs FOR Invoice = "paid"
```

APPEND MEMO: APPEND MEMO reads a text file into a memo field. The contents of the file are added to the end of any existing text in the memo field. If the OVERWRITE option is used, the contents of the file overwrite existing text in the memo field. The file should have an extension of .TXT, or the extension must be specified along with the filename. The syntax for this command is:

```
APPEND MEMO <memo field name> FROM <filename> [OVERWRITE]
```

Example:

```
APPEND MEMO review FROM myfile.txt
```

ASSIST: This command loads the menu-driven Control Center feature of dBASE IV. The syntax for this command is:

```
ASSIST
```

Example:

```
ASSIST
```

AVERAGE: This command averages expressions involving numeric fields. If the TO option is used, the results are stored to the memory variables specified in the variable list. If the TO ARRAY option is used, the results are stored in the named array. The syntax for this command is:

```
AVERAGE <list of fields> [<scope>] [FOR <condition> [WHILE <condition>] [TO <memvar list>]
[TO ARRAY array-name]
```

Example:

```
AVERAGE FOR SALESREP = "JOHNSON" TO GROSSAMT, NETAMT
```

BEGIN TRANSACTION: The BEGIN TRANSACTION and END TRANSACTION commands begin and end the recording of a transaction file. The transaction file maintains a record of all changes made to a database file. Use BEGIN TRANSACTION to begin recording all database file changes in a transaction log, then perform the desired operations for updating records. When the operations are complete, use END TRANSACTION to stop the transaction recording, and purge the transaction log. If an abnormal occurrence such as a power failure halts the process before the END TRANSACTION command is used, ROLLBACK can be used to restore the database files to their status before BEGIN TRANSACTION command was used. (See ROLLBACK.) The syntax for this command is:

```
BEGIN TRANSACTION
```

Example:

```
USE Sales EXCLUSIVE
ON ERROR ROLLBACK
BEGIN TRANSACTION
PACK
REPLACE ALL BONUS WITH BONUS + (BONUS * .05)
END TRANSACTION
CLEAR ALL
RETURN
```

BROWSE: This command provides the full-screen editing capability of a database. If no fields are specified, BROWSE displays all fields. The LOCK option locks a specified number of columns at the left side of the screen, while remaining columns are allowed to pan. FREEZE allows editing of only the named field. NOINIT forces BROWSE to use the settings in effect at the last use of BROWSE. NOFOLLOW can reposition the record pointer after a field's content is altered. NOMENU makes the Menu Bar inaccessible. WIDTH limits characters displayed for fields. With NOAPPEND, records can't be added to the current file using BROWSE. NODELETE prevents deletions with Control-U. NOCLEAR leaves the BROWSE display on the screen after the Browse mode is exited. NOEDIT prevents edits to records. FORMAT causes BROWSE to use any picture or function settings in effect due to an active format file. WINDOW causes the display to appear within a specified window. The syntax for this command is:

```
BROWSE [FIELDS <field list>] [LOCK <expression>] [FREEZE <field name>]
[NOINIT] [NOFOLLOW]
[NOMENU] [WIDTH <expression>] [NOAPPEND] [NODELETE] [NOCLEAR] [COMPRESS]
[NOEDIT] [FORMAT] [WINDOW <window-name>]
```

Example:

```
BROWSE FIELDS AMOUNT, STOCKNO, NAME, DESCRIPT LOCK 2
```

CALCULATE: CALCULATE uses standard financial and statistical functions to calculate amounts. The functions are defined as part of the options list. All records are processed until the condition is no longer true, or until the scope is completed. The syntax for this command is:

```
CALCULATE [scope] <options> [FOR<condition>] [WHILE <condition>][TO memvar list/
TO ARRAY array name>]
```

Use any of these functions within the options list:

AVG(<expN>)	Calculates the numerical average of value <expN>.
CNT()	Counts records in a database file. Any condition specified with the FOR clause must be met before the record will be counted.
MAX(<exp>)	Provides the maximum value in a field. <exp> is a field name or expression which translates to a field name.
MIN(<exp>)	Provides the minimum value in a field. <exp> is a field name or expression which translates to a field name.

NPV(<rate>,<flows>, <initial>)	Provides the net present value, where <rate> is the discount rate, <flows> is a series of signed periodic cash flow values, and <initial> is the initial investment.
STD(<exp>)	Provides the standard deviation of values stored in a database field. <exp> is a field name or expression which translates to a field name.
SUM(<exp)>	Provides the sum of values in a database field. <exp> is a field name or expression which translates to a field name.
VAR(<exp>)	Provides a variance of the values in a database field. <exp> is a field name or expression which translates to a field name. The value returned by VAR(<exp>) is a floating-point number.

Example:

```
USE PERSONS
SET TALK ON
CALCULATE MAX(SALARY), MIN(SALARY), VAR(SALARY)
```

CALL: This command executes an assembly-language (binary) routine. The routine must first be loaded into memory with the LOAD command (see LOAD). The WITH option is used to pass a parameter to the binary routine. The syntax for this command is:

```
CALL <module name> [WITH <expression>]
```

Example:

```
CALL stripbit
```

CANCEL: This command terminates execution of a command file and redisplays the dot prompt. The syntax for this command is:

```
CANCEL
```

Example:

```
CANCEL
```

CASE: See DO CASE.

CHANGE: This command allows full-screen editing of a record in the database. The CHANGE command is functionally identical to the EDIT command, but CHANGE allows the selection of specific fields for editing. If a list of fields is provided, only those fields can be edited. If no list is provided, all fields are available for editing. The syntax for this command is:

```
CHANGE [<scope>] [FIELDS <field list>] [FOR <condition> [WHILE <condition>]
```

Example:

```
CHANGE FIELDS AMOUNT, STOCKNO, GROSSPAY
```

CLEAR: This command erases the screen. The syntax for this command is:

```
CLEAR
```

Example:

```
CLOSE DATABASES
CLEAR
```

CLEAR ALL: This command closes all open files, releases all memory variables, and sets the current work area to 1. The syntax for this command is:

```
CLEAR ALL
```

Example:

```
CLEAR ALL
```

CLEAR FIELDS: This command cancels a fields list previously chosen with the SET FIELDS command. The syntax for this command is:

```
CLEAR FIELDS
```

Example:

```
CLEAR FIELDS
```

CLEAR GETS: This command clears current variables provided by GET from a READ access. The syntax for this command is:

```
CLEAR GETS
```

Example:

```
@5,5 SAY "Address?" GET ADDRESS
@6,5 SAY "City?" GET CITY
@7,5 SAY "State?" GET STATE
READ SAVE
CLEAR
SELECT 2
@8,5 SAY "Customer Number?" GET CNUMB
READ
CLOSE DATABASES
CLEAR GETS
```

CLEAR MEMORY: This command removes all memory variables. The syntax for this command is:

```
CLEAR MEMORY
```

Example:

```
CLEAR MEMORY
```

CLEAR MENUS: This command clears all bar menus, and deletes the bar menus from memory. The syntax for this command is:

```
CLEAR MENUS
```

Example:

```
CLEAR MENUS
```

CLEAR POPUPS: This command clears all popup menus, and deletes the bar menus from memory. The syntax for this command is:

```
CLEAR POPUPS
```

Example:

```
CLEAR POPUPS
```

CLEAR TYPEAHEAD: This command empties the typeahead buffer. (See SET TYPEAHEAD.)

CLOSE: This command closes a specific type of file. The file type can be ALTERNATE, DATABASES, FORMAT, INDEX, or PROCEDURE. If the ALL option is specified, all files of the named type are closed. The syntax for this command is:

```
CLOSE <file type> [ALL]
```

Example:

```
CLOSE DATABASES
CLOSE FORMAT
CLOSE INDEX
```

COMPILE: COMPILE loads a dBASE command (.PRG) file and creates an object (.DBO) file, which is an execute-only dBASE program. The syntax for this command is:

```
COMPILE <filename>
```

Example:

```
COMPILE mainmenu.prg
```

CONTINUE: This command continues a search begun by LOCATE. It finds the next record that meets the specific condition outlined with the LOCATE command. The syntax for this command is:

```
CONTINUE
```

Example:

```
@5,5 SAY "Last Name?" GET LAST
@6,5 SAY "First Name?" GET FIRST
READ
LOCATE FOR LAST = LNAME
IF FIRST <> FNAME
CONTINUE
<more commands...>
```

CONVERT: The CONVERT command converts a single-user database to a network-ready database. CONVERT adds a new field to the active database file. The field is used to store locking information used by dBASE operations when in multi-user (network) mode.

The new field in the database is named _dbaselock. It contains a numeric value of 16 as its default value, unless a different value has been entered with the optional TO clause. If TO is used, the numeric expression can range from 8 (which restricts the size of the network user name stored with each locked record or file to zero) to 24 (which allows a network user name of up to 16 characters). The syntax for this command is:

```
CONVERT [TO <expN>]
```

Example:

```
CONVERT TO 14
```

(In this case, the new field added to the active file will be able to store a network user name of up to 6 characters. dBASE will use the remaining 8 characters for network information.)

COPY FILE: This command creates a copy of any type of file. The syntax for this command is:

```
COPY FILE <source filename> TO <output filename>
```

Example:

```
COPY FILE TEST2.PRG TO TEST3.PRG
```

COPY INDEX: COPY INDEX converts .NDX (dBASE III/III-Plus style) index files to index tags in a .MDX (multiple index) file. If the TO clause is specified, the .NDX files are added as tags to the .MDX file named in the TO clause. If the TO clause is omitted, the .NDX index files are added as tags to the production .MDX file. The syntax for this command is:

```
COPY INDEX <.ndx files list> [TO .mdx filename]
```

Example:

```
COPY INDEX last, first, zipcode
```

COPY MEMO: COPY MEMO copies the contents of a memo field to a text file. Drive and path identifiers are optional in the filename. If the ADDITIVE clause is used, the text of the memo field is added to the end of an existing filename. If the ADDITIVE clause is omitted, any existing file with the same name is overwritten. The syntax for this command is:

```
COPY MEMO <memo field name> TO <filename> [ADDITIVE]
```

Example:

```
USE LITIGATE
SEEK "Smithers"
COPY MEMO trial TO A:COMMENTS.TXT
```

COPY STRUCTURE EXTENDED: This command creates a database that contains four fields and is a structural representation of the database in use when the COPY STRUCTURE EXTENDED command was entered. The file created with the COPY STRUCTURE EXTENDED command contains five fields: FIELD_NAME, FIELD_LEN, FIELD_TYPE, FIELD_DEC, and FIELD_IDX. The syntax for this command is:

```
COPY STRUCTURE TO <filename> EXTENDED
```

Example:

```
COPY TO DESIGN STRUCTURE EXTENDED
```

COPY STRUCTURE TO: This command copies the database structure of the file being used to a new database. If a list of fields is provided with the FIELDS option, only those fields will be included in the new database. The syntax for this command is:

```
COPY STRUCTURE TO <filename> [FIELDS <field list>]
```

Example:

```
COPY STRUCTURE TO TEMP2 FIELDS USER, OPTIONS, FLOOR, ROOM
```

COPY TAG: COPY TAG converts the tag information in a .MDX (multiple index) file to a dBASE-III style (.NDX) index file. If the TO clause is omitted, the .NDX file is given the same name as the active .MDX file. The syntax for this command is:

```
COPY TAG <tag name> [OF .MDX filename] TO <.NDX filename>
```

Example:

```
COPY TAG last_name TO names.ndx
```

COPY TO: This command copies part or all of a database to a specified file. A field list can be used to specify a list of fields that will be included in the file being created. The scope and FOR and WHILE <condition> options can be used to specify conditions that must apply before records are copied. The various TYPE options export non-dBASE IV files. The syntax for this command is:

```
COPY TO <filename> [<scope>] [FIELDS <field list>] [WHILE <condition>]
[FOR <condition>] [TYPE SDF/DELIMITED/WKS/SYLK/DIF/RPD/FWZ/DBASEII/DBMEMO3]
```

Example:

```
COPY TO RBASEFIL FIELDS LAST_NAME, COST, STOCKNO
```

COPY TO ARRAY: COPY TO ARRAY copies data from the fields of the active database into an array. For each record in the database, the first field is stored in the first column of the array, the second field in the second column, and so on. If the database has more fields than the array has columns, the contents of extra fields are ignored. If the array has more columns than the database has fields, the extra columns in the array are unchanged. Memo fields are not added to the array. The syntax for this command is:

```
COPY TO ARRAY <array name> [FIELDS <fields list>] [SCOPE]
[FOR <condition>] [WHILE <condition>]
```

Example:

```
USE PAYROLL
DECLARE Weeklies [10,8]
COPY TO ARRAY Weeklies NEXT 8
```

COUNT: This command totals the number of records that meet a specific condition or totals all records if condition and scope options are not used. If the TO option is used, the resultant total is stored as the specified memory variable. The syntax for this command is:

```
COUNT [<scope>] [WHILE <condition>] [FOR <condition>] [TO <memory variable>]
```

Example:

```
COUNT FOR SALESREP = "Steere" TO SNAME
```

CREATE: This command creates a new database file and specifies its structure. The syntax for this command is:

```
CREATE <filename>
```

Example:

```
CREATE PERSONS
```

CREATE APPLICATION: CREATE APPLICATION starts the Applications Generator. A filename with the .APP extension is created when the application is saved. If an application by the name specified in the command already exists, it is loaded into the Applications Generator. The syntax for this command is:

```
CREATE APPLICATION <filename>
```

Example:

```
CREATE APPLICATION Mailer
```

CREATE LABEL, MODIFY LABEL: This command creates or modifies a label form file for generating mailing labels. The syntax for this command is:

```
CREATE LABEL <filename>
MODIFY LABEL <filename>
```

Example:

```
MODIFY LABEL MAILERS
```

CREATE QUERY, MODIFY QUERY: This command creates a query file, or if the specified file exists, allows editing of the existing query file. Query files can be used to filter a database, hiding records that do not meet the conditions of the filter, or they can provide links between multiple files. The syntax for this command is:

```
CREATE QUERY <filename>
MODIFY QUERY <filename>
```

Example:

```
CREATE QUERY CUSTOMERS
```

CREATE REPORT, MODIFY REPORT: This command creates or modifies a report form file for generating reports. The syntax for this command is:

```
CREATE REPORT <filename>
MODIFY REPORT <filename>
```

Example:

```
MODIFY REPORT COMMISS
```

CREATE SCREEN, MODIFY SCREEN: This command creates a screen format file, or if specified file exists, allows editing of the existing screen format. The syntax for this command is:

```
CREATE SCREEN <filename>
MODIFY SCREEN <filename>
```

Example:

```
CREATE SCREEN TAXES
```

CREATE VIEW, MODIFY VIEW: This command is included to provide compatibility with dBASE III Plus. The command performs the same effect as CREATE QUERY or MODIFY QUERY. If the FROM ENVIRONMENT option is used with CREATE VIEW, a query file containing the names of all open databases, index files, and relational links will be created. The syntax for this command is:

```
CREATE VIEW <filename> [FROM ENVIRONMENT]
MODIFY VIEW <filename>
```

Example:

```
CREATE VIEW HOMES FROM ENVIRONMENT
```

DEACTIVATE MENU: DEACTIVATE MENU deactivates the active menu and clears the menu from the screen. The menu remains in memory until a RELEASE MENU command is issued, and it can be recalled with ACTIVATE MENU. The syntax for this command is:

```
DEACTIVATE MENU
```

Example:

```
DEACTIVATE MENU
```

DEACTIVATE POPUP: DEACTIVATE POPUP deactivates the active popup menu, and erases the menu from the screen. The menu remains in memory until a RELEASE POPUP command is issued, and it can be recalled to the screen with ACTIVATE POPUP. The syntax for this command is:

```
DEACTIVATE POPUP
```

Example:

```
DEACTIVATE POPUP
```

DEACTIVATE WINDOW: DEACTIVATE WINDOW deactivates the window(s) named within the <window name> clause, and clears them from the screen. The windows remain in memory until RELEASE WINDOW is used, and they can be restored to the screen with ACTIVATE WINDOW. If the ALL option is not used, the last window activated is deactivated. If a window is underlying the last window activated, it becomes the active window. If the ALL option is included, all active windows are deactivated. The syntax for this command is:

```
DEACTIVATE WINDOW <window name>/ALL
```

Example:

```
DEACTIVATE WINDOW
```

DEBUG: The DEBUG command starts the dBASE IV full-screen debugger. If a program is named with the command, that program is loaded into the Edit window of the debugger. The syntax for this command is:

```
DEBUG <program name> / <procedure name> [WITH parameter list]
```

Example:

```
DEBUG Mainmenu.PRG
```

DECLARE: DECLARE defines an array. Enter the array name and the dimensions of the array in the definition list. Array names may be up to 10 characters in length. Array dimensions consist of the row and column numbers. If a column number is omitted, dBASE creates a one-dimensional array. Where row and column numbers are provided, they must be separated by a comma, and dBASE creates a two-dimensional array. Note that arrays declared within programs are private unless declared public with the PUBLIC command. The syntax for this command is:

```
DECLARE <array name 1> [<no. of rows>,<no. of columns>]
[<array name 2>][<no. of rows>,<no. of columns>]
```

Example:

```
DECLARE ARRAY Salaries[10,4]
```

The above example declares a private array. An example which declares a public array follows:

```
PUBLIC ARRAY Salaries[10,4]
```

DEFINE BAR: DEFINE BAR defines a bar option in a popup menu. Line number identifies the line number within the popup menu; line 1 appears on the first line of the popup, line 2 on the second line of the popup, and so on. The text specified with PROMPT appears as text in the bar of the menu. The <popup name> is the name assigned to the previously defined popup menu. The MESSAGE option specifies optional text which is displayed in the message line when the specified bar is highlighted. The SKIP option causes the bar to be displayed but not to be selectable by the user. The syntax for this command is:

```
DEFINE BAR <line number> OF <popup name> PROMPT <expC>
[MESSAGE <expC>] [SKIP [FOR <condition>] [NOSPACE]]
```

Example:

```
DEFINE BAR Mailer FROM 4,15 TO 10,50
DEFINE BAR 1 OF Mailer PROMPT " Add records"
DEFINE BAR 2 OF Mailer PROMPT " Edit records"
DEFINE BAR 3 OF Mailer PROMPT " Delete records"
DEFINE BAR 4 OF Mailer PROMPT " Print reports"
DEFINE BAR 5 OF Mailer PROMPT " Quit system"
```

DEFINE BOX: DEFINE BOX defines a box which surrounds text in a report. Use the specified options in the command to mark the leftmost starting column, the rightmost ending column, the starting line for the top of the box, and the height of the box. The border definition string clause is used to specify a character which will appear as the box border; the default, if the option is omitted, is a single line. The syntax for this command is:

```
DEFINE BOX FROM <print column> TO <print column>
HEIGHT <exp> [AT LINE <print line>] [SINGLE/DOUBLE / <border
definition string>]
```

Example:

```
DEFINE BOX FROM 6 TO 65 HEIGHT 20 AT LINE 6
```

DEFINE MENU: DEFINE MENU defines a bar menu. If the MESSAGE option is included, the text of the message appears in the message line when the menu is displayed. (See ACTIVATE MENU.) The syntax for this command is:

```
DEFINE MENU <menu name> [MESSAGE <expC>]
```

Example:

```
DEFINE MENU Mailer
```

DEFINE PAD: DEFINE PAD defines a pad of a bar menu. The text specified with PROMPT is displayed within the menu pad. If the AT <row>,<col> clause is omitted, the first pad appears at the far left, and each successive pad is displayed one space to the right of the prior pad. Any text included with the MESSAGE option is displayed in the message line when that pad is highlighted within the menu. The syntax for this command is:

```
DEFINE PAD <pad name> OF <menu name> PROMPT <expC>
[AT <row>,<col>] [MESSAGE <expC>]
```

Example:

```
DEFINE MENU Mailer
DEFINE PAD Adder OF Mailer PROMPT "Add" MESSAGE "Add records"
DEFINE PAD Editor OF Mailer PROMPT "Edit" MESSAGE "Edit records"
DEFINE PAD Eraser OF Mailer PROMPT "Delete" MESSAGE "Delete records"
DEFINE PAD Printer OF Mailer PROMPT "Print" MESSAGE "Print reports"
DEFINE PAD Quit OF MainMenu PROMPT "Exit" MESSAGE "Quit system"
```

DEFINE POPUP: DEFINE POPUP defines a popup menu. Use the FROM and TO row and column coordinates to define the upper left and lower right corners of the popup menu. If the TO coordinate is omitted, dBASE will size the menu as needed to contain the prompts. The PROMPT FIELD, PROMPT FILE, and PROMPT STRUCTURE clauses are optional. These are used to display selection lists of the contents of database fields, lists of filenames, or lists of fieldnames from a database structure. The syntax for this command is:

```
DEFINE POPUP <popup name> FROM <row1>,<col1>
[TO <row2>,<col2>] [PROMPT FIELD <field name>/PROMPT FILES
[LIKE <skeleton>]/PROMPT STRUCTURE] [MESSAGE <expC>]
```

Example:

```
DEFINE POPUP Mailer FROM 5,10 TO 15,45
DEFINE POPUP Printer FROM 13,12 TO 35,27
```

DEFINE WINDOW: DEFINE WINDOW defines screen coordinates and display attributes for a window. Use the FROM and TO coordinates to plot the upper left and lower right corners of the window. The default border is a single-line box; use the DOUBLE, PANEL, NONE, or border definition character options to specify a different border for the window. (ASCII codes are used with the border definition option.) The syntax for this command is:

```
DEFINE WINDOW <window name> FROM <row1>,<col1>
TO <row2>,<col2> [DOUBLE/PANEL/NONE/<border definition string>]
[COLOR [<standard>][,<enhanced>][,<frame>]]
```

Example:

```
DEFINE WINDOW Lister FROM 5,5 TO 7,52 DOUBLE COLOR B/W
ACTIVATE WINDOW Lister
DISPLAY ALL last_name, first_name, salary, hireday
```

DELETE: This command marks certain records for deletion. The scope and FOR and WHILE <condition> options specify conditions that must apply before records are marked for deletion. (See also PACK.) The syntax for this command is:

```
DELETE [record number] [<scope>] [WHILE <condition>] [FOR <condition>]
```

Example:

```
DELETE ALL FOR AGE > 21 WHILE STATE = "AZ"
```

DELETE TAG: DELETE TAG either deletes the named tag from a multiple index file (if it is the named file within the command), or closes .NDX index files (if it is the named file). The syntax for this command is:

```
DELETE TAG <tag name 1> [OF <.MDX filename>]/<.NDX
filename1> [,<tag name 2> [OF <.MDX filename> ]/<.NDX filename 2>]
```

Example:

```
DELETE TAG Zipcode OF Mailer
```

DIR: This command displays a directory of all database files. If filenames or DOS wildcards are provided, specific files or types of files will be shown. The syntax for this command is:

```
DIR [<drive:>] [<path>\] [<skeleton>]
```

Example:

```
DIR *.PRG
```

This command will display all the program files for all databases.

DISPLAY: This command displays fields or records from the database that is active. The DISPLAY command pauses every 24 lines. The scope, fields, and FOR/WHILE options specify records and fields to be displayed; the OFF option stops the record number from being shown. The syntax for this command is:

```
DISPLAY [<scope>] [FIELDS <field list>] [WHILE <condition>] [FOR <condition>]
[<expressionlist>] [OFF]
```

Example:

```
DISPLAY NEXT 50 FOR COST > 3500 LAST_NAME, HIREDATE
```

DISPLAY FILES: This command performs a directory display in the same manner as the DIR command (see DIR).

DISPLAY HISTORY: This command displays commands stored within History. If the LAST option is used, the last X commands (X being a numeric variable) are displayed; otherwise, all commands stored in History are displayed. If the TO PRINT option is used, output will be simultaneously directed to the default printer. The syntax for this command is:

```
DISPLAY HISTORY [LAST X] [TO PRINT]
```

Example:

```
DISPLAY HISTORY LAST 13
```

DISPLAY MEMORY: This command displays size and contents of active memory variables. The display pauses every 24 lines. If the TO PRINT option is used, output will be simultaneously directed to the default printer. The syntax for this command is:

```
DISPLAY MEMORY [TO PRINT]
```

Example:

```
DISPLAY MEMORY TO PRINT
```

DISPLAY STATUS: This command displays information about currently active files and system settings. The display pauses every 24 lines. The status includes function key settings, ON/OFF status of SET commands, and names of open database and index files in work areas. The syntax for this command is:

```
DISPLAY STATUS [TO PRINT]
```

Example:

```
DISPLAY STATUS
```

DISPLAY STRUCTURE: This command displays the structure of the database in use. Display pauses every 24 lines. Structure shows names of fields, field types, field lengths, and number of decimal places. The syntax for this command is:

```
DISPLAY STRUCTURE [TO PRINT]
```

Example:

```
DISPLAY STRUCTURE
```

DISPLAY USERS: This command displays all current users running dBASE IV on a local-area network. The syntax for this command is:

```
DISPLAY USERS
```

Example:

```
DISPLAY USERS
```

DO: This command begins execution of a dBASE IV program (command file). Optional parameters can be passed to the command file using the WITH option. The syntax for this command is:

```
DO <program> [WITH <list of parameters>]
```

Example:

```
DO MYPROG2 WITH 2,5
```

DO CASE, CASE, OTHERWISE ENDCASE: This command chooses one path from among a number of possible paths within a program. All possible paths are identified by CASE statements, bracketed by DO CASE and ENDCASE statements. The first CASE statement evaluated as True is performed by the program. The syntax for this command is:

```
DO CASE
CASE
[OTHERWISE]
ENDCASE
```

Example:

```
DO CASE
     CASE CHOOSY = 1
         DO AddIt
     CASE CHOOSY = 2
         SET FORMAT TO MYFORM
         EDIT
     CASE CHOOSY = 3
         REPORT FORM MYREP TO PRINT
     CASE CHOOSY = 4
         QUIT
     OTHERWISE
         ? 'Invalid Choice!'
ENDCASE
```

DO WHILE, ENDDO: This command allows command statements to be repeated as a loop as long as a specified condition evaluates as true. The syntax for this command is:

```
DO WHILE
ENDDO
```

Example:

```
DO WHILE TIMER < 100
STORE 1 + TIMER TO TIMER
ENDDO
```

EDIT: This command permits full-screen editing of the database. PgUp and PgDn keys move the record pointer to prior and successive records for editing. If a record number is provided, editing will begin at that record. NOINIT forces EDIT to use the settings in effect at the last use of EDIT. NOFOLLOW causes movement between records to follow natural order, rather than the index order, as edits to the indexed field are changed. NOAPPEND, NOEDIT, and NODELETE prevent additions, edits, and deletions, respectively. NOMENU prevents access to the Edit Menu bar. The syntax for this command is:

```
EDIT [<scope>] [FIELDS <field list>] [WHILE <condition>] [FOR <condition>] [NOINIT]
[NOFOLLOW] [NOAPPEND] [NOMENU] [NOEDIT] [NODELETE]
```

Example:

```
EDIT RECORD 12
```

EJECT: This command sends a form feed command to the specified printer. The specified printer can be changed by means of the SET PRINTER command (see SET PRINTER). The syntax for this command is:

```
EJECT
```

Example:

```
WAIT "Press a key to print report and eject last sheet."
REPORT FORM MEMBERS TO PRINT
EJECT
```

EJECT PAGE: This command sends a form feed to the printer. The difference between EJECT PAGE and the EJECT command is that the form feed sent with EJECT PAGE is also sent to all destinations available with the ? command. The syntax for this command is:

```
EJECT PAGE
```

Example:

```
EJECT PAGE
```

END TRANSACTION: END TRANSACTION ends the recording of a transaction file. (See BEGIN TRANSACTION, ROLLBACK.) The syntax for this command is:

```
END TRANSACTION
```

For an example of the use of this command, see BEGIN TRANSACTION.

ERASE, DELETE FILE: This command deletes the named file from the directory. If an extension has been stored previously with the file, it must be provided as a part of the filename. Pathnames and drive designators can also be included to erase files that are not in the default directory. The syntax for this command is:

```
ERASE <filename>
```

Example:

```
ERASE FILE2.DBF
```

EXIT: This command ends a DO WHILE loop without halting execution of the program. Program execution continues at the command immediately following the ENDDO command. The syntax for this command is:

```
EXIT
```

Example:

```
EXIT
```

EXPORT TO: This command builds a database and accompanying screen form to be used with PFS:File, DBASEII, RapidFile, or Framework II. If used to export to PFS, the resulting PFS:File database uses all character fields. If a dBASE IV format file is open when the EXPORT TO command is used, the PFS:File screen form will be based on the design of the dBASE IV format file. RapidFile and FRAMEWORK II databases will share field type characteristics with the dBASE IV database, except for memo fields, which will not be exported. The syntax for this command is:

```
EXPORT TO <filename> TYPE PFS/DBASEII/FW2/RPD
```

Example:

```
EXPORT TO MEDICAL TYPE PFS
```

FIND: This command moves the record pointer to the first record having an index key matching the specified character string. If no such match is located, the record pointer is placed at the end of the file, and EOF() is set to True. The syntax for this command is:

```
FIND <character string>
```

Example:

```
FIND "Judie"
```

FUNCTION: FUNCTION identifies a procedure as a user-defined function. The syntax for this command is:

```
FUNCTION <procedure name>
```

Example:

```
FUNCTION Tax
PARAMETERS Cost, Rate
Totals = Cost + (Cost * Rate)
RETURN(Totals)
```

GO, GO BOTTOM, GO TOP, GOTO: This command moves the record pointer to a specified location. GO TOP and GO BOTTOM move the pointer to start and end of database, respectively. GO <X> or GOTO <X> will move the pointer to the record number specified by the numeric expression, X. The syntax for this command is:

```
GO <expression>
GOTO <expression>
```

Examples:

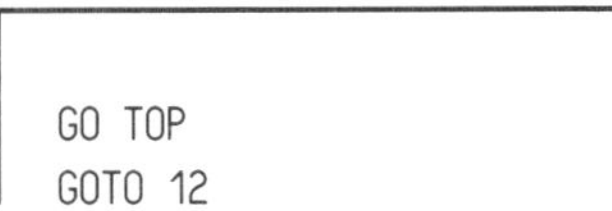

```
GO TOP
GOTO 12
```

HELP: This command displays an explanation of the specified dBASE IV command, function, or other information. Entering HELP followed by a valid command or function displays the help screen for that command or function. Entering HELP without a name displays a help menu. The syntax for this command is:

```
HELP [<command or function>]
```

Examples:

```
HELP LIST
HELP EOF()
```

IF, [ELSE], ENDIF: This command permits conditional processing of commands in a command file. If the condition identified by the IF statement is true, all commands between the IF and ENDIF are carried out. Otherwise, execution passes to the statement following the ENDIF command (unless the optional ELSE statement is used, in which case execution passes to the statements following the ELSE statement). The syntax for this command is:

```
IF <condition>
[ELSE]
ENDIF
```

Example:

```
IF LAST_NAME = TEMP
  ? LAST_NAME, CITY, STATE, PHONE_NUMB
ELSE
  ? "I can't find a match!"
ENDIF
```

IMPORT FROM: This command builds a dBASE IV database and accompanying format and view files that are based upon the contents of a PFS:File, DBASEII, RapidFile, Framework II, or Lotus 1-2-3 database. The resultant format file will imitate the layout of the PFS:File screen design. The syntax for this command is:

```
IMPORT FROM <filename> TYPE PFS/DBASEII/FW2/RPD/WKS
```

Example:

```
IMPORT FROM LEGAL TYPE PFS
```

INDEX ON: This command creates an index file based on a specified key field or expression. The expression can be a field, a list of fields, or a combination of fields and values. If TAG is used, the index is part of a multiple index (.MDX) file. If TO is used, the index is stored in a dBASE III-style (.NDX) file. If multiple records contain the same key field value, UNIQUE includes only the first record. The syntax for this command is:

```
INDEX ON <expression> TO <filename>/[UNIQUE] [DESCENDING] (or)
INDEX ON <expression> TAG <tag name> [UNIQUE] [DESCENDING]
```

Examples:

```
INDEX ON AMOUNT TO GROSSALE
INDEX ON (DATE() - HIREDATE) TO SENIORS
```

INPUT: This command waits for the user to enter data and stores the entry to a memory variable. If the response is enclosed in quotes, data will be stored as a character variable. If a number (without quotes) is provided, data will be stored as a numeric variable. If a valid expression is entered, the expression is first acted upon, and the results are stored to the appropriate type of variable. If an optional prompt is provided, the prompt will be displayed ahead of the cursor that waits for the user input. The syntax for this command is:

```
INPUT [<prompt>] TO <memory variable>
```

Example:

```
INPUT "Select an option from 1 to 4: " TO MENCHOICE
```

INSERT: This command adds a new record at a specific position in the database. The record will be inserted immediately following the current record, unless the BEFORE option is used. BEFORE inserts the record ahead of the current record. In either case, all records following the inserted record will be renumbered. The BLANK option inserts a blank record; otherwise, dBASE IV permits full-screen editing of the new record. The syntax for this command is:

```
INSERT [BLANK][BEFORE]
```

Example:

```
GO 10
INSERT BEFORE
```

JOIN WITH: This command builds a new database by duplicating chosen records and fields from two existing databases. The optional FOR condition specifies which records will be included. An optional list of fields limits fields that will be duplicated; if no list is provided, all fields will be duplicated. The syntax for this command is:

```
JOIN WITH <alias> TO <filename> FOR <condition> [FIELDS <list of fields>]
```

Example:

```
SELECT 2
USE SALES
SELECT 1
USE CUSTOMER
JOIN WITH SALES TO TEMP FOR TOTSALE >= 1000 FIELDS CUSTNO, NAME
```

LABEL FORM: This command prints mailing labels using a label form file. The FOR and WHILE <condition> options limit labels printed to a range of records. The SAMPLE option prints a sample label (actually a series of X's) prior to the printing of the first label. If the TO PRINT option is specified, output will be directed to the default print device. If the TO FILE option is specified, output will be stored in a disk file. The syntax for this command is:

```
LABEL FORM <filename> [SAMPLE] [<scope>] [FOR <condition>] [/WHILE <condition>]
[TO PRINT][TO FILE <filename>]
```

Example:

```
LABEL FORM MAILLIST FOR CITY = "Santa Barbara" TO PRINT
```

LIST: This command supplies a list of the records in the current database. A scope (Record No., NEXT X, ALL, or REST) can be used to limit the records that will be listed. The FOR and WHILE <condition> options can be used to further limit the list to a range of records. If a list of fields is specified, only those fields will be listed; otherwise, all fields are listed. The OFF option omits record numbers from the list. If the TO PRINT option is used, output will be simultaneously directed to the default printer. The TO FILE option directs the output to an ASCII text file. The syntax for this command is:

```
LIST [<scope>][FOR <condition>] [/WHILE <condition>][<field list>][OFF][TO PRINT]
[TO FILE <filename>]
```

Example:

```
LIST ALL FOR GROSSALE => 1000 ACCTNO, NAME, SALESREP
```

LIST FILES: This command performs a directory display in the same manner as the DIR command (see DIR).

LIST HISTORY: See Display History.

LIST MEMORY: This command lists names, sizes, and types of memory variables for the database in use. If the TO PRINT option is used, output will be simultaneously directed to the default printer. The TO FILE option directs the output to an ASCII text file. The syntax for this command is:

```
LIST MEMORY [TO PRINT] [TO FILE <filename>]
```

Example:

```
LIST MEMORY
```

LIST STATUS: This command lists information about currently active files and system settings. The status includes function key settings, ON/OFF status of SET commands, and names of open database and index files in respective work areas. If the TO PRINT option is used, output will be simultaneously directed to the default printer. The TO FILE option directs the output to an ASCII text file. The syntax for this command is:

```
LIST STATUS [TO PRINT] [TO FILE <filename>]
```

Example:

```
LIST STATUS
```

LIST STRUCTURE: This command lists the structure of the currently active database. The structure shows names of fields, field types, field lengths, and number of decimal places. If the TO PRINT option is used, output will be simultaneously directed to the default printer. The TO FILE option directs the output to an ASCII text file. Use IN ALIAS to list the structure of a file open in another work area. The syntax for this command is:

```
LIST STRUCTURE [TO PRINT] [TO FILE <filename>] [IN ALIAS alias-name]
```

Example:

```
LIST STRUCTURE
```

LIST USERS: This command lists all users currently logged on to the network installation of dBASE IV. The syntax for this command is:

```
LIST USERS
```

Example:

```
LIST USERS
```

LOAD: This command is used to load a binary (assembly-language) routine into memory. The routine must have an extension of .BIN, or the extension must be specified along with the filename. Once loaded, the routine can be executed with the CALL command (see CALL). The syntax for this command is:

```
LOAD <binary filename>
```

Example:

```
LOAD Stripbit
```

LOCATE: This command locates a record that matches the condition specified. A scope (Record No., NEXT X, ALL, or REST) can be used to limit the records that will be searched for the condition. The syntax for this command is:

```
LOCATE [<scope>] [FOR <condition>] [WHILE <condition>]
```

Example:

```
LOCATE NEXT 200 FOR GROSSAMT = 7295.68
```

LOGOUT: This command is used to log a user out from the network version of dBASE IV. The syntax for this command is:

```
LOGOUT
```

Example:

```
LOGOUT
```

LOOP: This command causes a loop back to the beginning of a DO WHILE loop. It is normally used as part of a conditional statement (IF . . . ENDIF or DO CASE), to prevent execution of commands following the LOOP command. The syntax for this command is:

```
LOOP
```

Example:

```
DO WHILE .NOT. EOF()
     IF INSTOCK < 20
          DO REORDER
     ENDIF
     IF INSTOCK < 10
          ? "Call in rush order for this record."
          ? STOCKNO, DESCRIPT, SUPPLIER
          STORE 15 + QUANTITY TO QUANTITY
          LOOP
     ENDIF
     SKIP
ENDDO
```

MODIFY APPLICATION: MODIFY APPLICATION starts the Applications Generator. The command has the same effect as CREATE APPLICATION. (See CREATE APPLICATION.) The syntax for this command is:

```
MODIFY APPLICATION <application name>
```

Example:

```
MODIFY APPLICATION Mainmenu
```

MODIFY COMMAND: This command invokes the dBASE IV processor to edit programs. If an alternate word processor has been specified in the CONFIG.DB file, that word processor will be run from DOS. The syntax for this command is:

```
MODIFY COMMAND <filename>
```

Example:

```
MODIFY COMMAND MYPROG
```

MODIFY LABEL: See CREATE LABEL.

MODIFY QUERY: See CREATE QUERY.

MODIFY REPORT: See CREATE REPORT.

MODIFY SCREEN: See CREATE SCREEN.

MODIFY STRUCTURE: This command changes the structure of the database in use. The syntax for this command is:

```
MODIFY STRUCTURE [<filename>]
```

Example:

```
MODIFY STRUCTURE
```

MODIFY VIEW: See CREATE VIEW.

MOVE WINDOW: MOVE WINDOW moves a pre-defined window to a new screen location. The syntax for this command is:

```
MOVE WINDOW <window name> TO <row>,<col>/BY <delta
row>,<delta column>
```

The example below moves the named window's left corner to row 12, column 30:

```
MOVE WINDOW Browser TO 12, 30
```

The next example moves the named window 8 lines down, and 3 lines to the right:

```
MOVE WINDOW Browser BY 8,3
```

NOTE, *: This command marks comment lines so they are not acted upon by a program. The syntax for this command is:

```
* [<expression>]
NOTE [<expression>]
```

Example:

```
NOTE Validate customer, salesrep, product numbers
CLEAR
@ 5,5 SAY "Verifying data...please wait..."
USE PRODUCT INDEX PRODUCT
SEEK MPRODID
IF EOF()
     * No such record found, so notify user
     * and back out of operation
     CLOSE DATABASES
     STORE .T. TO INVALID
     CLEAR
     ? CHR(7)
     @ 7,5 SAY "Invalid Product Number!"
```

ON ERROR: This command causes a specified command (usually a DO command to branch to another program) to be carried out when an error occurs within a program. The syntax for this command is:

```
ON ERROR <expression>
```

Examples:

```
ON ERROR DO FIXIT
ON ERROR ? "An error has occurred."
```

ON ESCAPE: This command causes a specified command (usually a DO command to branch to another program) to be carried out when the user presses Esc during program execution. The syntax for this command is:

```
ON ESCAPE <expression>
```

Example:

```
ON ESCAPE ? "Escape key is not a valid choice!"
```

ON KEY: This command causes a specified command (usually a DO command to branch to another program) to be carried out when the user presses any key. The syntax for this command is:

```
ON KEY <command>
```

Example:

```
DO WHILE .T.
     *Display date and time; wait for key
     CLEAR
     @ 5,5 SAY DATE()
     @ 7,5 SAY TIME()
     ON KEY DO MENU
ENDDO
```

ON PAD: ON PAD links a specified pad in a bar menu to a specific popup menu. When the pad is chosen from the bar menu, the associated popup menu appears. The syntax for this command is:

```
ON PAD <pad name> OF <menu name> [ACTIVATE POPUP <popup name>]
```

Example:

```
ON PAD Add OF Mailer ACTIVATE POPUP Adder
ON PAD Edit OF Mailer ACTIVATE POPUP Editor
ON PAD Print OF Mailer ACTIVATE POPUP Printer
```

ON PAGE: ON PAGE executes the command named after the ON PAGE command, each time the end of the page is reached. The page length is controlled by the system print variables when PRINTJOB is active (see PRINTJOB). The syntax for this command is:

```
ON PAGE [AT LINE <expN> <command>]
```

Example:

```
ON PAGE AT LINE 55 DO FOOTINGS
SET PRINT ON
LIST LAST_NAME, FIRST_NAME, COMMISSION, AMOUNT
(. . .more commands. . .)

*Procedure file begins here.*
PROCEDURE FOOTINGS
?
? " Sales listing- for Mid-Atlantic group."
EJECT
? " SALES LISTING "
?? DATE()
```

```
?
RETURN
```

ON READERROR: ON READERROR executes a named command, procedure, or program after detecting an error condition. ON READERROR is called as a result of improper responses to a VALID clause, improper entries when a RANGE clause is in effect, or improper date entries. The syntax for this command is:

```
ON READERROR [<command>]
```

Example:

```
ON READERROR DO EMESSAGE
```

ON SELECTION PAD: ON SELECTION PAD links a command, procedure, or program file to a pad in a bar menu. When the pad is chosen from the bar menu, the command, procedure, or program file named in the ON SELECTION statement is executed. The syntax for this command is:

```
ON SELECTION PAD <pad name> OF <menu name> [<command>]
```

Example:

```
ON SELECTION PAD Edit OF Mailer DO EDITOR
```

ON SELECTION POPUP: ON SELECTION POPUP names a command, procedure, or program file which executes when a selection is chosen from a popup menu. If no command or procedure is named, the active popup is deactivated. If the ALL clause is used, the command, procedure, or program file applies to all popups. The syntax for this command is:

```
ON SELECTION POPUP <popup name>/ALL [<command>]
```

Example:

```
ON SELECTION POPUP Printer DO Reports
```

PACK: This command removes records marked for deletion. It renumbers remaining records in the database. (See DELETE.) The syntax for this command is:

```
PACK
```

Example:

```
DELETE RECORD 7
PACK
```

PARAMETERS: This command passes parameters from one command file to another with the DO [WITH] command. The syntax for this command is:

```
PARAMETERS <parameter list>
```

Example:

```
*Program MAIN.PRG
INPUT "Social Security number? " TO NUMB
SEEK NUMB
IF .NOT. FOUND()
   DO CANTFIND WITH "Social Security Number"
ENDIF
<rest of commands...>

*Program CANTFIND.PRG
PARAMETER Noun
*Display the 'can't find it' message
CLEAR
? "This " + Noun + " does not exist in the database."
? "Return to the menu to select a function."
WAIT
RETURN
*End of CANTFIND.PRG
```

PLAY MACRO: PLAY MACRO plays a stored macro. The syntax for this command is:

```
PLAY MACRO <macro name>
```

Example:

```
PLAY MACRO MyMacro
```

PRINTJOB/ENDPRINTJOB: PRINTJOB puts stored print settings in effect for the duration of a print job, and activates the ON PAGE command (if ON PAGE was used earlier). The desired print settings are stored to the system printer memory variables before the PRINTJOB command is encountered. When PRINTJOB is executed, any starting codes stored to _pscodes are sent to the printer, a form feed is sent if _peject contains "BEFORE" or "BOTH", _pcolno is initialized at zero, and _plineno and ON PAGE are activated.

When printing is completed and ENDPRINTJOB is encountered, any ending print codes stored to _pecodes are sent to the printer. Also a form feed is sent if _peject contains "AFTER" or "BOTH"; the PRINTJOB command is repeated if the _pcopies variable contains more than 1 (that is, if more than one copy of the report is desired); and _plineno and ON PAGE are deactivated. The syntax for this command is:

```
PRINTJOB/<commands>/ENDPRINTJOB
```

Example:

```
*sets compressed print on for Epson with ESC code 018.
*does page eject before and after each report.
*spools three copies of report to printer.
_pecodes = 018
_peject = "BOTH"
_pcopies = 3
PRINTJOB
REPORT FORM Sales TO PRINT
END PRINTJOB
```

PRIVATE: This command creates memory variables that are not public to higher-level parts of a program. The syntax for this command is:

```
PRIVATE ALL [LIKE/EXCEPT <skeleton>] (or) PRIVATE <list>
```

Example:

```
PRIVATE HOURS, OVERTIME, TAXRATE
```

PROCEDURE: This command indicates the beginning of each procedure in a procedure file. The syntax for this command is:

```
PROCEDURE <name>
```

Example:

```
PROCEDURE FAIL1
   @2,10 SAY "You tried to enter a date outside of the valid range."
RETURN
**
PROCEDURE FAIL2
   @2,10 SAY "Are you using the correct disk?  Check and retry."
RETURN
**
PROCEDURE FAIL3
   @2,10 SAY "You tried to enter a salary outside of the valid range."
RETURN
```

PROTECT: PROTECT loads the menu-driven PROTECT utility, used to define security levels within the dBASE environment. The syntax for this command is:

```
PROTECT
```

Example:

```
PROTECT
```

PUBLIC ARRAY, PUBLIC MEMVAR LIST: This command declares memory variables or arrays as public; those variables are available to higher-level programs. The syntax for this command is:

```
PUBLIC [<memvar list>]/[ARRAY <array definition list>]
```

Example:

```
PUBLIC JANSALES, FEBSALES, MARSALES
```

QUIT: This command closes all open files and returns control to the operating system. The syntax for this command is:

```
QUIT
```

Example:

```
WAIT "Exit this program? Press E to exit, any other key for menu." TO TEMP
IF UPPER (TEMP) = "E"
     CLOSE DATABASES
     QUIT
ENDIF
RETURN TO MASTER
```

READ: This command permits full-screen data entry from a GET used with a field or memory variable. If the SAVE option is used, the GETs are not cleared following the READ command. The syntax for this command is:

```
READ [SAVE]
```

Example:

```
@ 2,2 SAY "Customer name?" GET CUST_NAME
READ
```

RECALL: This command restores records that have been marked for deletion. A scope (Record No., NEXT X, ALL, or REST) can be used to limit the records that will be recalled. The FOR and WHILE <condition> options can be used to further limit recalled records to a range of records. The syntax for this command is:

```
RECALL [<scope>][FOR <condition>] [WHILE <condition>]
```

Example:

```
GO 25
RECALL NEXT 15 FOR UPPER(LAST_NAME) = "GREGORY"
```

REINDEX: This command rebuilds open index files. The syntax for this command is:

```
REINDEX
```

Example:

```
REINDEX
```

RELEASE: This command erases memory variables from memory. Memory variables can be identified with a list, or ALL LIKE and ALL EXCEPT options can be used, with names or with wildcards, to specify variables to be released. MODULE removes a loaded module from memory. MENUS removes the named bar menus; POPUP removes the named popup menus; and WINDOW removes the named windows. The syntax for this command is:

```
RELEASE [:<memvar list>] [ALL [LIKE/EXCEPT <skeleton>]] [MODULE <module name>]
[MENUS <menu name>] [POPUP <popup name>] [WINDOW <window name>]
```

Examples:

```
RELEASE ALL EXCEPT *SALE
RELEASE ALL LIKE ???SALE
RELEASE GROSSSALE
```

RENAME: This command renames an existing file. If the old filename includes an extension, it must be provided. Path designations and drive designations can be provided, if the file is not located within the default drive and directory. The syntax for this command is:

```
RENAME <filename> TO <new filename>
```

Example:

```
RENAME C:FLNAME.DBF TO C:FILE1.DBF
```

REPLACE: This command replaces the contents of specific fields within a range of records with new values based on the expression provided. A scope (Record No., NEXT X, ALL, or REST) can be used to limit the records that will have fields replaced. The FOR and WHILE <condition> options can be used to further limit replacements to a range of records. Use the ADDITIVE option to build a memo field using the contents of character strings. The syntax for this command is:

```
REPLACE [<scope>] <field> WITH <expression> [,<field2> WITH <expression2>,...]
[FOR <condition>] [WHILE <condition>] [ADDITIVE]
```

Example:

```
REPLACE NEXT 250 SALEPRICE WITH SALEPRICE * 1.08
```

REPORT FORM: This command uses a report form file to generate a columnar report. (The report must have been created previously with the CREATE REPORT or MODIFY REPORT command.) A scope (Record No., NEXT X, ALL, or REST) can be used to limit the records that will appear in the report. The FOR and WHILE <condition> options can be used to further limit records printed to a range of records. The PLAIN option drops page numbers and system date from the report. The HEADING option, followed by character string, provides an additional header. The NOEJECT option cancels the form feed command that normally precedes a printed report. If the TO PRINT option is used, output will be simultaneously directed to the default printer. If TO FILE is used, output will be directed to a disk file. The syntax for this command is:

```
REPORT FORM <filename> [<scope>] [FOR <condition>] [WHILE <condition>] [PLAIN]
[HEADING <character string>] [NOEJECT] [TO PRINT] [TO FILE <filename>] [SUMMARY]
```

Example:

```
REPORT FORM SALES NOEJECT TO PRINT FOR AMT > 500
```

RESET: RESET strips the integrity flag from a database file. The integrity flag is normally removed by the END TRANSACTION command or by a successful ROLLBACK. If a successful ROLLBACK cannot be performed, use RESET to strip the integrity flag. The syntax for this command is:

```
RESET [IN <alias name>]
```

Example:

```
RESET
```

RESTORE FROM: This command restores memory variables from a memory variable (.MEM) file. If the ADDITIVE option is used, current memory variables will not be erased from memory when the new variables are read into memory. The syntax for this command is:

```
RESTORE FROM <filename> [ADDITIVE]
```

Example:

```
RESTORE FROM ERRFILE
```

RESTORE MACROS: RESTORE MACROS restores macros saved in a macro file to active memory. Any macros existing in memory which are assigned the same keys will be overwritten by the macros loaded with RESTORE MACROS. The syntax for this command is:

```
RESTORE MACROS FROM <macro filename>
```

Example:

```
RESTORE MACROS FROM MyMacros
```

RESTORE WINDOW: RESTORE WINDOW restores window definitions previously stored to a file with SAVE WINDOW (see SAVE WINDOW). The syntax for this command is:

```
RESTORE WINDOW <window name list>/ALL FROM <filename>
```

Example:

```
RESTORE WINDOW Screens
```

RESUME: This command resumes execution of a command file previously suspended, either when the user answers S to the "Cancel, Suspend, or Ignore?" prompt displayed at the time of a program error, or when a SUSPEND command has been placed within a program. The syntax for this command is:

```
RESUME
```

Example:

```
RESUME
```

RETRY: This command passes control to a higher-level program, at the same line that called the program containing the RETRY statement. Normally it is used within an error-trapping routine to return program control to the point of the error. The syntax for this command is:

```
RETRY
```

Example:

```
RETRY
```

RETURN: This command ends execution of a procedure or a command file. Program control returns to the next higher-level program. If there is no higher-level program, the dot prompt is displayed. The TO MASTER option can be specified to cause program control to return to the highest-level program (usually the Main Menu). Use <expression> to return a value from a user-defined function to a higher-level calling program. The syntax for this command is:

```
RETURN [TO MASTER] [<expression>]
```

Example:

```
RETURN
```

ROLLBACK: ROLLBACK restores the active database and any associated index files back to their original status before the BEGIN TRANSACTION command was encountered. (See BEGIN TRANSACTION.) The syntax for this command is:

```
ROLLBACK [<database name>]
```

Example:

```
ROLLBACK
```

RUN: This command runs an executable program from the DOS environment. The program can be any .COM, .EXE, or .BAT file, or any resident DOS command. Parameters can also be passed to the called program, if the called program normally accepts parameters. Upon completion of the program, batch file, or DOS command, control returns to dBASE IV. The syntax for this command is:

```
RUN <command>
```

Example:

```
RUN C:FORMAT A:/V/S
```

SAVE MACROS: SAVE MACROS stores macros currently in active memory to a macro file. The syntax for this command is:

```
SAVE MACROS TO <macro filename>
```

Example:

```
SAVE MACROS TO MyMacros
```

SAVE TO: This command stores memory variables in a file. Memory variables to be saved can be identified with a list, or ALL LIKE and ALL EXCEPT options can be used, with names or with wildcards, to specify variables to be saved. The syntax for this command is:

```
SAVE TO <variable filename> [ALL [LIKE/EXCEPT <skeleton>]]
```

Example:

```
SAVE TO MEMFILE ALL EXCEPT ???SOLD
```

SAVE WINDOW: SAVE WINDOW saves the windows named in <window list> to a disk file. If the ALL option is used, all windows in active memory are stored in the file. Use the RESTORE WINDOW command to restore the saved windows to memory. The syntax for this command is:

```
SAVE WINDOW <window list>/[ALL] TO <window filename>
```

Example:

```
SAVE WINDOW Browser, Editor TO Screens
```

SCAN: The SCAN and ENDSCAN commands form a repetitive loop, where all commands between the SCAN command and the ENDSCAN command are repeated for the condition named within the SCAN statement. The commands between SCAN and ENDSCAN will be processed for all records which meet the specified conditions. The syntax for this command is:

```
SCAN [<scope>] [FOR <condition>] [WHILE <condition>] [<commands. . .>]
     [LOOP]
     [<commands>]
```

```
    [EXIT]
ENDSCAN
```

Example:

```
USE SALES
SCAN FOR SALESCODE = "A"
     ? "Sales rep name is: " + SALESREP
     ? "Commission amount due is:"
     ? COMMISS
     ?
ENDSCAN
```

SEEK: This command moves the record pointer to the first record having an index key matching the specified expression. If no such match is located, the record pointer is placed at the end of the file, and EOF() is set to True. The syntax for this command is:

```
SEEK <expression>
```

Example:

```
SEEK CTOD("04/22/56")
```

SELECT: This command selects from among 10 possible work areas for opening of database and index files. A number of 1 to 10 can be specified, or alias names can be used. The syntax for this command is:

```
SELECT <n/alias>
```

Example:

```
SELECT 1
USE CUSTOMER
SELECT 2
USE SALES INDEX ACCOUNTS
```

SET: This command displays a menu-driven screen that can then be used to set various dBASE IV parameters. The syntax for this command is:

```
SET
```

Example:

```
SET
```

SET ALTERNATE OFF/ON: This command begins and ends storage of all keyboard entries and screen displays to the file named with the SET ALTERNATE TO command. This syntax for this command is:

```
SET ALTERNATE OFF/ON
```

Example:

```
SET ALTERNATE TO AUDIT
SET ALTERNATE ON
DISPLAY ALL
CLOSE ALTERNATE
```

SET ALTERNATE TO: This command creates a disk file that will contain all screen operations and keyboard responses, with the exception of full-screen (APPEND, EDIT, and so on) operations. (Also see SET ALTERNATE OFF/ON.) The syntax for this command is:

```
SET ALTERNATE TO <filename>
```

Example:

```
SET ALTERNATE TO LOG.TXT
```

SET AUTOSAVE ON/OFF: SET AUTOSAVE activates and deactivates the automatic save function after each I/O operation. If SET AUTOSAVE is ON, the chances of data loss due to power or hardware failure are greatly reduced. The default value for SET AUTOSAVE is OFF. The syntax for this command is:

```
SET AUTOSAVE ON / SET AUTOSAVE OFF
```

Example:

```
SET AUTOSAVE ON
```

SET BELL, SET BELL OFF/ON: This command controls whether a bell will be heard when entry fields are filled or when invalid responses are provided. The syntax for this command is:

```
SET BELL OFF/ON
```

Example:

```
SET BELL ON
```

SET BLOCKSIZE: SET BLOCKSIZE changes the block size used for storing data within memo fields. The default value of 1 is the only size compatible with dBASE III and dBASE III Plus. The value multiplied by 512 represents the actual size of the blocks, in bytes. Larger block sizes tend to speed performance when storing large amounts of text. The syntax for this command is:

```
SET BLOCKSIZE TO <expN>
```

Example:

```
SET BLOCKSIZE TO 4
```

SET BORDER: SET BORDER changes the default border from a single-line box to the type of border described. Use the SINGLE option to choose a single line, the DOUBLE option to choose a double line, the PANEL option to chooose a panel composed of the ASCII-219 character, and NONE to omit the border. The border definition string option should contain 8 ASCII values separated by commas. Value 1 specifies the top of the border; value 2 the bottom; values 3 and 4 the left and right sides; and values 5, 6, 7, and 8 the upper left, upper right, lower left, and lower right corners, respectively. The syntax for this command is:

```
SET BORDER TO [SINGLE/DOUBLE/PANEL/NONE/<border definition string>]
```

Example:

```
SET BORDER TO DOUBLE
```

SET CARRY OFF/ON: This command specifies whether entries will be duplicated from the previous record into a new record when the APPEND or INSERT command is used. The syntax for this command is:

```
SET CARRY OFF/ON
```

Examples:

```
SET CARRY ON
```

This entry duplicates fields from the previous record.

```
SET CARRY OFF
```

With this command, fields from the previous record are not duplicated.

SET CATALOG OFF/ON, SET CATALOG TO: This command creates a new catalog if none by the specified filename exists, or it opens an existing catalog if the catalog file exists. For files that are opened to be added to the catalog, the SET CATALOG ON command must then be executed. The syntax for this command is:

```
SET CATALOG OFF/ON
SET CATALOG TO <filename>
```

Examples:

```
SET CATALOG TO MASTER
SET CATALOG ON
```

SET CENTURY OFF/ON: This command turns on (or off) the display of dates with four-digit years. The syntax for this command is:

```
SET CENTURY OFF/ON
```

Example:

```
SET CENTURY ON
```

SET CLOCK ON/OFF, SET CLOCK TO: SET CLOCK specifies the location of the clock and whether the clock is displayed. SET CLOCK ON displays the clock, and SET CLOCK OFF hides the clock. The default location, if a location is not specified, is row 1, column 68. The syntax for this command is:

```
SET CLOCK ON/OFF
SET CLOCK TO <row>,<col>
```

Example:

```
SET CLOCK TO 21,10
SET CLOCK ON
```

SET COLOR ON/OFF, SET COLOR TO: This command sets the screen colors and intensity. The syntax for this command is:

```
SET COLOR TO <standard> [,<enhanced>][,<border>][, <background>]
```

Example:

```
SET COLOR TO W/B, GR/G
```

SET CONFIRM OFF/ON: This command controls the method of cursor advance between full-screen editing fields. The syntax for this command is:

```
SET CONFIRM OFF/ON
```

Examples:

```
SET CONFIRM ON
```

This command sets cursor movement so the user must press Return to move to next field.

```
SET CONFIRM OFF
```

This command sets the system so the cursor moves to next field when the field is filled or when Return is pressed.

SET CONSOLE OFF/ON: This command turns screen output off (or on). This command can be used within programs to hide operations normally viewed on the screen or to speed up program execution by temporarily disabling the screen. The syntax for this command is:

```
SET CONSOLE OFF/ON
```

Example:

```
SET CONSOLE OFF
REPORT FORM TOTSALE TO FILE TEXTFILE.TXT
SET CONSOLE ON
```

SET CURRENCY: SET CURRENCY changes the default currency symbol. A character expression containing 9 characters or less can be specified as the currency symbol. If a literal value is provided, it must be surrounded by quotes. The syntax for this command is:

```
SET CURRENCY TO [<expC>]
```

Example:

```
SET CURRENCY TO "f"
```

SET DATE: This command controls the date format for display of dates. Acceptable types are American, ANSI, British, Italian, French, German, Japan, USA, MDY, DMY, and YMD. American format is mm/dd/yy; ANSI is yy.mm.dd; British and French formats are dd/mm/yy; Italian format is dd-mm-yy; and German format is dd.mm.yy. Japan's format is yy/mm/dd; USA is mm/dd/yy. If the SET DATE command is not used, dBASE IV defaults to American display. The syntax for this command is:

```
SET DATE <type>
```

Example:

```
*Lire to Dollar Conversion Program
SET DATE ITALIAN
```

SET DEBUG OFF/ON: This command sends results of the SET ECHO command to the printer. The syntax for this command is:

```
SET DEBUG OFF/ON
```

Example:

```
SET DEBUG ON
SET ECHO ON
```

SET DECIMALS TO: This command sets the number of decimal places normally displayed as a result of calculations. The syntax for this command is:

```
SET DECIMALS TO <n>
```

Example:

```
SET DECIMALS TO 4
```

SET DEFAULT TO: This command sets the default drive. The syntax for this command is:

```
SET DEFAULT TO <drive:>
```

Example:

```
SET DEFAULT TO C:
```

SET DELETED OFF/ON: This command displays (or hides) records marked for deletion from processing by most dBASE IV commands. The syntax for this command is:

```
SET DELETED OFF/ON
```

Example:

```
*RECOVER.PRG restores deleted employee records
@5,5 SAY "Recover all deleted employee files? Y/N" GET ANS
READ
IF UPPER(ANS) = "Y"
     SET DELETED OFF
     RECALL ALL
ENDIF
```

SET DELIMITER OFF/ON: This command turns off (or on) delimiter characters specified with SET DELIMITER TO command. The syntax for this command is:

```
SET DELIMITER OFF/ON
```

Example:

```
SET DELIMITER OFF
```

SET DELIMITER TO: This command specifies characters to be used as the starting and ending delimiters for full-screen fields. Any character can be used. If one character is specified, that character is used as the beginning and ending delimiter. If two characters are used, the first character serves as the beginning delimiter, and the second character becomes the ending delimiter. The syntax for this command is:

```
SET DELIMITER TO [<character string>] [DEFAULT]
```

Example:

```
SET DELIMITER TO "{ }"
```

SET DESIGN ON/OFF: SET DESIGN activates and deactivates user access to the Design screens with Shift-F2. Use SET DESIGN OFF in your applications to keep end users from modifying forms, queries, etc. SET DESIGN OFF prevents design access with Shift-F2. SET DESIGN ON provides access to the design screens. The syntax for this command is:

```
SET DESIGN ON/SET DESIGN OFF
```

Example:

```
SET DESIGN OFF
```

SET DEVICE TO: This command specifies where the results of @ commands should be output. The default destination is the screen; a SET DEVICE TO PRINTER command reroutes output to the printer. Use the FILE option to route the output to a disk file. The syntax for this command is:

```
SET DEVICE TO PRINTER/SCREEN/FILE <filename>
```

Example:

```
SET DEVICE TO PRINTER
```

SET DEVELOPMENT ON/OFF: SET DEVELOPMENT ON is used to compare creation dates and times of source code (.PRG) files and compiled program (.DBO) files. This prevents an outdated .DBO file from being used when a program is run. SET DEVELOPMENT OFF tells dBASE to ignore any difference in directory dates and times between the .PRG file and an existing compiled (.DBO) file. The dBASE Editor deletes old .DBO files when a program is modified, so SET DEVELOPMENT ON is not necessary if the dBASE Editor is used to modify program files. If a different editor is used to create and modify program files, add SET DEVELOPMENT ON at or near the start of the program, or enter the command at the dot prompt. The default value of SET DEVELOPMENT is OFF. The syntax for this command is:

```
SET DEVELOPMENT ON/SET DEVELOPMENT OFF
```

Example:

```
SET DEVELOPMENT ON
```

SET DISPLAY TO: SET DISPLAY selects the desired monitor and sets the number of lines displayed. Note that the graphics hardware used must support the type chosen before the command will have any effect. The syntax for this command is:

```
SET DISPLAY TO MONO/COLOR/EGA25/EGA43/MONO43
```

Example:

```
SET DISPLAY TO EGA43
```

SET ECHO OFF/ON: This command determines whether commands within a program will be duplicated on—or "echoed" to—the screen during program execution. The SET ECHO command is a debugging tool primarily used with the SET DEBUG command (see SET DEBUG). The syntax for this command is:

```
SET ECHO OFF/ON
```

Example:

```
SET ECHO OFF
```

SET ENCRYPTION ON/OFF: This command, a network command, turns on or off the encryption of database files created from existing files. The syntax for this command is:

```
SET ENCRYPTION ON/OFF
```

Example:

```
SET ENCRYPTION ON
```

SET ESCAPE OFF/ON: This command sets the system to use (or not use) the Esc key to terminate program execution. The syntax for this command is:

```
SET ESCAPE OFF/ON
```

Example:

```
SET ESCAPE OFF
```

SET EXACT OFF/ON: This command sets the precision of comparisons between two character strings. If SET EXACT is ON, character strings must match precisely; if SET EXACT is OFF, only the first X characters of the larger string must match the smaller string with a length of X characters. The syntax for this command is:

```
SET EXACT OFF/ON
```

Example:

```
SET EXACT OFF
```

SET EXCLUSIVE ON/OFF: This command is a network command. When set to ON, it causes all subsequent databases opened to be opened in exclusive (non-sharable) mode. The syntax for this command is:

```
SET EXCLUSIVE ON/OFF
```

Example:

```
SET EXCLUSIVE ON
```

SET FIELDS OFF/ON; SET FIELDS TO: SET FIELDS TO specifies a list of fields that will be available to other dBASE IV commands. Once the list of fields has been specified, the list of fields is made active with the SET FIELDS ON command; the setting is canceled with the SET FIELDS OFF command. If the ALL option is used, all fields in the active database are made available. Use ADDITIVE to add the specified fields to a prior list of fields. The syntax for this command is:

```
SET FIELDS TO [<list of fields>] [ALL] [ADDITIVE]
```

Example:

```
SET FIELDS TO NAME, SOCSEC, PAYRATE
```

SET FILTER ON/OFF, SET FILTER TO: This command causes a database to appear as if it contains only records that meet a specific condition. All records not meeting the specified filter condition are excluded from most dBASE IV operations. The syntax for this command is:

```
SET FILTER TO [<condition>]/[FILE <filename>]
```

Example:

```
SET FILTER TO HIREDAY = CTOD("07/25/85")
```

SET FIXED OFF/ON: This command determines whether a specific number of decimal places will be displayed with all numeric output. It is used with the SET DECIMALS command (see SET DECIMALS). The syntax for this command is:

```
SET FIXED OFF/ON
```

Example:

```
SET DECIMALS TO 4
SET FIXED ON
```

SET FORMAT TO: This command opens a format file for use with full-screen commands. The syntax for this command is:

```
SET FORMAT TO <filename>
```

Example:

```
SET FORMAT TO FANCY
```

SET FULLPATH ON/OFF: This command, when off, suppresses the inclusion of file extensions in functions that return filenames. The syntax of this command is:

```
SET FULLPATH ON/OFF
```

Example:

```
SET FULLPATH ON
```

SET FUNCTION TO, SET FUNCTION ON/OFF: This command stores character strings in the function keys (to a maximum of 75 characters). The semicolon can be used to indicate a carriage return. The F1 function key cannot be reprogrammed with the SET FUNCTION command. The syntax for this command is:

```
SET FUNCTION <key #> TO <character string>
```

Example:

```
SET FUNCTION 2 TO "USE SALES;GO BOTTOM;EDIT"
```

SET HEADING OFF/ON: This command turns off (or on) the display of column headings that appear with LIST, DISPLAY, SUM, and AVERAGE commands. The syntax for this command is:

```
SET HEADING OFF/ON
```

Examples:

```
SET HEADING ON
SET HEADING OFF
```

SET HELP OFF/ON: This command determines whether the "Do you want some help?" prompt appears when an invalid command is entered. The syntax for this command is:

SET HELP OFF/ON

Example:

```
SET HELP OFF
```

SET HISTORY ON/OFF, SET HISTORY TO: This command specifies the number of previous commands to be stored within History. If no number is specified, a default value of 20 is assigned. The syntax for this command is:

SET HISTORY TO <numeric expression>

Example:

```
SET HISTORY TO 13
```

SET HOURS: SET HOURS sets the format for the time display to 12 (English) or 24 (military) hours. The syntax for this command is:

SET HOURS TO [12/24]

Example:

```
SET HOURS TO 24
```

SET INDEX TO: This command opens the index files named in the list. Up to seven index files can be opened at once by specifying more than one index filename. The syntax for this command is:

SET INDEX TO <index filename list>

Example:

```
SET INDEX TO CUSTOMER, SALESREP, REPID
```

SET INSTRUCT ON/OFF: SET INSTRUCT activates and deactivates the display of information boxes which are normally shown in BROWSE, EDIT, or other full-screen operations. SET INSTRUCT OFF hides the information boxes; SET INSTRUCT ON displays the boxes. The syntax for this command is:

```
SET INSTRUCT ON/SET INSTRUCT OFF
```

Example:

```
SET INSTRUCT ON
```

SET INTENSITY OFF/ON: This command sets reverse video on (or off) while full-screen operations are used. The syntax for this command is:

```
SET INTENSITY OFF/ON
```

Example:

```
SET INTENSITY ON
```

SET LOCK ON/OFF: SET LOCK activates and deactivates automatic file and record locking capabilities of dBASE IV, when installed on a local area network. The SET LOCK OFF statement disables automatic locking. The default value for SET LOCK is ON. The syntax for this command is:

```
SET LOCK ON/SET LOCK OFF
```

Example:

```
SET LOCK ON
```

SET MARGIN TO: This command sets the left margin that the printer will use. The value is in spaces for any printer. The default, if no value is specified, is zero. The syntax for this command is:

```
SET MARGIN TO <numeric expression>
```

Example:

```
SET MARGIN TO 15
```

SET MARK: SET MARK specifies a delimiter used to separate the month, day, and year of a date. The character expression must translate to a single character. If a literal character is supplied, it must be surrounded by quotes. The syntax for this command is:

```
SET MARK TO <expC>
```

Example:

```
SET MARK TO "\"
```

SET MEMOWIDTH TO: This command sets the width of the contents of memo fields when they are displayed or printed. The syntax for this command is:

```
SET MEMOWIDTH TO <numeric expression>
```

Example:

```
SET MEMOWIDTH TO 25
```

SET MENU ON/OFF: SET MENU is a valid (but non-operational) command, provided only to maintain compatibility with programs written in dBASE III PLUS. The command has no effect in dBASE IV. The syntax for this command is:

```
SET MENU ON/OFF
```

Example:

```
SET MENU ON
```

SET MESSAGE TO: This command specifies a message that appears at the bottom of the screen in place of the default message, "Enter a dBASE IV command." The syntax for this command is:

```
SET MESSAGE TO <character string or expression>
```

Example:

```
SET MESSAGE TO (DTOC())
```

SET NEAR ON/OFF: SET NEAR places the record pointer at the nearest record following an unsucessful SEEK or FIND operation. When SET NEAR is ON, the record pointer is placed at the next record following the expression that could not be found. When SET NEAR is OFF, the record pointer is placed at the end of the file if the expression is not found. The syntax for this command is:

```
SET NEAR ON/SET NEAR OFF
```

Example:

```
SET NEAR ON
```

SET ODOMETER: SET ODOMETER specifies how often commands which display a record count will update the screen display. The default value for SET ODOMETER is 1, and the maximum value is 200. The syntax for this command is:

```
SET ODOMETER TO [<expN>]
```

Example:

```
SET ODOMETER TO 20
```

SET ORDER TO: This command selects the controlling index tag or index file. The syntax of this command is:

```
SET ORDER TO [<expression>]
SET ORDER TO [TAG] <filename>/<.MDX tagname> [OF <.MDX filename>]
```

Example:

```
SET ORDER TO NAMES
```

SET PATH TO: This command specifies a DOS path to search if a file is not in the default directory. The syntax for this command is:

```
SET PATH TO <pathname>
```

Example:

```
SET PATH TO C:\DOS\SUPPLEM
```

SET POINT: SET POINT specifies the character used as the decimal point. The specified character expression can be a single character stored to a memory variable, or a single character surrounded by quotes. The syntax for this command is:

```
SET POINT TO <expC>
```

Example:

```
SET POINT TO "/"
```

SET PRECISION: SET PRECISION specifies the number of digits which dBASE IV uses for internal precision in math operations using fixed (type N) numbers. The default value of SET PRECISION is 16. Acceptable values range from 10 to 20. The syntax for this command is:

```
SET PRECISION TO <expN>
```

Example:

```
SET PRECISION TO 18
```

SET PRINT OFF/ON: This command echoes screen output to the printer in addition to the screen. The syntax for this command is:

```
SET PRINT OFF/ON
```

Example:

```
SET PRINT ON
```

SET PRINTER TO: This command specifies the DOS device that will be used as default printer. Standard DOS names (LPT1, LPT2, COM1, COM2) can be used. The syntax for this command is:

```
SET PRINTER TO LPT1/LPT2/COM1/COM2
```

Example:

```
SET PRINTER TO LPT2
```

SET PROCEDURE TO: This command opens the specified procedure file. The syntax for this command is:

```
SET PROCEDURE TO <procedure filename>
```

Example:

```
SET PROCEDURE TO Process1
```

SET REFRESH: SET REFRESH specifies the amount of time (in seconds) between screen refresh when in BROWSE or EDIT modes on a network. The minimum value is 0, and the maximum value is 3600 (one hour). The default is zero. The syntax for this command is:

```
SET REFRESH TO <expN>
```

Example:

```
SET REFRESH TO 30
```

SET RELATION TO: This command links the database in use to another database in a separate work area. The syntax for this command is:

```
SET RELATION TO <key>/RECNO()/<expression> INTO <alias>
```

Example:

```
SET RELATION TO CUSTOMER INTO SALES
```

SET REPROCESS: SET REPROCESS specifies the number of times that a retry operation will be attempted against a locked file or record before an error message is displayed. The minimum value is 1, and the maximum value is 32,000.

Any negative value may be entered; this causes the operation to be retried on an infinite basis. The syntax for this command is:

```
SET REPROCESS TO <expN>
```

Example:

```
SET REPROCESS TO 10
```

SET SAFETY OFF/ON: This command turns off (or on) the confirmation message that normally appears before files are overwritten. The syntax for this command is:

```
SET SAFETY OFF/ON
```

Example:

```
SET SAFETY OFF
```

SET SCOREBOARD ON/OFF: This command, when on, displays the keyboard indicators on line 0 if SET STATUS has been turned off. The syntax for this command is:

```
SET SCOREBOARD ON/OFF
```

Example:

```
SET SCOREBOARD ON
```

SET SEPARATOR: SET SEPARATOR specifies the symbol used to separate hundreds in numeric amounts. The default for SET SEPARATOR is the comma. The expression may be any single character stored to a variable, or any single character surrounded by quotes. The syntax for this command is:

```
SET SEPARATOR TO <expC>
```

Example:

```
SET SEPARATOR TO "*"
```

SET SKIP: SET SKIP command lets you access all records within a linked file that match a particular index key value. Use SET SKIP along with the SET RELATION command. The syntax for this command is:

```
SET SKIP TO [<alias name 1> [,<alias name 2>. . .]
```

Example:

```
SET SKIP TO Sales
```

SET SPACE ON/OFF: SET SPACE activates and deactivates the addition of a space between expressions printed with the ? and ?? commands. The default for SET SPACE is ON. The syntax for this command is:

```
SET SPACE ON/SET SPACE OFF
```

Example:

```
SET SPACE ON
USE SALES
GO 3
? last_name, first_name

Miller Larry

SET SPACE OFF
? last_name, first_name

MillerLarry
```

SET SQL ON/OFF: SET SQL enables or disables the Structured Query Language (SQL) mode of dBASE IV. The syntax for this command is:

```
SET SQL ON/SET SQL OFF
```

Example:

```
SET SQL ON
```

SET STATUS ON/OFF: This command turns on or off the status bar at the bottom of the screen. The syntax for this command is:

```
SET STATUS ON/OFF
```

Example:

```
SET STATUS ON
```

SET STEP OFF/ON: This command determines if execution of a command file will halt after each command. Normally it is used as a debugging aid. The syntax for this command is:

```
SET STEP OFF/ON
```

Example:

```
SET STEP OFF
```

SET TALK OFF/ON: This command turns off (or on) screen responses to most dBASE IV operations and calculations within a program. The syntax for this command is:

```
SET TALK OFF/ON
```

Example:

```
SET TALK ON
```

SET TITLE ON/OFF: SET TITLE activates and deactivates the catalog title prompt. The catalog title prompt normally appears when a new file is saved and SET CATALOG is ON. The syntax for this command is:

```
SET TITLE ON/SET TITLE OFF
```

Example:

```
SET TITLE ON
```

SET TRAP ON/OFF: SET TRAP activates and deactivates automatic startup of the program debugger in the event of a program error. When SET TRAP is

OFF, the debugger does not start automatically if a program error occurs. The syntax for this command is:

```
SET TRAP ON/SET TRAP OFF
```

Example:

```
SET TRAP OFF
```

SET TYPEAHEAD TO: This command changes the size of the typeahead buffer. Its default value is 20; valid entries are from 0 to 32,000. The syntax for this command is:

```
SET TYPEAHEAD TO <numeric expression>
```

Example:

```
SET TYPEAHEAD TO 500
```

SET UNIQUE OFF/ON: This command is used in combination with index files to create index files with no duplicate key expressions or fields. The syntax for this command is:

```
SET UNIQUE OFF/ON
```

Example:

```
SET UNIQUE ON
```

SET VIEW TO: This command selects the specified query (.QBE) or view (.VUE) file, opening all databases and associated files named within the query or view file. The syntax for this command is:

```
SET VIEW TO <filename>
```

Example:

```
SET VIEW TO GROUP5
```

SHOW MENU: SHOW MENU displays a menu without activating the menu. Use SHOW MENU while designing the menu, to check its appearance. The syntax for this command is:

```
SHOW MENU <menu name> [PAD <pad name>]
```

Example:

```
SHOW MENU Adder
```

SHOW POPUP: SHOW POPUP displays a popup menu without activating the menu. Use SHOW POPUP while designing the menu, to check its appearance. The syntax for this command is:

```
SHOW POPUP <popup name>
```

Example:

```
SHOW POPUP Printer
```

SKIP: This command moves the record pointer. If no numeric expression is supplied, SKIP moves the pointer forward by one record. Use IN alias-name to move the record pointer in a file open in another work area. The syntax for this command is:

```
SKIP [<numeric expression>] [IN <alias-name>]
```

Examples:

```
SKIP -2
SKIP 5
```

SORT TO: This command creates a sorted duplicate of a database. The new database will contain records arranged in the order specified by the fields listed. A scope (Record No., NEXT X, ALL, or REST) can be used to limit the records that will be included in the sorted database. The syntax for this command is:

```
SORT ON <field name>[/A][/C][/D][, <field name 2>[/A][/C][/D]...[, <field name 10>
[/A][/C][/D] TO <filename> [scope] [WHILE <condition>] [FOR <condition>]
```

Example:

```
SORT NEXT 200 TO MYFILE ON LAST_NAME + FIRST_NAME
```

STORE: This command stores a specified expression to the memory variable named. If the memory variable does not exist prior to the STORE command, an appropriate memory variable will be created. The ARRAY option stores the values to the named array. The syntax of this command is:

```
STORE <expression> TO [<memory variable list>]/[ARRAY <element-list>]
```

Example:

```
STORE GROSSTAX + GROSSALE TO FINALAMT
```

SUM: This command provides a total of expressions involving numeric fields. If the TO option is specified, totals are stored to the memory variables identified with TO; otherwise, totals are displayed on the screen. The FOR and WHILE <condition> options can be used to limit totals to include numeric fields from a range of records. The ARRAY option stores the values to the named array. The syntax for this command is:

```
SUM [<scope>] [<expression list>] TO [<memory variable list>] [FOR <condition>]
[/WHILE <condition>] [TO ARRAY <array-name>]
```

Example:

```
SUM GROSSTAX, NETTAX TO FIRST, SECOND
```

SUSPEND: This command suspends program execution while keeping files open and memory variables intact. It is used primarily for debugging purposes; execution can be restarted with the RESUME command. The syntax for this command is:

```
SUSPEND
```

Example:

```
SUSPEND
```

TEXT, ENDTEXT: This command displays all text that appears between the TEXT and ENDTEXT commands on the screen. The syntax for this command is:

```
TEXT
<character string(s)>
ENDTEXT
```

Example:

```
TEXT
Enter a selection:
(1) To use the deposition indexing system
(2) To search for a deposition witness
(3) To return to the previous menu
ENDTEXT
```

TOTAL TO: This command adds the numeric fields within the active database and creates a new database that contains a single record for each group of records in the original database. The single record shows the total for the records in the original database. The syntax for this command is:

```
TOTAL TO <filename> ON <key> [<scope>] [FIELDS <field list>] [FOR <condition>]
[WHILE <condition>]
```

Example:

```
USE PAYROLL
TOTAL TO FEES ON DOLLARS, LIRE, POUNDS
```

TYPE: This command displays the contents of a disk file. Use TO PRINT to route the output to the printer, TO FILE to route the output to another file. The syntax for this command is:

```
TYPE <filename> [TO PRINT] [TO FILE <filename>]
```

Example:

```
TYPE RECORDS.TXT
```

UNLOCK: This command, a network command, releases any file or record locks previously established in the current work area. Use the IN <alias> option to release locks in another work area. The syntax for this command is:

```
UNLOCK [ALL/IN <alias>]
```

Example:

```
UNLOCK
```

UPDATE: This command uses data from a specified database to make changes to the active database. The changes are made by matching records in both files on one key field. The syntax for this command is:

```
UPDATE [RANDOM] ON <key field> FROM <alias> REPLACE <field> WITH <expression>
[,<field2> WITH <expression2>...]
```

Example:

```
SELECT 2
     USE FINANCE
     SELECT 1
     USE EUROPEAN
     UPDATE ON LASTNAME FROM FINANCE REPLACE DOLLARS WITH FINANCE -> DOLLARS
```

USE: This command opens a database file and related index files in the chosen work area. If ? is used instead of a filename, a pick list of available filenames appears. The INDEX and ORDER options are used to specify open index files and active index tags. The IN option is used to open a file in a different work area. Use EXCLUSIVE on a local area network, when the file is to be opened for exclusive (non-shared) use. The syntax for this command is:

```
USE [<filename>] [/?] [INDEX <file list>] [ALIAS <alias>] [IN <work-area number>]
[ORDER <.ndx-filename/.mdx file-tag> [OF <.mdx name>]] [EXCLUSIVE]
```

Example:

```
USE FINANCE INDEX FEES,NAMES
```

WAIT: This command halts operation of a command file and displays an optional prompt until a key is pressed. If the TO option is used, the key pressed will be stored as a memory variable. The syntax for this command is:

```
WAIT [<prompt>] [TO <memory variable>]
```

Example:

```
WAIT "Enter choice now." TO CHOICE
```

ZAP: This command removes all records from a database file. ZAP is functionally identical to the DELETE ALL command that is immediately followed by a PACK command. However, ZAP operates faster than DELETE ALL and PACK. The syntax for this command is:

```
ZAP
```

Example:

```
ZAP
```

B

dBASE IV Function Summary

This appendix summarizes the commonly used dBASE IV functions. After each function's name, its purpose is detailed. Then the proper syntax for entering the function is shown, followed by an example of the function's use. For a similar summary of the dBASE IV commands, see Appendix A.

&: The & function is the macro substitution function. It is used to supply the contents of a memory variable containing a character expression, when dBASE would otherwise use the name of the variable itself. The optional period can be used as a terminator to clearly mark the end of the macro. The syntax for this function is:

```
& (<character expression>)
```

Example:

```
ACCEPT "Enter database file to use: " TO FNAME
ACCEPT "Enter .NDX index file to use: " TO NDXNAME
USE &FNAME.  INDEX &NDXNAME
```

ABS: The ABS function returns the absolute value of a numeric expression. The syntax for this function is:

```
ABS(<numeric expression>)
```

Example:

```
STORE —5 TO NUMB
? NUMB
—5
```

```
? ABS(NUMB)
5
```

ACCESS(): The ACCESS() function returns the access level of a user when running on a local area network. Use the PROTECT command to assign varying access levels to network users. The syntax for this function is:

```
ACCESS()
```

Example:

```
*Main program denies access if not authorized.
SET TALK OFF
SET BELL OFF
IF ACCESS() > 5
    CLEAR
    ? "You are NOT authorized to use this program!"
    ? "contact administrator for assistance."
    WAIT "Press a key to continue..."
    QUIT
ENDIF
CLEAR
TEXT
<...more commands...>
```

ACOS: The ACOS function returns the angle size, as measured in radians, for a given cosine value. (To convert radians to degrees, use the RTOD() function.) The value supplied to the numeric expression must be between −1 and +1. The syntax for this function is:

```
ACOS(<numeric expression>)
```

Example:

```
? ACOS(.707)
0.79
```

ALIAS: The ALIAS function returns the name of the specified work area. If no work area is specified, the ALIAS function returns the name of the current work area. The syntax for this function is:

```
ALIAS([<numeric expression>])
```

Example:

```
USE MAILER ALIAS MAILS
USE SALES IN 2
? ALIAS(2)
SALES
? ALIAS()
MAILS
```

ASC: This function converts a character, or the leftmost character in a character string, into its equivalent ASCII value. The syntax for this function is:

```
ASC(<character expression>)
```

Example:

```
. ? ASC("Nikki")
   78
```

ASIN: The ASIN function returns the angle, as measured in radians, for a given sine value. (To convert radians to degrees, use the RTOD() function.) The value supplied to the numeric expression must be between −1 and +1. The syntax for this function is:

```
ASIN(<numeric expression>)
```

Example:

```
? ASIN(.5)
0.52
```

AT: This function provides a numeric value indicating the starting position of a substring within a character string. The syntax for this function is:

```
AT(<substring>,<character string or expression>)
```

Example:

```
STORE "STRING INSIDE OF A STRING" TO TEXT
? AT("INSIDE OF",TEXT)
         8
```

ATAN: The ATAN function returns the angle, as measured in radians, for a given tangent value. (To convert radians to degrees, use the RTOD() function.)

The value specified by the numeric expression is the tangent of the angle. It can range between pi/2 and −pi/2. The syntax for this function is:

```
ATAN(<numeric expression>)
```

Example:

```
? ATAN(1.0)
0.79
```

ATN2: The ATN2 function returns the angle, as measured in radians, where the cosine and the sine of a given point are specified. Use <numeric expression 1> to specify the sine of the angle, and use <numeric expression 2> to specify the cosine of the angle. The value of <numeric expression 1>/<numeric expression 2> must range between pi and −pi. To convert the resulting value to degrees, use the RTOD() function. The syntax for this function is:

```
ATN2(<numeric expression 1>,<numeric expression 2>)
```

Example:

```
? ATN2(.5, .707)
0.62
```

BAR: The BAR function returns a number representing the most recently selected bar in a popup menu. If Esc was used to exit the menu, or if no menu is active, BAR() returns a value of zero. The syntax for this function is:

```
BAR()
```

Example:

```
PROCEDURE Printer
DO CASE
    CASE BAR() = 1
    REPORT FORM MAIL TO PRINT
    CASE BAR() = 2
    REPORT FORM PERSONS TO PRINT
    CASE BAR() = 3
    DO DETAIL
    CASE BAR() = 4
    RETURN
ENDCASE
```

BOF(): This function provides a logical True (.T.) if the record pointer is at the beginning of the database, and a logical False (.F.) if the record pointer is not at the beginning of the database. The syntax for this function is:

```
BOF()
```

Example:

```
GO TOP
SKIP -1
? BOF()
.T.
```

CALL: The CALL function is used to execute a binary routine loaded into memory with the LOAD command. The CALL function performs the same task as the CALL command, but the function can be used to execute and pass a value to the binary routine, and return a value (provided by the binary routine). <character expression> is the name of the routine, minus its extension. <memory variable> is the name of the variable which receives the value returned from the binary routine. The syntax for this function is:

```
CALL(<character expression>,<char expression>/<memvar name>)
```

Example:

```
*WRDCOUNT.BIN is a binary routine that counts words.*
STORE " " TO WORDS
? "Total words in the file are:"
? CALL("Wrdcount",words)
```

CDOW: This function provides the day of the week, in the form of a character expression, from a date expression. The syntax for this function is:

```
CDOW(<date expression>)
```

Example:

```
. store date() to today
 12/04/88
. ? CDOW(TODAY)
 Sunday
```

CEILING: The CEILING function returns the smallest integer greater than or equal to a numeric value. The syntax for this function is:

```
CEILING(<numeric expression>)
```

Example:

```
STORE 7.89 TO NUMB
? NUMB
7.89
? CEILING(NUMB)
8
```

CHANGE: This function returns a logical true if a record was changed after it was opened in a multi-user environment. The database must be updated with the CONVERT command before the CHANGE() function can be used. The syntax for this function is:

```
CHANGE()
```

Example:

```
? CHANGE()
.F.
```

CHR: This function converts a numeric expression containing a valid ASCII value to the equivalent character. The syntax for this function is:

```
CHR(<numeric expression>)
```

Example:

```
.? CHR(78)
 N
```

CMONTH: This function provides a character string containing the name of the month from a date expression. The syntax for this function is:

```
CMONTH(<date expression>)
```

Example:

```
? DATE()
12/04/88
? CMONTH(DATE())
```

```
December
```

COL: This function provides the current column location of the cursor. The syntax for this function is:

```
COL()
```

Example:

```
? COL()
25
```

A second example:

```
CLEAR
@ 5, 10 SAY "Account balance for: "
@ 5, COL + 1 SAY TRIM(LAST_NAME) + ": "
@ 5, COL + 1 SAY LTRIM(STR(BALANCE))
```

COMPLETED: This function returns a logical true when a transaction has been completed (see the commands BEGIN TRANSACTION, ROLLBACK in Appendix A). The syntax for this function is:

```
COMPLETED()
```

Example:

```
BEGIN TRANSACTION
REPLACE ALL BONUS WITH BONUS + (BONUS * .05)
END TRANSACTION
IF .NOT. COMPLETED()
    CLEAR
    ? "Error during transaction.  Please retry later."
    ? "One moment while transaction is rolled back..."
    ROLLBACK
    CLEAR
    RETURN TO MASTER
ENDIF
```

COS: This function returns a cosine value for an angle as measured in radians. The numeric expression supplied is the angle measured in radians. If the size is known in degrees, use the DTOR() function first to convert the size to radians, then use the COS() function. To convert the result back to degrees, use the RTOD() function. The syntax for this function is:

```
COS(<numeric expression>)
```

Example:

```
? COS(0.79)
0.70
```

CTOD: This function converts a character expression containing a string of characters formatted as a date into a date variable. The character string supplied by the expression can vary from "1/1/100" to "12/31/9999". The syntax for this function is:

```
CTOD(<character expression>)
```

Example:

```
. STORE CTOD("07/06/74") TO WEDDING
07/06/74
. DISPLAY MEMORY
WEDDING      pub   D  07/06/74
    1 variables defined,        9 bytes used
  255 variables available,   5991 bytes available
```

DATE(): This function provides the current date, in the form of a date variable. The syntax for this function is:

```
DATE()
```

Example:

```
. ? DATE()
12/04/88
```

DAY: This function provides a numeric expression equivalent to the day within a date expression. The syntax for this function is:

```
DAY(date expression)
```

Example:

```
? DATE()
12/04/88
? DAY(date())
4
```

DBF: This function provides the name of the currently active database file in the currently selected work area. The syntax for this function is:

```
DBF()
```

Example:

```
USE MAILER
? DBF()
C:MAILER.DBF
```

DELETED: This function provides a logical True (.T.) if the current record has been marked for deletion. The syntax for this function is:

```
DELETED()
```

Example:

```
USE MAILER
GO 5
DELETE
GO 2
? DELETED()
.F.
GO 5
? DELETED()
.T.
```

DIFFERENCE: This function returns a numeric value representing the difference between two character strings. The numeric value returned is a number between 0 and 4, and is calculated by converting both strings to equivalent SOUNDEX codes and comparing the two SOUNDEX codes. Two expressions that have no letters in common return a value of zero, while two expressions which are a close match phonetically return a value of 4. The syntax for this function is:

```
DIFFERENCE(<character exp 1>,<character exp 2>)
```

Example:

```
STORE "Jones" TO NAME1
STORE "Johnson" TO NAME2
STORE "Miller" TO NAME3
```

```
? DIFFERENCE(NAME1,NAME2)
3
? DIFFERENCE(NAME1,NAME3)
1
```

DISKSPACE: This function provides an integer value indicating the free space, in bytes, on the default disk drive. The syntax for this function is:

```
DISKSPACE()
```

Example:

```
? DISKSPACE()
   2234368
```

DMY: This function converts a valid date expression into a day-month-year format. The resultant format is DD-Month-YY if SET CENTURY is OFF, or DD-Month-YYYY if SET CENTURY is ON. The syntax for this function is:

```
DMY(<date expression>)
```

Example:

```
? DMY(DATE())
11 December 88
SET CENTURY ON
? DMY(DATE())
11 December 1988
```

DOW: This function provides a numeric value representing the day of the week from a date expression (Sunday is 1, Monday is 2, and so on). The syntax for this function is:

```
DOW(<date expression>)
```

Example:

```
? DATE()
12/05/88
? DOW (DATE())
2
```

DTOC: This function converts a date expression into a string of characters. The syntax for this function is:

```
DTOC(<date expression>)
```

Example:

```
. STORE DTOC(WEDDING) TO TEST
 07/06/74
.
. ? TEST
 07/06/74
.
. DISPLAY MEMORY
 WEDDING     pub   D  07/06/74
 TEST        pub   C  "07/06/74"
     2 variables defined,       19 bytes used
   254 variables available,   5981 bytes available
```

DTOR: This function converts a numeric value representing degrees of an angle into the equivalent angle size as measured in radians. The syntax for this function is:

```
DTOR(<numeric expression>)
```

Example:

```
? DTOR(90)
1.57
```

DTOS: This function converts a valid date expression into a character string in the format of CCYYMMDD, regardless of the SET DATE or SET CENTURY settings. The DTOS function is useful for maintaining proper chronological order when indexing on date fields. The syntax for this function is:

```
DTOS(<date expression>)
```

Example:

```
INDEX ON DTOS(HIRED) TAG HIREDAYS
```

EOF(): This function provides a logical True (.T.) if the record pointer is at the end of the database, and a logical False (.F.) if the record pointer is not at the end of the database. The syntax for this function is:

```
EOF()
```

Example:

```
USE MAILER
GO BOTTOM
?EOF()
.F.
SKIP
?EOF()
.T.
```

ERROR: This function provides a value that corresponds to a program error detected during the execution of a dBASE IV program. The syntax for this function is:

```
ERROR()
```

Example:

```
***PANIC.PRG is error trapping
CLEAR
DO CASE
    CASE CHOICE Error() = 1
         ? "Can't find that file. Do you have the proper"
         ? "disk in drive B? Verify correct disk and try again."
         WAIT
         RETRY
    CASE CHOICE Error() = 28
         <more commands>
```

EXP: This function provides an exponential value of a numeric expression. The syntax for this function is:

```
EXP(<numeric expression>)
```

Example:

```
? EXP(.5)
1.65
.
```

FIELD: This function provides the field name matching the numeric position of the field within the database structure. The syntax for this function is:

```
FIELD(<numeric expression>)
```

Example:

```
USE MAILER
? FIELD(3)
ADDRESS_1
? FIELD(5)
CITY
```

FILE: This function checks for the existence of a specified file. The filename must be enclosed in quotation marks or identified as a character variable. Any extension must be included as part of the filename. The syntax for this function is:

```
FILE(<filename>)
```

Example:

```
? FILE("MAILER.DBF")
.T.

? FILE("NOSUCH.TXT")
.F.
```

FIXED: This function converts floating numbers (type F, real floating point) to numeric (type N, binary coded decimal) numbers. Note that you may lose some levels of precision in the conversion process. The syntax for this function is:

```
FIXED(<numeric expression>)
```

Example:

```
SET DECIMALS TO 16
STORE PI() TO NUMB
? NUMB
3.1415926535897931
? FIXED(NUMB)
3.1415926535897930
```

FKLABEL: This function provides the name of the function key matching the numeric expression contained in the function. The syntax for this function is:

```
FKLABEL(<numeric expression>)
```

Example:

```
? FKLABEL(1)
F2
? FKLABEL(7)
F8
```

FKMAX: This function provides the number of programmable function keys present on the computer. On an IBM PC or AT compatible with 10 function keys, the FKMAX() function returns a value of 28, because F1 is not considered to be a programmable key by dBASE IV, and Shift-F10 is reserved for use with macros. Also, F11 and F12 are not programmable. The syntax for this function is:

```
FKMAX()
```

Example:

```
? FKMAX()
  28
```

FLOAT: This function converts numeric (type N, binary coded decimal) numbers to float (type F, real floating point) numbers. The syntax for this function is:

```
FLOAT(<numeric expression>)
```

Example:

```
? FLOAT(2.7995E09)
27995000000
```

FLOCK: This function locks a database file on a network, and returns a logical value of true if the attempted lock is successful. Use the optional [ALIAS] to lock a file in another work area. The syntax for this function is:

```
FLOCK([ALIAS])
```

Example:

```
USE MAILER
IF .NOT.  FLOCK()
    ? "Can't reindex file.  Someone else is using it."
```

```
    WAIT "Try again later.  Press any key..."
    RETURN
ELSE
    INDEX ON LAST_NAME TO NAMES
    UNLOCK
ENDIF
```

FLOOR: This function returns the largest integer less than or equal to the value specified by the expression. The syntax for this function is:

```
FLOOR(<numeric expression>)
```

Example:

```
STORE 5.87 TO NUMB
? NUMB
5.87
? FLOOR(NUMB)
5
```

FOUND: This function tests for the successful find of a record with a LOCATE, CONTINUE, SEEK, or FIND command. If the command used to search for the record is successful, the FOUND() function provides a logical value of True. The syntax for this function is:

```
FOUND()
```

Example:

```
USE MAILER INDEX NAMES
SEEK "Robinson"
?FOUND()
.T.
```

FV: This function returns the future value of an investment. <payment> is the payment amount and can be negative or positive. <rate> is a positive number representing the interest rate, compounded per period. <periods> is a number representing the number of payments. If the payments are compounded monthly and the interest rate is compounded yearly, divide the interest rate by 12 to obtain the monthly interest rate before using the function. The syntax for this function is:

```
FV(<payment>,<rate>,<periods>)
```

Example:

```
INPUT "Enter amount: " TO PMT
INPUT "Enter yearly interest rate: " TO YRINT
INPUT "Enter number of months: " TO MNTHS
INT = YRINT/12
? "Future value of investment is: "
?? FV(PMT,INT,MNTHS)
```

GETENV: This function provides the DOS environmental variable named in the character expression. The syntax for this function is:

```
GETENV(<character expression>)
```

Example:

```
? GETENV("path")
C:\PCWRITE
? GETENV("COMSPEC")
C:\COMMAND.COM
```

IIF: This function performs a conditional IF test of a logical expression and returns one of two expressions if the condition is true. The syntax for this function is:

```
IIF(<logical expression>,<expression 1>,<expression 2>)
```

Example:

```
BENEFITS = IIF(SALARIED = .T., .057*SALARY, 0)
```

INKEY: This function provides a numeric value representing the ASCII code for the keyboard key most recently pressed. If no key has been pressed, INKEY() returns zero as a value. The syntax for this function is:

```
INKEY()
```

Example:

```
*Following program displays results of INKEY function
STORE 0 TO KEY
DO WHILE KEY = 0
```

```
     STORE INKEY() TO KEY
ENDDO
? "The value of that key is: "
?? KEY
```

INT: This function converts a numeric expression to an integer. Rounding to a higher number does not occur; instead, all digits to the right of the decimal place are ignored. The syntax for this function is:

```
INT (<numeric expression>)
```

Example:

```
? INT(18.9995)
18
```

ISALPHA: This function evaluates a character expression and provides a logical True (.T.) if that expression begins with an alpha character. The syntax for this function is:

```
ISALPHA(<character expression>)
```

Example:

```
STORE "TX5400" TO FIRST
STORE "5400TX" TO SECOND

? ISALPHA(FIRST)
.T.

? ISALPHA(SECOND)
.F.
```

ISCOLOR: This function provides a logical True (.T.) if dBASE IV is running in color mode and a logical False (.F.) if dBASE IV is running in monochrome mode. The syntax for this function is:

```
ISCOLOR()
```

Example:

```
*Following program tests for color mode
USE CLIENTS
IF ISCOLOR()
```

```
   SET COLOR TO W/B, R/G
ENDIF
<rest of commands...>
```

ISLOWER: This function provides a logical True (.T.) if the expression begins with a lowercase alpha character. It provides a logical False (.F.) if the first character of the expression is a nonalpha character (any numeral, uppercase alpha character, or punctuation symbol). The syntax for this function is:

```
ISLOWER(<character expression>)
```

Example:

```
STORE "little words" TO FIRST
STORE "BIG WORDS" TO SECOND
STORE "10numbers" TO THIRD

? ISLOWER(FIRST)
 .T.

? ISLOWER(SECOND)
 .F.

? ISLOWER(THIRD)
 .F.
```

ISMARKED: This function returns a logical value of true if a database file is in the process of being changed, as indicated by the setting of a change marker contained in the file header. The marker is changed by the BEGIN TRANSACTION, END TRANSACTION, and ROLLBACK commands. BEGIN TRANSACTION sets the marker to TRUE, and END TRANSACTION and ROLLBACK set the marker to FALSE. If ISMARKED() returns a logical true, this indicates that a transaction is still in progress, or a successful ROLLBACK has not been completed. Use the optional alias to check the status of a file open in a different work area. The syntax for this function is:

```
ISMARKED([<alias>])
```

Example:

```
USE SALES
BEGIN TRANSACTION
REPLACE ALL PRICE WITH PRICE + (PRICE * .1)
? ISMARKED()
```

```
 .T.
END TRANSACTION
? ISMARKED()
 .F.
```

ISUPPER: This function provides a logical True (.T.) if the expression begins with an uppercase alpha character. It provides a logical False (.F.) if the first character of the expression is a nonalpha character (any numeral, lowercase alpha character, or punctuation symbol). The syntax for this function is:

```
ISUPPER(<character expression>)
```

Example:

```
STORE "little words" TO FIRST
STORE "BIG WORDS" TO SECOND
STORE "10numbers" TO THIRD

? ISUPPER(FIRST)
 .F.

? ISUPPER(SECOND)
 .T.

? ISUPPER(THIRD)
 .F.
```

KEY: This function returns the key expression for the specified index file. If a multiple index file is named, the numeric expression supplied in the function refers to the desired index tag in the multiple index file. If no index file is named, the numeric expression refers to the desired index among all open index files in the work area. Use the optional alias to return the index expression for an index open in a different work area. The syntax for this function is:

```
KEY([<.MDX filename>,] <numeric exp.> [,<alias>])
```

Example:

```
USE MAILER
INDEX ON LAST_NAME TO NAMES
INDEX ON ZIPCODE TO ZIPS
? KEY(2)
last_name
? KEY(1)
zipcode
```

LASTKEY: This function returns the ASCII value representing the last key pressed. The values returned are the same as those returned by the INKEY() function. The syntax for this function is:

```
LASTKEY()
```

Example:

```
*prints inventory listing.*
@ 5,5 SAY "Press F5 to HALT printing once started."
WAIT " Press any key to begin."
SET PRINT ON
?
? " Inventory listing"
?
DO WHILE .NOT.  EOF()
    ? ITEMNUMB
    ?? SPACE(10)
    ?? ITEMNAME
    ?? SPACE(10)
    ?? QUANTITY
    ?? SPACE(10)
    ?? ONHAND
    SKIP
    *check for press of F5 key.
    IF LASTKEY() = -4
        EXIT
    ENDIF
ENDDO
SET PRINT OFF
RETURN
```

LEFT: This function provides a character string containing the number of characters specified by the numeric expression, beginning with the leftmost character in the string. The syntax for this function is:

```
LEFT(<character expression>,<numeric expression>)
```

Example:

```
STORE "left and right parts" TO TEXT
? LEFT(TEXT, 8)
left and
```

LEN: This function provides a number indicating the length of a character string. The syntax for this function is:

```
LEN(<character expression>)
```

Example:

```
STORE "twenty-two characters!" TO WORD
? LEN(WORD)
22
```

LIKE: This function compares the pattern with the character string indicated by the expression. The function returns a logical value of true if the character string contained in the expression contains the characters indicated by the pattern. Wildcards * and ? can be used in the pattern. The LIKE function is commonly used with predicates in the SQL language. The syntax for this function is:

```
LIKE(<pattern>,<character expression>)
```

Example:

```
STORE "mayberry" TO NAME
? LIKE("may*",NAME)
  .T.
? LIKE("???ber??",NAME)
  .T.
? LIKE("mary",NAME)
  .F.
```

LINENO: This function returns the next line number to be executed within a command file or procedure file. This function can be used within the breakpoint window of the Debugger to halt the program at a specific line number. The syntax for this function is:

```
LINENO()
```

Example:

```
ON ERROR ? "Error at line number: " + STR(LINENO())
```

LKSYS: This function returns the name of a user who has locked a file or record, or the date or time of the lock. LKSYS(0) returns the time the lock was placed, and LKSYS(1) returns the date the lock was placed. LKSYS(2) returns the log-in name of the user who has locked the record. The syntax for this function is:

```
LKSYS(n)
```

Example:

```
IF .NOT. FLOCK()
     ? "File is already locked by: "
     ?? LKSYS(2)
ENDIF
```

LOCK: This function attempts a lock on a record, and returns a logical value of true if the lock attempt is successful. (The function is identical to the RLOCK function.) If the attempt is unsuccessful (that is, if the record or file is already locked), the function returns a logical false. The optional character expression list can contain a list of different records to lock (such as "3,25,72" to lock records 3, 25, and 72). If no list is used, the current record is locked. If a list is used and any one of the records cannot be locked, the function will return a logical false, and none of the records will be locked. Use the optional alias to lock records in a file open in a different work area.

Note that the type of lock placed by LOCK() is a shared lock. Other users may still access the locked record, but changes by other users will not be permitted until the record is unlocked with the UNLOCK command, or by closing the file. The syntax for this function is:

```
LOCK([<character exp.  list>,<alias>] / [<alias>])
```

Example:

```
SET EXCLUSIVE OFF
USE MAILER
SEEK FINDIT
IF FOUND()
     IF LOCK()
          EDIT
     ELSE
          ? "Record already locked by another."
          WAIT
     ENDIF
ELSE
     ? "Record not found."
     WAIT
ENDIF
```

LOG: This function provides the natural logarithm of a number. The syntax for this function is:

```
LOG(<numeric expression>)
```

Example:

```
? LOG(6.0)
1.79
```

LOG10: This function returns the common logarithm (to the base 10) of the number specified in the expression. The syntax for this function is:

```
LOG10(<numeric expression>)
```

Example:

```
? LOG10(4)
0.60
```

LOOKUP: This function searches for a specific record and returns a value from a named field in the database. <return field> and <expression to look for> can be any valid dBASE expressions. You can include an alias, to search a database in another work area. If an index is open, <search field> can contain a key expression. If no index is open, dBASE performs a locate (sequential search) to find the record. If no match is found, the record pointer is placed at the end of the file. The syntax for this function is:

```
LOOKUP(<return field>,<exp.  to look for>,<search field>)
```

Example:

```
ACCEPT "Name of person to display address for?" TO WHO
? "The address is: "
?? LOOKUP(ADDRESS, WHO, LAST_NAME)
```

LOWER: This function converts uppercase letters to lowercase. The LOWER function has no effect on lowercase letters, numbers, spaces, or punctuation marks. The syntax for this function is:

```
LOWER(<character expression>)
```

Example:

```
STORE LOWER("SMITH") TO TEST
? TEST
smith
```

LTRIM: This function strips leading blanks from a character string or expression. The syntax for this function is:

```
LTRIM(<character expression>)
```

Example:

```
STORE "     FIVE LEADING BLANKS" TO TEXT
     FIVE LEADING BLANKS
? TEXT
     FIVE LEADING BLANKS
? LTRIM(TEXT)
FIVE LEADING BLANKS
```

LUPDATE: This function provides a date expression containing the last update for the database in use. The syntax for this function is:

```
LUPDATE()
```

Example:

```
USE MAILER
? LUPDATE()
07/15/86
```

MAX: This function provides the maximum value of two numeric expressions. The syntax for this function is:

```
MAX (<numeric expression 1>,<numeric expression 2>)
```

Example:

```
USE SALES
GO 4
? MAX(PRICE, 200)
249.95
```

```
? MAX(PRICE, 400)
400.00
```

MDX: This function returns the filename of the multiple index file specified by the order number. The numeric expression specifies the position of the .MDX index file, as controlled by the SET INDEX TO command. Use the optional alias to return the filename of an .MDX file open in a different work area. The syntax for this function is:

```
MDX(<numeric expression> [,alias])
```

Example:

```
USE MAILER
SET ORDER TO ZIPS
INDEX ON CITY TAG CITIES OF TOWNS.MDX
? MDX(1)
C:MAILER.MDX
? MDX(2)
C:TOWNS.MDX
```

MDY: This function converts a valid date expression to a format of Month, DD, YY if SET CENTURY is OFF, or to a format of Month, DD, YYYY if SET CENTURY is ON. The automatic inclusion of a comma after the day makes the MDY() function useful for printing dates in a spelled- out format, as is used when writing checks. The syntax for this function is:

```
MDY(<date expression>)
```

Example:

```
? MDY(DATE())
December 12, 88
SET CENTURY ON
? MDY(DATE())
December 12, 1988
```

MEMLINES: This function returns the number of lines needed to display a memo field when SET MEMOWIDTH is in effect. The syntax for this function is:

```
MEMLINES(<memo field name>)
```

Example:

```
USE LITIGATE
GO 3
SET MEMOWIDTH TO 30
? MEMLINES(COMMENTS)
     9
? COMMENTS
Client originally complained
to hospital intern of severe
back pain.  Senior resident on
night staff duty at the time
failed to notice initial
muscular abrasions in X-rays
and prescribed pain relievers
for suspected muscle sprain.

SET MEMOWIDTH TO 50
? MEMLINES(COMMENTS)
      6

? COMMENTS
Client originally complained to hospital intern of
severe back pain.  Senior resident on night staff
duty at the time failed to notice initial muscular
abrasions in X-rays and prescribed pain relievers
for suspected muscle sprain.
```

MEMORY: This function returns the amount of free memory. Use this function to test for available memory before running external programs with the RUN or ! commands. The syntax for this function is:

```
MEMORY()
```

Example:

```
WAIT "Format floppies before backup? Y/N:" TO CHOICE
IF UPPER(CHOICE) = "Y"
    IF MEMORY() < 2048
        CLEAR
        ? "Not enough memory to run FORMAT."
        WAIT "Press any key..."
        RETURN
    ELSE
```

```
        RUN C:\DOS\FORMAT A:
    ENDIF
ENDIF
WAIT "Insert formatted disk in A, press a key..."
COPY NEXT 9999 TO A:BACKFILE.DBF
RETURN
```

MENU: This function returns a character string representing the name of the last activated menu. If no menu is active, MENU() returns a null string. The syntax for this function is:

```
MENU()
```

Example:

```
? MENU()
Printer
```

MESSAGE: This function returns a character string provided as an error message, in situations when dBASE IV detects an error in a program. The syntax for this function is:

```
MESSAGE()
```

Example:

```
? MESSAGE()
Too many files are open
```

MIN: This function provides the minimum value of two numeric expressions. The syntax for this function is:

```
MIN (<numeric expression 1>,<numeric expression 2>)
```

Example:

```
USE SALES
GO 4
? MIN(PRICE, 200)
200.00
? MIN(PRICE, 400)
249.95
```

MLINE: This function returns a line of text from a memo field. The line corresponds to a line of text that would be displayed under the current setting of the SET MEMOWIDTH command. The syntax for this function is:

```
MLINE(<memo field name>,<numeric expression>)
```

Example:

```
USE LITIGATE
GO 3
SET MEMOWIDTH TO 40
? COMMENTS
Client originally complained to hospital
intern of severe back pain.  Senior
resident on night staff duty at the time
failed to notice initial muscular
abrasions in X-rays and prescribed pain
relievers for suspected muscle sprain.

? MLINE(COMMENTS,2)
intern of severe back pain.  Senior
? MLINE(COMMENTS,4)
failed to notice initial muscular
```

MOD: This function provides the remainder of a division. The syntax for this function is:

```
MOD(<numeric expression-dividend>,<numeric expression-divisor>)
```

Example:

```
? MOD(16,4)
  0
? MOD(18,4)
  2
```

MONTH: This function provides a numeric expression equivalent to the month within a date expression. The syntax for this function is:

```
MONTH(date expression)
```

Example:

```
?DATE()
09/11/86
?MONTH(DATE())
9
```

NDX: This function provides the name of any open index file in the selected work area. The numeric expression is a value between 1 and 7. The value provided by the function indicates the position, in sequential order, of the index file; as an example, the second index file named would be number 2, the fourth index file named would be number 4, and so on. The syntax for this function is:

```
NDX(<numeric expression>)
```

Example:

```
USE APPLICAN INDEX LAST, RENT, ZIP
? ndx(1)
 C:last.ndx
? ndx(2)
 C:rent.ndx
? ndx(3)
 C:zip.ndx
```

NETWORK: This function returns a logical true when dBASE IV is running on a local area network. The syntax for this function is:

```
NETWORK()
```

Example:

```
SET TALK OFF
SET BELL OFF
IF NETWORK()
  SET EXCLUSIVE OFF
ENDIF
<...more commands...>
```

ORDER: This function returns the name of the controlling index for the active database. Use the optional alias to specify a database file open in another work area. The syntax for this function is:

```
ORDER([<alias>])
```

Example:

```
USE MAILER
SET ORDER TO ZIPS
? ORDER("Mailer")
ZIPS
```

```
SET ORDER TO NAMES
? ORDER("Mailer")
NAMES
```

OS: This function provides the name and version level of the operating system under which dBASE IV is running. The syntax for this function is:

```
OS()
```

Example:

```
? OS()
DOS 3.10
```

PAD: This function returns the name of the most recently chosen pad in a bar menu. If no menu is active, the PAD() function returns a null string. The syntax for this function is:

```
PAD()
```

Example:

```
? PAD()
Adder
```

PAYMENT: This function returns a payment amount of a loan, given the principal, interest rate, and periods. <principal> can be expressed as a positive or negative number. <rate> is the interest rate, expressed as a positive value. <periods> represents the number of periods (that is, payments) of the loan. If the payments are compounded monthly and the interest rate is compounded yearly, divide the interest rate by 12 to obtain the monthly interest rate before using the function. Note that fractional amounts are rounded to whole numbers. The syntax for this function is:

```
PAYMENT(<principal>,<rate>,<periods>)
```

Example:

```
INPUT "Enter loan balance: " TO PRINC
INPUT "Enter annual interest rate: " TO YRINT
INPUT "Enter number of monthly payments: " TO PMTS STORE YRINT/12 TO INT
? "Your payments wil be: "
?? PAYMENT(PRINC,INT,PMTS)
```

PCOL: This function provides current column position for the printer print-head. The syntax for this function is:

```
PCOL()
```

Example:

```
? PCOL()
    0
SET PRINT ON
@ 2,5 SAY "Test of printer."
SET PRINT OFF
? PCOL()
   15
```

PI: This function returns the approximate value of *pi* (3.14159). The syntax for this function is:

```
PI()
```

Example:

```
? PI()
3.14
SET DECIMALS TO 5
? PI()
3.14159
```

POPUP: This function returns the name of the last active popup menu. If no popup menu is active, the POPUP() function returns a null string. The syntax for this function is:

```
POPUP()
```

Example:

```
? POPUP()
Mainmenu
```

PRINTSTATUS: This function returns a logical value of true if the printer is ready to accept characters. The function will test the status of the last selected print device. The syntax for this function is:

```
PRINTSTATUS()
```

Example:

```
*print routine.*
WAIT "Ready printer, then press a key..."
IF .NOT.  PRINTSTATUS()
    WAIT "Printer NOT ready! Fix problem, try again. Press a key."
RETURN
ENDIF
REPORT FORM SALES TO PRINT
RETURN
```

PROGRAM: This function returns a character string representing the name of the program or procedure running when an error occurred. The syntax for this function is:

```
PROGRAM()
```

Example:

```
*Main program*
SET TALK OFF
SET BELL OFF
ON ERROR DO PANIC
SET ESCAPE OFF
<...more commands...>
 *Procedure File*
PROCEDURE PANIC
? "A program error has occurred."
? "on line number-"
?? LINENO()
? "Of the program or procedure named: "
?? PROGRAM()
?
? "Record this message, then contact"
? "your DP department for assistance."
WAIT
QUIT
```

PROMPT: This function returns a character string representing the most recently chosen option in a menu. If no menu is active, or if Esc is pressed to exit the menu, the function returns a null string. The syntax for this function is:

```
PROMPT()
```

Example:

```
? PROMPT()
Delete records
```

PROW: This function provides the current row position for the printer print-head. The syntax for this function is:

```
PROW()
```

Example:

```
? PROW()
    0
SET PRINT ON
@ 2,5 SAY "Test of printer."
SET PRINT OFF
? PROW()
    2
```

PV: This function returns the present value of, or the amount that must be invested at a given interest rate to earn, a known future value. <payment> is the payment amount, which can be negative or positive. <rate> is the interest rate, and <periods> is the number of payment periods. If the payments are compounded monthly and the interest rate is compounded yearly, divide the interest rate by 12 to obtain the monthly interest rate before using the function. The syntax for this function is:

```
PV(<payment>,<rate>,<periods>)
```

Example:

```
INPUT "Enter the payment amount:" TO PMT
INPUT "Enter the yearly interest rate: " TO YRINT
INPUT "Enter the number of monthly investments: " TO MNTHS
STORE YRINT/12 TO INT
? "Present value needed is: "
?? PV(PMT,INT,MNTHS)
```

RAND: This function returns a random number between 0 and 0.999999. The optional numeric expression can be included to provide a seed for generating the random number. A negative number may also be used in the expression, in which case the system clock is used as the seed for the random number. The syntax for this function is:

```
RAND([<numeric expression>])
```

Example:

```
? RAND()
0.47039
? RAND()
0.79907
? RAND()
0.89898
```

READKEY: This function provides a value representing the key pressed by the user to exit from a full-screen command (that is, APPEND or EDIT). The READKEY() function provides one of two possible values: a value between 0 and 36 if no changes were made to the data while the user was using the full-screen mode, or a value between 256 and 292 if changes were made to the data. The syntax for this function is:

```
READKEY()
```

Example:

```
APPEND BLANK
READ
*Test for user pressing Esc or Control-Q.  If so,
*delete the new record
IF READKEY() = 12
     DELETE
ENDIF
RETURN
```

This program uses READKEY() to test whether the user pressed the Esc key while using the APPEND command.

RECCOUNT: This function provides a numeric expression representing the total number of records in the active database. The syntax for this function is:

```
RECCOUNT()
```

Example:

```
USE MAILER
? RECCOUNT()
         8
```

```
USE C:LAWYERS
? "There are "
?? RECCOUNT()
?? "records in the database."
```

RECNO: This function provides a numeric value representing the position of the record pointer. The syntax for this function is:

```
RECNO()
```

Example:

```
GO 5
SKIP
? RECNO()
         6
```

RECSIZE: This function provides a numeric value indicating the size of each record in the database in use. The syntax for this function is:

```
RECSIZE()
```

Example:

```
USE MAILER
? RECSIZE()
        98
```

REPLICATE: This function causes repetition of the specified character expression. Characters are repeated the number of times identified within the numeric expression. The syntax for this function is:

```
REPLICATE(<character expression>,<numeric expression>)
```

Example:

```
STORE 10 TO FIRST
STORE 14 TO SECOND
STORE 22 TO THIRD

? REPLICATE("=",FIRST)
==========
? REPLICATE("*",SECOND)
**************
```

```
? REPLICATE("/",THIRD)
/////////////////////
```

RIGHT: This function provides a character string containing the number of characters specified by the numeric expression, beginning with the rightmost character in the string. The syntax for this function is:

```
RIGHT(<character expression>,<numeric expression>)
```

Example:

```
STORE "left and right" TO TEXT
? RIGHT(TEXT, 9)
and right
```

RLOCK: This function attempts a lock on a record and returns a logical value of true if the lock attempt is successful. (The function is identical to the LOCK function.) If the attempt is unsuccessful (that is, if the record or file is already locked), the function returns a logical false. The optional character expression list can contain a list of different records to lock (such as 3,25,72 to lock records 3, 25, and 72). If no list is used, the current record is locked. If a list is used and any one of the records cannot be locked, the function will return a logical false, and none of the records will be locked. Use the optional alias to lock records in a file open in a different work area. The syntax for this function is:

```
RLOCK([<character exp.  list>,<alias>] / [<alias>])
```

Note that the type of lock placed by RLOCK() is a shared lock. Other users may still access the locked record, but changes by other users will not be permitted until the record is unlocked with the UNLOCK command, or by closing the file.

Example:

```
SET EXCLUSIVE OFF
USE MAILER
SEEK FINDIT
IF FOUND()
     IF RLOCK()
          EDIT
     ELSE
          ? "Record already locked by another."
          WAIT
     ENDIF
ELSE
     ? "Record not found."
```

```
    WAIT
ENDIF
```

ROLLBACK: This function returns a logical value of true if the last ROLLBACK command was completed successfully. The syntax for this function is:

```
ROLLBACK()
```

Example:

```
BEGIN TRANSACTION
REPLACE ALL PRICE WITH PRICE + (PRICE * .05)
ROLLBACK

? ROLLBACK()
 .T.
```

ROUND: This function rounds off numbers, retaining the number of decimal places specified. The syntax for this function is:

```
ROUND(<numeric expression>,<number of decimal places>)
```

Example:

```
? ROUND(5.867,2)
5.870
```

ROW: This function provides the current row position of the cursor. The syntax for this function is:

```
ROW()
```

Example:

```
@ 5,5 SAY "Hello."
? ROW()

6
```

RTOD: This function converts radians, as expressed by the numeric expression, to degrees. The syntax for this function is:

```
RTOD(<numeric expression>)
```

Example:

```
STORE 4 * (PI()/2) TO RDS
? RTOD(RDS)
```

RTRIM: This function strips trailing spaces from a character string. The RTRIM function is identical to the TRIM function. The syntax for this function is:

```
RTRIM(<character expression>)
```

Example:

```
? RTRIM(FIRSTNAME) + " " + LASTNAME
Larry Miller
```

SEEK: This function returns a logical true if the search expression can be found in the active index. The function moves the record pointer and returns the logical value indicating whether the search term was found. If the search expression is not found in the index, the record pointer is placed at the end of the file, and the function returns a logical false. Use the optional alias to search for a record in a file open in a different work area. The syntax for this function is:

```
SEEK(<search expression> [,<alias>])
```

Example:

```
ACCEPT "Enter social security no.: " TO M_SOCSEC
IF SEEK(M_SOCSEC)
    EDIT
ELSE
    WAIT "No such record.  Press a key..."
ENDIF
```

SELECT: This function returns a numeric value indicating the highest unused work area. The syntax for this function is:

```
SELECT()
```

Example:

```
USE MAILER
USE CITIES IN 2
USE LITIGATE IN 3
```

```
? SELECT()
10
```

SET: This function returns a character string indicating the status of the SET command named within the function. The syntax for this function is:

```
SET(<character expression>)
```

Example:

```
SET BELL OFF
SET CARRY ON
SET MEMOWIDTH TO 30

? SET("bell")
OFF
? SET("carry")
ON
? SET("memowidth")
    30
```

SIGN: This function returns a numeric value which represents the sign of a numeric expression. The function returns a 1 if the expression contains a positive number, a −1 if the expression contains a negative number, and a 0 if the expression is a zero. The syntax for this function is:

```
SIGN(<numeric expression>)
```

Example:

```
X = 3
Y = -72.5
Z = 0

? SIGN(X)
1

? SIGN(Y)
-1

? SIGN(Z)
0
```

SIN: This function returns the sine of an angle, as measured in radians. The <numeric expression> supplied must be expressed in radians. If the size is known in degrees, use the DTOR() function first to convert the size to radians, then use the SIN() function. To convert the resulting value back to degrees, use the RTOD() function. The syntax for this function is:

```
SIN(<numeric expression>)
```

Example:

```
? SIN(3/2)
0.99749
```

SOUNDEX: This function returns a phonetic ("SOUNDEX") code for a given character expression. The code returned by the function is derived from the SOUNDEX algorithm, which is as follows:

1. The first letter of the character expression becomes the first character in the code.
2. All occurrences of the letters A, E, H, I, O, U, W, and Y are dropped.
3. The remaining letters are assigned a number according to the following:

b,f,p,v	1
c,g,j,k,q,s,x,z	2
d,t	3
l	4
m,n	5
r	6

4. When two or more adjacent letters have the same code, all but the first letter in the group are dropped.
5. A code in the format of "letter digit digit digit" is returned. If less than three digits are in the code, trailing zeros are added. If more than three digits are in the code, excess digits are dropped.
6. If the first character is not a letter, "0000" is returned as the code. If leading blanks exist in the character string, these are skipped. The calculation of the code stops at the first character that is not a letter.

The four-character code returned by the SOUNDEX() function can be useful for finding similar-sounding names, or for building an index to perform lookups based on the sound of a word. The syntax for this function is:

```
SOUNDEX(<character expression>)
```

Example:

```
USE MAILER
INDEX ON SOUNDEX(LAST_NAME) TO SOUNDLIK
ACCEPT "Enter last name to find:" TO ANS
```

```
FINDIT = SOUNDEX(ANS)
SEEK FINDIT
IF FOUND()
    EDIT
ELSE
    WAIT "No similar name found.  Press a key..."
ENDIF
```

SPACE: This function creates a character string containing a specified number of blank spaces. The numeric expression given can range from 1 to 254. The syntax for this function is:

```
SPACE(<numeric expression>)
```

Example:

```
STORE SPACE(15) TO GAP
? "System" + GAP + "Main" + GAP + "Menu"
System               Main               Menu
```

SQRT: This function calculates the square root of a numeric expression. The numeric expression must be a positive number. The syntax for this function is:

```
SQRT(<numeric expression>)
```

Example:

```
STORE 25 + 24 TO TEST
? SQRT(TEST)
7
```

STR: This function converts a numeric expression into a character string. The syntax for this function is:

```
STR(<numeric expression>[,<length>][,<no. of decimal places>])
```

Example:

```
STORE 7.75 to salary
? "Employee salary is: " + STR(SALARY)
```

STUFF: This function inserts or removes characters from any part of a character string. The syntax for this function is:

```
STUFF(<existing char. string>,<starting position>,<number of chars. to remove
from string>,<character string to insert>)
```

Example:

```
STORE "First Last" TO NAME
First Last
? STUFF(NAME,7,0,"Middle ")
First Middle Last
```

SUBSTR: This function extracts a portion of a character string from a character string. If the number of characters is not provided, the character expression produced by SUBSTR() will begin with the starting position specified and end with the last character of the character expression. The syntax for this function is:

```
SUBSTR(<character expression>,<starting position>[,<number of chars.>])
```

Example:

```
USE CLIENTS
GO 3
? PHONE
4156893212

STORE SUBSTR(PHONE,1,3) TO AREACODE
? AREACODE
415
```

TAG: This function returns a character string representing the name of an index (.NDX) file or index (.MDX) tag specified by the numeric expression. If a multiple index file name (.MDX) is not used, the function assumes that the numeric expression supplied refers to all open index files. Use the optional alias to refer to an index file open in a different work area. The syntax for this function is:

```
TAG([<.MDX filename>,] <numeric expression> [,<alias>])
```

Example:

```
USE MAILER
? TAG(2)
ZIPS
? TAG(1)
NAMES
```

TAN: This function returns the tangent of an angle as measured in radians. The numeric expression specified is the size of the angle, also measured in radians. If the size is known in degrees, use the DTOR() function first to convert to radians, then use the TAN() function. To convert the result back to degrees, use the RTOD() function. The syntax for this function is:

```
TAN(<numeric expression>)
```

Example:

```
INPUT "Degrees of the angle?" TO ANGLE
RDS = DTOR(ANGLE)
? "Tangent of the angle, in radians, is:"
?? TAN(RDS)
```

TIME(): This function provides the current time in the form of a character variable. The syntax for this function is:

```
TIME()
```

Example:

```
? TIME()
 22:09:29
```

TRANSFORM: This function formats alphanumerics with PICTURE options without requiring @ . . . SAY commands. The syntax for this function is:

```
TRANSFORM(<expression>,<character expression containing picture clause>)
```

Example:

```
GO 5
DISPLAY NEXT 3
Record#  LAST_NAME
      5  Miller              6  Canion              7  Roberts
DISPLAY NEXT 3 TRANSFORM(LAST_NAME, "@r X X X X X X X X X X")
Record#  TRANSFORM(LAST_NAME, "@r X X X X X X X X X X")
      5  M i l l e r             6  C a n i o n             7  R o b e r t s
```

TRIM: This function strips trailing spaces from a character string. The syntax for this function is:

```
TRIM(<character expression>)
```

Example:

```
? TRIM(FIRSTNAME) + " " + LASTNAME
Larry Miller
```

TYPE: This function provides a character indicating the type of expression. C denotes character expression, N denotes numeric expression, D denotes date expression, L denotes logical expression, and U denotes undefined expression. The syntax for this function is:

```
TYPE(<expression>)
```

Example:

```
STORE "words" TO WORD
STORE 45.67 TO NUMBER
STORE DATE() TO TODAY
STORE .T. TO LOGICS

? TYPE("WORD")
C
? TYPE("NUMBER")
N
? TYPE("TODAY")
D
? TYPE("LOGICS")
L
? TYPE("NOSUCH")
U
```

UPPER: This function converts lowercase letters to uppercase. The UPPER function has no effect on uppercase letters, numbers, spaces, or punctuation marks. The syntax for this function is:

```
UPPER(<character expression>)
```

Example:

```
STORE "rotunda" TO TEST
? UPPER(TEST)
ROTUNDA
```

USER: This function returns the log-in name of the user on a local area network. PROTECT must be used for this function to return the name; if PROTECT was not used, a null string ("") is returned. The syntax for this function is:

```
USER()
```

Example:

```
? USER()
ESMITH
```

VAL: This function converts strings of numeric characters into numeric expressions. If the character string begins with a non-numeric character that is not a space, the VAL function will provide a value of zero. The syntax for this function is:

```
VAL(<character expression>)
```

Example:

```
? VAL("3.14159")
3.14159
```

VARREAD: This function returns the name of the field or memory variable currently being edited. The function is useful when designing context-sensitive help systems, to display different help screens for different fields. The syntax for this function is:

```
VARREAD()
```

Example:

```
ON KEY LABEL F1 DO Helper
@ 5,5 SAY "Stock number?" GET STOCKNO
@ 7,5 SAY "Quantity?" GET QUANTITY
@ 9,5 SAY "Cost?" GET PRICE
READ

<...more commands...>

*Procedure file*
PROCEDURE HELPER
DEFINE WINDOW Helps FROM 5,5 TO 15,60 COLOR B/W
ACTIVATE WINDOW Helps
```

```
DO CASE
    CASE VARREAD() = "STOCKNO"
    ? "Enter a valid stock number for the item here."
    ? "Consult the Master Registry for valid numbers."

    CASE VARREAD() = "QUANTITY"
    ? "Enter the number of items in the inventory."
    ? "Enter a zero if no items are available."

    CASE VARREAD() = "PRICE"
    ? "See the Master Registry for current price list"
    ? "of all new items."
ENDCASE
WAIT
DEACTIVATE WINDOW Helps
RETURN
```

VERSION: This function provides a character string indicating the version of dBASE IV being used. The syntax for this function is:

```
VERSION()
```

Example:

```
? VERSION()
dBASE IV  version 1.0
```

YEAR: This function provides a numeric expression equivalent to the year within a date expression. The syntax for this function is:

```
YEAR(<date expression>)
```

Example:

```
? date()
12/04/88
? year(date())
 1988
```

C

Common Error Messages

Following are descriptions of the more common error messages displayed by dBASE IV, including their causes. Refer to your Ashton-Tate documentation if you encounter a message not described here. In cases where a number appears in parentheses next to the error message, this number is the value provided by the ERROR() function for that error.

```
ALIAS name already in use (24)
```

You attempted to use a file or an alias name for a work area that is already in use or that is reserved. dBASE IV reserves either names A through J or 1 through 10 as default alias names.

```
ALIAS not found (13)
```

You attempted to select an unnamed alias or an alias outside of the default alias range (A through J or 1 through 10).

```
All allowed slots have been filled
```

You have reached the maximum number of available indexes: 47 index tags in an .MDX file, or 10 separate (.NDX) index files.

```
Bad array dimensions (230)
```

You attempted to declare an array with more than the maximum of 1,023 elements, or you used an illegal value (such as a zero) when declaring the array expression.

```
Beginning of file encountered (38)
```

You attempted to move the record pointer above the beginning of the file.

```
Cannot clear menu in use (176)
```

You attempted to recover menu memory with CLEAR MENU or RELEASE MENU while the menu is still active. Use DEACTIVATE MENU first.

```
Cannot clear popup in use (177)
```

You attempted to recover popup memory with CLEAR POPUP or RELEASE POPUP while the popup menu is still active. Use DEACTIVATE POPUP first.

```
Cannot close database when transaction is in progress (185)
```

You attempted to close a database after a BEGIN TRANSACTION and before an END TRANSACTION or a ROLLBACK. Issue an END TRANSACTION or a ROLLBACK command, then close the file.

```
Cannot close index files when transaction is in progress (187)
```

You attempted to close an index file after a BEGIN TRANSACTION and before an END TRANSACTION or a ROLLBACK. Issue an END TRANSACTION or a ROLLBACK command, then close the file.

```
Cannot erase a file which is open (89)
```

You attempted to erase an open file. Close the file, then issue the ERASE or DELETE FILE command.

```
Cannot erase a read-only file (336)
```

You are attempting to erase a file for which you have read-only access. In single-user mode, use the DOS ATTRIB command to change file access; on a network, contact your network administrator.

```
Cannot write to read-only file
```

You attempted to write to a file that has been set to read-only by the operating system. Use the DOS ATTRIB command or the appropriate network system software command to change the read-only status of the file.

```
Command not allowed in PRS programs (265)
```

The command you are attempting to use is invalid in the SQL mode of dBASE IV.

```
CONTINUE without LOCATE (42)
```

The program executed a CONTINUE before executing a LOCATE command.

```
Current print driver does not support quality (331)
```

The printer driver currently in use does not support special fonts or letter-quality printing.

```
Cyclic Relation (44)
```

A series of SET RELATION commands have created an endless loop, where a database in the chain of linked databases relates back to the database currently selected.

```
Database encrypted (131)
```

You are attempting to use a database that has been encrypted by the PROTECT utility of dBASE (network installation of dBASE IV). Either you have no security clearance to use the file, or you are attempting to open the file with a single-user installation of dBASE IV.

```
Database not indexed (26)
```

You attempted to use a SEEK or FIND command while an index file was not open or did not exist; or, a relation into an unindexed database was attempted.

```
Data type mismatch (9)
```

You attempted to mix conflicting data types (that is, you attempted to make combinations of character and numeric strings without an appropriate conversion function).

```
.DBT file cannot be opened (41)
```

A memo field (.DBT) file cannot be found to accompany a corresponding database file.

```
Disk full when writing file: <filename> (56)
```

You attempted to write a file to a full disk.

```
Disk is write-protected
```

You are attempting to write to a write-protected floppy disk. Remove the write-protect tab.

```
End-of-file encountered (4)
```

You attempted to move the record pointer past the end of a database; or, you used a FIND or SEEK command on an incomplete or corrupted index; or, the database file has been damaged.

```
Field name is already in use
```

You attempted to reuse an existent field name during a CREATE or MODIFY STRUCTURE.

```
File already exists (7)
```

You attempted to rename a file to the same name as an existing file.

```
File does not exist (1)
```

You attempted to open a nonexistent file.

```
File in use by another (108)
```

The file you are attempting to access has been opened for exclusive use by another user.

```
File must be opened in exclusive mode (110)
```

You are attempting a command which requires the file to be open in non-shared mode. Close the file, use SET EXCLUSIVE ON, and open the file.

```
Index damaged.  Do REINDEX before using data (114)
```

The associated index file has been damaged. Rebuild the index.

```
Index file does not match database (19)
```

The index file opened does not correspond to the database in use.

```
Insufficient memory (43)
```

The computer does not have sufficient memory remaining to perform the requested operation. Exit dBASE IV and change the CONFIG.SYS file specifications or release any memory-resident software currently stored in the system.

```
Invalid Lotus 1-2-3 version 2.0 Spreadsheet (297)
```

You are attempting to import a Lotus worksheet that is not in version 2.0 format. Convert the worksheet to version 2.0 format before importing it to dBASE IV.

```
Lock table is full (217)
```

You have reached the maximum of 50 possible record locks.

```
MDX file doesn't match database (207)
```

The multiple index file does not match the database currently in use.

```
Mismatched DO WHILE and ENDDO (246)
```

The program contains an extra ENDDO or is missing a DO WHILE statement.

```
No database in USE.  Enter file name: (52)
```

A command was executed that requires a database file to be open, and no file was open at the time of the command.

```
No more windows available (213)
```

You have reached the maximum of 20 possible windows.

```
Not a dBASE database (15)
```

The database file header has been damaged, or the file is not a dBASE IV or dBASE III database.

```
Not enough disk space (275)
```

Insufficient disk space remains to perform a sort operation.

```
Not enough records to sort (277)
```

You are attempting to sort a database containing less than 2 records.

```
Operation with logical field invalid (90)
```

You are attempting to use SORT or INDEX on a logical field.

```
Operation with memo field invalid (34)
```

You are attempting to use SORT or INDEX on a memo field.

```
Printer not ready (125)
```

The printer is not connected, or turned on, or on-line.

```
Record is in use by another (109)
```

On a networked system, the record you are trying to use has been locked by another user of dBASE Administrator.

```
Record is not in index (20)
```

You attempted to move the record pointer to a record that is not contained in the index. If the record exists, reindex the index file.

```
Record is out of range (5)
```

You attempted to move the record pointer to a record that does not exist.

```
Relation record in use by another
```

You are attempting to set a relation to a file which is in exclusive use by another user.

```
Syntax error (10)
```

The program contains a misspelled or misworded command.

```
Syntax error in (contents/field/group) expression
```

An error was made in the design of an expression within a report form or label form; or, you attempted to use a report or label form containing memory variables that are not available.

```
Too many files are open (6)
```

You attempted to open more than the DOS-supported maximum number of files (DOS allows 99 files, but dBASE IV uses 5 files). Or, the boot disk or start-up directory does not contain a CONFIG.SYS file that specifies sufficient files (normally FILES = 20).

```
Too many indexes (28)
```

You have reached the maximum of 10 index (.NDX) files, or 47 multiple index (.MDX) files.

```
Unable to load COMMAND.COM (92)
```

You attempted to enter a RUN command (or use an external word processor through the CONFIG.DB file), and the file COMMAND.COM could not be found where it was originally loaded or specified by the DOS COMSPEC command.

```
Unable to LOCK (129)
```

You are attempting to lock a record that is in use by another.

```
Unauthorized access level (133)
```

You attempted to access a file or a field that has been made unavailable to your access level by the PROTECT utility.

```
Unauthorized login (132)
```

Three unsuccessful tries were made to enter a valid user name, group name, and password to log onto a protected dBASE IV installation.

```
Unbalanced parenthesis (8)
```

An expression or filter within the program contains an unmatched number of starting and ending parentheses.

```
*** Unrecognized command verb (16)
```

A command line starts with a word that is not a valid dBASE IV command.

```
Unrecognized phrase/keyword in command (36)
```

A program statement contains an invalid word (often a misspelling).

```
Unterminated string (35)
```

A string is missing a terminator (usually quotation marks).

```
Variable not found (12)
```

The program has attempted to use a memory variable or field name that does not exist or is not available.

```
WINDOW has not been defined (214)
```

You are attempting to activate a window that does not exist. Use DEFINE WINDOW first.

```
Wrong number of parameters (94)
```

A DO WITH statement and the corresponding PARAMETERS statement do not contain the same number of parameters.

D

System Memory Variables

This appendix contains a listing of the system memory variables. These variables control the appearance of printed text. They can be set from the Report Generator menu options, from the dot prompt, or from within your programs and procedures. To set the variables from the dot prompt or within a program, enter the variable name, the assignment statement (=), and the desired value, as in these examples:

```
_alignment = "center"
_pcopies = 3
_wrap = .T.
_pdriver = "HPJET.pr2"
```

_alignment = "left"/"center"/"right": Controls alignment for output produced by the ? and ?? commands when _wrap is .T.

_box = .T./.F.: Specifies whether boxes defined with DEFINEBOX will be printed.

_indent = <numeric expression>: Specifies an indentation for the first line of each paragraph printed using the ? command when _wrap is set to .T. The value of <numeric expression> can range from 0 to 254, but must be less than the _rmargin setting.

_lmargin = <numeric expression>: Specifies a left margin for text printed with the ? command when _wrap is set to .T.

_padvance = "formfeed"/"linefeeds": Specifies whether form feeds or line feeds should be used to advance pages in the printer.

_pageno = <numeric expression>: Specifies a beginning page number for the print job. The numeric expression can range from 1 to 32,767.

_pbpage = <numeric expression>: Names a specific starting page to begin printing within a document. The value specified in the numeric expression can range from 1 to 32,767, and can be less than or equal to the value of _pepage.

_pcolno = <numeric expression>: Specifies starting column position at which the printhead will be located before printing begins. The value of the numeric expression can range from 0 to the value of _rmargin if _wrap is .T., or from 0 to the value of (_pwidth − _poffset) if _wrap is .F.

_pcopies = <numeric expression>: Specifies the number of printed copies of a report desired. The value of the numeric expression can range from 1 to 32,767.

_pdriver = "printer driver filename": Specifies the desired printer driver or returns the name of the current printer driver.

_pecode = <character expression>: Specifies ending control codes for a print job. Escape codes may be specified as {ESC} or {27} followed by the desired letter.

_peject = "before"/"after"/"both"/"none": Specifies whether a form feed should be sent to the printer before starting a print job, after completing the print job, both before and after, or not at all.

_pepage = <numeric expression>: Specifies the last page of a report to be printed. The value of the numeric expression can range from 1 to 32,767.

_pform = "print form filename"/(" "/filename): Activates desired print form file, or returns the name of the current print form file.

_plength = <numeric expression>: Specifies the desired page length. The value of the numeric expression can range from 1 to 32,767.

_plineno = <numeric expression>: Sets the line number to the specified line within the page. The value of the numeric expression can range from 0 to 32,767, but must be less than the value of _plength.

_ploffset = <numeric expression>: Specifies the desired page length offset. The value of the numeric expression can range from 0 to 254.

_ppitch = "pica"/"elite"/"condensed"/"default": Specifies the desired printer pitch, or returns the currently defined printer pitch.

_pquality = .T./.F.: Sets print quality to draft (.F.) or quality (.T.) print.

_pscode = <character expression>: Specifies the beginning control codes for a print job. Escape codes may be specified as {ESC} or {27} followed by the desired letter.

_pspacing = 1/2/3: Specifies the desired line spacing as 1 (single), 2 (double), or 3 (triple). The default value is single spacing.

_pwait = .T./.F.: Specifies whether printer should print continuously (.F.), or should pause between form feeds (.T.) and display a prompt to insert paper.

_rmargin = <numeric expression>: Specifies a right margin for text printed with the ? command when _wrap is set to .T. The value specified by the numeric expression can range from 1 to 255.

_tabs = <character expression>: Sets one or more tabs, where the tabs are listed as ascending numbers separated by commas (such as 5,15,25,55). A maximum of 30 tabs can be included in the list.

_wrap = .T./.F.: Specifies whether word wrap will be on (.T.) or off (.F.). Note that this option must be set to On for the _alignment, _indent, _lmargin, and _rmargin system memory variables to work.

Index

C

D

E

F

G

H

I

L

M

N

O

P

Q

R

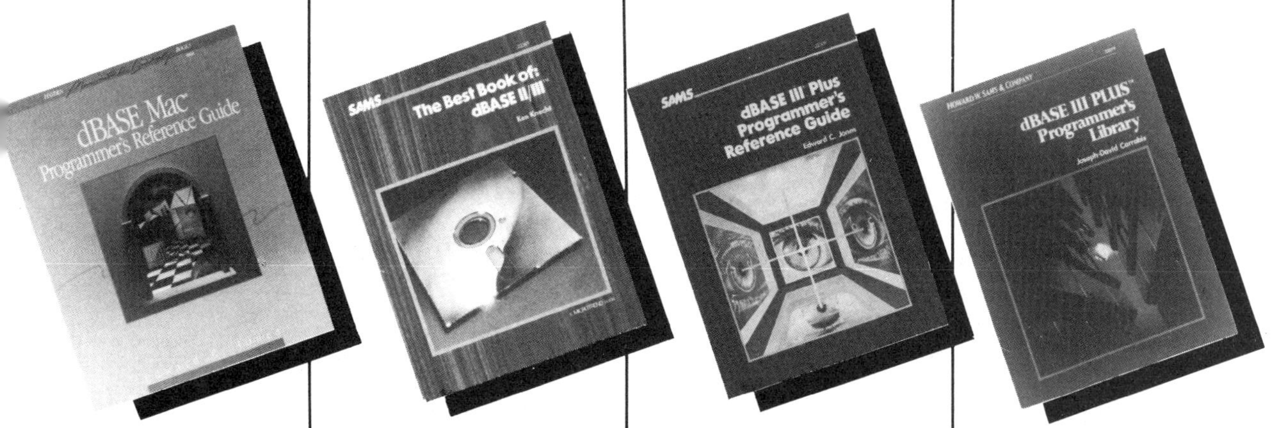

dBASE Mac® Programmer's Reference Guide
Edward C. Jones

This detailed guide for using and programming in dBASE for the Macintosh® was written especially for those who need to take full advantage of the program's available power.

This book highlights programming applications using modular code to develop complete applications for any purpose. It provides a detailed explanation of how to use the relational powers of the software, as well as how to add and edit records with full error tracking and data verification, system design, and file transfer from DOS.

Current DOS dBASE users will learn how to take advantage of the unique Macintosh graphical interface when they program or use dBASE Mac.

Topics covered include:

- Creating and Modifying Files
- Working with Display Views
- Managing Data
- Working with Related Files
- Building Applications
- System Design
- Procedural Flow in a dBASE Mac Procedure
- Adding and Modifying Records Under Procedural Control
- User Input and Output
- dBASE Mac for dBASE III Programmers
- Sample/Design Applications
- Appendix: dBASE Mac Commands

300 Pages, 7¾ x 9¼, Softbound
ISBN: 0-672-48416-1
No. 48416, $19.95

The Best Book of: dBASE II® /III®
Ken Knecht

For readers who already know how a data base performs, this time-saving guide explores the tricks that make dBASE II and dBASE III respond to their needs. In an effort to get the most out of dBASE II and dBASE III and apply these systems to specific business needs, it describes how to detect and correct errors, sort files, create new and useful programs, and manipulate data. The conversational style makes this book easy-to-read and an enjoyable, rewarding way to master dBASE II/III.

Topics covered include:

- Getting Started
- Creating a Simple Database
- More About dBASE II Data
- Dealing with the Entire Database
- Creating Reports
- dBASE II Command Files
- Advanced Programming
- An Annotated Program
- Quickcode
- Putting Quickcode to Work
- dGRAPH
- dBASE II—In Conclusion
- Introducing dBASE III—System and Program Specifications
- More dBASE III—Report, Variables, Label Commands, New Functions, The File Conversion Program

256 Pages, 7½ x 9¾, Softbound
ISBN: 0-672-22349-X
No. 22349, $21.95

dBASE III PLUS™ Programmer's Reference Guide
Ed Jones

Offering a unique approach to dBASE III PLUS, this book provides such options as menu design, instructions for restructuring programs for added speed, and sample turnkey applications for tracking inventory.

It is a complete reference guide to the many new programming features of this software package.

This reference guide explains in detail how dBASE commands are used for creating a database, adding and editing records, displaying data, and other introductory aspects of this powerful programming language.

Topics covered include:

- Introduction to dBASE III PLUS
- Programming Basics
- Program Flow
- Memory Variables
- System Design
- User Input and Output
- Adding and Modifying Records
- Managing the Database
- Debugging Strategies
- Programming for Network Users
- Command Reference

448 Pages, 7½ x 9¾, Softbound
ISBN: 0-672-22509-3
No. 22509, $19.95

dBASE III PLUS™ Programmer's Library
Joseph-David Carrabis

Written for intermediate to advanced programmers, this book shows how to quickly build a library of dBASE III PLUS code that can be reused many times with only minor modifications. The author reveals universal patterns for editing, adding, deleting, finding, and transferring records in databases, so that dBASE III PLUS tools can be adapted to a variety of applications.

The book has two major parts: The first provides kernels of code that can be used in applications as varied as dental records keeping, fundraising, small business management, and newsletter subscription systems. The second part shows the code necessary to handle such systems, and how kernels and modular programming help you set them up.

Topics covered include:

- What Is a Library?
- The Basic Kernels of Code
- Database Designs
- Advanced Kernels
- Inventory Systems
- Client/Personnel Record Keeping
- Subscription and General Accounting Systems
- Appendices: Clipper Versions of dBASE III Plus Listings, and dBASE III Plus Commands, Functions, and Abbreviations

536 Pages, 7½ x 9¾, Softbound
ISBN: 0-672-22579-4
No. 22579, $21.95

Visit your local book retailer or call
800-428-SAMS.

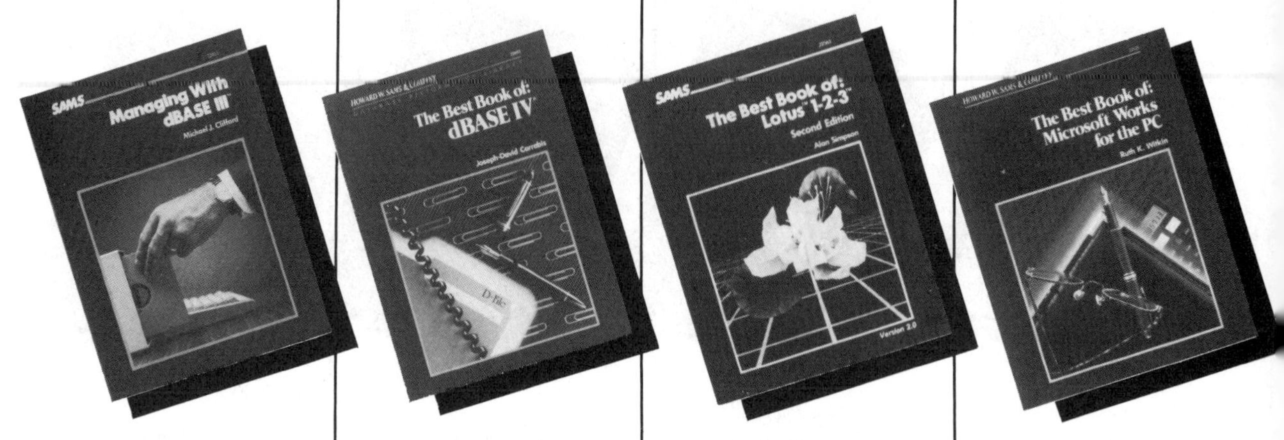

Managing With dBASE III®

Michael J. Clifford

This book takes a personal, practical approach to this popular software. It explains such features as dBASE III, memo and date fields, filters and paths, the new PICTURE and RANGE statements, and the SET RELATION TO method of linking files. It also gives programming strategies for using dBASE III to control inventory, manage accounts payable and receivable, update client files, and produce business graphics.

Topics covered include:

- Basic Concepts and Organization
- Setting the Stage
- Tracking Prospects and Maintaining Clients
- Using the MAILFORM System
- Installing MAILFORM
- The Stages of an Application Program: A Technical Tutorial
- Using the INVENT System
- Installing INVENT
- Using the INVOICE System
- Installing INVOICE
- Using the PAYBILLS System
- Installing PAYBILLS
- Working with Numbers: A Technical Tutorial
- Using the EXPENSE System
- Installing EXPENSE
- Initializing Programs with INIT
- The Date and Duration Toolkit
- dPLOT: The Graphics Toolkit
- The Three P's of Programming: A Technical Tutorial
- Appendices: So You've

412 Pages, 7½ x 9¾, Softbound
ISBN: 0-672-22455-0
No. 22455, $22.95

The Best Book of: dBASE IV®

Joseph-David Carrabis

This book features in-depth coverage of all major features of dBASE IV including the new user visual interface, the dBASE IV Control Center. Each operation is presented step-by-step, along with an illustrated sample application designed to make the reader comfortable enough with dBASE IV to shut off its automatic features and operate with the new interface.

The book also covers Query by Example (QBE) template programming for custom applications. It shows how to convert dBASE III PLUS applications into the dBASE IV environment and features detailed explanations of what each interface does, how it does it, and how the reader can perform the same tasks with or without the benefit of the user interface.

Topics covered include:

- Introduction to Database Management Systems and dBASE IV
- The dBASE IV Interface System
- Designing Databases
- Knowing What to Index and When
- Creating a Rolodex
- Getting Information from the Rolodex
- Modifying the Rolodex
- Linking Databases
- Changing the Rolodex into an Information Manager
- Getting Help When You Need It
- Automating the Information Manager

608 Pages, 7½ x 9¾, Softbound
ISBN: 0-672-22652-9
No. 22652, $22.95

The Best Book of: Lotus® 1-2-3®, Second Edition

Alan Simpson

This is *the* book for beginning 1-2-3 users. Written as a tutorial, this book steps readers through the various functions of the program and shows them how to use Version 2.0 in today's business environment.

Divided into four sections—worksheets, graphics, database management, and macro—each chapter within a section is designed to allow newcomers to be productive right away. With each new chapter, the users' skills are honed for faster and more spontaneous use of the software.

Topics covered include:

- Creating and Worksheet
- Functions and Formulas
- Formatting the Worksheet
- Copying Ranges
- Editing, Displaying, and Managing Worksheet Files
- Practical Examples
- Creating Graphs and Printing Graphs
- Database Management and Sorting
- Tables and Statistics
- Macros
- Custom Menus

350 Pages, 7½ x 9¾, Softbound
ISBN: 0-672-22563-8
No. 22563, $21.95

The Best Book of: Microsoft® Works for the PC

Ruth K. Witkin

This step-by-step guide uses a combination of in-depth explanations and hands-on tutorials to show the business professional or home user how to apply the software to enhance both business and personal productivity.

Clearly written and easy to understand, this book explains how to use such varied applications as the word processor with mail merge, the spreadsheet with charting, the database with reporting, communications, and integration. For each application the author provides a detailed overview of the hows and whys followed by practical examples that guide the reader easily from idea to finished product. Quick-reference charts, summaries, and end-of-chapter questions and answers enhance the learning process.

Topics covered include:

- Spreadsheet Essentials
- Exploring the Spreadsheet Menus
- About Formulas and Functions
- Charting Your Spreadsheet
- Exploring the Chart Menus
- Database Essentials
- Filling a Database
- Exploring the Database Menus
- Word Processor Essentials
- Exploring the Word Processor Menus
- Integration Essentials
- Communications Essentials
- Exploring the Communications Menus

350 Pages, 7½ x 9¾, Softbound
ISBN: 0-672-22626-X
No. 22626, $21.95

Visit your local book retailer or call
800-428-SAMS.

To Order Companion Diskettes

The sample applications in Chapter 19, along with most programs and procedures in *dBASE IV Programmer's Reference Guide,* are available on disk. The disk also contains a collection of useful dBASE IV utilities and user-defined functions. Included are a perpetual calendar, calculator, notepad, and other desktop utilities, written completely in dBASE IV. The 5¼" diskette is prepared for IBM-compatible computers running under DOS 2.1 or higher and formatted to 360K. The 3½" diskette is prepared for IBM-compatible computers running under DOS 3.1 or higher and formatted to 720K.

The diskette may be purchased with check or money order. Purchase price includes shipping and handling. Make checks and money orders payable to J.E.J.A. Software. (No cash, please.) Foreign orders should be payable in U.S. funds.

Send this form with your payment to:

J.E.J.A. Software
P.O. Box 1834
Herndon, VA 22070

Howard W. Sams & Company assumes no liability with respect to the use or accuracy of the information contained on these diskettes.

Diskette Order Form

Jones, *dBASE IV Programmer's Reference Guide,* #22654

(Please print)

Name ______________________ Company ______________________

Address ____

City ______________________ State ______________ Zip __________

Country ______________________ Phone (____)______________________

Place of Book Purchase ____________________________________

5¼" Disk (DOS 2.1 or higher)

Quantity: __________ @$15 U.S. Total: $__________
@$18 Canadian
@$20 Foreign

3½" Disk (DOS 3.1 or higher)

Quantity: __________ @$15 U.S. Total: $__________
@$18 Canadian
@$20 Foreign

(Virginia residents add 5% sales tax.) $__________

Total enclosed: $__________

Method of Payment: Check#______________ M.O.#______________

All orders will be shipped U.S. Postal Service First Class. Please allow six weeks for delivery. Orders can be shipped Federal Express at the purchaser's expense.